Working with dBASE Mac

Pushing Productivity to the Limit

Rusel DeMaria and George Fontaine

BRADY
New York

Simon & Schuster, Inc.
Gulf + Western Building
One Gulf + Western Plaza
New York, NY 10023

DISTRIBUTED BY PRENTICE HALL TRADE

Manufactured in the United States of America

1 2 3 4 5 6 7 8 9 10

Library of Congress Cataloging-in-Publication Data

DeMaria, Rusel, 1948–
Working with dBase Mac.

Includes index.
1. Data base management. 2. dBASE Mac (Computer program) I. Fontaine, George R., 1960–
II. Title.
QA76.9.D3D455 1988 005.75′65 88–6111
ISBN 0-13-939760-4

Dedication

To our wives and families.

Acknowledgments

We want to thank the following people, whose contributions to our efforts have been salutary:

From Brady Books:

Janice Mandel
Meagan Calogeras
Maryjane Wraga
Michael Mellin

From Ashton-Tate—all of you helped us tremendously:

Tim Mitchell
Dennis Cohen
Larry Colker
Bill Jordan
Quinn Wildman
Kent Irwin
Ron Arons
Malcolm Hobbs

and especially Tom Bodine for technical review and for his great contribution of the NewCheck Project as well as numerous tips.

Limits of Liability and Disclaimer of Warranty

Trademarks

CONTENTS

Preface xix

Introduction xxi
What Is in this Book? xxi
Who Can Use this Book? xxiii
How To Use this Book xxiii
Recommended Hardware xxiv
Conventions Used in this Book xxiv

PART I
THE TUTORIAL

Chapter 1
Database Concepts 3
Overview 3
Introducing Databases 3
The Computer Advantage 5
Relational Databases 6
Field Types 8
Displaying and Reporting 9
Programming 10
Database Design 10

Chapter 2
A Quick Application 12
Overview 12
Loading dBASE Mac 13
Creating the File 13

Adding Data to the File 18
Viewing the Data 24
Mailing Labels 26
Summary 34

Chapter 3
dBASE Mac Structures 35
dBASE Mac Specifications 36
Ways to Communicate with dBASE Mac 36
Need Help? 38
Types of Files 39
Field Types 39
Field Data Types 39
Structure Window 41
Relationships 42
Preferences 43
Views 43
View Types 43
Define Hierarchy 45
Layout 46
Sorting and Selecting Records 50
Perform and Use 50
Procedures 50
The Project as an Application 52
Summary 52

Chapter 4
Creating dBASE Mac Files 53
Using the Tutorial 53
Overview 54
Special Instructions 54
Ways to Start dBASE Mac 54
Starting dBASE Mac 54
Creating a File 55
The Key Field 56
Defining Other Fields 57
Multivalued Fields and Sets 58
How Sets Work 59
Pattern Matching 60
Pattern Matching for the Phone Field 61
The Structure Window 65
The Palette 66
Selection—A Choices Field 67
A Quick View Form 68
Data Entry 70

Viewing Data 76
Deleting a View 77
Creating the Checkbook File 77
An Auto-Sequencing Key Field—Transaction Number 78
Field 2—Date—A Date Field 79
Field 3—Type—A Choices Field 81
Field 4—Check Number—A Numeric Field 83
Field 5—Description—A Text Field 85
Field 6—Check Amount—A Dollar Field 85
Field 7—Deposit Amount—A Dollar Field 86
Field 8—Memo—A Text Field 86
Field 9—Tax—A Logical Field 87
Field 10—Counter—A Memory Field 88
Field 11—Balance—A Memory Field 89
Field 12—Tot Check—A Memory Field 89
Field 13—Tot Dep—A Memory Field 90
Posting Data 90
Summary 92

Chapter 5
Creating Relationships 94
Overview 94
Creating a Relational System 94
A Timecard Project 94
Related Files—An Employee File 95
Employee Pic—A Graphics Field 97
Using Picture This . . . Desk Accessory 100
Amount Paid—A Number Field 101
Salary Earned—A Number Field 102
Current Amount Due—A Formula Field 102
Related Files—The Hourly Rates File 105
Related Files—The Timecard File 106
Timecard Number—A Key Field 106
Date—A Date Field 107
Two Time Fields—Time In and Time Out 108
Time Arithmetic—The Total Hours Field 110
Posting Amount—A Posting Field 112
Total Due—A Formula Field 112
Saving the Project 113
What Is a Relationship? 113
Creating Relationships 115
Finishing the Total Due Field 118
Posting to Another File 119
Creating an Index File 121
Removing a Field 129

Removing and Modifying Relationships 132
Saving Your Work and Quitting 133
Summary 133

Chapter 6
Creating Views—Hierarchies 135
Overview 135
The Define Hierarchy Palette 136
Mailing Labels Revisited 136
Creating a View Field 138
Procedures in the Hierarchy—Checkbook Entry 141
Creating a Hierarchy with Relationships 151
Summary 154

Chapter 7
Creating Layouts 155
Overview 155
The Define Layout Palette 155
Creating Mailing Label Forms 156
Working with a Column View 161
The Checkbook Layout 166
Show/Hide Hierarchy—Finishing Touches 172
Optional Graphics 176
Laying Out the Timecard 177
Hiding the Grid 180
Reducing the Form 180
Groups 181
Display Only Fields 181
Other Ideas 182
Summary 183

Chapter 8
Adding Records, Sorting, and Selecting 184
Overview 184
The Use Mode Palette 184
Manipulating Data in Form Views 185
Adding Data to Checkbook 186
Use vs. Perform and Use 186
Adding Records to Timecard 189
The Employee File 190
The Hourly Rates File 192
Sorting Records 196
The Sort Palette 196
Sorting 196

Special Instructions 197
Sort Example 198
Sorting a Multilevel Hierarchy 200
Sorting Rules 205
Selecting Records 205
The Define Selection Palette 205
Selecting Records 205
Optional Exercises 208
Using Snapshots 209
Summary 210

Chapter 9
Printing And Reporting With dBASE Mac 211
Overview 211
Printing to Document a Project 211
The Structure Window 212
Printing View Definitions 213
Printing Reports 214
Breaks 215
Accumulating Totals 217
A Cash Flow Report 218
MultiMail—Using Multivalued Fields 221
Multivalued Mailing Labels 222
Summary 225

Chapter 10
Procedures, The Custom Palette, and Custom Menus . . . 227
Overview 227
The Procedural Interface 228
Procedures 228
Elements of the Procedural Interface 230
Dialog Boxes 232
Dialog Box in a View Pre-Processor Procedure 232
Turn Trace On 236
Customizing the Palette 238
Removing an Icon 239
Adding an Icon 239
Finishing Touches—Custom Menus 240
Protecting a Project 244
Completing MultiMail 246
A Context-Sensitive Help System 248
Final Touches to MultiMail 257
Summary 258

Chapter 11
Transfer Views and Foreign Files 260
Overview 260
Transfer View 260
The Transfer View Layout 262
Transfer View—A Date Timecard File 266
Using the Date Transfer File 268
Deleting Selected Records 273
Batch Processing—An Inventory Example 275
Foreign Files 276
Creating a Foreign File Structure for Export 277
Creating a Transfer View to a Foreign File Structure 281
Importing Foreign Text Data into dBASE Mac 284
Importing dBASE II, dBASE III, and dBASE III Plus Files 286
Summary 286

Chapter 12
Finishing Touches—Romancing the Checkbook 288
Overview 288
The NewCheck Project—How Does It Work? 289
The Budget File 290
The Transactions File 292
The Items File 295
The Globals File 297
Relating the Files 297
Entering Budgets 298
The Main Menu View 303
Enter Transactions View 306
List Transaction View 321
Modify Transactions View 325
Reconcile View 334
Income Statement View 339
The States Project 349
Optimizing File Performance 357
Understanding File Statistics 357
Optimizing File Performances 359
Summary 360

Part II dBASE Mac Reference

dBASE Mac Reference 363
About dBASE Mac 363
Add Button 363
Add Field 363

Align to Grid 364
Apple Menu 364
Bring to Front 364
Change Field 365
Change File 365
Choices Field 367
Clear 370
Close DataFile 370
Close Project 370
Close View 371
Copy 371
Custom Menus 371
Cut 372
DataFile Menu 373
Data Type Field 373
Date Field 373
Define Selections 376
Define Sorts 377
Delete <name> 378
Delete File 379
Delete Record Procedure 379
Delete View 379
Design Menu 379
Dialog Boxes 380
Display Options 382
Duplicate File 383
Duplicate View 384
Edit Menu 385
Explode 385
Export 387
Field Definition 388
File Types and File Icons 389
File Size 390
Foreign File 390
Form Size 392
Formula Fields 393
Globals File 394
Graphic Fields 394
Help 398
Hierarchy 398
Icons and Pointers 402
Index Files 405
Insert <name> 407
Internal Index 407
Key Field 408

Layout 410
Logical Data Type 416
Memory Field 417
Menus 417
Modulo 418
Multivalued Fields 418
New File 420
New Project 420
New Record Procedure 420
New View 421
Next <name> 421
Number Fields 421
Open File 424
Open Project 424
Page Breaks 425
Page Setup 425
Palette 426
Paste 430
Perform and Use 430
Picture This. . . 431
Post-Processor 431
Posting 432
Pre-Processor 433
Preferences 433
Print 434
Prior <name> 436
Procedural Interface 436
Project Menu 442
Protect Project 443
Quick Create 444
Quit 444
Reduce to Fit 445
Relationships 445
Remove Field 448
Reorganize File 449
Reports 449
Restore Field 450
Revert 450
Rulers 450
Save 451
Save Us 451
Select All 451
Send to Back 451
Separation 451
Show Path 451

Show Procedure 452
Show Selections 452
Show Statistics 452
Show/Hide Grid 452
Show/Hide Palette 452
Snapshot 452
Structure Window 453
Tablets 454
Text Data Type 455
Time Field 456
Transfer View 457
Turn Trace On 461
Undo 462
Use 462
VMFF 463
View Menu 463
View Type 463
Windows Menu 464
Write Record Procedure 464

Part III Applications

Chapter 13
Introducing Applications 467
Applications Development 468
Designing an Application 468
The Applications Chapters 469

Chapter 14
A Comparative View of dBASE Mac and dBASE III and a Questionnaire Application 470
Comparing dBASE Mac and dBASE III 470
The Questionnaire Application 471
dBASE III File Listing 471
dBASE Mac Project Listing 501
Conclusion 518

Chapter 15
The MultiMail Project 519
MultiMail Project Listing 520

Chapter 16
The Checkbook Project 544

Checkbook Project Listing 545

Chapter 17
The Personnel Project 558
Timecard Revisited 558
Payroll Listing 560

Chapter 18
Freelance 613
The Tickler 613
Freelance Listing 615

Appendix A
Macintosh Conventions, Tips, and Techniques 647
Introduction to the Mac 647
Basic Equipment 647
Basic Terms and Techniques 649
The Cursor 649
The Finder 649
Icons 649
Mouse Techniques 649
Menus and Dialog Boxes 650
Desk Accessories and Fonts 651
Working with Windows 651
Working with HFS 652
File Naming Conventions 653
Edit Commands 654

Appendix B
Using the Keyboard and Other Tricks 655
The Keyboard 655
Other Tips 657

Appendix C
Other Resources 659
dBASE Toolbox 659
Getting the Picture 659
Operating Systems, Networks, and Add-Ons 660
Add-On Drives 662
Mac-VAX Connectivity 665
Mac-UNIX Connectivity 667
Mac-IBM Mainframe Connectivity 667
Other Sources 668

dBASE Mac/dBASE III Plus File Sharing 668
Exchanging Files Between dBASE III Plus and dBASE Mac 668
Importing the dBASE III Plus File into dBASE Mac 669
To Edit/Append Records in dBASE Mac 669
To Move Data Between dBASE Mac and dBASE III Plus 670

Index 673

PREFACE

dBASE Mac is a complex database product very different from its IBM cousins. With a heavy reliance on the Macintosh interface and a more localized programming approach, it presents unique challenges in the conceptualization and application of ideas. Like the other dBASE products, dBASE Mac can be used in a variety of ways.

Working with dBASE Mac is a powerful tool designed to help you get the most out of your database. Because it is a tutorial, a reference, and an application guide, this book is probably all you'll need to plumb the depths of dBASE Mac. Whether you are a computer novice, an experienced Mac user, a recent convert from the IBM world, or some combination of the above, you will be able to gain insight and information from this book.

Use it to learn dBASE Mac. The tutorial in Part I takes you from the very basic concepts of databases through complex procedures while you create several complete applications.

Use it as a reference. Part II is a complete alphabetical reference to dBASE Mac. Use it to find out how to use a command or procedure while you are developing your applications.

Use it as an application guide. Part III contains several complete application listings. Use these as guides to your own applications, or copy them without modification if they work for you.

Working with dBASE Mac is a versatile book. You can use it as you see fit, depending on your needs and your level of knowledge. Anyone, from novice to expert, can learn from this book.

INTRODUCTION

Welcome to dBASE Mac. Welcome to *Working with dBASE Mac.* You have in your hands the result of many months of involvement with dBASE Mac. Perhaps, like us, you first heard rumors that Ashton-Tate was creating a database product for the Macintosh more than a year (or two) ago. And, like us, you waited to see what the company with the most successful IBM database would do with the Mac.

We became so curious that we began digging around with friends and colleagues and got a look at an early beta copy of the program. We saw it for only a few minutes, but we could tell that dBASE Mac was going to depart from the programming-only style that had always typified dBASE products in the past.

We saw one thing immediately: dBASE Mac was truly a Macintosh product, and, as such, was probably going to appeal to a new group of database users. With that insight, the idea for this book was born.

Having read multitudinous user manuals, we knew that *Working with dBASE Mac* would have to be clear, organized, and complete, that it would need many examples and graphics, and that it should be application oriented—something that most user manuals are not.

We think we have created a book that anyone interested in dBASE Mac can use. Without hesitation, we recommend this book to computer novices and experienced users alike. The result of many months of involvement with dBASE Mac is in your hands. May it serve you well!

What Is In This Book?

Working with dBASE Mac is divided into three parts. Each part serves a unique purpose.

Part I contains twelve chapters. Chapter 1 introduces the idea that a database is a common, everyday item in our lives, and defines some of the terms and concepts of computer databases. Chapter 2 is a complete, by-the-numbers guide to creating a usable mailing label application. Just follow the instructions to create your first application. Chapter 3 is very special. It introduces the main concepts and structural elements of dBASE Mac in a single chapter. Use Chapter 3 to give you an overview of dBASE Mac.

Chapter 4 begins the applications development tutorial. You will recreate the file structure of the mailing label program from Chapter 2, but with some differences and with complete explanations of what you are doing. You will create the file structure of a more complex application, a personal Checkbook Project.

Chapter 5 introduces the third of the tutorial applications—a Timecard Project for tracking employee's hours and earned wages. The Timecard Project introduces several new files, and you learn about creating relationships between files, including one-way and two-way relationships and indexes. Moving toward a completed project, Chapter 6 introduces views, and shows how to create view hierarchies for the MultiMail, Checkbook, and Timecard projects.

Chapter 7 introduces the view layout. Here is where you begin to use the many graphic and visual elements of dBASE Mac. You begin by recreating the mailing labels from Chapter 2, then a more complex data entry screen for the Checkbook. You will lay out the Timecard Entry screen.

In Chapter 8, you begin data entry into the Checkbook and Timecard projects. You get to see the effects of special procedures created in earlier chapters, and you have the opportunity to catch a glimpse of the power to come. You'll learn to Sort the records in your databases, to Select specific records, and we'll take a look at Snapshots, too.

In Chapter 9, you explore printing with dBASE Mac. First you learn to print the various file, field, and view definitions as well as the layout and Structure Window graphics. You'll see reporting with dBASE Mac and create a simple report from the Timecard Project. You'll create a cash flow report from the Checkbook Project.

Chapter 10 introduces the dBASE Mac Procedural Interface. You'll learn where and when to write procedures, what kinds of procedures you can write, and what kinds of commands and functions are available. You'll create a simple procedure for a Checkbook data entry view and a more complex procedure to automate the selection of a city in the MultiMail project. Next, you'll create a context-sensitive help application and controlling menu structure for the MultiMail application—beginning the creation of a self-running turn-key system. You'll learn how to modify the Palette, and how to create Custom Menus and Protect a project to create a turnkey system.

Chapter 11 introduces the Transfer View, a method for moving and reorganizing data between files. You'll use the Transfer View to create a special new file for the Timecard Project, and you'll use that file to create a statistical report using the Timecard data. We also discuss batch processing with Transfer Views, and introduce foreign files and detail the basic methods for creating them. You'll export data from the Checkbook file to an ASCII file, and then import the ASCII data back into dBASE Mac. You'll also learn about importing dBASE II and III files.

Chapter 12 concludes the tutorial. You'll use all that you have learned to create a truly sophisticated NewCheck Project. NewCheck includes budgets and split transactions, error checking procedures, a procedure for reconciling the Checkbook, and, finally, a procedure for producing income statements for any time period. The last part concludes the tutorial with a look at how to maximize the efficiency of your files.

Part II of *Working with dBASE Mac* is an alphabetical reference to the commands and features of the program. Use this reference as a day-to-day guide to using dBASE Mac.

Part III consists of five chapters. Chapter 13 introduces the Applications section of dBASE Mac. It discusses the methods used to document and re-create applications, and it states the goals of the Applications section of the book.

Chapter 14 is a special chapter that creates the same application, a questionnaire, in both dBASE III and dBASE Mac. The dBASE III code is fully annotated to provide dBASE III users with an easy conversion between the two programs.

Chapter 15 contains the complete final listing for the MultiMail project created in the tutorial. Chapter 16 contains the complete listing for the Checkbook Project.

Chapter 17 contains some ideas for additions to the Timecard Project as well as a complete listing of a modified version of that project.

Appendix A is a brief guide to using the Macintosh. It is especially aimed at the new user or converts from other systems.

Appendix B lists the various keyboard commands available in dBASE Mac, and also suggests some interesting Macintosh tips and techniques.

Appendix C lists some special resources you might need to make complete use of dBASE Mac.

Who Can Use This Book?

You can use this book if you:

- Are a new Mac user looking for a good database product
- Have purchased dBASE Mac and want to get the most out of it
- Are thinking about purchasing dBASE Mac
- Are an IBM user who wants to make use of the unique features available in dBASE Mac
- Are a dBASE II or dBASE III programmer and want to know what dBASE Mac is all about

How To Use This Book

Working with dBASE Mac is organized in a unique manner. Anyone can get what he or she wants from it without reading everything. To get the most from this book, read this section.

Special ways to use this book:

- For new Mac users, first read Appendix A, then begin with Part I, Chapter One.
- For converts from other systems who are already familiar with database concepts, read Appendix A, then begin with Part I, Chapter One. Later, read Appendices B and C.

- If you are a dBASE III programmer, Part III, Chapter Two is of special interest to you.
- If you already have a working knowledge of dBASE Mac, you may still learn something by reading Part I, Chapter Three and Chapters Ten through Twelve, and by working with the Applications in Part III. You can use the Reference in Part II as needed.

The tutorial can be read two ways. You can follow along, chapter by chapter. That is the best way. Or you can begin one application and skip to the next chapter where that application is further developed. A message will guide you to the next chapter where the application is continued.

Recommended Hardware

You can use dBASE Mac with a Mac Plus and dual floppy disks. We recommend, however, that you use a hard disk system to get the most out of the program. Also, performance is much more delightful on a supercharged SE or a Mac II.

Conventions Used In This Book

For an understanding of basic Macintosh terminology, see Appendix A. If you understand these basic Macintosh terms and techniques, there is nothing very tricky or confusing about the way this book is written.

PART I

THE TUTORIAL

1

DATABASE CONCEPTS

Overview

Chapter 1 looks at databases as a common and familiar part of our lives, and uses ordinary items like a telephone number card file and a telephone book to illustrate database principals. Database terminology is introduced, and certain concepts unique to dBASE Mac are illustrated throughout the chapter.

The first part of this chapter is for the newcomer to databases. It explains in simple, mostly nontechnical terms what a database is. The second part of the chapter may be of interest to newcomers and experienced users alike because it hints at the unique qualities of dBASE Mac.

Introducing Databases

Databases have actually been around for a long time. The first shepherd who inventoried his flock by making scratches on a rock was, in effect, creating a database. Medieval lords who kept tax rolls on their serfs were also keeping a database. Scientists like Galileo and da Vinci kept organized records to support their findings. Wine makers kept records of vintages and quantities. Kings kept records of their royal wealth. All these lists and records were databases.

Databases are very familiar in modern life as well. A telephone book—which is really an alphabetical collection of names, addresses, and phone numbers—is a database.

Next to your telephone you may have a card file. Look at how it is organized. First there is the file itself—a collection of individual cards sorted alphabetically (probably by last name). Each card contains complete information about one individual. On each card are separate bits of information: name, address, phone number, and maybe a note or two about the person.

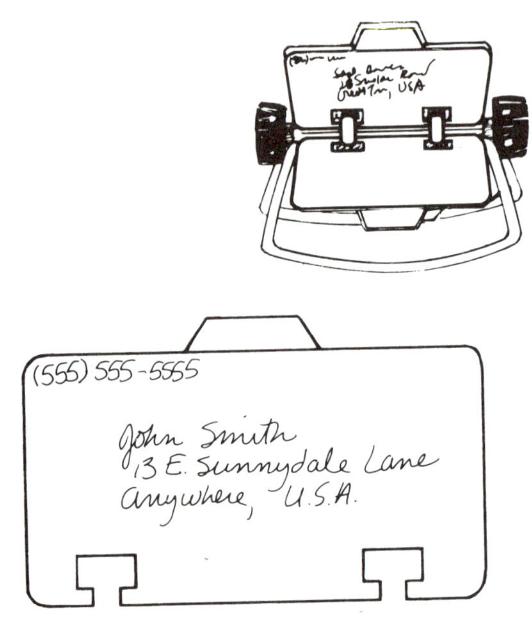

Figure 1-1 Card File Graphics.

If you look at the card file as a database, then you really only need to learn a few new terms to grasp what a computer database is.

Computers keep files, too. Where the card file is a collection of cards, a database **file** is a collection of individual **records**. Database records, like card file cards, contain complete information about a single event or thing.

Separate entries tend to be the same from card to card. For instance, each card contains a name (first, last, and possibly a middle initial), probably an address (street address, city, state, zip code), and almost certainly a phone number.

In the computer database, each separate element of the record is called a **field**. A field might be a first or last name, a city, state, or zip code; or it might be a date, an amount owed, even a calculation of sales tax on an invoice total.

In summary, a computer database is a collection of fields that make each record, and a collection of records that make a file.

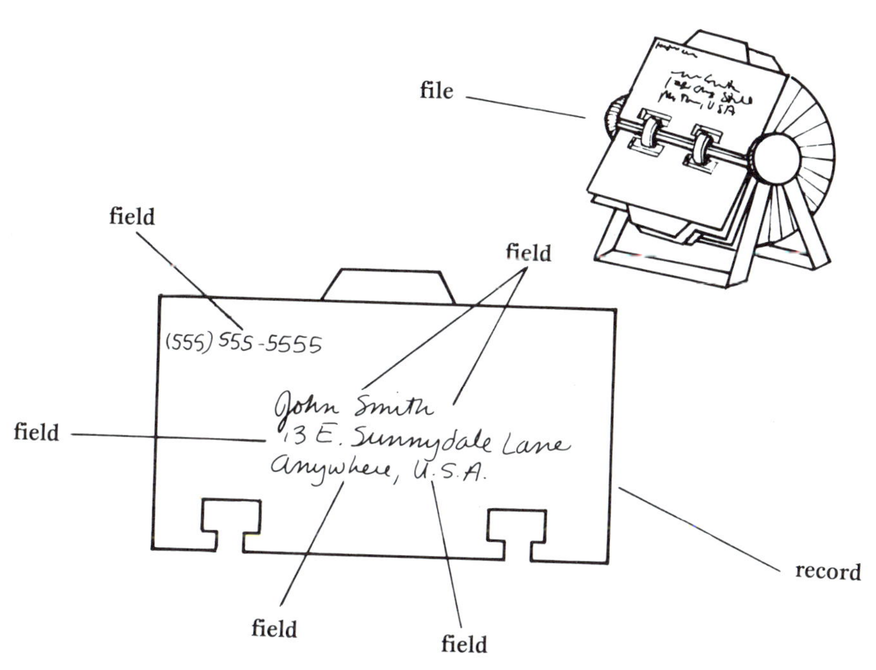

Figure 1-2 Diagram of Fields Records File.

The Computer Advantage

Computer databases begin to differ from noncomputer databases in the way they perform. Computer databases are **dynamic**. You can **sort** information in a computer database in many different ways. In addition, you can change information, calculate mathematical formulas, and manipulate information almost without limit and with ease.

Imagine trying to reorganize your card file so that it was sorted by the city each person lived in, or the state. It would take you a long time to remove the cards, sort them, and then replace them in the new order. A computer database can accomplish the same result in seconds. Sorting a computer database is usually a simple task of deciding which field is to be sorted, and whether it should be **ascending** (A to Z) or **descending** (Z to A).

You can also design multilevel sorts. Imagine that you want to sort a mailing list first by state, and then, within each state, you want to sort by zip code. The state field is the **primary sort field**. The zip code field is the **secondary sort field**. If necessary, you can sort a computer database to many levels.

State	Zip Code	Last Name	First Name	Street	City
CA	90502	Goodman	Bob	2560 Blue Ave.	Torrance
CA	91722	Condie	Steve	676 Legal Lane	Covina
CA	91722	Fern	Mel	2160 Rose St.	Covina
CA	91722	Fern	Melvina	2160 Rose St.	Covina
CA	94704	Bach	John	418 Brandenbe...	Berkeley
CA	94704	Goodman	James	123 Rose Ave.	Berkeley
CA	94704	Shakespeare	Bill	19 W. Avon Pl.	Berkeley
CA	94706	Smith	John	124 Maple Street	Glenview
NY	10018	Moto	Esther	1218 Secret Dr...	New York
NY	10018	Moto	Frank	1218 Secret Dr...	New York
NY	10023	Bacon	Frank	32 Covington St.	New York
NY	10075	Bacon	William	84 W. 89th	New York
NY	11378	Sandeine	Bart	15 Benthys St.	Maspeth
UT	84057	Keats	John	61 Songbird Lane	Orem
UT	84167	Shelly	Mary	13 Science Dr.	Provo

Figure 1-3 Sort and Subsort Graphic.

In addition to sorting information, a computer database can instantly extract specific information—all the people in your list whose first name is Joe, for instance, or those who live on Maple Street (or those people whose first name is Joe AND live on Maple Street). The criteria by which the computer chooses specific records is called the **selection criteria** or the **filter**. Selection criteria often use logical operators to define selections. For instance, to find all people with the first name Joe, you might instruct the database to find if "First Name = Joe". But if you wanted to find all people whose names began with P, Q, or R, you might write "First Name > O AND First Name < S". This reads First Name is greater than O (P is greater than O), AND First Name is less than S (R is less than S). Names like Penelope, Robert, and Quincy would be found, but Sam, Annabelle, and Xavier would not.

A computer database containing your financial records could tell you instantly how much you paid last year on heating bills, what the average monthly payment was, and what months you paid the largest and the smallest bills. A business database program could tell you what items were in inventory and automatically set reorder points for items whose stock was low.

When you perform calculations on information in a database, you use a combination of standard mathematical operations and field names. For instance, to calculate the tax on a sub-total, you might write the **formula**, "Sub-Total * Tax Rate" (or "Sub-Total * .06" if your tax rate is six percent).

Relational Databases

Computer database files can also share information between them. Imagine being able to look in your checkbook register (another database) and have the card file or phone book automatically open to display the address and phone number of each payee. Or you might look in your card file and see a list of all checks written to a particular person over the last year. A computer database can perform this sort of cross-referencing quickly and easily.

Computer databases that share information between files are called **relational databases.** In a relational database you keep separate files that are linked by common information.

A simple example of a relational database is a parts ordering application. Suppose you own the Progresso Hardware Store, and you use the computer to reorder items from inventory. You have a file called Inventory that contains a list of parts. Each part in the inventory has a unique part number, description, cost, and so on.

Inventory

Part Number	Part Name	Cost	Price
100	5" Screwdriver	0.94	150.00
110	8" Screwdriver	1.28	2.14
120	5" Philips	0.96	1.64
130	8" Philips	1.31	2.23
140	Socket Wrench set	39.52	97.50
150	Small Pliers	1.48	2.75
160	Large Pliers	2.25	4.09
170	Vice Grip Pliers	5.77	7.88

Figure 1-4 Inventory Table.

Another file is called Order Forms. Each order form is actually one record in the file. One of the fields on the Order Forms file is called Part Number. Other fields share information with the Inventory file, such as cost of part, description, and so on.

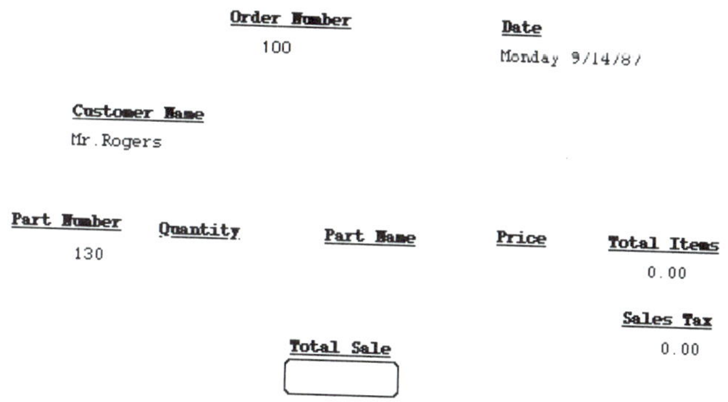

Figure 1-5 Parts Order Form Graphic.

When you enter a part number on the order form, the relational database looks for that same number in the Inventory file. When it finds a match, it retrieves the pertinent information and inserts it in appropriate fields on the Order form.

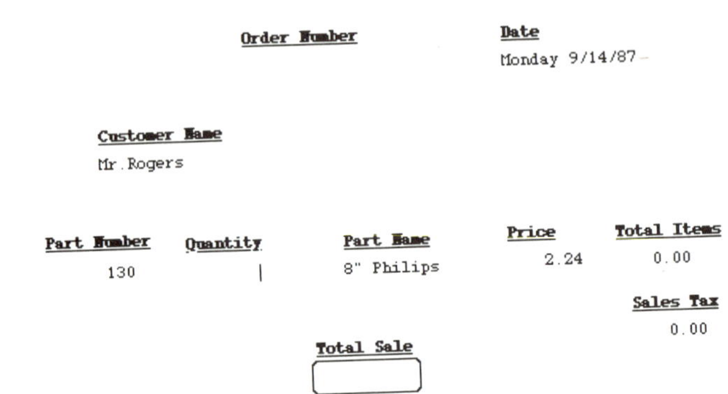

Figure 1-6 Filled-In Graphic.

You have only to fill out the quantity to order. A special **formula** field then calculates the Quantity Ordered times the Cost of the item to produce the Amount of the total order.

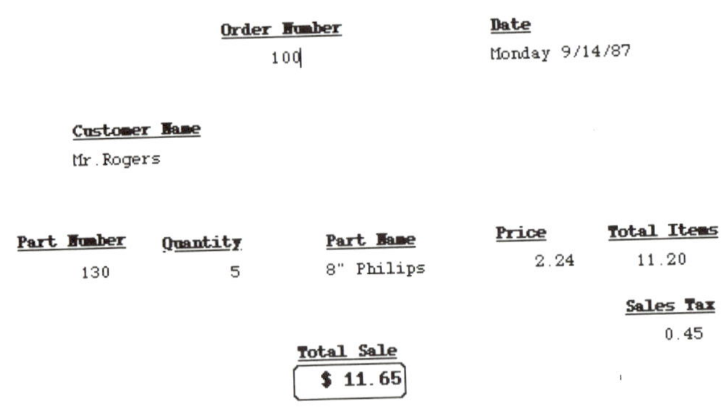

Figure 1-7 Calculated Graphic.

You might have another database structure that retrieves the vendor name and address from a relationship created between the parts in the Inventory file and the vendors in the Vendor file. Thus, by inserting a part number on the order form, the program might fill in the part information and the vendor information automatically.

Field Types

A computer database needs to know something about the information contained in a field. For instance, the computer treats text (which it calls **strings**) differently from the way it treats numbers.

Some databases have special kinds of fields for dates, time, and other kinds of information. Such special fields only accept information in valid **formats**. For instance, a date field could not accept a street address or an invalid date (Dec. 32, 1961, for instance). A number field usually cannot accept anything but numbers (and sometimes symbols for currency). Text fields usually can accept any input, but cannot perform mathematical calculations on numbers.

Input to any field can be limited or controlled by means of **edit masks**. An edit mask may limit input to certain types of characters (text only, numbers only, etc.), or it may allow the insertion of default, or automatic, information. For instance, a date field may allow you to type in only numbers (i.e., 021487), inserting the slashes automatically (result: 02/14/87). Edit masks are useful because they make data input easier, and they often help prevent typographical errors. dBASE Mac calls edit masks **matching patterns**, and can include them as part of a field's definition.

dBASE Mac has some additional types of fields called **Memory Fields, Formula Fields, Graphic Fields, Choices Fields,** and **Logical Fields**. For more on dBASE Mac field types, see Chapter 3, **dBASE Mac Structures**, or see Part II, **dBASE Mac Reference**.

In most databases, each field contains one, and only one, piece of information. For instance, the telephone number field in the card file example would contain just one telephone number. But many people and businesses have more than one number. dBASE Mac allows what are called **multivalued** fields.

Multivalued fields can contain many distinct items. In the case of the phone number, each record in the file could contain several phone numbers—if you make the phone number field multivalued.

Another unique feature offered by dBASE Mac is a way to line up the values in two or more multivalued fields within the same record by putting them in **sets**. Sets cause individual occurences within two or more multivalued fields to become associated with each other for each individual record.

Displaying and Reporting

The information in a database is only useful if you can display and print it the way you need it. There are essentially two ways to display information—as a **list** (several records) or as a **form** (one record at a time). When you display the contents of a database in list format, you see the values of each field listed in columns, side by side. For this reason, a list format is often called a **columnar** format. In a columnar format, each record is represented in a single row of the list. In a database form, only one record is displayed on screen. Forms can contain a great amount of information, and can be organized like paper forms. They offer greater flexibility in displaying information whereas a columnar format allows you to view many records at one time.

dBASE Mac calls each display format a **view**. The arrangement of fields and other elements (fixed text, boxes and other graphics, etc.) is called a layout. dBASE Mac allows both column- and form-type layouts.

The output, or report, is the proverbial bottom-line. It may be all the contact with a database that many people will ever have. They may have no interest in field types or file relations. They judge a database largely by how well it provides the information they need. The report is the medium for providing that information.

Reports, like database display, are based on lists or forms. A list-based report might be a parts list, an employee list, a sales transaction report, the phone book, or a check register. A form-based report might be a 1040 form, an invoice, a card-file card, or an individual printed check.

Reports can include summary information like totals, subtotals, averages, and other statistical information. You can instruct the database to print out information in discrete units. For instance, suppose you were printing out a summary of monthly sales, and you wanted the summary organized by salesperson with subtotals for each. You would first sort the file by salesperson, then instruct the database to print a subtotal whenever the salesperson's name changed. In computer terms, you would instruct the database to issue a **control break** each time the value of the Salesperson field changed.

Reporting and displaying database information is generally handled through layout and form generators. dBASE Mac includes a powerful layout section that utilizes the graphic ability of the Macintosh. For more on layouts, see Chapter 3, "dBASE Mac Structures," and Chapter 7, "Creating Layouts."

Programming

The role of programming in database design depends on the database software you use. Some database software is almost entirely programming oriented. To create anything, you must be able to write a set of computer instructions—a program.

Other database software lacks a programming language altogether. Although it may be easier to work with such a program initially, you may not be able to perform some tasks due to limitations within the database.

dBASE Mac uses programming for certain aspects of application development. For instance, you use a program to create specialized error checking and to control program flow. You can also use programs (called **procedures**) to perform very complex series of events displaying dialog boxes and offering many choices to the user. All of the applications in this book use procedures to automate certain processes, to control program flow, or to maintain data integrity. For instance, one procedure helps you find mailing list records for certain cities. Another helps you reconcile your checkbook.

One very important use of procedures is to help create an application that anyone can use easily, without having to know the database commands themselves. This is especially important in office situations where many people may need to use a database, but not all of them will understand how the software works. An application that can be used by anyone without really having to use the design portion of the database software is called a **turnkey system**. You can use dBASE Mac to create turnkey systems through the use of procedures and views.

Database Design

Designing a database can be complex. You must decide what information is needed, how much can be calculated from other data, how to organize it, and how to relate information in several files (in a relational system). In addition, you must design data input forms, data retrieval views, sorts, selections, formulas, controlling procedures, and reports.

There are several ways to approach database design. Some are very methodical, others are "seat of the pants" methods. One good way is to work backwards, starting with the reports you will need to create. Knowing what data will be needed on reports can often help you assess what data will be needed within the database, as well as how that information might be structured. This method is especially useful when you are converting a paper-based system to a computer system. You may be able to create a close simulation of the paper system input and output methods while taking advantage of the computer's increased speed and convenience features.

You should also look at the input side. If you know what information you generally record, that may be another good place to start. Remember that the computer can perform calculations for you, so you may only need to enter the raw data—letting the computer take over much of your former work.

In a relational database like dBASE Mac, you can divide data in logical ways. One of the clearest examples of a relational database can be seen in a small retail invoicing system. For instance, you might create one file of employee names and addresses, another for vendors, and a third for customers. Still other files might contain inventory information, and possibly discount rate tables for quantity orders. An invoice file might then use information from several of these files in creating an individual invoice. The salesperson's name is drawn from the employee file, the customer's name, address, and credit information are from the customer file, the product information from inventory, and the discount rate from the discount table based on the quantity of the purchase. Another relationship, between inventory and vendor files, is used when filling out purchase orders.

Other applications may be best if data are divided into related files. Determining the best method depends on how the data are to be used. Sometimes a table of information is used to modify other information (as is the case with the discount rate table mentioned above). The data in a file may be used in many other ways. For instance, the employee file mentioned above is used to provide the salesperson's name to the invoice, but it is also used by payroll and personnel applications, and to produce mailing labels.

In any case, there is no one right way. Whatever works best for you is the best way. It takes experimentation to achieve optimal results. A program like dBASE Mac leaves a lot of room for experimentation, and certainly you are ready to begin. In Chapter Two, you'll get a chance to develop a simple dBASE Mac application, called a **project**. Enough theory, already. It's time to get started!

2

A QUICK APPLICATION

Overview

Chapter 2 is for the impatient and intuitive reader. You will create a mailing label application in dBASE Mac. This is a hands-on chapter, and you should perform the steps that follow on your computer.

Because this is still an introductory chapter, you will be asked to perform many unfamiliar dBASE Mac commands. There will be very little explanation of these commands. That comes later. But you will have the opportunity to see the program in action.

Creating a dBASE Mac application involves several specific steps:

1. Loading dBASE Mac
2. Creating the File(s)
3. Adding Data to the File(s)
4. Viewing the Data
5. Reporting

Follow the procedures outlined for each step to create a finished application. A detailed tutorial with full explanations of all procedures is presented in Chapters 4 through 12.

> NOTE: If you are new to the Mac, you may want to review Appendix A, "Macintosh Tips and Techniques," since some knowledge of Mac procedures is assumed in this chapter and the chapters that follow.

dBASE Mac

Loading dBASE Mac

To begin dBASE Mac, double-click the dBASE Mac icon on the Finder.

If this is the first time you have opened dBASE Mac, fill in the requested information, including the serial number from your master disk. Use the **Tab** key to move from field to field. When you have entered all the data, press **Return**.

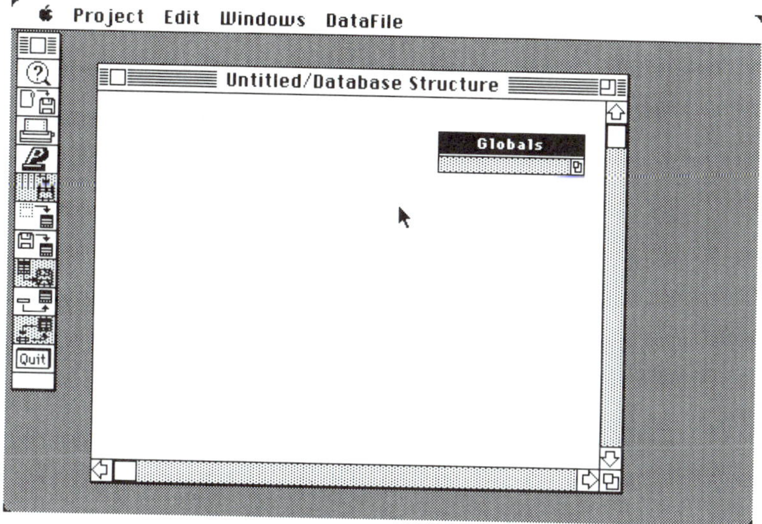

Figure 2-1 New Structure Window Graphic.

After the program has loaded, you will see the Structure Window. At the top of the window should be a label that says "Untitled." This indicates that you have opened a new dBASE Mac application.

Creating the File

Creating a file involves creating a file structure, then creating and defining the individual fields in the file.

1. Open the DataFile menu and select New. . . .

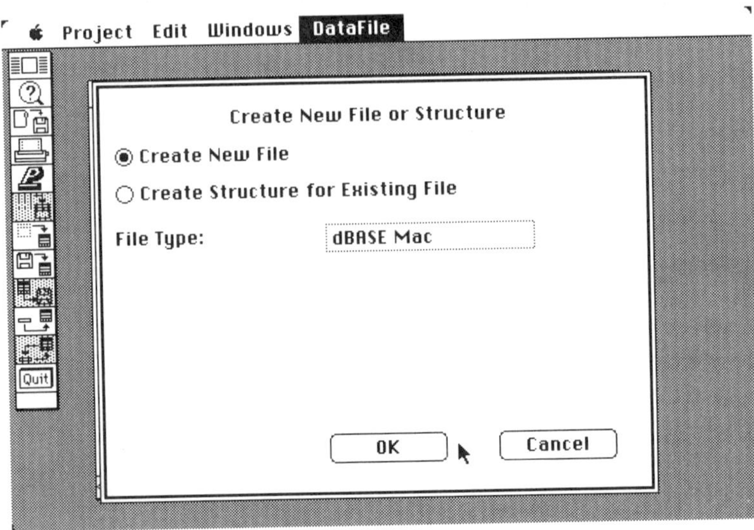

Figure 2-2 New File Dialog Box 1 Graphic.

2. You want to leave the information on the initial dialog box unchanged, so click **OK**, or press **Return**.

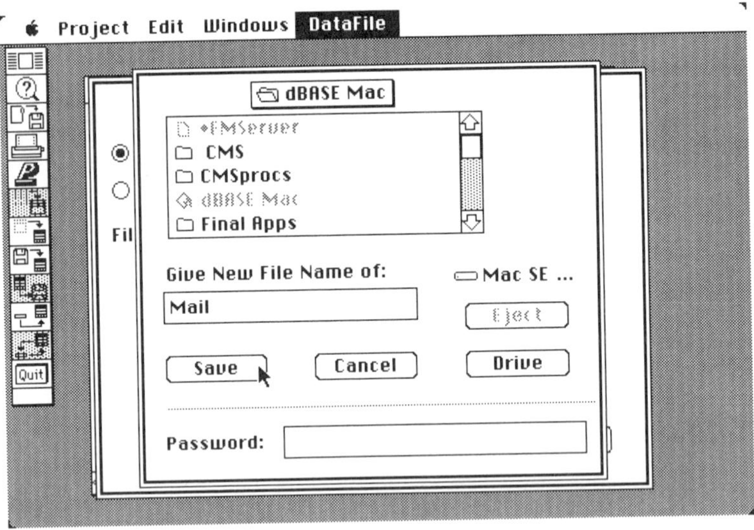

Figure 2-3 Name File Dialog Box Graphic

3. The dialog box that follows contains a text box for the file name. Type *Mail*.

4. Click **Save** or press **Return** to accept the title and leave the rest of the dialog box unchanged.

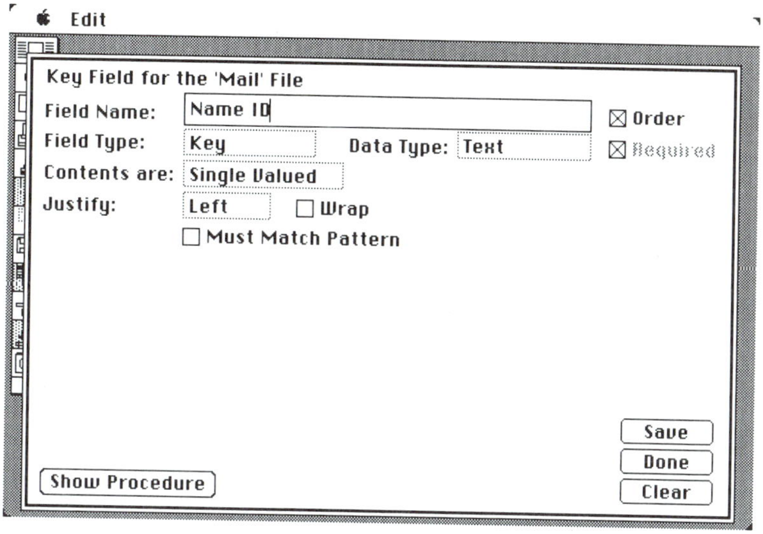

Figure 2-4 Key Field Definition Graphic.

The next dialog box is the Key field definition box. The Key field is necessary to allow dBASE Mac to identify individual records within a database. The first field created must be the Key field of the file. The first step in defining a Key field is to give it a name:

5. Type "Name ID"

6. Leave the rest of the box unchanged. At the bottom-right corner, click **Save** or press **Enter** to save the Key Field definition.

What follows is a series of field definition boxes. The fields in the Mail file are simple Text fields. You need only name and save each field definition. Follow the directions to finish the field definitions:

HINT: You may press the **Enter** key instead of clicking the **Save** button. There is a difference between the **Enter** key and the **Return** key in this instance.

7. Type "First Name" and click **Save**.

8. Type "Last Name" and click **Save**.

9. Type "Street" and click **Save**.

10. Type "City" and click **Save**.

11. Type "State" and click **Save**.

12. Type “Zip Code” and click **Save.**
13. Type “Phone Number” and click **Save.**
14. Now click **Done.**

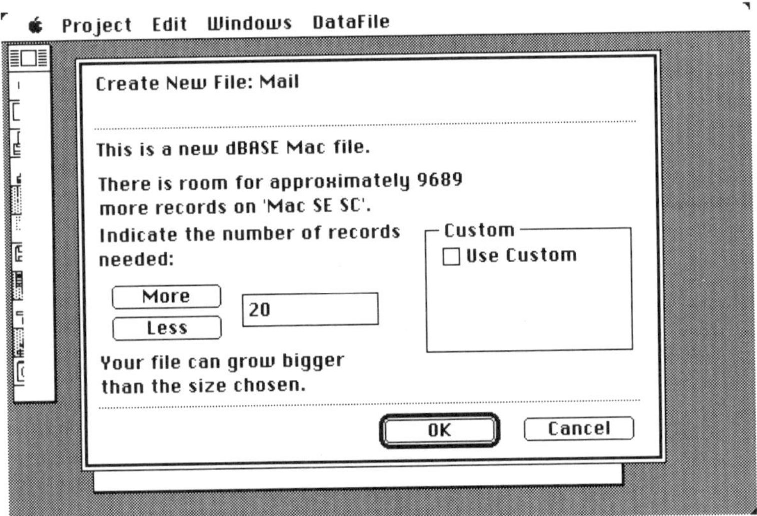

Figure 2-5 Set File Size Dialog Box.

dBASE Mac wants you to estimate the size of your file. Space is allocated on the current disk drive to accomodate the number of records you estimate. Don't worry, though. You'll be able to add as many records as you need.

15. This dialog box asks you to approximate the number of records your new file will contain. For now, enter 20 and press **Return** or click **OK.**

You should return to the Structure Window after a moment. Note the new file on the screen.

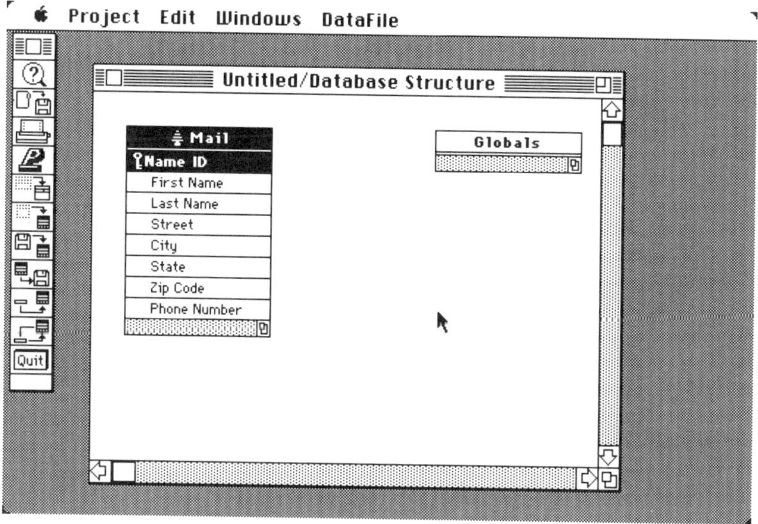

Figure 2-6 Structure Window with Mail File.

You can add a field after completing the initial definitions. Suppose you forgot to include a Comments field.

16. Open the DataFile menu and select Add Field. The familiar field creation box appears.

17. Type "Comments", click the Wrap check box, and click **Save**.

    The Wrap checkbox allows you to create a field with the same text wrapping qualities as a word processor. This kind of field is often used to contain free-form text entries.

18. Click **Done**.

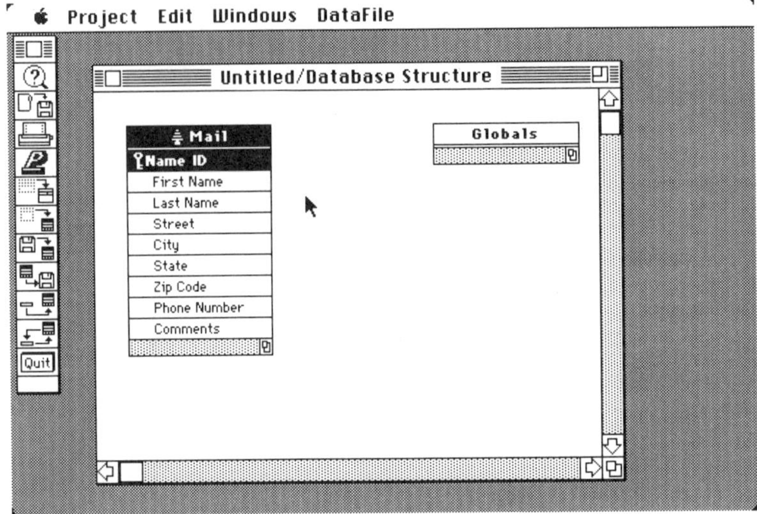

Figure 2-7 Structure with Comments Added Graphic.

The new field, Comments, has been added to the Mail file.

Summary:

1. Select New. . . from the DataFile menu.
2. Click **OK** or press **Return**.
3. Type "Mail"
4. Click **Save** or press **Return**.
5. Type "Name ID"
6. Click **Save** or press **Enter**.
7. Type "First Name" and click **Save**.
8. Type "Last Name" and click **Save**.
9. Type "Street" and click **Save**.
10. Type "City" and click **Save**.
11. Type "State" and click **Save**.
12. Type "Zip Code" and click **Save**.
13. Type "Phone Number" and click **Save**.
14. Click **Done**.
15. Enter *20,* then click **OK** or press **Return**.
16. Select Add Field from the DataFile menu.
17. Type *Comments,* click the Wrap check box, and click **Save**.
18. Click **Done**.

Adding Data to the File

Now that you have created a file structure, you must enter data. To do so, you will need a data entry form that contains all the fields in the file. A data entry form is a specific type of Form view. To create a Form view:

1. Open the Windows menu and select New View. . .

NOTE: If New View is dimmed, click once on the word *Mail* at the top of the file structure, then try again.

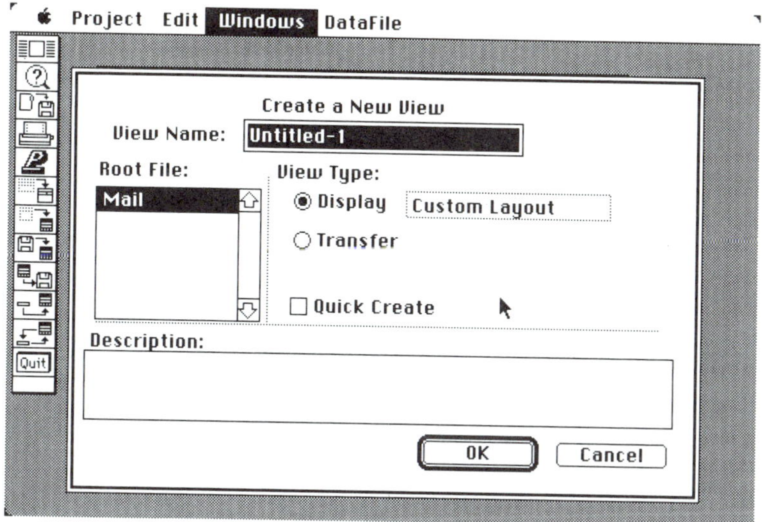

Figure 2-8 New View Dialog Box.

2. Enter a view name.

   Type "Mail List Entry"

3. Place the cursor where it says Custom Layout and press and hold the mouse button. Notice that a pop-up menu appears. Drag the mouse down until Form Layout is highlighted, then let go. The window should close, still displaying Form Layout. If it did not, try again.

4. Click the mouse in the box next to the words *Quick Create* (or anywhere on the words *Quick Create*). An X should appear in the box.

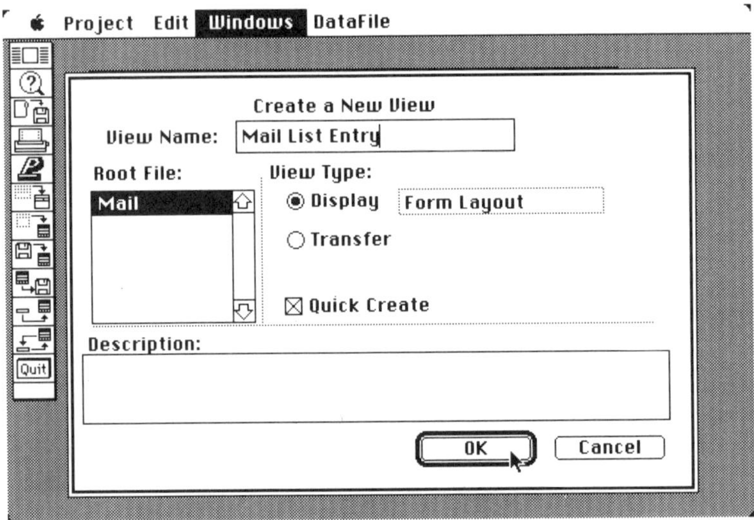

Figure 2-9 Create Form View Graphic.

5. If your screen looks like the screen in Figure 2-9, click **OK** or press **Return.**

   After a few moments you should see a list of fields from the Mail File.

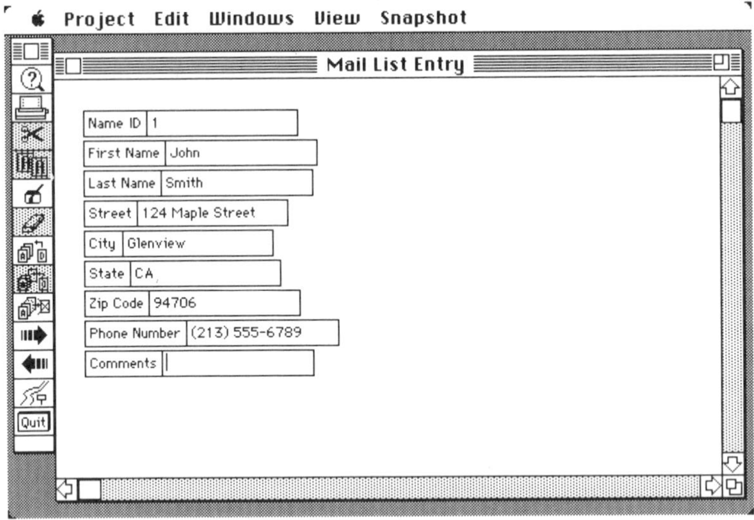

Figure 2-10 Mail Form Layout Graphic.

6. Begin filling out the first record. Press the **Tab** key after each entry. Do not type the quotes.

Type "1" (press **Tab**)
Type "John"
Type "Smith"
Type "124 Maple Street"
Type "Glenview"
Type "CA"
Type "94706"
Type "(213) 555-6789"

Leave the Comments field blank. You have just filled in the information for a record. To tell the program to save the record, press the **Enter** key.

Fill in the following names and addresses. Remember to press **Tab** after each entry, and to press **Enter** after each record is complete. You can, if you wish, enter information into the Comments field. (The Comments field is completely optional, and leaving it blank won't make any difference at this point.) You will use these names and addresses later in the tutorial.

Name ID: **2**
First Name: **Mel**
Last Name: **Fern**
Street: **2160 Rose Ave.**
City: **Covina**
State: **CA**
Zip Code: **91722**
Telephone: **(818)555-1212**

Name ID: **3**
First Name: **Frank**
Last Name: **Bacon**
Street: **32 Covington**
City: **New York**
State: **NY**
Zip Code: **10023**
Telephone: **(212)555-6789**

Name ID: **4**
First Name: **Bill**
Last Name: **Shakespeare**
Street: **19 W. Avon Pl.**
City: **Berkeley**
State: **CA**
Zip Code: **94704**
Telephone: **(415)555-6543**

Name ID:	5
First Name:	Frank
Last Name:	Moto
Street:	1218 Secret Drive
City:	New York
State:	NY
Zip Code:	10018
Telephone:	(212)555-9988

Name ID:	6
First Name:	Steve
Last Name:	Condie
Street:	676 Legal Lane
City:	Covina
State:	CA
Zip Code:	91722
Telephone:	(818)555-6767

Name ID:	7
First Name:	Bart
Last Name:	Sandeine
Street:	15 Benthys St.
City:	Maspeth
State:	NY
Zip Code:	11378
Telephone:	(718)555-1213

Name ID:	8
First Name:	Bob
Last Name:	Goodman
Street:	2560 Blue Ave.
City:	Torrance
State:	CA
Zip Code:	90502
Telephone:	(213)555-8686

Name ID:	9
First Name:	John
Last Name:	Keats
Street:	61 Songbird Lane
City:	Orem
State:	UT
Zip Code:	84057
Telephone:	(801)555-6868

Name ID:	10
First Name:	Mary
Last Name:	Shelly
Street:	13 Science Dr.
City:	Provo
State:	UT
Zip Code:	84167
Telephone:	(801)555-1313

Name ID:	11
First Name:	John
Last Name:	Bach
Street:	418 Brandenburg Ave.
City:	Berkeley
State:	CA
Zip Code:	94704
Telephone:	(415)555-2435

Name ID:	12
First Name:	William
Last Name:	Bacon
Street:	84 W. 89th
City:	New York
State:	NY
Zip Code:	10075
Telephone:	(212)555-3213

Name ID:	13
First Name:	James
Last Name:	Goodman
Street:	123 Rose Ave.
City:	Berkeley
State:	CA
Zip Code:	94704
Telephone:	(415)555-4343

Name ID:	14
First Name:	Esther
Last Name:	Moto
Street:	1218 Secret Dr.
City:	New York
State:	NY
Zip Code:	10018
Telephone:	(212)555-9988

Name ID:	**15**
First Name:	**Melvina**
Last Name:	**Fern**
Street:	**2160 Rose Ave.**
City:	**Covina**
State:	**CA**
Zip Code:	**91722**
Telephone:	**(818)555-1212**

Summary:

1. Select New View. . . from the Windows menu.
2. Type "Mail List Entry"
3. Select Form Layout from pop-up menu.
4. Click the Quick Create checkbox.
5. Click **OK** or press **Return**.
6. Fill in records. Press **Tab** to move between fields and **Enter** after each record.

Viewing the Data

After you have entered some data into your new file, you may want to see the records together. To see the information all together, create a Column view.

1. Open the Windows menu and select New View. . .
2. Name the view "Mailing List Columns".
3. Complete the dialog box the way you did before, but this time, select Columnar Layout from the pop-up menu.
4. Click the Quick Create checkbox.

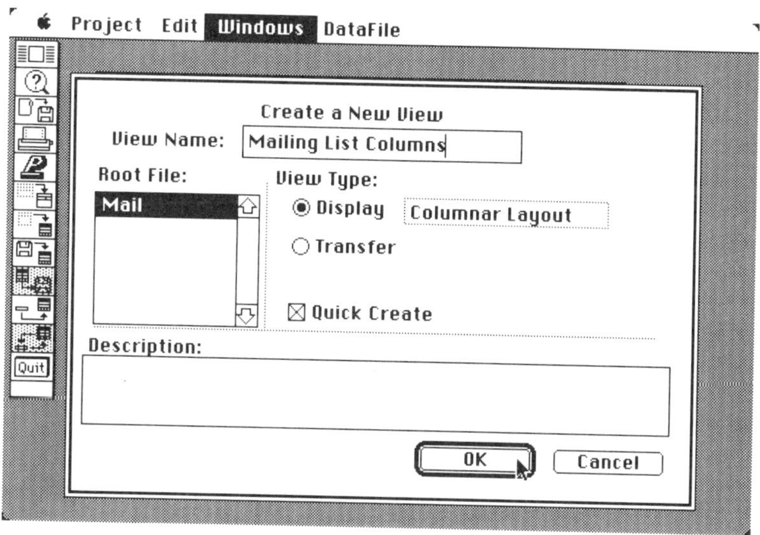

Figure 2-11 Column Quick Create Graphic.

5. If your screen looks like the one in Figure 2-11, press **Return** or click **OK**.

   A Column view appears on the screen.

6. To see your records, open the View menu and select Perform and Use View. dBASE Mac will load all your records into memory and display them on the screen.

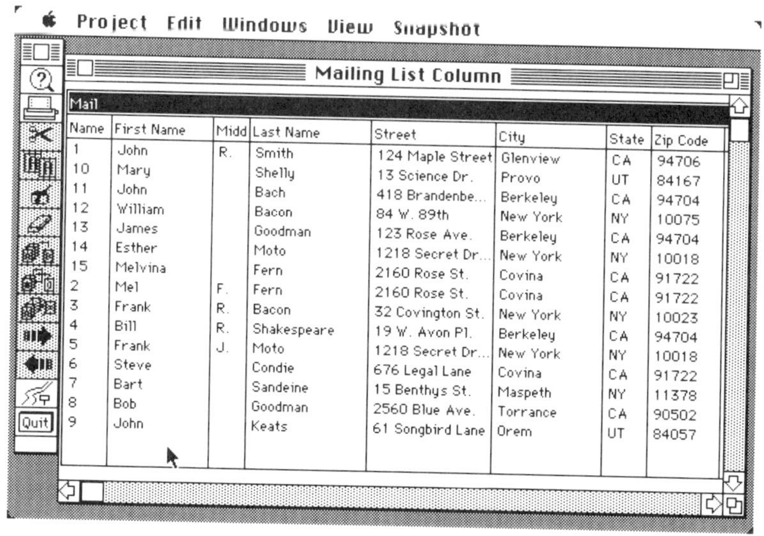

Name	First Name	Midd	Last Name	Street	City	State	Zip Code
1	John	R.	Smith	124 Maple Street	Glenview	CA	94706
10	Mary		Shelly	13 Science Dr.	Provo	UT	84167
11	John		Bach	418 Brandenbe...	Berkeley	CA	94704
12	William		Bacon	84 W. 89th	New York	NY	10075
13	James		Goodman	123 Rose Ave.	Berkeley	CA	94704
14	Esther		Moto	1218 Secret Dr...	New York	NY	10018
15	Melvina		Fern	2160 Rose St.	Covina	CA	91722
2	Mel	F.	Fern	2160 Rose St.	Covina	CA	91722
3	Frank	R.	Bacon	32 Covington St.	New York	NY	10023
4	Bill	R.	Shakespeare	19 W. Avon Pl.	Berkeley	CA	94704
5	Frank	J.	Moto	1218 Secret Dr...	New York	NY	10018
6	Steve		Condie	676 Legal Lane	Covina	CA	91722
7	Bart		Sandeine	15 Benthys St.	Maspeth	NY	11378
8	Bob		Goodman	2560 Blue Ave.	Torrance	CA	90502
9	John		Keats	61 Songbird Lane	Orem	UT	84057

Figure 2-12 Column View Graphic.

In later chapters you will learn how to modify the appearance of the Form and Column views.

Summary:

1. Select New View. . . from the Windows menu.
2. Type "Mailing List Columns"
3. Select Columnar layout
4. Click the Quick Create check box.
5. Click **OK** or press **Return**.
6. Select Perform and Use View from the View menu or click the Perform and Use icon in the palette.

Mailing Labels

The main purpose of this application is to print mailing labels. To do that, you must create another view. This time you will not use the Quick Create option, but will create the view hierarchy and layout from beginning to end. The view hierarchy is used to select those fields to include in a view. The layout places the selected fields in appropriate positions for display and printing.

1. Select New View. . . from the Windows Menu.

   Although you need not change anything, be sure the words *Custom Layout* are displayed in the View Type: pop-up menu.

2. Name the view "Mailing Labels" and press **Return** or click **OK**.

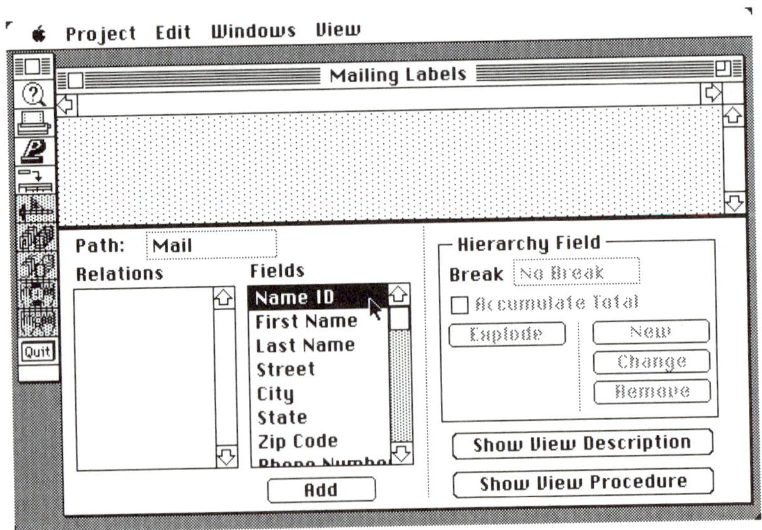

Figure 2-13 Hierarchy Definition Screen.

3. The Define Hierarchy screen appears. At the bottom of the screen is a list box that contains all the field names for the Mail file.

4. Click the Mouse on Name ID in the field list box. Then click **Add** (or double-click the Name ID field). Note that the Name ID field appears at the top of the screen.

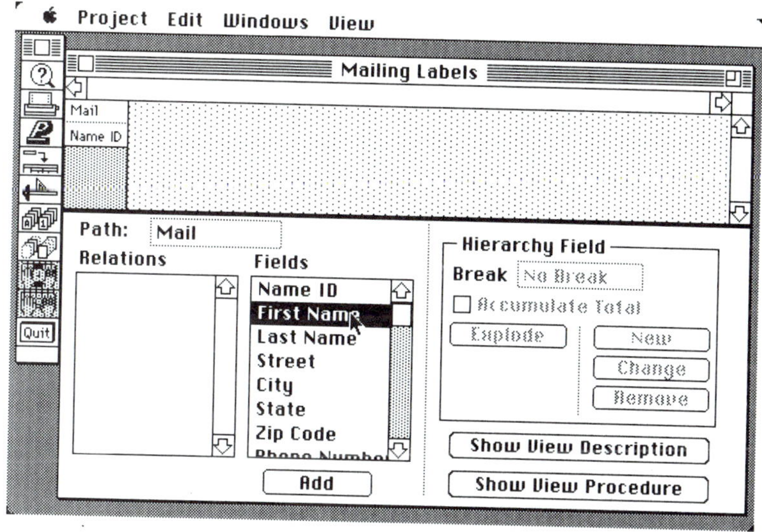

Figure 2-14 Hierarchy With Name ID Added.

5. Now click on each of the field names in turn and click **Add** (or double-click each name).

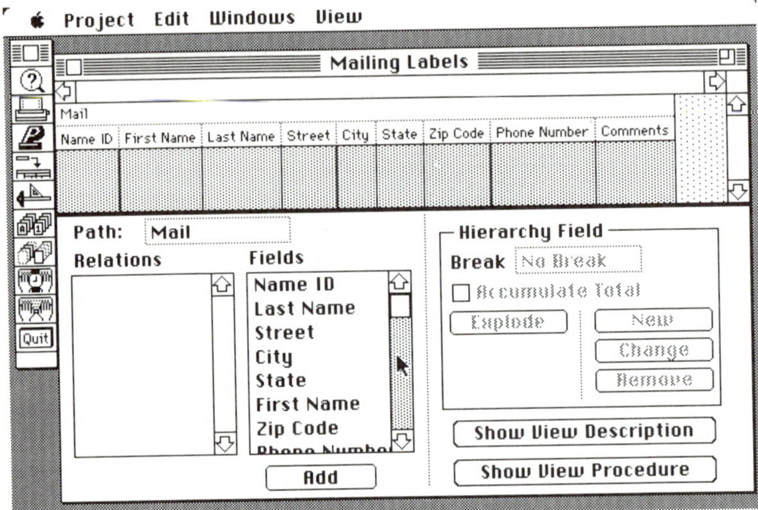

Figure 2-15 Completed Hierarchy Graphic.

Your screen should look like the screen in Figure 2-15.

6. Now you will have to create two special fields, called View Fields. They are specific to the current view only.

   a. Click the **New** button on the right side of the screen.

NOTE: If the **New** button is dimmed, click once on the Name ID field in the hierarchy (see Figure 2-15), then click **New**.

   A new field dialog box appears. Call this field Full Name.

   b. Type "Full Name"

   c. Click on the **Show Formula** button.

   A new dialog box appears.

   On the formula screen you will create a formula that displays the first and last names without extra spaces between them.

7. Double-click on First Name in the field list box, then type :" ": (colon quote space quote colon). Now double-click on Last Name. The resulting formula should read:

```
{First Name•Mail}:" ":{Last Name•Mail}
```

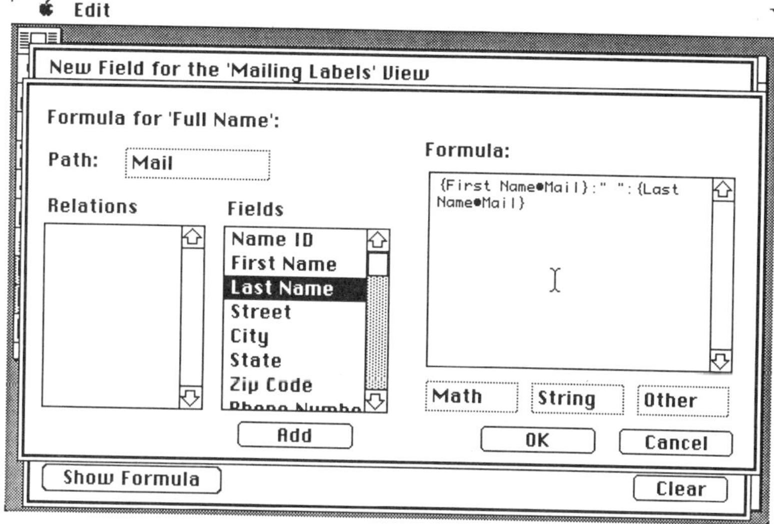

Figure 2-16 Formula Screen Graphic.

8. If your screen looks exactly like the screen in Figure 2-16, click **OK** or press **Return**.

9. Now click **Save** or press **Enter** to save the Full Name field definition.

Next you will create a special view field to concatenate (string together) the City, State, and Zip Code fields.

10. Name the next field *Address,* then click **Show Formula.**

11. Double-click City, type :", ": and double-click State. Type :" ": again and then double-click Zip Code. The formula should read:

```
{City•Mail}:", ":{State•Mail}:" ":{Zip Code•Mail}
```

Don't forget the comma!

12. Click **OK** or press **Enter.**

13. Click **Save,** then **Done** to return to the hierarchy screen.

You have just created a view hierarchy.

14. Now select Layout View from the View menu.

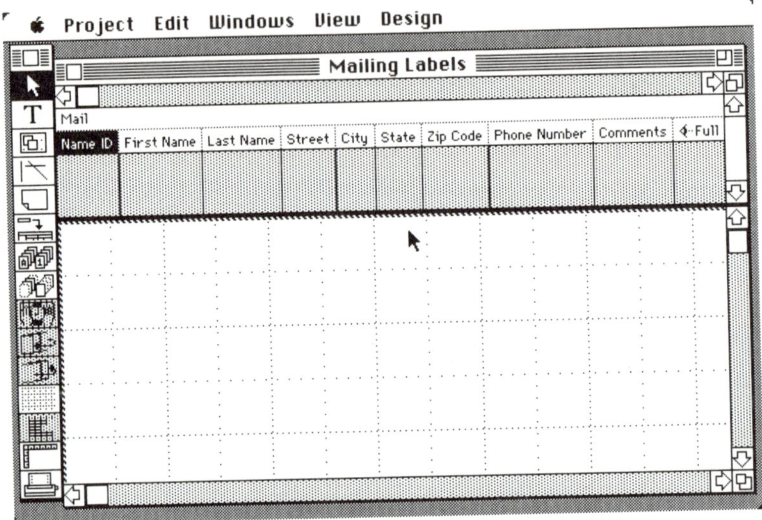

Figure 2-17 Layout View Graphic.

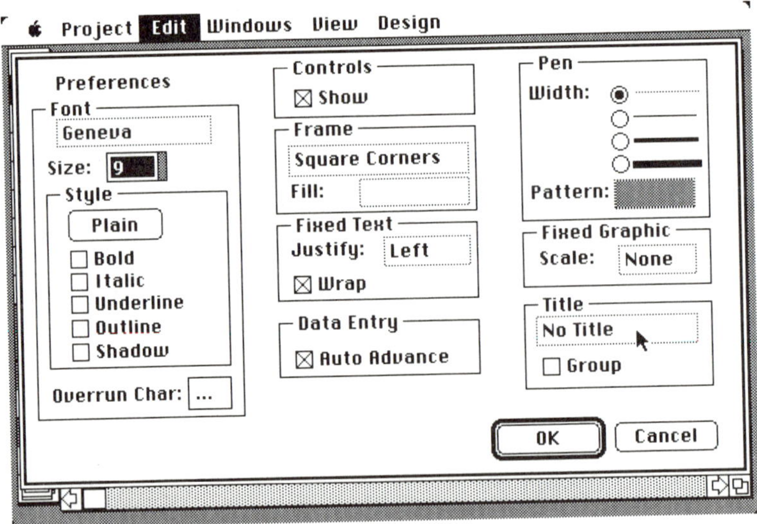

Figure 2-18 Preferences Graphic.

15. At the top of the screen you will see the hierarchy you just created. Before you begin to design the layout, open Preferences. . . from the Edit menu.

Change the **Pen Width** choice to the thin grey box (the one at the top-right corner of the dialog box). Then, under Titles, select "No Title". The screen should look just like the screen in Figure 2-18. Click **OK**, or press **Enter**.

Now you need to tell dBASE Mac what size to make the labels, and how many should print across the page.

16. Open the Form Size option from the Design menu. A pop-up menu contains various possible widths and lengths. Select a size that conforms to the size of your labels, such as 3 inches × 1-7/16 inches.
17. How many labels will you print across a single page? Enter that number in the **Number of Forms Across Page** text box.
18. Click **OK** or press **Enter** to return to the layout screen.
19. You should be back at the layout screen. Now highlight the Full Name field in the hierarchy and drag it down onto the design area (the gridded area below the hierarchy).

NOTE: You may have to scroll over to the Full Name and Address fields. To do so, use the scroll bar at the top of the screen.

20. Next highlight the Street field and drag it down beneath the Full Name field. Try to line it up the way you would like to see it on a mailing label.
21. Finally, drag down the Address field and place it beneath the Street field.

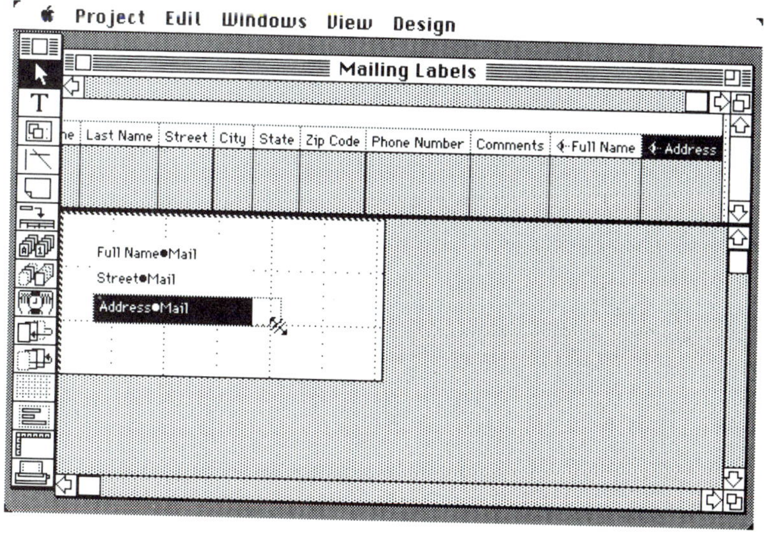

Figure 2-19 Sizing the Fields Graphic.

NOTE: You may need to resize the fields. To do so, click once on the field you wish to size and then place the cursor at the lower-right corner of the field. The cursor shape changes as in Figure 2-19. Drag the mouse to lengthen the fields.

HINT: To lengthen all the fields at once, click anywhere on the form outside the fields, then drag a box around all of them. When they are all highlighted, size one field. All the fields will be sized at the same time.

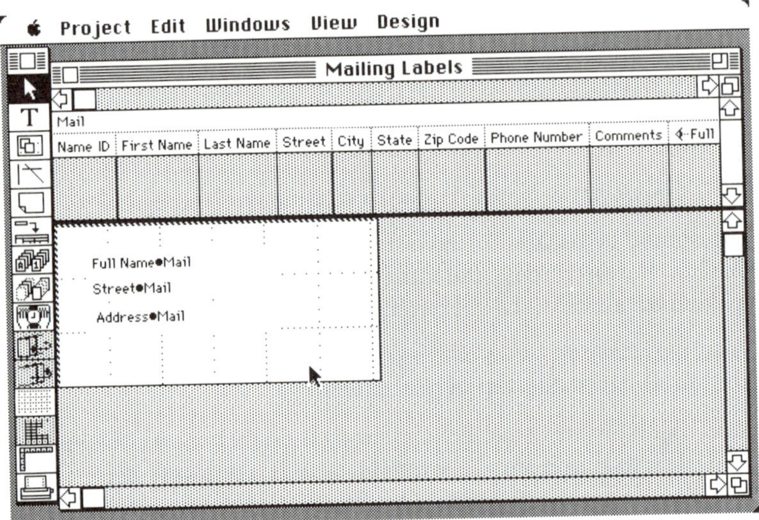

Figure 2-20 Layout Graphic.

The screen should look like the one in Figure 2-20.

22. Now select Perform and Use View from the View menu, or from the Palette.

23. Select Print Report from the Projects menu. *Be sure your printer is on,* fill in the printer dialog box, and click **OK**.

You have just created your first dBASE Mac application. To save the work you have done, select **Save** from the Projects menu and call the application, Mailing List Project. Click **OK**.

In the future, to load the Mailing List Project, double click the Mailing List Project icon on the Finder desktop.

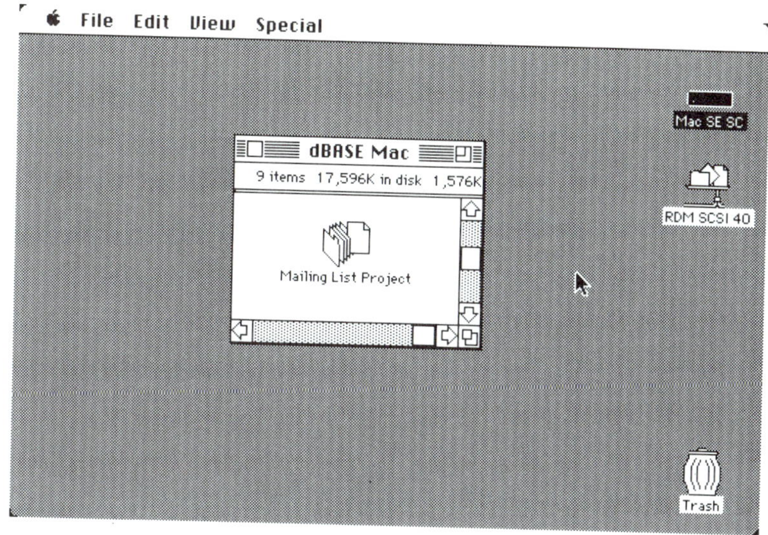

Figure 2-21 Finder Showing Mailing List Project Icon.

Summary:

1. Select New View. . . from the Windows menu.
2. Type "Mailing Labels" and click **OK** or press **Return**.
3. Examine Define Hierarchy screen.
4. Click on Name ID in the field list box, then click **Add**.
5. Click on each name in turn, then click **Add**
6. If necessary, click once on the Name ID field bar.
   a. Click **New**.
   b. Type "Full Name"
   c. Click **Show Formula**.
7. a. Double-click First Name in the field list box.
   b. Type :" ": (colon quote space quote colon)
   c. Double-click Last Name in the field list box.
8. Click **OK** or press **Return**.
9. Click **Save** or press **Enter**.
10. Type "Address" and click **Show Formula**.
11. a. Double-click City.
    b. Type :", ": (colon quote comma space quote colon).
    c. Double-click State.
    d. Type :" ": (colon quote space quote colon)
    e. Double-click Zip Code.
12. Click **OK** or press **Enter**;
13. a. Click **Save** (**Enter**).
    b. Click **Done** (**Enter**).
14. Select Layout View from the View menu.

15. a. Open Preferences. . . from the Edit Menu.
    b. Change **Pen Width** to thinnest choice.
    c. Under Titles, select No Title.
    d. Click **OK** or press **Enter**.
16. Select Form Size from the Design menu. Select a size.
17. Enter number of labels in Number of Forms Across Page box.
18. Click **OK** or press **Enter**.
19. Click on Full Name and drag it onto the layout area.
20. Drag and align the Street field.
21. Drag and align the Address field.
22. Select Perform and Use from the View menu (or from the Palette).
23. Make sure printer is on. Select Print Report from the Project menu. Click **OK** when ready to print.

Summary

In Chapter 2 you have created a complete and useful dBASE Mac application in five basic steps. The main elements of a dBASE application are:

1. Loading dBASE Mac.
2. Creating the File(s).
3. Adding Data to the File(s).
4. Viewing the Data.
5. Reporting.

To create a view, you must:

1. Name the view.
2. Define the view type.
3. Create the hierarchy.
4. Create the layout.
5. Perform or Use the view.

Chapter 3 contains an overview of the structures that comprise the dBASE Mac program. Read this chapter to gain an understanding of the various parts of the program you will be using. Chapter 4 begins the hands-on tutorial with complete explanations and step-by-step procedures.

3

dBASE MAC STRUCTURES

Chapter 3 presents an overview of the entire dBASE Mac program, concentrating on special structural elements. An understanding of the structure of a dBASE Mac application is essential to full utilization of the program. Use this chapter as a very short reference section. For further information on each topic, see Part II, **dBASE Mac Reference**, and work through the tutorial that begins in Chapter 4.

This chapter is a "what is" chapter. It tells you about the structural elements in dBASE Mac. It is not a "how to" chapter. It does not attempt to tell you how to use these elements. You will learn to use them beginning in Chapter 4.

- dBASE Mac applications are built on a foundation of database files. Information flow is controlled in part through interfile relationships. Entering, viewing, moving, and reporting data are handled through dBASE Mac Views. Each view is made up of a hierarchy definition, a layout, and associated procedures.
- Procedures play an important role in the control of the data and the display. There are several types of procedures.
- An entire collection of files, relationships, views, and procedures is called a **project**. Opening a project icon from the Finder opens all associated files, relationships, and so on.

Project

NOTE: Any individual file may be used by more than one project.

dBASE Mac Specifications

A database program like dBASE Mac is more than just a collection of commands and structures. It is a gestalt, an entire collection of features and options that, taken as a whole, becomes a distinct product with its own strengths and weaknesses.

On the other hand, a database program is also a set of raw capabilities that determine its limits. This section is designed to present the quantitative dBASE Mac.

- Maximum of sixteen files open simultaneously.

NOTE: A theoretical limit of twenty-six open files exists, but sixteen is the practical limit. This figure may vary as Graphic fields, views, and indexes are added to the project.

- Maximum file size is limited to disk space available.
- Maximum number of records per file is limited by disk space available.
- Maximum 32,000 byte record size (theoretical limit).
- Maximum 32,000 byte field size (theoretical limit).
- Maximum 16,000 fields per record (theoretical limit).
- Maximum 16,000 occurrences per field (multivalued fields) (theoretical limit).
- Maximum 255 characters per multi-valued occurrence or single valued field.
- Number of sort levels is eight per sort definition criterion.
- Nineteen digits numerical precision (including decimal point).
- Report widths limited to: 48 inches x 96 inches (same as Mac Draw).
- Recognizes five file types: dBASE Mac, ASCII text, dBASE II, dBASE III, and dBASE III PLUS.
- Seven field data types: Text, Number, Date, Time, Graphic, Logical, and Choices.
- One hundred sixteen commands or functions in Procedural Interface.

Ways to Communicate with dBASE Mac

Menus Menus are familiar to all Macintosh users. The pull-down menus in dBASE Mac operate just the same as the menus in other applications. The basic technique is to place the mouse over the menu heading desired, then press the button and drag the cursor to highlight the desired command. Release the button to execute the command.

Another kind of menu is the pop-up menu. This may be less familiar. It looks just like a text box, but its edges are grey, signifying that there is information contained beyond the borders of the box. To view the pop-up menu's contents, click on the contents of the box, then drag the cursor to the desired selection. Pop-up boxes are very common throughout dBASE Mac.

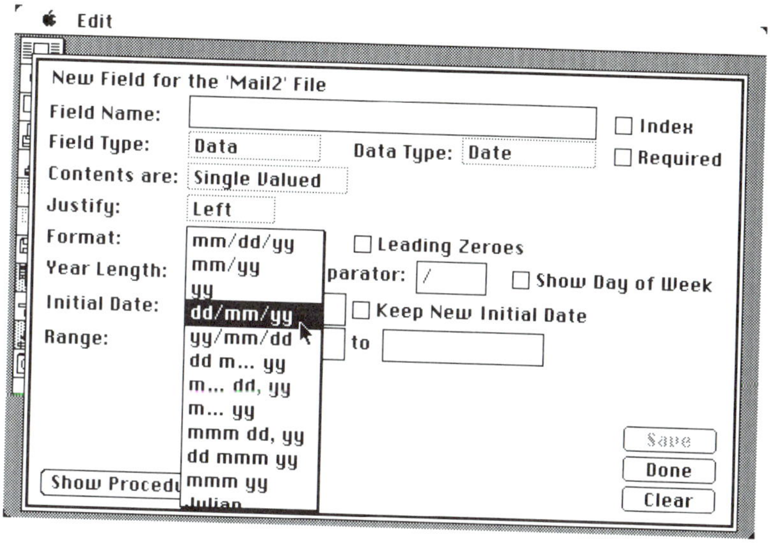

Figure 3-1 Pop-up Menu Graphic.

Dialog Boxes Throughout dBASE Mac, dialog boxes are used to interact with the user. These can be simple boxes asking you to confirm an action by clicking on one of two buttons, or they can be complex forms with many different elements. Dialog boxes can have buttons, check boxes, radio buttons, text boxes, and pop-up menus.

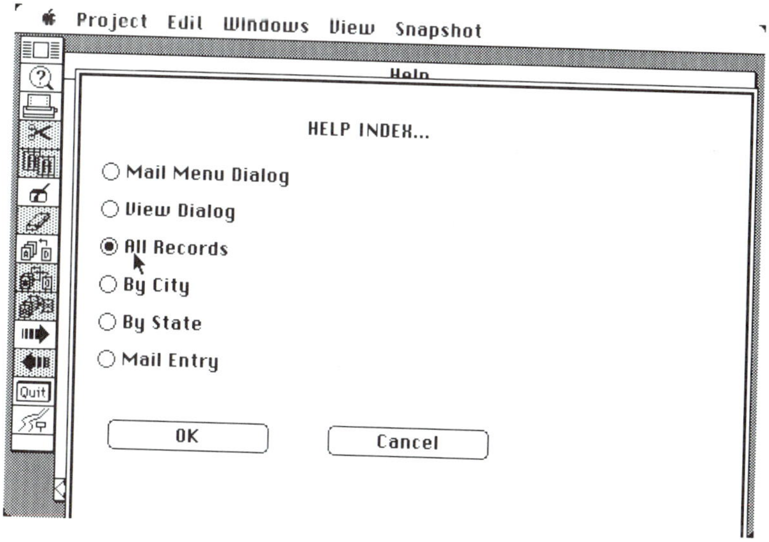

Figure 3-2 Button Graphic.

Buttons Buttons are special controls that execute immediately when they are clicked. The standard **OK** and **Cancel** buttons in most Macintosh applications are good examples.

Radio Buttons Radio buttons are small, round buttons that allow you to select options or values in a dialog box. Only one radio button in a set of radio buttons can be clicked at one time.

Checkboxes Checkboxes are used to select certain values or options. Several checkboxes can be clicked in one dialog box. The difference between radio buttons and checkboxes is that only one radio button in a set of associated buttons can be chosen. Any number of checkboxes may be selected.

Edit Text Boxes Text boxes allow you to enter text directly. A standard text cursor is displayed in text boxes, and you can move the insertion point from one text box to another by pressing **Tab**.

The Palette The Palette is a special window containing icons, most of which echo commands from the main menus. Learning to use the Palette effectively can speed up your interaction with dBASE Mac. You can modify, add, or delete the Palette icons. The default Palette is different for each section of dBASE Mac.

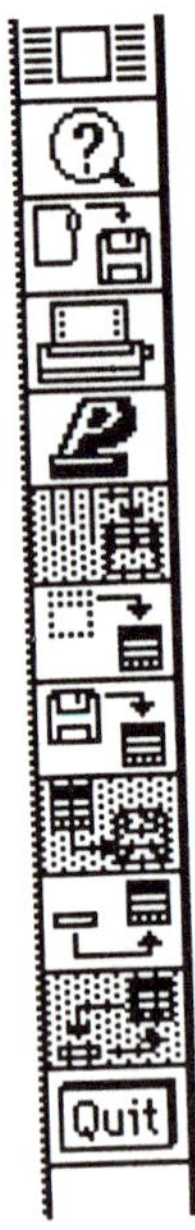

Figure 3-3 Sample Palette Graphic.

Need Help?

dBASE Mac Help is available from the Apple menu as a Desk Accessory. Select the topic that interests you from the Topic list, then read the associated text. Help is available during most operations.

Types of Files

dBASE Mac creates its own unique file types. In addition, it can utilize so-called foreign files—ASCII text files, and dBASE II and dBASE III files.

Whatever the file type, you must create a structure. If the file is foreign, you must define record size (fixed or variable), field delimiters, and end-of-record markers.

The most important part of the file structure is the field definition. Within the field definition you create a framework for the data you will process.

You can create four field types and seven data types.

Field Types

Key Field A unique field type reserved exclusively for the first field defined. The Key field contains only unique entries and is used by dBASE Mac to identify each record. A Key field can be a Text, Number, Time, or Date data type.

Data Field A field that contains ordinary data to be saved for each record in the file. Each Data field contains one or more values to be saved with the current record.

Formula Field A field that contains the results of some calculation process involving other fields and constants. Formula fields may contain results of string concatenation (combining text), numeric calculation, or even calculations on times or dates. A Formula field is evaluated at the time the fields it references are displayed, printed, or modified.

Memory Field A field that contains one value for the entire file, not just for one record. A Memory field may be used to hold a running balance, as a counter field (for sequential numbering), or as a place holder referenced while processing any record in the entire file. Memory fields are most useful for passing information from one view or file to another. A special type of Memory field—the Globals Memory field—resides in the Globals file. Information in a Globals Memory field is available to any file or view in the project.

Field Data Types

Text Field Text fields can accept letters, numbers, or symbols. Text fields commonly contain names, addresses, comments, and so on. They can also take seemingly numeric data like phone numbers, zip codes, and even dates and times. Text fields can use pattern matching to validate the data entered, and to make data entry easier by automatically adding constant data (like the slashes in a date, i.e., 8/12/87). They can also be set to wrap, center, left- or right-justify text within a data entry or display box.

Number Field Stores numeric data that need to be treated as numbers—such as dollar amounts, quantities of items, ages, and so on. Number fields can be formatted for several different display options. Number fields cannot accept nonnumeric entries like letters or symbols other than special symbols for currency. You can Post number field values to other fields. Use Posting with Memory fields or other Numeric fields to accumulate values positively or negatively.

Date Field Stores date information. Date fields can be set up to display data in a variety of formats. Many date formats are mutually compatible, so that a date entered in a format different from the one designated in the field definition will be automatically changed. Use caution when entering dates that may not be compatible. For a chart listing compatible and noncompatible formats, see the dBASE Mac User Manual.

Time Field Stores time information. Time fields, like Date fields, can be set up to display information in different formats. All time formats are compatible, but not all formats contain the same amount of information. Therefore, converting between formats may cause loss of minutes or seconds from the time value if the internal value is not used.

Graphic Field Stores graphic information. Graphic fields can store pictures and graphs entered by means of the Clipboard. You can use the Picture This. . . desk accessory or any other picture grabbing Desk Accessory to capture graphics, then paste them into a graphics field. You can set the display size, and also select various scaling options for Graphics fields.

Logical Field Stores one of two possible internal values: either "T" for true or "F" for false. These values are represented by the external field definition as logical pairs such as Yes/No, On/Off, True/False, and so on. You can set your own custom values or select from the preset values. Logical fields may be used in procedures or formulas as follows:

```
IF {logical field} THEN
```

which causes the true portion of the IF statement to execute if the value in the Logical field is True (On, Yes, etc.), and does not if the value is False (Off, No, etc.). Logical fields can display as a checkbox, pop-up windows, text boxes, or horizontal or vertical radio buttons.

Choices Field Stores the value selected from a list of possible predefined choices. Choices fields can display as pop-up windows, horizontal or vertical radio buttons, or a text input area. Keyboard entry is not allowed in a choice field unless the format is a text area, in which case the keyboard entry must exactly match one of the valid choices.

Any Field Data Type can be multivalued. This means that the field can store more than one value per record. Examples of multivalued fields include phone lists where some people on the list have more than one phone number, or a field containing the names of someone's children, which would often contain more than one value. One of the most important uses of multivalued fields is in Pointer fields, which are special fields created to contain information for related files.

The following table illustrates what kinds of data types the four field types can contain:

Field Type	Data Type
Key	Text, Numeric, Date, Time
Data	Any
Formula	Any
Memory	Any

Structure Window

Whenever you finish defining a file, you return to the Database Structure Window. The Structure Window graphically displays the file structures for a dBASE Mac project. Each file is represented by its own box. Each field is represented as a band within the box.

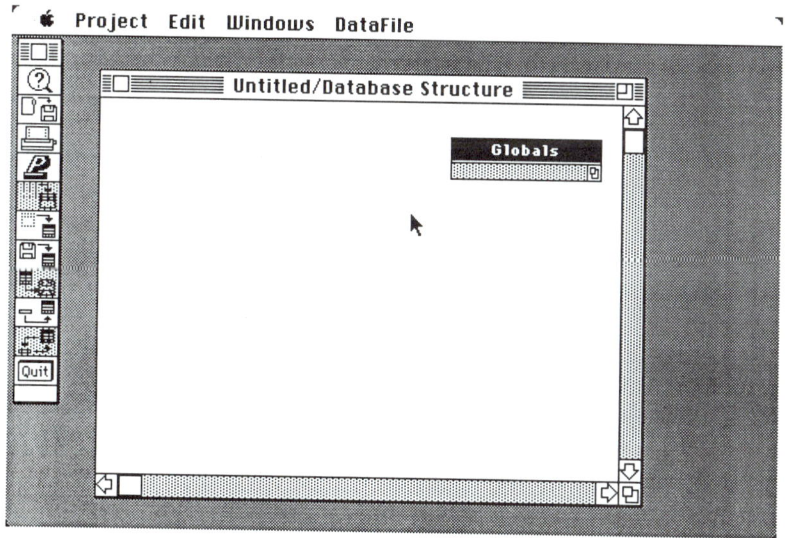

Figure 3-4 Structure Window Graphic.

The Globals file is always present on the Structure Window (although you may choose to hide it beyond the visible window boundries or behind another file on the Structure Window). The Globals file is used for special Memory fields that may pass values between all parts of a project. For instance, a Global Memory field can contain values that all views can use. Common uses of Global Memory fields are to accumulate temporary totals, or to pass information from one view to another.

Relationships

After creating files in an application, you will often want to make it possible for them to share information. On the Structure Window, you can define the structures that allow such sharing. File relationships allow many sophisticated operations involving shared information.

There are basically two kinds of relationships: one-way and two-way.

In a two-way relationship, a pointer field is created in each of the related files, and a two-way arrow is drawn connecting the pointer fields. Data are shared between the two related files in both directions.

In a one-way relationship, only the file that must retrieve information from the other has a pointer field. If you think of the two files as source and destination, it is the destination file that contains the pointer field. A one-way arrow links the pointer field with the source file. Since a one-way relationship only passes information in one direction, the source file does not need a pointer field.

The Pointer field contains Key field values from corresponding records in the related file. Through the Key field value, dBASE Mac can locate any information for corresponding records in the related file. That is why they are called pointer fields—they point out the key value to access related information.

NOTE: The Pointer field occurs as the title bar in a view hierarchy. The title bar will be seen in view hierarchies on the Define Hierarchy or the Layout View screens. More on that later.

External Index files are files with special relationships created to sort file data on a specific field other than a Key field. The External Index file initially contains two fields: the original Key field and the indexed field (which is the new Key of the Index file). The Key field values are ordered according to an ascending alphabetical or numeric sort of the indexed field. You can add other fields to an External Index file, or even establish relationships with other files.

When a new record is added to a file, any External Index files associated with that file also gain a new record automatically if a value was entered in the indexed field of the new record. Any changes to information in an indexed field are automatically updated in the External Index file. This kind of automatic updating is unique to the External Index file, and does not occur in one- or two-way relationships.

Index files can, in fact, sort and maintain similar data from more than one file. Thus, you could keep an index of names from a customer and vendor file. This index would contain Key field values from both files, and they would be sorted alphabetically according to the names from both files. A master list of both customers and vendors would be easy to create using such an Index file.

NOTE: You can also create an internal index on any field from the field definition dialog box. The internal index is used to improve efficiency while sorting/selecting on a particular field. In some circumstances, this internal index is sufficient, but both types of indexing have unique uses, as mentioned above.

Preferences

Selecting the Preferences. . . option on the Edit menu opens a dialog box of display settings. These include fonts and font sizes, special effects (**bold**, *italic*, etc.), and other settings to control the size, shape, and kind of boxes to use with display elements, the background pattern for the boxes, the position of titles, and so on. Any settings selected in the Preferences. . . dialog box affect the entire project. To modify settings for individual display elements in a layout, see Display Options, below.

Views

Of all the structures in dBASE Mac, Views can be the most complex and the most powerful, and they are essential for any data processing. It is through the views that all file data are entered, modified, moved, sorted, selected, deleted, browsed through, and printed out. Views define what information is to be displayed and printed, what operations to perform on the data, and how the data are to look.

View Types

There are two basic types of view: Display View and Transfer View. Display Views are used to enter, modify, and browse through file information, and to create reports. Transfer Views are used to move information between files and are generally good vehicles for batch processing—without observing the data. Transfer Views can also be used to call other views and projects.

When you create a new view, you first determine if it is a Display or Transfer View. There are three kinds of Display View: Form views, Column views, and Custom views.

Form View In a Form view, each field is displayed separately as a data entry/display element. You can enter and modify information on a record-by-record basis.

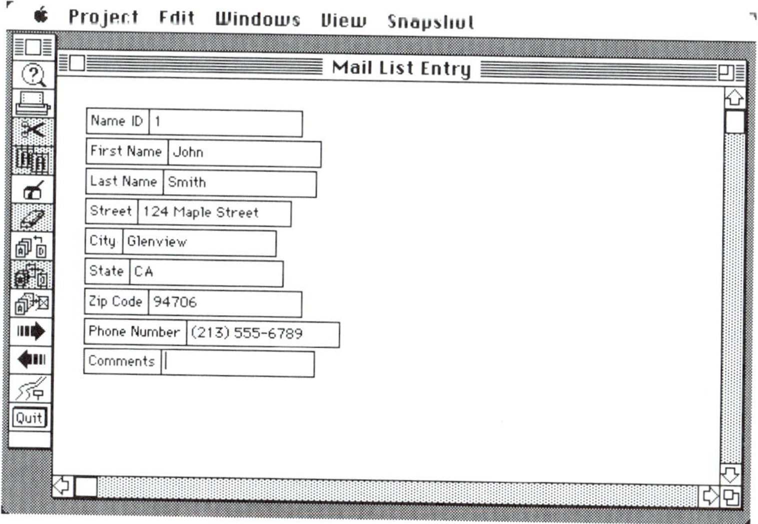

Figure 3-5 Form View Graphic.

Column View A Column view is a tabular listing of all the records in a file (depending on whether Selection criteria are in use, limiting the number of records displayed). You cannot enter or modify records in a Column view. The advantage of a Column view is the ability to see all file information at once. Column views are used to create tabular reports.

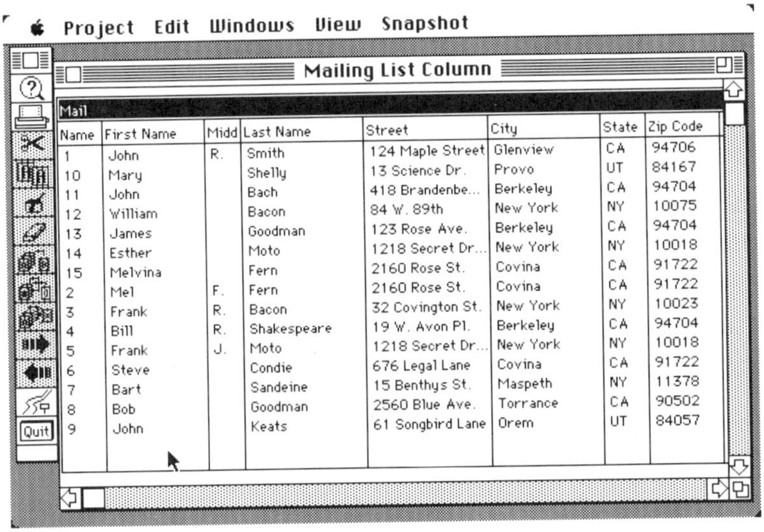

Project Edit Windows View Snapshot

Mailing List Column

Mail

Name	First Name	Midd	Last Name	Street	City	State	Zip Code
1	John	R.	Smith	124 Maple Street	Glenview	CA	94706
10	Mary		Shelly	13 Science Dr.	Provo	UT	84167
11	John		Bach	418 Brandenbe...	Berkeley	CA	94704
12	William		Bacon	84 W. 89th	New York	NY	10075
13	James		Goodman	123 Rose Ave.	Berkeley	CA	94704
14	Esther		Moto	1218 Secret Dr...	New York	NY	10018
15	Melvina		Fern	2160 Rose St.	Covina	CA	91722
2	Mel	F.	Fern	2160 Rose St.	Covina	CA	91722
3	Frank	R.	Bacon	32 Covington St.	New York	NY	10023
4	Bill	R.	Shakespeare	19 W. Avon Pl.	Berkeley	CA	94704
5	Frank	J.	Moto	1218 Secret Dr...	New York	NY	10018
6	Steve		Condie	676 Legal Lane	Covina	CA	91722
7	Bart		Sandeine	15 Benthys St.	Maspeth	NY	11378
8	Bob		Goodman	2560 Blue Ave.	Torrance	CA	90502
9	John		Keats	61 Songbird Lane	Orem	UT	84057

Quit

Figure 3-6 Column View Graphic.

Custom View Form and Column views are very specific types of views. As soon as you modify one of them, it becomes, to dBASE Mac, a Custom view. A Custom view can contain both Form and Column elements. Thus, you can display a tabular list of some fields as a reference while you perform data entry. Custom views allow greater versatility. Also, where the Form and Column views automatically create a default layout, no layout is created when you first create a Custom view.

Transfer View Transfer Views are used to move data between files. You can use a Transfer View to update records from separate files, combining the information from several files into one. You can also reroute the contents of specific fields to other fields in a new file. You could, for instance, create a new record in the Destination file for each record in a Source file—with the contents of a particular Data field becoming the Key field values in the Destination file. You can also use a Transfer View to modify and write records back to the same file, using the same file as both Source and Destination.

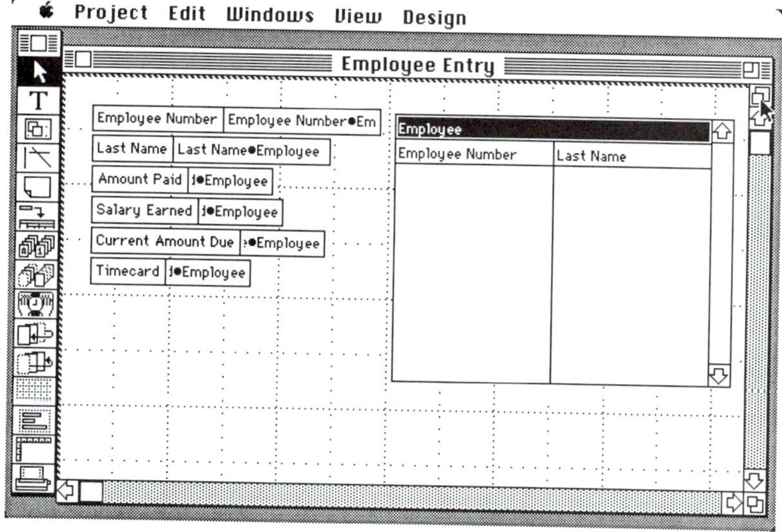

Figure 3-7 Custom View Graphic.

Define Hierarchy

Once their type has been determined, all views are created mainly in a two-step process: hierarchy and layout. The first step is to define the hierarchy—the fields that will be used in the view and the precedence by which those fields may be processed for some operations. The hierarchy determines the path by which data are accessed.

In addition, you can create View fields—fields specific to the current View. These can be Formula or Memory fields. Their position within the hierarchy may have significance.

While creating the hierarchy definition, you create a Path for the data from related files. The Path is the complete route dBASE Mac takes to retrieve data, and includes all file relationships used. A path for a field called First Name in a file called Names would read:

```
{First Name•Names}
```

The path for that same field called by a relationship between the Names file and a file called Invoices would read:

```
{First Name•Names•Invoices}
```

Invoices is the primary file (called the Root File). It contains a relationship with Names (in this case a sub-file) through which it retrieves the First Name field. The full path reads as above.

NOTE: Often, the pointer field has the same name as the file to which it belongs, but the pointer field can have any name you wish. Therefore, in the examples above, the pointer field and the file name are the same. This will not always be true, but the path designation will contain the pointer field names occurring between the field name and the root file designation.

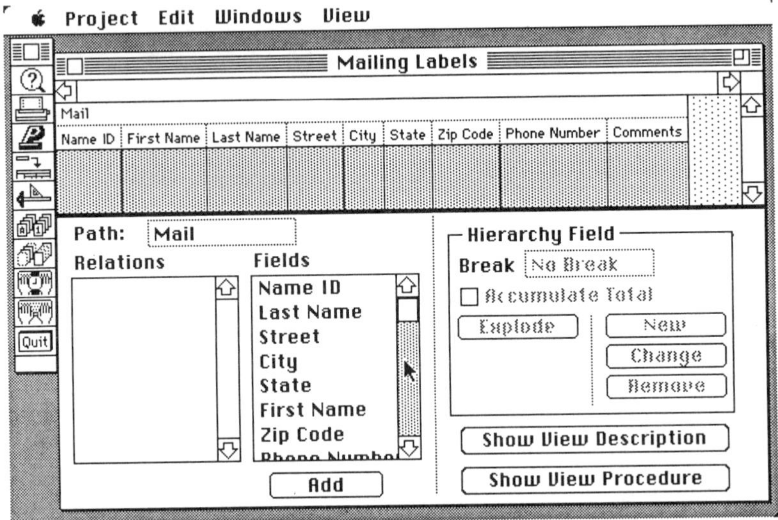

Figure 3-8 Hierarchy Screen Graphic.

To add fields to the hierarchy, select them from the field list while in the Define Hierarchy mode. To add a file to the Path, select a related file from the file list. To choose an alternative Path, open the Path pop-up window, and select the Path level you wish.

You can also set break conditions and total definitions for individual fields. These breaks and totals will appear in the printed reports where control breaks occur.

Layout

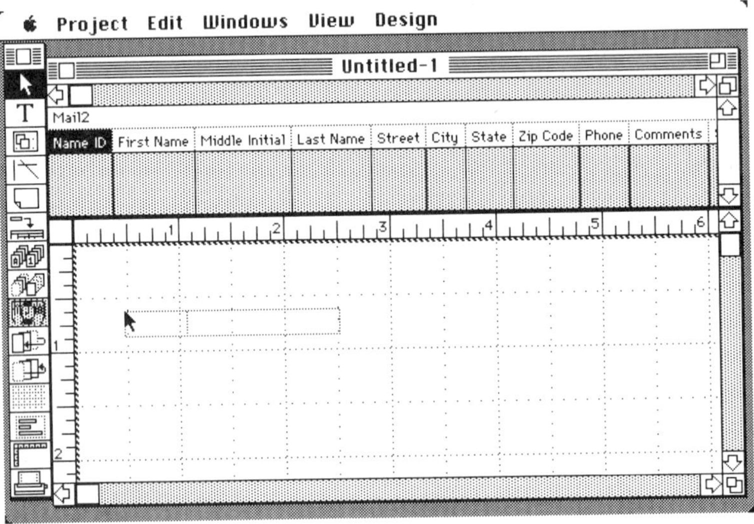

Figure 3-9 Layout Graphic.

The second process in defining a view is to define the Layout. The Layout controls the appearance of the view. On the design area of the Layout, you can position and size the columns and data boxes of a Display view. You can also modify the font and other display characteristics.

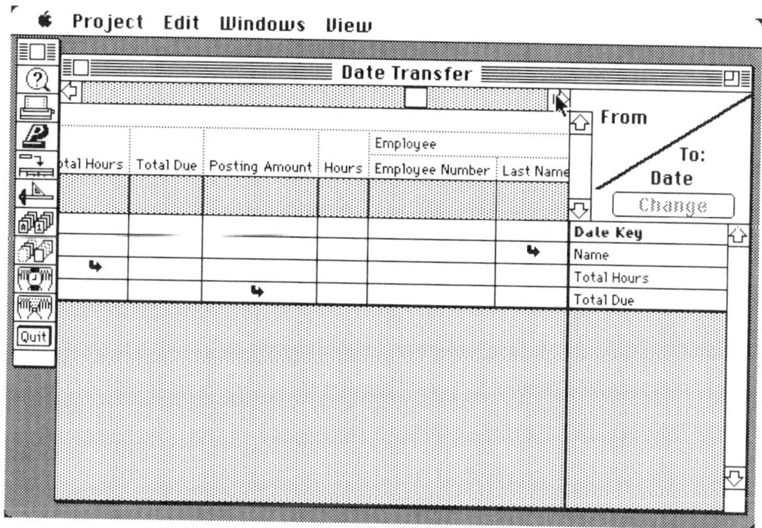

Figure 3-10 Transfer Layout Graphic.

The Layout for a Transfer View is quite different. The Transfer View Layout is used to determine which field data from a Source file will be mapped to which fields in the Destination file. The Layout also determines whether the data transfer will update records, replace records, delete all existing records, or append new records.

To design a Form view, drag fields from the Layout hierarchy onto the design area. In addition, you can place text and graphics anywhere on the design area. To create a Column view, highlight the title bar (pointer field) of any file in the Layout hierarchy, then highlight (Shift click) the desired fields underneath it. Drag the highlighted elements onto the design area.

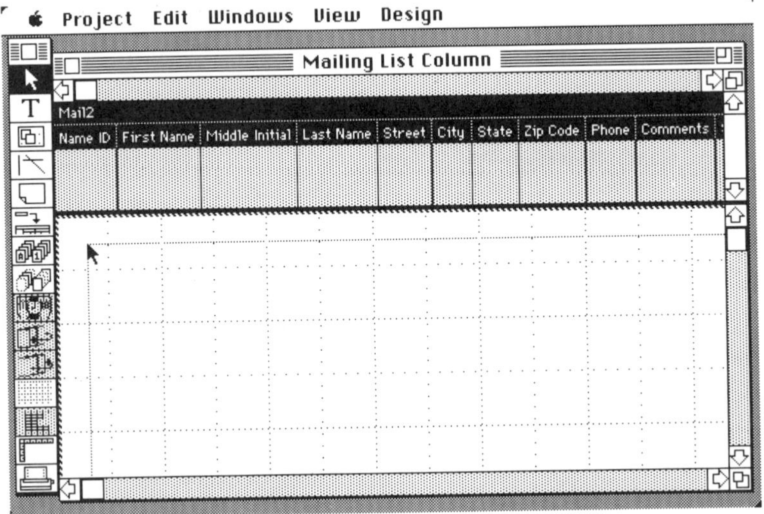

Figure 3-11 Create Column Graphic.

There are several aids to layout design. These include Rulers, Grids, Grouping, Tablets, Form Size, and Display Options.

Rulers The Ruler is turned on or off from the Design menu. You can set one of three standard or metric rulers. When you set the Ruler on, it displays across the top and down the left side of the design area.

Grids If you Turn On Grid, elements placed on the design area will automatically line up with an invisible gridwork. The Grid is either one-eighth of an inch or one centimeter, depending on the Ruler setting.

Grouping You can select several elements on the design area, and then select the Group command in the Design menu. The elements will then act as one item when you move or resize them. To separate the elements again, highlight the group and then select Ungroup from the Design menu. Grouping is also used to control the order of data entry.

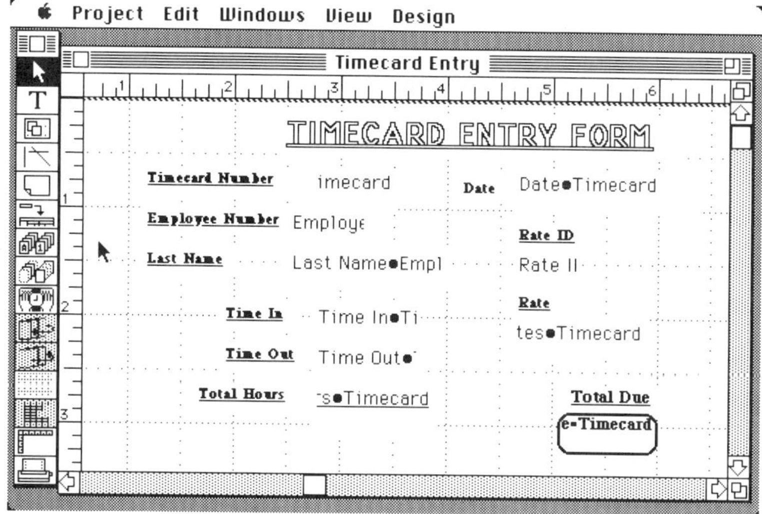

Figure 3-12 Ruler Graphic.

Tablets A Tablet is a special layout element that allows you to produce multipage displays on the Macintosh screen. Like the Scrapbook, Tablets can contain many pages, which you leaf through one at a time. In addition, you can control the display of any individual Tablet page by creating selection criteria. Thus, a page only appears if its selection criteria are met. You create a Tablet by selecting the Tablet cursor from the Palette and drawing a box in the design area.

Form Size You can change the size of the form for the current view. Select Form Size from the Design menu and define the width and length of the form. You may do so manually or select from among several preset choices. In addition, you may select how many forms are to print across a page. This is especially helpful when printing mailing labels with more than one label across the paper. Form size is different from Page Size. You select the Page Size in the normal way from the Page Setup selection in the Projects menu.

Display Options Selecting Display Options from the Design menu presents a special dialog box very similar to the Preferences dialog box found in the Edit menu. The main difference is that the Display Options affect only the currently highlighted display elements in the current layout. At the bottom of the Display Options screen is a Show Selections button. Pressing this reveals a dialog box for setting the selection criteria for Tablet pages.

Sorting and Selecting Records

In addition to the hierarchy and the layout, there are special selection modules for each view that allow you to sort and select records. On the Sort definition screen, you choose the fields on which to sort, and whether to sort records in ascending or in descending order. Sorting will be performed on the records starting with the first field selected, and moving down the list. Thus, if you sort on zip codes, then on last names, you will get all names alphabetically sorted within each zip code, and the whole file sorted by zip code.

Selecting records is similar to sorting. On a separate screen, you define the criteria for selection. You can create any kind of criterion you wish. You can select for all names equal to Smith, or all names less than Smith, or all names equal to Smith and living in San Francisco. You can use any valid criteria you wish to select records, including limited wildcards (characters used to represent missing characters). dBASE Mac uses ellipses to represent missing characters (i.e., Sm. . .th represents Smith, Smyth, Smoth, or even Smooth). The elipses only work with the MATCHES operator from the Procedural Interface.

Only selected records will appear on the screen when you Use the view, or on a report if you print the view report.

Perform and Use

After you have defined a hierarchy, a layout, and any Sort or Selection criteria, you can Perform and Use a view. When you do this, dBASE Mac sorts and selects if necessary, builds a list of key values according to sort and selection criteria, and then activates the Use mode. The Use mode is the interactive mode for a view. It displays all currently selected records in a Column view, or displays the first record in a Form view. If you have a sort in effect, the records will be in sorted order. If you have a selection in effect, only those records that meet the selection criteria will appear.

If you do not wish to have dBASE Mac verify and update all records, you can choose Use View. This will activate the Use mode of the view without verifying or updating the data. Sometimes you will need to Perform the view to update the values of the currently selected records. For instance, if you have a Form and a Column view, and you add records to the Form view, you will need to Perform the Column view to see the added records. If you only Use the view, the new records will not appear.

Procedures

Procedures are special programs you write to control the flow of data, to prompt and interact with the user of your projects, and to verify and error-check your applications. Procedures use the dBASE Mac Procedural Interface (PI). Some aspects of the PI are used during creation of Formula fields, selection records, or selection Tablet pages.

There are several types of procedures, and they occur at several points in the program.

Pre-Processor A Pre-Processor procedure is invoked before entering a view or field. This is a good way to prompt a user for preliminary information—through a custom dialog box. You might also use a Pre-Processor to allow the user to select a particular operation to perform and, based on the selection, activate a different view or even a new project. Pre-Processors are used frequently to initialize values in a field or record.

Post-Processor A Post-Processor is invoked upon exiting a view or field. Post-Processors can be used to create dialog boxes that require the user to verify his or her entries before continuing, or to perform an automatic check that the data in the field is correct. In the case of a view-based Post-Processor, that procedure is invoked only after modifying the contents of the field and physically leaving the field. A file-based field Post-Processor is, in addition, invoked when the contents are modified via a procedure.

New Record A New Record processor is attached to a file or view pointer field. It is invoked whenever a new record command is issued from the keyboard or the Edit menu, or when the New Record command is encountered in a procedure, or when a New Record is invoked in a Transfer View. A NEW(SELF) is required to complete the action. You might use the New Record to prompt for information that affects the new record.

Write Record A Write Record processor is attached to a particular file or pointer field in a view. It is activated whenever a Write Record command is issued from the keyboard (by pressing **Enter**) or from another procedure (from the Write command), or whenever a record is written during the processing of a Transfer View. A Write Record procedure might be used to prompt the user to verify his decision to write the record, or it might be used to process information from the record at the time of writing it. If a Write Record procedure is associated with a file or view, it must contain a WRITE(SELF) command, or the actual writing of the record will not be completed.

Delete Record A Delete Record procedure is attached to a particular file or pointer field in a view. It activates whenever a Delete Record command is issued from the keyboard, from the Edit menu, or from a procedure (when the Delete command is encountered). Delete Record procedures can be used to prompt the user for verification of deletion, or for updating information in other files and fields that might be affected by the deletion. If a Delete Record procedure is associated with a file or view, it must contain a DELETE(SELF) command, or the record will not be deleted.

Procedures can occur in several locations:

Procedure	Location
Pre-Processor	View, Fields in Views
Post-Processor	File Fields, Views, Fields in Views
Add Record	File, Pointer Field in View
Write Record	File, Pointer Field in View
Delete Record	File, Pointer Field in View

The Project as an Application

Finally, after you put all the elements together, you can customize a dBASE Mac project through Custom Menus. The function of this feature is to determine which views may be accessed directly. To invoke Custom Menus, you must Protect the project by selecting Protect from the Project menu and entering a password. Once a project is protected, it cannot be modified until it is unprotected using the password. After you have finished all the file, field, view, and procedure definitions, you can protect a project to create a turnkey application.

Passwords You can use passwords to protect different parts of a project. You can password-protect files or the entire project. Field or view password protection is accomplished through the Procedural Interface.

Descriptions You can add descriptive text to views if necessary in the Show View Description dialog.

Summary

It may seem that there are many aspects to this program, and many new terms and techniques to learn. But these ideas soon become second nature. By following the step-by-step instructions in the chapters that follow, you will gain experience and insight into how these many elements combine to make a fully functional dBASE Mac application.

For more detailed information about dBASE Mac, you can look up any of these program aspects in Part II, dBASE Mac Reference.

4

CREATING dBASE MAC FILES

Using the Tutorial

Chapter 4 is the first in a series of tutorial chapters, to be read with the computer running and dBASE Mac on the screen. Each chapter focuses on a different aspect of dBASE Mac. Three applications illustrate the different parts of the program—a Mailing List, a Checkbook, and a Timecard Project.

If you completed the example in Chapter 2, you have already created a Mailing List project. You can use that version of the project for simple mailing list applications. However, a slightly different, and more interesting version of this project in Chapter 4 illustrates multivalued fields. The simple mailing list from Chapter 2 could be modified to be just like the one illustrated in this tutorial, but we recommend that you work through the tutorial, step by step, to better understand the basic underlying principles of dBASE Mac. Later in the Tutorial, each project will be used in examples.

The Checkbook Project also begins in Chapter 4. The Timecard Project begins in Chapter 5.

You may prefer to work through each project from beginning to end. The tutorials are structured so that you can do that. For instance, you can begin with the Mailing List project you created in Chapter 2, then create the MultiMail project in the first part of this chapter, then skip to Chapter 6 to create the Mailing Label hierarchy, then on to Chapter 7 to create the layout, and so on. You could then return to Chapter 4 and work through the examples for the Checkbook Project, then on to Chapters 6 and 7 to continue. For a guide to project flow, see How To Use This Book in the Introduction.

Each project in the Tutorial section has different characteristics, and you will find it valuable to look at each of them. Whether you do each Tutorial chapter in order, or whether you complete each project one at a time is a matter of personal preference.

We feel, however, that each chapter and project builds on the previous information, and recommend completing each chapter in turn.

Overview

After designing a database, the first step in creating it is to create the file structures. Chapter 4 shows in detail how to create dBASE Mac file structures, a process that involves determining the file type, then defining the fields (and their characteristics) that make up the file.

Fields can be of several types and formats depending on the kind of data they contain. Chapter 4 looks closely at many of the different file and data types.

Some fields can send data automatically to other fields. This is called Posting. Chapter 4 begins the process of creating Posting fields.

Special Instructions

Even though the Mailing List project in Chapter 2 is very similar to the MultiMail project that follows, please follow the instructions in this chapter to build the new project. You'll find it has some interesting features, and all the steps are explained. By the time you finish the next two chapters, you should be accomplished at file creation and field definitions.

You could duplicate the Mail file either from the Finder or within dBASE Mac (the Duplicate File option from the DataFile menu), but you would have to modify the resulting duplicate file in several ways. It's easier to follow the instructions in this chapter.

> NOTE: The Duplicate File option is handy—as you'll see later in the Tutorial—and allows you to duplicate with or without the file's records.

Ways to Start dBASE Mac

You can use one of three different icons to start a dBASE Mac session.

dBASE Mac

1. Double-clicking the dBASE Mac icon begins dBASE Mac with a new, untitled project.

File

2. Double-clicking a file icon opens dBASE Mac with the selected file on the dBASE Mac Structure Window and an untitled project becomes active. (Shift clicking on several file icons, then double-clicking, opens an untitled project with all highlighted files on the Structure Window.)

Project

3. Double-clicking a project icon opens dBASE Mac with an entire project just as it was when last saved—including all files, relationships, and views.

Starting dBASE Mac

Double-click the dBASE Mac icon. After the disclaimer you will see the opening dBASE Mac screen—the Structure Window.

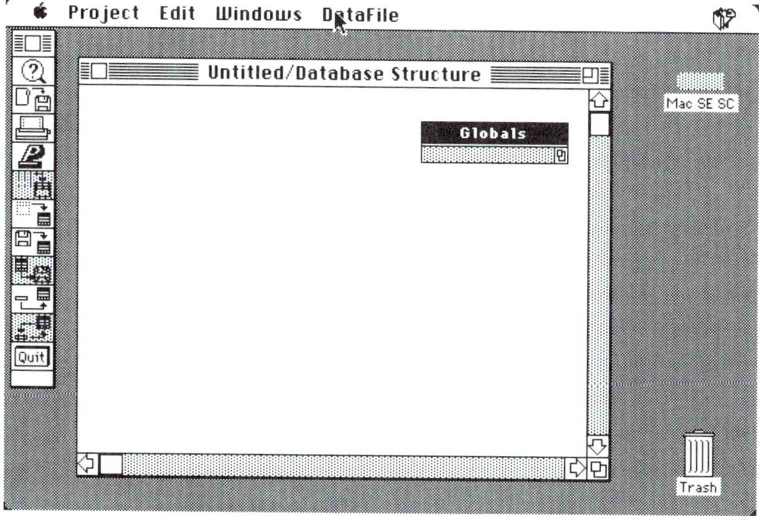

Figure 4-1 New Structure Window Graphic.

Before you examine the opening screen, put something on it. Create a file.

Creating a File

First, design the file. Plan the kinds of information you will need to include. This first file is a mailing list, similar to the one created in Chapter 2.

The first field defined is the Key field. Each entry in the Key field must be unique, so choose a value that is nonrepetitive. Don't choose the last name field as the Key because there may be more than one person with the same last name. You can use a mnemonic code, or a sequential number series.

After the Key field, the entries will be pretty standard:

first name; middle initial; last name
street address
city; state; zip code
phone
comments

NOTE: For optimum performance, especially in large databases, use a Numeric Key field.

Suppose some of the people on your mailing list have more than one address and phone number. You will see how dBASE Mac can handle such a situation using multivalued fields and sets.

1. To begin, open the DataFile menu and select New. . .
2. On the dialog box that appears next, click **OK** or press **Return** to leave it set to a dBASE Mac type file.

The next dialog box has a text area for the name of the file.

3. Type "Mail2" (without quote marks). Click **Save** or press **Return**.

NOTE: See Appendix A for more on Macintosh file naming conventions.

Skip the password selection for now. Press **Return** or click **Save** to save the file name and move on to field definition.

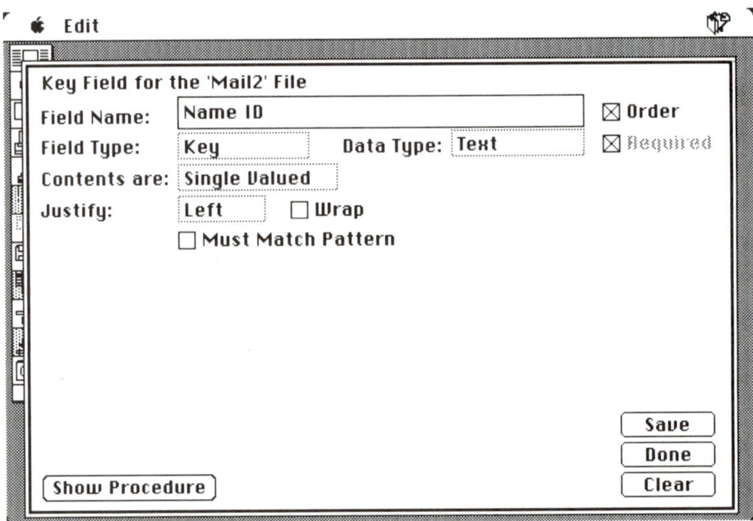

Figure 4-2 Key Field Definition Screen Graphic

The Key Field

The first field defined must be the Key field. Your screen should be displaying the Key field definition dialog. Notice that the Field Type: box is already filled in as Key. Also, the Required checkbox is checked. This means that you must enter a Key field value or dBASE Mac can not process the record.

- Take a moment to look at the pop-up menus. Pop-up menus are the dotted-line boxes. Hold down the mouse button over each of these menus. You'll notice that several choices are dimmed, meaning that they are not currently available. Notice that Key fields can be Text, Numeric, Date, or Time data types, but not Choices, Logical, or Graphics. Leave the Data Type set to Text.
- The Order box is unique to the Key field. Check-marking the Order box causes the program to retrieve records in Key order. If you do not check the Order box, dBASE Mac determines the order of your records based on internal filing criteria.

Click the mouse in the Field Name box to be sure the text cursor is there. You should see a blinking vertical line (called the I-beam cursor). This is the standard Macintosh text cursor. To name the field,

4. Type "Name ID"

Leave the rest of the Key field the way it is.

5. Click **Save**, or press **Return**.

The Key field is defined. The next dialog box that appears is for a standard field. Summary:

1. Select New. . . from the DataFile menu.
2. Click **OK** or press **Return**.
3. Type "Mail2"; click **Save** or press **Return**.
4. Type "Name ID"
5. Click **Save** or press **Return**.

Defining Other Fields

The screen for defining other fields is similar to the Key field definition screen. Begin by filling in the field name:

Type "First Name"

The Field Type: pop-up menu offers several choices now, but this file will only use Data fields. The next section of this chapter will look at other field types.

Now look at the Data Type: pop-up. Again, although there are several choices, this file uses only Text data types. The next section of this chapter will look at other data types.

If you want to require that each record contain a first name, check the Required box.

The steps to create the First Name field are:

1. Type "First Name"
2. Check Required (optional).
3. Click **Save** or press **Return**.

That's all there is to it!

To create the Middle Initial and Last Name fields, follow the same procedure again, but substitute the appropriate field names:

1. Type "Middle Initial"
2. Click **Save** or press **Return**.
3. Type "Last Name"
4. Check Required (optional).

Look at the checkbox marked Index. If you check the Index box, dBASE Mac creates an internal index of the field. This internal index is used to speed up sorts and selections. You can create an index on a Text, Number, Date, Time, Choices, or Logical field—in fact, any field but a Graphics field.

However, internal indexes can greatly increase file size, and should be used where a field might often be the subject of sorts and selections. In Chapter 5 you will see another kind of index, an External Index, which can be used to create an indexed relationship across two or more files.

To create the Last Name field:

1. Check the Index checkbox for the Last Name field.
2. Click **Save** or press **Return.**

Multivalued Fields and Sets

The next four fields are address fields. These are Street, City, State, and Zip Code. Start with Street.

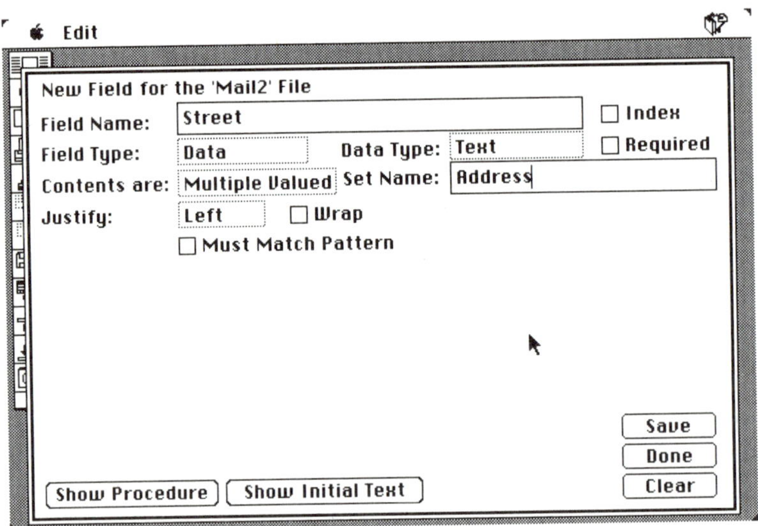

Fig. 4-3 Multivalued Graphic with Set.

After you **Save** the Last Name field:

1. Type "Street" to name the first address field.

   Street addresses usually contain numbers and alphabetical characters. Some may even contain symbols (i.e., #5 instead of Apt. 5). This kind of field is called a Text field even though it may contain numbers, so leave the Data Type set as Text.

RULE: The basic test for determining whether a field containing numbers should be Text or Numeric is: Do you plan to use the numbers in a calculation or other mathematical process? Since you can accurately sort numbers even in a Text field, the only reasons a field needs to be Numeric are if the numbers it contains will be used mathematically or if a particular numeric format (i.e., $21.00) should be placed on the value.

Back to the address fields. You remember that some of the names on your list have multiple addresses.

2. Open the Contents are: pop-up and select Multiple Valued.

   A multivalued field can contain more than one entry per record. A Set links each value in a multivalued field with the corresponding values in other fields in the Set.

Notice that a box entitled Set Name: has appeared.

3. Type "Address" to name the Set.

4. **Save** the Street field.

To summarize:

1. Type "Street"
2. Select Multiple Valued from Contents are: pop-up.
3. Type "Address" in the Set Name: text box.
4. Click **Save**.

To create the City, State, and Zip Code fields, follow exactly the same procedures you used to create Street, but substitute the appropriate names (City, State, Zip Code) in the Field Name: text box. Remember to type "Address" in the Set Name: box of each field.

NOTE: Again, as with the Street field, use Text data type for the Zip Code. You won't be using it in calculations, so treat it as Text:

1. Type "City"
2. Select Multiple Valued from the Contents are: pop-up.
3. Type "Address" in the Set Name: text box.
4. Click **Save**.
5. Type "State"
6. Select Multiple Valued from the Contents are: pop-up.
7. Type "Address" in the Set Name: text box.
8. Click **Save**.
9. Type "Zip Code"
10. Select Multiple Valued from the Contents are: pop-up.
11. Type "Address" in the Set Name: text box.
12. Click **Save**.

How Sets Work

Sets allow you to associate multiple values in fields with each other. In this case, you are going to associate several street addresses with their City, State, and Zip Code values.

Suppose your friend, Joe Miller, has a house in New York and another in Florida. His New York address is:

232 Sycamore Ave.
White Plains, NY 10072

His Florida address is:

3365 Palm Drive
Coral Gables, FL 99999

The multivalued fields then contain:

Street:	**232 Sycamore Ave.** **3365 Palm Drive**
City:	**New York** **Coral Gables**
State:	**NY** **FL**
Zip Code:	**10072** **99999**

The Set named Address keeps the first street address, city, state, and zip together; the second street address, city, state, and zip together; and so on.

Pattern Matching

The next field to define is the Phone field. After you **Save** the Zip Code field,

1. Type "Phone"

Since a telephone number is another example of a field that contains numbers, but not for calculation, the Phone field is a Text field.

Assume that each person on your list has one phone number per address. If that is true, can you guess how to associate each Phone number with its address? Use a multivalued field and place the Phone field in the Address Set.

Telephone numbers have a standard appearance, or format. Most numbers are written (*nnn*) *nnn-nnnn*, where *n* stands for any number. Wherever a particular format is required, you can use Must Match Patterns to facilitate data input and to verify that the format is properly followed.

Unlike most databases, dBASE Mac allows you to define several matching pattern possibilities.

2. Click on the Must Match Patterns box.

A data entry box appears. Here you can define the patterns for the Phone field.

Before defining these patterns, look at the symbols used in pattern matching:

Symbol	Meaning
a	any alphabetical character
n	any number
x	any character
1-99 (a, n, or x)	match the character the specified number of times
∞(a,n, or x)	match a, n, or x any number of times (Option 5 for the infinity symbol)
\'text'	match the text in single quotes exactly
any text	accept only data input that exactly matches the text, except a, n, x, or ~
~character	accept the data whether or not it contains the character following the tilde (Option-N). If the data entered does not contain the character, it is inserted at that position.
~\'text'	accept the data whether or not it contains the text in single quotes that follows the tilde. If the data entered does not contain the text in single quotes, it is inserted at that position.

Pattern Matching for the Phone Field

Suppose that many of the entries in your mailing list will be local numbers, and you don't want to type the area code for them. The first pattern you define should be the one that will be followed most frequently. You could write the pattern:

nnn-nnnn

You could also write that:

3n-4n

You can make data input easier if you use the tilde (~) to make typing the dash optional:

3n~-4n

- The tilde can be produced by holding down the Option key and pressing the letter *n*. On some keyboards, it can be produced by using the shifted accent key above the **Tab** key.

To type the example above:

Type "3n Option-n - 4n" (no quotes and no spaces)

- In pattern matching, the tilde means "if the following character is not entered, then enter it automatically."

Look how the tilde might be used in entering a phone number with area code:

~(3n~)~ 3n~-4n

Using the pattern above, if you enter 8005554321, the program will turn that into (800) 555-4321.

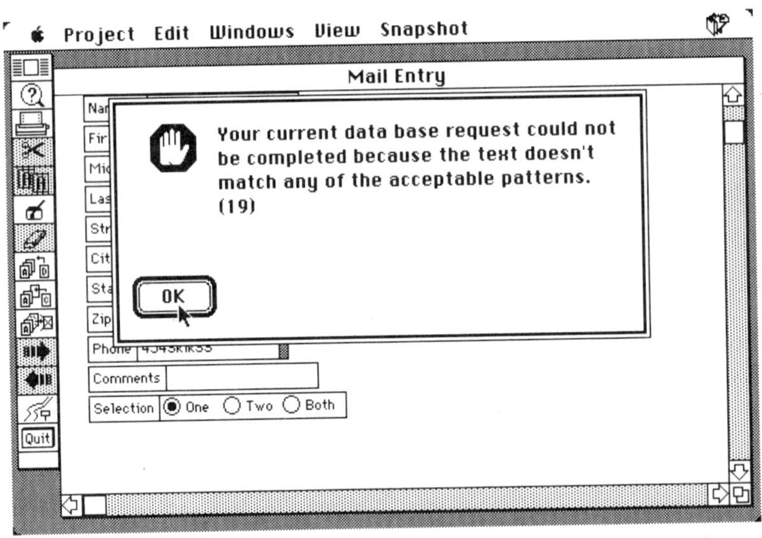

Figure 4-4 Pattern Matching Error Dialog Graphic

Matching patterns can help speed up data entry. It can also prevent erroneous information from making its way into your files. For instance, if you enter 800345ty56 using the pattern defined above, the program will beep at you and display the message screen in Figure 4-4.

Other variations on the phone number patterns might include country codes for international dialing, long distance service numbers, or extensions.

3. To fill in the pattern matching for the Phone field, type the following patterns. Press **Return** after each pattern to move to the next line.

 3n~-4n
 ~(3n~)~ 3n~-4n
 3n~-4n~ ~"Ext."~ 3n
 ~(3n~)~ 3n~-4n~ ~"Ext."~ 3n

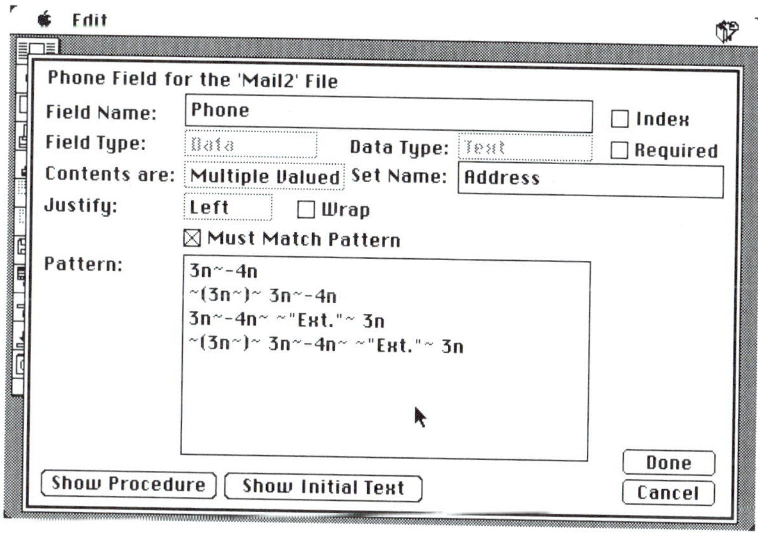

Figure 4-5 Completed Phone Field Graphic.

NOTE: You may return later to change, modify, add, or delete the patterns you have defined.

NOTE: To speed up processing, enter the most frequently used patterns first. dBASE Mac scans the pattern list in order until it finds a match.

When you are finished defining the Phone field, click **Save**.
To enter the Phone field:

1. Type "Phone" in the Field Name: box.
2. Click on the Must Match Patterns checkbox.
3. Type the patterns listed above in the text box.
4. Click **Save**.

You have now defined most of the Mail2 file. Before defining the last field, return to the Structure Window. To return to the Structure Window, click **Done**.

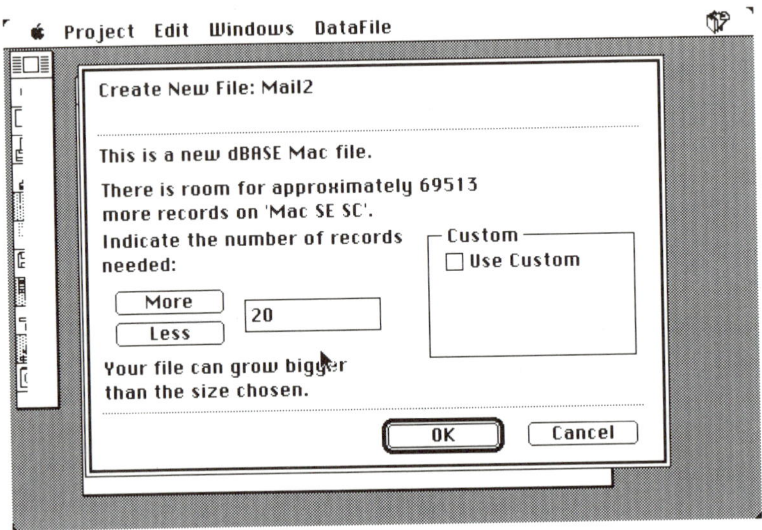

Figure 4-6 Allocating File Space Graphic.

After a few moments, the program asks you to estimate the number of records your file will contain. Near the top of the screen you will see an approximation of the number of records the present data disk can hold. Unless you are using floppy disks, or the estimated number of records is very close to the number you expect to enter, you needn't worry about this too much. Just use the More or Less buttons to display a number that is close to the expected size of your file, or type the number directly in the text box. If you eventually enter more records than this number, the program will adjust automatically.

- When dBASE Mac estimates file size it approximates the size of a record and creates a disk file large enough to accomodate the number of records expected. The file can grow larger, but this method safeguards your data and makes sure that you will have the minimum amount of space required.

The Structure Window

Click **OK** after selecting the size for your file.

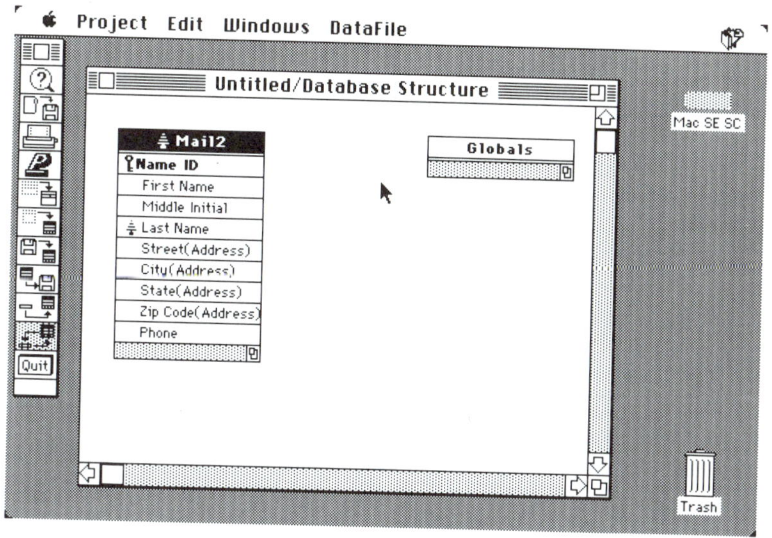

Figure 4-7 Mailing List Structure Window Graphic.

Wait while the program allocates disk space for the file. As soon as disk space has been allocated, the program returns to the Database Structure Window—the same window you saw when you first opened the program, but with a difference. Do you recognize your Mail2 file?

Examine the screen of the Structures Window. At the top it should read, "Untitled/Database Structure". Inside the window you will see two file listings, Globals and Mail2.

Examine Mail2. The fields you just created appear stacked upon each other. The Key field, Name ID, has a key symbol next to it and is at the top of the stack. The Mail2 file title and Last Name both have a small tree symbol next to them. This means they are indexed using the internal index (the Order box on the Key field is also an index). The tree stands for B-tree, an indexing technique.

NOTE: You can remove the indexing from a field by unchecking the Index or Order checkbox during a Change Field session.

Can you see any other significant information on the Structure Window? Look at the City field. Notice that it and the other fields in the Address Set contain the word (Address) after the field name. The parentheses indicate that the field is multivalued. The name of the Set, if any, appears inside the parentheses. In fields with longer names you will not be able to read the Set name.

Later, in the other applications in this book, you will see different symbols next to field names to indicate Formula and Memory fields. Watch for them.

If you move the mouse pointer to the small box at the bottom right corner of Mail2, then press and hold the mouse button, you can resize the window by moving the mouse. Try it now. You can close the file structure so that some of the field names are hidden, or widen it to display the entire field names of the longer entries. When you are finished, leave the file open so you can see all the field names.

You can also change the order of the fields in the file box. Click on a field (say First Name), and place the cursor on the left edge of the field box. The cursor should change to two vertical arrows. Now drag the field box below the Last Name field. When you release the mouse button the field will be in a new position. If you save a project (see below), the new position will also be saved.

HINT: You can move any file box on the Structure Window by dragging it with the title bar at the top. You can also hold down the **Option** key and drag a file by any part of the file structure.

The Palette

To the left of the Structure Window is the Structure Window Palette. The Palette offers an easy, icon-oriented approach to the main commands in dBASE Mac. Learning the meaning of the various icons can save you time while using the program. The Palette changes from one part of dBASE Mac to another. Look at the Structure Window Palette.

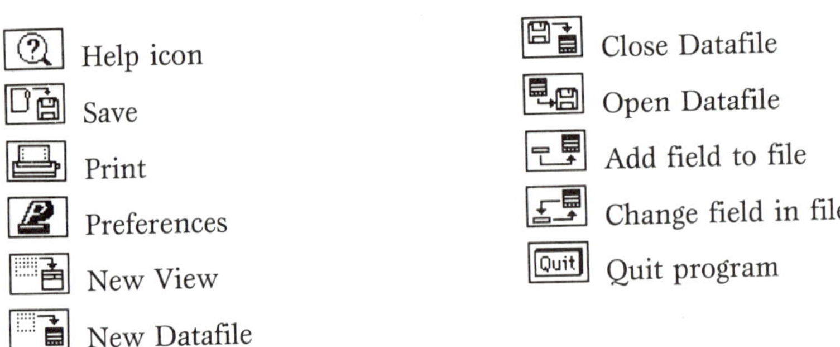

Use one of these icons now to add two fields to the Mail2 file.

1. Click on the Add Field icon.

   In a moment the familiar field definition screen appears.

   Type "Comments"

2. Name the new field.

   Leave the Comments field as Data and Text. The only modification you will make is to click on the Wrap checkbox.

3. Click the Wrap checkbox.

Later you can use the Wrap feature to add free-form text into the Comments field. The text will wrap, much the way it does in a word processor.

4. Click **Save**.

5. Now click **Save**, then **Done**.

You will return to the Structure Window. Notice that the Comments field now appears at the end of the Mail2 file.

You are going to add one more field to the file. This one, Selections, will be used later for some special processing of the multivalued fields.

Selection – A Choices Field

To create the Selection field:

1. While still on the Structure Window, open the DataFile menu again and select Add Field.

2. Type "Selection"

3. Select Choices from the Data Type: pop-up.

4. Under Format: select Horizontal Buttons.

5. Enter the choices in the Choices: text box. Press **Return** after each entry:

   One
   Two
   Both

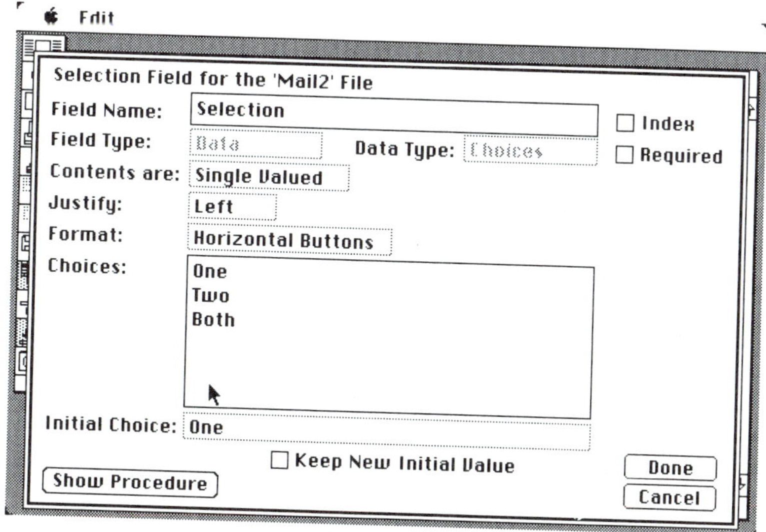

Figure 4-7a. Selection Field Definition Graphic.

6. Click **Save** then **Done** to complete the definition.

The Selection field will be used later to help select a current address from the two in the multivalued field.

It's a good idea to save your work in progress. In dBASE Mac your file is automatically saved when you create it, but many other aspects of your work are not saved. In fact, new views or modifications to existing views are only saved with the project. New fields in the Globals file, relationships, and any files added to the Structure Window during a particular session are also saved as part of the current project. Therefore, you must save your work as a project.

To Save a project, pull down the Projects menu and select Save or Save As (see the discussions on Save and Save As in Part II, dBase Mac reference). Or click on the Save icon from the Palette. If this is the first time you have saved the project, or if you selected Save As, you will be prompted to enter a project name.

Type "MultiMail"

The disk drive will spin a few moments, then the pointer will return. Now you can continue your work.

NOTE: If you run into problems later, or if you make a mistake you can't correct, select Revert to Saved from the Projects menu to return your project to this point.

If you would like to quit now, you can do so by clicking on the Quit icon, or by opening the Projects menu and selecting Quit. If you have made any changes to your project since the last time you saved it, you will be asked whether you want to save those changes or not. Click **Yes** if you want to save changes. If you have made no changes you will not be prompted.

1. Click on the Quit icon,
   or
   Select Quit from the Projects menu
2. Click on the **Yes** button (if desired).

→ MultiMail continues in Chapter 6.

A Quick View Form

In the next sections, you will create a Form view and a Column view using dBASE Mac's Quick Create feature. Views are included in this chapter to give you a greater feeling for dBASE Mac, and to allow you to enter and view some multivalued data. A more complete treatment of views begins in Chapter 6.

If you elected to Quit at the end of the last section, you will need to start a project again. To do this, double-click on the project icon labeled "MultiMail". dBASE Mac will open, and you should see the Structures Window with the Mail2 file on it.

Click once anywhere on the Mail2 file to be sure it is the active file. The file name bar at the top should be dark.

NOTE: dBASE Mac will always highlight one file in a project when you first begin. If there is only one file, then it will be highlighted when the project is opened. If there are several files in a project, then the file that was highlighted when the project was last Saved will be highlighted the next time it is opened.

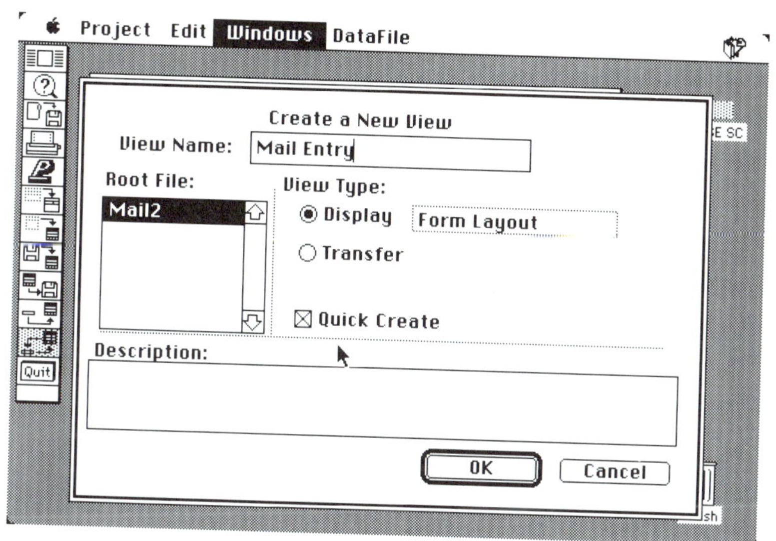

Figure 4-8 Create New View Graphic.

1. Now open the Windows menu and select New View... or click on the New View icon in the Palette.

   Type "Mail Entry"

2. Fill in the name.
3. Be sure the Mail2 file is highlighted in the Root File: menu to the left of the dialog box.
4. Click on the pop-up menu and select Form Layout.
5. Click on the Quick Create box.

   Check to see that your screen looks exactly like the screen in Figure 4-8.

6. Click **OK**

After a few moments, the Mail Entry form should appear on the screen. Each of the fields from the Mail2 file is represented by a label and an empty box in which you can enter data.

To enter the following data, type only the words in bold print. Type the entries exactly as they appear on the page. Press the **Tab** key to move the cursor between fields. To add another occurrence in a multivalued field, press **Command-A** (hold the Command key and press the letter A).

- **Use Command-A to add additional data to a multivalued field. Once an additional occurrence or item has been added to a multivalued field, all fields in the same Set will have a new, blank corresponding occurrence or item. Select values in a multivalued field by moving the mouse pointer to the end of the field and opening the pop-up menu there. Select the value you wish to display. All fields in the same Set will display associated records.**

To enter values for address and phone, type in all the first set of values, then press **Command-A** (only once) while in any of the fields in the Address Set, then fill in the second set of values.

Data Entry

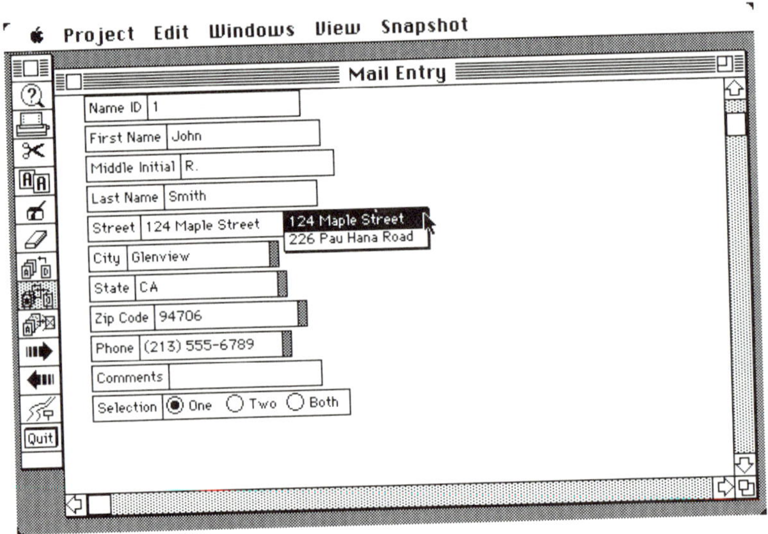

Figure 4-9 Enter Data Graphic.

Name ID:	**1**
First Name:	**John**
Middle Initial:	**R.**
Last Name:	**Smith**
Street:	**124 Maple Street**
	226 Pau Hana Road
City:	**Glenview**
	Kailua

State:	**CA**
	HI
Zip Code:	**94706**
	96789
Phone:	**2135556789**
	8085552345

Notice that you did not type parentheses, spaces, or dashes into the phone numbers, but they appear anyway. That is the result of the Must Match Patterns you created using the tilde (~).

Notice also that when a multivalued field contains data, a small box at the right of the field box turns dark. This box operates like a pop-up window, allowing you to open a list of all the multivalued field's contents. Click the mouse pointer on the multivalued pop-up selector, then select any occurrence of a multivalued field by dragging the mouse to that occurrence and releasing the button. Notice what happens to the other fields in the Set when you select a new occurrence in any one of the fields in the Set. Because all values in a Set are linked, displaying one value automatically displays them all.

Skip the Comments field for now, or enter data into it if you desire.

Now press the **Enter** key to save the record.

- To complete the processing of a record and save the results, you must press the **Enter** key.

Now enter the following names and addresses using **Tab** to move between fields, **Command-A** to set a new multivalued occurrence, and **Enter** to complete each record:

Name ID:	**2**
First Name:	**Mel**
Middle Initial:	**F.**
Last Name:	**Fern**
Street:	**2160 Rose St.**
	13 Science Dr.
City:	**Covina**
	Provo
State:	**CA**
	UT
Zip Code:	**91722**
	84167
Phone:	**8185551212**
	8015551313

Name ID:	**3**
First Name:	**Frank**
Middle Initial:	**R.**
Last Name:	**Bacon**
Street:	**32 Covington St.**
	61 Songbird Lane

City:	**New York**
	Orem
State:	**NY**
	UT
Zip Code:	**10023**
	84057
Phone:	**2125556789**
	8015556868

Name ID:	**4**
First Name:	**Bill**
Middle Initial:	**R.**
Last Name:	**Shakespeare**
Street:	**19 W. Avon Pl.**
	2560 Blue Ave.
City:	**Berkeley**
	Torrance
State:	**CA**
	CA
Zip Code:	**94704**
	90502
Phone:	**4155556543**
	2135558686

Name ID:	**5**
First Name:	**Frank**
Middle Initial:	**J.**
Last Name:	**Moto**
Street:	**1218 Secret Drive**
	676 Legal Ave.
City:	**New York**
	Covina
State:	**NY**
	CA
Zip Code:	**10018**
	91722
Phone:	**2125559988**
	8185556767

NOTE: To scroll through the records once you have entered a few, press **Command-P** to move backward (to the previous record) or **Command-N** to move to the next record. You can also open the Edit menu and select Prior or Next, or use the arrow icons on the Palette. To find a particular record, type its Key field value in the Name ID field box, then press **Tab**. If the Key field value that you type matches an existing record, that record will become the current record. If no match is found, a blank record is presented. Filling in the blank record and pressing **Enter** will create a new record with the current Key Field value.

HINT: Pressing **Shift-Tab** will move backward through the fields of the current record, and using **Option-Tab** will retrieve the current record and cause the cursor (insertion point) to remain in the Key field. Use **Option-Tab** when searching for a specific record and entering Key field values to find it. That way, if you don't find it, you can just enter another key value.

Name ID:	**6**
First Name:	**Steve**
Last Name:	**Condie**
Street:	**676 Legal Lane**
	56 Margaret Lane
City:	**Covina**
	Mathew
State:	**CA**
	CA
Zip Code:	**91722**
	94111
Telephone:	**8185556967**
	4155556567

Name ID:	**7**
First Name:	**Bart**
Last Name:	**Sandeine**
Street:	**15 Benthys St.**
	125 Ambition Ave.
City:	**Maspeth**
	Unbridled
State:	**NY**
	TX
Zip Code:	**11378**
	50955
Telephone:	**7185551213**
	7145559876

Name ID:	**8**
First Name:	**Bob**
Last Name:	**Goodman**
Street:	**2560 Blue Ave.**
	3984 Brandon Blvd.
City:	**Torrance**
	E. Modem
State:	**CA**
	OR

Zip Code: 90502
93434
Telephone: 2135558686
5035556923

Name ID: 9
First Name: John
Last Name: Keats
Street: 61 Songbird Lane
545 Ozymandius St.
City: Orem
Skylark
State: UT
NM
Zip Code: 84057
30949
Telephone: 8015556868
5055550096

Name ID: 10
First Name: Mary
Last Name: Shelly
Street: 13 Science Dr.
26 Frankie Alley
City: Provo
South Bavaria
State: UT
NY
Zip Code: 84167
21222
Telephone: 8015551313
2125551311

Name ID: 11
First Name: John
Last Name: Bach
Street: 418 Brandenburg Ave.
16 Canon Lane
City: Berkeley
Fugal City
State: CA
AZ
Zip Code: 94704
43445

Telephone:	4155552435
	6025559933

Name ID:	12
First Name:	William
Last Name:	Bacon
Street:	84 W. 89th
	7 Manuscript Ct.
City:	New York
	Writer's Block
State:	NY
	FL
Zip Code:	10075
	22033
Telephone:	2125553213
	8135553432

Name ID:	13
First Name:	James
Last Name:	Goodman
Street:	123 Rose Ave.
	8789 Samaritan Dr.
City:	Berkeley
	Omaha
State:	CA
	NE
Zip Code:	94704
	50059
Telephone:	4155554343
	4025556231

Name ID:	14
First Name:	Esther
Last Name:	Moto
Street:	1218 Secret Drive
	676 Legal Ave.
City:	New York
	Covina
State:	NY
	CA
Zip Code:	10018
	91722
Phone:	2125559988
	8185556767

Name ID:	15
First Name:	Melvina
Last Name:	Fern
Street:	2160 Rose St.
	13 Science Dr.
City:	Covina
	Provo
State:	CA
	UT
Zip Code:	91722
	84167
Phone:	8185551212
	8015551313

Viewing Data

When you have finished entering the sample data into your file, you may want to see all the records at one time. To do so you will create another view, called a Column view. Again, you will use the Quick Create feature to simplify the process.

1. Open the Windows menu and select New View. . .
2. Type "Mailing List Columns" to Name the view.
3. In the View Type pop-up menu, select Columnar Layout.
4. Check the Quick Create checkbox.

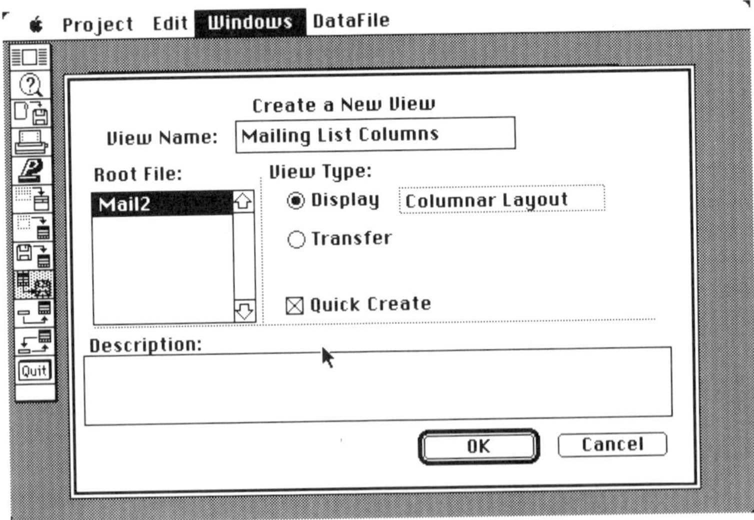

Figure 4-10 Quick Create Column View Screen.

5. If your screen looks like the screen above (Figure 4-10), then click **OK** to create the view.

After a few moments, the screen should display several columns. Select Perform and Use from the View menu or from the Palette. dBASE Mac will process and then display all the records in the file. If the data extend off the bottom or the right of the screen, use the scroll bars at the bottom and to the right of the window to see fields or records that are not displayed. Notice how multiple entries are displayed.

Deleting a View

What happens if you no longer want a view? Simple. You delete it. While still looking at the Mailing List Columns view, open the View menu and select Delete View. A dialog box will ask you to confirm that you want to delete the view. Click **Yes**. That's all there is to it.

> WARNING: A deleted view cannot be undeleted. However, if you really make a tragic mistake, you may be able to recover the view by selecting Revert from the Project menu. This will load the project in its last-saved form. Any changes you have made to the views or file relations since the time the project was saved will be lost. However, the view you deleted will be recovered assuming it was ever saved with the project. Obviously, if you just created the view during a dBASE Mac session and never saved the project, any deleted view stays deleted.

Oh, but don't worry. You'll get another look at Mailing List Columns in Chapter 7 where you'll learn a lot more about Columnar views.

Now you have created a simple file. You have used mulitvalued fields and pattern matching, and you have created a Form view and a Column view, and you have deleted the Column view. In the next section of Chapter 4 you will begin a more ambitious application. This application, a personal checkbook manager, uses several other kinds of fields.

If you wish to stop now, Quit and Save the current project. If you did not save it before, call it "MultiMail". MultiMail continues at the beginning of chapter 6.

In the next section, you will begin a checkbook project. The Checkbook uses Text fields, Numeric fields, Memory fields, Choices and Logical Fields.

Creating the Checkbook File

If you Quit dBASE Mac at the end of the last session, start the program again by double-clicking on the dBASE Mac icon.

If you did not Quit dBASE Mac at the end of the last session, you will still have the MultiMail project on the screen. To save the MultiMail project, select Close from the Projects menu. You will be prompted to save changes. Click **OK** to save any changes you have made since the last time you saved the project. When the mouse cursor reappears, you should see the dBASE Mac menus, and a small Palette window, but no

Structure Window. Open the Projects menu and select New. This will create a new, untitled project. Now you may proceed with the next application.

To create the Checkbook file:

1. Open the DataFile menu and choose New. . .
2. Click **OK** on the next screen to choose a dBASE Mac type file.
3. Now name the new file. Type "Checkbook" and click **Save.**

An Auto-Sequencing Key Field – Transaction Number

You should now see the Key field definition screen. The Key field for the checkbook will be a special kind of Number field. Call it Transaction Number.

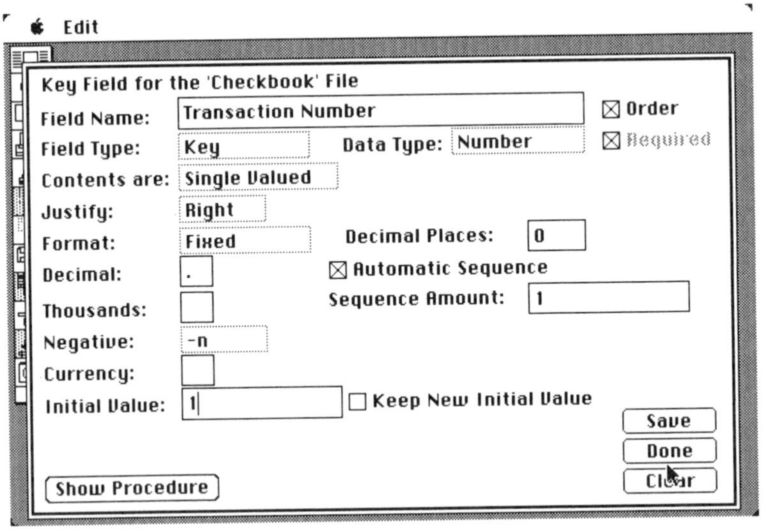

Figure 4-11 Key Field Definition Screen.

1. Type "Transaction Number" to name the field.
2. Select Number from the Data Type: pop-up.

   Notice that a whole new set of options appears. Take a look at the new options. For a complete treatment of these options, see Numeric Field in the Reference.

3. Now **Tab** once. The cursor should move to the Decimal Places: box, highlighting the default value of 2.

   Type "0"

   The 2 should be replaced by a zero.

4. Now click in the Automatic Sequence check box

NOTE: Automatic Sequence causes dBASE Mac to increase the Key value by a preset amount for each new record. It is only available with Numeric Key fields. If you use Automatic Sequence, you may override the auto-sequence manually, and of course you can enter Key field values to call up existing records.

Notice that some new options appear when you check Automatic Sequence. Sequence Amount determines the amount of change made in the value of the Key field for each new record. A value of one adds one to each Key field value as you add new records.

Initial Value is the starting value for the Key field. If you want to start at a certain number, insert that number in the Initial Value box.

Check the Keep New Initial Value box if you want to retain the value from the last record entered. In the case of an Automatic Sequence field, this box is meaningless.

5. Enter an Initial Value of 1.

   Note that the Order checkbox is checked. This instructs dBASE Mac to keep an internal index on the Key field, keeping records in Key field order.

6. Click **Save** to save the Key field definition.

Summary:

1. Type "Transaction Number"
2. Select Number from the Data Type: pop-up.
3. Press **Tab** and type 0 (zero).
4. Click the Automatic Sequence checkbox.
5. Enter an Initial Value of 1.
6. Click **Save**.

Field 2—Date—A Date Field

The next field in the Checkbook file is a Date field. To create a Date field:

1. Type "Date"

2. Select Date from the Data Type: pop-up. Notice that several new options appear.

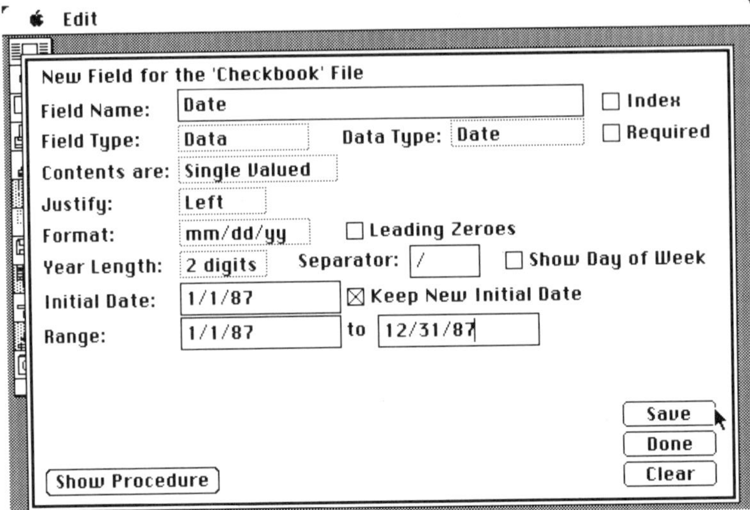

Figure 4-12 Date Field Definition Screen

The Format: pop-up contains a list of valid date formats. You can choose the one you wish to use. For now, leave the Format unchanged.

You can choose to display the year as a 2-digit number, or as a 4-digit number. For now, leave it a 2-digit number.

The Separator is the character that separates parts of the date. The Separator option only appears when you choose a format that needs it. Try choosing some of the other formats from the Format: pop-up. When you are finished, return to the top option (mm/dd/yy). A slash is the default separator, but you may choose to use a space or a dash, or other valid character. For now, leave the Separator unchanged.

Click the Leading Zeros check box if you want dates to display as 01/05/87 instead of 1/5/87. For now, leave it unchanged.

You can click the Show Days of Week box to display dates with days of the week, for example, Monday, 1/5/87.

If you want the program to begin with a particular date, enter that date in the Initial Date text box. For this application, you will enter an initial date of "1/1/87"

3. **Tab** to the Initial Date text box and type "1/1/87"

4. Click the Keep New Initial Date checkbox if you wish the program to keep the last entered date and forward it to the next record. For the Checkbook application, check the Keep New Initial Date box.

NOTE: Using Keep New Initial Date in this case causes the program to consider the most recently entered date as a default. Therefore, when you enter several transactions for the same day, you will not have to re-enter the date for each transaction.

The Range boxes let you define a minimum and a maximum range for your date entries. This is useful if, for instance, you want to be sure that no entries are accidentally entered for the wrong year. Use the Range box to make the Checkbook accept only entries for 1987.

5. **Tab** to the first Range text box and type "1/1/87"

6. **Tab** to the Second Range text box and type "12/31/87"

Any entries before or after 1987 will not be accepted.

7. Click **Save** to save the Date field definition.

Summary:

1. Type "Date".
2. Select Date from the Data Type: pop-up.
3. **Tab** to the Initial Date text box and enter "1/1/87"
4. Click the Keep New Initial Date check box.
5. **Tab** to the initial Range text box and enter "1/1/87'
6. **Tab** to the second Range text box and enter "12/31/87"
7. Click **Save**.

Field 3—Type—A Choices Field

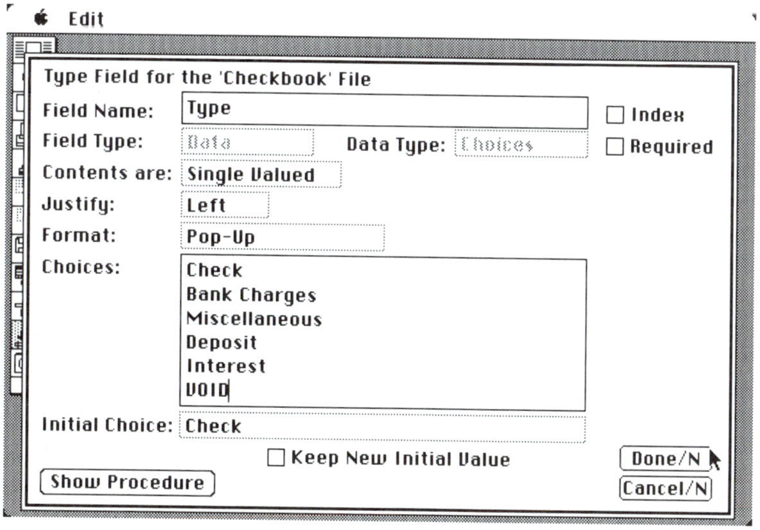

Figure 4-13 Choices Field Graphic.

The next field is a special one that determines the type of transaction you wish to enter. Each entry in the checkbook can be one of several set types of transaction—check, deposit, bank charge, interest, or perhaps a miscellaneous charge. Because there is a finite number of choices, you can use a Choices field.

NOTE: Choices fields can hold up to 8,000 choices, although any number greater than about 20 or 30 may become awkward due to the great amount of scrolling that will be necessary to reach some of the entries. One application in this book uses a Choices field to contain each of the fifty states. (Choices fields can contain up to 8,000 total characters per field, and each choice can be up to 255 characters in length.)

1. Enter "Type" as the name of the field.

2. Open the Data Type: pop-up and select Choices.

3. Open the Format: pop-up and examine the possibilities. You can select a pop-up menu, horizontal or vertical buttons, or a text box. For now, select Pop-Up as the format. Later you can change the format if you wish.

NOTE: Even after saving a field definition, you can still return to change any part of the field except the Field Type and the Data Type. Double-click the field name on the Structure Window or highlight the field you wish to modify and select Change Field from the DataFile menu to return to the field definition screen.

4. The Choices box is where you will enter the available options for this field. After you type each option, press the **Return** key to move to the next position.

   Type "Check" (Ret)
   Type "Bank Charges" (Ret)
   Type "Miscellaneous" (Ret)
   Type "Deposit" (Ret)
   Type "Interest"
   Type "VOID"

   Notice that Check is the default initial value. You can change the Initial Value by selecting from the pop-up. (Note that the borders of the Initial Value box are grey, meaning that it is a pop-up.) Since checks are the most common transactions, leave Check as the Initial Value and click on the Keep New Initial Value checkbox.

NOTE: You may wonder about the order chosen for the choices. Notice that similar types are grouped together. Checks, Bank Charges, and Miscellaneous transactions all subtract from the checking account balance. Deposits and Interest add to the balance. Later, when you sort data, this order will become more important (see Chapter 8).

6. If your screen looks just like the one in Figure 4-13 click **Save** to save the field definition.

Summary:

1. Enter "Type"
2. Select Choices from the Data Type: pop-up.
3. Select a Format (use Pop-Up).
4. Enter each choice and press **Return**:

   Check
   Bank Charges
   Miscellaneous
   Deposit
   Interest
   VOID

5. Check Keep New Initial Value.
6. Click **Save**.

Field 4—Check Number—A Numeric Field

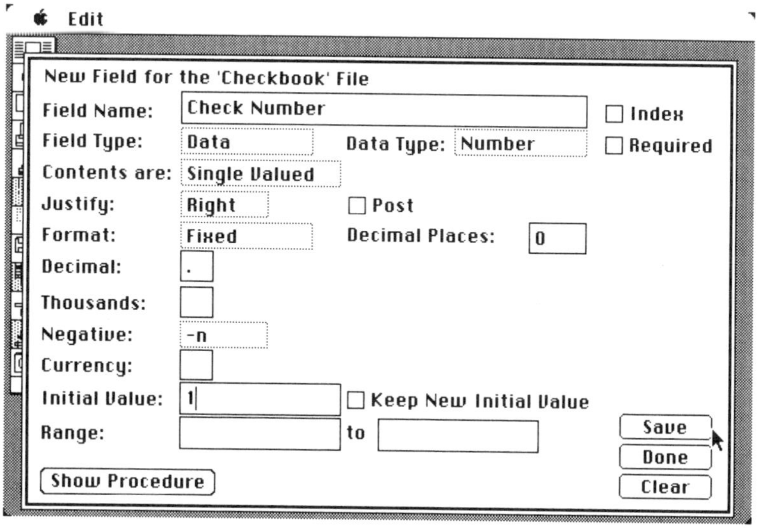

Figure 4-14 Check Number Field Definition Graphic.

The next field is the Check Number field. This field must be a Numeric field because it will be incremented for each new check.

1. Type "Check Number" to name the field.

2. Select Number from the Data Type: pop-up.

NOTE: In most of the fields you have defined until now, the Justify: option has always defaulted to Left. This means that all field values have aligned with the left margin of the field box. Number fields traditionally align to the right to keep decimal places even. Thus, the default justification for a number field is Right.

The Format: pop-up for a Number field contains two choices: Fixed and Floating. Both refer to the number of places after the decimal point. A Fixed format always displays the same number of places after the decimal point. For instance, when you are displaying dollar amounts, you may always want to display the cents column, even if its value is zero. You never want to display more than two decimal places, however. By selecting Fixed and setting the number of decimal places to 2, you assure that all data for the current field will display with two decimal places.

If, on the other hand, you are displaying data that need greater accuracy, you can set the format to Floating, which will display the numbers to the greatest amount of decimal accuracy the program can provide. dBASE Mac can display up to ninteen digits. By setting a high number of decimal places, and a Floating format, you assure the greatest accuracy.

3. Leave the Format set to Fixed and **Tab** to the Decimal Places: box. Notice that the present contents of the box are highlighted. Type a zero (0) to indicate no decimal places. If you use the mouse to move to the box, the contents are not automatically highlighted.

NOTE: To replace the contents of any box, drag the mouse across the box, highlighting the contents, then type in the replacement information.

4. Leave the Decimal:, Thousands:, Negative:, and Currency: boxes unchanged. The decimal point, the format for negative numbers, and the currency symbol don't apply to the Check Number field. You want to leave the Thousands: value blank. You don't want to display a comma in a four-digit check number!

5. For the Initial Value, you might want to type in the number of the first check you expect to enter. For this exercise, enter the number one (1). Leave the Keep New Initial Value box blank.

6. You may wish to enter a range for your check numbers, but for now leave the Range values blank.

7. Click **Save** to save the field definition.

Summary:

1. Type "Check Number"
2. Select Number from the Data Type: pop-up.
3. **Tab** to the Decimal Places text box and enter 0 (zero).
4. **Tab** past the other options to Initial Value.
5. Enter 1.
6. Leave the Range blank.
7. Click **Save**.

Field 5—Description—A Text Field

The Description field is a simple text field used to provide information about the transaction—name of the payee for a check, source of a deposit, other notes, and so on.

1. Type "Description" to name the field.
2. Click **Save** to save the field definition.

The next two fields are amount fields. In this application you will use two different fields, one for checks and charges, and another for deposits. You will use these two fields in a special way during data input (see Chapter 6).

Field 6—Check Amount—A Dollar Field

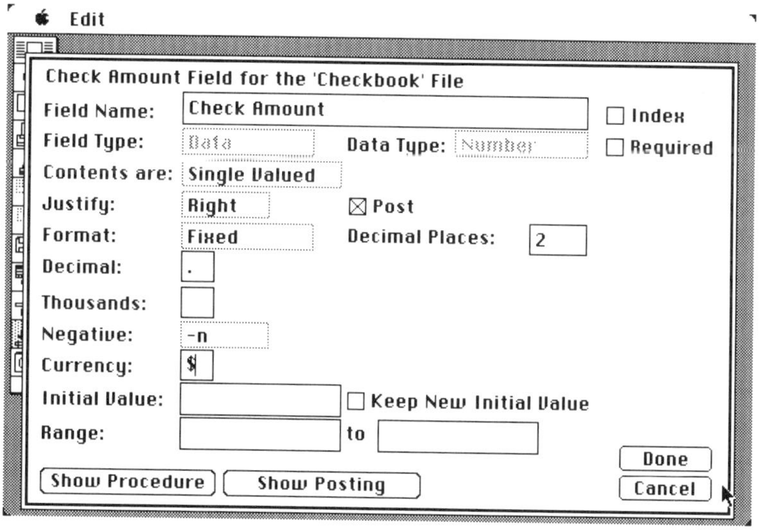

Edit
Check Amount Field for the 'Checkbook' File
Field Name: Check Amount
Index
Field Type: Data
Data Type: Number
Required
Contents are: Single Valued
Justify: Right
Post
Format: Fixed
Decimal Places: 2
Decimal: .
Thousands:
Negative: -n
Currency: $
Initial Value:
Keep New Initial Value
Range: to
Done
Show Procedure
Show Posting
Cancel

Fig. 4-15 Dollar Field Graphic.

1. Type "Check Amount" to name the field.
2. Select Number from the Data Type: pop-up.

3. Check the Post checkbox. Notice that a new button appears called Show Posting. You will come back to that later.

4. Leave everything else unchanged except the Currency: box. **Tab** to the Currency: box or click on it, then type a dollar sign ($) in that box.

TIP: To create a dollar-formatted field, create a Number field and enter the dollar sign in the Currency: box. That's all there is to it. The dollar field can be a Formula, Memory, or a Data field.

5. Click **Save** to save the field definition.

Field 7—Deposit Amount—a Dollar Field

1. Type "Deposit Amount" to name the field.

2. Select Number from the Data Type: pop-up.

3. Check the Post checkbox.

4. Leave everything else unchanged except the Currency: box. Type a dollar sign ($) in the Currency: box.

5. Click **Save** to save the field definition.

Field 8—Memo—A Text Field

Since the Description field only shows a limited amount of information about each transaction, you may want to add a Memo field for more complete explanations. The Memo field will allow you to describe your transactions in as much detail as you wish.

1. Type "Memo" to name the field.

2. Click on the Wrap checkbox.

3. Select Multiple Valued from the Contents Are: pop-up.

   Making this a Wrapping field allows you to enter long descriptions, if necessary, without worrying about formatting the text you enter.

4. Click **Save**.

Field 9 – Tax – A Logical Field

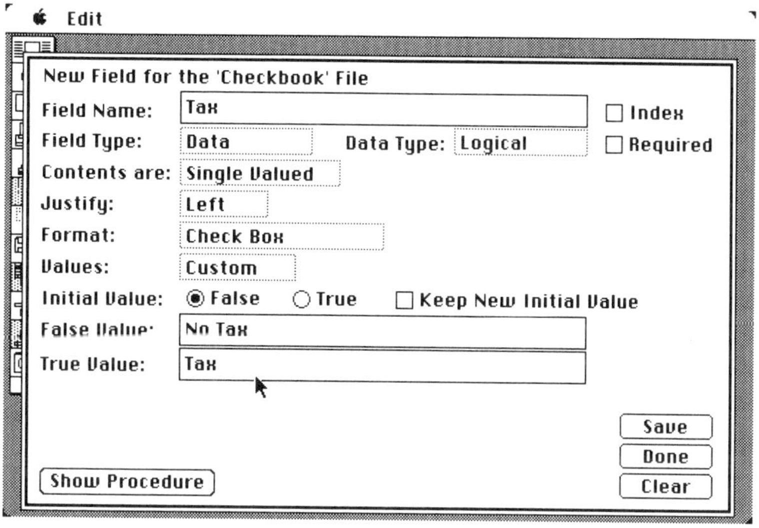

Fig. 4-16 Logic Field Graphic

You may wish to note whether a particular transaction has tax implications or not. The best way to do so is to create a Logical Field called Tax.

1. Type "Tax" to name the field.

2. Select Logical from the Data Type: pop-up

3. Open the Format: pop-up and examine the choices available. You can have the same basic choices of format as the Choices field with the addition of the Checkbox. Select Checkbox.

   Look at the list of choices available in the Values: pop-up. None of the preset values, with the possible exception of the No/Yes choice, look appropriate for the Tax field.

4. You could select No/Yes, but for this application, select the Custom value to define your own. Notice that two new text entry boxes appear.

5. Leave the Initial Value set at False.

   In the case of a Checkbox, the false value is the value of the box when it is not checked. A true value is the value of a box that has been checked.

6. Type "No Tax" for the False Value.

When you are using a Checkbox format for a logical field, only the True value will appear, so the False value is optional. When using other format options, the False value is important.

7. Type "Tax" for the True Value.

8. Click **Save** to save the Tax field definition.

Summary:

1. Type "Tax"
2. Select Logical from the Data Type: pop-up.
3. Select Checkbox from the Format pop-up.
4. Select Custom from the Values: pop-up.
5. Leave Initial Value as False.
6. Enter "No Tax" in the False Value: text box.
7. Enter "Tax" in the True Value: text box.
8. Click **Save**.

Field 10—Counter—A Memory Field

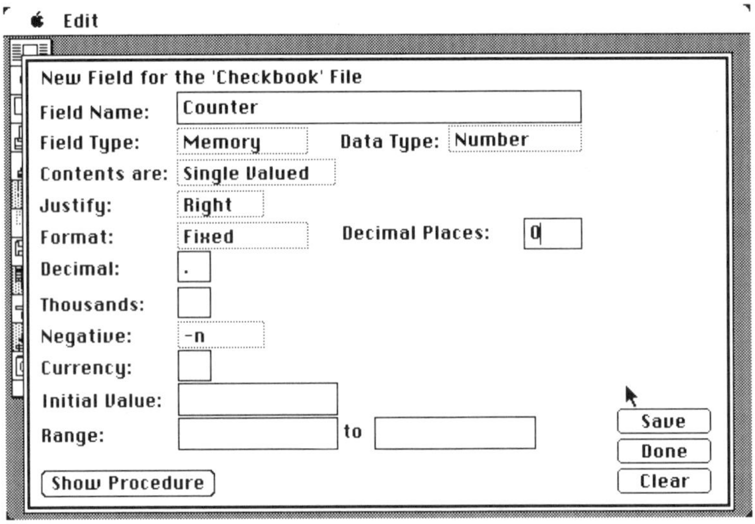

Fig. 4-17 Counter Field Graphic.

The Check Number field presents a problem. Because it is not a Key field, it does not have an Automatic Sequencing option. Therefore, you need a way to make it incremental. Additionally, not all transactions are going to be checks, so you don't want the Check Number field to be incremental for each transaction. To solve the problem, create a special field to keep track of the current check number. Call this field Counter.

1. Type "Counter" to name the field.
2. Select Memory from the Field Type: pop-up.
3. Select Number from the Data Type: pop-up.
4. Set Decimal Places: to zero (0).
5. Important: Set the Initial Value of this field to 1 (or to the number you want to start your checks with). Do not leave Initial Value blank.
6. Click **Save** to save the Counter field.

Memory fields store data for the whole file. Therefore, the value in the Counter field will always remain regardless of the current record being processed. In the next chapter, you will create a procedure that uses the values in the Type and Counter fields to determine (1) if the Check Number field should be incremented, and (2) how to calculate its value.

Field 11—Balance—Memory Field

The Balance field is a Numeric Memory field that keeps a running balance of your checking account. You will Post the amounts from the Check Amount and Deposit Amount fields in the Checkbook file to the Balance field.

1. Type "Balance" to name the field
2. Select Memory from the Field Type: pop-up.
3. Select Number from the Data Type: pop-up.
4. Enter a dollar sign in the Currency: box.
5. Click **Save** to save the file.
6. Click **Done** to return to the Structure Window.

The next two memory fields are used to keep a running balance of all checks and deposits. This is useful information to have, and can be kept easily in the Checkbook Project.

Field 12—Tot Check—A Memory Field

1. Type "Tot Check" to name the field
2. Select Memory from the Field Type: pop-up.
3. Select Number from the Data Type: pop-up.
4. Enter a dollar sign in the Currency: box.
5. Click **Save** to save the file.
6. Click **Done** to return to the Structure Window.

Field 13—Tot Dep—A Memory Field

1. Type "Tot Dep" to name the field.
2. Select Memory from the Field Type: pop-up.
3. Select Number from the Data Type: pop-up.
4. Enter a dollar sign in the Currency: box.
5. Click **Save** to save the file.
6. Click **Done** to return to the Structure Window.
7. At the file creation dialog box, estimate about twenty records for the file size and click **OK**.

Posting Data

To complete the file definition, you need to change the definitions for the Check Amount and the Deposit Amount fields. The Check Amount and Deposit Amount fields use the memory fields you just defined within their definitions (for posting) so, until you defined the memory fields, Check Amount and Deposit Amount could not be completed.

The easiest way to change a field definition is to double-click on the field name on the Structure Window. You can also highlight the field name by clicking on it once, then select Change Field from the DataFile menu. In either case, return to the field definition screen.

1. Double-click the Check Amount field.
2. Click once on the Show Posting button.

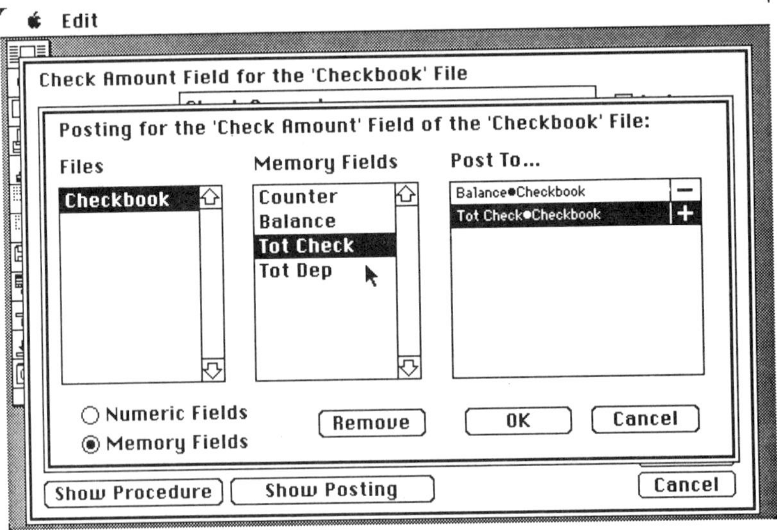

Figure 4-18 Posting Graphic.

Notice toward the bottom-left corner of the screen, there are two buttons—Numeric Fields and Memory Fields.

3. Select the Memory Fields button by clicking on it once.
4. Under Files, you will see the entry for Checkbook. Select Checkbook.
5. Select Balance from the Memory Fields column.
6. Under Post To: you should see the words Balance•Checkbook and then a large plus sign. Since you want to subtract all checks and charges, click once on the plus sign to change it to a minus sign.
7. Now select the Tot Checks field.

   This time leave the plus sign alone. This posting will accumulate a total of each check written.
8. If your screen looks like the one in Figure 4-18, click **OK** to save the Posting information.
9. Now click **Done** to save the new field definition for the Check Amount field. If you had changed your mind, you could have clicked **Cancel** to cancel the changes you made.

HINT: In the next step, you will repeat the procedure for the Deposit Amount field. Instead of clicking **Done** here, you can use a special feature of dBASE Mac to go directly to the Deposit Amount Change Field dialog box. Press and hold the **Command** key. Notice that /N appears. If you click **Done** now, when the **Command** key is pressed and the /N is visible, the current field definition will be saved, and you will move to the next field. Holding down the **Option** key displays a /P and moves to the previous field.

So, when changing file field definitions:

Option-Done moves to the previous record.
Command-Done moves to the next record.

If you did not use the **Command-Done** method outlined in the Hint, you need to repeat the procedure for the Deposit Amount field. Otherwise, begin with Step 2:

1. Double-click the Deposit Amount field.
2. Click once on the Show Posting button.
3. Select the Memory fields button by clicking on it once.
4. Under Files, select Checkbook.
5. Select Balance from the Memory fields column.

6. Under Post To: you should see the words Balance•Checkbook and then a large plus sign. Since you want to add all deposits, leave the plus sign unchanged.

7. Select the Tot Dep field and leave the plus sign unchanged.

8. Click **OK** to save the Posting information.

9. Now click **Done** to save the new field definition for the Check Amount field. If you had changed your mind, you could have clicked **Cancel** to cancel the changes you made.

NOTE: You might think that the Globals file would be a good place to keep the running balance because any view or field can access data in Global Memory fields. But Global field contents are not saved unless you save the project, and you will not necessarily save a project every time you use it. File Memory fields, like other file data, are saved independently from the project.

Congratulations. You have just completed the basic definition for the Checkbook file. In the chapters that follow you will complete the project and see how it all works. You will be adding several additional fields and views to the Checkbook Project, and learning several ways to manipulate data in dBASE Mac.

At this point you may want to take a break. If you wish to Quit, click on the Palette Quit icon (or select Quit from the Project menu). When the prompt appears asking if you wish to save changes, click **Yes**. Name the project "Checkbook Project". You will return to the Finder.

→ Checkbook continues in Chapter 6.

Summary

In Chapter 4 you have learned to open dBASE Mac from the Finder in several ways.

Also:

You learned to create new files and save new projects.

You learned to create different field and data types:

- Automatically Sequencing Key fields
- Data fields
- Memory fields
- Date fields
- Text fields
- Multivalued fields
- Sets
- Pattern matched fields
- Number fields
- Currency format fields
- Posting fields
- Logical fields

You also created two Quick views—one a Form view and the other a Column view.

You learned to enter new records and to enter and manipulate multiple occurrences in multivalued fields.

You learned how Sets work.

By now you should find it easy to create new files and fields. In the next chapter you will begin the Timecard Project. The Timecard Project is a multifile project that utilizes relational capabilities.

5

CREATING RELATIONSHIPS

Overview

Chapter 5 introduces the concept of relational files. These are files that can share information by means of special fields called pointer fields. A relationship is like a pipeline for information in that it acts as a conduit that must be shared between files. You can have one-way or two-way relationships.

Chapter 5 also introduces a personnel management application called Timecard Project. The Timecard Project uses three files: an Employee file, a Timecard file, and an Hourly Rate file. You will use this project through the next few chapters of the Tutorial.

In addition to relational files, Chapter 5 introduces several new types of fields: Time fields, Formula fields, and Graphic fields.

Creating a Relational System

A Timecard Project

The first relational system you will create is a timecard system to keep track of hours and salaries earned by employees who work on a timeclock. This simplified application, the Timecard Project, will contain three files: an Employee file, a Timecard file, and an Hourly Rate file. In addition, the Timecard Project contains an Index file.

The Timecard Project illustrates two of the three basic types of relationships—one-way and two-way. A two-way relationship links data from the Employee file to the Timecard file, and vice versa. Timecard is linked via a one-way relationship with Hourly Rates. (Indexes are illustrated later in the chapter by another small application.)

Specifically, you link each record in the Timecard file to an employee's ID number—a one-to-one relationship. At the same time, each Employee record contains a multivalued field listing all Timecards for that employee by their Key field values—a one-to-many relationship.

To illustrate the concept of one-to-one as opposed to one-to-many, look at the following chart:

Timecard 1	Joe
Timecard 2	Jane
Timecard 3	Joe
Timecard 4	Sam
Timecard 5	Joe
Timecard 6	Jane

Each timecard links with one, and only one, employee. But now look at the employee's records:

Jane	Timecard 2
	Timecard 6
Joe	Timecard 1
	Timecard 3
	Timecard 5
Sam	Timecard 4

Each employee record can contain references to several timecards—a one-to-many relationship (one employee to many timesheets).

The total salary earned for a particular timecard is computed and, using the relationship, then Posted back to the Employee file—to a field called Salary Earned. dBASE Mac's Post option allows you to add or subtract the values from a Numeric Data field in one file to the values in a Numeric or Memory field in another file. Another field in the Employee file contains the amount paid to the Employee, and a Formula field subtracts the Amount Paid from the Salary Earned to produce the Current Amount Due field.

A one-way relationship links data from the Hourly Rate file to the Timecard file. By selecting one of several hourly rates, you determine the amount of salary accrued. Since different timecards might have different salary rates, this system allows you to control the actual amount earned in any pay period. Since information is drawn from the Hourly Rates file, but no information need be returned to it, the relationship is a one-way relationship. In some applications, the Hourly Rate file might be referred to as a lookup table. Another common application for a lookup table (hence a one-way relationship) is a tax rate table.

Related Files—An Employee File

In this section, you will create an Employee database that contains only the information necessary for this application. Other data could be added to the file (and should be in a complete personnel application), but to avoid excessive effort, the application in this chapter is kept as simple as possible. For instance, in most personnel applications, the employee number would be a social security number. Other information such as hire date, evaluations, family and work history, and so on, would be included.

The Employee file contains the following fields:

Employee Number (Key field)
Last Name
Employee Pic
Amount Paid
Salary Earned
Current Amount Due

There are two new types of fields in this file. The Employee Pic is a Graphics field, and the Amount Due is a Formula field.

To create the Employee file:

1. Select New. . . from the DataFile menu.

2. Leave the type of file set to dBASE Mac and click **OK**.

3. Name the file. Type "Employee" and click **Save**.

Next create the Key field:

1. Name the Key field. Type "Employee Number"

2. Click **Save** to save the field

(You can create an Automatic Sequencing Number field as you did in Chapter 4, but it is not necessary. Often, in a personnel database, a Social Security Number is used as an Employee ID. You may wish to structure your personnel file that way. If you do, remember that you can make data entry much easier if you create a pattern match as follows:

3n~-2n~-4n

If you wish to create an Automatic Sequencing Key field instead (for convenience in doing the exercise), follow the directions in Chapter 4, or later in this chapter in the definition of the Timecard file.)

The next field is the Last Name field:

1. Type "Last Name" to name the field.

   In this case, you may often wish to produce reports sorted by Last Name. So you should click on the Index checkbox. This will speed up sorting by Last Name.

2. Click the Index checkbox.

3. Click **Save** to save the field.

Employee Pic—A Graphics Field

Graphics fields are used to incorporate graphics into specific records. You can also create fixed graphics that are independent of the records (used in layouts; see Chapter 7). The difference between a fixed graphic and a graphic field is that each picture in a graphic field may be dynamically updated and, unless the graphic field is a Memory field, each graphic is associated with a single record. Also, graphic fields can be multivalued. Fixed graphics are placed on forms and do not change. An example of a fixed graphic is a company logo placed at the top of a report.

In the Employee file, the graphic field might contain actual digitized pictures of your employees created with a digitizing camera, scanner, or a low-cost scanning device such as Thunderscan™.

(Even though you may have no intention of creating such an application, please follow the procedure for creating a Graphics field. Later you will have an opportunity to delete the field.)

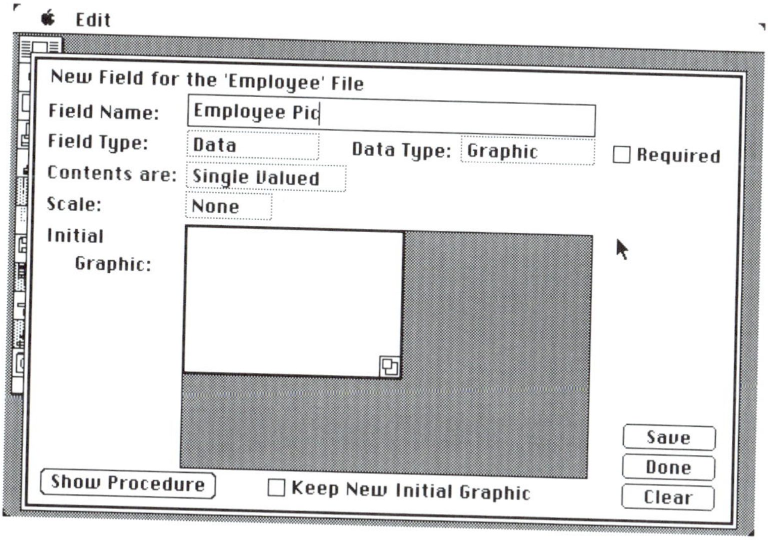

Figure 5-1 Graphic Field Definition Graphic.

To create a Graphics field:

1. Type "Employee Pic" to name the field.

2. Select Graphic from the Data Type: pop-up.

   Notice that a graphic window appears on the screen. The larger, grey area represents the maximum initial size the graphic can be when you first place it on a layout. However, the graphic can be made larger at a later time. The smaller box represents the current size of the graphic image. To make the initial graphic size larger or smaller, drag the small double box in the lower-right corner of the graphic image box to change its size.

Edit
New Field for the 'Employee' File
Field Name:
Employee Pic
Field Type:
Data
Data Type:
Graphic
Required
Contents are:
Single Valued
Scale:
None
Initial
Graphic:
Save
Done
Clear
Show Procedure
Keep New Initial Graphic

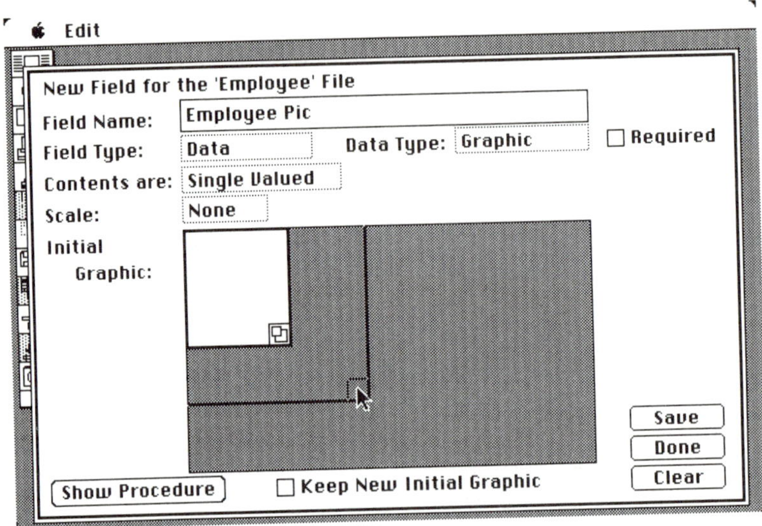

Figure 5-2 Graphic Change Size Graphic.

3. The Scale pop-up contains four choices: None, Width, Height, and Both. You can use the Scale menu to adjust the display of the graphic image to fit in the size box you create. If you choose None, whatever part of the image that fits within the box will appear. The rest will be cut off.

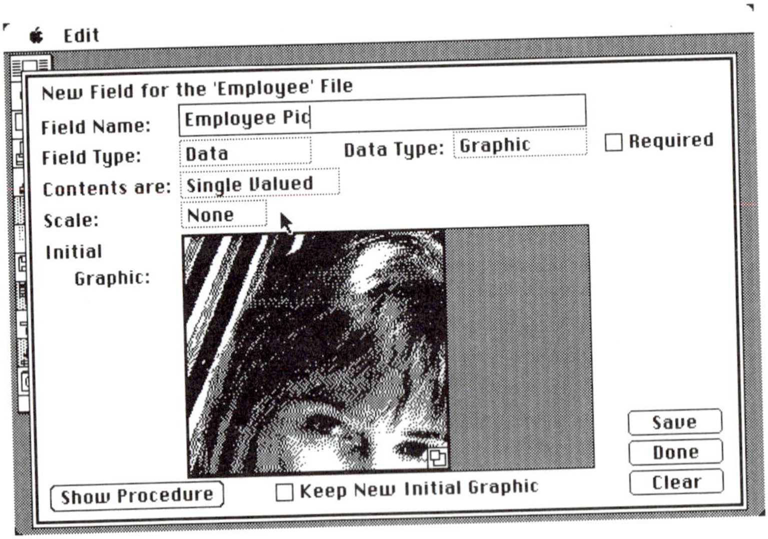

Edit
New Field for the 'Employee' File
Field Name:
Employee Pic
Field Type:
Data
Data Type:
Graphic
Required
Contents are:
Single Valued
Scale:
None
Initial
Graphic:
Save
Done
Clear
Show Procedure
Keep New Initial Graphic

Figure 5-3 None Scaling.

Edit
New Field for the 'Employee' File
Field Name:
Employee Pic
Field Type:
Data
Data Type:
Graphic
Required
Contents are:
Single Valued
Scale:
Width
Initial Graphic:
Save
Done
Clear
Show Procedure
Keep New Initial Graphic

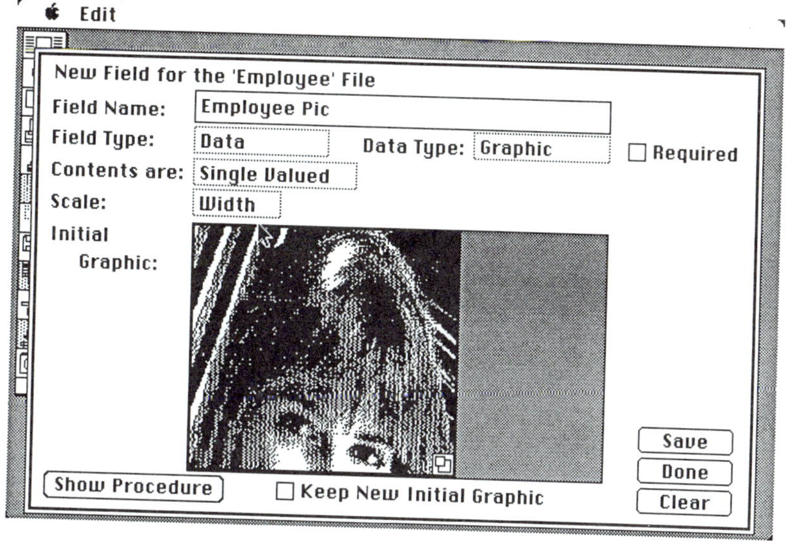

Figure 5-4 Width Scaling.

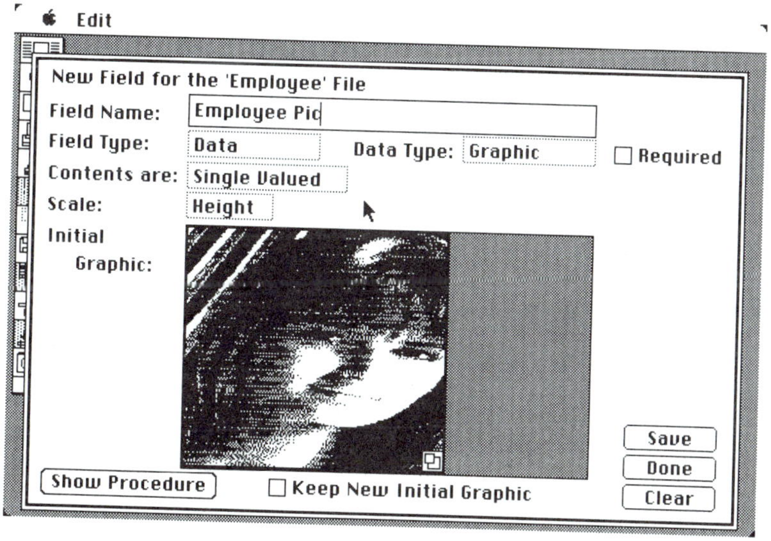

Edit
New Field for the 'Employee' File
Field Name:
Employee Pic
Field Type:
Data
Data Type:
Graphic
Required
Contents are:
Single Valued
Scale:
Height
Initial Graphic:
Save
Done
Clear
Show Procedure
Keep New Initial Graphic

Figure 5-5 Height Scaling.

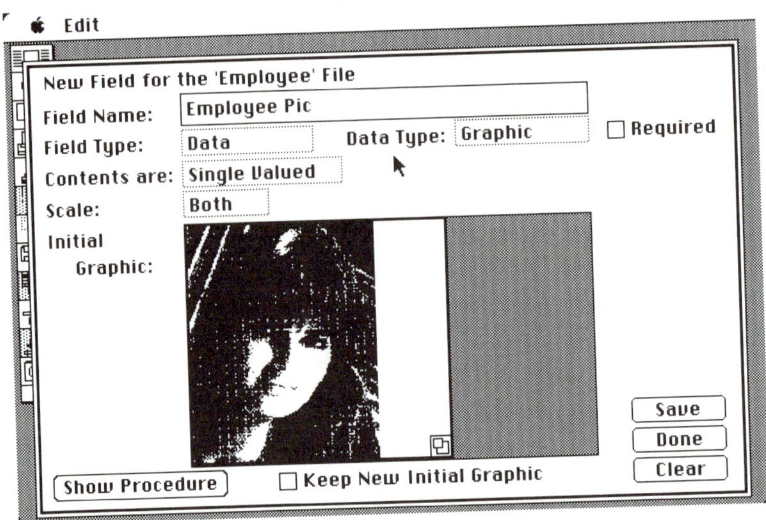

Figure 5-6 Both Scaling.

Selecting one of the other options causes the picture to be shrunk, if necessary, to fit into the graphic image box. Selecting Width causes the picture to be scaled to fit the width of the image box. Selecting Height causes the picture to be scaled to fit the length of the image box. Selecting Both causes the picture to be scaled to fit entirely within the graphic image box.

Using Picture This. . . Desk Accessory

When you load dBASE Mac, you automatically load two Desk Accessories (DA)—Help, and Picture This. . . . Picture This. . . allows you to grab parts of pictures from existing MacPaint compatible graphics (including SuperPaint and FullPaint images, and entire libraries of clip art).

- When you first open the Picture This. . . DA, you will be presented with a list of files in the current directory. Find the graphics files you need (changing folders if necessary), then double-click or highlight and click Open.
- Drag the mouse to select the part of the picture you want to grab, then **Command-C**, or Copy from the Edit menu, to copy the image into the Clipboard.
- Close the Picture This. . . window and select a Graphic field or Fixed Graphic box on the layout.

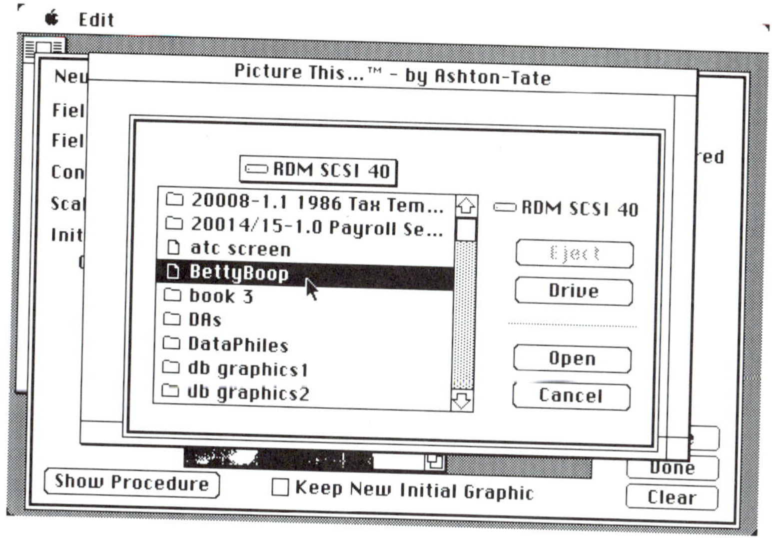

Figure 5-7 Picture This. . . Dialog Box.

- Press **Command-V** or Paste from the Edit menu to insert the graphic into the Graphic field or Fixed Graphic.

HINT: If you don't have any graphics, but you want to try the scaling options, you can create a MacPaint compatible picture of the current screen by pressing **Command-Shift-3**. The picture file thus created will appear on the desktop as Screen 0. You can create ten such screen shots, numbered Screen 0 to Screen 9. To create more than ten, you must rename one or more of the original ten.

You can keep an archive of pictures in the Scrapbook or other location if you wish. With an image in the graphic image box, you can experiment with sizing and scaling.

When you are finished experimenting with the Employee Pic field, click **Save** to save the field definition.

Amount Paid—A Number Field

The next field is the Amount Paid field. This is a currency format field. To create its definition:

1. Type "Amount Paid"
2. Select Number from the Data Type: pop-up.
3. Tab or mouse down to the Currency: box and enter a dollar sign ($).

4. Click **Save** to save the field definition.

Amount Paid will contain the total amount paid to a particular employee to date.

Salary Earned—A Number Field

Next is the Salary Earned field. Salary Earned derives from the amounts in the individual Timecard records. Each record posts its total to the Salary Earned field. To create the Salary Earned field:

1. Type "Salary Earned"
2. Select Number from the Data Type: pop-up.
3. Tab or mouse down to the Currency: box and enter a dollar sign ($).
4. Click **Save** to save the field definition.

Current Amount Due—A Formula Field

The final field is the Current Amount Due field. This tells you at a glance how much is still owed any employee. Current Amount Due is a calculated field based on the amount of Salary Earned less any Amount Paid. To create this field:

1. Type "Current Amount Due"
2. Select Formula from the Field Type: pop-up.

   Notice that the button that normally reads "Show Procedure" now reads "Show Formula."

3. Select Number from the Data Type: pop-up.
4. Tab or mouse down to the Currency: box and enter a dollar sign ($).
5. Click the Show Formula button.

   At this point stop and examine the Formula dialog box. At the top of the screen you should see "Formula for 'Current Amount Due':". Below that the Path should read "Employee." The Path represents the levels of the hierarchy in the view (the pointer fields by which dBASE Mac retrieves the data). As you will see in future chapters, the Path can contain references to many related files. For now, leave the Path alone.

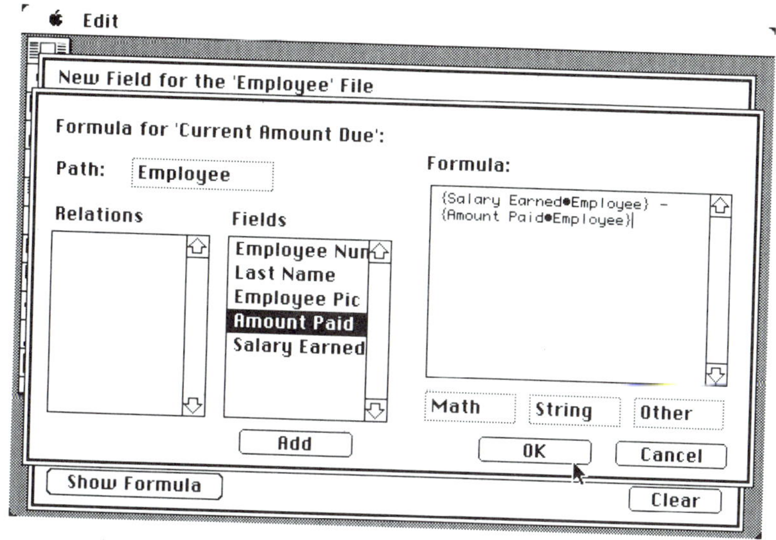

Figure 5-8 Formula Screen Graphic.

Since the Employee file is the only file that exists so far in this project, the Relations list box will contain no entries. If there were some other files with valid relationships to the Employee file, pointers to these files would be listed in the Relations list box.

The Fields list box displays a list of the fields you have just defined in the Employee file. The fields listed in the list box are always the fields for the file at the current level of the path. You can add field names to a formula by clicking on the field name and then clicking the **Add** button, or by double-clicking the field name.

6. Select Salary Earned and click **Add**, or double-click Salary Earned.

Notice that the full path of Salary Earned is displayed in the Formula: box. The path reads {Salary Earned•Employee}. Notice that the field name is first, followed by the file name. Also notice the curly brackets. All field names and field paths must be contained within the curly brackets.

Now open the Math pop-up menu by pressing and holding the mouse button with the cursor over the word *Math*. Notice that a pop-up menu of mathematical operators appears.

HINT: If you open a pop-up and change your mind about making a selection, drag the mouse off to the right or left until no option is highlighted, then let go of the mouse button.

Look at each of the three formula buttons—Math, String, and Other. These are the dBASE Mac commands you can use when defining a formula for a Formula field.

7. Open the Math pop-up and select the minus sign (−).
8. Now select and Add (or double-click) Amount Paid to add it to the formula. The formula now reads:

```
{Salary Earned•Employee} - {Amount Paid•Employee}
```

When you click **OK**, dBASE Mac first verifies that the syntax, or language, you have used is correct, and that all path references are valid. Then it closes the dialog box and returns to the field definition screen.

9. Click **OK** and watch as the program verifies the formula and returns you to the field definition screen.
10. Click **Save** to save the field definition.
11. That is all you need to define for the Employee file, so complete the definition by clicking **Done**.
12. Estimate the file size (enter 20) and click **OK** to complete the file definition and return to the Structure Window.

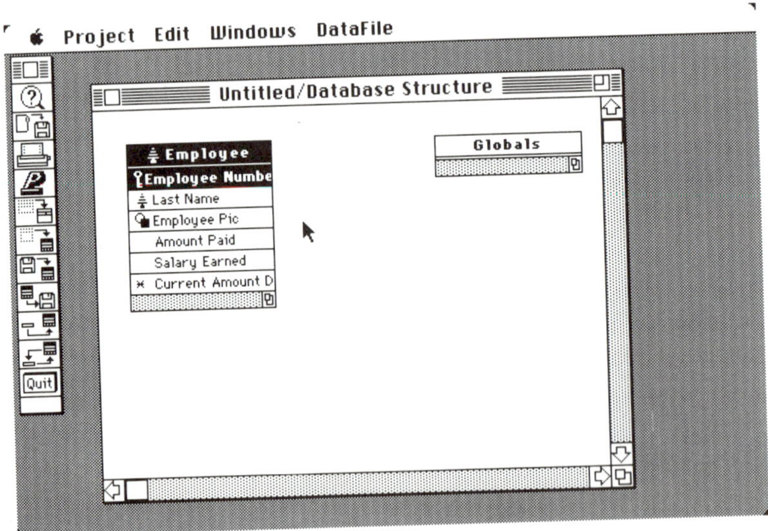

Figure 5-9 Employee Structure Window Graphic.

Notice that the Graphics field and the Formula field are marked specially on the Structure Window. Notice that the indexed Last Name field is also marked to indicate that it is indexed (as does the file as a whole because the Order box is checked in the Key field definition).

Related Files—The Hourly Rates File

To create a list of rates, you need only three fields: a Key field, a Rate Name field, and a Rate field. The Hourly Rates is a special kind of file, sometimes called a lookup file because it is used to contain tables of information that other files may need to look up. Other common lookup files might be a tax rate file and a file of price discounts based on various order quantities.

To create the Hourly Rates file, first be sure that the Structure Window is showing.

1. Select New. . . from the DataFile menu.
2. Click **OK** to make this a dBASE Mac file.
3. Type "Hourly Rates" to name the file.
4. Click **Save** to continue

The Key field definition screen for the Hourly Rates file appears. To define the Key field:

1. Type "Rate ID".
2. Click **Save.**

To create the Rate Name field:

1. Type "Rate Name"
2. Click **Save.**

The next field is a currency field.

1. Type "Rate" to name the field.
2. Select Number from the Data Type: pop-up.
3. Tab or mouse down to the Currency: box and enter a dollar sign ($).
4. Click **Save.**
5. Click **Done.**
6. Estimate file size (enter 10) and click **OK.**

When you return to the Structure Window you'll probably notice that the Hourly Rates file is placed on top of the Employee file. To move it to another place on the window, drag it by the title bar. Drag it down and to the right to an empty area.

NOTE: You can reposition any file on the Structure Window. Remember that the window is larger than a single screen, so if your files begin to seem too crowded, simply move them down or to the right.

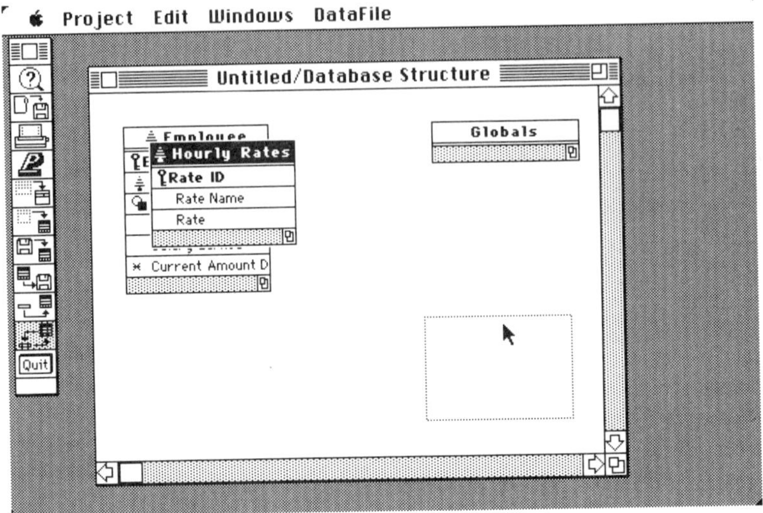

Figure 5-10 Moving the Hourly Rates File Graphic.

That's all there is to creating the Hourly Rates file.

Related Files—The Timecard File

The Timecard file is the heart of this application. By entering only a few items, you can update an employee's records easily. The Timecard file contains the following fields: Timecard Number, Date, Time in, Time Out, Total Hours, Total Due, and Posting Amount.

Time In and Time Out are Time fields. Total Hours is a formula field that subtracts Time In from Time Out. You will see that Time fields (and Date fields) can be used in arithmetic operations.

Total Due gives the total amount of salary earned for the current timecard record by multiplying the Total Hours by the hourly Rate taken from the Hourly Rates file. This amount is then written to a Numeric field (Posting Amount) and Posted to the Salary Earned field in the Employee file.

To create the Timecard file:

1. Select New. . . from the DataFile menu.
2. Click **OK** to make this a dBASE Mac file.
3. Type "Timecard" to name the file.
4. Click **Save.**

Timecard Number—A Key Field

The Key field for the Timecard file should be an automatic sequencing number file such as you created in Chapter 4. To create the Key field:

1. Type "Timecard Number"

2. Select Number from the Data Type: pop-up.

3. **Tab** to the Decimal Places box and enter zero (0).

4. Check the Automatic Sequence checkbox.

   You use the Automatic Sequence to control the record numbering. Because the timecards are in fixed order, you don't want to be able to change their numbering. If you were using a different system of timecards that was not compatible with the Automatic Sequence, you would not use the Automatic Sequence option. You could, however, create procedures to carry out your own auto number scheme in much the same way you will in the Checkbook Project.

4. Enter an Initial Value of 1.

5. Click **Save** to save the Key field definition.

Date—A Date Field

The Date field is next. Each Timecard record must have a date.

1. Type "Date" to name the field.

2. Select Date from the Data Type: pop-up.

3. Leave the format unchanged, but check the Show Day of Week checkbox.

4. Check the Required checkbox.

5. Because you may process several timecards from the same date in a single session, check the Keep New Initial Date check box. This assures that the last-used date will be carried over to the next record you enter.

6. Click **Save** to save the Date field definition.

You check the Required checkbox because each Timecard record must have a date. This prevents anyone from entering a record and leaving off the date. dBASE Mac will give a warning message if you attempt to enter a record without filling in a Required field.

TIP: Within a procedure or formula, you can represent the current date (from the Macintosh internal calendar) with the DAYS function. For instance, setting a Date field equal to DAYS sets it to the current date. You can also perform arithmetic using dates. For instance, if you had an application that automatically sent out past-due statements after 30 or 60 days, you could use a procedure like the following (where Date Field1 is set to DAYS, and Date Field2 is the original billing date:

```
IF {Date Field1•File} - {Date Field2•File} = 30
THEN
     PRINT("Statement")
```

Similarly, you can set a time field equal to the current time using the SECONDS function. You can use Time fields in formulas and procedural equations as well. Here's an interesting use of the Time field. Suppose you want to display the current time in other time zones. You would write a procedure that added or subtracted from the current time. For each hour of difference, you would add or subtract 3,600 (seconds). For instance, to calculate the time in California starting with Eastern Standard Time (three hours later), you would enter the following formula:

```
{Time Field•File} = Seconds
CATime = {Time Field•File} - 10800
```

Two Time Fields—Time In and Time Out

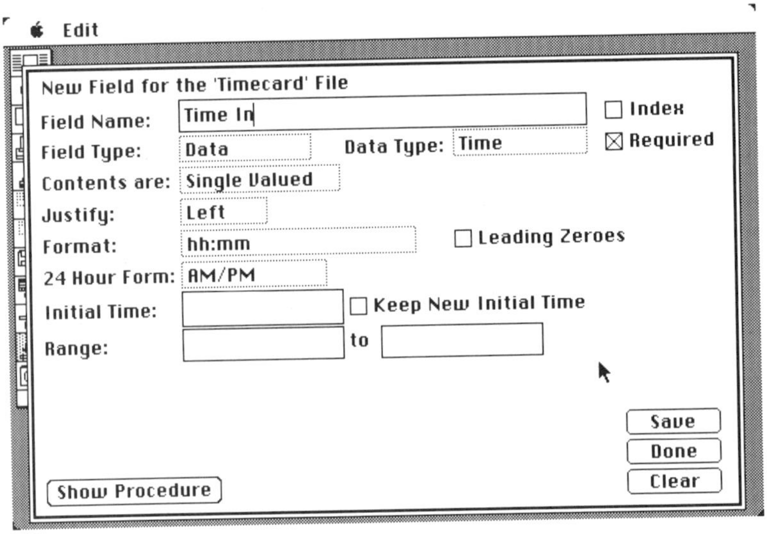

Figure 5-11 Time Field Graphic.

Time fields are much like Date fields. They can be displayed in a variety of formats, and they can be used directly in mathematical operations. You can enter Time fields as 24-hour time, 12-hour time, or AM/PM times. The program will automatically convert times entered in a format other than the one set for a field. For instance, a field set for 24-hour time would convert the entry "2 pm" to "14:00:00." Likewise, if the field is set as an AM/PM time, an entry of "18:31:56" would be converted to "6:31:56 PM."

1. Type "Time In" to name the field.
2. Select Time from the Data Type: pop-up.

   Look at the formats available in the Format: pop-up. Since you won't be concerned with the number of seconds on the Timecard, choose the hh:mm format to show only hours and minutes.

3. Select hh:mm from the Format: pop-up.
4. Select AM/PM from the 24-Hour Form: pop-up. (You can choose any of the formats; they're all interchangeable.)
5. Optionally, you might check the Show Leading Zeros check box, depending on whether you prefer to see times written as "2:09 PM" or '02:09 PM."
6. Check the Required checkbox.
7. Leave the rest of the dialog box unchanged. Click **Save** to save the Time In field definition.

To create the Time Out field, follow the same procedure as above:

1. Type "Time Out" to name the field.
2. Select Time from the Data Type: pop-up.
3. Select hh:mm from the Format: pop-up.
4. Select AM/PM from the 24-Hour Form: pop-up.
5. Optionally, check the Show Leading Zeros checkbox.
6. Check the Required checkbox
7. Leave the rest of the dialog box unchanged. Click **Save** to save the Time Out field definition.

Time Arithmetic—The Total Hours Field

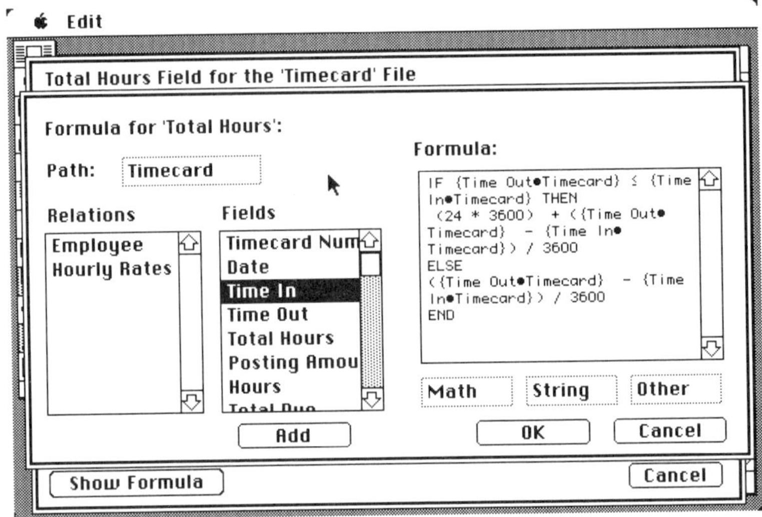

Figure 5-12 Total Hours Graphic.

Total Hours is a formula field that subtracts the value of Time In from the value of Time Out. The formula is relatively simple. You will simply enter:

```
IF {Time Out•Timecard} ≤ {Time In•Timecard} THEN
     (24 * 3600) + ({Time Out•Timecard} - {Time
           In•Timecard}) \ 3600
      ELSE
           ({Time Out•Timecard} \ {Time In•Timecard})
\ 3600
      END
```

Because dBASE Mac keeps all internal times as seconds since midnight, you need to divide by 3600 to obtain the number of hours between two times. Also, you need to check if the two hours fall on opposite sides of midnight, hence the IF statement (if Time Out is less than Time In, then midnight must fall in between). Use the parentheses to order the processing so that the subtraction occurs before the division and for greater clarity.

To create the Total Hours field:

1. Type "Total Hours".
2. Choose Formula from the Field Type: pop-up.
3. Choose Number from the Data Type: pop-up.
4. Leave the Decimal Places set to 2.
5. Click the Show Formula button.

Although you can type in the formula by hand, the easiest way to enter the formula is to use the shortcuts provided by dBASE Mac:

6. Open the Other pop-up menu and select the IF command. Notice that the IF-THEN-ELSE-END structure is added for you.
7. Now double-click the Time Out field name from the list titled Fields.
8. Select the less than or equals operator (≤) from the Other pop-up.
9. Double-click Time In to add it to the formula.
10. Now click once on the line below the THEN and choose the parentheses (). Notice that the cursor remains within the two parentheses in the formula text box.
11. Enter 24.
12. Choose the * operator from the Math pop-up.
13. Enter 3600, then click past the right parenthesis mark.
14. Choose the + operator from the Math pop-up.
15. Choose the parentheses again.
16. Double-click the Time Out field name to enter it in the formula.
17. Open the Math pop-up and select the minus sign (-).
18. Double-click the Time In field name to enter it after the minus sign.
19. Click the mouse cursor once to the right of the parenthesis.

NOTE: When dBASE Mac stores time values, it stores the number of seconds since midnight. Therefore, when you subtract one value from another, the result is given in seconds. Since there are 60 seconds each minute, and 60 minutes per hour, there are 3600 (60 * 60) seconds per hour. Therefore, you must divide the result of the calculation by 3600.

20. Open the Math pop-up and select the division symbol (/).
21. Type in the number "3600".

    Now you will save yourself some keystrokes.

22. Highlight the portion of the formula you just entered— the portion that reads ({Time Out•Timecard} - {Time In•Timecard}) / 3600—and press **Command-C** to copy that portion to the Clipboard.
23. Click once on the line following the ELSE statement.
24. Press **Command-V** to paste the contents of the Clipboard into the formula.

Your formula should read:

```
IF {Time Out•Timecard} ≤ {Time In•Timecard} THEN
     (24 * 3600) + ({Time Out•Timecard} - {Time
     In•Timecard}) \ 3600
ELSE
     ({Time Out•Timecard} - {Time In•Timecard}) \
     3600
END
```

25. If the formula is correct, click **OK** to validate and then save the formula. You will return to the field definition screen.

26. Click **Save** to save the Total Hours field definition.

Posting Amount—A Posting Field

You will use the Posting Amount field to post the results of the Total Due formula field (defined next) to the Employee file. Formula fields cannot post, and so you must create an intermediate field to pass on the posting data.

1. Type "Posting Amount" to name the field.
2. Select Number from the Data Type: pop-up.
3. Tab or mouse to the Currency box and type a dollar sign ($).
4. Click in the Posting checkbox.
5. Click **Save** to save the file definition.

Total Due—A Formula Field

The Total Due field is a Formula field that derives the amount of salary earned from the hourly rate and the total number of hours worked. This field depends on a relationship with another file for its formula. Since you cannot Post from a formula field, the result of the formula is assigned (in a procedure) to the Posting Amount field. The record is then written.

1. Type "Total Due".
2. Select Formula from the Field Type: pop-up.
3. Select Number from the Data Type: pop-up.
4. Tab or mouse down to the Currency: box and enter a dollar sign ($).

NOTE: To finish defining this file, you will need to use relationship links created in the next section of this chapter. For now you will leave the definition unfinished. In the next section, you will complete the file definition after creating the necessary relationship.

5. Click **Save** to save the Total Due field definition.
6. Click **Done**.

7. Estimate the file size (enter 25) and click **OK** to return to the Structure Window.

You can move the Timecard file to a new location on the Structure Window as you did with the Hourly Rates file.

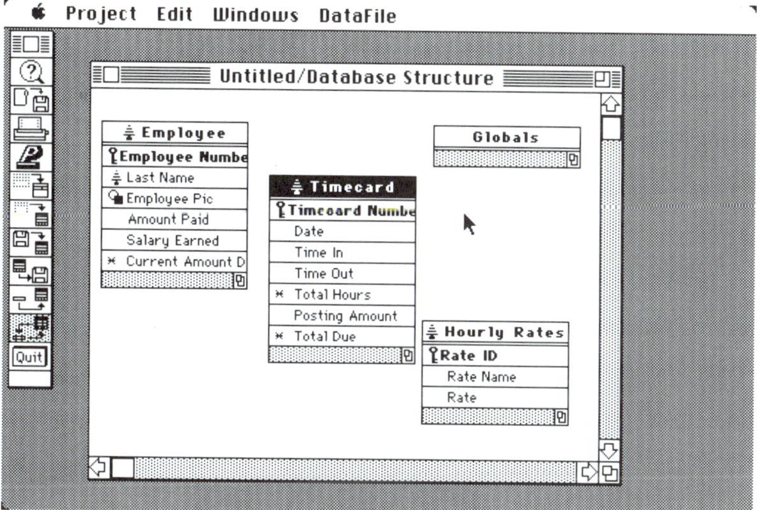

Figure 5-13 Structure Window Graphic.

Saving the Project

Before continuing with the Timecard application, you should save your work. To save the project in progress, open the Project menu and select Save (or use the Save icon on the Palette). Since this is the first time you have saved this project, a dialog box will appear asking you to name the project.

- Type "Timecard Project" and click **Save** (or press **Return**).

After the disk drive has stopped spinning and the normal mouse cursor returns, you can proceed with the tutorial. If you wish to Quit now, select Quit from the Project menu, or click the Quit icon on the Palette. When you wish to return to this tutorial, double-click the Timecard Project icon on the Finder.

What Is a Relationship?

A relationship is a link created between two files. That link is established on an identifying field—the Key field. When a relationship is created between any two files, dBASE Mac creates a special field called a Pointer field. The Pointer field is often a multivalued field (although it can be single-valued) that contains one or more Key field values from records in the related file. These Key field values serve as identifiers to relate a record in one file with one or more records in the related file.

In a simple example, suppose you have a list of composers in one file, and a list of musical works in another file:

Composer	Work
Bach	Yesterday
Beethoven	Michelle
Brahms	Moonlight Sonata
The Beatles	Toccata and Fugue in Dm
Mozart	Jesu, Joy of Man's Desire
	Ninth Symphony
	Brahm's Lullaby
	Magic Flute

Using a two-way relationship between the two files, each musical work would contain a single reference to its composer in the Composer file, but each composer would have several references in the Works file. Bach would have "Toccata and Fugue in Dm" and "Jesu, Joy of Man's Desire." The Beatles would have "Yesterday" and "Michelle." These would be listed in the Pointer field by their Key field values, but any part of the record for any of the Works could be retrieved.

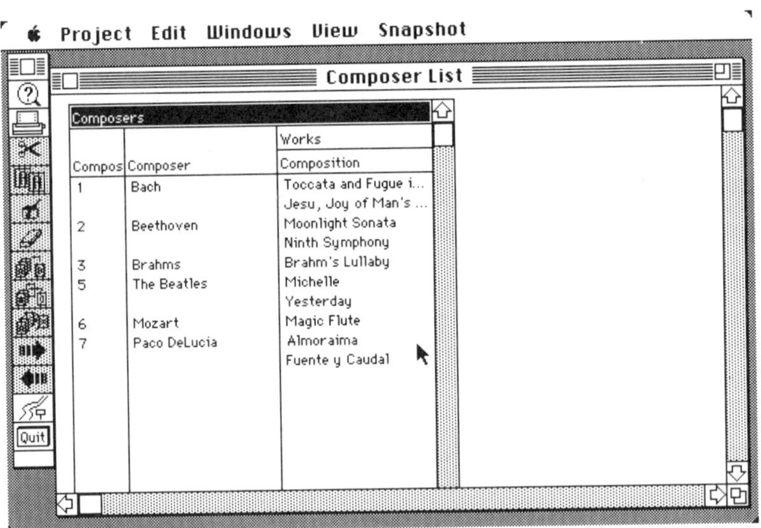

Figure 5-14 Graphic of This Relation.

In two-way relationships (only) dBASE Mac dynamically maintains the information in the pointer fields. Thus, if you enter a new composition by Bach in the Works file, a pointer to that composition is automatically added to the Composer's file (specifically to Bach's record).

NOTE: Because these links are maintained dynamically, it is easiest to create all relationships before you begin data entry. If you begin entering data before your relationships are defined, you may have to go back and manually bring the Pointer fields up to date.

Creating Relationships

Now that you have defined the files for the Timecard Project, it is time to create the relationships between them. Before you create a relationship, you need to decide what kind you need. Do both files need to access data from each other, or is one of the files for information only? Basically, it depends on the flow of data. Does information flow in both directions? If so, you need to create a two-way relationship. If not, a one-way relationship will do.

Look at the Timecard file. It will need to draw information from the Employee file (name and ID of the employee). It will also need to return information to the Employee file (Posting the Posting Amount to the Salary Earned field). Thus a two-way relationship is needed.

On the other hand, although the Timecard file needs information from the Hourly Rates file (the Rate itself), it does not need to return any information to that file. Can you think of any useful information that the Hourly Rates file could obtain from the Timecard file? In this case a one-way relationship is sufficient.

To create interfile relationships, you drag fields from one file to another. For instance, to create a two-way relationship, drag the Key Field of one file onto the field area of another file.

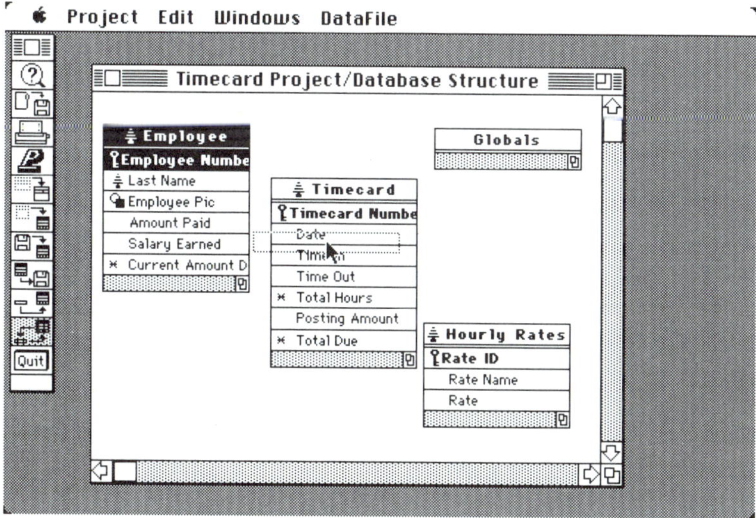

Figure 5-15 Creating Two-Way Relationship Graphic.

A dialog box appears asking if you wish to create a two-way relationship between the two files. Click **OK** to create the relationship. dBASE Mac then creates two new fields, one in each file. These are the pointer fields. When they are first created, pointer fields are named after related files, but you can change the name to more closely represent the purpose they serve.

To create a relationship between the Employee file and the Timecard file, you can drag either Key field onto the field area of the other file. For this exercise, drag the Timecard Key field onto the Employee file. The following dialog box should appear:

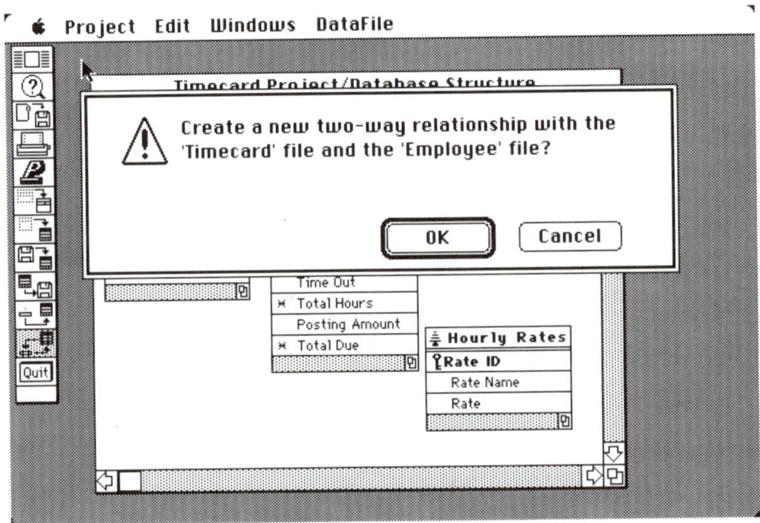

Figure 5-16 Two-Way Relationship Dialog Box Graphic.

Click **OK** to create the two-way relationship. The Structure Window reappears and you should see the new pointer fields in the Employee and the Timecard files. Note that pointer fields are labeled with an arrow, and contain parentheses to tell you that they are multivalued. A double-headed arrow is drawn between the two files, representing the flow of data between them.

That's all there is to creating a two-way relationship.

NOTE: Pointer fields can be in sets. To place a pointer field in a set, double-click the Pointer field and enter the set name in the appropriate text box. Placing a Pointer field within a set allows you to associate specific multivalued occurrences in the current file with specific records in a related file. However, this practice is not recommended and won't be useful in all situations. Use Pointer fields in sets with care.

(The NewCheck project in Chapter 12 uses a special intermediate file specifically to avoid the use of multivalued pointer fields in sets when working with budgets and

split transactions. Although you haven't reached that chapter yet, you may want to refer to that file structure later as an alternative to multivalued Pointer fields in sets. The intermediate file structure works better and creates a smoother database design than one that we had previously attempted—using multivalued budget Pointers in a set in the checkbook file.)

To create a one-way relationship, you follow the same basic procedure, but this time you drag the Key field of one file onto the title bar of the other. Think of one file as a reference file, and another as the destination file. The reference file contains information necessary to the destination file. To create a relationship in which data flow from the reference to the destination file, drag the Key field of the reference file onto the title bar of the destination file.

HINT: In a two-way relationship, both files contain pointer fields. In a one-way relationship, only the destination file contains a Pointer field. There is an easy way to remember how to create a one-way relationship. You are dragging a Key field from one file to another. Data will flow in that same direction. The Pointer field that will be created represents the Key field you are dragging, so, in a sense, the Key field you drag over becomes the Pointer field. As long as you remember that information flows in the same direction as you move the Key field, you should not become confused when creating one-way relationships.

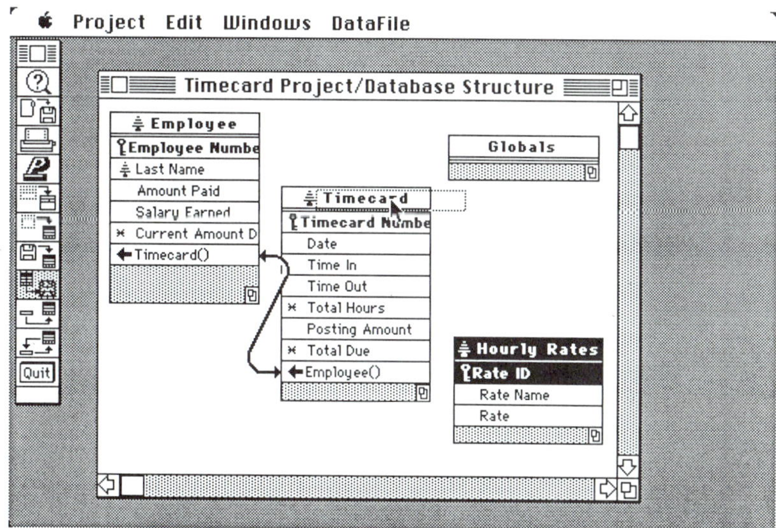

Figure 5-17 Creating a One-Way Relationship Graphic.

To create a one-way relationship between the Timecard file and the Hourly Rate file, then, drag the Key field from the Hourly Rate file onto the title bar of the Timecard file. Information will flow from the Hourly Rate file to the Timecard file. A new Pointer field, Hourly Rate, will be created in the Timecard file.

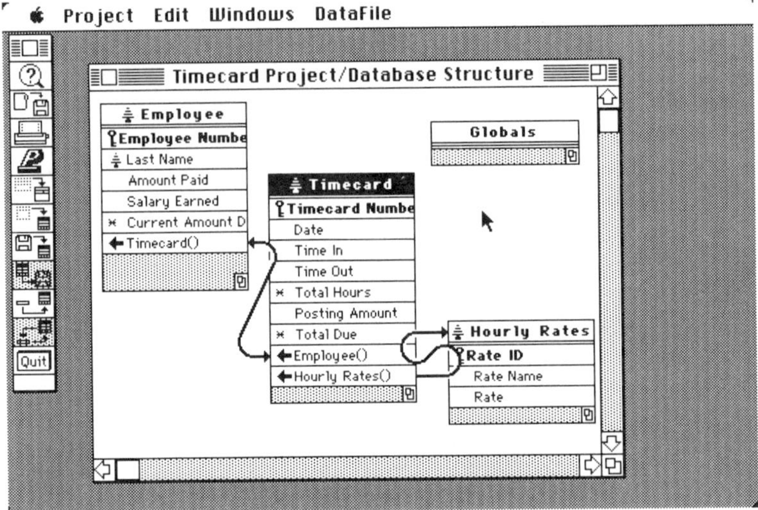

Figure 5-18 Structure Window with Relations Graphic.

Drag the Timecard file to the middle of the screen with the Employee file to its left and the Hourly Rate file to its right. Note that the relationship arrows always point to their Pointer fields, no matter where you place the files. Your screen should look basically like the screen in Figure 5-18, above. If it does not, go back over the steps in this chapter. Otherwise, continue with the Tutorial.

Finishing the Total Due Field

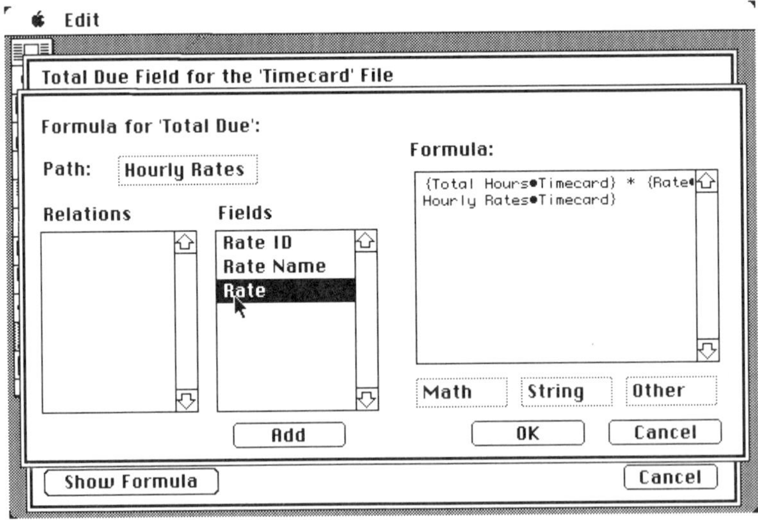

Figure 5-19 Total Due Graphic.

Remember you left the Total Due field in the Timecard file unfinished. Now, open the Total Due field definition by double-clicking on the Total Due field on the Structure Window (or highlight Total Due and select Change Field from the DataFile menu).

When the field definition dialog box reappears, click on Show Formula. Here you will create the formula that calculates the total amount due on each timecard.

The formula multiplies the number of total hours derived in the formula field, Total Hours, times the hourly rate. But there is no Hourly Rate field in the Timecard file. Here you must use one of the relationships you just defined. You can see why you couldn't create this formula before—there were no relationships!

To create the formula:

1. Double-click the Total Hours field.

2. Open the Math pop-up and select the multiply symbol (*).

3. In the Relations list box click once on Hourly Rate.

   When you click on a file name in the Relations box, you add that name to the Path. Notice that the Fields list box changes to display the fields in the Hourly Rate file. Now open the Path pop-up. Notice that it now reads Timecard first, then Hourly Rate. Highlight Timecard in the Path pop-up and close the window by releasing the mouse button. Notice that the Fields box returns to the fields in the Timecard file.

   By selecting a file higher in the Path pop-up, you change the Path. Open the Path pop-up again. Notice that only Timecard appears. Now click once on Hourly Rate again in the Relations list box. Open the Path pop-up again. The Path has changed again. The Fields box has changed again. If you ever get unexpected results, it could be that your Path is inaccurate. You can check and, if neccessary, correct the Path any time by opening the Path pop-up.

4. The fields from the Hourly Rate file should be in the Fields list box. Double-click the Rate field.

   The formula should now read:

   ```
   {Total Hours•Timecard} * {Rate•Hourly Rate•Timecard}
   ```

   Notice that the full Path name is included in the formula.

5. That's all there is to the Total Due formula, so click **OK** to verify and then save the formula, returning to the field definition screen. Click **Done** to save the changes you made.

Posting to Another File

NOTE: For now it may not make much sense, but the Posting Amount field will contain the results of the Total Due formula in a Numeric field. The value will be placed in the Posting Amount field through a Write Record procedure—a procedure that takes effect whenever the record is written to disk. Posting then occurs after the Write Record procedure is completed. This is necessary because you cannot Post from a Formula field. Since you want to Post the Total Due to the Employee file, you need to pass the results of the formula to a Numeric field.

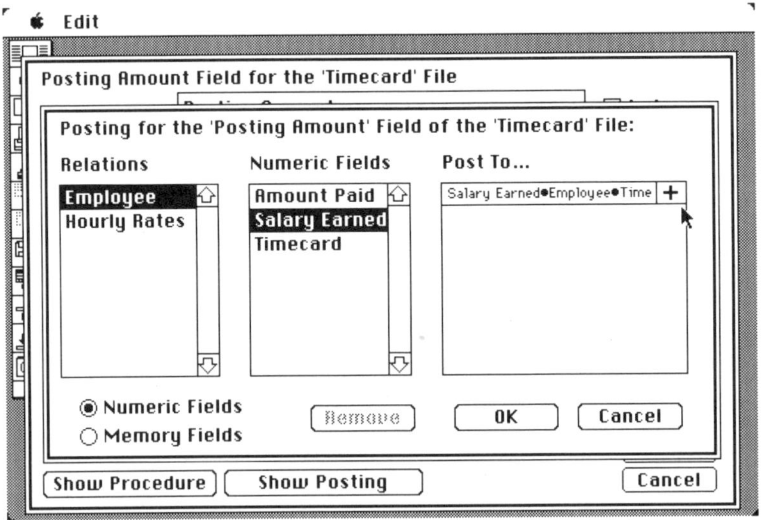

Figure 5-20 Posting Graphic.

You want to add the value of the Posting Amount field to the Salary Earned field in the Employee file. Again, this could not be done until the two-way relationship between Employee and Timecard was established.

1. Open the field definition for the Posting Amount field by double-clicking on Posting Amount.

2. Check the Post: checkbox if it is not already checked.

3. Click on Show Posting.

4. Click once on the Employee file in the Relations list.

5. Click once on the Salary Earned field in the Number Fields list.

   The relations list shows all files related to Timecard. Once you select a related file, all Numeric fields in that file are listed in the Numeric Fields list. By selecting one of these fields, you tell dBASE Mac to Post information to that file. Notice in the Post To: list, the field listed has the Path {Salary Earned•Employee•Timecard}. If you click on the large plus sign to the right of the Path name, it changes to a minus. You can Post by adding to another file, or by subtracting. For now, leave the plus sign. (If you changed it to a minus, click again to change back to a plus.)

NOTE: You can also Post to Memory fields. To do so, select Memory Fields at the bottom of the screen. The Numeric Fields list changes to read Memory Fields, and the names of available Memory fields will display in the list box.

That's all you have to do to Post the value from the Total Due field to the Salary Earned field.

6. Click **OK** to accept the posting information.
7. When you return to the field definition screen, click **Done** to save the Total Due field definition and return to the structure Window.

NOTE: Since you are only changing a field definition, you don't have to estimate file size again.

To continue with the next section, Close this project and Save the changes. If you had not saved the project previously, you will be asked to name the project. Call it "Timecard Project."

→ Timecard continues later in this chapter.

Creating an Index File

An index is a special kind of relationship that keeps the values from a particular field in sorted order. When you create an External Index file, dBASE Mac actually creates a new file. The External Index file Key field contains the values from the indexed field and a pointer field with the corresponding Key field values from the indexed file. The External Index file orders its records by the indexed field. This means that it alphabetically or numerically sorts the indexed field and all the records accordingly. You can add other fields to an External Index file, including Formula and Memory fields. You can also establish relationships from an Index file to other files.

One of the unique abilities of the Index file is that it automatically creates a new record each time a new value is added to the field on which it is indexed. For instance, in a name file that is indexed on Last Name, if you add the name Johanas to the main file, the Index file also creates a record for the name Johanas and places it in the proper alphabetical position. Furthermore, if you change the information in an indexed field, it is also dynamically updated. Suppose Ms. Johanas gets married and changes her name to Zebeck. When you enter the change of name in the main file by updating the Last Name field, the Index file automatically changes the reference from Johanas to Zebeck and places it in its new sorted position.

To illustrate the value of Index files, a small detour is in order. In this section you will create a mini-application showing how a multiple index file might be used in a specialized setting. Along the way, you'll get a preview of some of the procedures illustrated in detail in the next two chapters.

Suppose you have a business with two warehouses. Because the warehouses service different geographical areas, they both may stock the same items. For various practical and bookkeeping reasons, you have determined that the best way to keep track of the stock in each warehouse is in a separate file. But sometimes you want to see how much total inventory you have for each item. To do this, you create an index file that links the values from the two separate warehouse files.

To begin, create the two files. For this example, keep them very simple. Each file will contain a Part Number Key field, a Part Name, a Quantity On Hand value, a Cost field, and a Formula field that calculates Stock Value.

By now, you should know how to create a file and simple field definitions. To create the file for the Rockport warehouse, first make sure that you have dBASE Mac running and that any other applications are closed. Then:

1. Choose New... from the DataFile menu, then click **OK** at the first dialog box.
2. Type "Rockport" to name the file.
3. Click **Save**.
4. Call the Key field "Part Number"

   You can use Automatic Sequencing if you wish. To do so, be sure the Data Type is Number.
5. Click **Save**.
6. The next field is "Part Name", a Text field.
7. Click **Save**.
8. Now create a Number field with zero decimal places called 'Quantity On Hand"
9. Click **Save**.
10. Create a currency type field (Number, two decimal places, dollar sign) and call it Cost.
11. Click **Save**.
12. Create a Formula field called "Stock Value"
13. Enter the following formula (you'll need to click the Show Formula button):

    ```
    {Cost•Rockport} * {Quantity On Hand•Rockport}
    ```
14. Click **OK**. Click **Save**. Click **Done**.

That completes the Rockport warehouse file. Now create another warehouse file—this time for the warehouse in Montrachet. To do so, you could follow exactly the same steps you just completed, but substitute Montrachet everywhere you had Rockport above.

On the other hand, you could use Duplicate File from the DataFile menu. If you do, you will be asked to name the new file (call it Montrachet) and then the file will be duplicated. The new file will not automatically appear in the Structure Window; you will have to Open the Montrachet file using the Open command in the DataFile menu.

NOTE: In this instance, if you were to enter data into the Rockport file first, then copy it with all its records, your Montrachet file would also contain all the duplicate records. You could then go back over them to modify the Quantity On Hand field for the Montrachet warehouse.

If you used the Duplicate File option, there is one more step to take. You will need to open the Stock Value field in the Montrachet file (double-click it) and then click the Show Formula button. Notice that the formula still refers to the Rockport fields. Change each occurrence of the word Rockport to Montrachet. Click **OK**, then **Done**.

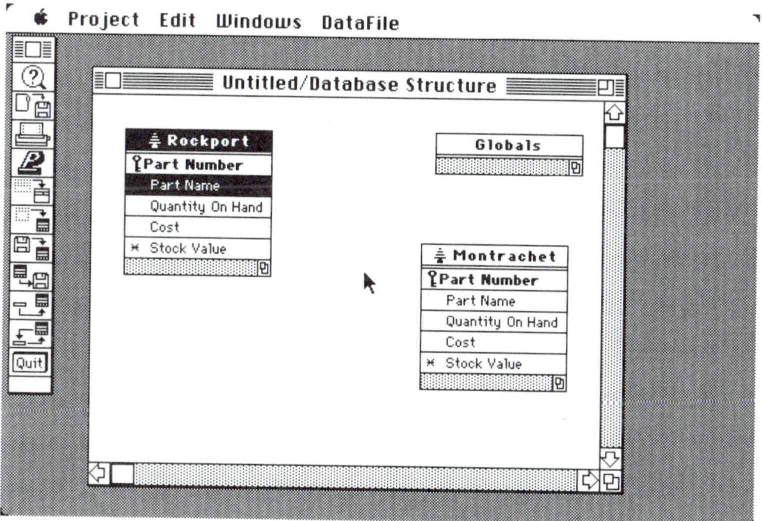

Figure 5-21 Rockport and Montrachet Graphic.

Have you finished creating the Montrachet file? If so, your Structure Window should look like the one in Figure 5-21. Now it is time to create the Index file:

NOTE: Due to the dynamic maintenance that dBASE Mac performs, it is best to create the Index file before data entry. You can bring an Index file up-to-date manually if necessary (by entering new values through a data input form), but you'll find that method much more time-consuming. In addition, mistakes made during manual entry of index data could introduce inaccuracies into the index file.

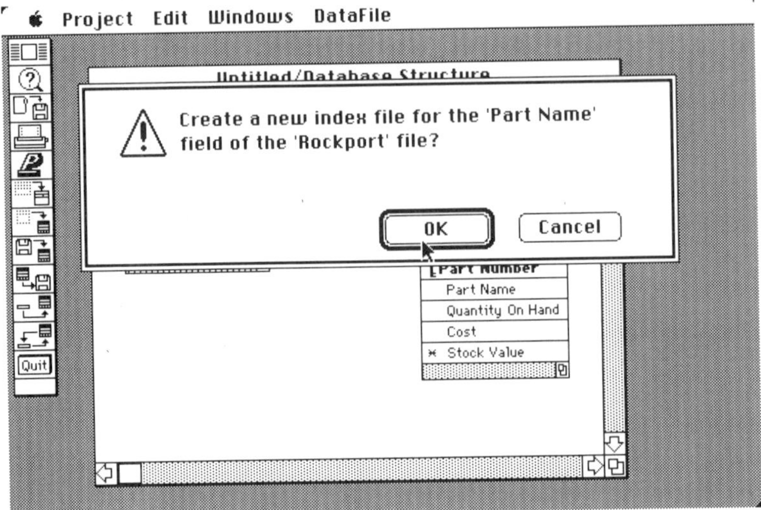

Figure 5-22 Index Alert Box.

1. Click once on the Part Name field in the Rockport file, and then drag that field onto an empty area of the Structure Window.
2. When you release the mouse, an alert box will appear as in Figure 5-22. Click **OK**.

   You will be asked to name the Index file. Call it "Part Index" and click **OK**. After a moment a new file will appear on the Structure Window where you dragged the Part Name field.
3. Now drag the Part Name field from the Montrachet file onto the Part Index file. Another dialog box appears asking if you want to add the new index to the Part Index file. Click **OK**.

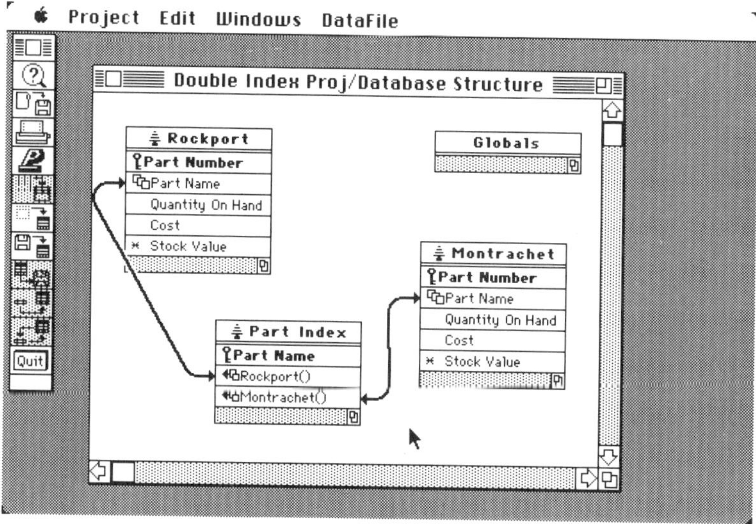

Figure 5-23 Final Structure Window Graphic.

Notice that the Part Index file contains a key field called Part Name, and two pointer fields called Rockport and Montrachet. Notice also that two-way relationships exist between the main files and the Index file. You will use these relationships later.

Now you need to create data entry views for Rockport and Montrachet. To do so, click once on the file for which you wish to create a view, then select New. . . from the Windows menu. You can name the views anything you wish; make them Form Views and use the Quick Create option. Once you have created the Views, enter the following data:

In the Rockport file enter:

Part Number: **1**
Part Name: **Widget**
Quantity On Hand: **15**
Cost: **12.49**

Part Number: **2**
Part Name: **Gizmo**
Quantity On Hand: **23**
Cost: **16.78**

Part Number: **3**
Part Name: **Glue**

Quantity On Hand: **122**
Cost: **1.67**

Now, in the Montrachet file, create a Form View, and enter:

Part Number: **1**
Part Name: **Widget**
Quantity On Hand: **4**
Cost: **12.49**

Part Number: **2**
Part Name: **Gizmo**
Quantity On Hand: **43**
Cost: **16.78**

Part Number: **3**
Part Name: **Glue**
Quantity On Hand: **64**
Cost: **1.67**

The data you just entered in the two files were automatically indexed in the Part Index file. Now you need to create a view that looks at the data, and helps you see what you have in the two warehouses. In the steps that follow, you will work with the Define Hierarchy screen. You will learn more about this part of dBASE Mac in Chapter 6. For now, follow the steps indicated:

1. Click once on the Part Index file to be sure it is selected, then select New View. . . from the Windows menu.

2. Call this view "Inventory Totals" and make it a Custom View. Be sure that the Part Index file is the selected file, and click the Quick Create checkbox.

   After you click **OK**, you will be at the Layout View screen. Open the View menu and select Define Hierarchy. Notice that the available fields are Part Name, Rockport, and Montrachet. Notice also that both Rockport and Montrachet are listed in the Relations list box on the left.

3. Click once on Rockport in the Relations list box and add Quantity On Hand, Cost, and Stock Value to the Hierarchy.

NOTE: To add a field to the hierarchy, double-click the name in the Fields list box, or click once to highlight and then click the **Add** button beneath the list.

4. Open the Path pop-up and select Part Index.

5. Now click once on Montrachet in the Relations list and add Quantity On Hand, Cost, and Stock Value to the Hierarchy.

   Next you will add a special Formula field to the view. This field will add the Stock Value fields from Rockport and Montrachet to provide a total value.

6. Click once on the Part Name field in the Hierarchy.

NOTE: It is important that you choose the level at which to create a Formula field. If you choose the root level of the Hierarchy, you will create a field that cannot be displayed in a column format. To create a view field at the same level as Part Name, click once on Part Name, then click the **New** button.

7. Click the **New** button.

   A new field dialog appears. It defaults to a Text Formula field.

8. Name the field "Total Quantity"

9. Make this field a Number field with zero decimal places.

10. Click Show Formula.

11. Click once on Rockport in the Relations list.

12. Double-click on Quantity On Hand.

13. Select the plus sign from the Math pop-up or type +.

14. Open the Path pop-up and select Part Index.

15. Click once on Montrachet in the Relations list.

16. Double-click Quantity On Hand.

    The formula should read:

    ```
    {Quantity On Hand•Rockport•Part Index} + {Quantity
    On Hand•Montrachet•Part Index}
    ```

17. If the formula looks correct, click **OK**, then click **Save**.

Now you want to create another View field called Total Value. Follow the above procedure, but this time the field should be a Numeric field with two decimal places and a dollar sign in the Currency field. The formula will read:

```
{Stock Value•Rockport•Part Index} + {Stock
Value•Montrachet•Part Index}
```

Project Edit Windows View
Inventory Totals
Part Name.ndx
Rockport
Montrachet
Part Name
Quantity On Hand
Cost
Stock Value
Quantity On Hand
Cost
Stock Value
Total Qua
Path: Part Name.ndx
Relations
Rockport
Montrachet
Fields
Part Name
Rockport
Montrachet
Add
Hierarchy Field
Break
No Break
Accumulate Total
Explode
New
Change
Remove
Show View Description
Show View Procedure
Quit

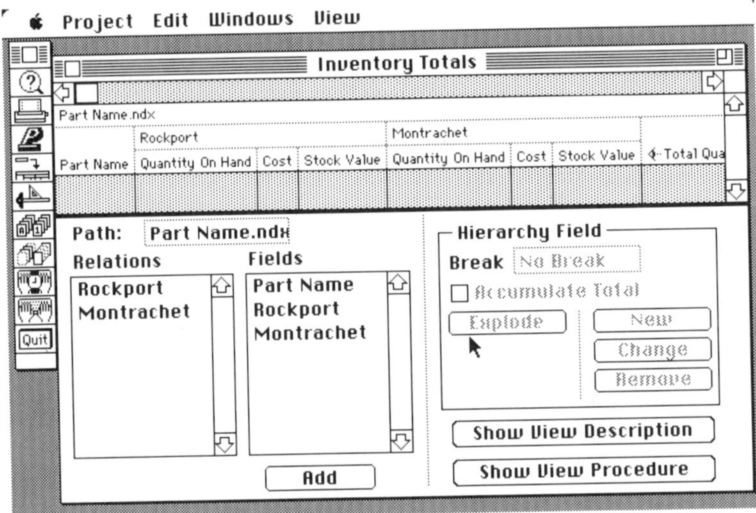

Figure 5-24 Finished Hierarchy.

After you have created the Total Value field, your hierarchy should look like the one in Figure 5-24. Now it is time to create the layout.

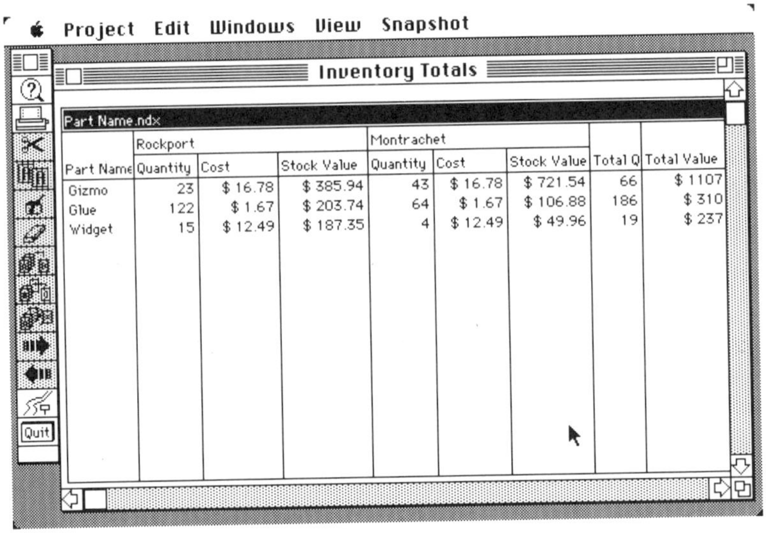

Project Edit Windows View Snapshot
Inventory Totals
Part Name.ndx
Rockport
Montrachet
Part Name
Quantity
Cost
Stock Value
Quantity
Cost
Stock Value
Total Q
Total Value
Gizmo
23
$ 16.78
$ 385.94
43
$ 16.78
$ 721.54
66
$ 1107
Glue
122
$ 1.67
$ 203.74
64
$ 1.67
$ 106.88
186
$ 310
Widget
15
$ 12.49
$ 187.35
4
$ 12.49
$ 49.96
19
$ 237
Quit

Figure 5-25 Finished View Display.

The layout for the Inventory Totals view will be simple.

1. Select Layout View from the View menu or from the Palette.

2. **Command** click the Part Index title bar, then hold down the **Option** key while you drag the fields onto the layout area to create a set of columns.

3. Resize the columns if you wish.

NOTE: To resize the columns, click on a column, then place the cursor on the line dividing two columns. Click and drag to make the column wider or narrower. For this view, you might want to make the Part Name column narrower and all the dollar field columns wider. You can return to the Layout View screen whenever you wish to change the layout, so if you aren't satisfied with the column widths the first time you Perform the view, return to the Layout View screen and resize them, then Use the view to see the results.

4. Select Perform and Use from the View menu or from the Palette, and examine the results.

You might also wish to return to the Define Hierarchy screen and set up Totals and Breaks for this report. You'll learn how to do that in Chapter 9. For now, though, you have an idea how an Index file can be used.

HINT: If this were a real application, you might notice that all the basic inventory records had to be entered twice. That is not efficient. However, duplicating the Rockport file after entering data, then adding the Montrachet Part Name to the index would work much better. You would have to re-enter the Quantity On Hand data for Montrachet, but that's all. Another way to duplicate a file's contents involves a Transfer View (which you'll see in Chapter 11.)

If you wish to work with this application again, Save it as a project for later, then close it. If you are finished with it, you can return to the Finder and throw away the Rockport, Montrachet, and Part Index files. To continue with this chapter, you should reload the Timecard Project.

Removing a Field

If you do not have the Timecard Project on your screen, load it now.

Remember the graphic field you defined at the beginning of this chapter? It is not essential to the application. You can easily remove it, or any field, from a file by highlighting the field to remove, then selecting Remove Field from the DataFile menu.

A dialog box will ask for confirmation that you wish to remove the field. Click **OK** to complete the process.

NOTE: Removing a field will prevent dBASE Mac from opening any projects that contain views referring to that field. Use caution when removing fields from projects that are active.

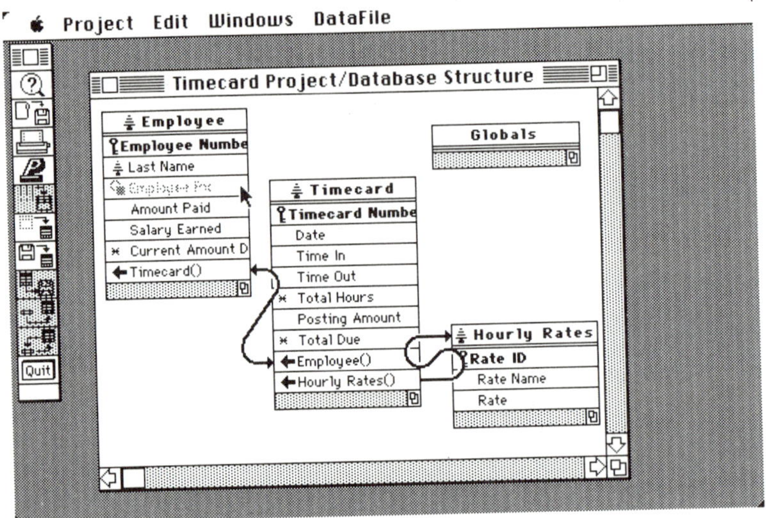

Figure 5-26 Removed Field Before Reorganization Graphic.

When you return to the Structure Window, you will notice that the field is still present in the file defintion, but it is dimmed. You can still Restore that field by selecting Restore Field from the DataFile menu.

NOTE: Restoring a Posting or an Indexed field can cause dBASE Mac to save erroneous and/or irretrievable data in a file. Also, restoring a field after you have processed other records may leave the data in some records incomplete. Restoring a field deactivates the Required option. If the restored field is required, you must update any new records, then set the Required option back by selecting Change Field and checking the Required checkbox.

If you wish to remove a field permanently, you must first use the Remove Field command, then Reorganize the file.

To Reorganize a file, choose Change File from the DataFile menu.

Don't worry about all the other options available in the Change File dialog box. Click the Reorganize File button. Once again estimate the number of records your file will contain, and click **OK** (or press **Return**). Then click **Done**. After a few moments, you will return to the Structure Window. The field you Removed will be gone.

To remove the Employee Pic field:

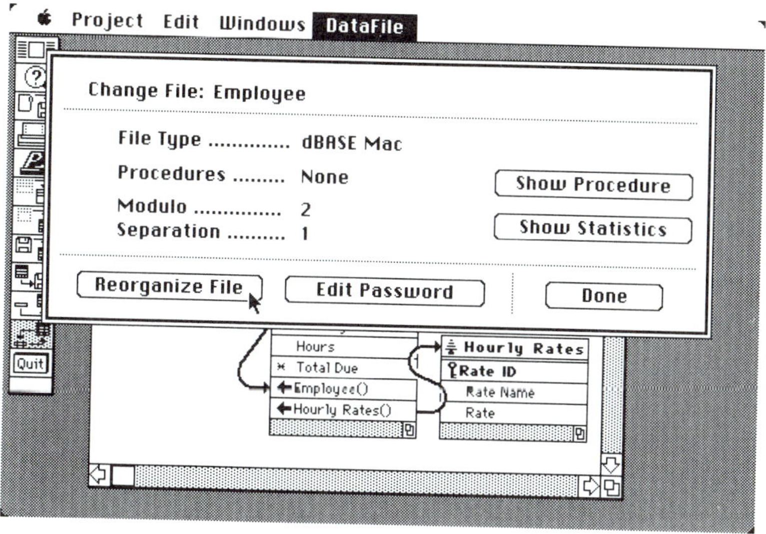

Figure 5-27 Change File Dialog Graphic.

1. Highlight the Employee Pic field on the Structure Window.
2. Select Remove Field from the DataFile menu.
3. Click **OK** to confirm the removal.
4. Select Change File from the DataFile menu.
5. Click the Reorganize File button.
6. Enter a number. Enter 25 for now.
7. Click **OK.** Click **Done.**

You have now permanently removed the Employee Pic field from the Employee file. Any data that might have been in that field are now lost forever. (Of course there were no data in that field because you haven't yet entered any in the Employee file.)

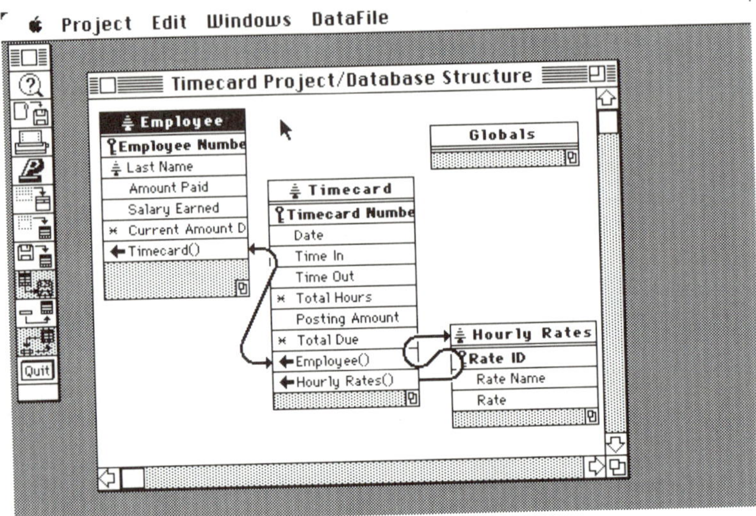

Figure 5-28 Final Structure Window Graphic.

Removing and Modifying Relationships

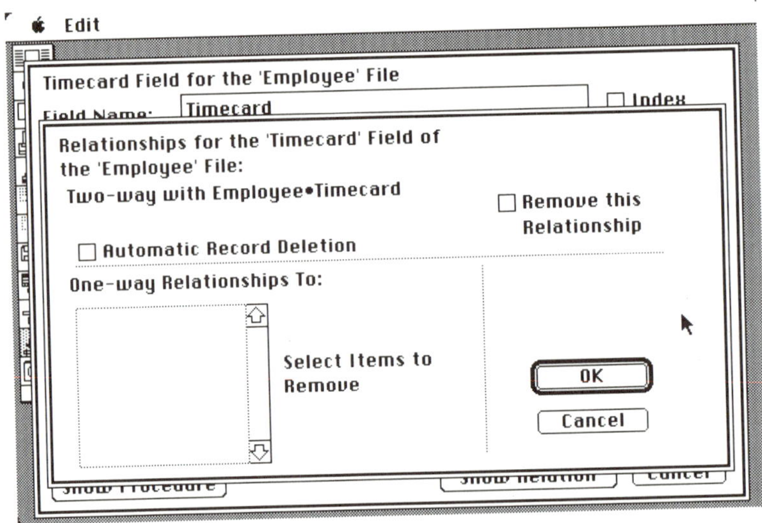

Figure 5-29 Show Relations Graphic.

- To remove a relationship, you must be at the Structure Window. First double-click (or highlight and Change) a pointer field.
  On the field definition dialog screen, you will see a button labeled, Show Relations.
- Click the Show Relations button to see the field's relationships.

- To remove a two-way relationship, click in the Remove this Relationship check box.

NOTE: Removing a two-way relationship from one pointer field converts it into a one-way relationship. To eliminate the relationship completely, open the other pointer field and select the one-way relationship to remove (see below).

- To remove a one-way relationship, click once on any existing one-way relationships (listed under One-way Relationships To:). When you click **OK**, the relationship(s) will be removed. You can also remove the Pointer field to end the relationship.

The Automatic Record Deletion checkbox is not involved in relationship removal, but has to do with how two-way relationships work. When you check Automatic Record Deletion, you tell dBASE Mac to remove any records in a file if all pointers to those records are eliminated from the related file.

As an example, suppose you had a Voucher file made up of records for special expenses that your employees incur—special travel or material vouchers, perhaps. Vouchers has a two-way relationship with Employee. When a voucher record is entered, an employee's Key field number is entered in the Pointer field of the Voucher file. Whenever one of these vouchers is paid off, the voucher's Key field value is removed from the Pointer field in the Employee record. If Automatic Record Deletion is set, the record for the voucher would also be removed.

Saving Your Work and Quitting

You have now completed the definition of the fields, relationships, and index for the Timecard Project. In the next few chapters you will complete this project, creating hierarchies, data entry forms, sorts, selections, and reports.

For now, save your work by selecting Save from the Project menu (or click on the Save icon in the Palette).

You may wish to Quit now. To do so, select Quit from the Project menu (or click on Quit in the Palette).

→ Timecard continues in Chapter 6.

Summary

In Chapter 5 you learned about relationships. You learned to identify one-to-one and one-to-many relationships.

In two-way relationships, data are shared in two directions.

One-way relationships are relationships in which only one file has access to data in another.

Graphics fields can be sized and scaled.

Graphics can be imported via the Picture This. . . DA or the Scrapbook.

You learned about Formula fields and Time fields.

You learned how to perform date and time arithmetic.

Formula fields can't post, so you created a Numeric field to contain the result of a formula.

You created one-way, two-way, and indexed relationships.

You removed a field and reorganized a file.

You learned how to remove or modify a relationship.

In the next chapter, you will begin to work with views. Views are the link that you have with the data in your files. Without views, you can't enter, modify, browse, sort, select, or print your data. Chapter 6 begins with the Define Hierarchy screen where you set up the relationships and data retrieval order of a view. In the hierarchy you also create procedures, special fields for the current view, and special conditions for reports.

6

CREATING VIEWS—HIERARCHIES

Overview

After creating file structures and relationships, you need to be able to enter and manipulate data in the files. dBASE Mac allows you to design the forms you will use to work with your files. These forms are called views.

Creating a view is essentially a two-step process—the first step being to create the hierarchy. The second step, the layout, will be covered in Chapter 7.

The hierarchy tells dBASE Mac what files and fields to include in the view, and in what order to process them. Hierarchy definition determines the scope and capabilities of a view.

You can create special procedures attached to the fields in the view or to the view itself.

You can also create special fields in the hierarchy. These fields are called View Fields and they are often Formula fields that use information from other fields in the hierarchy. View Fields must be either Formula or Memory field types.

Finally, you can create special attributes for reports. These attributes include breaks, totals, and exploded views—a special kind of hierarchy that involves a recursive file relationship.

In Chapter 6, you will create hierarchies for the Mailing List project from Chapter 2, for a Checkbook data entry form in the Checkbook Project, and for the Timecard Project data entry forms. Since the Mailing List and the Checkbook projects have no relationships, their hierarchies are fairly simple to create. However, all the hierarchies contain procedures. The Timecard hierarchy contains relationships.

The Define Hierarchy Palette

Help

Print

Preferences

Define Hierarchy

Layout View

Define Sorts

Define Selections

Perform and Use View

Use View

Quit Project

Mailing Labels Revisited

If you followed the instructions in Chapter 4, you should have created a project called MultiMail. You also entered some data and produced a Column view of that data. If you had started with the application in Chapter 2, you have also created a Mailing Label view. In this chapter you will recreate the Mailing Label view. This chapter provides much more detail on the hows and the whys of view creation, so we recommend that you perform all the steps again.

- Open the MultiMail project by double-clicking on the MultiMail project icon.

If you are already in dBASE Mac, close any active project by selecting Close from the Project menu and clicking **Yes** to Save Changes. Then select Open from the Project menu and select MultiMail. If you don't see the MultiMail project, perhaps you need to open a different folder or drive.

- When the project loads, it should be just as it was the last time you saved it.
- If the Structure Window is not currently displayed, open the Windows menu and select Structure Window.

You are going to create a new Mailing Label view just like the one in Chapter 2. The first part of the procedure is familiar:

1. Open the Windows menu and select New View. . .
2. Type "Labels-2" to name the view.
3. Select Custom from the View Type: pop-up.
4. Click **OK**.

The next screen that appears is the Define Hierarchy screen. At the top is the view name "Labels-2." Beneath the name is an area for the hierarchy files and fields. Here is where you will build the hierarchy.

The Path pop-up is much like the Path menu you saw in Chapter 5 during formula definitions. The Relations and Fields list boxes are also much like those on the formula definition screen.

You can add file fields to a hierarchy by highlighting the field name in the Fields list box and clicking **Add**, or by double-clicking the field name. If you try to add the same field twice at the same hierarchy level, the program will beep and issue an error dialog upon the third attempt.

To see how adding fields to the hierarchy works, begin adding the fields from the MultiMail file to the hierarchy.

1. Click on Name ID in the Fields list box. Then click on **Add** (or double-click the Name ID field). Note that the Name ID field appears at the top of the screen as the first entry in the hierarchy.
2. Now click on each of the field names in turn and click on **Add** (or double-click each name).

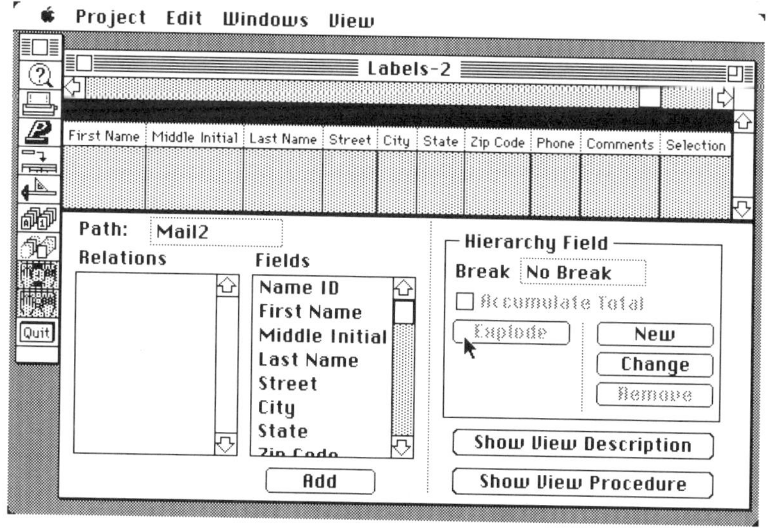

Figure 6-1 Completed Hierarchy Graphic.

Your screen should look like the one in Figure 6-1.

The long bar titled Mail2 is the view's root pointer field, the file's title bar. All fields listed beneath that bar are from the Mail2 file. In a relational or multilevel hierarchy, there can be other files identified by other title bars (pointer fields). You will see that kind of hierarchy later in this chapter. Beneath the title bar, each field is identified by its own label.

NOTE: The title bar in a hierarchy has special qualities. At the highest level of the hierarchy it is known as the Root. Other title bars are called Pointer fields. A Pointer field represents the path for all fields at that level of the hierarchy. You can attach procedures to the Pointer field just as you would to the file using the Change File command. The Pointer field can contain New Record, Delete Record, and/or Write Record procedures. Only a Pointer field or the 'Root' can contain the New, Write, and Delete Record procedures in a View. In a multilevel hierarchy (one that has fields from several related files) the title bar for each file is also the Pointer field for that file. The name of a subordinate title bar (one below the Root) is derived from the Pointer field, and is not necessarily the same as the name of the file itself.

To remove a field from the hierarchy, highlight the field, and click the **Remove** button.

NOTE: You cannot remove a field from the hierarchy if it is present in the layout design area. To remove such a field, you must first remove it from the layout, then from the hierarchy.

To remove all the fields, highlight the Title bar, then click **Remove**.

TIP: To highlight all the fields, you can **Shift**-Click each field in the hierarchy, or you can **Command**-Click the title bar (holding down the **Command** key and clicking).

If you double-click a field label bar within the hierarchy, or if you highlight the field label bar and click the **Change** button, you will open a field definition dialog box just like the ones you filled out when you first defined the field. Any changes you make to this dialog box will affect the field *for the current view only!* The result is called a View Modified File Field (or VMFF). A VMFF has a separate and distinct definition from that of the original file field until the VMFF is reverted using the **Revert** button in the Change Field dialog box.

Creating a View Field

Imagine that you are creating mailing labels. Place the name fields as follows:

First Name   Middle Initial   Last Name

When that line prints, it might read:

Robert   J.   Foxworth

or

Bill   Jameson

Notice that there are extraneous spaces between words, depending on the length of the first name and the presence or absence of a middle initial. A report or label printed based on that sort of information would be unattractive and hard to read.

To correct the problem, you need to create a view field. This field will eliminate the extra spaces or, to put it another way, the field will concatenate two or more fields. Concatenation is the process whereby you string one value at the end of another.

To create the Full Name view field, first click on any field below the Root title bar (i.e., Name ID, Last Name, etc.). This is very important, because the view fields you create here must be at the same level of the hierarchy as the other fields. By clicking on one of the fields at that hierarchy, you tell dBASE Mac you want to create the field there.

1. Click on **New** (the button on the right side of the Define Hierarchy screen). If the **New** button is dimmed, click once on a field underneath the Mail2 title bar in the hierarchy, then click the **New** button.

2. A familiar field definition screen soon appears. Type "Full name" to name the field.

   View fields can be either Formula fields or Memory fields. In either case, they store information for the current view only. The program defaults to the Formula field type.

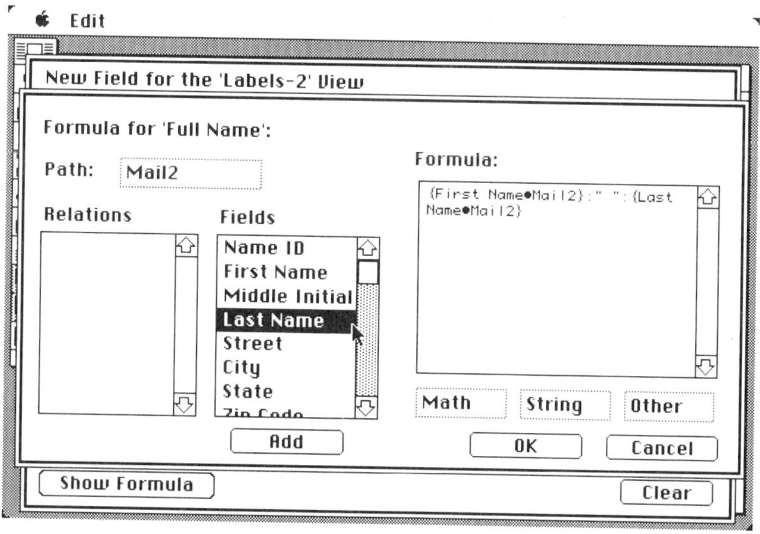

Figure 6-2 Formula Screen Graphic.

3. The Full Name field is a Formula field. To define the formula, click the Show Formula button.

The Formula definition screen is the same screen you saw in Chapter 5 when defining a Formula field. Notice the Path pop-up, the File and Fields list boxes, and the various function pop-up menus (Math, String, and Other).

4. Click First Name and then click **Add** (or double-click First Name). The formula should read:

```
{First Name•Mail2}
```

5. Now open the String pop-up menu. Select the colon (:). The colon is a symbol that connects (concatenates) formula elements.

6. Next, open the String menu and select the double quotes (" "). Whatever is between quotation marks is considered a constant in the formula. It will always appear in the formula's result.

7. Type a space inside the quotes. By typing a space, you separate the two fields by one space. If you did not type the space, the fields would run into each other, for example, BillJameson.

8. Click once to place the cursor outside the quotes, then open the String menu and select another colon (:).

9. Finally select and **Add** (or double-click) Last Name from the Fields list box.

10. The formula should read:

```
{First Name•Mail2}:" ":{Last Name•Mail2}
```

This formula concatenates a space to the First Name field, then concatenates the Last Name to the space.

11. To accept the formula definition, click **OK**. dBASE Mac will verify the syntax and return to the field definition.

The City, State, and Zip Code fields will not print perfectly in labels because the City field can vary in length. Therefore, you will now create another formula that concatenates these three fields.

1. Type "Address" to name the new field.

2. Click Show Formula.

3. The formula for the Address view field is:

```
{City•Mail2}:", ":{State•Mail2}:", "{Zip Code•Mail2}
```

4. Create the formula above by double-clicking the field names and selecting the colon and the quotation marks from the String menu. Optionally, you can type the whole thing from the keyboard if you wish.

(Don't forget the comma and space within the first set of quotes, and the space within the second set.)

5. Click **OK** to validate the syntax and return to the field definition

6. Click **Done** to save the Address field definition.

WARNING: The Full Name and Address fields must be at the same level as the Name ID, Last Name, and City, fields. If they are not, click on them in turn and Remove them. You will have to recreate them after first clicking on one of the fields below the title bar. If you do this step incorrectly, later procedures will not work at all.

In Chapter 7 you will create the layout for this view. For now, save the work you have just done by selecting Save from the Project menu.

If you wish to continue with this chapter, select Close from the Project menu, then go on.

If you wish to Quit now, select Quit from the Project menu or click on the Quit icon in the Palette. If you did not save your work, do so now.

→ MultiMail continues in Chapter 7

Procedures in the Hierarchy—Checkbook Entry

You may have Quit dBASE Mac at the end of the last section. If so, load the Checkbook project by double-clicking the Checkbook Project icon from the Finder. After a few moments you should see the Structure Window for the Checkbook Project appear on the screen.

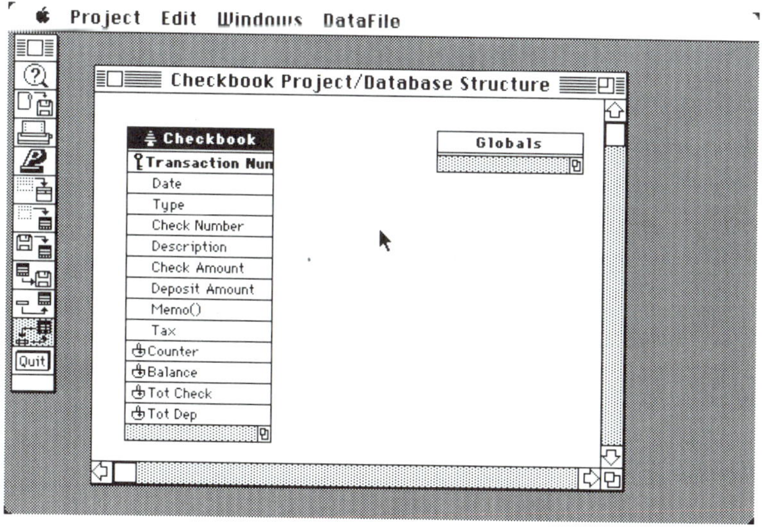

Figure 6-3 Checkbook Structure Window Graphic.

If you did not Quit dBASE Mac at the end of the last chapter, Close any active project by selecting Close from the Projects menu. Save any changes you may have made, if you wish. Now select Open from the Projects Menu and select the Checkbook Project. (If you don't see the Checkbook Project, be sure you are in the proper folder or disk. If necessary, change folders or disks to find the Checkbook Project. See Appendix A if you don't know how to change folders or disks.)

The Checkbook Project presents some new challenges. Remember the Counter field? You need to use the Counter field to update the Check Number field. You will also need to check the Type field to see if the current transaction is a check (or VOID) or not. In addition, you'll need to check if the current record is a new record or an old one. You wouldn't want the Check Number to change when you were modifying an old record! You will perform all these operations within a procedure attached to the Check Number field. You will also use a procedure to update the Balance field, and another to update the Counter field.

To create a new view for the Checkbook file:

1. Open the Windows menu and select New View. . .

2. In the dialog box that follows, type "Checkbook Entry" to name the new view.

3. Click **OK** to continue.

Note that dBASE Mac defaults to Display View. All data entry and browsing views are Display Views. You will learn about Transfer Views in Chapter 11.

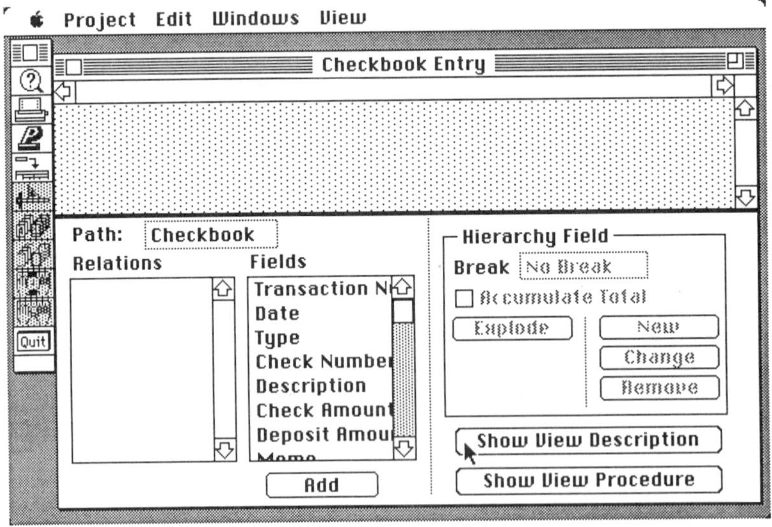

Figure 6-4 Hierarchy Screen Graphic.

1. Double-click (or click and **Add**) the Transaction Number field.

   Notice that the file identifier appears, and below that the field Transaction Number.

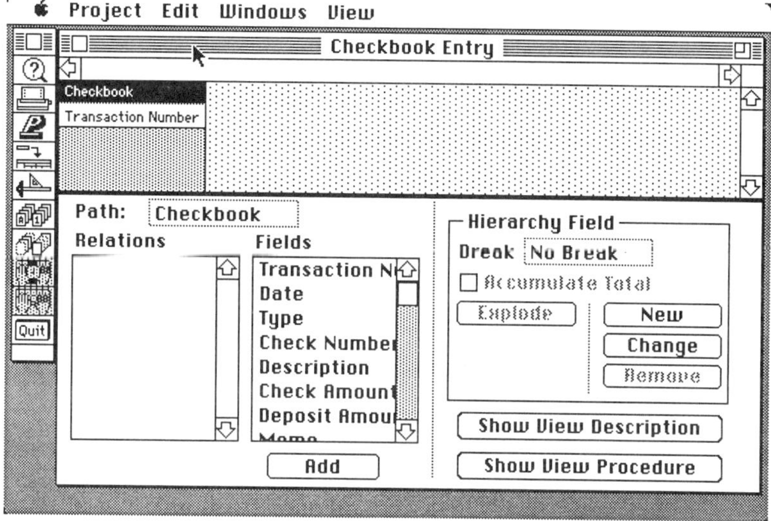

Figure 6-5 First Hierarchy Graphic.

2. Now add the other fields, one after another.

   a. To add the Memory fields—Balance, Counter, Tot Check, and Tot Dep—you'll need to open the Path pop-up, select Globals, then, in the Relations box, click on Checkbook. Now the Memory fields will appear. Notice that Memory fields are under the Globals path, even though they were created as part of the Checkbook file. Add each Memory field to the hierarchy.

When you have finished, the screen should look like the one in Figure 6-6.

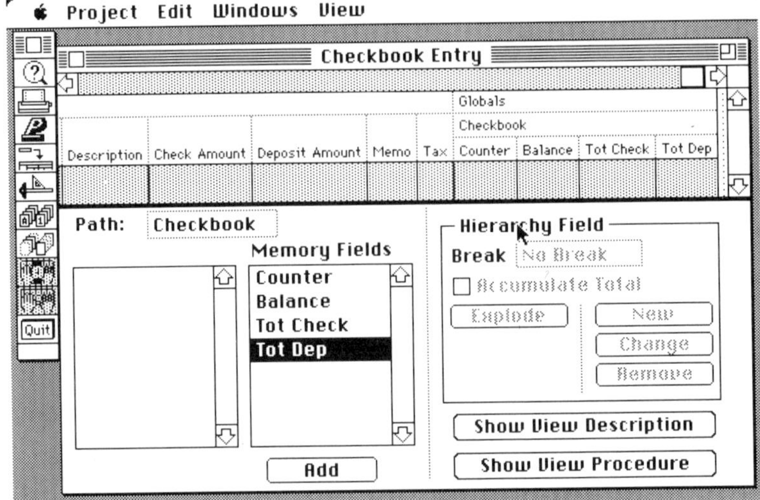

Figure 6-6 Finished Hierarchy Graphic with Memory Fields

Procedures were described in Chapter 3. Now you will have an opportunity to create a procedure that updates the Check Number field.

3. Click on the Check Number field in the hierarchy (not in the Field List).

   There are two ways to modify a field in a hierarchy. You can double-click it, or you can highlight it and click on the **Change** button.

4. Double-click or Change the Check Number field.

5. You should be in the Check Number field definition screen. Click Show View Procedure.

   You will create a Pre-Processor procedure on the Check Number field. You want a Pre-Processor because you want the procedure to run before the cursor enters the Check Number field. This Pre-Processor will control the sequencing of the Check Number field. It will increase the Check Number only if the value of the Type field is Check and if the record is new.

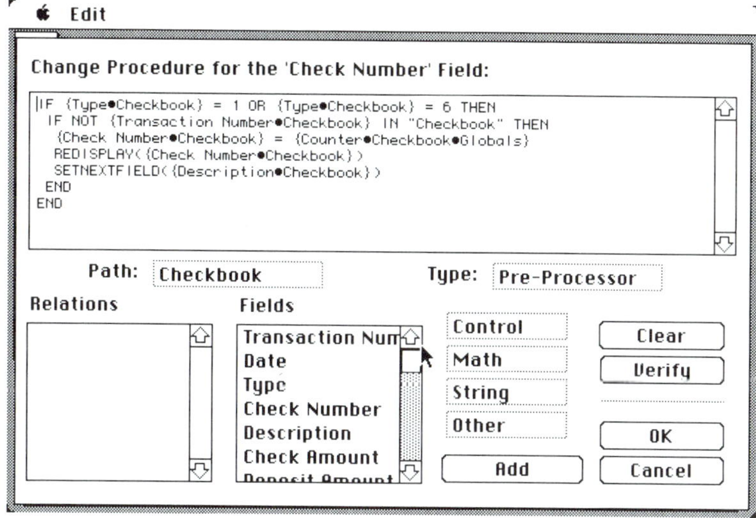

Figure 6-7 Procedure Graphic.

NOTE: Pre means before. A Pre-Processor Procedure is invoked before you **Tab** or mouse into the field or open a view it is attached to. In this case, the Pre-Processor attached to the Check Number field will be invoked after you select a transaction type, enter the Date, and **Tab** into the Check Number field. Conversely, a Post-Processor is invoked after you leave the field or view to which it is attached.

Before you begin to create a procedure, look at the procedure definition screen. It is similar to the formula definition screen, but also different. Notice that the procedure itself is written in a wide text box in the top part of the window. Beneath the text box is the familiar Path: pop-up, and beneath that are the familiar Relations: and Fields: list boxes.

To the right side of the Path: pop-up is another pop-up labeled Type:. This pop-up controls the procedure type. Notice that it is presently set to Pre-Processor. The Show Procedure definition screen always defaults to the first active procedure type. So if you last created a Pre-Processor, that will be the processor type first displayed when you open the Show Procedure dialog box.

6. Open the Type: pop-up and select Pre-Processor if it is not already selected.

   Now you are ready to begin defining the procedure for the Type field. Although you could use the keyboard to enter the entire procedure, dBASE Mac offers some short cuts.

   Notice the four pop-ups labeled Control, Math, String, and Other. You may remember Math, String, and Other from the formula definition. Control is new, however. Open the Control pop-up and examine the available commands. You will use some of these commands later in the tutorial but, for now, just look. *To exit the pop-up without selecting a command, pull the mouse off to the side of the pop-up window (either right or left) and then release the button.*

   One other button deserves mention—the **Verify** button. Remember that dBASE Mac verifies the syntax of Formula fields when you click **OK**? In a procedure, you can press the Verify button at any time to check the syntax of your procedure without having to save it at that point.

7. Begin the procedure by opening the Control pop-up and selecting IF (for IF. . . .THEN).

   Notice that all the key words for the command are entered into the procedure text box. The cursor is placed after the IF statement.

   What must happen when the value in the Type field is Check or a VOID check? The Check Number field must be updated. You are using the Counter field to hold the current check number. (You will see how the Counter field is updated later). If the value in the Type field is not Check, then the Check Number field should be left alone.

8. Enter the following procedure:

```
IF {Type•Checkbook} = 1 OR {Type•Checkbook} = 6 THEN
      IF NOT {Transaction Number•Checkbook} IN "Checkbook" THEN
           {Check Number•Checkbook} =
{Counter•Checkbook•Globals}
           REDISPLAY({Check Number•Checkbook})
           SETNEXTFIELD({Description•Checkbook})
      END
END
```

   Remember, you can add field names from the Fields list box. Double-click the field name, or click and **Add**. The equals sign (=) can be added from the Other pop-up.

NOTE: dBASE Mac keeps the values of Choice fields as numbers. The first choice is 1, the second is 2, and so on. Also, dBASE Mac procedures and formulas reference the internal representation of field values by default, unless otherwise instructed. Therefore, when you refer to values from Choice fields in procedures and formulas, you can use numeric representations. In the example above, typing 1 represents the first choice in the Type field, Check.

NOTE: An alternative to writing the procedure above uses the FORMAT command. FORMAT will return the "external" format of a field (as defined in the field definition) instead of the "internal" format used by dBASE Mac. Using the FORMAT command, the syntax for the procedure above reads:

```
IF FORMAT({Type•Checkbook}) = "Check" THEN
```

Notice that the field path is contained in parentheses, and that the field value is in quotes.

```
IF NOT {Transaction Number•Checkbook} IN "Checkbook" THEN
```

The second line in the procedure uses the IN command to determine if the current value of Transaction Number (the Key field) is already stored in the Checkbook file. If it is not, that means that this is a new record. If it is already there, then, obviously, it is an old record.

The REDISPLAY command updates the on-screen display of the field's current contents. This is sometimes necessary when the field value has been changed within a procedure.

9. Click the **Verify** button to check the syntax of the procedure. If it accepts the procedure, then click **OK** to save the procedure and return to the field definition screen. Click **Done** to save the changes you have made and return to the Define Hierarchy screen.

NOTE: The Check Number field has a special symbol on it now, which indicates that this field has been modified. The Check Number field in the view is no longer considered by dBASE Mac to be a file field, but is now a View Modified File Field (VMFF). If you return to the Check Number definition screen and select the **Revert** button, it will display a dialog box that will allow you to return the field to its file field status, eliminating any modifications that have been made to it in the view.

Remember, the procedure you just created is only valid within the Checkbook Entry view.

Now that you have used the Counter field to update the Check Number field, you will need a way to increase the value in the Counter field. You don't want this to happen more than once per record, and you only want to increase the value in the Counter field if the transaction was a Check.

Handling VOID transactions can be more of a problem in this application. For the purpose of this tutorial, you won't be able to modify a VOID check or change an existing check to VOID because the steps necessary to do this are complex and beyond the scope of this level of the tutorial. For this application, you will enter procedures to prevent changing transaction types and also to prevent changing VOIDed check amounts.

With some ingenuity, you may figure out a way to compensate for changes in transaction type and their effects on Posting. You will probably have to use Global fields to flag various conditions and carefully monitor the changes in the Check Amount and/or Deposit Amount values.

For now, double-click on the Type field in the hierarchy, click on Show Procedure, open the Type: pop-up and select Post-Processor, and enter the following Post-Processor on the Type field:

```
IF {Transaction Number•Checkbook} IN "Checkbook" THEN
   ALERT("You can't change a transaction type once it
has
been entered into the file." STOP)
ELSE
ACCEPT
END
```

Click **OK** and then **Done** to complete the modification to the Type field.

Next, double-click on the Check Amount field, click the Show Procedure button, open the Type: pop-up and select Post-Processor, and enter the following Post-Processor to the Check Amount field:

```
IF {Transaction Number•Checkbook} IN "Checkbook" AND
{Type•Checkbook} = 6 THEN
   ALERT("You can't change the value in a VOIDed
check.",STOP}
   ELSE ACCEPT
   END
```

Click **OK** and **Done** when you are finished.

NOTE: A field Post-Processor only activates if the value in the field changes. Therefore, these Post-Processors will not be activated unless you attempt to change the values in the field. The first line of each of the procedures above checks to see if the record already exists in the file (if it does not, then it is a new record, and you can change the values at will). The ACCEPT command must be encountered or the field value will not be accepted. Notice that in the program flow, after each ALERT box, there is no ACCEPT command. Therefore, along those branches of the procedure, the changed value in a field will not be allowed. The field will revert back to its original value. This will become very clear in Chapter 6 when you begin to enter data into the Checkbook Entry view.

Now you can enter the Write Procedure for the Root of the view:

NOTE: A Write Record procedure is only invoked when the **Enter** key is pressed, when a WRITE command is encountered in a procedure, or when a Transfer View is writing records. After you enter information into the fields of a record, press **Enter** to save the record. At that time, a Write Record procedure is invoked.

In a view, you can only create a Write Record procedure in the Root or a subordinate file Pointer field of a hierarchy. To create the Write Record procedure:

1. Double-click on the Root (it reads "Checkbook" at the top of the hierarchy).
2. Click on the Show Procedure button.
3. Open the Type: pop-up and select Write Record.
4. Enter the following procedure:

```
\** Checkbook Entry Write Record procedure **\
IF NOT {Transaction Number•Checkbook} IN "Checkbook" THEN
    IF {Type•Checkbook} = 1 OR
       {Type•Checkbook} = 6 THEN
         {Counter•Checkbook•Globals} =
{Counter•Checkbook•Globals} + 1
         END
\** Add the VOID check amount back into the Balance field
and subtract it from the Tot Checks field **\
         IF {Type•Checkbook} = 6 THEN
              {Balance•Checkbook•Globals} =
{Balance•Checkbook•Globals} + {Check Amount•Checkbook}
              {Tot Checks•Checkbook•Globals} = {Tot
Checks•Checkbook•Globals} - {Check Amount•Checkbook}
         END
END
WRITE(SELF)
REDISPLAY({Checkbook•Globals})
```

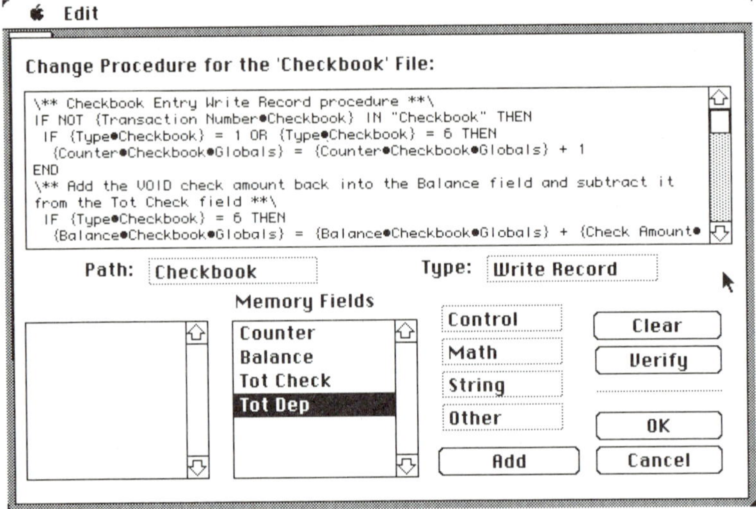

Figure 6-8 Write Record Procedure Graphic.

Select IF. . .THEN from the Control pop-up, = from the Other pop-up, and + from the Math pop-up. IN, WRITE, SELF, and REDISPLAY can be found under the Other menu. Double-click the field names from the Fields list box. If you make a mistake, you can erase it by backspacing over it or highlighting and correcting. If you want to start over, click **Clear** to remove the entire procedure and start over.

NOTE: Even though the Balance, Tot Checks, and Tot Dep fields are all file Memory fields (in the Checkbook file), you add them to a procedure by opening the Globals file from the Path pop-up and then clicking on Checkbook in the Relations list. Finally, you can click and select **Add** or double-click the appropriate field name to add it to the procedure line.

The procedure above first checks if the record already exists. If not, it checks to see if the transaction is a Check or VOID. If so, it adds one to the Counter field. Then it looks to see if the transaction was VOID (Type = 6) and, if so, modifies the Balance and Tot Checks fields. Then, because a Write Record procedure disables the automatic saving of the record, you must use the WRITE(SELF) command to complete the process.

The REDISPLAY(Checkbook•Globals}) command then updates the display of the three memory fields to show the effects of the posting. If an old record is modified, the posting will make an adjustment to the posted records so that the net effect will be accurate. For instance, in the case of a check that was originally $50 and is modified to be $100, the posting will in effect add $50 to the Balance and Tot Checks fields, then subtract $100, keeping the figures accurate.

Note that a single REDISPLAY command updates all three memory fields. That is because any REDISPLAY command updates all fields at the level specified. If the command had read REDISPLAY({Checkbook}) the display of all fields in the view would have been updated, since Checkbook is the Root.

5. Click **Verify** and, if all is well, click **OK**.

6. Click **Done** to save the changes and return to the Define Hierarchy screen.

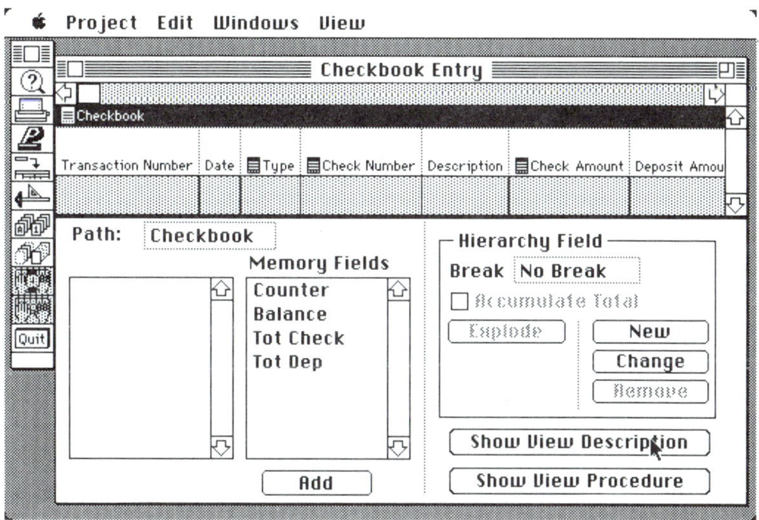

Figure 6-9 Completed Hierarchy Graphic.

That completes the Checkbook Entry hierarchy. This is a brief introduction to procedures. In future chapters you will work with more procedures to control various aspects of your dBASE Mac applications. You will also get to see these procedures in action. For now, though, you'll have to be patient because each step in the creation process takes time.

You will continue with the layout for this view in Chapter 7. If your screen looks just like the one in Figure 6-9 select Close from the Project menu. At the prompt, click **OK** to save changes.

Now, if you wish, continue with the next section of the Tutorial, or Quit to return to the Finder.

→ Checkbook continues in Chapter 7.

Creating a Hierarchy with Relationships

Begin the Timecard project by double-clicking the project icon on the Finder. If you are already in dBASE Mac, Close any active projects, then select Open from the Project menu.

In the dialog box, select Timecard Project. In a few moments you should see the three files you created in Chapter 5—complete with Index file and relationships.

1. Highlight the Timecard file by clicking the mouse once anywhere on the file.
2. Now select New View... from the Windows menu.
3. Type "Timecard Entry" to name the view.
4. Double check that the file highlighted in the Root File: list box is Timecard. If it is not, click once on the name Timecard in the Root File: list box.
5. Click **OK** to accept the Display View format and move to the Define Hierarchy screen.

The hierarchy for the Timecard Entry view is in some ways more complex than the one created for the Checkbook Entry. Examine the information needed to process a timecard. Besides the basic timecard information, you also need the name of the employee (from the Employee file), and you will need the hourly rate to calculate the total due for each timecard. The hourly rate is drawn from the Hourly Rate file.

To build the Timecard Entry hierarchy:

1. Add the fields to the hierarchy by the double-click or the click and **Add** method. Begin with Timecard Number, then add Date, Time In, Time Out, Total Hours, Total Due, and Posting Amount.
2. To add the fields from the Employee file, you must change the path. Click once on Employee in the Relations list box. The Path pop-up now reads:

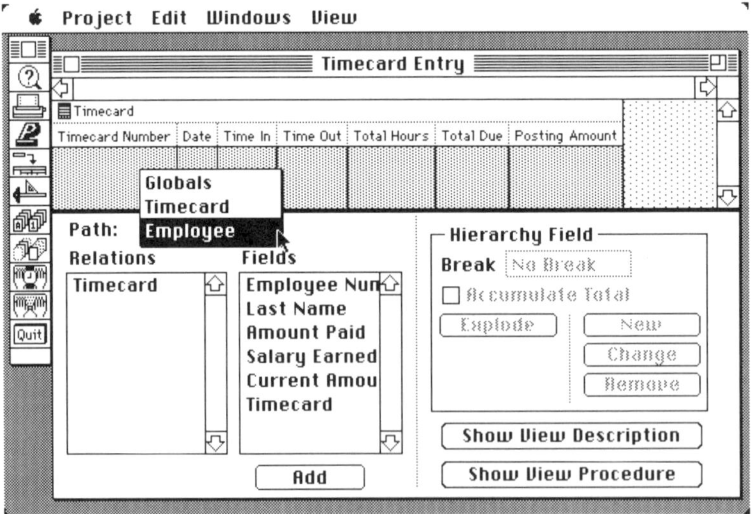

Figure 6-10 Pop-up Graphic (Timecard,Employee).

3. Add the Employee ID and Last Name fields to the hierarchy.

   Notice the new Pointer Field that has been added below the Timecard level. Each successive level of a Path is represented by a new Pointer Field. Under the Employee Pointer Field are the two fields, Employee ID and Last Name.

4. Time to change the Path again. You want to add the fields from the Hourly Rates file. Before adding Hourly Rates to the Path, however, you need to change the current path to the level above Employee. To do so, open the Path: pop-up and select Timecard. By doing so, you change the current Path up one level.

5. Now select Hourly Rates from the Relations list box.

6. Add the Rate ID and Rate fields to the hierarchy. Notice the new pointer field and the fields beneath it.

NOTE: If you had not changed the Path up one level, you would have had to access the Hourly Rates file by going through the Timecard file again. The Path would have read {Timecard•Employee•Timecard•Hourly Rate}. Obviously, that makes no sense. The program would have to search through Timecard, then Employee, then Timecard again. Removing Employee from the path shortens it and prevents loops, repetition, and possible program confusion. Always pay attention to the Path and keep it as short as possible.

The next step will assure that the Hours and Posting Amounts fields are equated with the appropriate Formula fields.

1. Double-click on the Root (the Timecard title bar).

   The title bar is a Pointer field in the view hierarchy. On this field you can place New, Delete, and Write Record procedures. You'll learn more about these procedures in later chapters.

2. Click on the Show Procedure button.

3. Open the Procedure Type: pop-up and select Write Record.

4. Enter the following procedure:

```
REDISPLAY({Timecard})
{Posting Amount•Timecard} = {Total Due•Timecard}
WRITE(SELF)
```

   This procedure assigns the current amount of the Total Due formula field to the Posting Amount field before writing the record. The Posting Amount field then Posts to the Employee field when the record is written.

5. Click **Verify** to check that the procedure has no errors.

6. If all is well, click **OK**.

That completes the Timecard Entry hierarchy. You will create the layout for this view in Chapter 7.

Save the project by selecting Save from the Project menu, or clicking the Save icon from the Palette. Now Close the Timecard Project or Quit.

→ Timecard continues in Chapter 7.

Summary

In Chapter 6, you learned how to create both simple hierarchies with no relationships and more complex multifile hierarchies.

You learned to create special view fields, concatenation formulas, a Post-Processor procedure, and a Write Record procedure.

You learned about the view Pointer field and about using the **Verify** button to confirm syntax in a procedure.

You learned about changing the Path and adding related files and fields to a view.

7

CREATING LAYOUTS

Overview

Chapter 7 introduces the visual side of creating views. After defining the Hierarchy, you will generally proceed to the Layout. In this chapter, you will create views in three projects—the MultiMail Project from Chapter 4, and, using the hierarchies created in Chapter 6, the Checkbook Project, and the Timecard Project.

Layouts are created on the design area of the Layout Window. You can place fixed text and graphics, individual file and view fields, and columnar listings of file data. You can customize the appearance of various layout elements, including changing the font and size, the special effects (bold, italic, etc.), presence and position of titles, boxes, background, and so on.

You can have more than one form per printed page. The Form Size controls allow you to set the size of each printed form, as well as the number of forms to print across a page.

One unique aspect of layouts is the Tablet. Tablets are special multipage displays available on a single layout form. You control the display of specific Tablet pages by linking them with specific conditions. The Checkbook Project uses Tablets to control the display of different forms for checks, deposits, and other transactions.

The Define Layout Palette

The default Palette for the layout contains several unique icons and commands. Five of the icons—Selection, Fixed Text, Fixed Graphic, Line, and Tablet—have no command menu equivalents and cannot be removed or modified. The other icons, with the exception of Perform and Use View and Print, are also unique to the layout. They represent menu commands that will be discussed in this chapter. You can use them interchangeably with the menu commands during the Tutorial.

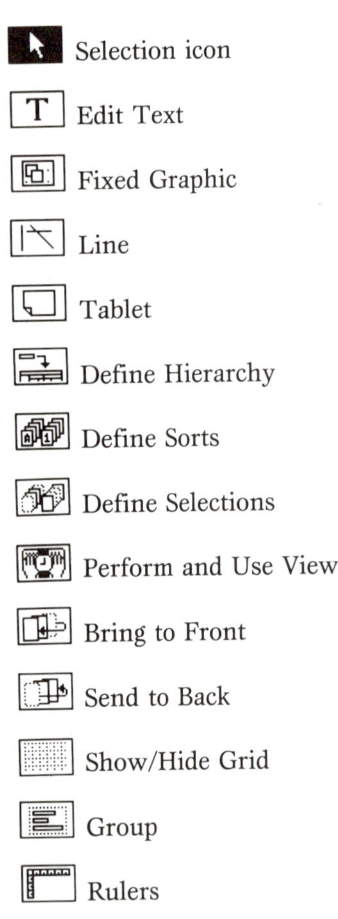

Creating Mailing Label Forms

Load the MultiMail project by (1) double-clicking the MultiMail project icon on the Finder, or (2) Closing any active projects within dBASE Mac and then Opening MultiMail.

In Chapter 6 you created the hierarchy for a view called Labels-2. That hierarchy screen should be displayed now. If it is not, select Labels-2 from the Windows menu.

In this section you will recreate the mailing label layout that you created in Chapter 2. First, re-acquaint yourself with the hierarchy for the Labels-2 view. Remember the special view fields, Full Name and Address?

Now select the Layout icon from the Palette, or select Layout View from the View menu. Notice that the hierarchy is still at the top of the screen. Beneath the hierarchy is the design area. Anything placed on the design area becomes part of the layout.

Whenever you begin to create a layout, you should envision the finished result first. Try to imagine the position of each field. Try to imagine the appearance of the fields.

Do you want them to have boxes around them? Do you want them to display with a different font, or some special effect? Do you want special titles or graphics? If necessary, design the layout's appearance on a piece of paper before you begin. You may save yourself some steps by planning ahead.

In the case of the mailing label, you want only the name and address. You don't want the Key field, and you don't want the boxes around the fields.

> NOTE: If you do not include the Key field in the layout, you will not be able to use that layout to retrieve records manually via key values. You will be able to print out reports of a layout without a Key field, however.

Before you begin putting fields onto the design area, select the significant display characteristics that you desire by setting Preferences.

> NOTE: Remember, Preferences affects all views in the current project. Later, to change display characteristics for individual design elements, you will select Display Options from the Design menu.

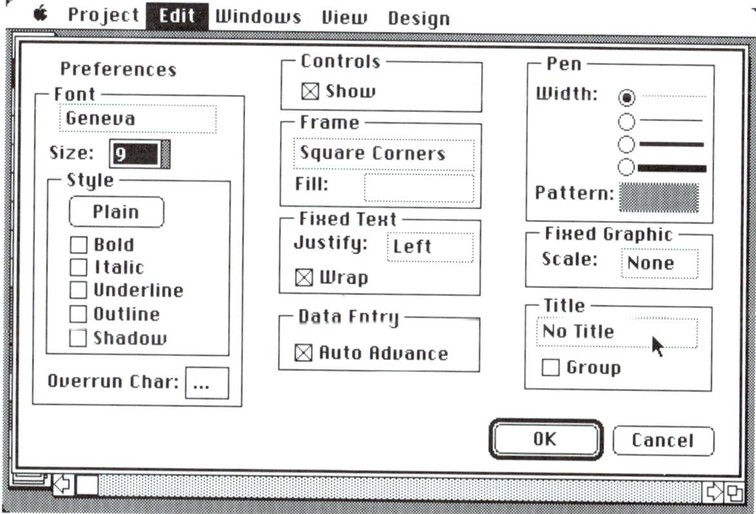

Figure 7-1 Preferences Graphic.

1. Open Preferences. . . from the Edit menu.

2. Change the Pen Width choice to the thin grey box (the one at the top-right corner of the dialog box).

   Changing the Pen Width to the minimum setting eliminates boxes around fields.

3. Under Titles, select No Title.

Normally when you drag a field onto the design area, it has a field title attached. You can have that title display above the field, below it, to the right or to the left. If you select None, as you did above, no titles will display.

NOTE: If you want to create a new default setting for fonts, font sizes, or special effects (bold, italic, etc.), set those options now. (You will still be able to modify individual display elements through Display Options.)

Sometimes labels will print out better in bold face, especially on dot matrix printers with old ribbons. Or you may wish to use a special font to make the labels more readable, or more decorative.

4. Click **OK** to save the changes in the Preferences screen.

NOTE: The changes you just made through Preferences could also have been done through Display Options. With Display Options, you would have (1) dragged fields onto the design area; (2) removed all titles by highlighting them and pressing **Backspace**; (3) highlighted the display elements you wished to change; then (4) opened the Display Options dialog box and set the font, font size, pen width, and so on for the currently highlighted field elements. Obviously, whenever possible, working with a default, Preferences setting is easier.

Before placing any fields on the design area, you should set the form size. If you place fields or other design elements outside the area you plan to use, you will be unable to set the form size because dBASE Mac will not create a form size that might cut off existing design elements. Therefore, it is better to set the form size for the mailing labels before you place the layout elements.

5. Open the Form Size option from the Design menu. A pop-up menu contains various possible widths and lengths. You can select from the menu, or enter values for width and length in the appropriate text boxes. Select a size that conforms to the size of your labels, for example, 3 inches by 11/16 inches.

   You can print several forms across a single page. Many mailing labels are sold with two or more labels across. How many labels you can print across a page depends on the width of your paper, the number of labels, and the page-width setting under Page Setup in the Project menu.

6. For now, enter 2 in the Number of Forms Across Page text box. This will print two labels across a page. (If you plan to use one-up labels,

enter a 1. If you have other kinds of labels, enter the appropriate number in the text box.)

7. Click **OK** to return to the layout screen.
8. Highlight the Full Name field in the hierarchy and drag it down onto the design area.

   To create a form type field in a layout, highlight the field name in the hierarchy and drag it into position on the design area.

9. Now highlight the Street field and drag it down beneath the Full Name field. Try to line it up the way you would like to see it on a mailing label.

   Perhaps the fields are not lining up just the way you want them to. dBASE Mac provides a helpful tool for aligning layout elements—the Grid.

10. Select Turn Grid On from the Design menu.

NOTE: Turn Grid On/Off is a toggle command. It changes its value each time it is selected. When you select Turn Grid On, the next time you open the Design menu, the command will read Turn Grid Off. Whenever the command reads Turn Grid Off, the grid is on.

11. Now that the Grid is on, highlight the two existing layout elements. You can do this by clicking on the first element, then holding the **Shift** key and clicking on the second, or by drawing a box around the two elements (clicking and dragging the mouse around them). After both elements are highlighted, select Align to Grid from the Design menu. The highlighted layout elements will align with the invisible grid lines.

    Try clicking on one of the fields on the display area. Move it around. You should notice that it moves in an uneven motion instead of the usual smooth motion that you're used to on a Mac. The unevenness occurs as the field icon moves to, and aligns with, each invisible grid line. Place the field where you want it. Now move the other field until it is aligned with the first. Using the Grid, you can easily place layout elements accurately and neatly with respect to each other.

12. Drag the Address field down, and place it beneath the Street field.

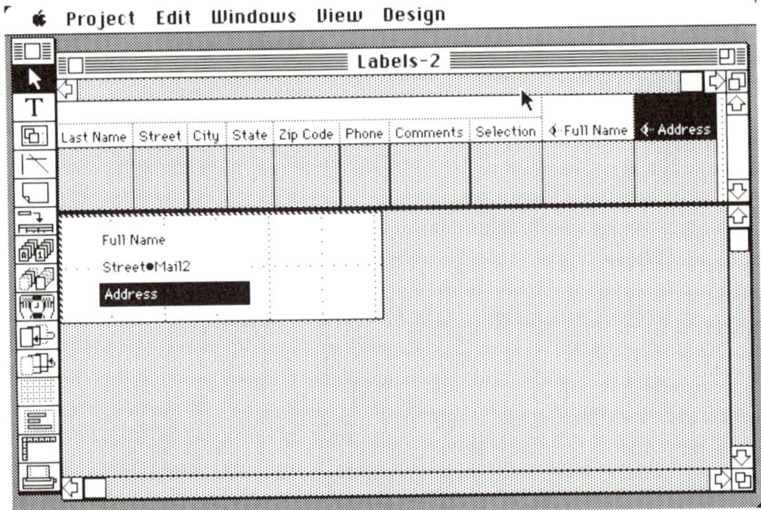

Figure 7-2 Layout Graphic.

The screen should look like the one in Figure 7-2.

NOTE: You may have to lengthen the fields. To do so, click once on a field to highlight it, then place the cursor at the lower-right corner. When the cursor changes shape, drag to the right. To re-size all three fields at one time, highlight all three by dragging a selection box around them, or **Shift**-click each one, then size one to size all.

You can use dBASE Mac's graphics and special effects to create different kinds of mailing labels for different purposes. Look at our examples in Figure 7-3.

That completes the layout for the mailing labels. If you wish to continue with the Tutorial, click the Save icon on the Palette or select Save from the Project menu, then go on to the next section.

If you wish to stop now, select Quit from the Project menu or click on the Quit icon in the Palette. Click **Yes** to save changes you have made in the Mailing List Project.

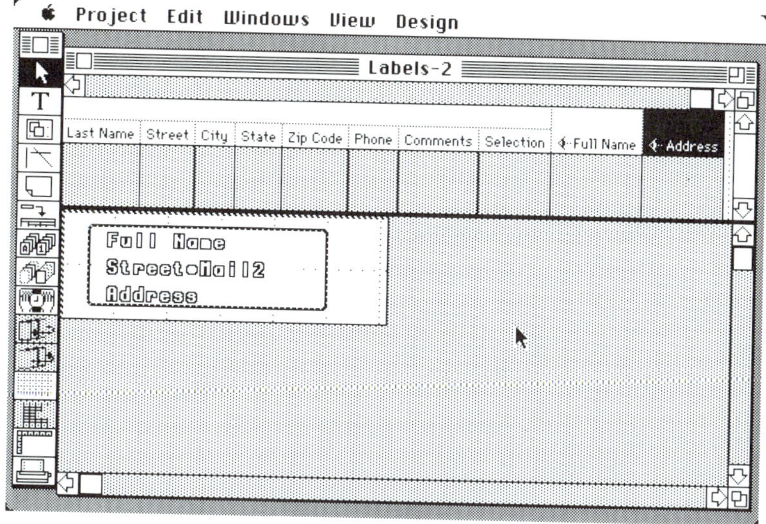

Figure 7-3 Different Mailing Label Format Graphic.

Working with a Column View

You can get a good look at your mailing list if you use dBASE Mac's Column view. The Column view displays all records in a tabular format. Although you cannot edit or add data directly to a Column view, you can browse through the records, print them, sort, and select using Column views.

In Chapter 2 and again in Chapter 4, you created a Column view using Quick Create. For practice, delete that view now (if you didn't delete it before) and create a new Column view. To delete the existing view:

1. Open the Windows menu and select Mailing List Column.
2. Open the View menu and select Delete View.
3. A dialog box asks you to confirm your choice. Click **Yes** to confirm.

That's all there is to deleting a view. Any procedures or view fields created with that view as well as all formatting, fixed text and graphics will be deleted permanently. (You can retrieve lost information, even a deleted view, if you use the Revert to Saved command from the Project menu. This command will return your project to the state it was in when last saved).

NOTE: Before you begin the next part of the exercise, change the Preferences settings back to their default values. To do so, select Preferences. . . from the

Edit menu and change the Pen Width to the second line from the top, then change No Titles to Place on Left.

To create a new Column view of your list of names and addresses:

1. Select New View. . . from the Windows menu.
2. Type "Mailing List Column" to name the view.
3. Select Columnar Layout from the View Type pop-up.

   If you want to include all fields in the Column view, the easiest way to create the view is with the Quick Create option you used in Chapter 2. But for this exercise, do not use Quick Create.
4. Click **OK**
5. Quickly create a hierarchy for the Mailing List Column view. Double-click or click and **Add** each field.

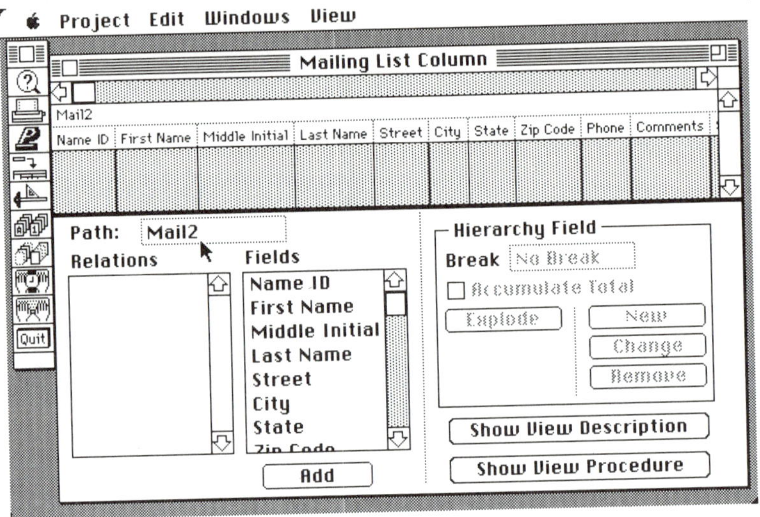

Figure 7-4 Mailing List Column Hierarchy.

6. Now click the Layout icon on the hierarchy or select Layout View from the View menu.

NOTE: Notice that the columns are already created. When you select Columnar from the View Type pop-up, the columns are created for you.

NOTE: If the columns were not created, you could create them by highlighting each field that you wanted in the layout along with the title bar (pointer field or Root) above it, then dragging them onto the design area. The quick way to highlight all the fields under a title bar is to hold the **Command** key and click on the title bar.

HINT: What would happen if you tried to create columns on the layout for all the fields in a large file? Depending on your form size, you might get an error message saying that your form size is too small to accommodate all the fields. But using the default columns from a Columnar view type circumvents the problem. Another way to fit many columns into a layout involves using the **Option** key. You can instruct dBASE Mac to fit all fields of a columnar element into the current size of the view window by holding down the **Option** key while you drag the fields from the hierarchy. The resulting columns may be narrower, but they can be adjusted later.

The length and width of the columnar elements dragged down with the **Option** key will be completely on-screen. This is of benefit for browsing records, but may not be useful for printing reports. Locking down the **Caps Lock** key while **Option**-dragging the columnar elements fits the elements to the current page size (according to the layout definition).

NOTE: You can move the whole column display at any time by dragging using its title bar (which in this case reads "Mail2"). You can also remove any fields you don't want to include in the display. To do so, click on the field's title on the layout, then press the **Backspace** key. The column will be removed from the layout. In this case, you will want to remove the Comments field.

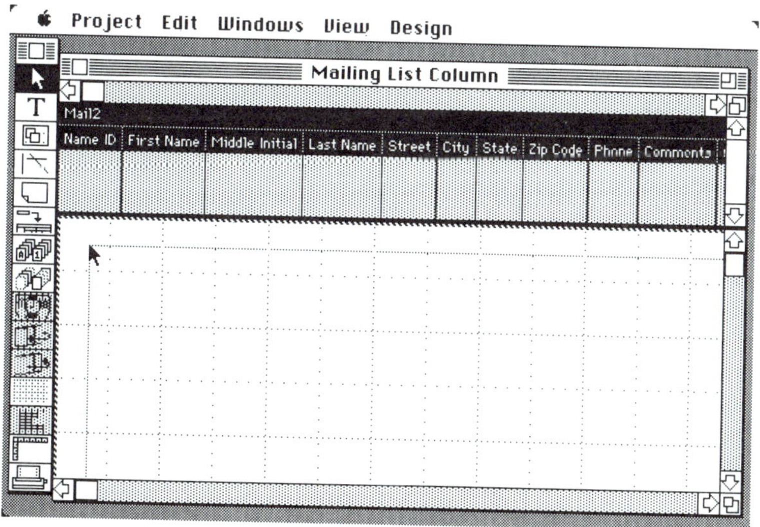

Figure 7-5 Creating Column View Graphic.

All text fields default to the same width. In many cases these fields are too wide, and for greater readability and convenience you should shrink any columns that are too wide.

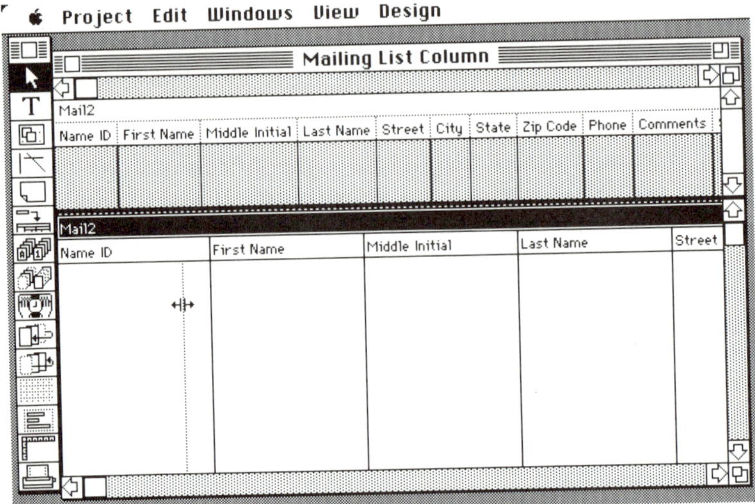

Figure 7-6 Shrinking Column Graphic.

9. To shrink a column, position the cursor on a dividing line between two columns. It should change to two vertical lines with arrows. When the cursor changes, drag it in the direction you wish to move the affected column. When you release the mouse, the screen will redraw in the new proportions.

   You can also change the position of column elements. To move a column, select it, then drag it to the desired position. dBASE Mac determines the postion of the column based on its position in the hierarchy.

RULE: Placing columns follows the rules of the hierarchy closely.

1. If you place the column on a field or title bar at the same or higher level, the field is placed to the left of that field or title bar.
2. If you place the column on a title bar at the same hierarchy level, the column is placed to the left of that title bar, even if it contains several fields beneath it. A variant of that rule is that placing the column on the Root places the column to the extreme left of the layout.
3. If you place the column on a title bar at a lower hierarchy level, the column is placed to the right of that title bar even if it contains several fields beneath it.
4. If you place a column on top of a field title at the same level, the column is placed to the right of that column.
5. If you place a column on top of a field title at a lower level, the column is placed to the right of the column, even splitting the title bar.

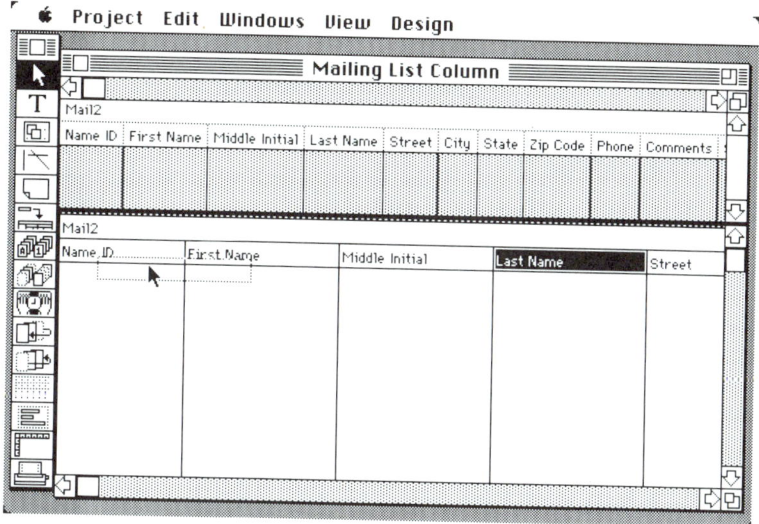

Figure 7-7 Moving Columns Graphic.

10. Highlight the Last Name column and drag it onto the Name ID column. The Last Name column should now appear to the left of the First Name.

If the list is long or wide when you use a Column view to view data, you can use the scroll bar to see more of the data.

You could add titles, change headings, and otherwise modify the Column view if you wished. For now, though, leave the view as it is.

NOTE: Unless you set the minimum Pen Width in the Preferences dialog box (in the Edit menu), Column views always display boxes around titles and display lists. You can eliminate boxes around any element in a Column view by selecting that element, double-clicking (or selecting Display Options from the Design menu) and selecting the thinnest Pen Width setting. You can also set new fonts, font sizes, and other effects on the elements of the display, the same way you would a Form view. Remember, if you increase the font size, the display will be wider. Some Column views may become too wide with larger font sizes.

If you wish to continue with the Tutorial, open the Project menu and select Close. Click **Yes** to save changes made in the MultiMail Project.

If you wish to stop now, select Quit from the Project menu or click on the Quit icon in the Palette.

→ MultiMail continues in Chapter 8.

The Checkbook Layout

Open the Checkbook Project by (1) double-clicking the Checkbook Project icon on the Finder, or (2) selecting Open from the Project menu in dBASE Mac and selecting Checkbook Project from the list of projects available.

If you followed the Tutorial in Chapter 6, the Checkbook Project should open to the Checkbook Entry hierarchy you created in that chapter. If, for some reason, the Checkbook Entry view is not active, open the Windows menu and select Checkbook Entry.

To move from the hierarchy to the layout, click once on the Layout view icon in the Palette, or open the View menu and select Layout View.

Before you begin creating the Checkbook Entry form, think about the process you follow when you maintain a manual ledger:

- You first determine if the transaction is a check, deposit, or other type of transaction.
- Next, if the transaction is a check, you enter the next check number in sequence. If the transaction is not a check, you may enter something, or leave the check number area blank.
- Now you enter the date of the transaction, the description, and the amount. You may or may not include other notes about the transaction.

Your dBASE Mac Checkbook Project follows essentially the same pattern:

- First, the Transaction Number (the Key field) is increased by one for each transaction using the Automatic Sequence option.
- Next you select the type of transaction from the Type Choices field.
- Now here is where dBASE Mac becomes your helper. Once you choose the Type of transaction, dBASE Mac will choose the appropriate form to fill in. You will use the special abilities of Tablets and Show Selections to create the logic behind this choice.

NOTE: Tablets are multipage, on-screen layout elements whose display is controlled using special criteria defined in Show Selections. In the Checkbook Project, the appropriate Tablet page will display for each transaction type.

Begin creating the layout:

1. Drag the Transaction Number down and place it in the upper-left corner of the design area, perhaps just slightly in from the upper-left corner.

2. Now drag down the Type field and place it beneath the Transaction Number field.

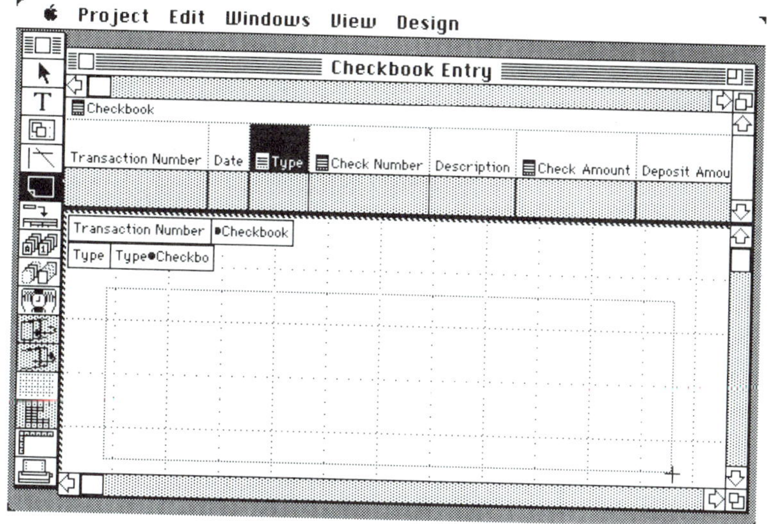

Figure 7-8 Creating Tablet Graphic.

3. Now choose the Tablet icon from the Palette by clicking once.
4. Place the cursor about half-way down the design area and to the left-hand side, then press and hold the mouse. Now drag the mouse down and to the right (create a box about the size and shape of a bank check). Now release the mouse button.

HINT: In the normal layout display, to see other parts of a layout that are off the screen, you can use the scroll bars to bring other sections into view, but there is an easier way. With the cursor on any blank part of the design area, press and hold the **Option** key. Notice that the cursor changes into a hand. Drag the hand to bring other parts of the layout into view. Notice that the scroll bars move as you drag the hand. Also, you can resize the Tablet box or move it after it is created, so don't worry about making it exactly right the first time.

NOTE: The box you have just created is a Tablet. At the bottom-left corner of the Tablet are two small triangular shapes. These are the page flippers. For the moment, do not try to flip the pages.

The first Tablet page you will create is the check. What fields do you need to include when you enter a check? You need the Date, the Check Number, the Description, the Check Amount, the Tax field, and the Memo field.

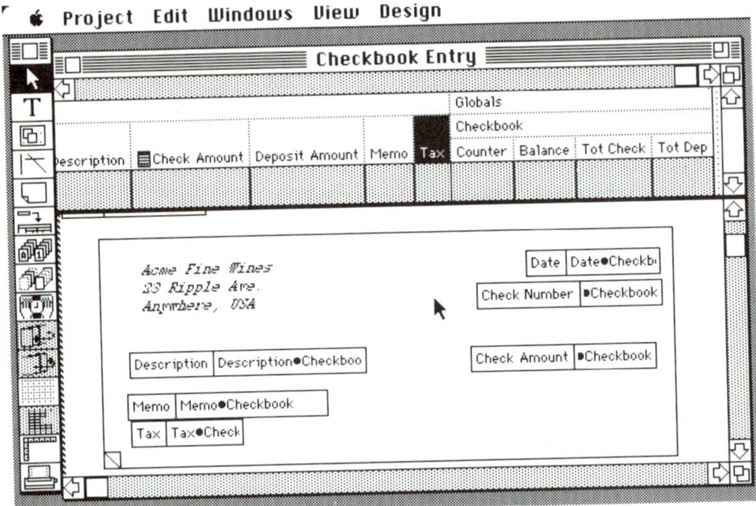

Figure 7-9 Check Tablet Page Graphic.

5. One at a time, drag the necessary fields onto the Tablet page. Place them, wherever possible, in the same approximate positions that you would find them in a real check (see Figure 7-9). (Remember to use the Check Amount field.)

NOTE: You might like to place some identifying text on the check page. To do so, select the Fixed Text icon from the Palette (the icon shaped like a T) and then click on the check page. Type whatever you like there. When you are finished, select the arrow icon from the Palette. You may want to remove any boxes from the text (using Display Options and the minimum Pen Width), and you may want to use a different font, font size, or special effect.

When you have completed the placement of the fields for the check page, create the selection criteria for that page. You could create another page and return to create the selection criteria, but it may be preferable to create the criteria for each page as it is completed.

6. To create the selection criteria, click once anywhere in the Tablet page where there is no field. The whole page should become highlighted. Now double-click the page, or select Display Options from the Design menu.

7. A dialog box very similar to the Preferences dialog box will appear. At the bottom of this dialog box is the Show Selections button. Click once on Show Selections.

   The Show Selections dialog box is similar to the Formula definition. There is a Path pop-up, a Relations list, and a Fields list. Special pop-up menus for Math, String, and Other appear at the bottom of the screen, and the formula for the selection is placed in the Show If. . . formula box.

   The selection criteria for a check are based on the value of the Type field. dBASE Mac keeps all values in a Choice field in numeric order. This means that Check occupies position number one, Bank Charge occupies position number two, and so on. In a formula or procedure, you can refer to the position number for a choice field value.

8. The selection criteria for the check page are:

   ```
   {Type•Checkbook} = 1 OR {Type•Checkbook} = 6
   ```

   Enter the selection criteria by double-clicking Type in the Fields list, typing the rest of the formula, or selecting the equals sign from the Other pop-up and typing a 1, then type OR and add the field name and equals sign and type 6.

9. Click **OK**. dBASE Mac validates the syntax and saves the selection criterion, finally returning you to the Display Options dialog box.

10. Click **OK** once more to return to the design area.

11. Now it's time to create another Tablet page. Click once on the upper triangle at the bottom-left corner of the Tablet. The page you just created should disappear, revealing a blank page.

NOTE: Think of page flippers as pages in a book or magazine. Think of the upper triangle as the edge of the current page. Click it to move forward to the next page. Think of the lower triangle as the edge of the page behind the current one. Click it to move to the previous page.

The next page will be for deposits. Deposits don't need all the same information that checks do. You will need Date, Description, Deposit Amount, Tax, and maybe the Memo field.

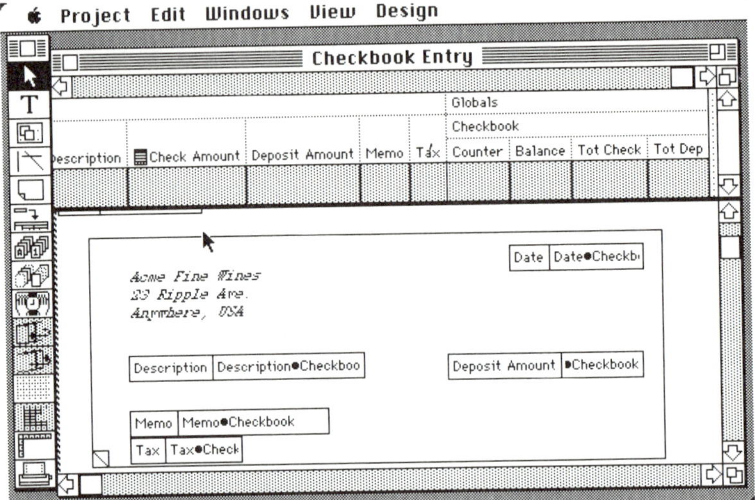

Figure 7-10 Deposit Page Graphic.

12. Drag the Date, Description, Deposit Amount, Tax, and (optionally) Memo fields onto the blank Tablet page. Align them as they would be on a real deposit slip, wherever possible.

HINT: Although it shouldn't happen, it has been our experience that Tablets sometimes "bleed through" when using early versions of dBASE Mac. This means that a field from a nonselected tablet page might show on a different page. This is not supposed to happen, and does not happen consistently, but one trick can help avoid the situation should you encounter it. When you position the same field on several different pages, place them in exactly the same position. That way, even if there is a bleed-through effect, it won't be noticed. It won't affect the data in the file in any case.

HINT: If you plan to place the same Fixed Text or Fixed Graphics on several layout pages, you can use the Clipboard to duplicate them. To duplicate the text you entered on the check page, move the check page (using the page flipper) and select the Text icon again. Now highlight the text you entered, then press **Command-C** (for copy) or select Copy from the Edit menu. Now select the arrow icon, flip the page back to the deposit page, and then select the Text icon again. Click where you want the text and select Paste from the Edit menu. The text will be pasted in. However any Display Options will have to be set once again. Also, you may have to resize the text, depending on what options you used on it.

13. Now double-click on a blank spot on the Tablet page to activate the Display Options dialog box for the current Tablet page.

14. Click Show Selections.

15. Enter the following selection criteria under Show If. . .

```
{Type•Checkbook} = 4 OR {Type•Checkbook} = 5
```

These selection criteria instruct dBASE Mac to show the Tablet page if the transaction type is Deposit or Interest, both of which can share the same input form.

16. Click **OK** to save the selection criterion, and then click **OK** again to return to the design area.

You need to create one more page—this one for bank charges and miscellaneous charges. Here you need the Date, Description, Check Amount, Tax, and Memo fields.

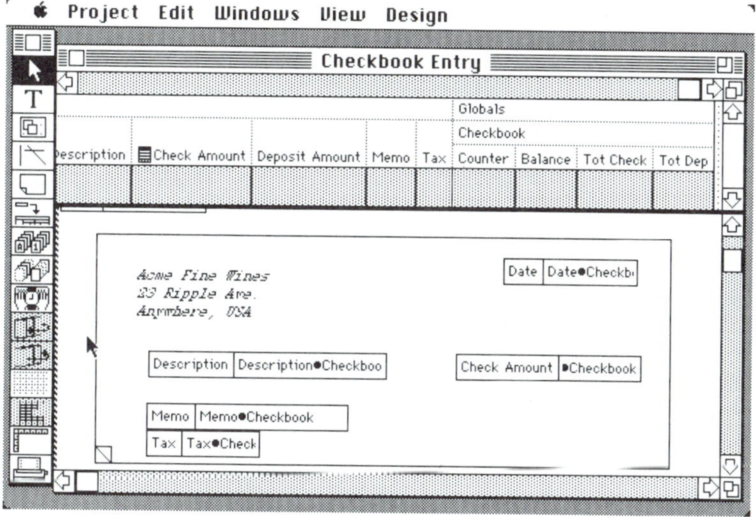

Figure 7-11 Third Tablet Page Graphic.

17. Click on the upper triangle to flip to a new, blank page. Drag the Date, Description, Check Amount, Tax, and Memo fields onto the page, and position them as you wish.

HINT: Since you already copied the Fixed Text into the Clipboard, now you only need to create a text element and Paste it again.

18. Double-click on a blank area of the Tablet page to open the Display Options, then click Show Selections.

19. Enter the criteria for Show If. . .

```
{Type•Checkbook} = 2 OR {Type•Checkbook} = 3
```

20. Click **OK** to return to the Display Options dialog, then **OK** again.

You can now flip back through the Tablet pages by clicking on the bottom triangle. Check to see that your three pages are correct.

Finally, place the Balance field at the top of the page (or, optionally, below the Tablet pages). You can also place the Tot Checks and Tot Dep fields on the layout below the Balance field if you wish. These two Memory fields are really unnecessary, but they provide an interesting window into your financial activities.

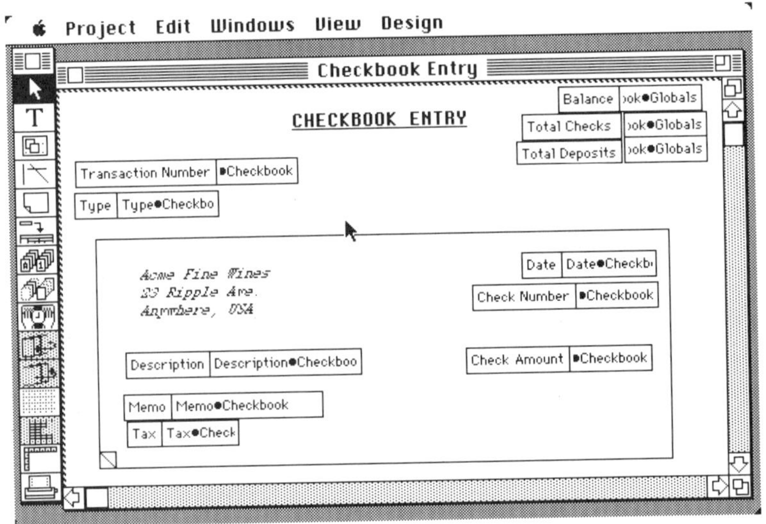

Figure 7-12 Finished Layout Graphic.

Show/Hide Hierarchy—Finishing Touches

Next you will add a little something extra. First, make some more room.

1. Click once in the small box in the upper-right corner of the hierarchy. The Show/Hide Hierarchy box is just above the scroll bar on the right, and below the Zoom control box (the standard Macintosh control to Zoom the screen to full or partial size). Since you have added all the fields you need, you can hide the hierarchy.

   Notice that the contents of the design area move to the top of the screen, and that a new area is displayed below. You can click the box again to replace the hierarchy.

2. Next, make some room at the top of the form. Click and hold the mouse button at the top-left corner of the design area. Now drag the mouse diagonally toward the lower-right corner until the selection box surrounds all the fields and the Tablet. Release the mouse button. All the layout elements should be highlighted. (Another way to highlight all the elements on a layout is to choose Select All from the Edit menu.)

3. Now click on any highlighted element and drag downward. The outline of all the fields and the Tablet should move down. Make about an inch of space at the top.

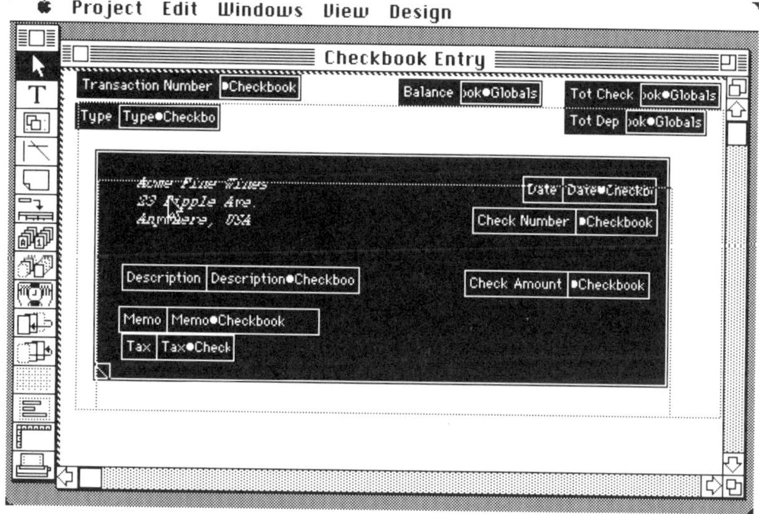

Figure 7-13 Moving the Whole Lot Graphic.

Now you will add some fixed text to make a clearer and more attractive form.

4. Click once on the Fixed Text icon in the Palette.

5. Now position the cursor at the top of the design area. Set the **Caps Lock** button on your keyboard down. Type "CHECKBOOK ENTRY"

6. Now select the pointer icon again. Release Caps Lock.

Notice that the text you just entered appears just like any other design element. You can change its position or appearance the same way you would any other element of the design.

7. Double-click anywhere on the words CHECKBOOK ENTRY to open the Display Options.

8. Select a font that you like—something appropriate to the title of your checkbook maintenance view. (You may like something fancy, or something plain. It's up to you.)

9. Now change the size of the font to 12 or 14. You want the title to show clearly.

10. Next select Bold and Underlined from the special effects.

11. Finally select the smallest pen width.

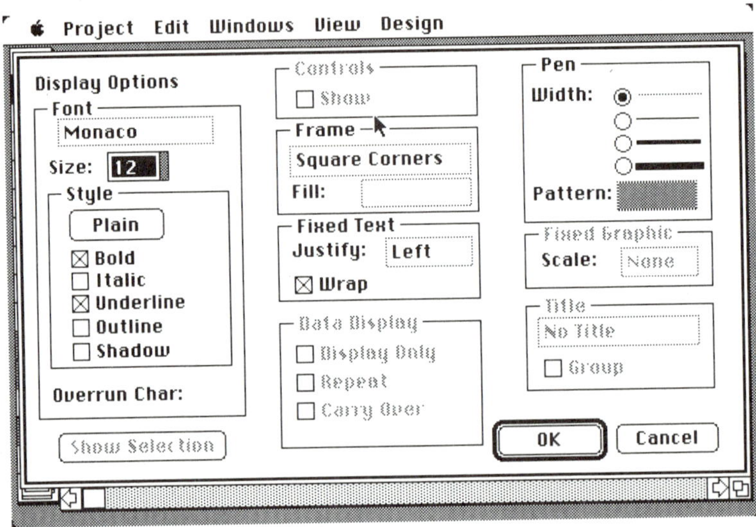

Figure 7-14 Display Options Graphic.

NOTE ON THE MAC II: dBASE Mac can create color layouts. Color settings are found in the Preferences and Display Options dialogs under Fill and Pattern (at the bottom of the list. Although color is not normally a big part of Mac programming, you can add some splash to your programs with color—assuming you have a Mac II or some other way to display color on a Mac).

12. Click **OK** to save the new options

    Click on a blank spot on the design area. Notice that your fixed text looks different now. It probably has been cut off so that only part of it is showing. You can change the size of any design element by highlighting that element, then moving the cursor to the lower-right corner. The cursor changes shape to a pair of diagonal lines with arrows. Drag the design element to the desired size and shape.

13. Size the fixed text to display the both words. Move it if necessary to center it.

Now that you have created the title, you know how to add fixed text to your layout. You might also add labels to each of the Tablet pages. For instance, the Check page might be labeled as such, and the Deposit and the Bank Charges/Miscellaneous page might be labeled for easy identification. Of course you can change the display of any of the other fields and titles by using the same methods used above to modify the fixed text.

To make the Checkbook Entry layout more attractive, try using different fonts and other effects, eliminating the boxes around fields, and applying some creative design to the layout. One suggestion is to highlight the Description, Check Amount, Deposit Amount, and Memo fields, then double-click to open Display Options. Now select the upper Pen Width (the thinnest) to eliminate the box around the field. Then click in the Underlined checkbox under Style. Now, when you enter these field values, the results will be underlined. Do the same with any other field. You might try setting off the field titles or reorganizing the entire layout. Experiment with Display Options to see what combinations work best for you.

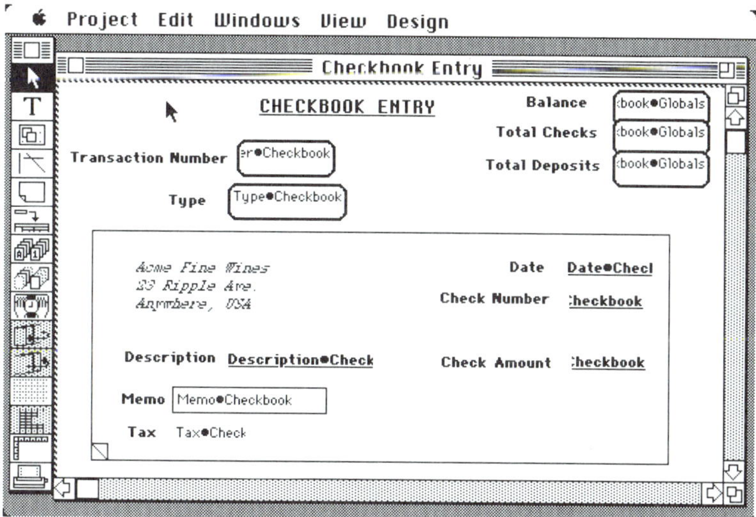

Figure 7-15 Finished Check Page.

Finally, you don't want to modify the Balance, Tot Checks, or Tot Dep fields. You might highlight them and select Display Only from the Display Options dialog. You might want to change the field titles for Tot Checks and Tot Dep to something more like English. You can do so by highlighting the existing title boxes and pressing **Backspace**. Then enter Fixed Text items with more appropriate titles. Now move back to the Define Hierarchy screen and double-click on the Balance field in the hierarchy to open the Change Field dialog box. Enter the following short Pre-Processor procedure to the Balance field:

```
SETNEXTFIELD({Transaction Number•Checkbook})
```

This prevents the cursor from entering the Memory fields.

NOTE: If you decided to place the Memory fields underneath the Tablet pages, then you should use SETNEXTFIELD({Transaction Number•Checkbook}) to move to the top of the form.

Optional Graphics

You could make the checkbook page even fancier by placing a digitized check image on the Tablet page. The following steps are completely optional, but illustrate some new concepts—Fixed Graphics and Bring to Front/Send to Back.

- First, you need to digitize one of your checks using Thunderscan(TM) or one of many scanners on the market.
- Or you might use your artistic talents to draw a check image in a paint or drawing program like MacPaint or MacDraw.
- Now that you have a check image in a picture file, re-open the Checkbook Project.
- Select the Fixed Graphic icon from the Palette. The cursor becomes a cross shape.
- Position the cursor at the top-left corner of the check Tablet page, and drag diagonally down to the bottom-right corner. A dotted box should surround the check page. Be sure that it doesn't extend past the Tablet or leave much room within it.
- When you let go of the mouse, the Tablet will turn completely black, and you will not see your fields any more. Don't worry, they're still there.

At this point, you can adjust the size and/or position of the box if it isn't just right. You do this the same way you move and size any layout element. Position the cursor at the bottom-right corner of the Fixed Graphic box. The cursor will change shape to display two lines and diagonal arrows. You can drag the corner of the box to adjust its size. You can move the entire box by clicking on it once, then dragging it wherever you wish to place it.

- Now, from within the layout, select the Picture This. . . Desk Accessory from the Apple menu.
- Open the file that contains the image of the check.
- Drag the mouse around the image to select it
- Press **Command-C** or select Copy to copy an image of the check into the Clipboard.
- Close Picture This. . . by selecting Quit from the Picture menu.
- Select the Fixed Graphic box you created a few steps ago.
- Press **Command-V** or Paste.
  The checkbook image will appear in the graphic field.
- Now, select Send to Back from the Palette or the Design menu
- The fields you inserted earlier reappear.

NOTE: You can stack layout elements on top of each other. Select Send to Back to place an element on the bottom of the stack. Select Bring to Front to place an element on top.

The chances are that your checkbook image and the fields in the Tablet do not immediately create a satisfactory image. You may want to modify the Tablet or the fields to improve the display.

NOTE: When you create your final application, it would be better to create the graphic first, size it to your liking, then create the Tablet and place the fields in their appropriate places. For the purposes of this Tutorial, the above method will work. If you did follow the procedures above, and you don't like the results, you can remove the Fixed Graphic by clicking on it and pressing **Backspace**.

When you are satisfied with the appearance of your layout, save the project by selecting Save from the Project menu.

If you wish to continue with the next layout, Close the project and answer **Yes** to save changes.

If you wish to take a break now, select Quit from the Project menu or Exit from the Palette.

→ Checkbook continues in Chapter 9.

Laying Out the Timecard

To begin the layout for the Timecard Entry view, first load the Timecard Project.

If dBASE Mac is active, Close any active projects, then Open the Timecard Project.

To load the project from the Finder, double-click the Timecard Project icon.

The Timecard Entry hierarchy should still be active on your screen. If not, open the Windows menu and select Timecard Entry.

Briefly review the hierarchy you created in Chapter 6.

Now select Layout View from the View menu. To create a simple layout for this view, you might drag each field onto the design area and position it to your liking.

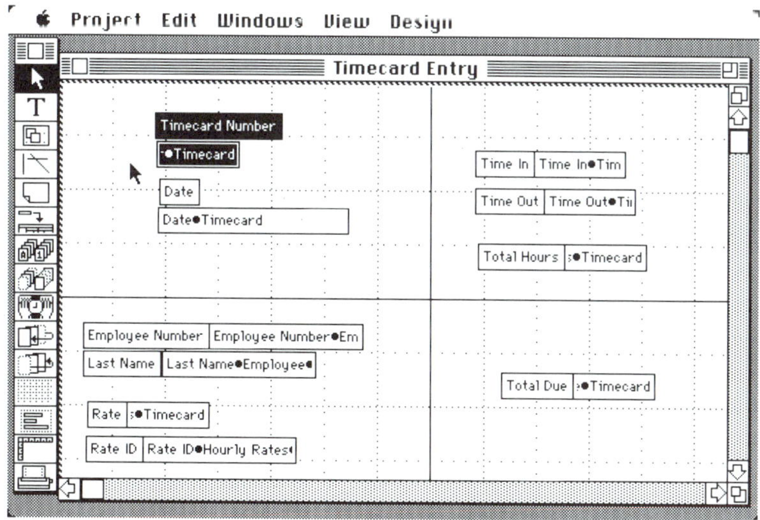

Figure 7-16 Simple Layout Graphic.

On the other hand, a little time spent improving the looks of the layout might pay off later by setting it apart and giving it some style. It will also make a more impressive printout.

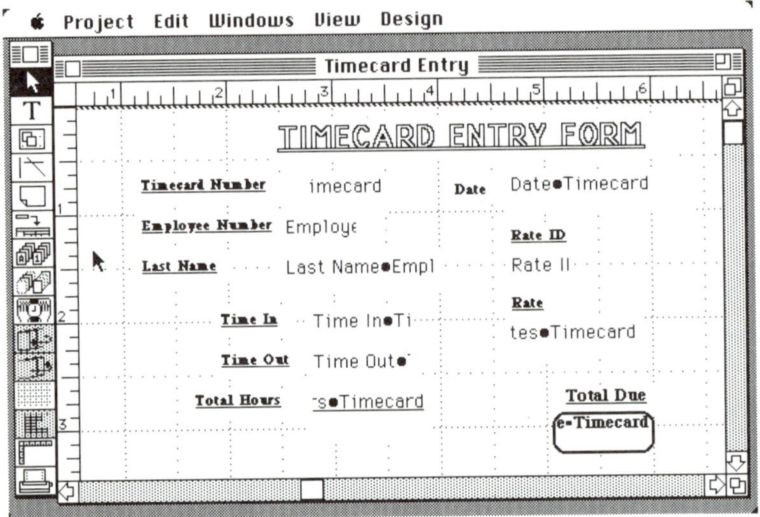

Figure 7-17 Finished Layout Graphic.

1. Before you begin bringing the fields onto the design area, select Turn Grid On from the Design menu. This will help you place the fields more precisely.

2. Next, select Rulers from the Design menu. Set the size to one-eighth inch and click the Show Rulers checkbox. When you click **OK**, you will return to the layout view. Notice the rulers that appear along the upper and left edges. You can use them to further line up your work.

NOTE: You can use Rulers to help create accurate layouts. Rulers are especially useful when you are working with pre-printed forms and need to align field data in exact positions.

NOTE: Rulers can be scaled in one of three standard scales, or one of three metric scales.

Suppose you want the timesheets to print out two to a page. You need to set the form size.

3. Select Form Size from the Design menu. Set a size approximately eight inches wide by five inches in length. Since normal paper is 11 inches long, this should be about right. Click **OK** to return to the layout view.

   If you scroll downward on the design area, you will notice that the form has become smaller. This is the new form size you have set. If you position your fields and other layout elements with this total form in mind, the form will be attractive and balanced when printed out.

4. Now select the fixed text icon. Position the cursor about one-quarter inch from the top of the design area and about three inches from the left edge. Type the title "Timecard Entry" and use Display Options to select appropriate fonts and special effects to make the view title stand out.

5. Finally, drag each field onto the design area (except Posting Amount). It really doesn't matter where you place them at first, but it is easier to place them close to their final positions.

   The Posting Amount field must be in the hierarchy to be processed, but it does not need to be on the layout, since it contains the same value as the Total Due field. Remember, if you need to remove a field from the design area, highlight it and press **Backspace**.

HINT: If you drag one field onto another, they overlap. You can use this overlapping effect in some forms since the active field always moves to the top of a stack during data entry or modification.

   You should have the following fields and their titles on the layout screen: Transaction Number, Date, Employee ID, Last Name, Rate ID, Rate, Time In, Time Out, Total Hours, and Total Due.

6. Now change Display Options for all the titles. Click up at the top-left corner near the Transaction Number title. Drag the mouse down to select the other titles beneath it. Now, holding the **Shift** key down, draw a box around the titles on the right side of the screen. When you are done, only the field titles should be highlighted.

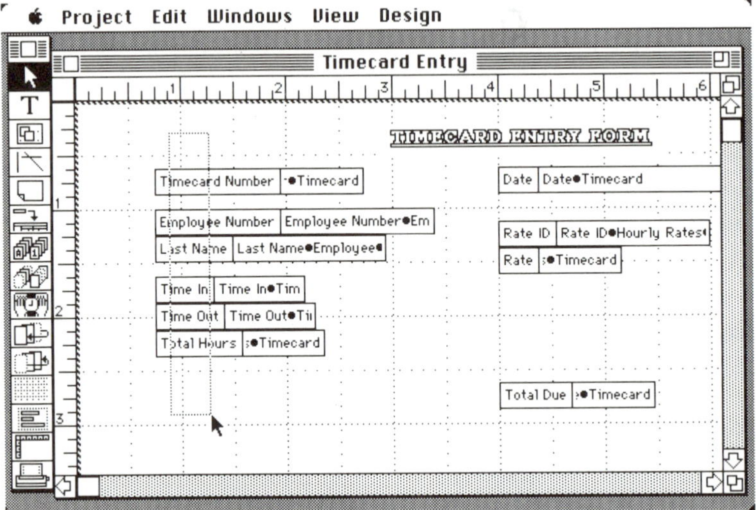

Figure 7-18 Selecting Titles Graphic.

7. Double-click any one of the highlighted titles to open the Display Options dialog.

8. Select a font, font size, and special effect if desired. You might want to underline the titles to set them off. If you want to eliminate the boxes around the titles, set the pen width to its minimum setting.

   When you are done setting the Display Options, click **OK** to return to the design area.

   You can change the Display Options for all field data the same way. Remember, using group selections is a quick way to work with many layout elements at once (also see Groups, below).

Hiding the Grid

When you are finished placing the fields and other design elements on the screen, you can remove the large grid lines to display the form in a way that more closely resembles its final appearance. Select Show/Hide Grid from the Palette or Hide Grid from the Design menu. The grid lines will disappear.

> NOTE: Hiding the Grid does not turn the Grid off, nor does it disable the Align to Grid option. It only removes the large grid that normally covers the design area.

Reducing the Form

Do you want to see how the size of your view and the positions of the design elements will display on a printed page? You can select Reduce to Fit to see a reduced image of the form on a page mock-up. Use Reduce to Fit to check that fields are properly positioned, graphics and titles look balanced, and that the whole form will print properly. Click the mouse to return to the layout screen.

> HINT: Sometimes the most balanced form on paper, or in the Reduce to Fit view, is not the most balanced on the Mac screen at its default position. Use the scroll bars to line up the form to its most advantageous position on the screen, regardless of its position on the total form. If you leave it in that position, it will display that way when in the Use mode. (Don't forget to hide the hierarchy when you are positioning the layout. The hierarchy will not be present in Use mode.)

Groups

Another way to work with several elements at once is to use the Group command from the Design menu.

Use the Group command to work with the field data. First select all field data the same way you did the titles. When all fields are highlighted, select Group from the Design menu.

From now on, selecting any field data element will select them all. Try it. Click once on a blank spot in the design area. The fields should no longer be highlighted. Now click any field. They should all be highlighted again. Try dragging a field to a new position. They all move. If you did move these elements from their position, replace them now.

Try resizing one field. Place the cursor at the bottom-right corner of any field element until the cursor changes to two diagonal lines with arrows. Now drag the corner. Notice that all fields change size.

Grouping the data field elements was an exercise but, for various reasons, you don't want to leave them all grouped. First, you may want to work with field elements individually and, second, Group has other uses.

The Group command has an even more important purpose than aiding in the design process. It allows you to control the processing order of data entry. Ordinarily, when you enter data on a form, dBASE Mac moves automatically left to right and down the screen. This means that you may find yourself entering data in a nonlogical order from time to time. For instance, in the Timecard Entry form, you might prefer to process the Timecard Number, then the Date, then the Employee Number, then the Time In and Time Out fields. But the Rate ID field is to the left of the Employee Number, so the natural order of processing would go there next. You could use a SETNEXTFIELD command to control the processing order, but an easier way is to group all the fields that you want to process first. Fields outside the group will be processed next.

You can group nonadjacent fields, causing the cursor to move through the entire group before continuing with the next field outside the current group. Experiment with various types of grouping to see what works for you.

Display Only Fields

Several kinds of fields do not require data entry. Obviously Formula fields derive their values from calculations based on other field contents. Likewise, certain kinds of fields are called lookup fields. These fields derive their values from other files and do not require data entry by keyboard.

Two fields in the Timecard Entry view use information from other files. The Last Name and Rate fields will be filled in automatically when you enter a value in the Employee ID and Rate ID fields respectively. Therefore, you do not want anyone entering or changing the data in those fields. You want to view the data these lookup fields display, but in no way interact with it. For best results, you should add a SETNEXTFIELD Pre-Processor to the Last Name and Rate fields—preventing the cursor from entering them at all, but you can set them as Display Only as well.

NOTE: If you were allowed to change information in the Last Name or the Rate fields, pressing **Enter** with the insertion point in one of those fields would write new records to their associated files, but would not write the information for files higher in the hierarchy (like the Root file, Timecard) However, if you press **Command-Enter**, the values in all files will be changed, meaning that you can enter a complete record from any field using **Command-Enter**.

1. To set the Last Name and Rate fields to Display Only, first click on the Last Name field to highlight it. Next **Shift**-click on the Rate field, then double-click the Rate field to open the Display Options dialog box.

2. The checkbox for Display Only is under the box titled Data Display. Click on that box and then click **OK** to prevent data entry into the highlighted layout elements.

NOTE: The Repeat box will repeat field contents in a multipage columnar report where the current field contents overflow the page. The Carry Over checkbox causes the contents of the previous record to be placed in the current record for the highlighted fields. This overrides the Keep New Initial Value checkbox in the field definition.

- Now add SETNEXTFIELD Pre-Processors to the Last Name and Rate fields by returning to the Define Hierarchy screen and adding the Pre-Processor. The Last Name procedure should set the next field to Time In. The Rate procedure should set the next field to Timecard Number if you used the grouping example explained earlier. Otherwise, it should set the next field to whatever field the cursor normally enters after the Rate field.

Other Ideas

Instead of setting all field titles to the same font and size, and all field data likewise, you might use some of the other effects for special purposes. For instance, in the Timecard Entry view, you might put a thin box around the Time In and Time Out data, and a thick box around the Total Due data. For Total Due select a different pattern (the one with diagonal stripes works well) and a thick box to really set off the amount.

You can experiment freely with layouts. There is no way you can harm your files or data. The best way to find out what works is to try many different kinds of designs and features. Since the layout features of dBASE Mac are so versatile, you should be able to create a wide variety of different looks and kinds of data entry forms, as well as a great number of report layouts.

→ Timecard continues in Chapter 8.

Summary

The Layout section of dBASE Mac is the most feature-rich section of the program. There are many ways to manipulate the appearance of your forms and reports.

Fortunately, layouts are most conducive to experimentation, and are easily changed and rearranged.

Chapter 7 illustrates many of the features of the Layout:

Add form elements to a view.
Change the size of a Form view using Form Size.
Select number of forms across page.
Use Preferences to select default settings.
Use the Grid to align design elements.
Turn the Grid on or off.
Hide the Grid.
Add column elements to a view.
Move and Resize columns in Column views.
Remove boxes and titles in Column and in Form views.
Create Tablets and Show Selection criteria.
Create Fixed Text and Fixed Graphic elements.
Use Picture This. . . to import graphics.
Bring to Front and Send to Back to contol stacking design elements.
Create overlapping design elements.
Use Rulers for more accurate layouts.
Use Groups as a design aid and also to control data processing later.
Select fields for Display Only, Carry Over, or Repeat.

The basic definition of the three projects in this tutorial is done. Now it is time to put them to some use, to see how data can be entered, modified, and printed out.

In the next chapter you will enter data into the Checkbook and Timecard projects. Once you have data in the files, you will learn ways to manipulate and browse through that data in a Form view.

You will also learn how to change the order of the records by setting Sort criteria, and how to choose certain records to display using Selection criteria.

8

ADDING RECORDS, SORTING, AND SELECTING

Overview

In Chapter 8 you finally begin to see the procedures and relationships you have developed in action. You will begin entering data in the Checkbook and Timecard projects.

After the data have been entered, you will begin to see how to sort the data in your files and select specific records.

The Use Mode Palette

Each of the special Edit menu commands mentioned in the next section has a Palette icon equivalent. The default Use mode Palette contains the following icons:

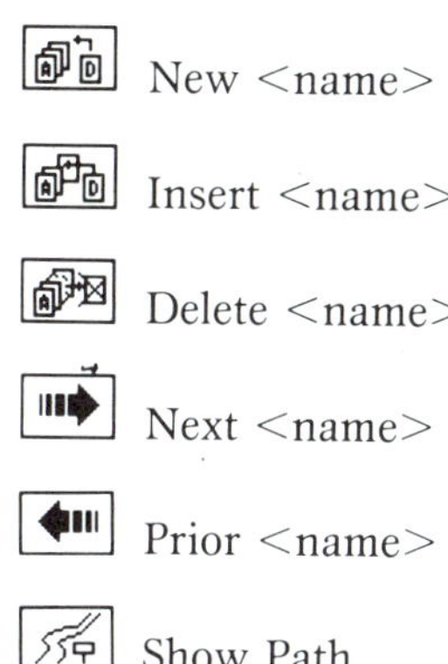

The Path icon displays the full path of a field, the number of occurrences in a multivalued field, and the position of the currently selected occurrence.

Manipulating Data in Form Views

When you are entering and modifying data in Form views, you will sometimes have to do more than simply add and **Enter** records. Sometimes you may have to delete whole records, or specific occurrences in multivalued fields. You may want to insert a new occurrence in a particular position in a multivalued field or set.

Several Edit menu commands control the data in a Form view. In addition to the standard Macintosh commands—Cut, Copy, Paste, Clear, and Select All—dBASE Mac adds some new commands: **New <name>**, **Insert <name>**, **Delete <name>**, **Next <name>**, and **Prior <name>**. All of these are commands that change with the context. The value of **<name>** changes depending on where the cursor is.

New <name> displays a new, blank record in an open file if the cursor is in the Key field or any single valued file field. In this case, **<name>** is the file name. If the cursor is in a multivalued field, **New <name>** adds an occurrence to the multivalued field, and **<name>** is the field name. If the cursor is in the pointer field of a relationship, it adds another blank occurrence to the multivalued field just as it would with any other multivalued field.

Insert <name> Inserts a new occurrence in a multivalued field. Use **Insert <name>** to create a new occurrence at the current position of the mutlivalued field. **New <name>** adds a new occurrence at the end of the list.

Delete <name> If the pointer is in the Key field or any single valued file field, **Delete <name>** removes the record. If the cursor is in a multivalued field, **Delete <name>** removes the current occurrence in the multivalued field or all fields in the Set.

WARNING: Be careful when you Delete records. They cannot be recovered. Also beware of deleting multivalued occurrences within Sets. All the data for that occurrence in each of the fields in the Set will be removed. If you only want to remove the *value* from an occurrence in an individual field—not the entire occurrence—use **Backspace** or Cut.

Next <name> retrieves the next record, if any, in the current file if the cursor is in a Key field or other single valued file field. Otherwise it scrolls to the next occurrence within a multivalued field. **Next <name>** will retrieve records that meet the current sort and selection criteria in sorted order. Any Snapshots (see later in this chapter), Indexes, or other data selection rules in effect are followed.

Prior <name> retrieves the previous record, if any, in the current file if the cursor is in a Key field or other single valued file field. Otherwise it scrolls to the previous occurrence within a multivalued field. **Next <name>** will retrieve records that meet the current sort and selection criteria in sorted order. Any Snapshots, Indexes, or other data selection rules in effect are followed.

Adding Data to Checkbook

Load the Checkbook Project by (1) double-clicking the Checkbook Project icon on the Finder, or (2) Closing any other active dBASE Mac projects, choosing Open from the Project menu and selecting Checkbook Project.

If you saved the Checkbook Project after creating the layout for Checkbook Entry, then that view should be active. Now it is time to use the view.

To use a view, you can select either Use or Perform and Use from the Palette or the View menu.

Use vs. Perform and Use

Perform and Use creates a memory-resident list of key values matching the sort and selection criteria of a view and creating what is called Work File. Perform and Use positions all selected Key field values in memory and positions the first record in the file on the current form.

NOTE: The Work File is usually a memory resident list of key values, although sometimes these values will be saved in a temporary file on the disk. In the event of a system crash or other mishap, these temporary files may be left on the desktop. You can simply throw them in the trash. They are worthless to you, and are only the result of dBASE Mac being unable to complete its housekeeping chores.

Selecting Use accesses the Use mode of a view, but does not update the records or display the first record on the form. Use presents the current Form view with a blank record. If the view is a Column view, it displays any records that have been previously retrieved with Perform and Use. If you know that no changes have been made to files associated with a particular view, Use is a quicker way to call it. It is also the appropriate command to use when entering new data into a Form view. However, Perform and Use offers the security of knowing that the display of all data is up to date, especially in Column type views and reports.

NOTE: Perform does not actually update the data, only the list of keys by which the data are accessed.

Since you are about to add records to the Checkbook file, you can select Use from the View menu, or click the Use icon from the Palette. The layout you created in Chapter 7 is still visible, but now it is in the Use mode. Now you can begin to enter data. Use the **Tab** key to move from field to field. Type in the data listed below and press **Enter** after each record.

NOTE: To make selections in a Choices field, you can select using the mouse, or you can press the **Spacebar** to move from one choice to another. Press **Tab** to move to the next field. Also press the **Spacebar** to select or deselect the Tax check box (or click the mouse in the checkbox).

NOTE: Remember that the Transaction Number field is an Automatic Sequence field, so you won't have to put anything in that field. To begin a new record when the Transaction Number field is blank, choose Add Transaction Number from the Edit menu or type **Command-A**. **Command-A** is the preferred way to begin a new record. It is better than just typing in a new Key field value. During a lengthy session of data entry, a new record is automatically initiated in the file whenever you write the last record. This is true if Auto Advance is checked in the Preferences menu. Auto Advance is the default setting that comes with dBASE Mac. If you don't want a new record initiated whenever you write a record to the file, you can change the status of Auto Advance.

To have something to work with in the Checkbook file, add the following records. You should choose the transaction type from the Type field, then enter the appropriate information for each record. Also, any data you wish to enter in the Memo field is optional:

Transaction Number:	**1**
Type:	**Deposit**
Date:	**01/01/87**
Description:	**Initial Deposit**
Check Amount:	
Deposit Amount:	**$1000.00**
Tax:	**No**

Transaction Number:	**2**
Type:	**Check**
Date:	**01/02/87**
Description:	**Nick's Market**
Check Amount:	**$25.66**
Deposit Amount:	
Tax:	**No**

Transaction Number:	3
Type:	Check
Date:	01/02/87
Description:	Sam's Paper Supply
Check Amount:	$34.92
Deposit Amount:	
Tax:	Yes

Transaction Number:	4
Type:	Interest
Date:	01/05/87
Description:	Interest Payment
Check Amount:	
Deposit Amount:	$12.32
Tax:	Yes

Transaction Number:	5
Type:	Bank Charge
Date:	01/07/87
Description:	New Checks
Check Amount:	$7.00
Deposit Amount:	
Tax:	No

Transaction Number:	6
Type:	Check
Date:	01/15/87
Description:	Joe Landlord
Check Amount:	$650.00
Deposit Amount:	
Tax:	No

Transaction Number:	7
Type:	Miscellaneous
Date:	01/16/87
Description:	Bank Machine Withdrawal
Check Amount:	$120.00
Deposit Amount:	
Tax:	No

Transaction Number:	8
Type:	Deposit
Date:	01/18/87
Description:	Paycheck

Check Amount:	
Deposit Amount:	**$1500.00**
Tax:	**Yes**
Transaction Number:	**9**
Type:	**Check**
Date:	**01/18/87**
Description:	**Auto License**
Check Amount:	**$59.39**
Deposit Amount:	
Tax:	**Yes**
Transaction Number:	**10**
Type:	**Check**
Date:	**01/22/87**
Description:	**Computer Market**
Check Amount:	**$350.00**
Deposit Amount:	
Tax:	**Yes**

If you wish, go back to one of the records you just entered and modify the amount entered. When you press **Enter** to save the modifications, notice the changes to the Balance and other Memory fields. Also notice on checks that the Check Number does not change when you modify an existing record. (Remember the procedure you entered in Chapter 6?)

Now that you have entered the data listed above, Close the Checkbook Project and load the Timecard Project. Continue entering data in the Timecard Entry view.

Adding Records to Timecard

If you do not have the Timecard Project active, load it now. The Timecard Entry view layout should be active. Before you enter data into the Timecard Entry view, you need to add some employee records to the Employee file, and some pay rates to the Hourly Rates file.

The Employee File

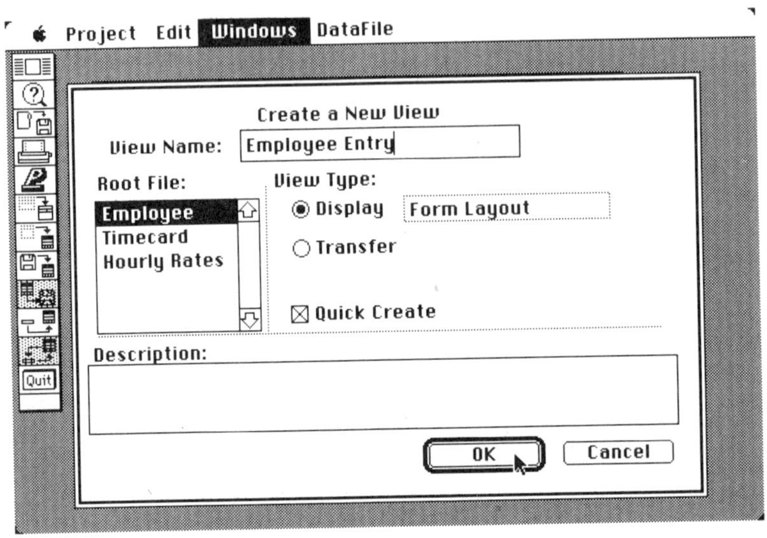

Figure 8-1 Employee Quick View Create Graphic.

Create a new view for Employee.

- Select New View . . . from the Windows menu.
- Be sure to highlight the Employee file in the file list.
- Type "Employee Entry" to name the view.
- Select Form Type and check Quick Create.
- Click **OK**.

Want to try something new?

1. Select Layout View from the View menu.

2. Click once on the Employee title bar.

3. Now **Shift**-click on the Employee Number and Last Name fields in the hierarchy.

4. Drag the Employee title bar onto the layout and position the dotted box to the right of the fields.

5. Resize the Employee Number field, making it smaller, and reposition the columns by dragging the title bar. Place the columns off to the side.

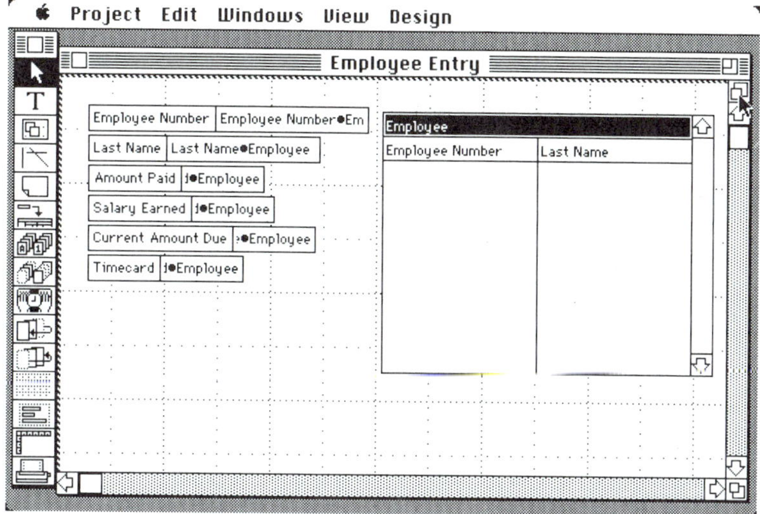

Figure 8-2 Layout Graphic.

The layout you have just created has an interesting use. Below you will find some records to enter into the Employee file. Enter the first two or three records, then select Perform and Use from the View menu. Watch the column part of the view. The records you have just entered will appear there. In each data entry session, you will be able to check all the existing records through the Column view.

NOTE: You can create a mixed view like the one above for any view. However, the view will process more slowly because of the columns. Also, you can scroll the column information if there is more than will fit on the screen, but you must click once to activate the columns. To return to the form fields, you must click on that part of the view.

NOTE: A view can contain both column and form elements, but you must be careful to set up the view with the appropriate hierarchy for best results. Experiment with different hierarchies and different layouts to determine what will produce intelligible results and what will not. Once a Column or Form view is modified, it becomes a Custom view.

Now enter the following records:

Employee Number: **1**
Last Name: **Smith**
Amount Paid: **$1485.00**

Employee Number: **2**
Last Name: **Fern**
Amount Paid: **$248.00**

Employee Number: 3
Last Name: **Bacon**
Amount Paid: **$1225.00**

Perform and Use the view. Notice the change in the column part of the view.

Employee Number: 4
Last Name: **Shakespeare**
Amount Paid: **$36.00**

Employee Number: 5
Last Name: **Moto**
Amount Paid: **$564.00**

Employee Number: 6
Last Name: **Condie**
Amount Paid: **$1865.00**

Remember to **Tab** between fields and press **Enter** after each record.

Perform and Use again to update the columns. When you are finished, close the view by clicking on the close box (in the upper-left corner).

The Hourly Rates File

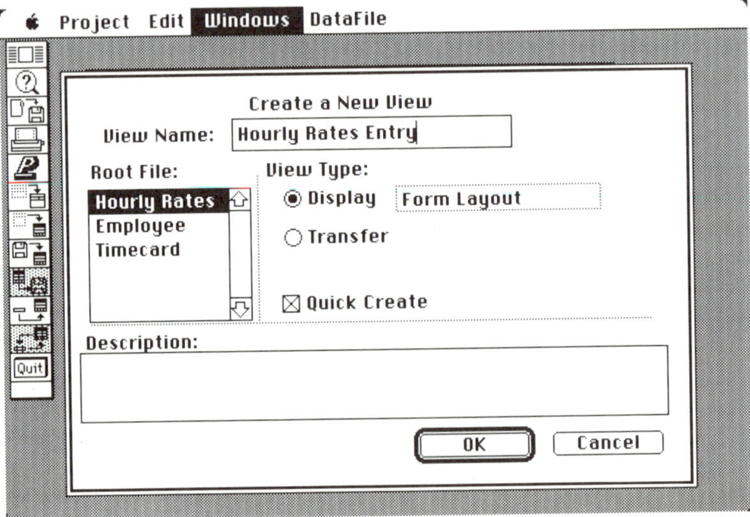

Figure 8-3 Hourly Rates Quick View Create Graphic.

Next you want to enter some pay rates. To do so,

- Select New View. . . from the Windows menu.
- Name the view Hourly Rates Entry.
- Select Form from the Type pop-up.
- Be sure the root file is Hourly Rates.
- Check the Quick Create box and click **OK**.

Enter the following information into the Hourly Rates file:

Rate ID:	**a**
Description:	**Basic Pay**
Rate:	**$3.65**
Rate ID:	**b**
Description:	**Grade II**
Rate:	**$5.65**
Rate ID:	**c**
Description:	**Grade III**
Rate:	**$8.65**
Rate ID:	**d**
Description:	**Overtime**
Rate:	**$10.50**
Rate ID:	**e**
Description:	**Hazard Pay**
Rate:	**$35.85**

Remember to **Tab** between fields and press **Enter** after each record. When you are finished, close the view.

Now you want to activate the Timecard Entry view. Open the Windows menu. Notice that the names of all your views are listed beneath the Structure Window entry. Select Timecard Entry.

The last time you used Timecard Entry, you left it in the layout. Therefore, it will be in layout when you open it now.

NOTE: dBASE Mac remembers how you left a view the last time you used it. If you left it in Use mode, it will be in Use mode the next time you activate it.

Select Use from the Palette or from the View menu. Now the view is ready to receive information.

Like the Checkbook Entry view, the Timecard Entry view uses Automatic Sequencing on the Key field, so you will not have to enter each new Transaction Number. Enter a Date (the program keeps the date from the previous record), an Employee Number (the Last Name fills in automatically), a Rate ID (the Rate fills in), a Time In, and a Time Out.

NOTE: When you enter times, you can enter the time in virtually any valid format. For instance, you can enter 15:30 to mean 3:30 PM, or vice versa. To enter 7:00 AM, you need only enter 7. Experiment with this feature. dBASE Mac will not accept anything invalid, and if you enter a mistaken value, simply correct it by backspacing, highlighting, or **Tabbing** back to the field and correcting.

After you have entered the time values, the Total Hours and the Total Due will calculate and display. Note that you can't change the value in a Formula field. The only way to do that is to change the value in one of the fields it uses for calculation.

NOTE: Pressing **Enter** saves the current record information for the current level of the insertion point. If you press **Command-Enter**, you enter information for all files in the view. In this case, if you were allowed to enter a new rate in the Rate field, or a new name in the Last Name field, pressing **Command-Enter** would update the new information to all files.

Transaction Number: **1**
Date: **01/05/87**
Employee Number: **3**
Time In: **8:00**
Time Out: **17:00**
Rate ID: **b**

Transaction Number: **2**
Date: **01/05/87**
Employee Number: **1**
Time In: **8:00**
Time Out: **17:00**
Rate ID: **a**

Transaction Number: **3**
Date: **01/05/87**
Employee Number: **2**
Time In: **8:30**
Time Out: **17:30**
Rate ID: **c**

Transaction Number: **4**
Date: **01/05/87**
Employee Number: **4**
Time In: **8:30**
Time Out: **17:30**
Rate ID: **c**

Transaction Number:	5
Date:	01/05/87
Employee Number:	5
Time In:	17:30
Time Out:	20:45
Rate ID:	d

Transaction Number:	6
Date:	01/06/87
Employee Number:	6
Time In:	11:30
Time Out:	14:22
Rate ID:	e

Transaction Number:	7
Date:	01/06/87
Employee Number:	1
Time In:	8:00
Time Out:	17:00
Rate ID:	a

Transaction Number:	8
Date:	01/06/87
Employee Number:	2
Time In:	8:30
Time Out:	17:30
Rate ID:	c

Transaction Number:	9
Date:	01/06/87
Employee Number:	3
Time In:	8:00
Time Out:	17:00
Rate ID:	b

Transaction Number:	10
Date:	01/06/87
Employee Number:	5
Time In:	8:30
Time Out:	17:30
Rate ID:	c

Transaction Number:	11
Date:	01/06/87
Employee Number:	4

Time In:	8:30
Time Out:	17:30
Rate ID:	c
Transaction Number:	12
Date:	01/06/87
Employee Number:	6
Time In:	12:30
Time Out:	16:17
Rate ID:	e

Remember to **Tab** between fields and press **Enter** after each record.

Sorting Records

The Sort Palette

The default Palette in the Define Sorts screen contains the following icons:

 Help

 Print

 Preferences

 Define Hierarchy

 Layout View

 Sort

 Select

 Perform and Use

 Use

Quit

Sorting

dBASE Mac will sort the records in a file by their Key field values, but only if the Ordered checkbox in the field definition is checked (that is the default). This can be useful in maintaining records for files whose data is sequential according to the Key field (like the Checkbook and Timecard files). However, you will often want to display and report the data in some other order, and often the Key field values do not relate to the most logical ordering of the file. Also, causing the file to be kept in Key field order takes a little longer, so for speedier responses, you may elect not to use that feature at all.

Sorting a view is easy with dBASE Mac. You can create sort criteria any time after the hierarchy has been defined, although you may prefer to set up the layout first.

When you are ready to define the sort criteria, simply select Sort from the View menu. The top of the sort dialog box contains the hierarchy. Beneath that are the by-now familiar Relations and Fields list boxes. To the right is the list box where the sort criteria will actually appear.

To create a sort, click once on a field in the hierarchy on which to sort. A list of associated fields and relations will appear. As with other dialog boxes, you can double-click or click and **Add** to place a field within the sort criteria list.

> NOTE: You can also sort a multivalued field by clicking on it in the hierarchy and then selecting that field to sort. You cannot, however, sort a file using a multivalued field as the sort criterion.

Designing a sort is generally easy. What do you want to sort? Do you want to subsort the sort? For instance, you might sort a name and address list by state. But then, within the state, you might want to sort all the Zip Codes. Then within each Zip Code, you might sort by last name. This is a three-level sort. State is the primary, Zip Code the secondary, and Last Name the third and final sort criterion. (Sorting by Zip Code first and Last Name second would yield similar results, but this three-level sort places the results in alphabetical order by State.)

Try creating a three-level sort like the one described above in the Mailing List project from Chapter 2. If the Mailing List project is not currently active, Open it now.

> NOTE: You can perform this sort exercise with the MultiMail project, but the results will be confusing because the address fields are multivalued. However, you will be able to do some other interesting procedures with MultiMail later in the Tutorial. If you did not create the Mailing List project in Chapter 2, you should create it now (although you don't have to create the Label view).

Special Instructions

If you did not create the Mailing List project in Chapter 2, there is an easy way to perform this exercise. First load MultiMail, and highlight the Mail2 file on the Structure Window, then choose Duplicate File from the DataFile menu. Be sure that the records will be duplicated with the file (look at the checkbox entitled Copy Existing Records and be sure it is checked). Name the file "Mail" and click **OK**.

You could Open the Mail file now (from the DataFile menu) to add it to the MultiMail project, but a better way would be to Close MultiMail and select New from the Project menu to begin a new project. Open the Mail file to add it to the Untitled project.

Create a simple Quick Create Form view for the Mail file. Scroll through each record, select either occurrence of the address set and type **Command-D** to delete the selected occurrence. It doesn't matter which occurrence you delete, as long as you end up with only one occurrence per record. Now move to the next record and repeat the process. Be sure the cursor is inside one of the fields from the Address set when you perform the deletion.

Now you will have to change each multivalued field to a single valued field. Move back to the Structure Window, double-click on the Street field, and set the Contents Are: pop-up to Single Valued.

Move to the next field definition dialog box by holding the **Command** key and clicking **Done/N**. Proceed to change each multivalued field to a single valued one.

When you have completed the last step, create a Quick Create Columnar view. Call it "Mailing List Column." Now you're ready to proceed with the sort example below. When you complete the exercise, you may save the project, or Close it without saving. If you do not wish to retain this project, you will probably also want to throw the Mail file you just created in the Trash as well.

Sort Example

1. Select the Mailing List Column view from the Windows menu.

Depending on where you left the view last, you may be in Use mode, or in the layout (or even the hierarchy).

NOTE: When you open the Windows menu, you can see several things. First, you see all available views, including the Structure view. Second you can tell at a glance which views are currently open. Open views are displayed in hollow letters. The view that is currently active has a checkmark next to it. To close an open view, simply click on its close window box at the upper-left corner.

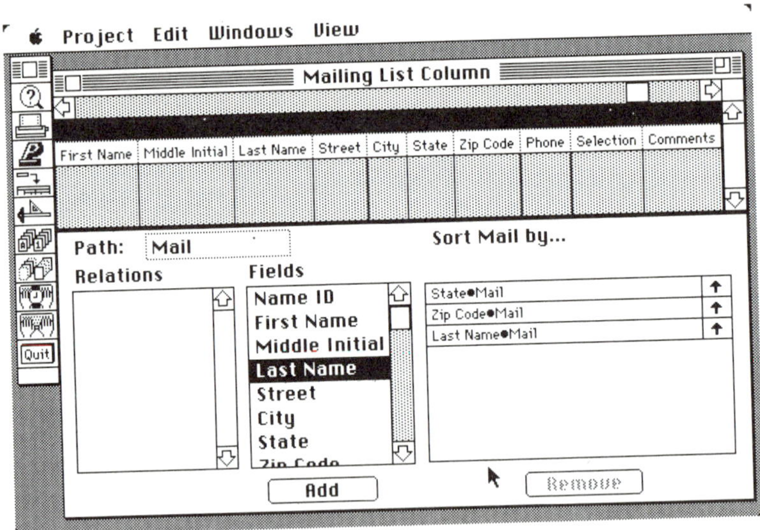

Figure 8-4 Sort Critieria.

2. To set sort criteria, select Define Sorts from the View menu.

3. Click once on the Mail title bar in the Hierarchy. A list of available fields should appear in the Fields list box.

4. Double-click (or click and **Add**) the State field.

The State field appears in the Sort By. . . box. Notice the arrow pointing upward. This means that the sort will be in ascending order. If you want a descending sort, click once on the arrow to change its direction.

5. Now Add the Zip Code field to the sort.

6. Finally, add the Last Name field.

That's all there is to the sort selection. To remove any sort criterion, simply highlight it and click **Remove**. When you are finished, select Perform and Use from the View menu or click the Perform and Use icon in the Palette.

TIP: You can change the order of the sort criteria easily. Suppose you wanted to sort by Last Name, then by State and Zip. To do so, drag the Last Name sort criterion over the State criterion. Last Name will move to the top of the list.

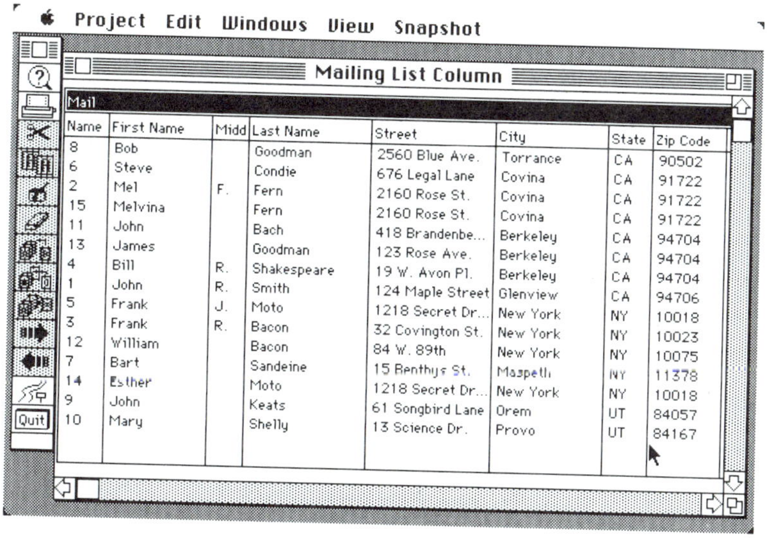

Name	First Name	Midd	Last Name	Street	City	State	Zip Code
8	Bob		Goodman	2560 Blue Ave.	Torrance	CA	90502
6	Steve		Condie	676 Legal Lane	Covina	CA	91722
2	Mel	F.	Fern	2160 Rose St.	Covina	CA	91722
15	Melvina		Fern	2160 Rose St.	Covina	CA	91722
11	John		Bach	418 Brandenbe...	Berkeley	CA	94704
13	James		Goodman	123 Rose Ave.	Berkeley	CA	94704
4	Bill	R.	Shakespeare	19 W. Avon Pl.	Berkeley	CA	94704
1	John	R.	Smith	124 Maple Street	Glenview	CA	94706
5	Frank	J.	Moto	1218 Secret Dr...	New York	NY	10018
3	Frank	R.	Bacon	32 Covington St.	New York	NY	10023
12	William		Bacon	84 W. 89th	New York	NY	10075
7	Bart		Sandeine	15 Benthys St.	Maspeth	NY	11378
14	Esther		Moto	1218 Secret Dr...	New York	NY	10018
9	John		Keats	61 Songbird Lane	Orem	UT	84057
10	Mary		Shelly	13 Science Dr.	Provo	UT	84167

Figure 8-5 Sorted Column View Graphic.

The sort you have just created will stay in effect for this view until you change it. Now suppose you left this view and moved to your data entry view to enter a few new names and addresses. When you return to the Mail List Column view, do you suppose the new information would be in sorted order?

Actually, the new data will not appear in the Column view until you Perform and Use again. Then it will, indeed, be placed in sorted order.

NOTE: Remember, if you do data entry in a Form view, you must Perform and Use a Columnar view to update it with the new records. If you simply Use the view, it will not reflect the new data.

You can try any number of sorts. Change, add, remove, or redesign the sort criteria. It doesn't affect the actual data in the file, and when the sort criteria are all removed, dBASE Mac returns the file to its original order.

You might try some other sorts. For instance, create a Column view in the Checkbook Project and sort by Type, then by Date, then by Description. This will give you a list of all transactions by transaction type, ordered by the date, and transactions for the same date will be ordered by the value of the Description field. (See Chapter 9 for an example of such a view.)

NOTE: Sorting on a Choices field results in data sorted according to the order the choices were defined, not alphabetically.

For the next section, close the Mailing List project and Open the Timecard Project. Activate the Timecard Entry view if it isn't already activated.

→ MultiMail continues in Chapter 9.

Sorting a Multilevel Hierarchy

You can sort a more complex type of view, one that contains data from different files. To use the Timecard Project as an example, you will need to create a new view for that project.

The new view should be a Columnar view so that you will be able to see the data all together after they have been sorted.

But wait! Before you create a new view, think about what you will want it to do. Basically it is going to display the data from the Timecard in a Column format. Therefore, instead of following the entire sequence of creating a new view, you can save yourself some work by choosing Duplicate View from the View menu.

To create a Column view for Timecard:

1. Select Duplicate View. . . from the View menu.

   The view name defaults to Copy of Timecard Entry.

2. Rename the view "Timecard Column".

3. Set the View Type pop-up to Columnar.

4. Click **OK** to move to the Define Hierarchy screen.

Notice that the hierarchy is already filled in. This has saved you some time and effort.

5. Select Layout View from the Palette or from the View menu.

NOTE: Duplicating a view does not duplicate the layout. If you had left the View Type as Custom, the view would be empty. Because you selected a Columnar View Type, each field in the hierarchy automatically produces a column in the layout. However, you may not want all columns in the layout.

6. To remove the Employee Number column, scroll over to it (using the scroll bar at the bottom of the screen), and click once inside the column to highlight it. Then press the **Backspace** or **Delete** key. The column will disappear and the other columns will move to fill in the space. Now remove the Posting Amount and Hours fields.

NOTE: If you change your mind about removing a column and wish to replace it, you will have to recreate the columns. You cannot add a column to an existing columnar layout. To replace the columns, first clear the entire layout by selecting the Root—the title bar highest in the hierarchy (in the current view it would be Timecard)—and press **Backspace.** All the columns should be removed. Then **Command** click the Root and **Shift**-click any fields you do NOT want to include in the layout. Drag the title bar onto the layout and position the dotted box where you want the columns to be. When you release the mouse, the column view will be replaced.

TIP: Remember, if all the columns do not fit on the current form, hold the **Option** key down (with or without **Caps Lock**) as you drag the fields from the hierarchy onto the layout.

7. (Optional) If you wish to create a view title, drag the title bar of the columns down to make room. Select the Text icon and type a title. To eliminate the title bar at the top of the columns, select the Arrow icon, and move the mouse cursor over the line beneath the title bar. When it changes shape, click and drag upward until the title bar is invisible.

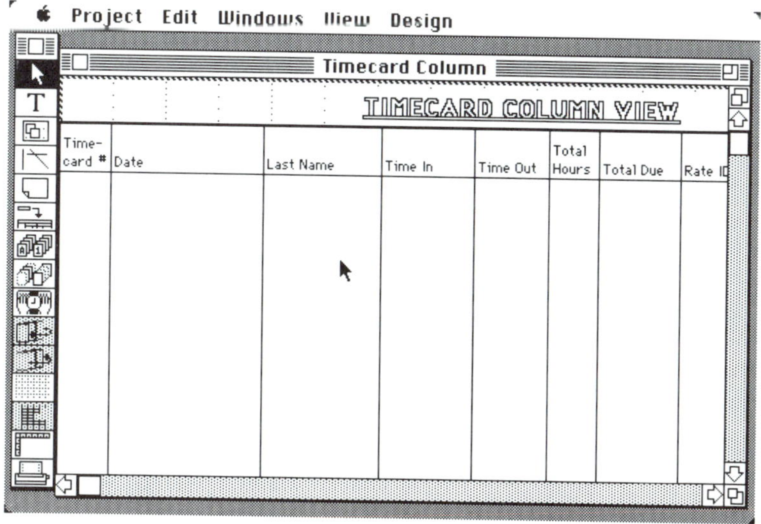

Figure 8-6 Finished Timecard Column View Graphic.

8. You may wish to resize various elements, and you may also wish to change the order of the fields by moving some to new positions. Once you have completed the arrangement of the columns and any other layout design, you can move on to Perform and Use.

TIP: If you resize the Total Hours field to its minimum size, the words Total Hours in the columns title will not completely display. Try this: Click on the Text icon in the Palette, then position the text cursor just after the word Total. Press the **Return** key. Now the words Total Hours should display in two lines in the narrow column. You can modify any titles using similar techniques.

TIP: Here's another idea. Look at the Last Name field. Notice how the entire hierarchy is represented there. Position the cursor at the bottom of the Employee title box. When the cursor changes shape, you can drag the bottom of the box upward until the entire box disappears. (If the cursor does not change shape, click once anywhere in the column display to activate it, then try again.) Now you will have the title Last Name by itself. You can hide any title bar if you wish.

When you select Perform and Use from the Palette or from the View menu, dBASE Mac selects the key values for the records based on the sort and selection criteria, and then displays them in the current view. You should see all the records displayed down the columns of the view you just created.

Suppose you want to sort the records in this view by Date:

1. To begin, select Sort from the View menu.

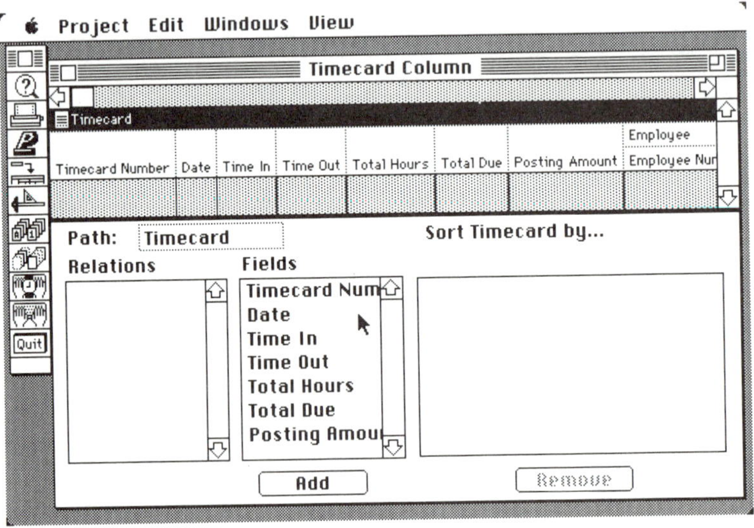

Figure 8-7 Sort Selection Screen Graphic.

2. The Sort selection screen appears. Click once on the Timecard title bar to display the available fields.

NOTE: You click on an item at the level where you wish the sort to take place. Any files and fields below that level will be displayed according to that sort. In the case of a view with multiple levels, you can sort specific fields below the root level without affecting the higher levels of the view.

The fields from the Timecard file reappear in the Files list.

3. Double-click (or click and **Add**) the Date field. The Date field will appear in the sort criteria list.

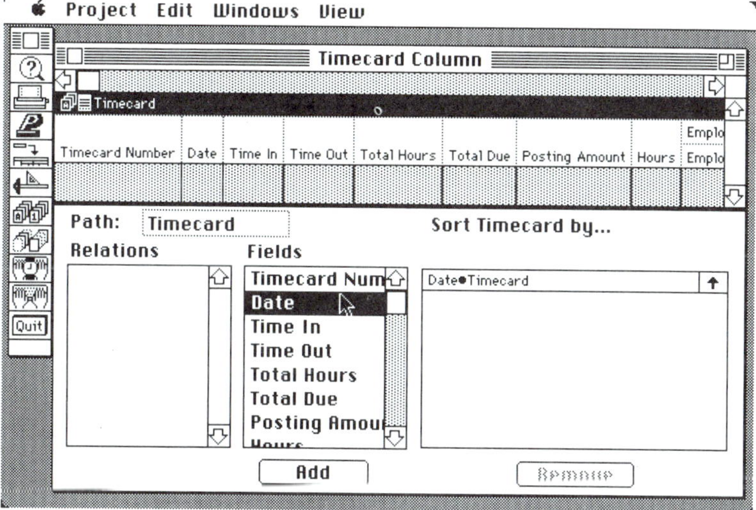

Figure 8-8 Finished Sort Graphic.

4. Perform and Use the view. You should see your data, now sorted by Date.

A more useful report would show all timecards sorted first by Employee, then by Date. To create such a sort, you will need to create another view.

1. Select New View. . . from the Windows menu.

2. Name the new view "Employee Sort" and be sure that the Employee file is highlighted.

   This sort will use the Employee file as the root file. Therefore, it must be selected as the Root when you create the view.

3. Click **OK**.

4. Add the following fields to the hierarchy: From the Employee file—Employee Number, Last Name; from the Timecard file—Timecard Number, Date, Total Hours, Total Due; from the Hourly Rates file—Rate ID, Rate.
5. Move to the Define Sorts screen by selecting Define Sorts from the View menu or from the Palette.
6. Click once on the Employee title bar in the hierarchy. The sort definition should read "Sort Employee by . . ."
7. Double-click on Last Name. You should see the Last Name field become the first criterion in the sort list.
8. Now, in the hierarchy, click on the Timecard title bar (one level below Employee). The definition should now read "Sort Timecard by . . ."
9. Double-click the Date field to define it as a sort criterion.
10. Move to Layout View.
11. Click the Employee title bar and **Shift** click the following fields: Last Name, Timecard Number, Date, Total Hours, Total Due, and Rate. Drag the selected fields onto the layout to form columns and modify the resulting display as you wish.
12. Perform and Use the view.

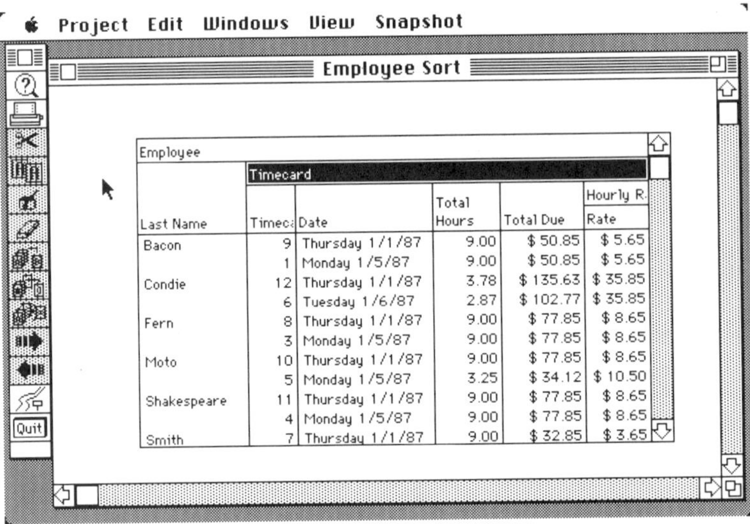

Employee	Timecard				Hourly R.
Last Name	Timeca	Date	Total Hours	Total Due	Rate
Bacon	9	Thursday 1/1/87	9.00	$ 50.85	$ 5.65
	1	Monday 1/5/87	9.00	$ 50.85	$ 5.65
Condie	12	Thursday 1/1/87	3.78	$ 135.63	$ 35.85
	6	Tuesday 1/6/87	2.87	$ 102.77	$ 35.85
Fern	8	Thursday 1/1/87	9.00	$ 77.85	$ 8.65
	3	Monday 1/5/87	9.00	$ 77.85	$ 8.65
Moto	10	Thursday 1/1/87	9.00	$ 77.85	$ 8.65
	5	Monday 1/5/87	3.25	$ 34.12	$ 10.50
Shakespeare	11	Thursday 1/1/87	9.00	$ 77.85	$ 8.65
	4	Monday 1/5/87	9.00	$ 77.85	$ 8.65
Smith	7	Thursday 1/1/87	9.00	$ 32.85	$ 3.65

Figure 8-9 Employee Sort Graphic.

Notice that employees are listed in alphabetical order. Within each employee listing, each timecard is listed by date. Later, when you learn about reports, you will be able to create a break condition on the Last Name field to create subtotals for each Employee, and grand totals for Total Hours and Total Due.

> NOTE: Notice that there are two scroll bars showing when you Use this view. Experiment with the effects of the inner scroll bar when you click on the Employee title bar, then click on the Timecard title bar and scroll. You'll notice that the inner scroll bar responds to the selected level of the column hierarchy.

Sorting Rules

1. You cannot sort a file based on the contents of a multivalued field.
2. You can, however, sort a multivalued field's contents.
3. You can sort using fields at the current level of the hierarchy. You cannot include subfields in a sort.
4. To create sorts that affect different levels of a hierarchy, create separate sort criteria for each level.
5. Sorts at higher levels of the hierarchy take precedence.
6. You can sort a file using a field that is not on the layout, as long as it is in the hierarchy.
7. You can drag sort criteria to change their processing order.
8. When you sort on a Choices field, the results are ordered according to the Choices as defined in the field definition, not in alphabetical order.

Selecting Records

The Define Selection Palette

The Define Selections screen has the same default Palette as the Define Hierarchy and the Define Sort screens.

Selecting Records

While you sort records to change the order in which they are displayed and printed, you use Selection criteria to limit those records that are displayed and/or printed to specific records. For instance, in a database of employee names and addresses, you might use the Define Selection feature to show only those records that contain data for people who live in California, or for people who live in New York, or records containing data for people who do not live in California or New York. There are many ways to select records.

Record selection is governed by rules that you define on a formula-like screen. These rules often use similar syntax. For instance, to find all records in the Employee file where the State field contained the value CA, you would write:

```
{State•Employee} = "CA"
```

To select all employees with salaries below a certain amount, you might write:

```
{Salary•Employee} < 20000
```

These are simple selections. How about all employees who live in California and make less than $20,000?

```
{State•Employee} = "CA" AND {Salary•Employee} < 20000
```

Once you perform a Selection, you will only view those records that meet the criteria you have set up. Any reports you print or views you display will show only those selected records. Once you remove the selection criteria, all records will be available again.

Some database programs call the selection criteria *filters*. Think of selections as filtering out unwanted records and only passing through the records that meet your current needs.

If you are continuing from the last section of the Tutorial, the Timecard Project should be active. If it is not, close any existing projects and Open the Timecard Project now.

There are many different ways to select data from the Timecards. For instance, you could select by a certain Rate to see who is drawing overtime pay. Or you could select for specific dates to examine your payroll for a specific period. You might select only those records whose Total Due fields show an amount higher than a certain amount.

To Select records, you should still have the Employee Sort view active.

1. Select Define Selections from the View menu.

2. The Selection definition screen should look familiar. It is similar to a formula or procedure definition screen. The hierarchy, the Path pop-up, the Relations list, and the Files list are all familiar by now.

   To create the Selection criteria, enter conditions in the Show If. . . text area. You can use the same methods used when entering formulas and procedures.

3. To select all Employee records where Total Hours are greater than eight, click on the Employee title bar, then enter the following formula under "Show Employee if . . .":

   ```
   {Total Hours•Timecard•Employee} > 8
   ```

   Use the shortcuts you have already learned, or type in the formula from the keyboard. Remember that Total Hours is found under the Timecard file through a relationship.

Return to the view by selecting Perform and Use from the Palette or from the View menu. Notice that only employees who have worked more than eight hours in any timecard are displayed. But all the timecards under those employees are displayed, even if they don't have Total Hours greater than eight.

NOTE: With Sorts and Selections, you can select what level of the hierarchy to use. The higher the level, the more general the effect of the Sort or Selection. In this case, if you highlight the Employee title bar, any selections will affect the whole view. For example, if you highlight the Employee title bar and then select for all Total Hours greater than eight, only those records in which Total Hours comes out higher than eight will display. However, if you highlight the Timecard title bar and create the same criterion, all Employee records will display, but the Timecard fields will only display for those records that meet the criterion. But a combination of the two selections will yield the results you are after.

1. Return to the Define Selections screen.

2. Highlight the Timecard title bar, and enter the same formula again.

3. Be sure the selection reads:

```
Show Timecard If . . .
{Total Hours•Timecard•Employee} > 8
```

4. Perform and Use the view to see the result.

You can combine selection criteria in other ways, too. For instance, select all records where Total Hours is greater than eight and the Hourly Rate is greater than $6.00 per hour.

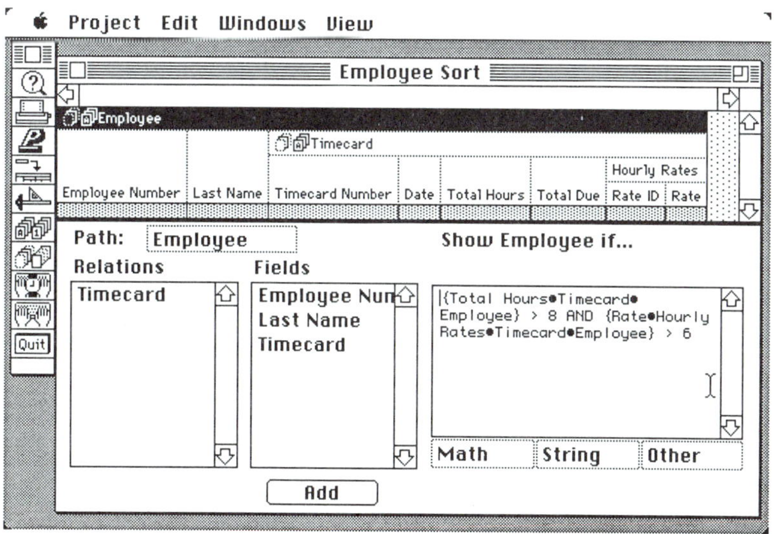

Figure 8-10 Selection Graphic.

1. Select Define Selections.
2. Highlight the Timecard title bar.
3. Enter the formula:

```
{Total Hours•Timecard•Employee} > 8 AND
{Rate•Hourly Rates•Timecard•Employee} > 6
```

4. Now highlight the part of the selection that begins with AND and press **Command-C** to copy it to the Clipboard.
5. Click once on the Employee title bar.
6. Place the cursor at the end of the existing selection (after the 8), click once, press the **Spacebar**, and then press **Command-V** to paste the contents of the Clipboard. The selection should be the same as the selection above.

Perform and Use to see the result. Notice that by setting the sort criteria on the Employee file (the Root File) and on the Timecard subfile, the report shows only the data that meet the criteria. You can try different combinations of selection criteria to look for other results.

NOTE: You can erase any selection criterion by highlighting the appropriate title in the hierarchy, then selecting the criteria and pressing **Backspace** or **Delete**. The selection will no longer be in effect when you Perform and Use the view next.

HINT: As you can see, the easiest way to duplicate the Selection criteria for different files is to highlight the formula, then use **Command-C** (Copy) to place a copy in the Clipboard. Then you can Paste the formula wherever you want it.

NOTE: If you create Selection criteria at one level of a hierarchy, then select another level, the text box will blank to allow you to define new criteria. However, if you select the former hierarchy level, the original Selection criteria will return to the box. Although this is convenient, do not make the mistake of thinking that the criteria are inactive. The criteria at the higher level of the hierarchy take precedence. When in doubt, erase any extra criteria you may have created before defining new ones.

Optional Exercises

Try some selections with the Checkbook Project. For instance, you might select all records in which the Tax field has been checked. The syntax for such a selection formula using a logical field is simply to enter the field name. For instance, under Select Checkbook If... enter the formula "{Tax•Checkbook}". ("IF Logical Field" is the same as saying "IF Logical Field is True".)

Another interesting use of sorts and selections is to select only check transactions ({Type•Checkbook} = 1) and then sort by Check Amount. This gives you a listing of all checks written in descending order, from largest to smallest.

Using Snapshots

Sometimes you might create a combination of sort and selection criteria that are particularly useful. You could recreate these criteria in another view, but there is an easier way to recreate a set of sort and selection criteria—by using Snapshots.

A Snapshot is a frozen moment in the life of your database. It is an ordered listing of the Key field values for a particular view at a particular moment. Since it is nothing more than a list of Key field values, it can be used in any view for which those Key field values would be valid.

To use Snapshots, Perform and Use a view with selection and sort criteria defined. Now open the Snapshot menu. Notice the possible commands—Take, Use . . ., Save, Save As, Close.

Select Take Snapshot to freeze the moment. Now dBASE Mac is holding in memory a frozen picture of your current data as represented by the order of Key field values.

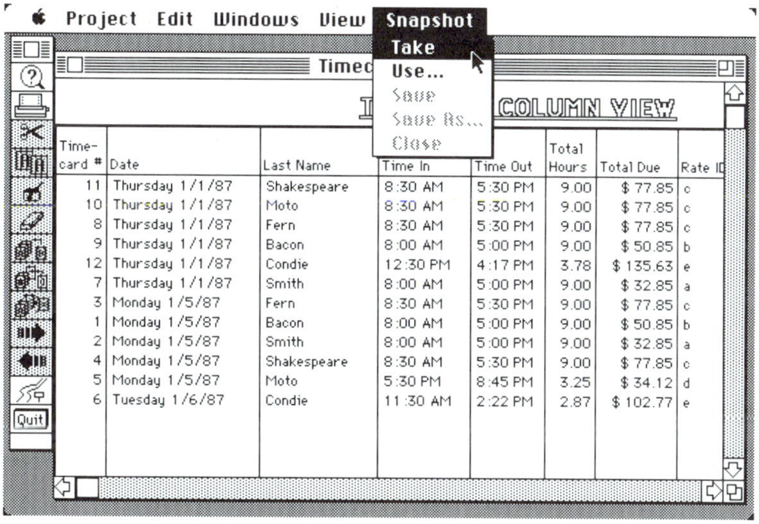

Project Edit Windows View Snapshot
Take
Use...
Save
Save As...
Close
COLUMN VIEW

Time-card #	Date	Last Name	Time In	Time Out	Total Hours	Total Due	Rate ID
11	Thursday 1/1/87	Shakespeare	8:30 AM	5:30 PM	9.00	$ 77.85	c
10	Thursday 1/1/87	Moto	8:30 AM	5:30 PM	9.00	$ 77.85	c
8	Thursday 1/1/87	Fern	8:30 AM	5:30 PM	9.00	$ 77.85	c
9	Thursday 1/1/87	Bacon	8:00 AM	5:00 PM	9.00	$ 50.85	b
12	Thursday 1/1/87	Condie	12:30 PM	4:17 PM	3.78	$ 135.63	e
7	Thursday 1/1/87	Smith	8:00 AM	5:00 PM	9.00	$ 32.85	a
3	Monday 1/5/87	Fern	8:30 AM	5:30 PM	9.00	$ 77.85	c
1	Monday 1/5/87	Bacon	8:00 AM	5:00 PM	9.00	$ 50.85	b
2	Monday 1/5/87	Smith	8:00 AM	5:00 PM	9.00	$ 32.85	a
4	Monday 1/5/87	Shakespeare	8:30 AM	5:30 PM	9.00	$ 77.85	c
5	Monday 1/5/87	Moto	5:30 PM	8:45 PM	3.25	$ 34.12	d
6	Tuesday 1/6/87	Condie	11:30 AM	2:22 PM	2.87	$ 102.77	e

Figure 8-11 Save Snapshot Graphic.

Next, Save the Snapshot. Give it a name at the prompt. Enter information in the Description text box if you wish. Now the Snapshot is saved in a special file on your current disk (or whatever disk or folder you chose to save it to).

You can also resave a Snapshot under a different name using Save As . . .

To reorder a current view in Snapshot order, choose Use. . . from the Snapshot menu. You will be presented with a choice of possible Snapshots. Choose the one you want to implement. The Snapshot will be used to reorder and reselect your current data. The Snapshot will stay in effect until you Close it, or until you replace it by Taking or Using another Snapshot.

NOTE: If you choose Close from the Snapshot menu before you Save your current Snapshot, you will be prompted to do so if you wish.

Using the Sort and Selection example from the Timecard Project, create a Snapshot of those criteria.

1. Perform and Use the Timecard Column view with the sort criteria in effect (sorted by Date).
2. Select Take from the Snapshot menu.
3. Now select Save from the Snapshot menu and type "TimeSnap1" to name the Snapshot.
4. Now Close the Snapshot.
5. Select Timecard Entry from the Windows menu.
6. Select Use . . . from the Snapshot menu.
7. Select TimeSnap1 from the list menu that appears.
8. Browse through the records in the file. Use the arrows on the Palette to move from record to record. The records are in the same order as they were in the Timecard Column view when you took the Snapshot.

You might also try removing the sort and selection criteria from the Timecard Column view, then Using the Snapshot to recreate the same effect.

Use Snapshots whenever you wish to recreate a particular set of Sort and Selection criteria.

→ Timecard continues in Chapter 9.

Summary

In Chapter 8 you entered data in the remaining projects. You saw how to Use a view and how to Perform and Use.

The Edit menu and the Use mode Palette contain commands to help manipulate the data in a Form view. These commands include the standard Macintosh Cut, Copy, Paste, and so on, and also commands to **Add** and **Delete** records and occurrences in multivalued fields, **Insert** occurrences in multivalued fields, and retrieve Next and Prior records in the Root File of a Form view or occurrences in a multivalued field.

You can sort Column views in multilayered sorts. You can sort at different levels of the hierarchy.

You can select records using many of the same operators and mathematical functions that you use in formulas and procedures. You can select at different levels of the hierarchy and create complex sort criteria.

Take Snapshots to freeze the Key field values of a file in a particular order, as determined by current sorts and selections. Use the Snapshot in the same view, or in any view that uses the same Key field values.

9

PRINTING AND REPORTING WITH dBASE MAC

Overview

Chapter 9 deals largely with the printed results of dBASE Mac projects. Some printing is done to document the various field, file, and view structures. Other printing is performed to produce final reports from the data in your project. What will happen when you select a Print command depends on where you are in the program

You can print from the Structure Window. You can print the Structure Window image itself, a file structure definition, or a field definition.

From the Define Hierarchy screen you can print a detailed description of each field in the hierarchy. Field definitions include procedure listings. You can also print entire view listing with all procedures.

From the Define Sort screen, you print the sort criteria. From the Define Selections screen, you print selection criteria.

From the Layout View screen, you can print your layout design.

From Use mode in any view you can print a report.

Reports in Column views allow certain special conditions called Breaks. They also have the ability to display accumulated totals on printed reports.

Executing a report prints out the contents of the view as defined by the current Selection criteria, and as sorted by the current Sort criteria.

Printing to Document a Project

You can use various print commands throughout dBASE Mac to archive the definition of your project. Use these printouts to study your project structurally, or to help someone else recreate your work. Later in this book you will find examples of projects that are largely made up of file and view definition printouts.

The Structure Window

A good place to start printing is on the Structure Window. You can produce three types of printout from the Structure Window:

1. A graphic printout of the Structure Window.
2. A definition for a single field.
3. A definition for an entire file.

You determine what printout you will receive by highlighting various parts of the Structure Window. For instance, to print out a field definition for a specific field, click once on the field name, then select the Print icon from the Palette, or select Print Field Definition from the Project menu.

In the same way, if you highlight the title bar of a file, then select Print File Definition from the Project menu (or select the Printer icon in the Palette), you will print out a definition for each field in your file.

Clicking on the Structure Window in such a way as to remove all file or field highlighting, then selecting Print Structure Window, will print a graphic image of the current Structure Window, complete with relational arrows, and so on.

> NOTE: You can also create a Mac Paint type file of any Mac screen by pressing **Command-Shift-3**. The first file created will be called Screen 0. Subsequent files will be named Screen 1 through Screen 9. You can only create ten such files. If you wish to create more, rename the first files before taking more such "screen shots."

> NOTE: Before you continue with this chapter, be sure your printer is hooked up and turned on.

Load the Timecard Project. (Double-click the Timecard Project icon, or select Open from within dBASE Mac and select Timecard Project.)

Now click once on the Timecard file to highlight it, then open the Project menu and select Print File Structure. Complete the Printer dialog box and then wait while the printer produces the report.

At the top of the page is Report Name: File Structure. The current time and date are taken from the internal Mac memory and inserted as part of the header in the upper-right corner of the report.

Next is File Name: Timecard and File Type: dBASE Mac.

Beneath the header information are the field definitions. These definitions give you all the specifics about each field. You should be able to recreate the fields completely from this printout.

Look at the first field definition—for Transaction Number.

```
Field Name:          Transaction Number
Field Type:          Key, Ordered    Data Type: Number  Required
Jusify:              Right
Format:              Fixed               Decimal Places: 0
Decimal:             .                         Thousands:
Negative:            -n                        Currency:
Auto Sequenced By:   1
Initial Value:       1
```

All the information in the field definitions printout is familiar from the field definition dialog box. Any procedures or formulas attached to the field will also be printed (look at the definitions for Total Hours and Total Due).

Relationships are also defined. Look at Employee, which reads

Relations: Two-way with Employee

and Rates, which reads

Relations: One-way with Hourly Rates

Printouts of other field definitions might include information not shown on the Timecard printout. (If you want to see some other examples of field definition printouts, print the Checkbook file definition, or look at Part III, Applications, to see several detailed printouts.)

If you highlight a single field on the Structure Window, you can print a definition for that field alone. The printed definition is the same as the definition printed in the file definition printout.

Finally, you can print a graphic image of the Structure Window by clicking on a blank spot in the Structure Window (thereby removing any highlighted files or fields), then selecting Print Structure Window from the Project menu (or selecting the Printer icon from the Palette).

Printing View Definitions

You can print the definition of a view from the Define Hierarchy screen. The view definition printout is similar to the file definition printout available from the Structure Window, but it shows all the fields in the current hierarchy. A printout of the view definition can include view fields and fields from related files. All procedures and formulas attached to the fields in the hierarchy are listed.

Select the Timecard Entry view from the Windows menu. If it does not currently display the Define Hierarchy screen, select Define Hierarchy from the Palette or from the View menu.

Be sure your printer is on and ready to go, then select Print View Definition from the Project menu. Wait while the view definition for Timecard Entry is printed.

The header for a view definition printout tells you a lot about the printout.

```
Report Name: View Definition                           6/25/87  2:25 pm
                                                                Page 1
Project Name:   Timecard Project
View Name:  Timecard Entry   View Type:  Display, Custom Layout
File Name:  Timecard         Tile Type:  dBASE Mac
```

Information about the current project, view, and Root File is in the view definition header. In addition, sort and selection criteria are given for the root level of the view hierarchy. This information is followed by the field descriptions.

In a relational view, the Access Path is defined. The Access Path defines the source file for the fields that follow. The Timecard Entry view definition printout begins with Access Path: Timecard. This means that the fields following the Access Path entry come from the Timecard file.

The field definitions in the view definition printout follow the same format as the field definitions in the file definition printout. Therefore, it should be easy to read them. Notice that if a field was originally defined with a formula, procedure, or posting, that information is carried over to the field definition in the view. Look at the definitions for Total Hours and Total Due. Look also at Posting Total for an example of a posting field. Other fields in a view may have procedures and other changes that were not defined in the original file, but were added or modified in the view.

The view definition printout follows the hierarchy closely. When it reaches a new pointer field, it sets the new Access Path designation and then describes sorts, selections, and the fields in that path. Look at the way the program handles the Employee file and the Hourly Rates file. By paying attention to the Access Path and the field definitions, you should be able to use the information to recreate a view hierarchy.

If you have any sort or selection criteria active, you can print them out by themselves. Move to the Define Sorts or the Define Selections screen and select Print Sort Definition, or Print Selection Definition as appropriate. The current sort or selection criteria will print out.

Finally, move to the Layout screen. Here, when you select Print Layout from the Project menu (or the Printer icon in the Palette), you print a graphic representation of the current layout.

> NOTE: Printing the current layout does not print such information as Show Selections from Tablets, groups, Display Only fields, or other Display Options. The best way to notate these features is to mark the printout by hand. The Display Options are the only project features you can't archive in the definition printouts.

Printing Reports

You can print reports from the Use mode of any view, but you may prefer to use some views for data entry and modification, and other views for printing reports.

There are two basic kinds of reports you can print. One is based around a Column view; the other is based around a Form view. The Mailing Labels you created in Chapter 2 and again in Chapter 7 are examples of a Form view report. If you print the Timecard Entry screen as a report, it will also print as a Form view report.

A report based on a Form view prints one form for each currently selected record, in the current sort order. What this means is that only those records that meet the current selection criteria will print in the report, and they will print in the sorted order. One form prints for each record.

> NOTE: When you print a Form view containing multivalued fields with multiple entries, a separate form prints for each occurrence in the multivalued field. See how the MultiMail project handles multivalued fields and reporting later in this chapter.

> NOTE: When you print a form report that contains multiple Tablet pages, only those pages that meet selection criteria for each individual form record will print. However, if you have multiple pages that meet selection criteria, a separate form will print for each page.

A column-based report prints each currently selected record in sorted order in a tabular listing. Each field in the report occupies a column, and the report prints the listing of records all on the same page, or on several pages if the report is long.

The two basic report formats are intended to meet varied reporting needs. Form reports are good for mailing labels, and for complex forms such as medical billing, personnel forms, or even 1040 tax forms.

Column reports are good for listing a lot of information. You might use a column format to create a balance sheet or an income statement, a listing of specific transactions, or a comprehensive name and address list.

You can set special conditions on columnar reports. These conditions include three kinds of Breaks and two kinds of Accumulated Totals.

Breaks

In a columnar report, you can set Break conditions. Breaks are specific events that occur when the value in a selected field changes.

The easiest way to observe the effect of a break is to print out a report using breaks. With the Timecard Project active:

1. Select Timecard Column from the Windows menu.
2. Select Define Sorts from the View menu or from the Palette.
3. Click once on the Timecard title bar if necessary to bring up the field names in the Fields list box.
4. The current sort should be by Date.
5. Now that you have defined the sort criterion, select Define Hierarchy from the View menu or from the Palette.
6. Click once on the Date field in the hierarchy.
7. Now open the Breaks pop-up and select Line Break.

Notice the break symbol that is placed next to the field name in the hierarchy.

8. Perform and Use the view by selecting Perform and Use from the View menu or from the Palette.

9. Print the report by selecting the Printer icon from the Palette, or select Print Report from the Project menu.

NOTE: Depending on how you sized the columns in your view, and how many columns you have, the report may be wider than the paper size you are using. If it is wider, those columns that won't fit on the first page will be printed on a second page. However, it is often preferable to print all the columns on one page. There are two ways to tell if you are going over the page size. One is to scroll over to the right. You'll notice a grey line going vertically down the page. That represents the end of the current page. The other way to tell how something will fit when printed is to return to the Layout View screen and select Reduce to Fit. You will see immediately whether your layout will fit on the page or not.

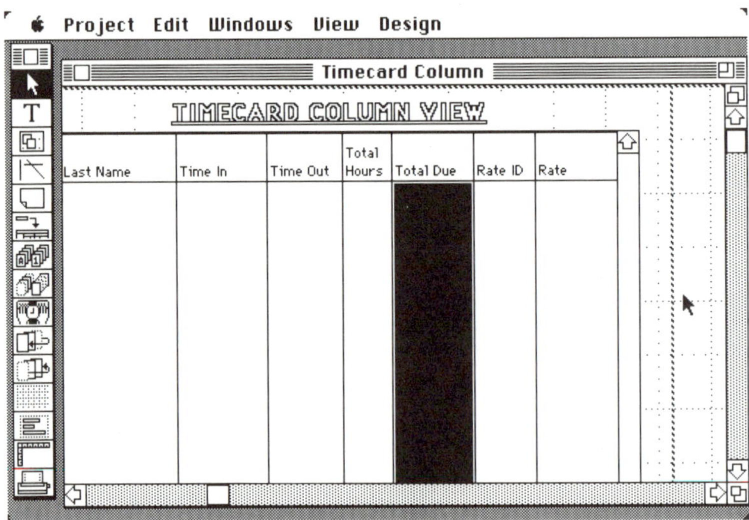

Figure 9-1 Page Ending Layout Graphic.

Now notice that when the Date changes, the program inserts a line to separate the records. Breaks are effective when the field used to determine the break is ordered in some way. If the field is not in any particular order, then the breaks will make no sense.

Variations on the Line Break include Blank Line Break (which inserts a blank line at each Break), and Page Break (which inserts a form feed at each Break—starting a new page).

Accumulating Totals

You can print two kinds of totals in a report. One adds the values in a Numeric field. The other counts the number of occurrences in a non-numeric field. You can Accumulate Totals with or without Breaks. If you use Breaks, a new total will be entered at each Break, and a grand total will be entered at the end of the report. Otherwise only the grand total will be placed in the report.

To mark a field for totals, highlight the field in the Define Hierarchy screen, then click the Accumulate Totals checkbox. A sum symbol is placed next to the field name in the hierarchy to signify that it is a totaling field.

Using the Break example above:

1. Return to the Define Hierarchy screen and select the Total Hours field.

2. Click the Accumulate Totals checkbox.

3. Now do the same with the Total Due field.

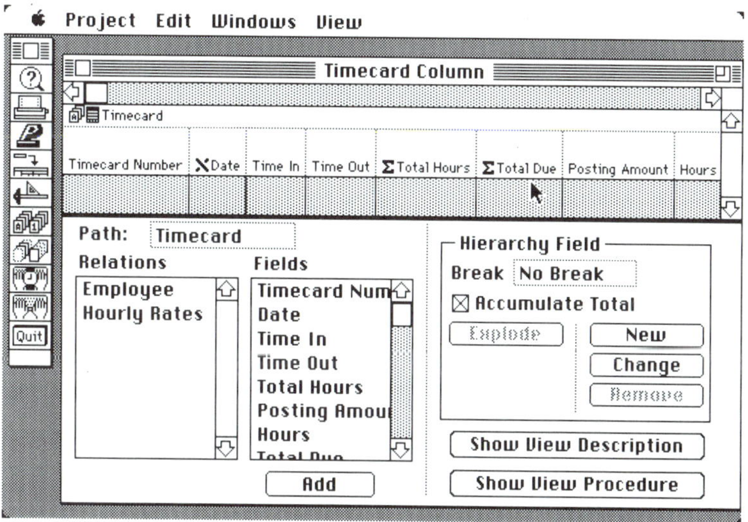

Figure 9-2 Accumulate Totals Definition Graphic.

NOTE: Leave the Date field as a Break field.

You might also set either the Date field or the Last Name field to Accumulate Totals. The Date field will give you a total of all timecards issued for each day, plus a grand total. The Last Name field will give you a total of employees who have turned in timecards for each day.

4. Perform and Use the view.

5. Print the report.

Notice that the Numeric fields (Total Hours and Total Due) display totals for each Break (Daily Totals) and for the grand total (Report Total). The totals under Last Name are counts of the number of records for each break (the number of occurrences of Last Name—also the number of timecards issued for each day), and a total count of the number of records in the report (total number of timecards issued).

You could also create a report using the Employee Sort view. Eliminate the selection criteria you created earlier in this chapter, and then create a Break condition on Last Name. Now Accumulate Totals for the Total Due fields and the Total Hours field. The resulting report will show subtotals for each employee as well as grand totals.

→ Timecard continues in Chapter 10.

A Cash Flow Report

You can use Breaks and Accumulate Totals to produce a variety of different reports. In the Checkbook Project, you could produce columnar lists of transactions sorted by Date or by Type (or by Type, then Date). You could also use selections to filter the file and display only a particular transaction Type, then sort and print that information.

To create a modified Cash Flow Report for the Checkbook Project:

1. Load the Checkbook Project (if necessary, Close and Save the current project first).
2. Create a Column view called "Cash Flow."

REMINDER: This is a Column view, so don't forget to set the View Type pop-up to Columnar.

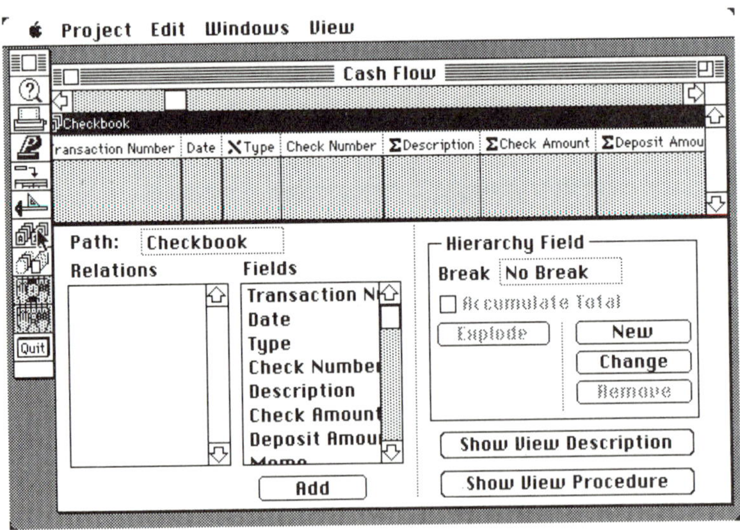

Figure 9-3 Hierarchy Graphic.

3. Add the following fields to the hierarchy; Transaction Number, Type, Date, Description, Check Number, Check Amount, Deposit Amount, and Tax.

4. Click once on the Type field in the hierarchy.

5. Select Blank Line Break from the Break pop-up.

6. Select the Check Amount field and check the Accumulate Totals checkbox. Repeat the procedure with the Deposit Amount and Description fields. (Description will give you a count of the records).

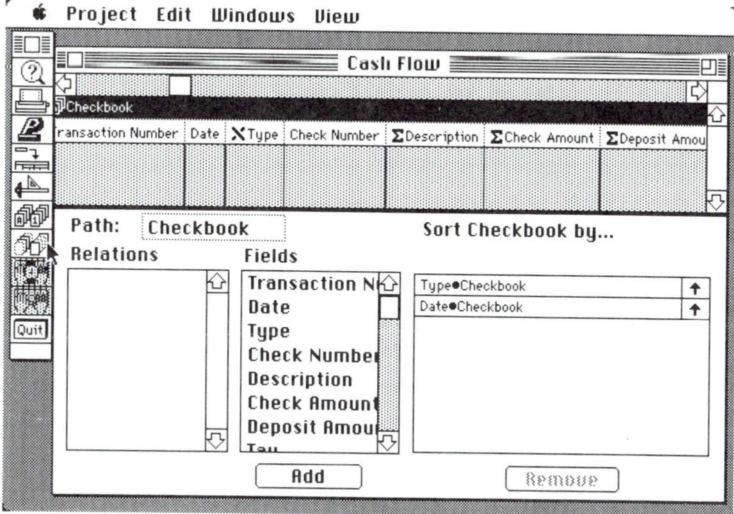

Figure 9-4 Sort Definition Graphic.

7. Select Define Sorts from the Palette or from the View menu

8. Double-click Type from the Fields list box. Then double-click the Date field. This sets up Type as the first sort field and Date as the second.

NOTE: When you sort on a Choice field, the sort is performed on the numeric position of the Choice field values. It will not be alphabetical unless the choices in the Choice field have been entered in alphabetical order. In the case of the Type field from the Checkbook Project, the choices are in order of function, such as all debits together and all credits together.

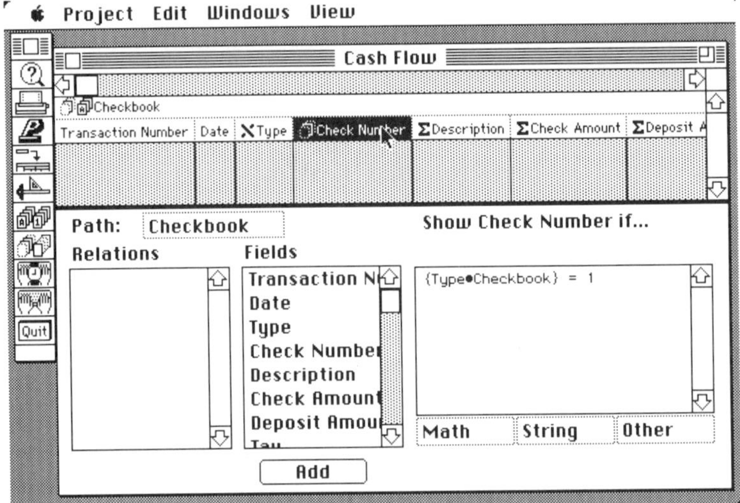

Figure 9-5 Selection Graphic.

9. Now that the sort is defined, select Define Selection from the Palette or from the View menu.

10. Click once on the Check Number field. The selection box should read "Show Check Number If:"

11. Double-click (or click and **Add**) the Type field in the Fields list box.

12. Select the equals sign from the Other pop-up (or type the equals).

13. Type the number 1. The formula should read:

```
{Type•Checkbook} = 1
```

The purpose of this selection criterion is to display a check number only for transactions that are checks. If the Type does not equal Check (number one in the Choice field) then no check number will be displayed. If you don't do this, erroneous check numbers might display next to other records such as deposits and bank charges.

14. Next, click on the Checkbook title bar and enter the following criterion under Show Checkbook if . . .

```
{Type•Checkbook} ≠ 6
```

This prevents VOIDed checks from being included in the report.

15. Move to the Layout View screen and adjust the columns so that the data will display the way you want them to, and also stay on one page.

16. Now Perform and Use the view.

17. Now print the view by selecting the Printer icon from the Palette or by selecting Print Report from the Project menu.

Notice that the contents of the file are sorted by Type and by Date, and that check numbers only show next to checks. No VOID checks should appear.

HINT: For a more attractive display, try moving to the Layout View screen, and choosing Select All to highlight the entire set of columns. Now double-click anywhere on the highlighted layout or choose Display Options from the Design menu. Change the Pen Size to its minimum value to eliminate the boxes around the columns, and choose other fonts and special effects as needed. You may have to make some adjustments depending on your printer and the size of the paper you are using. Experiment with the layout to make it as attractive as you can. You could also add the Balance field to the top of the report.

Notice the subtotals after each break. By adding together the Check, Bank Charges, and Miscellaneous totals, you get a complete total of money going out of your account. By adding Deposits and Interest, you get an incoming total.

Procedures are the subject of Chapter 10. In that chapter you will see some of the more common uses for procedures.

→ Checkbook concludes in Chapter 11. NewCheck begins in Chapter 12.

MultiMail—Using Multivalued Fields

In this section, you will work with the multivalued fields in the MultiMail project from Chapter 4.

First, Close any active projects and Open the MultiMail project.

Next you will use the Selection field you created in Chapter 4 to create a default address for each record.

You should activate the Mail Entry view in Use mode.

- To begin with, browse through the records you added in previous chapters. Find the first record by clicking on the right facing arrow in the Palette when the Name ID field is blank, or pressing **Command-P** until you reach the first record. (In this case, you know the first record has a key value of 1, so you can enter the number 1 in the Name ID field and press **Tab**.) Next select a value—One, Two, or Both—for each record and press **Enter** to save the changed record. It doesn't matter what value you choose. Just be sure to have several of each choice in the file.

NOTE: As you Enter each record, the next record will automatically display. If the next record does not display, it means that you have disabled the Auto Advance feature under Preferences. To set Auto Advance back on, select Preferences. . . from the Edit menu and click on the Auto Advance checkbox. Then, whenever you Enter a record, the next record will display.

The following steps will create a selection formula that allows you to display a current address for each person in your MultiMail list.

In theory, you should be able to select which address should be considered current for any individual. The choices are One, Two, or Both. You will use selection criteria to determine which address to display.

1. Open the Mailing List Columns view, and move to the Define Selections screen.

2. Click once on the Street field in the hierarchy. The selection criterion screen should read "Show Street if . . ."

3. Although it is not one of the available choices in the pop-up command menus, you can use the CASE statement in selections. Type in the formula that follows using, shortcuts wherever possible:

```
CASE {Selection•Mail2} OF
    WHEN 1 DO
        {Street•Mail2} = {Street•Mail2}[1]
    WHEN 2 DO
        {Street•Mail2} = {Street•Mail2}[2]
    OTHERWISE
        "T"
END
```

This selection works because the multivalued fields in the address are combined in the Address set. Using the Selection field to select a particular occurrence level of Street forces the other fields to follow suit. Notice that the way to refer to a particular occurrence level in a multivalued field is with the square brackets, that is, {Street•Mail2}[2] represents the second occurrence in the multivalued field.

To see the result of this selection, Perform and Use the view.

Multivalued Mailing Labels

Printing the mailing labels in the MultiMail project presents a few problems. What you want the report to do is print out labels only for the specific addresses that you have chosen using the Selection field. Therefore, if the Selection is One, you want to print a label for the first address only. If the Selection is Two, you want to print the second address, and if the Selection is Both, you want to print a label for each address.

Ordinarily, when you print a multivalued field, all occurrences will print unless specifically limited. In this case, you must find a way to cause the appropriate occurrence to print.

Back in Chapter 6, you created the Labels-2 view. If you remember, you created two view fields to combine or concatenate other fields. Now you will need to further modify one of those fields:

1. Open the Labels-2 view.

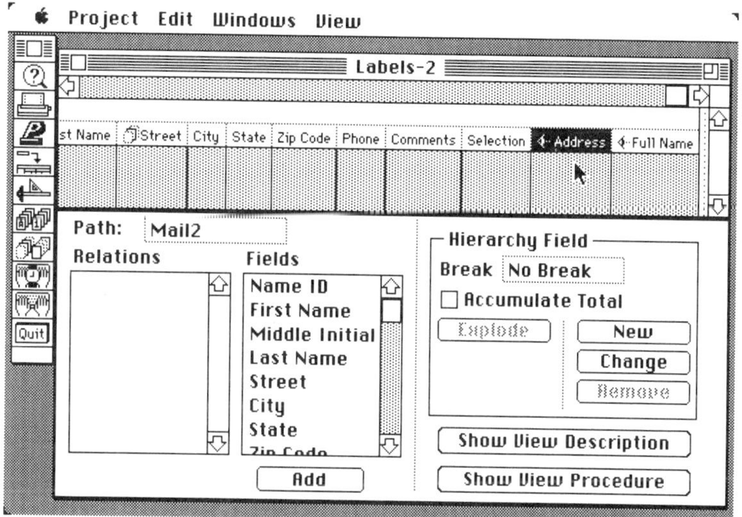

Figure 9-6 Labels-2 Hierarchy.

2. If it is not at the Define Hierarchy screen, move to that screen.

   To modify a field in the hierarchy, you can highlight it and click on the **Change** button, or double click the field in the hierarchy.

3. Find the field named Address in the hierarchy and double click.

   Be sure it is at the same level as the other fields. It should be below the Mail2 title bar. If it is not, go back to Chapter 6 and review the procedure for creating the Full Name and Address fields.

4. Open the Contents Are: pop-up and set the Address field to Multiple Valued.

5. In the Set Name box, type "Address"

   What you have just done is make the Address field a part of the Address set.

6. Click **Done**.

Next, you will use Selections to determine the occurrence level of the Street field. Since the Street field and the Address field are now in the same set, they will always display the same occurrence level.

1. Move to the Define Selections screen.

2. Click once on the Street field.

   The Selections should read "Show Street if . . ."

   Remember the formula you just entered for the Mailing Column view above? You will use it again now. If you prefer, you can open Mailing Column view, move to the Define Selections screen, then highlight and Copy (**Command-C**) the selection formula. Otherwise, enter it as follows:

3. Enter the following formula:

```
CASE {Selection•Mail2} OF
    WHEN 1 DO
        {Street•Mail2} = {Street•Mail2}[1]
    WHEN 2 DO
        {Street•Mail2} = {Stree•tMail2}[2]
    OTHERWISE
        "T"
END
```

   In order to process the multivalued Address field properly, dBASE Mac needs the Key field to be present on the layout. In an ordinary mailing list, this would not be necessary, but in this case it is. However, you don't want the Key field (Name ID) to print on each label. In the next step, you will place the Key field on the layout in such a way that it does not display.

1. Move to the Layout View screen.

2. Drag the Name ID field anywhere onto the label form.

NOTE:Depending on your current Preferences settings, the field may include a field title and a box. Eliminate the field title, if necessary, by clicking on the field title element alone (you may have to click elsewhere first, then click on the field title), then pressing **Backspace** or **Delete** to remove the title element. If there is a box around the field data element, double-click it to enter the Display Options dialog box and select the thinnest Pen Size, then click **OK** to return to the layout. The box should be gone.

3. If it is not highlighted already, click once on the Name ID field, then place the mouse cursor at the lower-right edge of the field. The cursor should change into two diagonal lines with arrows, indicating that you can change the size of the highlighted element.

4. Drag the mouse upward and to the left until the Name ID field is a small square or dot.

5. Drag the small square or dot on top of one of the other layout elements, near the left edge.

6. Select Send to Back from the Design menu. The dot should disappear.

   Now, when you print the mailing labels, the Key field will not print.

7. Finally, Perform and Use the view to set the selections.

NOTE: Be sure your printer is on before proceeding with the next step.

8. Now Select Print from the Palette or from the Project menu. Fill in the printer dialog box and click **OK**.

   The resulting printout should produce mailing labels that follow the Selection field value. If Selection equals One, then the first street and address should print, and only one label should print. If Selection equals Two, then the second street and address should print, and only one label should print. If Selection equals Both, then two labels should print—one for each address.

   If the report does not perform as expected, go back over the preceding steps. If necessary go back to Chapters Six and Seven to be sure the hierarchy and layout of the view were correctly created.

→ MultiMail continues in Chapter 10.

Summary

There are two kinds of printing in dBASE Mac:

1. Printing file, field, and view definitions.
2. Printing Reports.

You can print a file definition report by highlighting the file's title on the Structure Window and selecting Print from the Palette or the Project menu.

You can print a field definition report by highlighting a field on the Structure Window and selecting Print from the Palette or the Project menu.

You can print the Structure Window graphic by clicking on a blank space in the Structure Window and selecting Print, or by pressing **Command-Shift-3** to make a graphic file of the screen.

You can print a view definition report from the Define Hierarchy screen.

You can print a Sort criteria report from the Define Sorts screen.

You can print a Selection criteria report from the Define Selections screen.

You can print a graphic image of the layout from the Layout View screen.

You can print a report in Use mode.

Reports can be columnar or form-based.

Columnar reports can contain Breaks and can Accumulate Totals for individual fields.

You can mix form and columnar elements in a report.

You can use multivalued fields along with selections and sets to produce sophisticated conditional reports.

In Chapter 9 you examined printing. In Chapter 10, you will look at the dBASE Mac Procedural Interface (PI).

10

PROCEDURES, THE CUSTOM PALETTE, AND CUSTOM MENUS

Overview

Putting the finishing touches on a dBASE Mac project often entails using procedures to smooth the interfaces between user and program. Procedures are often used to create dialog boxes offering choices to the user, or they may control the entire project. Simple procedures are often used to perform such tasks as cursor movement or data entry validation.

There are several different types of procedure, and they can occur at different levels of the program: at the file level, at the view level, or at the field level. Each procedure is used for a different purpose.

The five kinds of procedure are: Pre-Processor, Post-Processor, New Record, Delete Record, and Write Record. You have already worked with some of these procedure types in the Checkbook Project. In Chapter 10 you will learn more about how they are used.

Throughout this tutorial, you have seen the Palette change from one part of the program to another. In Chapter 10, you will learn how to modify the Palette to meet your specific needs.

In addition to the procedures, there are some other ways to customize a project. Custom Menus are user-created menus that can be used to call views. By grouping specific views under a Custom Menu, you can contribute to the clarity and organizational control of a project.

Custom Menus take effect when you Protect a project. You do this by assigning a password to the project. Once the password is assigned, no one can modify the structure of the project without first re-entering that password. A protected project can be completely controlled by procedures and views—thus creating a turnkey system.

The Procedural Interface

Procedures

dBASE Mac contains a sophisticated programming language called the Procedural Interface (PI). You have already used this programming language in earlier chapters in the Tutorial. Formulas created in formula fields use a subset of the PI. You also wrote some procedures in the Checkbook Project to control the Check Number field and the new record determination. You've also written several Write Record procedures already.

There are five different types of procedure:

Pre-Processor Pre stands for before. A Pre-Processor is a procedure that takes effect at the beginning of an operation. For instance, if the Pre-Processor is attached to a view, the procedure is run when you first Use the view—before any other operation takes place. A typical view Pre-Processor might be used to initialize, or preset, certain values in the view, or to select certain records before data display. If the Pre-Processor is attached to a field, in a data entry form for instance, it is run at the time the insertion point enters that field.

Post-Processor Post stands for after. A Post-Processor is a procedure that takes effect after an operation is complete. For instance, a Post-Processor attached to a view will take place when you exit the view. Typically this would be a procedure that performs some validation function or that performs some operation on the data in the view. For instance, the Post-Processor might invoke a report view and print the new data after you close a data entry view. A Post-Processor attached to a field in a view is run when the value in that field has been changed and after the cursor leaves it. A file field Post-Processor is also invoked when a different value is assigned to that field in a procedure. A simple, but typical, Post-Processor would be used to validate the accuracy of data entered into a particular field. A Post-Processor requires an ACCEPT statement to complete its actions.

New Record A New Record procedure is invoked whenever a new record is added to a file, when a NEW command is encountered in a procedure, or when a new record is added during processing a Transfer View. You can attach a New Record procedure to a file through the Change File dialog box, or to a view through the Pointer Field. A typical use of a New Record procedure is for initializing data only when a record is first added. A New Record procedure offers specialized control when initializing/clearing fields for a new record to be entered, and is not invoked when you modify an existing record. If a New Record procedure is used, it must contain the statement NEW(SELF) to complete the initialization of a new record.

REMINDER: Title bars in the hierarchy are Pointer Fields.

Delete Record A Delete Record procedure is invoked only when a Delete command is issued from the keyboard or a menu, or when a DELETE command is encountered in a procedure. Commonly a Delete Record procedure warns you that you are about to delete the record, and gives you a chance to back out of the operation. Another use of the Delete Record procedure occurs when certain values in a record are linked through procedures to fields in other files or views. When you delete an existing record, it may require some adjustment to those associated values. By using a Delete Record procedure, you can be sure that all associated fields are kept up to date. To complete the operation, any Delete Record procedure requires the command DELETE(SELF).

Write Record The Write Record procedure, if present, is invoked whenever the appropriate command is entered via keyboard, menu, or procedure. Typically, pressing **Enter** to finish processing a record will invoke a Write Record procedure. Write Record procedures are also invoked whenever a record is written during the processing of a Transfer View. While the New Record procedure is invoked only when a new record is added to the file, a Write Record procedure is invoked whenever a record is written—whether it is a new record or a recently modified one. A Write Record procedure requires the command WRITE(SELF) to complete writing of the current record.

REMINDER: New, Write, and Delete Record procedures disable the normal operation of dBASE Mac. To complete these procedures, you must use the appropriate command, using the SELF parameter as the argument, that is, NEW(SELF), WRITE(SELF), or DELETE(SELF). If the appropriate command is not encountered in the procedure, the operation (New, Write, or Delete) will not occur.

Procedures can be created in several places—file, view, file field, or View Modified File Fields (VMFF).

File Procedures You can create New, Delete, and Write Record procedures for an entire file. For instance, a New Record procedure created as a file procedure is invoked whenever a new record is added to the file—regardless of the view. File Procedures are especially useful when more than one view can control record entry, deletion, and/or modification.

File Field Procedures Most fields (except Formula fields) can contain Post-Processors. If you enter a procedure in a file field (starting from the Structure Window), that procedure takes place wherever the field is modified, because when you modify the contents of the field manually or via a procedure assignment, the file field Post-Processor procedure is invoked automatically (in addition to any procedures added to the field within the view).

View Procedures You can attach a Pre-Processor or a Post-Processor to a view. View Procedures are created by clicking the Show Procedures button on the Define Hierarchy screen. Typically a View Pre-Processor might be used to display a dialog box offering choices to the user. The user may then have the opportunity to initialize the data, choose Selection criteria, or pass control to another view or even another project, through the Pre-Processor dialog box.

View Modified File Field Procedures File Field Procedures are accessed in addition to procedures attached to fields within views. A field is technically considered a File Field until it is modified in some way within a view hierarchy; then it becomes a View Modified File Field (VMFF). VMFFs can contain Pre-Processor and/or Post-Processor types. Pointer Fields (title bars) can also contain New, Delete, and Write Record procedures. A procedure attached to a VMFF is valid only for that view. This type of procedure is useful within views that perform very specific functions. For instance, in the Checkbook Entry view, the procedures that control the Check Number are not necessary in other views that display or modify the data. The Check Number need only be defined once for each check record. In other views, the Check Number field should be Display Only to prevent modification in other views.

NOTE: In the discussion above, the term *View Modified File Field,* or VMFF, refers to any field that has been modified within a view hierarchy. Fields that have not been Changed remain File fields. A View field is a field created specifically in that view using the New command on the Define Hierarchy screen.

Elements of the Procedural Interface

As in any programming language, the dBASE Mac Procedural Interface (PI) contains several types of elements. These include constants, variables, expressions, functions, and commands. What follows here is a very brief description of these elements.

Constants Constants are values that do not change during the running of a procedure. These constants can be numbers, strings (text), dates, times, or logical values. All constants must be enclosed in quotation marks, with the exception of numbers. Number constants may optionally exclude the use of quotation marks.

"Ashton-Tate"—a string constant.
101—a numeric constant
"12/31/79"—a date constant
"8:30 AM"—a time constant
"T"—a logical constant meaning True

Variables Although fields are not technically variables, you can use field names as arguments within many commands. You must use the proper syntax and include the full path name, that is, {Description•Checkbook}. To designate the occurence number in a multivalued field, enclose the number in brackets after the path, for example, {Description•Checkbook}[3]. Field names can be used freely, in procedures, as if they were variables. In some cases, Memory fields can be used as global variables for transferring data between procedures and views.

The other type of variable is called a **local variable**. You can define a local variable easily. Simply create a label for the variable and assign it a value. For example Test_Total = 3000 sets the new variable Test_Total equal to 3000. You can use the variable anywhere within the current procedure. A local variable exists within the current procedure only. Its value is not carried over to other procedures. Notice that blank spaces are not allowed in local variable names.

Local variables can contain data in one- or two-dimensional arrays. Arrays are to local variables what multivalued fields are to single valued fields. A one-dimensional array contains separate occurences of values within a local variable. Notate the fourth occurence in the array as Test_Total[4].

> HINT: You can use a variable as the occurence number, that is Test_Total[i] where i is a local variable. Thus you can use a procedure to add values sequentially to the array.

Two-dimensional arrays are actually data tables. Like a spreadsheet, these arrays are organized in rows and columns. For instance, to assign the value 1500 to the third row, ninth column of an array, the code reads, Test_Total[3,9] = 1500.

You can use arrays in many of the same ways that you would use multivalued fields. Arrays are especially useful for performing statistical analysis that otherwise could only be performed on the contents of a multivalued field.

Expressions and Functions The expressions used in dBASE Mac programming fall into four categories: mathematical, string, logical, or Date/Time. Expressions use constants, variables, functions and even other expressions to evaluate information and return a constant as the result.

A large number of operators are available to create expressions. These operators and functions are found in the pop-up menus on formula, procedure, and selection criterion dialog boxes. They range from mathematical operators (+, −, *,/, etc.) to functions like Sum, Standard Deviation (STD), Variance, (VAR), Sine (SIN), Square Root (SQRT), and so on, to specialized financial functions (COMPOUND and ANNUITY).

There are specialized text or string operators like SUBSTR, UPPER, or LENGTH, and logical and date/time functions as well.

Commands Linking and controlling these procedural elements are commands. Commands include conditional commands (IF...THEN...ELSE and CASE), repeating commands (LOOP, REPEAT, WHILE, etc.), and various commands to control views and projects (PROJECT, USE, PERFORM, SETNEXTVIEW, EXIT, etc.). Finally there are commands that control communication with the user (DIALOG, BUTTON, RADIOLIST, EDITTEXT, etc.).

For more information on programming dBASE Mac, see also Chapter 12 Part II, dBASE Mac Reference; and Part III, Applications.

Dialog Boxes

One of the most common procedures involves the dialog boxes. You are already very familiar with dialog boxes. Almost all Macintosh applications—including dBASE Mac—use dialog boxes. dBASE Mac has a sophisticated set of commands that allow you to create all kinds of dialog boxes. You can create boxes that act as prompts and warnings, boxes to confirm an action (**OK** and **Cancel** boxes), boxes that allow the user to choose from several options, and even boxes that allow the user to enter specific data to be acted upon by the program.

To create a dialog box, you must determine the top-left corner of the box and the bottom-right corner. You measure the screen in pixels. Thus, a typical box might have the coordinates 100, 100, 250, 400. This means that the upper-left corner of the box is at row 100, column 100. The lower-right corner is at row 250, column 400.

> NOTE: The Macintosh screen measures 512 pixels across and 342 pixels vertically. There are 72 pixels to the inch. The upper-left corner of the screen is row 0, column 0.

Dialog boxes can contain Buttons, Radio Buttons, Fixed Text, Fixed Graphics, Check Boxes, and Edit Text boxes.

> TIP: There is help for those who don't want to calculate the exact positions of buttons, text, graphics, checkboxes, and so forth. Kent Irwin of Ashton-Tate's Product Support has written a wonderful desk accessory called dBASE Toolbox. With dBASE Toolbox you can graphically create dialog boxes using the techniques similar to those used when creating a layout. The resulting template can be turned instantly into a dialog procedure script. You can also cut and paste a dialog box script from an application, test and modify it with dBASE Toolbox, then cut and paste it back into the original application. This product is currently available on popular BBS systems, however Ashton-Tate will probably bundle the DA utility with the next release of dBASE Mac. Be sure to update if you are using an old version. Oh, and thanks, Kent.

Dialog Box in a View Pre-Processor Procedure

The following procedure shows how to use Buttons, Radio Buttons, Fixed Text, Edit Text, and a local variable (called Choose). It uses a view Pre-Processor to allow you to pre-select records in the MultiMail project according to the value in the City field. It uses a Global field to pass variable information from the procedure to the Define Selections part of the view. (This selection procedure will work equally well with the single valued Mailing List project.)

1. Open the MultiMail project if it is not already active.
2. Select the Globals file.
3. Choose Add field from the DataFile menu.
4. Call the field "Selections"

5. Click **Save**, then **Done** to return to the Structure Window.

The Selections field will be used later to pass selection criteria to the Define Selections screen.

6. Now open the Windows menu and select Mailing List Columns.
7. Select Duplicate View from the View menu. Name the new view "By City". Select the Columnar view type. Click **OK**.

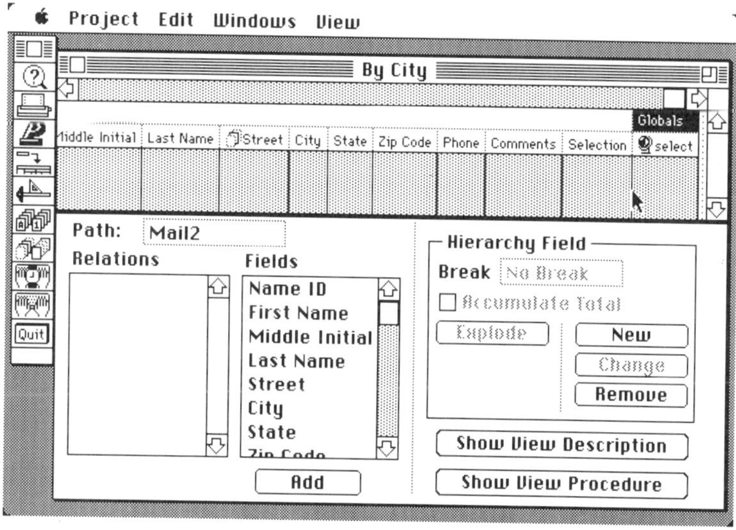

Figure 10-1 Hierarchy Graphic with Globals Path.

8. You will be in the By City view now. Move to the Define Hierarchy screen, open the Path pop-up and select Globals.
9. Now add the Selections field to the hierarchy.
10. Move to the Define Selections screen.
11. Click once on the Mail2 title bar. The selection should read "Show Mail2 if. . ."
12. Enter the following selection criterion:

```
{City•Mail2} = {Selections•Globals}
```

Next you will create a new view. This view will ultimately be used to control the entire MultiMail project:

1. Open the Windows menu and select New. . .
2. Name the new view "Mail Menu" and leave it a Custom View.

3. Add all the fields from MultiMail to the hierarchy, then add the Selections field from the Globals file.

4. Click the Show View Procedure button on the Define Hierarchy screen.

Enter the following procedure. Use the four procedural language pop-up menus to select and enter commands. Text bracketed by backslashes (\) represents comments. Comments are added for clarity. You can leave them out if you wish. If you make a mistake, you can reposition the cursor using the mouse. To erase part of the procedure, highlight that part and press **Backspace**. Be careful to include all punctuation exactly as it appears here (using the pop-up command menus whenever possible will help you keep the syntax accurate).

```
\ **Auto Selection Pre-Processor** \
REPEAT
  DIALOG 100,100,250,400
   BUTTON 1,125,20,145,130,"OK"
   BUTTON 2,125,170,145,280,"Cancel"
  FIXEDTEXT 20,25,40,380,"SELECTING BY CITY"
  RADIOLIST 1,1
   RADIOBUTTON 50,55,65,380,"All Records"
   RADIOBUTTON 70,55,85,380,"Selected Records"
  END
 END

 \ **If the user doesn't press the "Cancel" button
 **\
 IF BUTTONVALUE(1) THEN
    Choose = RADIOVALUE(1)
    \ **The user has decided to select a City. A new
    dialog box appears** \
    IF Choose = 2 THEN
        {Selections•Globals} = " "
        DIALOG 100,100,250,400
        BUTTON 1,125,20,145,130,"OK"
        BUTTON 2,125,170,145,280,"Cancel"
        FIXEDTEXT 20,105,40,280,"Enter the city:"
        EDITTEXT 1,50,25,65,280,{Selections•Globals}
       END
       IF BUTTONVALUE(1) THEN
           \ **Assign what the user has typed
        to the Globals field **\
            {Selections•Globals} =
          TEXTVALUE(1)
            \ **Perform the view to initialize
          the selection** \
           PERFORM ("By City",MODAL)
       END
   ELSE
      SETNEXTVIEW("Mail List Column")
      EXIT
```

```
                END
            END
        UNTIL BUTTONVALUE(2)
        END
        SETNEXTVIEW("Mail Entry")
        EXIT
```

Some of the command lines in the procedure above require explanation.

BUTTON 1,125,20,145,130,"OK" The BUTTON command creates a button like the standard **OK** or **Cancel** buttons common to Macintosh applications. The first number is the button number, the next four numbers represent the coordinates of the button within the dialog box. The text in quotes is the text that will appear within the button.

> NOTE: The coordinates of a dialog box are measured from the top-left corner of the Macintosh screen (0,0). All components of a dialog box are positioned relative to the top-left corner of the dialog box itself! Be sure to position Buttons, Radio Buttons, text, and other dialog box elements in their places relative to the upper corner of the box, not the Mac screen.

The DIALOG command must end with an END statement. Notice that the two BUTTON commands, the FIXEDTEXT command, and the whole RADIOLIST subclause are contained within the first dialog box.

FIXEDTEXT is self-explanatory. Position the text relative to the upper-left corner of the dialog box, then indicate the text content within quotes.

RADIOLIST 1,1, etc. This clause creates a list of button choices. The RADIOLIST command initializes the set of choices. The first number following the RADIOLIST command is the identification number of this radiolist (relative to other radiolists) within the dialog box. The second number indicates which radiobutton is to be preselected when you run the procedure. The radiobuttons are placed at coordinates relative to the upper-left corner of the dialog box, and their text messages are indicated in quotes. The RADIOLIST command must end with an END statement.

IF BUTTONVALUE(1) means "If Button 1 is pressed."

Choose = RADIOVALUE(1) sets the local variable called "Choose" equal to the number of the radiobutton pressed in Radiolist number one. If the first button is clicked, then Choose = 1. If the second button is clicked, then Choose = 2.

EDITTEXT 1,50,25,65,280,{Selections•Globals} The EDITTEXT command allows you to enter data directly into a procedure. The first number represents the number of the EDITTEXT box relative to other such boxes in the dialog box. Then follows the coordinate expression. The final entry is the path that designates the field value that the EDITTEXT box initially displays (this could also be text in quotes or a local variable).

TEXTVALUE(1) is the text entered in EDITTEXT box number one. This value is then transferred into the Global field, Selections. If no value is typed into the text box, then TEXTVALUE(1) will return the Initial Value defined for the EDITTEXT item's initial (default) value.

The PERFORM command is the same as selecting Perform and Use from the Palette or from the View menu. However, the PERFORM command has several optional parameters:

PERFORM (view name [,MODAL][,INIT]) The MODAL parameter disables the Palette and the menus during performance of the view.

The INIT parameter runs any Pre-Processor attached to the view (see below).

The EXIT command leaves the view. If you select **Cancel** in the initial dialog box, the program will leave the view and return to the previous position within the project.

- When you are finished with the Pre-Processor, click **Verify** to check for errors. If you encounter no errors, go on to the next step.

Now, when you run the Pre-Processor, you enter a city name into the EDITTEXT box. It is then transferred into the Selections field, which is used in the selection criterion when the By City view is Performed. When you exit the By City view, you re-enter the Repeat loop of the Mail Menu view which re-displays the initial dialog box.

HINT: There are shortcuts to programming dBASE Mac. Any procedure can be Cut, Copied, and Pasted like any standard Macintosh data. Therefore, you can Cut parts of a program from one procedure and Paste those parts into another. For code that you use often (like standard dialog boxes, error checking routines, etc.) you can keep a file of procedures in a word processor, in the Scrapbook, or in a Desk Accessory like Mock Write or Notepad. Since the DAs are always accessible from within dBASE Mac, you can use them to Cut and Paste standard procedures.

TIP: Before this view will work, you must put something in the layout. It does not have to be a field, however, and we suggest placing a Fixed Text element at a position behind the dialog box, then typing a space in it. Eliminate any box around the text element, and the screen will always appear blank behind the dialog box. Alternately, you can place a Fixed Graphic on the layout, perhaps a company logo or some other graphic figure. Since there are times when the layout surface will show up during execution of the view, this makes the application seem more professional and more interesting.

NOTE: There is an exception to the above rule about the layout. In the next chapter, you will place a Pre-Processor on a field element in a view. In order to execute a procedure attached to a field, the insertion point must enter that field, so the field must be on the layout. The first field on the layout (meaning the one most toward the upper left) is the one the insertion point enters first.

Turn Trace On

When you are writing procedures, you may need help finding bugs or mistakes in the code. dBASE Mac has a built-in Trace function that allows you to see the code being executed as it is run. To activate the Trace function, select Turn Trace On from the View menu.

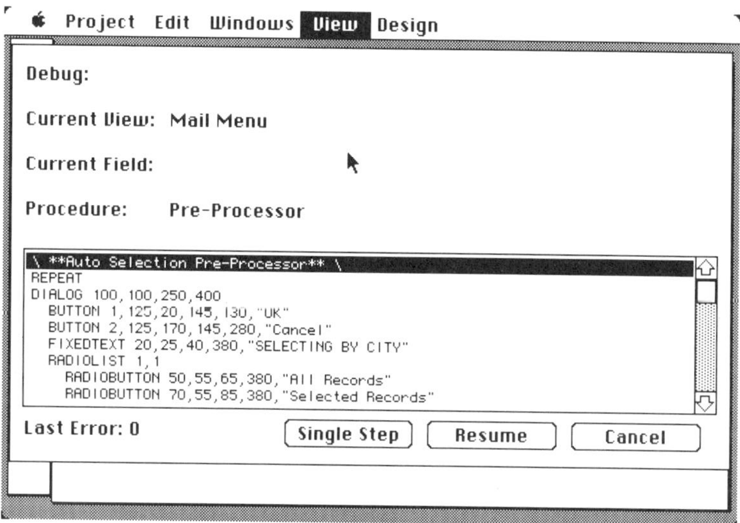

Figure 10-2 Trace Dialog Box Graphic.

When you perform a procedure with Trace on, a dialog box appears as the procedure begins. The dialog box displays the current view, the current field being processed, and part of the current procedure with the active line highlighted. You can select Single Step to step through the procedure one line at a time, or you can select Resume to continue through the entire procedure. Trace will stop the procedure if it encounters an error. The Last Error number represents a dBASE Mac error (listed in the back of the dBASE Mac manual).

Stopping a procedure:

> You can place preset stopping points in a procedure with the BREAK command. Then, when you select Resume (with Trace on), the procedure will continue uninterrupted until it encounters the BREAK; then it will stop. From the BREAK, you can go back to Single Step mode. This is useful for bypassing parts of procedures that you know are correct.
>
> There are two ways to interrupt a procedure. When you enter or leave a view or field that has a procedure attached, holding the **Shift** and **Option** keys down will cause a dialog box to appear, giving you the option of cancelling the execution of the current procedure before it executes.
>
> If a procedure gets stuck in an endless loop, you can press the **Command** key and the period key together to break out of the loop and stop the procedure from running.

Trace is especially helpful in determining the actual order of processing within a procedure. If you are unsure whether an IF statement is correctly interpreting data, or whether one of the repeating commands like LOOP, REPEAT, or WHILE is performing as expected, you can watch the program flow in the Single Step mode to determine the order of processing.

Trace follows program flow. If one procedure calls another, Trace will continue to operate on the new procedure. When the calling procedure resumes, Trace will follow.

To disable the Trace function, choose Turn Trace Off from the View menu.

Customizing the Palette

The Palette occurs in the Structure Window, Define Hierarchy, Define Sorts, Define Selections, Layout View, and Use modes of a project. Each mode has its own default Palette. Each Tutorial chapter includes a section that defines the default Palette. In this section you will learn to modify the Palette to your needs.

The Palette is actually a collection of icons that represent menu commands. Think of each icon as a command attached to a graphic.

> NOTE: Most menu items have a default Palette icon. For a complete list of available icons, see Part II, dBASE Mac Reference, under **Palette**.

There are several ways to modify the Palette. You can change the icon graphic, change the menu command for a specific icon, add or remove icons, or even create your own Palette icons.

If you are continuing from the previous section of the Tutorial, you should have the MultiMail active. If you do not, Open MultiMail now.

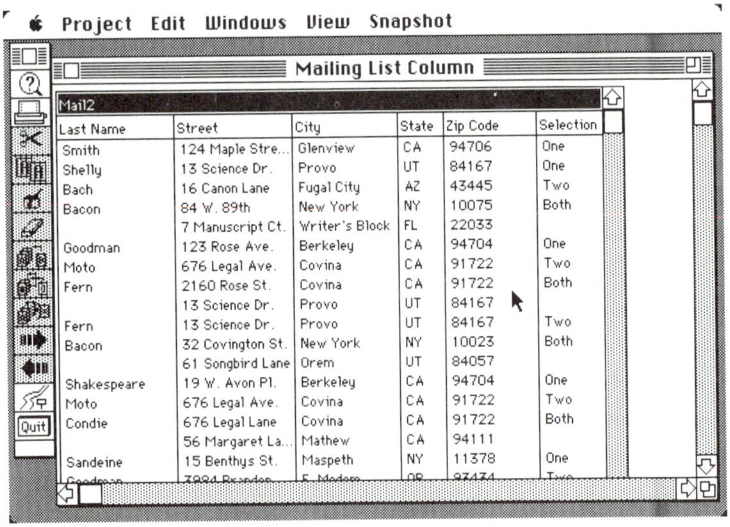

Figure 10-3 Mailing List Column Graphic.

Perform and Use the Mailing List Column view. You should be in the Column view displaying the Mail2 records.

Removing an Icon

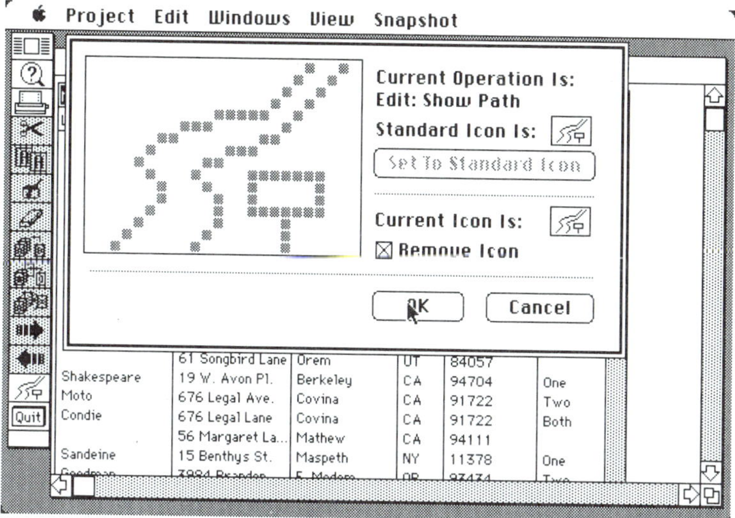

Figure 10-4 Palette Modification Dialog Box Graphic.

To remove an icon from any Palette:

1. Hold the **Command** key down and click on the icon you wish to remove.
2. Click in the Remove Icon check box.
3. Click **OK** to return to the current view or screen. The icon you selected will be gone.

Try removing the Path icon from the Palette.

1. **Command**-click on the Path icon.
2. Click in the Remove Icon checkbox.
3. Click **OK**.

The Path icon should be gone.

Adding an Icon

To add an icon to the Palette:

1. Hold down the **Command** key and click on the blank space at the bottom of the Palette.

NOTE: If there is no blank space at the bottom of the Palette, the Palette is full. You will need to remove an icon (or replace it with a new one).

2. Choose the command you wish to include in the Palette. You can choose the command normally, from the menus or by using its keyboard equivalent, if any. In this case, select Show Path from the Edit menu.

3. If you click Set To Standard Icon, then the dBASE Mac default icon for that command will appear in the small box labeled Current Icon Is: and also in the larger graphic box. (Check the Standard Icon Is: box to see what it will look like before clicking the button). If you decide to show the standard icon for the Show Path command, it will look just like the icon you removed in the previous section (**Removing an Icon**).

You can modify the large image by positioning the mouse over any part of the image and clicking. Clicking on a white space turns it black. Clicking on a black space turns it white. If you are familiar with MacPaint, this graphic operates just like Fat Bits. Try clicking on a white space and dragging the mouse.

You can also draw an icon from scratch, ignoring the standard icon entirely. To do so, do not click the Set To Standard Icon button.

4. When you are finished with the icon, click **OK** to return to the active view and accept the choices you have made. Click **Cancel** if you change your mind.

NOTE: You can change an icon's command by **Command**-clicking the icon, then selecting a new command for the existing icon. Click **OK** to keep the new command. You can also replace an icon by **Command**-clicking the icon, then changing the command and selecting the standard icon for the new command. Click **OK** and the previous icon will be replaced by the new one.

Five icons in the Layout View do not have menu or keyboard command equivalents. These are Selection, Fixed Text, Fixed Graphic, Line, and Tablet. You can modify their icons if you wish, but you cannot change their command definitions or remove them from the Palette.

You may find that you often use certain commands that are missing from the default Palette in particular areas of the program. You might, for instance, add the Perform and Use icon to the Use mode for Column views. Then, if you switch between data entry and the Column view, you can update the records quickly. Other icons that come in handy in the Use mode are the Sort and Select icons. When you are developing a view, adding the Define Hierarchy and/or the Layout View icons to the Use mode Palette may be helpful.

MultiMail concludes later in this chapter.

Finishing Touches—Custom Menus

After you have defined all the files, fields, views, and procedures that make up a project, you may want to create an independently running application. You can do this using Custom Menus and by Protecting the project.

Custom Menus allow you to polish the look of your project. Each Custom Menu consists of a menu title and a series of view names.

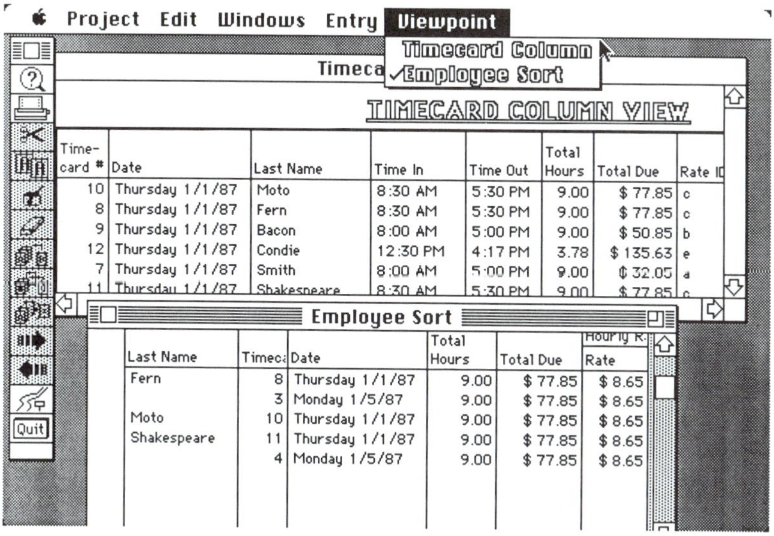

Figure 10-5 Custom Menus Graphic.

If you wish to control the project completely through Custom Menus, you can hide the Windows menu. If you hide the Windows menu, the only menus that will appear during execution of your project are the Apple menu, Project, Edit, and your Custom Menus.

Custom Menus must be created while in the Layout View. Thus, you create Custom Menus from within a particular view.

> NOTE: Even though you must create the Custom Menus within a view, they operate on the whole project. It doesn't matter at all which view you use to create the Custom Menus. They won't be activated until the current project is Protected, and then they will remain active until you remove the Protected status from the project, regardless of where they were created. (To learn how to Protect a project, see the next section).

Open the Timecard Project. If necessary, Close any active project first. Now select any view. For this exercise, select the Hourly Rates Entry view (activate it from the Windows menu). From the View menu, select Layout View.

To create a Custom Menu:

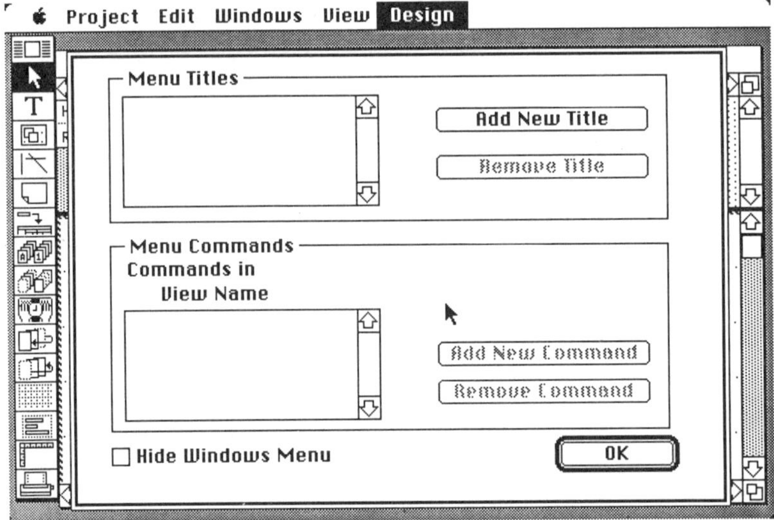

Figure 10-6 Custom View Dialog Box Graphic.

1. In the Layout View, select Custom Menus from the Design menu.

   Notice that the Custom Menu dialog box is divided into two sections, one called Menu Titles, the other, Menu Commands. Menu Titles are the actual labels that will appear at the top of the screen. Edit, Project, and Windows are examples of menu titles in dBASE Mac. Menu Commands are view names like Timecard Entry and Timecard Columns.

2. Create a menu title. Click on Add New Title. A new dialog box appears. In the text box, type "Entry" as your first title.

3. Click **OK** to accept the title.

   The new title, Entry, now appears in the list box beneath Menu Titles.

4. To add a command to the title, you must first highlight that title. Click once on Entry in the Menu Titles list box.

5. Click Add New Command.

6. A new dialog box containing a list of available views appears. Click on the view name you wish to include under that currently selected menu title. Click on Hourly Rates Entry.

7. Click **OK**.

8. The Menu Commands list box now displays the name of the Menu Title currently selected. Hourly Rates Entry appears in the list.

9. Add Employee Entry and then Timecard Entry to the Menu Commands list by following steps 5 through 7 for each view name.

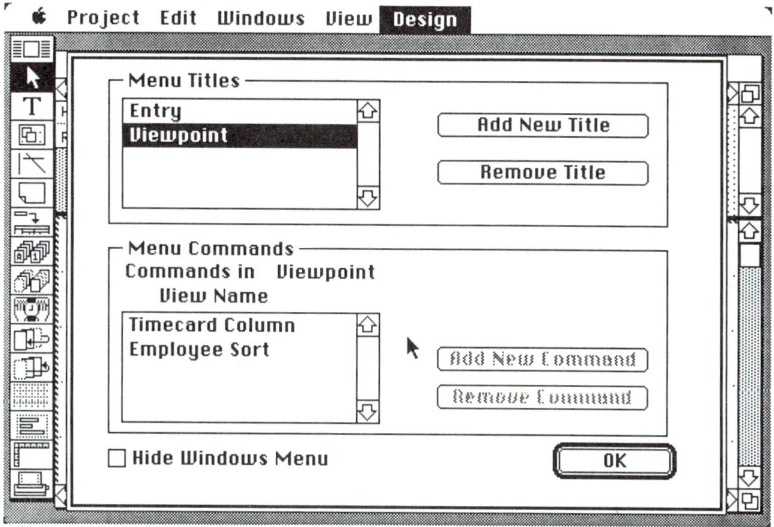

Figure 10-7 Custom Menus Graphic with Views.

10. Now that you have entered some titles into the Entry menu, add a new Menu Title. Click on Add New Title.

11. Fill in the name of the next menu. Type "Viewpoint".

HINT: If you plan to create a large number of Custom Menu titles, you may want to keep the title short. There is only so much room at the top of the Mac screen, and dBASE Mac will only use those titles that can fit there.

12. Click **OK**.

    The title, Viewpoint, now appears beneath Entry.

13. Highlight Viewpoint and click Add New Command.

14. Add Timecard Column and Employee Sort to the Menu Commands list.

NOTE: Before you exit the Custom Menus dialog box, you can check the Hide Windows checkbox. If you do so, the Windows menu will not be displayed in a protected project. Any views that are not included in one of the Custom Menus will be inaccessible during the operation of the protected project when the Hide Window Menu checkbox is checked.

You have now defined two Custom Menus. To complete the process, Click **OK**. You will return to the Hourly Rates Entry view hierarchy.

REMINDER: It does not matter which view you use to create Custom Menu. You used Hourly Rates Entry, but you could as easily have used Timecard Entry or Employee Entry or Employee Sort. In fact, if you open the Custom Menu dialog box in any other view, the same selections you just made will appear. Custom Menus are project-wide in effect.

You won't see any difference in your project yet. The Custom Menus you just created will not appear until you protect the project.

Protecting a Project

Protecting a project is easy. You simply select Protect from the Project menu and enter a password.

NOTE: You will need to remember the password you use or you will not be able to make any changes in the project. A protected project does not allow modifications to be made to the structures of files, views, or procedures. To make any changes you must select Modify from the Project menu and enter the password you used to Protect the project.

To Protect a project:

1. Still in the Timecard Project, select Protect from the Project menu.
2. Enter a password in the text box that appears. Enter "Timepass"
3. Click **OK**.

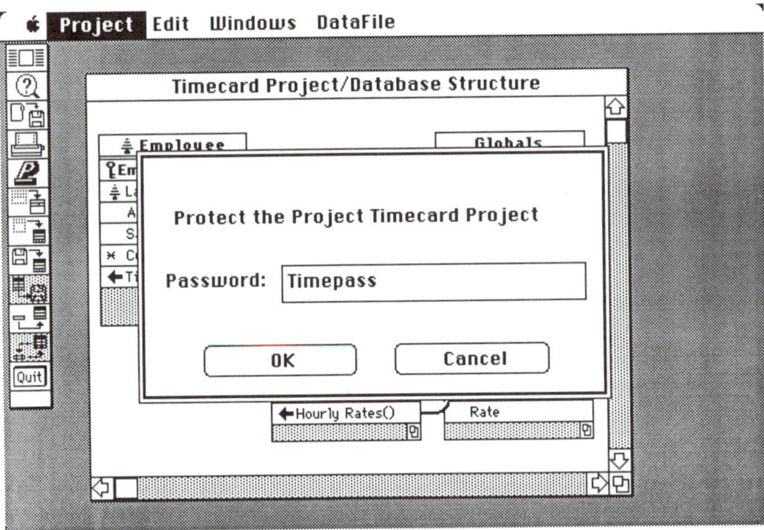

Figure 10-8 Protecting from Save As Dialog Graphic.

You can also Protect a project when you first Save the project, or any time you use Save As. . . to save a new version of the current project. A checkbox at the bottom of the file-naming dialog box asks if you want to Save As Protected. If you check that box, you will be able to assign a password to the project before it is saved. When you retrieve the project, it will be in Protected mode.

NOTE: If any of the views in the current project cannot be performed for some reason (most commonly because no layout has been defined), an error message will appear. You can only protect a project if all views are performable.

NOTE: In a protected project, the View menu is suppressed. The Windows menu contains the command Perform View. . . . If you think you will have to perform any views in a protected project, be sure to include the Windows menu or add the Perform and Use icon to the Use Mode Palette. Adding Perform and Use to the Palette of any view in the Use Mode will add it to all views in Use Mode. Another common way to Perform columnar views is to create a controlling view to actually Perform the columnar view. This is often accomplished in conjunction with a dialog box menu that allows you to select the view to Perform.

NOTE: Other View menu selections are suppressed entirely when a project is protected. You will not be able to enter the Structure Window, the Layout View, or the Define Hierarchy screen in a protected project. Also, Define Sorts and Define Selections are suppressed in a protected project. You cannot set up new sort or selection criteria in a protected project, so you will have to anticipate those kinds of reporting needs in advance, or unprotect the project to make modifications.

NOTE: If you end up creating a lot of views for different purposes, you may exceed the limit of sixteen views per project. Also, the number of files and views open can affect the maximum number of views available. You can create another project to contain any extra views. The PROJECT command in the Procedural Interface calls and activates another project. The syntax is PROJECT("project name"). Whenever a PROJECT command is encountered, the program closes the current project and activates the new project named in the command.

TIP: If you call another project, but you want to pass specific values from the calling project to the new project, you can use file Memory fields to do so. You might even create a special file that can be used as a "messenger file" between projects. File Memory fields are excellent for this purpose.

If you leave a view in Layout View or the Define Hierarchy, Sorts, or Selections screens, it will be placed in Use Mode when activated in a protected project.

NOTE: You can use protected projects to provide a smooth interface to the user of your projects. You can also use them to prevent user-modification of the project. But remember, you can password protect any project or file on an individual basis. Sometimes you may wish to allow users access to the entire project, but only protect specific views and/or fields (through procedures).

You can create passwords for files at any time. Use them as you need them, or not at all. Create procedures to password protect specific fields or views.

NOTE: As of this writing, Ashton-Tate had not released the runtime version of dBASE Mac. However, dBASE Mac Runtime is due to be released by the time this book ships. Only Protected projects will work with dBASE Mac Runtime.

→ Timecard continues in Chapter 11.

Completing MultiMail

If you wish to create a completed application, the instructions below will help you turn the MultiMail application into a turnkey system. You will need to create some additional views and one additional file, add some Pre-Processors and Post-Processors to various views, rewrite the Mail Menu procedure, develop a context-sensitive help system, create Custom Menus, and, finally, protect the MultiMail project.

This section contains several major steps that take the MultiMail project from a simple application to one that hints at something sophisticated. You can use some of the ideas outlined here to help you develop more interesting and useful applications in your own business.

The instructions in this section will assume your knowledge of what has been done before, and will, therefore, be brief:

- Duplicate the By City view, call the new view "By State", make it a Columnar layout, and change its selection criterion to read:

```
{State•Mail2} = {Selections•Globals}
```

- Adjust the columns on the layout of the By State view.
- Add the following Post-Processor to By City, By State, Mail Entry, Labels-2, and Mailing List Column views:

```
EXIT
```

  (That's simply the single command, EXIT, as a view Post-Processor.)

- Replace the Mail Menu procedure created earlier in this chapter with the following procedure (you'll notice that some of it is the same, but there are many differences as well):

```
REPEAT
\ **Auto Selection Pre-Processor** \
  DIALOG 100,100,250,400
   BUTTON 1,125,20,145,130,"OK"
   BUTTON 2,125,170,145,280,"Cancel"
   FIXEDTEXT 20,25,40,190,"MAIL MENU"
   RADIOLIST 1,1
    RADIOBUTTON 50,55,65,380,"Enter Records"
    RADIOBUTTON 70,55,85,380,"View Records"
    RADIOBUTTON 90,55,105,380,"Print Labels"
   END
```

```
 END

\ **If the user doesn't press the "Cancel" button **\
  IF BUTTONVALUE(1) THEN
  CASE RADIOVALUE(1) OF
   WHEN 1 DO
    USE ("Mail Entry")
   WHEN 2 DO
    REPEAT
     DIALOG 100,100,250,400
      BUTTON 1,125,20,145,130,"OK"
      BUTTON 3,125,170,145,280,"Cancel"
      FIXEDTEXT 20,25,40,190,"VIEWING RECORDS"
      RADIOLIST 1,1
       RADIOBUTTON 50,55,65,380,"All Records"
       RADIOBUTTON 70,55,85,380,"By City"
       RADIOBUTTON 90,55,105,380,"By State"
      END
     END

\ **If the user doesn't press the "Cancel" button **\
    IF BUTTONVALUE(1) THEN
     CASE RADIOVALUE(1) OF
      WHEN 1 DO
       PERFORM("Mailing List Column 5", MODAL)
      WHEN 2 DO
       {Selections•Globals} = " "
       DIALOG 100,100,250,400
        BUTTON 1,125,20,145,130,"OK"
        BUTTON 3,125,170,145,280,"Cancel"
        FIXEDTEXT 20,105,40,280,"Enter the city:"
        EDITTEXT 1,50,25,65,280,
        {Selections•Globals}
       END
       IF BUTTONVALUE(1) THEN
 \ **Assign what the user has typed to the Globals field **
\
        {Selections•Globals} = TEXTVALUE(1)
\ **Perform the view to initialize the selection** \
          PERFORM ("By City",MODAL)
       END
        WHEN 3 DO
         {Selections•Globals} = " "
         DIALOG 100,100,250,400
           BUTTON 1,125,20,145,130,"OK"
           BUTTON 3,125,170,145,280,"Cancel"
           FIXEDTEXT 20,105,40,280,"Enter the state:"
           EDITTEXT 1,50,25,65,280,
           {Selections•Globals}
        END
        IF BUTTONVALUE(1) THEN
 \ **Assign what the user has typed to the Globals field **\
         {Selections•Globals} = TEXTVALUE(1)
\ **Perform the view to initialize the selection** \
```

```
                PERFORM("By State",MODAL)
              END
             END
            END
           UNTIL BUTTONVALUE(3)
           END
          WHEN 3 DO
           PRINT("Labels-2")
         END
        END
      UNTIL BUTTONVALUE(2)
      END
      SETNEXTVIEW("Mail Entry")
      EXIT
```

The Mail Menu procedure allows you to enter new records, view records in several ways, and even print out mailing labels. It by no means exhausts the possibilities of a mailing list program. Feel free to add your own wrinkles to it. To find out what the Pre-Processor you entered does, the best way is to experiment. You'll soon understand what it does and, probably, why.

NOTE: Some operations may not perform completely to your satisfaction, especially with MultiMail's multivalued fields (in particular the selections on city and state that will not limit themselves to the current record as defined by the Selections field). You'll find that if you customize the Mailing List Project (which uses single valued fields) in the same way, the selections will be more meaningful. Since this is a tutorial on dBASE Mac, we have tried to show you some of the more obscure possibilities. When you finalize your own work, you can draw from these examples to create applications that do exactly what you want them to do.

HINT: If you plan to customize the Mailing List Project, use Copy and Paste to move the Mail Menu Pre-Processor to a new view in the Mailing List Project. You can either Copy it to the Clipboard, then Close MultiMail, open Mailing List, and Paste it in; or you can Copy it from the Clipboard to a word processor or other text editing program. Using Switcher or MultiFinder will make that task even easier.

A Context-Sensitive Help System

To add a context-sensitive help system to any application gives you greater latitude in developing applications for other users. There are several ways to create help systems in dBASE Mac. This is just one alternative, but it is one with some degree of effectiveness.

This help system uses its own file, the Help Mail file. This file contains two fields, Help ID and Help Text. You will see how you can use the Help Text file in a dialog box to display the help information, and how to create a system that allows users to browse the help screens, or select from a help index. The system also knows where it was called from and immediately displays the appropriate screen when called.

Implementing this help system in an application is fairly laborious because Help buttons will have to be inserted into all dialog boxes, and help text written for each eventuality. Because this could be a huge job, we have decided to show only a limited sort of help application here. Every aspect of the help system is demonstrated, but only a few examples are included. This will make it much easier to follow the examples.

To begin:

1. Create a new file called Help Mail.

2. Name the Key field "Help ID" and make it an Auto Sequencing Numeric field with zero decimal places. Enter an Initial Value of 1. Click **Save**.

3. Name the next field "Help Text." It should be a Text field and the Wrap checkbox should be checked. Click **Save**.

4. Click **Done** and estimate about ten records for the file size.

5. With the Help Mail file still selected on the Structure Window, create a new Quick Create Form view. (Help Mail should be the Root File.) Name the view "Help Entry."

6. Move to Layout view and resize the Help Text field. Make the field about 1 1/2 inches deep and about 3 1/2 inches wide.

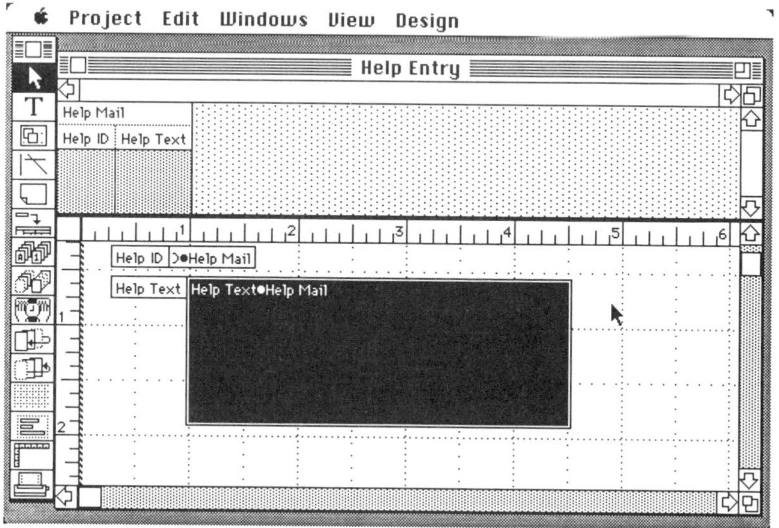

Figure 10-9 Help Entry Layout.

7. Use Help Entry and add the following records. (These are suggestions only. You can add any text you wish. Just remember that you cannot add more than 255 characters per field):

Help ID: 1

Help Text:

On this dialog box you can select to view or enter new records. You can also print out mailing labels. Select the appropriate radio button to begin processing.

MORE...

Help ID: 2

Help Text:

If you choose the View Records option, a new dialog box offers three new choices:

All Records, By City, and By State.

END SECTION

Help ID: 3

Help Text:

Selecting All Records will display a Column view of the entire file.

MORE...

Help ID: 4

Help Text:

Selecting By City will display a dialog box on which you can enter a city name. Enter the city name exactly as it appears in your records.

MORE...

Help ID: 5

Help Text:

Selecting By State allows you to enter a state abbreviation. A Column view will display showing those records that match the state.

END SECTION

Help ID: 6

Help Text:

On the Mail Entry view, you can enter records to the mailing list. Remember that Command-A will add a new record. If the cursor is in a multivalued field, it will add a new occurrence to the Address set.

Now that you've entered some help screen information, it is time to create the help view itself:

1. Duplicate the Help Entry view and call the copy "Help."
2. Move to the Layout view screen of the Help view and drag the Help ID field onto the layout. In this case, the Help ID field needs to be on the layout. You can still remove any box around the field, then resize till it is very small. Place a Fixed Graphic over it to hide it during those times when the dialog boxes are changing.
3. Return to the Structure Window and select the Globals file.
4. Add a Numeric file to the Globals file. Call it "Help Level."
7. Return to the Help view and move to the Define Hierarchy screen.
8. Add the Global file, Help Level, to the hierarchy. (Don't forget the Path pop-up.)
9. Double-click on the Help ID field in the hierarchy to open the change field dialog.
10. Click on Show Procedure and enter the following Pre-Processor:

```
\Help ID Pre-Processor_Main Help Engine **\
REPEAT
 SETBROWSE({Help ID•Help Mail},{Help Level•Globals})
 REDISPLAY({Help Text•Help Mail})
 DIALOG 30,50,330,450
  BUTTON 90,260,150,280,240,"Exit"
  BUTTON 10,175,70,195,180,"Next"
  BUTTON 20,175,220,195,330,"Previous"
  BUTTON 50,225,150,245,240,"Help Index"
  FIXEDTEXT 20,150,40,260,"HELP SCREENS. . ."
  EDITTEXT 1,50,25,150,375,{Help Text•Help Mail}
 END
 IF BUTTONVALUE(50) THEN
 DIALOG 50,50,350,500
  BUTTON 1,225,20,245,130,"OK"
  BUTTON 2,225,170,245,280,"Cancel"
  FIXEDTEXT 20,150,40,260,"HELP INDEX. . ."
  RADIOLIST 1,1
   RADIOBUTTON 50,10,70,140,"Mail Menu Dialog"
   RADIOBUTTON 75,10,95,120,"View Dialog"
   RADIOBUTTON 100,10,120,120,"All Records"
   RADIOBUTTON 125,10,145,120,"By City"
   RADIOBUTTON 150,10,170,120,"By State"
   RADIOBUTTON 175,10,195,120,"Mail Entry"
```

```
  END
 END
  {Help Level•Globals} = RADIOVALUE(1)
  END
  IF BUTTONVALUE(10) THEN
   {Help Level•Globals} = {Help Level•Globals} + 1
  END
  IF BUTTONVALUE(20) THEN
   {Help Level•Globals} = {Help Level•Globals} - 1
  END
 UNTIL BUTTONVALUE(90)
 END
 EXIT
```

This system works by using the {Help Level•Globals} value to set the appropriate record in the Help file and to display the appropriate Help Text entry in the dialog box. So, whenever you add a new help item to a dialog box in any view, you assign Help Level a number that corresponds to the record number in the Help Mail file. The procedure then sets the Help file to the appropriate record and displays its corresponding Help Text field. The Next and Previous buttons operate very simply inside the REPEAT loop to increment or decrement the Help Level.

The Help Index is always available within the Help view. Each Radiobutton in the Help Index sets Help Level to a different value, returning you to the help screen of your choice. The EXIT command will cause the procedure to exit to the calling view. Thus, you can use Help from any view or procedure without getting lost.

Finally, to implement this simplified help system, you'll have to make some modifications to the Mail Menu Pre-Processor. The entire procedure is printed below. The new parts are in bold text. It shouldn't be difficult to add the new lines to the existing procedure. Before you do so, however, be sure to add the Help Level field to the hierarchy.

> NOTE: Before you begin to work with Mail Menu, you will have to stop execution of the view Pre-Processor. To do so, press the **Option** and **Shift** keys while you select the view. A dialog box will appear allowing you to stop execution of the Pre-Processor.

```
REPEAT
\**Auto Selection Pre-Processor**\
 DIALOG 100,100,250,400
  BUTTON 1,125,20,145,130,"OK"
  BUTTON 2,125,170,145,280,"Cancel"
  BUTTON 90,20,200,40,250,'HELP'
  FIXEDTEXT 20,25,40,190,"MAIL MENU"
  RADIOLIST 1,1
   RADIOBUTTON 50,55,65,380,"Enter Records"
   RADIOBUTTON 70,55,85,380,"View Records"
   RADIOBUTTON 90,55,105,380,"Print Labels"
  END
 END
```

```
   IF BUTTONVALUE(90) THEN
     {Help Level•Globals}  1
     PERFORM('Help',MODAL)
   END
\ **If the user doesn't press the "Cancel" button **\
  IF BUTTONVALUE(1) THEN
   CASE RADIOVALUE(1) OF
    WHEN 1 DO
     USE ("Mail Entry")
    WHEN 2 DO
     REPEAT
      DIALOG 100,100,250,400
       BUTTON 1,125,20,145,130,"OK"
       BUTTON 3,125,170,145,280,"Cancel"
       BUTTON 90,20,200,40,250,'HELP'
       FIXEDTEXT 20,25,40,190,"VIEWING RECORDS"
       RADIOLIST 1,1
        RADIOBUTTON 50,55,65,380,"All Records"
        RADIOBUTTON 70,55,85,380,"By City"
        RADIOBUTTON 90,55,105,380,"By State"
       END
      END
      IF BUTTONVALUE(90) THEN
          CASE RADIOVALUE(1) OF
          WHEN 1 DO
           {Help Level•Globals} = 3
           PERFORM('Help',MODAL)
          WHEN 2 DO
           {Help Level•Globals} = 4
          PERFORM('Help',MODAL)
         OTHERWISE
          {Help Level•Globals} = 5
          PERFORM('Help',MODAL)
         END
        END
\ **If the user doesn't press the "Cancel" button **\
      IF BUTTONVALUE(1) THEN
       CASE RADIOVALUE(1) OF
        WHEN 1 DO
         PERFORM("Mailing List Column", MODAL)
        WHEN 2 DO
         {Selections•Globals} = " "
         DIALOG 100,100,250,400
          BUTTON 1,125,20,145,130,"OK"
          BUTTON 3,125,170,145,280,"Cancel"
          FIXEDTEXT 20,105,40,280,"Enter the city:"
          EDITTEXT 1,50,25,65,280,{Selections•Globals}
         END
 \ **Assign what the user has typed to the Globals field **\
        {Selections•Globals} = TEXTVALUE(1)
\ **Perform the view to initialize the selection** \
         PERFORM ("By City",MODAL)
        WHEN 3 DO
         {Selections•Globals} = " "
```

```
            DIALOG 100,100,250,400
             BUTTON 1,125,20,145,130,"OK"
             BUTTON 3,125,170,145,280,"Cancel"
             FIXEDTEXT 20,105,40,280,"Enter the state:"
             EDITTEXT 1,50,25,65,280,{Selections•Globals}
            END
     **Assign what the user has typed to the Globals field **\
            {Selections•Globals} = TEXTVALUE(1)
\  **Perform the view to initialize the selection** \
PERFORM("By State",MODAL)
          END
         END
        UNTIL BUTTONVALUE(3)
        END
       WHEN 3 DO
        PRINT("Labels-2")
      END
     END
    UNTIL BUTTONVALUE(2)
    END
    SETNEXTVIEW("Mail Entry")
    EXIT
```

Notice how the CASE statement tests the value of the Radiobuttons and sets the Help Level accordingly.

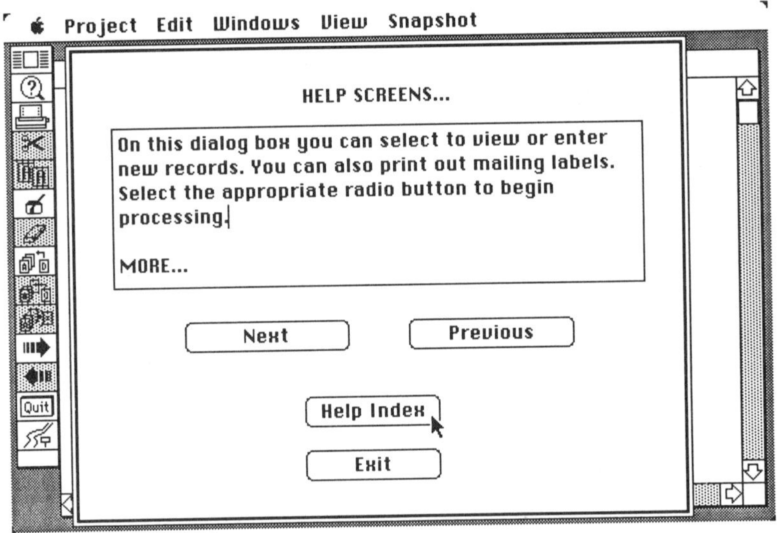

Figure 10-10 Sample Help Screen.

To test these procedures, Use the Mail Menu view and click on the Help button. You can experiment from there to see how it works. Add, change, or modify the help screens as you wish. Create new ones, or add the whole system to another application. That's what it's for.

Often you may want to include a help option on a layout screen—for instance, during data entry. There is a way to accomplish this, but it involves some trickery. What you do is create a Fixed Text entry that says "HELP" on the layout. Then, on top of that text, place a graphic "button" with no Fill (from the Display Options dialog). You needn't actually place a graphic in the graphics box, just round the edges and darken the lines (also from the Display Options dialog box). The text will show through the "button." Now attach a Pre-Processor to the graphic so that when the user clicks on it, it calls the help system. Of course, you set the Help Level to the appropriate level for the current layout.

To create a graphic layout help button:

1. Move to the Define Hierarchy screen of the Mail Entry view.

NOTE: The EXIT Post-Processor will send you out of the view if you don't hold down **Option** and **Shift** when you select Define Hierarchy from the View menu. You can return to the view in the Define Hierarchy mode, however.

2. Create a new view field called "Graph Help." It should be a Memory field, Graphics type. You can presize it to be fairly small, but don't worry: You'll be able to size it on the layout later.

3. Move to Layout View.

4. Now create a Fixed Text element by clicking on the Fixed Text icon in the Palette and then clicking on the layout to position the text cursor. Type "HELP."

   You can make the text element any size, font, or other effect you want. You can leave a box around it or remove it. Use Display Options to make the text look the way you want it to.

5. Now drag the Graph Help field from the hierarchy onto the layout. Double click it to open the Display Options dialog.

6. Open the Fill pop-up and drag it all the way to the top to the item called None. Click on Display Only.

7. Choose a heavy Pen Size to draw a thick box around the field. If you are using a Mac II, you might choose a color fill pattern for the pen (the color selections are at the bottom of the pattern list). Also, you might like to place a rounded frame around the graphic. To do so, select one of the corner settings under the Frame heading.

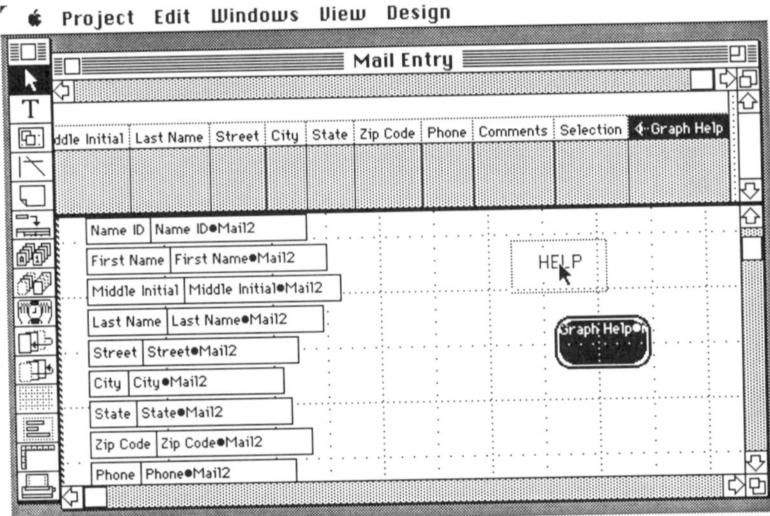

Figure 10-11 Placing the Graphic Field on the Text.

8. Click **OK** to return to the layout and drag the Graph Help field over the Fixed Text you created before. Size the Graph Help field to fit nicely around the text.

9. Return to the Define Hierarchy screen and add the Help Level field to the hierarchy. Then add the following Pre-Processor to the Graph Help file:

```
{Help Level•Globals} = 6
PERFORM("Help",MODAL)
SETNEXTFIELD({Name ID•Mail2})
```

Now that you have added the Pre-Processor (and clicked **OK** and **Done**), there is one more thing to do. You don't want the cursor to enter the Help button accidentally, so you must control the movement of the cursor during record entry. To do so requires two extra modifications:

1. Create a new Graphics Memory view field and call it "Dummy Field."

2. Add the following Pre-Processor to the Dummy Field:

```
SETNEXTFIELD({Name ID•Mail2})
```

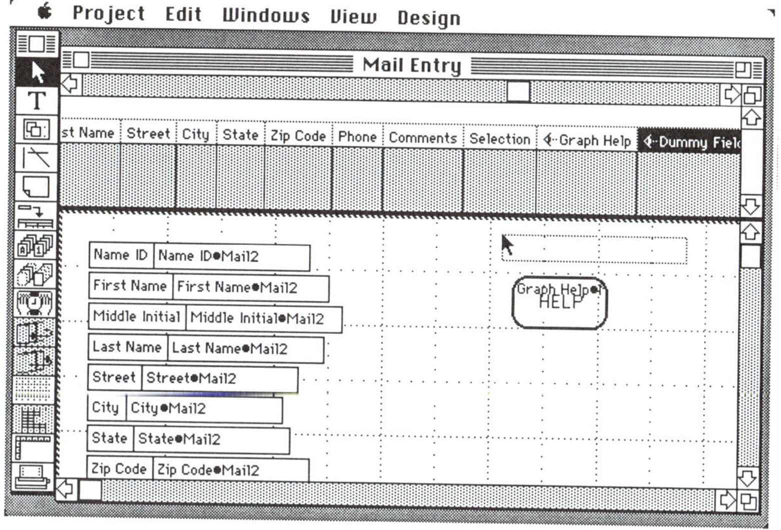

Figure 10-12 Placing the Dummy Field.

3. Move to Layout View and drag the Dummy Field onto the layout just above the Help button, but below the level of the Name ID field.

4. Use Display Options to set the Dummy Field as follows: Fill = None, Pen Size = minimum.

5. Next highlight all the Mail Entry fields except the Help button and the Dummy field. You can highlight the fields by dragging a box around them or by **Shift**-clicking.

6. Select Group from the Design menu.

   Now, when you enter data or browse through the fields, the cursor will move through the grouped fields first. When it leaves the group, it will encounter the Dummy field Pre-Processor and move on to the Mail ID field. Help will only be invoked when you click on the Help button with the mouse.

Final Touches to MultiMail

Now that you have entered the Mail Menu procedure and the help system, it is time to create Custom Menus. You can add any menus you wish, but you must add the Mail Menu view to the project before it is protected, or it won't do much. If you like, you can also add Mailing List Columns and Mail Entry to the Custom Menu. To run the Help screens as a stand-alone system, add Help to the Custom Menus as well.

> NOTE: Before you protect the project, Perform and Use the Mailing List Column view. Then close it. If you do not do so, it will not display anything when opened from the MultiMail menu. If you have not checked the Hide Windows

Menu checkbox, a Perform View option is available. Sometimes it is better to leave the Windows menu available, but then the views not included in the Custom Menus will be available through the Windows menu. This is often not desired.

1. Activate any view and enter the Layout View screen.
2. Select Custom Menus from the Design menu.
3. Click on Add New Title and fill in a menu name, for instance "MultiMail."

   Notice that the name MultiMail appears in the Menu Titles list.
4. Click on MultiMail to highlight it if it is not already highlighted.
5. Click on Add New Command.
6. Select Mail Menu from the list that appears. Click **OK**.

   Note that Mail Menu appears in the Command list.
7. Now add, in turn, Mailing List Columns, Mail Entry, and Help.
8. Click on the Hide Windows Menu checkbox.
9. Click **OK** to finish the Custom Menu definition.

   Finally, protect the application by selecting Protect from the Project menu and entering a password of your choice. We recommend using something you will be sure to remember at first (like the word, *Password* or *Sesame*). Once you have completed work on the project, change the password to something more private.

Congratulations! You have completed the first of the three tutorial applications. Play with the project in Protected mode. See what you might like to add to it. See what this application suggests to you about other uses you might have for dBASE Mac.

You should have a pretty good idea how to use dBASE Mac by now. In Chapter 11, you'll get a look at Transfer views and Foreign files. Then, in Chapter 12, you'll get a chance to look at a revamped Checkbook project.

Summary

Chapter 10 covers a lot of ground. It introduces the Procedural Interface and presents its major elements. Then it presents some procedures and explanations of them. Finally, modifying the Palette, Custom Menus, and Protecting projects are discussed.

Key information presented includes:

Programming dBASE Mac involves using special procedures that are invoked at different times and places within the application.

There are five basic kinds of procedure: Pre-Processor, Post-Processor, New Record, Write Record, and Delete Record.

Procedures can take place on a file, in a field, in a view, or in a VMFF.

The PI contains several key elements. These are: constants, variables, expressions, functions, and commands.

Local variables are valid only for the current procedure and can contain one- or two-dimensional arrays.

The main method for communicating with the user is through dialog boxes.

Dialog boxes can contain a variety of information including buttons, radiolists, check boxes, text edit boxes, fixed text, and fixed graphics.

You can use the Trace command to observe program flow and look for logical errors in the program. The Trace command will return certain error codes that can be looked up in the back of the dBASE Mac manual.

You can remove, change, or replace Palette icons.

You can create Custom Menus to control program flow. Custom menus take effect when a project is created.

To create a Protected project, open the Project menu, select Protect, and give the project a password. No one can modify the project without the password.

11

TRANSFER VIEWS AND FOREIGN FILES

Overview

Chapter 11 introduces the Transfer View, by which data can be moved from one file to another, with several types of modifications along the way. You can use Transfer Views in several ways—to create new files with Key field values derived from other fields in the source file, to move the values of a collection of single valued fields into one multivalued field or vice versa, to update values in records via addition or replacement, and more.

Foreign files are information sources from outside dBASE Mac. These data may be derived from word processors, spreadsheets, or other databases like dBASE III (and other IBM PC type databases) or Helix, Reflex, Omnis, and other Mac databases. In Chapter 11 you will learn the rules for importing foreign files.

Transfer View

The Transfer View is used for various purposes, all of which involve the movement, or transfer, of information from one file to another (or the modification and sending of information back to the original file). To use the Transfer View, you must have a Source file and a Destination file. The Source can use data from several files linked through a view hierarchy. The Destination file must be a single file.

Before you can begin a Transfer View, both files must exist. In some cases you will need to create a new file structure to act as Destination file. In other cases, particularly when using the Update function of the Transfer View, you may already have both files.

You already know how to create a new file, and you already know how to create a hierarchy. However, the layout of a Transfer View is very different from the layout of a Display View.

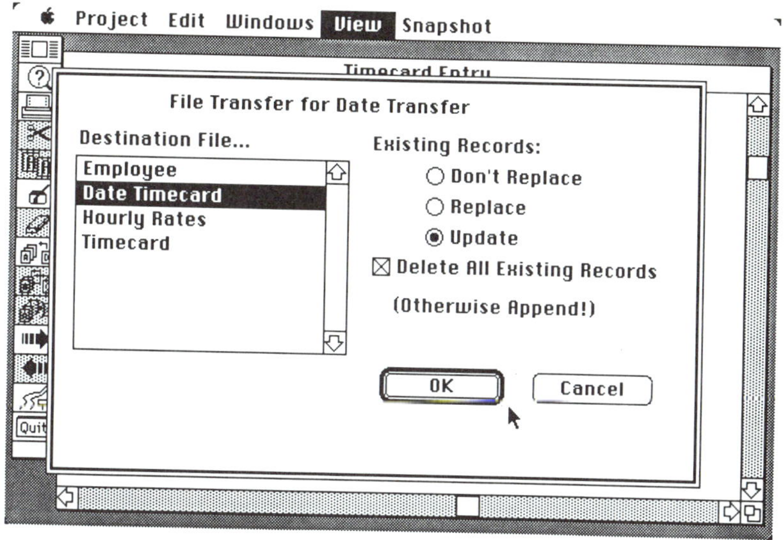

Figure 11-1 Transfer View Select Destination File Graphic.

When you select the Transfer View radio button on the New View... dialog box and click **OK**, a new dialog box appears. In the list box are all the available files. Select one file as the Destination file.

NOTE: You can even select the Source file as the Destination file if you wish to transfer information from one field to another.

On the right side of the Destination file selection dialog box are three radio buttons and a checkbox. These represent the different ways the Transfer View has of dealing with existing records in the Destination file.

Don't Replace If you select Don't Replace, the Transfer View skips any records in the Destination file that have the same Key field value as records in the Source file. No data are changed in those records, but new records will be created in the Destination file where no match is found.

Replace If you select Replace, the Transfer View will replace selected field contents for each record it encounters with the same Key field value. Unmatched Key field values create new records in the Destination file just as with Don't Replace.

Update If you select Update, the Transfer View will update selected field information in the Destination file based on the contents of the Source fields. Update actually offers three possible options that are available in the Transfer View Layout (see below).

Delete All Existing Records The single checkbox in the dialog box allows you to clear an entire file of existing records before the transfer takes place. If there are incorrect data in the Destination file, that need to be completely replaced by the data in the Source file, it may be a good idea to check the Delete All Existing Records checkbox.

NOTE: These options are preset. However, you can use processors in a Transfer View just as you can in a Display View. Use these processors to further refine the transfer process and/or create conditional transfers.

After you select the Destination file and the options for handling existing records, click **OK** to move to the Define Hierarchy screen. The Transfer View hierarchy is created exactly like any Display View hierarchy.

TIP: You can choose Duplicate View to use an existing hierarchy in a Transfer View. So if you have a view that uses a complex hierarchy, you can select Duplicate View from the View menu and select the Transfer View radio button. You then proceed normally with the Destination file definition dialog, but when you click **OK**, the hierarchy will be a duplicate of the original view hierarchy. (If you do duplicate a view, remember that you also duplicate the procedures attached to that view and to its fields. You may need to **Clear** these processors before continuing with the transfer).

The Transfer View Layout

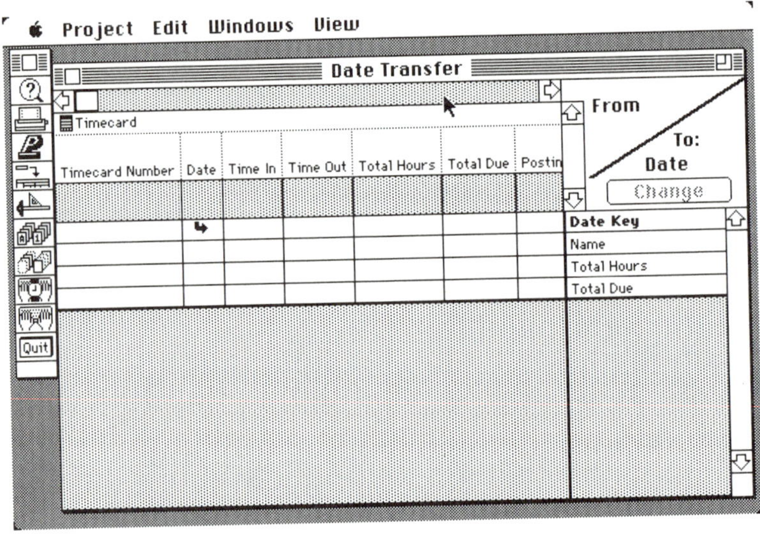

Figure 11-2 Transfer Layout View Graphic.

When you select the Layout icon from the Palette, or Layout View from the View menu, you move to the Transfer View layout screen.

Unlike the Display View layout, the Transfer View is not terribly complex. It consists of a grid made up of Source fields in the columns and Destination fields in the rows. A grid is formed by the intersections of Source and Destination fields.

Click in any position in the grid to select the fields that determine the transfer. An arrow appears in the grid box signifying the transfer from Source field to Destination field. No arrow will appear if the two files are incompatible. For instance, you couldn't transfer text information into a Number field or a Date field, nor could you transfer information between a Graphics field and any other kind. Also, you can't transfer Formula or Memory fields. In addition to the obvious compatibility rules governed by data types, several other rules govern the Transfer View:

Table 11-1 Transferring Data in Transfer View.

Source Field	Destination Field
Single valued	Single valued Multivalued
Multivalued	Multivalued Key field
Several single valued	Multivalued Key Field Single valued (foreign)

NOTE: When transferring several single valued fields to one Destination field, the effect depends on the type of Destination field. If you transfer several single valued fields to a Key field, a new record is created for each unique single field value. When transferring several single valued fields to a multivalued field, the values in the single valued fields are appended to the multivalued field. When transferring several single valued fields to one single valued field, a new record is created for each single field value in the Source file (this only operates when transferring to a foreign text file).

If you selected Update when choosing the Destination file, you can select any Destination field on the layout, then click the Change button to open the Update options dialog.

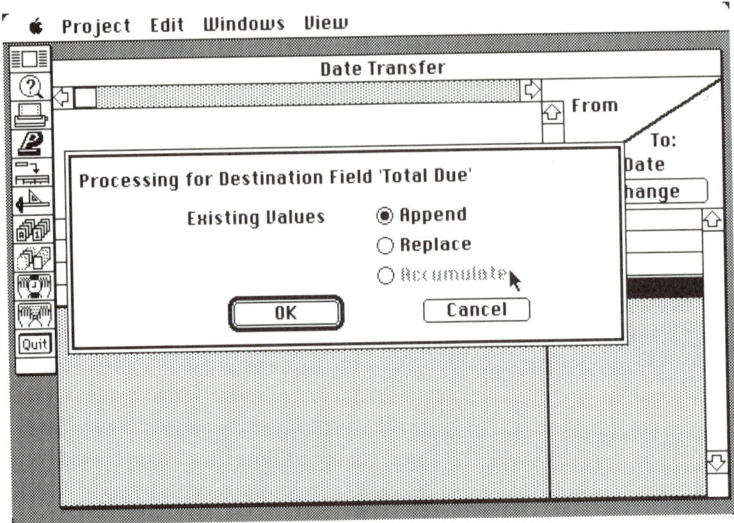

Figure 11-3 Update Options Dialog Graphic.

Append Choosing the Append option adds all Source field values as new occurrences within a multivalued field array. If the Destination field is not multivalued, Append is dimmed and not available.

Replace Replace is the default selection. Choosing Replace instructs the Transfer View to replace all Destination field values with Source field values.

Accumulate Choosing Accumulate will add values from the Source field to the current value in the Destination field. You can only select Accumulate if the Destination field is a single valued Numeric Data field.

You might use Append to add new occurrences to a multivalued set. For instance, if another worker had entered new data into a file compatible with your master file, you could use the Transfer View with Update and Append active to add occurrences to a Set in the master file. You might use Accumulate the same way, to take compatible file information and add results. For instance, if you have people compiling separate monthly reports, use the Transfer View with Update and Accumulate to prepare a yearly report from the monthly records. Those already familiar with batch processing procedures should feel comfortable with these options.

To execute the Transfer View, Perform and Use the view. The program will display a dialog box showing the number of records processed. If at any time you wish to pause or cancel the transfer, click the **Suspend** button. You will then be given the option to **Resume** or **Cancel** the transfer.

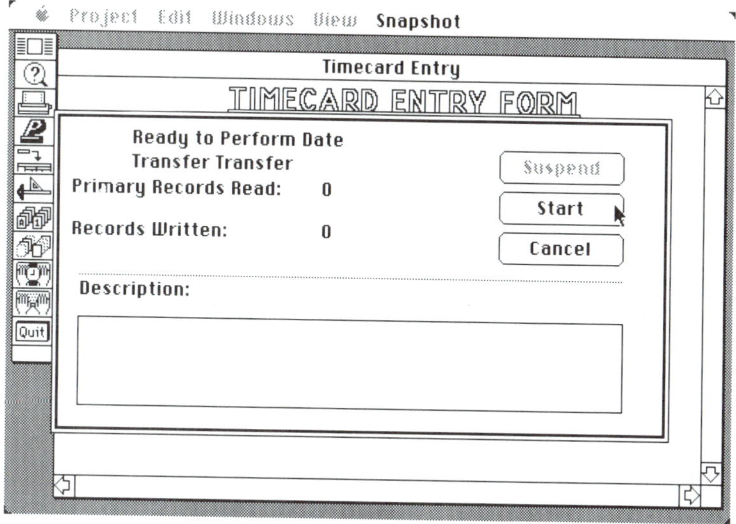

Figure 11-4 Transfer Perform Dialog Graphic.

NOTE: You can also select Use View from the View menu. Click **Start** to begin the transfer if you selected Use View instead of Perform and Use View.

You can attach a view Pre-Processor or Post-Processor to a Transfer View. These procedures are designed to operate as they normally would in any other view.

WARNING: In dBASE Mac, Version 1.0, there is a bug that causes Post-Processors attached to Transfer Views to execute twice. If you must use a Post-Processor attached to a Transfer View, you will need to create it in such a way as to avoid data conflicts due to this.

TIP: File procedures operate in Transfer Views. This means that if a Post-Processor is attached to a field at the file level, it will execute during the processing of a Transfer View. Likewise, a New, Write, or Delete Record procedure attached to a file (through the Change File dialog) will also execute. You can control some of the functions of the transfer by using these kinds of procedures. The drawback is that they must be at the file level. You cannot create view level procedures to execute during a transfer. You can, however, create sorts and selections on a Transfer View. You'll see an example of a selection on a Transfer View later in the chapter.

Transfer View—A Date Timecard File

Suppose you want to keep the information in the Timecard Project in a special file that contains daily totals. You can create reports to do daily totals, but there are some advantages you can gain from creating a special file with the Date as Key field, and other information in multivalued fields. With the Transfer View it's easy to create such a file.

First create the Date Timecard file:

1. Select New. . . from the DataFile menu.
2. Click **OK** to create a new dBASE Mac type file.
3. Type "Date Timecard" to name the file.
4. Click **Save**.
5. Type "Date Key" to name the Key field.
6. Select Date from the Data Type: pop-up.
7. The Order checkbox should be checked.
8. Click **Save**.

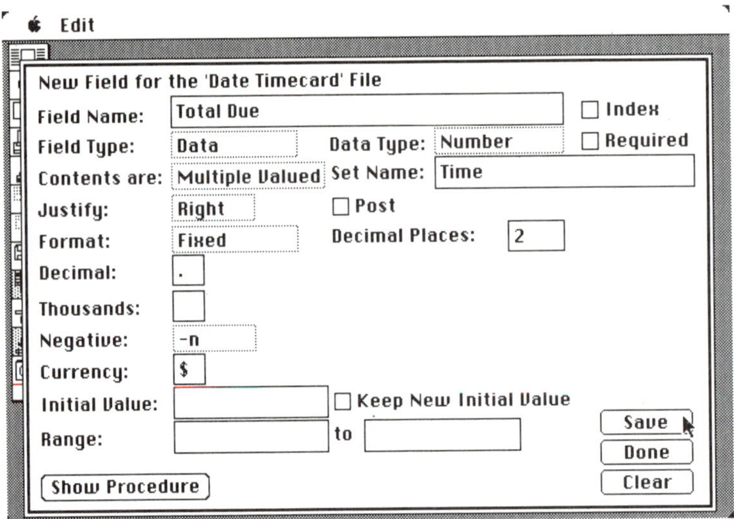

Figure 11-5 Multivalued Field in Time Set Graphic.

9. Now enter a field called Name. It should be multivalued in a Set called Time. Click **Save** when you have defined the Set name.
10. Add a Numeric field called Total Hours, zero decimal places, multivalued in the Time set.

11. Add a Numeric currency field called Total Due, multivalued in the Time set.

12. To make things interesting, add a field called Daily Total. This should be a Numeric currency Formula field.

13. Click Show Formula and enter the following formula:

```
SUM({Total Due•Date Timecard})
```

14. Click **OK** to close the formula dialog and then click **Save** to save the file.

15. Click **Done** to return to the Structure Window.

16. Estimate the number of records. Enter a small number for now. Enter 10 and click **OK**.

Now you have created the Destination file for the Transfer View. Next you will duplicate the Timecard Entry view and prepare to perform the transfer:

1. Activate the Timecard Entry view by selecting it from the Windows menu.

2. Choose Duplicate View from the View menu.

3. Type "Date Transfer" to name the view.

4. Click on the Transfer View radio button. (Be sure the Timecard file is the Root File—it should appear in the list box labeled Root File.) Click **OK**.

5. Next Choose a Destination file (select Date Timecard from the list in the box labelled Destination File . . .).

   Since there are no records yet in the Date Timecard file, it won't matter what selections you make for handling existing records. But to allow the names and totals to add to the multivalued fields in Date Timecard, you need to select Update (and later Append).

6. Select Update. You might also select Delete All Existing Records to clear the file each time you use the Tranfer.

7. When you click **OK**, you will move to the hierarchy screen. The hierarchy from the Timecard Entry view is reproduced here. You shouldn't have to make any modifications.

8. Finally select Layout View from the View menu or the Palette.

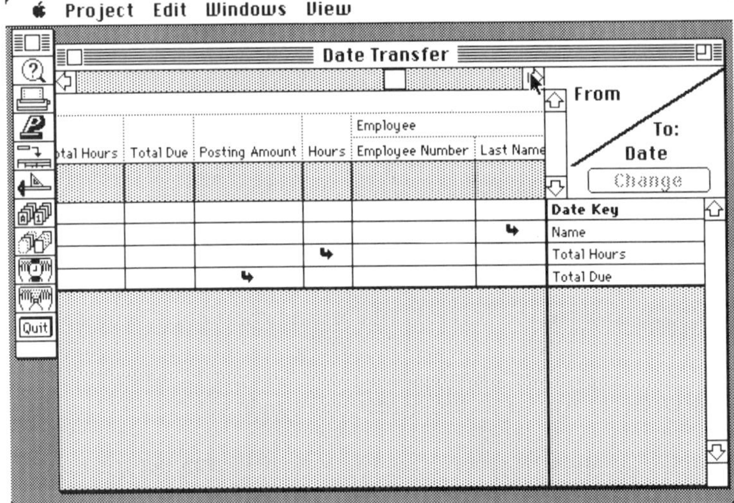

Figure 11-6 Transfer Layout for Date Timecard Graphic.

9. Click in the grid box that links Date in the Timecard file and Date Key in the Date Timecard file.
10. Click in the intersection box that links Last Name with Name, Total Hours with Total Hours, and Posting Amount with Total Due.
11. Now click once on Name under the Destination column. The **Change** button should change from grey to black.
12. Click **Change**.
13. Select Append.
14. Repeat steps 11 through 13 for the Total Hours and Total Due fields.
15. That completes the Layout. Perform and Use the view to complete the transfer.

Using the Date Transfer File

Because totals from each Timecard record are now contained in daily multivalued fields, you can perform statistical analysis on the data. It is also easier to write procedures that analyze records from specific time periods. To retrieve daily statistical information is as easy as creating view fields that evaluate the multivalued field in question. For instance a Formula field created in the view to perform a standard deviation test on the number of hours worked by each employee would contain the following simple formula:

```
STD({Total Due•Date Timecard})
```

This kind of statistical work can only be performed on a multivalued field or a local variable array.

To evaluate the information for a particular time period longer than one day, you might write a longer procedure. The following procedure will first prompt you for the dates, then will evaluate the information in the file and return the results to specific files.

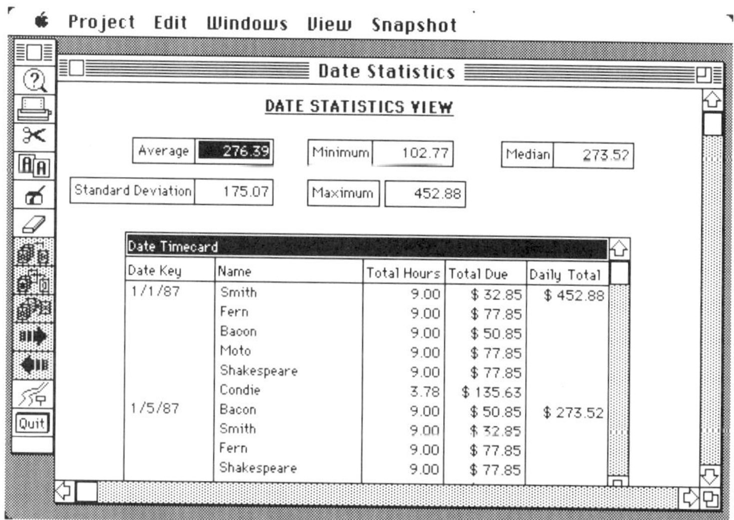

Figure 11-7 Date Statistics Column View Graphic.

- To begin, you will need to create a new Columnar view using the Date Timecard file as the Root File.
- Call the view "Date Statistics"
- Add all the Date Timecard fields to the hierarchy.
- Move to the Structure Window and click once on the Globals file.
- Create two Global Memory fields called Criterion and Criterion1. Make them Date fields.
- Now create a Numeric Global Memory field for each statistical function you wish to test: Average, Standard Deviation, Minimum, Maximum, Median, and so on. These should be Numeric currency type Memory fields.
- Back at the Define Hierarchy screen for the Date Statistics view, add Criterion and Criterion1 to the hierarchy. Remember, you need to open the Path pop-up and select Globals to add Global Memory fields to the hierarchy.
- Now add each statistical Global Memory field to the hierarchy.
- Open the Define Selections screen, click once on the Date Timecard title bar, and enter the following selection rule:

```
{Date Key•Date Timecard} ≥ {Criterion•Globals} AND {Date
Key•Date Timecard} ≤ {Criterion1•Globals}
```

- Move to Layout View and create form elements at the top of the screen for each statistical function. Then, below them, drag the Date Timecard fields down as columns (remember, you can highlight all the Date Timecard fields by clicking on the title bar, then **Command**-clicking).

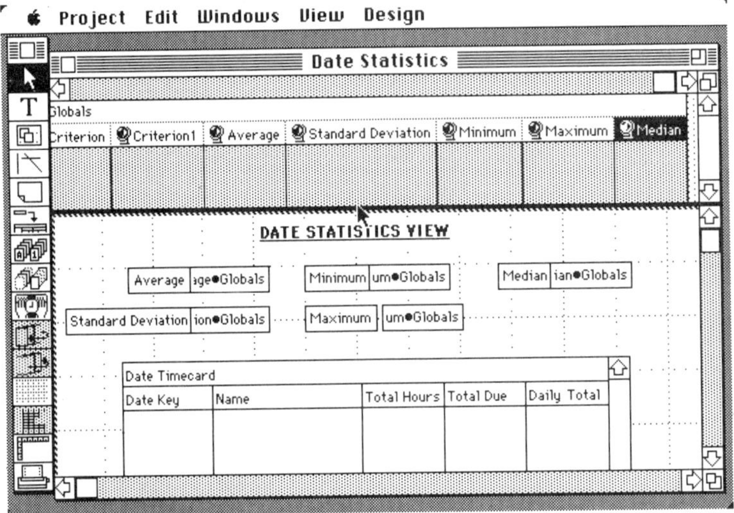

Figure 11-8 Date Statistics Layout.

- Now Duplicate the Date Statistics view twice. Call the first copy "Do Statistics" and the second "Print Statistics".
- In the Print Statistics view, open Layout View and recreate the view you created for Date Statistics (with the memory field form elements and the Date Timecard columns).

All other features of the Print Statistics view will be the same as those of the Date Statistics view, but you might consider adding some other touches. For instance, you can add automatic page numbering and the current date to the top of the report using the **Option-Shift-P** and **Option-Shift-D** combinations inside a Fixed Text element on the layout (see Figure 11-9).

- Move to the Do Statistics view, and activate the Layout View.
- Drag the Date Key field onto the layout as a form element. Shrink the Date Key field to its minimum size and, if you wish, hide it beneath a blank graphic as you did before in the MultiMail project.

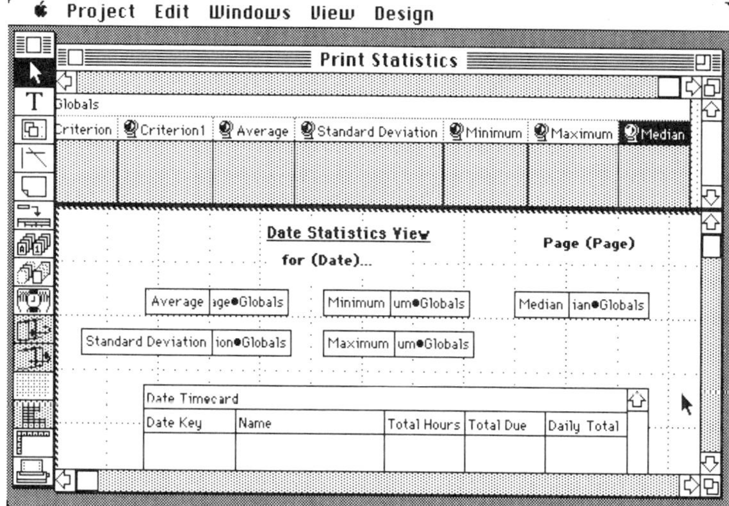

Figure 11-9 Print Statistics Layout.

- Return to the Define Hierarchy screen.
- Select Show View Procedure and enter the following Pre-Processor:

```
\** Do Statistics Pre-Processor-Set Date Range **\
LOOP
  ALERT("In the dialog box that follows, please enter the
  beginning date and the ending date for the period you wish
  to examine. Click Cancel to exit",STOP)
 LOOP
  DIALOG 50,100,350,400
   BUTTON 1,225,20,245,130,"OK"
   BUTTON 2,225,170,245,280,"Cancel"
   FIXEDTEXT 20,25,40,380,"DATE STATISTICS"
   FIXEDTEXT 60,55,75,380,"Enter Beginning Date
(mm\dd\yy):"
   EDITTEXT 1, 90,55,110,155,""
  FIXEDTEXT 120,55,140,380,""Enter Ending Date
(mm\dd\yy):"
   EDITTEXT 2, 150,55,170,155,""
 END
  n1 = INTERNAL(TEXTVALUE(1),{Date Key•Date Timecard})
 e1 = ERROR
  n2 = INTERNAL(TEXTVALUE(2),{Date Key•Date Timecard})
 e2 = ERROR
 WHEN (e2 = 0 AND e1 = 0) OR BUTTONVALUE(2)
  LEAVE
```

```
   ALERT("An invalid date has been entered. Please re-
enter.",STOP)
 END
WHEN BUTTONVALUE(2) LEAVE
 {Criterion•Globals} = n1
 {Criterion1•Globals} = n2
 PERFORM("Date Statistics",INIT,MODAL)
END
SETNEXTVIEW("Timecard Entry")
EXIT
```

- When you have finished entering the procedure, check it with the **Verify** button, then click **OK** when it is all right.

This procedure allows you to set a starting and an ending date for statistical analysis of the daily timecard data. It also shows an example of how to use the INTERNAL command to set the value of a text entry to the format of an existing field. In this case, the date entered in the dialog box is given the format of the Date Key field using the INTERNAL command. Without the format, dBASE Mac would treat the entry as simple text, but formatted, it is treated as a date field.

In the next steps, an error-checking routine determines if the entries are valid dates. If they are not, an Alert box informs the user, and the loop repeats. Otherwise the procedure continues by setting the Global Memory fields equal to the formatted variables, then performing the Date Statistics view.

- Before running this procedure, you need to return to the Date Statistics view. You should be at the Define Hierarchy screen.
- In the hierarchy, choose the statistical field that first appears on your layout (this will be the one at the top left of the layout screen). In our example, the first field is Average.
- Double-click the statistical field and then click on the Show Procedure button.
- Enter the following Pre-Processor:

```
\** Do Statistics-Average field Pre-Processor **\
i = 1
LOOP
 T[i] = {Daily Total•Date Timecard}
 i = i +1
WHEN  ENDOF ({Date Timecard})
 LEAVE
 NEXTBROWSE({Date Key•Date Timecard})
END
{Average•Globals} = AVG(T)
{Standard Deviation•Globals} = STD(T)
{Maximum•Globals} = MAX(T)
{Minimum•Globals} = MIN(T)
{Median•Globals} = MED(T)
```

This Pre-Processor actually computes the necessary statistics and assigns them to the Globals Memory fields.

- When you have completed the procedure, click **Verify** to check the results, then click **OK** when you are sure that everything is all right.
- Click **Done**.
- Finally, click the Show View Procedure button.
- Enter the following Post-Processor:

```
\Do Statistics Post-Processor-Print Report? **\
DIALOG 100,100,250,400
  BUTTON 1,125,20,145,130,"Yes"
  BUTTON 2,125,170,145,280,"No"
 FIXEDTEXT 20,25,40,380,"PRINT REPORT?"
END
IF BUTTONVALUE(1) THEN
  PRINT("Print Statistics")
ELSE
 EXIT
END
```

- Finally, return to the Do Statistics view and Use the view.

Turn Trace On to check the flow of the procedures. Also, remember that you can prevent a procedure from executing by holding **Option** and **Shift** down together when you perform an operation that would normally call the procedure. To interrupt an already running procedure, type **Command** and the period key.

When you Perform this view, you will enter a beginning and ending date. The procedure will then Perform Date Statistics, selecting the records that occur within these dates. The Pre Processor on the first statistical field will compile the totals for each record into local array variable T. Then the statistical fields you created are equated with statistical calculations on the array. Finally, when you exit the Date Statistics view, you may choose to print the report or return to Do Statistics to choose another time period.

You may find other uses of the Date Statistics type of view, and many other ways to use the Transfer View. This example only looks at pay amounts. You might also modify the procedures to perform statistics on the hours worked as well.

> TIP: Another use of the Transfer View occurs when you want to clear a file of all records. Simply make the same file the Source and Destination of a Transfer View and, on the layout, select the intersection of Key field to Key field. Check the Delete All Existing Records checkbox and Perform the transfer. Within seconds you will have an empty file.

Deleting Selected Records

Here's another way to use the Transfer View. Suppose you want to delete specific records based on some selection criteria. There are several ways to do this, including writing a complex Post-Processor on a Transfer View or deleting records one at a time. But a simple way to delete selected records involves using a Duplicate File and a Transfer View.

Removing "B" from the Database

Basically, the technique involves duplicating the file, then transferring the records you want to keep to the duplicate file. Then you transfer those records back to the original file, using the Delete All Existing Records option first. Here is a step-by-step approach to the procedure:

- Duplicate the file that contains the records you want to delete. Don't duplicate the records. There is a checkbox that allows you to duplicate records. Be sure it is not checked.
- Open the duplicate file (using Open from the DataFile menu) to add it to the Structure Window.
- Create a Transfer View with the original file as the Source file and the duplicate file as the Destination file.
- Create a one-to-one transfer on the layout—Key field to Key field, and so on.
- Create selection criteria on the Transfer View that selects the records you want to *keep*. For instance, if you want to delete all the records where the last name begins with a letter greater than M, your selection

criterion should read 'Last Name < N" because those are the records you want to keep.

- Now perform the transfer with the Replace option on (and optionally with the Delete All Existing Records checked). The duplicate file will now contain only the records you want to keep.
- Create another Transfer View, this time with the duplicate file as the Source and the original file as the Destination.
- Create a one-to-one field layout, use Replace, and check the Delete All Existing Records box.

NOTE: This Transfer View is going to erase all the existing records in your original file. It might be a good idea to have a backup in case you make a mistake or something happens during the tranfer.

- Now transfer from the duplicate file to the original. The records you didn't want will be gone.

Although it seems somewhat complicated, in reality this doesn't take very long, and it works very well. You could even automate it all from a procedure very simply.

→ That concludes the Timecard Project.

Another common use of the Transfer View is in batch processing.

Batch Processing—An Inventory Example

Batch processing is a method by which people in different places can process data for the same file separately, then add the new data to the existing file. It is also a safe way to enter or modify data for a master file before incorporating it. Batch processing also allows specific information from different files to be added to a master file.

Inventory files often have to be updated frequently. New purchase orders are received and inventory restocked, while simultaneously inventory is going out in the form of sales. Although you won't create such an inventory file in this Tutorial, imagine the way you might use a Transfer View to update inventories from purchase orders and invoices:

Acme Widgets has just entered the world of dBASE Mac. They have happily installed a Mac in the Sales Office, the Purchasing Department, and the Stock Room.

In the Sales Office, Julie, the Sales Manager processes all the daily invoices. She enters the usual data—customer, part number, amount, puchase price, taxes. She might use Define Selections to create a subset of the Invoices file that just displays today's list. Then she might use a Transfer View to create a new file containing just those invoices. Since she probably does this every day, the Transfer View will be set up to erase all existing records first.

Meanwhile, in the Purchasing Department, Omar marks existing Purchase Orders as received. He selects all outstanding purchase orders and marks the ones that have been received today. Omar creates a new, selected daily Purchase Order file with a Transfer View similar to Julie's.

Bob heads the Stock Room. Bright and early in the morning he receives the Purchase Order and Invoice that Omar and Julie updated yesterday. He logs in the new inventory items, checking them against the Purchase Order information received from Omar. He makes any corrections, then runs a simple Transfer View to update the master inventory list from the Purchase Order file, and another from the Invoices file.

Using the Purchase Order file as a Source file and the Inventory file as the Destination, Bob selects the Update option. He then selects the grid box that links Quantity Received with Quantity On Hand. Clicking the Change button, he selects the Accumulate option. To process the records correctly, he selects the grid box that links Item Number from the Purchase Order file with Item Number in the Inventory (the Key field). For each matching Item Number, the Quantity Received will be added to the Quantity On Hand.

Then, using the Invoices file as a Source file and the Inventory file again as the Destination file, Bob selects the Update option, the grid box that links Quantity Sold with Quantity On Hand. In this case, a Pre-Processor on the Quantity Sold field sets it to a negative number, that is {Quantity Sold•Invoices} = – {Quantity Sold•Invoices}. Selecting the Accumulate option causes the Quantity Sold to be subtracted from the Quantity On Hand. Linking Item Number from the Invoices file and Item Number from the Inventory file completes the transfer layout.

Bob sends the updated inventory up to Julie who now has accurate information about the current status of each item. He runs another copy over to Omar along with an updated copy of the Purchase Orders file. Omar now uses a Transfer View to update any changes Bob may have made to the Purchase Order file. Then he can use the updated inventory file to examine possible re-orders needed. He can also compare yesterday's Purchase Orders with Bob's corrections to find any shortages or overages in yesterday's orders.

This example is a bit fanciful and simplistic, but it illustrates a possible use of batch processing and Transfer View updating.

Foreign Files

Sometimes you may wish to use information originally entered in another program, or you may wish to send data from dBASE Mac to another program. dBASE Mac calls such files foreign text files. You may import information from spreadsheets, word processors, or other databases using foreign text file structures. You can also export data from dBASE Mac to these types of fields. You can use foreign files in projects the same way you would use a dBASE Mac file, with some limitations (see below).

You may already have some data from another application that you wish to import into dBASE Mac but, in case you don't, you will have the opportunity to export some of the data from this Tutorial to a foreign file. Then you can use that data to import back into dBASE Mac. When you are finished with the Tutorial, you may wish to try importing your own data.

There are three ways to export data from dBASE Mac to a foreign text file: (1) Use the Export command under the DataFile menu, (2) Use a Transfer View, (3) Use the

Print to Disk command in a Column view or a Custom view with only columnar elements. The most versatile method is to use the Transfer View, but often the simple Export or Print to Disk options will perform admirably. In the case of the Transfer View, you will have to create a special foreign text file structure. In the case of the Export command, the structure is created automatically, and in the case of the Print to Disk option, no structure is needed.

There are two ways to import data from a foreign text file into a form dBASE Mac can use: (1) Use a Transfer View, or (2) Use the Import command under the DataFile menu. In either case you will need to create a foreign text file structure. Creating a foreign text file structure is much the same as creating a dBASE Mac file, but there are some differences.

Before you begin to create a foreign file, you must understand some of the structural elements in a database file.

Record Terminator Records are usually handled internally in dBASE Mac, but foreign files use special characters called Record Terminators. The Record Terminator is a character that is used to mark the end of a particular record. Usually the Record Terminator is a Carriage Return (**Return** on the keyboard). However the Record Terminator can also be a single blank line (single-line feed), a Carriage Return (CR) followed by a blank line (CR followed by line feed), or a blank line followed by a Carriage Return (single-line feed followed by CR).

Field Size There are two ways dBASE Mac can work with the size of a field. Some fields are fixed in length. These are called Fixed Length Fields. For instance, the Name field in a foreign file may be always fifteen characters long. In this case, dBASE Mac will always know where the field begins and ends. Other fields may be of varying lengths. These are called Variable Length Fields. Like the Record Terminator, Variable Length Fields use a Field Terminator. In dBASE Mac foreign files, you can use one of six characters to terminate a Variable Length Field: comma (,), slash (/), period (.), colon (:), tab, or space.

dBASE Mac foreign files are not as versatile as normal dBASE Mac fields. They can't contain graphics or multivalued fields. As a consequence, you can't have a two-way relationship between a foreign file and another file in dBASE Mac because pointer fields are multivalued. You can, however, create a one-way relationship between the foreign file and a dBASE Mac file.

Creating a Foreign File Structure for Export

To continue with this section, load the Checkbook Project.

Suppose you want to take a look at your financial information in a spreadsheet like Excel, and combine the information from your checkbook with some other data you already had in the spreadsheet. The first step in exporting the data is to create a foreign text file structure for the dBASE Mac data. Although this could be more easily accomplished using the Export command, it is important to know how to create the structure yourself, so for this example we'll use the "manual" method.

To create a foreign structure:

1. First go to the Structure Window by selecting Structure Window from the Windows menu.

2. Select New. . . from the DataFile menu.

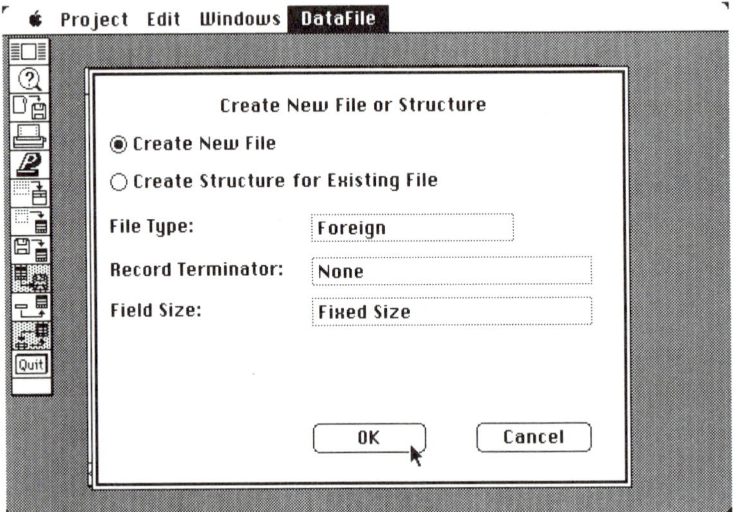

Figure 11-10 Create New File Dialog for Foreign Graphic.

3. On the Create New File Structure dialog, select Create New File, then open the File Type: pop-up and select Foreign.

   The default selections for Record Terminator and Field Size are None and Fixed Size. Notice that these are both in pop-up menus.

4. Select Variable Size, Delimited from the Field Size: pop-up.

5. Look at the options in the Record Terminator and Field Delimiter pop-ups. Accept the default settings of Carriage Return and Comma (,).

NOTE: Excel uses Tabs as field terminators, but many programs use commas.

6. Click **OK**.

7. Name the file "Text Out" and click **Save**.

   A field definition dialog box appears. This is the Record Number field. It is the Key field for the foreign file. You can change the name of this field if you wish, but otherwise you should leave it unchanged.

NOTE: The Record Number field of a foreign file has to be a Numeric Key field.

Since the Transaction Number field (the Key field) is an Auto Sequencing field, the values in the Record Number field should be the same as those in the Transaction Number field.

8. Rename the Record Number field by typing "Transaction Number", then save the field definition by clicking **Save**.

The next field definition dialog appears. Now you will define the rest of the fields from the Checkbook file.

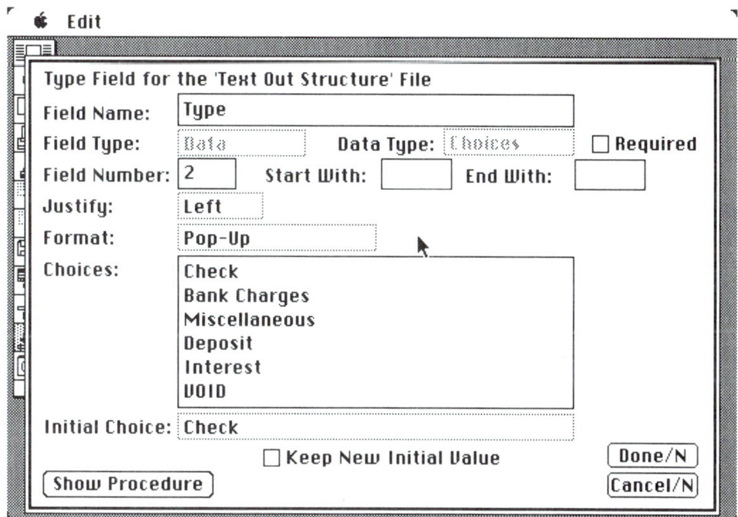

Figure 11-11 Foreign Field Definition Screen.

9. Name the next field Type. Leave it set to Data and Text.

NOTE: You could create a Choices field here, and add the same choices that you had in the original Type field. If you do so, you will be able to use the foreign text file in a Form view the same way you use the normal dBASE Mac file. However, remember that foreign files cannot be multivalued or contain graphics. Otherwise, the full range of data types is available.

Notice the three new boxes beneath the Field Type and Data Type pop-ups. These are Field Number, Start With, and End With.

The Field Number: box must contain a unique number to represent the position of the field within the foreign file. You can change the Field Number if you wish, but dBASE Mac automatically increments the number for each field. It is therefore preferable to organize your fields before creating the field definitions. Then you enter the fields in order without having to modify the Field Number. When creating a file definition for an existing file, the Field Number identifies the position occupied by the data for that field as determined by the delimiter character.

You may need to define some initial characters to fit the format of an outside program. Start With: and End With: allow you to define characters that will be placed before and after every entry to that field. These characters appear in the written file only. They are added to the field data when the record is written, and stripped off when it is read by dBASE Mac. If dBASE Mac encounters the End With character before the end of the data in a field, that field will be truncated, and the rest of the field data will be ignored.

10. Save the Type field without changing anything.
11. Enter the following field definitions:

Name	Type	Field Number
Date	Date	2
Check # (Decimal Places = 0)	Number	3
Description	Text	4
Check Amount (Currency = $)	Number	5
Deposit Amount (Currency = $)	Number	6
Tax (No/Yes)	Logical	7

12. Click **Done**, to return to the Structure Window. (Notice that you don't have to estimate the file size. dBASE Mac automatically creates space for the file.)

Back on the Structure Window, you should see the Text Out Structure you just created. You could create a Form view and manually enter data into this file, but you created it to receive the data already contained in Checkbook. Therefore, you will use a Transfer View to send the data over.

Creating a Transfer View to a Foreign File Structure

You've already created Transfer Views earlier in this chapter. The one you will create now is very simple:

1. Click once on the Checkbook file to highlight it.
2. Select New View. . . from the Windows menu.
3. Name the view Check Transfer.
4. Select the Transfer radio button.
5. To save time, click the Quick Create checkbox.
6. Select Text Out Structure as the Destination file.
7. Select Replace and check the Delete All Existing Records checkbox.

   You want to delete existing records because you may use this Transfer View periodically to send new data from the Checkbook file to the spreadsheet (or any other outside file). Remember that you can use sorts and selections to prepare the data for the Transfer View. You won't always be sending all the data from the file.

WARNING: If you check the Delete All Existing Records checkbox, be sure you have designated the right Source and Destination files. You could end up deleting all your records if you are not careful. The best way to prevent such disasters is to keep current backups of your data.

8. Click **OK.**

   Because you selected a Quick Create view, you won't have to define the hierarchy. The program moves directly to the Transfer View layout screen.

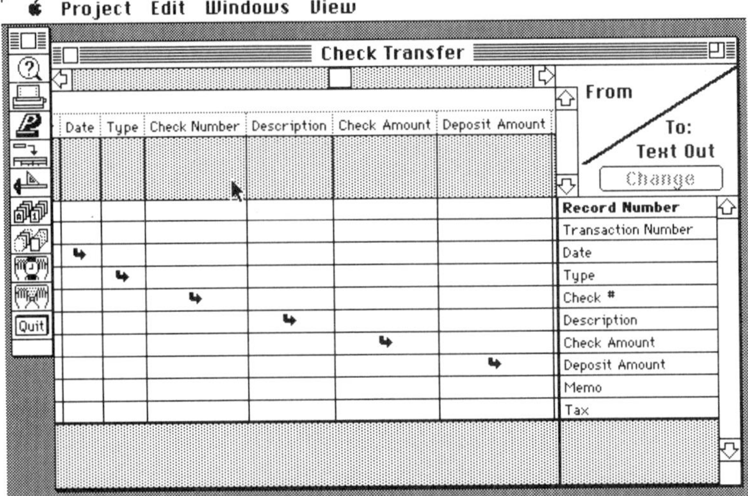

Figure 11-12 Layout Screen Graphic.

9. Lay out the transfer. Click the intersections between Type and Type, Date and Date, Check Number and Check #, Description and Description, Check Amount and Check Amount, Deposit Amount and Deposit Amount, and Tax and Tax. You need not click the intersection between Transaction Number and Transaction Number.

   You may scroll the hierarchy to select many of the fields. Use the scroll bar at the top of the screen to move the hidden parts of the hierarchy into view.

10. Perform and Use the view to send the data to the foreign structure. If you want to pause during the transfer, click **Suspend**. If you want to cancel the operation, click **Suspend** and then **Cancel**. Otherwise, click **Resume** to continue.

Now you have a foreign text file with data from the Checkbook. You can create a view to examine the records in the new file if you wish. Or you can exit the program and try experimenting with importing the text data into one of your other programs.

The export procedure you just performed was somewhat lengthy. Now, for contrast, see how easy the Export command is:

1. Click once on the Checkbook file in the Structure Window.

2. Select Export from the DataFile menu.

3. This time, use the default settings of Carriage Return and Tab. Click OK.

4. Name the file "Text Out-2".

5. When you click **OK**, dBASE Mac will create a file structure for the foreign file automatically.

6. Now click Start to begin the export of the records.

TIP: If you click **Cancel** at this point, the records will not be exported, but the file structure will appear in the Structure Window. As you will see, there may be times when you will want to back out of the Export procedure here.

Now use a word processor to examine the two text files, Text Out and Text Out-2. You will see an interesting distinction. Text Out, which was created with a Transfer View, is in Key field order. If you had defined sort criteria for the Transfer View, the records would be in sorted order. On the other hand, the Text Out-2 file, which was created with the Export command, is in seemingly random order. That is because they are output in the order that dBASE Mac uses to keep them internally (technically in hash order).

Because you may prefer to have the records output in a controlled order, you may wish to use Export to create the file structure, then use a Transfer View to actually transfer the records.

Another reason to use a Transfer View has to do with multivalued fields. The Export command only exports the first value of a multivalued field, but with a Transfer View you can control the transfer to create new records for multivalued fields.

NOTE: Text files are ASCII standard files. They can be read and imported by a great variety of programs, not only on the Macintosh, but on IBM PCs and other systems. You should be able to import the data into word processors, text-based desk accessories like Notepad+ (part of Borland's Sidekick), or MockWrite. You should also be able to use this data with spreadsheets and other databases. With the Apple File Exchange, you should be able to convert a variety of file types between the Mac and other program environments.

Finally, take a look at the third kind of export—the Print to Disk command.

1. Open the Cash Flow view you created in Chapter 9.

2. Select Print to Disk from the Project menu.

3. Name the output file. Call it "Cash.txt"

4. dBASE Mac will Perform the view if necessary, then output the records.

If you examine the resulting text file, you will find that the records have been output with a Tab for the Field Delimiter and a Carriage Return as a Record Terminator. The records will be in sorted order, and will correspond with any selections in place on the view. Multivalued fields, if present, will display the same way they do in the Column view. In fact, the text file created with Print to Disk is pretty much a duplication of the Column view.

Importing Foreign Text Data into dBASE Mac

NOTE: For the next exercise you will need a word processor or other program that can edit an ASCII document.

Now suppose the file you just created was actually created by another application. You want to import the information from the Text Out file. You can import data into dBASE Mac by creating a new foreign text file structure just as you did in the previous section. You can then import records to a dBASE Mac file using Import from the DataFile menu, or by using a Transfer View.

The quickest way to create a file structure for an existing text file is by creating a Header Record in the text file itself. The only requirement is that the Field Length be set to Variable.

Before you create the dBASE Mac foreign file structure, you need to create the Header Record in the text file you just created. One way to do this is to open the text file data in a word processor or other program that can edit ASCII files. Most word-based programs on the Mac can open ASCII files, as can many programs on the IBM PC.

- If you are still in dBASE Mac, Quit the program and Save changes.

Look on the desktop in your dBASE Mac folder. You should see two new icons—Text Out Structure and a document icon called Text Out. The document icon is the one you will open with your word processor or other program.

- In some cases, double-clicking the Text Out document icon will load the appropriate application.
- If not, load the application you wish to use to edit the file, then Open the Text Out file using the application's procedures.

Once you load Text Out, you should see the Checkbook records:

```
1,Deposit,01\01\87,,Initial  Deposit,,$  1000.00,False
2,Check,01\02\87,1,Nick's    Market,$   25.66,,False
3, Check,01\02\87,2,Sam's    Paper Supply,$     34.92,,False
```

. . . and so on.

Notice that the logical fields display as True or False.

Now you will enter the Header Record. Header Records indicate to dBASE Mac the field type and field name to create for each field position. Use special characters to designate the field type:

Character	Data Type
None	Text
#	Number
@	Date

!	Time
~	Logical

NOTE: You can't create a Header Record to import Graphics or Choices data types. If you wish to create a foriegn file structure that contains Choices fields, you will have to create the structure manually (see section above). Foreign files can't contain Graphics fields.

- To create a Header Record in the Text Out file, first make a space at the top of the file by positioning the cursor on the first character of the first line. Press Return to make a new line and place the cursor on it.
- Type the following information:

```
#TransNum,Type,@Date,#ChkNum,Description,#ChkAmt,
#DepAmt,~Tax
```

- Now **Save** the file and exit the text editing program.
- Reload the Checkbook Project.

To create the foreign file structure:

1. From the Structure Window select New... from the DataFile menu.
2. Click the Create Structure for Existing File radio button.

   Notice that the File Type: pop-up changes to display Foreign.
3. Choose Variable Size, Delimited from the Field Size: pop-up.
4. Accept the default values for Record Terminator (Carriage Return) and Field Delimiter (comma (,)).
5. Click the Create Structure Using First Record checkbox. This instructs dBASE Mac to use the Header Record.
6. Click **OK.**
7. Name the file "Text In".
8. Click **OK.**

   After a few moments, the new file structure should appear in the Structure Window.

Now you can use the data contained in the foreign file in your project. You can use a Transfer View to move it into a dBASE Mac type file, but the easiest way is to use the Import command. Or use the text file without transferring the data. If you do not transfer the data, however, you will be unable to create an Index file from the foreign file, or any two-way relations or multivalued fields. You can create reports, Form views, procedures, and so on that use the foreign file.

To use the Import command, highlight the foreign structure, then select Import from the DataFile menu. Now name a new dBASE Mac file, and within moments a new file will be created.

If you have followed the instructions in this section, your Checkbook Project must look pretty messy by now. The best way to clean it up is to Close it without saving the changes. If you do so, none of the added file structures will remain with the project. You can then return to the Finder and throw the text files in the Trash when you are finished with them.

Importing dBASE II, dBASE III, and dBASE III PLUS Files

Earlier in the chapter, when you selected Create Structure for Existing File, the File Type pop-up defaulted to Foreign. If you opened the pop-up, you would have notice some additional choices had appeared—dBASE II and dBASE III.

dBASE Mac can load a dBASE II or dBASE III .DBF file directly to a dBASE Mac type file.

- After you select New . . . from the DataFile menu and check the Create Structure for Existing File, select dBASE II or dBASE III from the File Type pop-up (whichever is appropriate).
- Click **OK**.
- A dialog box opens to allow you to select the .DBF file.
- Double-click the file name, or highlight and click **OK**.

Without further ado, the dBASE Mac file structure is placed on the Structure Window.

NOTE: For those who anticipate using files from dBASE II, III, or III PLUS, there are several ways to transfer the data. One way is by modem. Another way is to use one of the networks that can link IBM PCs and Macintoshes. TOPS from Centram Systems is a good, inexpensive network that makes such file sharing easy. For bigger offices, AppleShare offers powerful networking between IBM PCs and Macintoshes. Other very effective methods include Daynafile, Quickshare, and Laplink Mac. For more, see Appendix C.

Summary

Chapter 11 introduces the Transfer View. Using Transfer Views, you can move data between dBASE Mac files, in and out of foreign text files (ASCII files), and out of dBASE II, III, and III PLUS files.

Transfer Views use a Source file and a Destination file.

You can choose from several options that govern the transfer: Replace, Don't Replace, Update, Append, and Accumulate.

You can also use procedures in the Transfer View hierarchy to further modify the transfer.

You set up the transfer on a special grid, the Transfer View layout.

You can start and stop the transfer during operation.

When working with foreign files, you must define the Record Terminator, the Field Terminator, and the Field Size.

There are several valid options available for Record Terminator and for Field Terminator.

File Size is either Fixed or Variable.

Foreign files are ordered numerically by Record Number.

Fields in foreign files have a position number that identifies their order in the record.

You can create a Header Record to automate the creation of a file structure when importing foreign files into dBASE Mac.

Foreign files have two icons on the Finder screen. One is for the file structure, the other contains the ASCII data.

In Chapter 12, you will look at ways to finish an application, including error trapping procedures. You will create a new, improved Checkbook Project called NewCheck and learn some basic information about dBASE Mac file structure maintenance.

12

FINISHING TOUCHES—ROMANCING THE CHECKBOOK

Overview

In the preceding chapters you have created three dBASE Mac projects (and one mini-application). You have defined files, fields, views, and procedures. You have also made Custom Menus and Protected projects. You have seen and tried every part of dBASE Mac, and you have some working projects to show for it.

In essence, you are ready to go it alone now. But this chapter is for the adventurous—the explorer who wants to see a little bit more. In collaboration with Tom Bodine of Ashton-Tate's Test Group, we have designed a new application—a checkbook system that goes far beyond what we've done up to this point. This system has a complete set of budget categories, handles split check transactions, and includes a reconciliation routine.

We're deeply indebted to Tom for his insight into dBASE Mac. He's shared much of that insight in creating this project and developing the excellent procedures that comprise it. (Tom also wrote the checkbook application that comes as a sample with dBASE Mac, but together, we've gone beyond that application.)

There's a lot to learn in this chapter, but there is a lot to do, too. Since this is the finale of the Tutorial—the graduation exercise, so to speak—we are going to let you be on your own while creating the project. We will provide you with all the dBASE Mac printouts of file structure, view definitions, and layouts. You'll be on your own to create the application.

It's worth it. Don't be put off by the amount of work it takes. You'll find this project full of surprises and programming niceties. We hope you'll dive into it feet first. After all you've done, much of it should be elementary. But as it comes together, you'll have an opportunity to learn some very useful tricks.

Chapter 12 assumes that you have worked through the previous chapters, and that you have a good working knowledge of basic dBASE Mac procedures, such as creating new fields and new views, and adding procedures to fields and views.

The NewCheck Project—How Does It Work?

NewCheck takes a very different approach from that of the Checkbook Project you worked on in earlier chapters. Some parts of it will be familiar, but many of them will be different. Much of the design of NewCheck was dictated by the need to perform detailed transaction processing on split checks and budgets.

NewCheck uses three files: Budget, Items, and Transactions. The Transactions file is similar to the Checkbook file from the Checkbook Project, but it is also different, both in structure and in conception.

Transaction is linked through a two-way relationship with Items, the main processing file of the application. Items, in turn, is linked to Budgets through a two-way relationship.

Basically, when you enter a transaction, a new transaction number is assigned in the Transaction file. The transaction type, date, and check number (if it is a check) are entered in the Transactions file, but the item description is entered in the Items file. Also, the Transaction Amount is placed through a calculation into either the Withdrawal Amount or the Deposit Amount field (depending on the transaction type, of course). Withdrawal Amount and Deposit Amount then post to the appropriate budget category and to the Balance field (a Memory field in the Transactions file).

What makes this system interesting is when you enter a split transaction. In this case, there is one transaction, one check number, but several line items associated with them through the relationship. In addition, each line item is associated with a separate budget category.

As you will see, the procedures included with this application demonstrate how records are written to files and carefully manipulate the processing order.

Several views are associated with this application. There is a Main Menu view that allows you to call all the other views. There are Budget Entry and Budget Listing views to work with the budgets. There is an Enter Transaction view for entering new transactions, and a Modify Transactions view for changing existing transactions. In addition, there are views to List Transactions, print a simple Income Statement, and even Reconcile the checkbook against your bank statement.

In the next section, create the file structures listed below. You have seen these printouts before. They are the printouts that dBASE Mac creates to describe files, fields, and views. All the information you need is there. For instance, look at the Budget file listing. It tells you that the file name is Budget, that it has a two-way relationship with Items (which you will create later, of course), and that it is made up of fields called Budget ID#, Budget Name, Budget Type, Monthly Budget, Actual Budget, and Trial Budget. The Items field at the end of the listing is the pointer field to the Items file. *You don't want to create that.* It will be created when you create the relationship.

When you complete the file definitions, estimate about ten records for the Budget file and about twenty for the Transaction file. Estimate about fifty records for the Items file. (If you plan to use this application for your own data, you may want to estimate higher numbers for the files.)

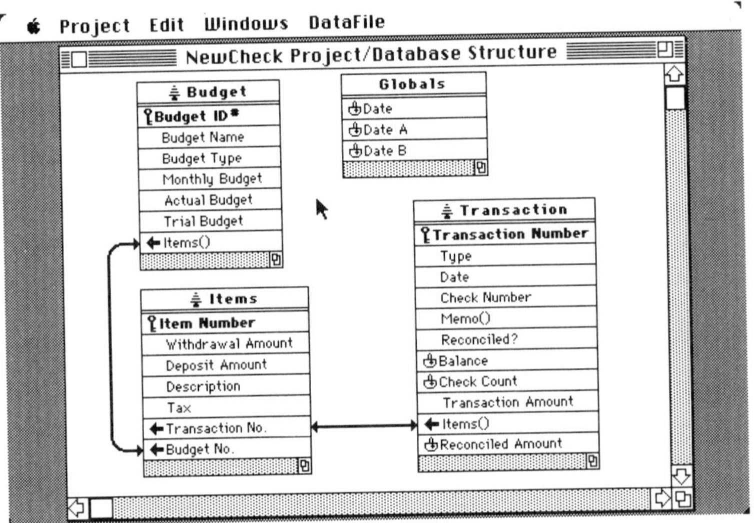

Figure 12-1 Structure Window for NewCheck.

The Budget File

In this section, you will create the basic file structure for the NewCheck project.

Report Name:	File Structure			10/30/87 4:43 PM
				Page 1
File Name:	Budget	File Type:	dBASE Mac	

Field Name:	Budget ID#			
Field Type:	Key, Ordered	Data Type:	Number	Required
Justify:	Right			
Format:	Fixed	Decimal Places:	0	
Decimal:	.	Thousands:		
Negative:	-n	Currency:		
Initial Value:	1			

Field Name:	Budget Name		
Field Type:	Data	Data Type:	Text
Contents are:	Single Valued		
Justify:	Left		

Field Name:	Budget Type		
Field Type:	Data	Data Type:	Choices
Contents are:	Single Valued		
Justify:	Left		
Format:	Pop-Up		
Values:	Per Inc		
	Bus Inc		
	Per Exp		
	Bus Exp		
Initial Value:	Per Inc		

Field Name:	Monthly Budget		
Field Type:	Data	Data Type:	Number
Contents are:	Single Valued		
Justify:	Right		
Format:	Fixed	Decimal Places:	2
Decimal:	.	Thousands:	
Negative:	-n	Currency:	$

Field Name:	Actual Budget		
Field Type:	Data	Data Type:	Number
Contents are:	Single Valued		
Justify:	Right		
Format:	Fixed	Decimal Places:	2
Decimal:	.	Thousands:	
Negative:	-n	Currency:	$

Field Name:	Trial Budget		
Field Type:	Data	Data Type:	Number
Contents are:	Single Valued		
Justify:	Right		
Format:	Fixed	Decimal Places:	2
Decimal:	.	Thousands:	
Negative:	-n	Currency:	$

Report Name:	File Structure			10/30/87 4:43 PM
				Page 2
File Name:	Budget	File Type:	dBASE Mac	
Field Name:	Items			
Field Type:	Data	Data Type:	Number	
Contents are:	Multiple Valued			
Justify:	Right			
Format:	Fixed	Decimal Places:	0	
Decimal:	.	Thousands:		
Negative:	-n	Currency:		
Relations:	Two-way with Items			

The Transactions File

You should have no trouble creating this file. It is in many ways similar to the Checkbook file you created in Chapter 4. Take a note of the Range setting for the Transaction Amount field. It is set from $0.00 to . . . (elipsis). The three dots represent a wildcard value and mean that the Transaction Amount can be up to any amount. Be sure to set the Initial Value of Check Count to zero, and Balance to zero (unless you wish the application to begin with an initial balance).

Notice also that Balance, Check Count, and Reconciled Amount are all Memory fields. The Items field is a Pointer field. *Do not enter the Items field.* It is a Pointer field and will be entered when you create the relationship with the items file.

Report Name:	File Structure			10/30/87 4:43 PM
				Page 1
File Name:	Transaction	File Type:	dBASE Mac	
Field Name:	Transaction Number			
Field Type:	Key, Ordered	Data Type:	Number	Required
Justify:	Right			
Format:	Fixed	Decimal Places:	0	
Decimal:	.	Thousands:		
Negative:	-n	Currency:		
Auto Sequenced By:	1			
Initial Value:	10			
Field Name:	Type			
Field Type:	Data	Data Type:	Choices	
Contents are:	Single Valued			
Justify:	Left			
Format:	Pop-Up			
Values:	Check			
	Bank Ch			
	Misc Ck			
	Deposit			
	Interest			
	Split Ck			
	VOID			
Initial Value:	Check			
Field Name:	Date			
Field Type:	Data	Data Type:	Date	
Contents are:	Single Valued			
Justify:	Left			
Format:	mm/dd/yy			
Year Length:	2	Separator:	/	
Field Name:	Check Number			
Field Type:	Data	Data Type:	Number	
Contents are:	Single Valued			
Justify:	Right			
Format:	Fixed	Decimal Places:	0	
Decimal:	.	Thousands:		
Negative:	-n	Currency:		
Field Name:	Memo			
Field Type:	Data	Data Type:	Text	
Contents are:	Multiple Valued			
Justify:	Left			
Field Name:	Reconciled?			
Field Type:	Data	Data Type:	Logical	
Contents are:	Single Valued			
Justify:	Left			

Report Name:	File Structure			10/30/87 4:43 PM Page 2
File Name:	Transaction	File Type:	dBASE Mac	
Format:	Check Box			
Values:	No/Yes			
Initial Value:	No			
Field Name:	Balance			
Field Type:	Memory	Data Type:	Number	
Contents are:	Single Valued			
Justify:	Right			
Format:	Fixed	Decimal Places:	2	
Decimal:	.	Thousands:		
Negative:	-n	Currency:	$	
Initial Value:	$ 515.00			
Field Name:	Check Count			
Field Type:	Memory	Data Type:	Number	
Contents are:	Single Valued			
Justify:	Right			
Format:	Fixed	Decimal Places:	0	
Decimal:	.	Thousands:		
Negative:	-n	Currency:		
Initial Value:	5			
Field Name:	Transaction Amount			
Field Type:	Data	Data Type:	Number	Required
Contents are:	Single Valued			
Justify:	Right			
Format:	Fixed	Decimal Places:	2	
Decimal:	.	Thousands:		
Negative:	-n	Currency:	$	
Range:	$ 0.00 To ...			
Field Name:	Items			
Field Type:	Data	Data Type:	Number	
Contents are:	Multiple Valued			
Justify:	Right			
Format:	Fixed	Decimal Places:	0	
Decimal:	.	Thousands:		
Negative:	-n	Currency:		
Relations:	Two-way with Items			
Field Name:	Reconciled Amount			
Field Type:	Memory	Data Type:	Number	
Contents are:	Single Valued			
Justify:	Right			
Format:	Fixed	Decimal Places:	2	
Decimal:	.	Thousands:		
Negative:	-n	Currency:	$	

Report Name:	File Structure			10/30/87	4:43 PM
				Page 3	
File Name:	Transaction	File Type:	dBASE Mac		
Initial Value:	$ 0.00				

The Items File

Next, enter the Items file. Notice on the listing that Withdrawal Amount posts positive amounts to Actual Budget and negative amounts to Balance. Deposit Amount posts positive to both Actual Budget and Balance.

Remember, you can't enter the posting until you have created the file relationships (that's the next step after creating the files).

Also notice that the Transaction No. and Budget No. fields are Pointer fields. *You cannot enter them at this time.*

Report Name:	File Structure			10/30/87 4:46 PM
				Page 1
File Name:	Items	File Type:	dBASE Mac	

Field Name:	Item Number			
Field Type:	Key, Ordered	Data Type:	Number	Required
Justify:	Right			
Format:	Fixed	Decimal Places:	0	
Decimal:	.	Thousands:		
Negative:	-n	Currency:		
Auto Sequenced By:	1			
Initial Value:	23			

Field Name:	Withdrawal Amount		
Field Type:	Data	Data Type:	Number
Contents are:	Single Valued		
Justify:	Right		
Format:	Fixed	Decimal Places:	2
Decimal:	.	Thousands:	
Negative:	-n	Currency:	$
Post To:	Add to: Actual Budget•Budget		
	Subtract from: Balance•Transaction		

Field Name:	Deposit Amount		
Field Type:	Data	Data Type:	Number
Contents are:	Single Valued		
Justify:	Right		
Format:	Fixed	Decimal Places:	2
Decimal:	.	Thousands:	
Negative:	-n	Currency:	$
Post To:	Add to: Balance•Transaction		
	Add to: Actual Budget•Budget		

Field Name:	Description		
Field Type:	Data	Data Type:	Text
Contents are:	Single Valued		
Justify:	Left		

Field Name:	Tax		
Field Type:	Data	Data Type:	Logical
Contents are:	Single Valued		
Justify:	Left		
Format:	Check Box		
Values:	No/Yes		
Initial Value:	No		

Field Name:	Transaction No.		
Field Type:	Data	Data Type:	Number
Contents are:	Single Valued		
Justify:	Right		
Format:	Fixed	Decimal Places:	0

Report Name:	File Structure			10/30/87 4:46 PM
				Page 2
File Name:	Items	File Type:	dBASE Mac	
Decimal:	.	Thousands:		
Negative:	-n	Currency:		
Relations:	Two-way with Transaction			
Field Name:	Budget No.			
Field Type:	Data	Data Type:	Number	Required
Contents are:	Single Valued			
Justify:	Right			
Format:	Fixed	Decimal Places:	0	
Decimal:	.	Thousands:		
Negative:	-n	Currency:		
Relations:	Two-way with Budget			

The Globals File

Add the following fields to the Globals file—Date, Date A, and Date B. All three are Date fields.

Relating the Files

Now that you have created all three files, it is time to create the relationships between them. First, position the files on the Structure Window where you want them to be. Drag the Transaction Number field onto the Items file. Check to be sure that the dialog box indicates a two-way relationship between Items and Transactions. If so, click **OK** to create the relationship.

Now drag the Budget Number field onto the Items file. Again, confirm that the relationship is correct, then click **OK**.

Now double-click the Transaction Number-pointer field in the Items file (the field that was just created), and change its name to "Transaction No." Change the Contents Are: to Single Valued. Click **Command-Done/N** and change the Budget Number field name to "Budget No." and change the contents to Single Valued. Click **Done**.

You want the Pointer fields to be single valued because each item will point to one transaction and to one budget.

Now go back to the Withdrawal Amount and Deposit Amount fields and enter the posting information (to Actual Budget and Balance).

Entering Budgets

The following is a Budget Entry view description.

Report Name:	View Definition		10/30/87 4:47 PM Page 1
Project Name:	NewCheck Project		
View Name:	Budget Entry	View Type:	Display, Custom Layout
Root File:	Budget	File Type:	dBASE Mac

NOTE: You'll notice how the entries for the Choices Field Budget Type are underlined. Also, the word "modified" occurs on the field definition. dBASE Mac does this to indicate that the underlined items have been modified from the original File Field definitions.

Report Name:	View Definition		10/30/87	4:47 PM
			Page 2	
Project Name:	NewCheck Project			
View Name:	Budget Entry	View Type:	Display, Custom Layout	
File Name:	Budget	File Type:	dBASE Mac	

Access Path:	Budget			

Field Name:	Budget ID#			
Field Type:	Key, Ordered	Data Type:	Number	Required
Justify:	Right			
Format:	Fixed	Decimal Places:	0	
Decimal:	.	Thousands:		
Negative:	-n	Currency:		
Initial Value:	1			

Field Name:	Budget Name			
Field Type:	Data	Data Type:	Text	
Contents are:	Single Valued			
Justify:	Left			

Field Name:	Budget Type			Modified
Field Type:	Data	Data Type:	Choices	
Contents are:	Single Valued			
Justify:	Left			
Format:	Pop-Up			
Values:	Personal Income			
	Business Income			
	Personal Expense			
	Business Expense			
Initial Value:	Personal Income			

Field Name:	Monthly Budget			
Field Type:	Data	Data Type:	Number	
Contents are:	Single Valued			
Justify:	Right			
Format:	Fixed	Decimal Places:	2	
Decimal:	.	Thousands:		
Negative:	-n	Currency:	$	

Field Name:	Actual Budget			
Field Type:	Data	Data Type:	Number	
Contents are:	Single Valued			
Justify:	Right			
Format:	Fixed	Decimal Places:	2	
Decimal:	.	Thousands:		
Negative:	-n	Currency:	$	

Field Name:	Trial Budget			
Field Type:	Data	Data Type:	Number	
Contents are:	Single Valued			
Justify:	Right			

Report Name:	View Definition		10/30/87 4:47 PM Page 3
Project Name:	NewCheck Project		
View Name:	Budget Entry	View Type:	Display, Custom Layout
File Name:	Budget	File Type:	dBASE Mac
Format:	Fixed	Decimal Places:	2
Decimal:	.	Thousands:	
Negative:	-n	Currency:	$
Field Name:	Items		
Field Type:	Data	Data Type:	Number
Contents are:	Multiple Valued		
Justify:	Right		
Format:	Fixed	Decimal Places:	0
Decimal:	.	Thousands:	
Negative:	-n	Currency:	
Relations:	Two-way with Items		

Create the Form view called Budget Entry (see listing) for the Budget file and enter the following records or use data of your own:

Budget ID#	**1**
Budget Name	**Food**
Budget Type	**Personal Expense**
Monthly Budget	**$400.00**
Budget ID#	**2**
Budget Name	**Rent**
Budget Type	**Personal Expense**
Monthly Budget	**$350.00**
Budget ID#	**3**
Budget Name	**Clothing**
Budget Type	**Personal Expense**
Monthly Budget	**$150.00**
Budget ID#	**4**
Budget Name	**Salary**
Budget Type	**Business Income**
Monthly Budget	**$1500.00**

Budget ID#	**5**
Budget Name	**Commissions**
Budget Type	**Business Income**
Monthly Budget	**$1000.00**

Budget ID#	**6**
Budget Name	**Interest**
Budget Type	**Personal Income**
Monthly Budget	**$100.00**

Budget ID#	**7**
Budget Name	**Dividends**
Budget Type	**Personal Income**
Monthly Budget	**$200.00**

Budget ID#	**8**
Budget Name	**Travel Expense**
Budget Type	**Business Expense**
Monthly Budget	**$50.00**

Budget ID#	**9**
Budget Name	**Supplies**
Budget Type	**Business Expense**
Monthly Budget	**$200.00**

Budget ID#	**10**
Budget Name	**Misc. Expense**
Budget Type	**Business Expense**
Monthly Budget	**$100.00**

Next, create the Budget Listing view.

Report Name:	View Definition		10/30/87	4:48 PM
			Page 1	
Project Name:	NewCheck Project			
View Name:	Budget Listing	View Type:	Display, Custom Layout	
Root File:	Budget	File Type:	dBASE Mac	

Report Name:	View Definition		10/30/87	4:48 PM
			Page 2	
Project Name:	NewCheck Project			
View Name:	Budget Listing	View Type:	Display, Custom Layout	
File Name:	Budget	File Type:	dBASE Mac	

Access Path:	Budget			
Field Name:	Budget ID#			
Field Type:	Key, Ordered	Data Type:	Number	Required
Justify:	Right			
Format:	Fixed	Decimal Places:	0	
Decimal:	.	Thousands:		
Negative:	-n	Currency:		
Initial Value:	1			
Field Name:	Budget Name			
Field Type:	Data	Data Type:	Text	
Contents are:	Single Valued			
Justify:	Left			
Field Name:	Budget Type			Modified
Field Type:	Data	Data Type:	Choices	
Contents are:	Single Valued			
Justify:	Left			
Format:	Pop-Up			
Values:	Personal Income			
	Business Income			
	Personal Expense			
	Business Expense			
Initial Value:	Personal Income			
Field Name:	Monthly Budget			
Field Type:	Data	Data Type:	Number	
Contents are:	Single Valued			
Justify:	Right			
Format:	Fixed	Decimal Places:	2	
Decimal:	.	Thousands:		
Negative:	-n	Currency:	$	
Field Name:	Actual Budget			
Field Type:	Data	Data Type:	Number	
Contents are:	Single Valued			
Justify:	Right			
Format:	Fixed	Decimal Places:	2	
Decimal:	.	Thousands:		
Negative:	-n	Currency:	$	
Field Name:	Trial Budget			
Field Type:	Data	Data Type:	Number	
Contents are:	Single Valued			
Justify:	Right			

Report Name:	View Definition		10/30/87 4:48 PM
			Page 3
Project Name:	NewCheck Project		
View Name:	Budget Listing	View Type:	Display, Custom Layout
File Name:	Budget	File Type:	dBASE Mac
Format:	Fixed	Decimal Places:	2
Decimal:	.	Thousands:	
Negative:	-n	Currency:	$
Field Name:	Items		
Field Type:	Data	Data Type:	Number
Contents are:	Multiple Valued		
Justify:	Right		
Format:	Fixed	Decimal Places:	0
Decimal:	.	Thousands:	
Negative:	-n	Currency:	
Relations:	Two-way with Items		

Perform and Use Budget Listing to see the data.

The Main Menu View

After you complete work on the Budget file, it's time to begin creating the application structure. The Main Menu view is used to call all the other views in the project. Even though you haven't created most of the views yet, create the view that follows. Note that its hierarchy contains only two fields—Transaction Number and Balance.

The procedure listed at the beginning of the view listing is a view Pre-Processor. Enter it by clicking the Show View Processor button.

Note also that the layout is the kind of layout you created in Chapters 10 and 11 with the blank space in a text field. Notice also that the window has been squeezed down to its minimum size and the scroll bars have been removed using the Hide Scroll Bars option under the Design menu in Layout View.

```
Report Name:   View Definition                                      10/30/87   4:48 PM
                                                                    Page 1
Project Name:  NewCheck Project
View Name:     Main Menu                    View Type:     Display, Custom Layout
-----------------------------------------------------------------------------------
Procedure:
 Pre-Processor LOOP
               DIALOG 40,90,310,415
                  BUTTON 1,220,58,240,108,"OK"
                  BUTTON 2,220,213,240,263,"Exit"
                  FIXEDTEXT 10,75,25,320,"---Checkbook Application---"
                  FIXEDTEXT 250,40,265,400,"current checkbook balance is: ":
                                FORMAT({Balance•Transaction•Globals})
                 RADIOLIST 1,1
                    RADIOBUTTON 40,77,55,230,"Enter Transactions"
                    RADIOBUTTON 65,77,80,230,"Modify Transactions"
                    RADIOBUTTON 90,77,105,230,"Maintain Budgets"
                    RADIOBUTTON 115,77,130,230,"Budget Listing"
                    RADIOBUTTON 140,77,155,230,"Bank Reconciliation"
                    RADIOBUTTON 165,77,180,230,"Income Statement"
                    RADIOBUTTON 190,77,205,230,"List Transactions"
                 END
               END
               WHEN BUTTONVALUE(2) LEAVE

                 CASE RADIOVALUE(1) OF
                   WHEN 1 DO USE("Enter Transactions",INIT)
                   WHEN 2 DO USE("Modify Transactions",INIT)
                   WHEN 3 DO USE("Budget Entry",INIT,MODAL)
                   WHEN 4 DO PERFORM("Budget Listing",INIT)
                   WHEN 5 DO PERFORM("Reconcile",INIT,MODAL)
                   WHEN 6 DO PERFORM("Income Statement",INIT)
                   WHEN 7 DO PERFORM("List Transactions",INIT)
                 END
               END
               EXIT
-----------------------------------------------------------------------------------
Root File:     Transaction                  File Type:     dBASE Mac
-----------------------------------------------------------------------------------
File Name:     Globals                      File Type:     Globals
```

Note: Solid lines represent new pages in the report printout. Initial value for Balance Field is arbitrary.

Report Name:	View Definition		10/30/87	4:48 PM
			Page 2	
Project Name:	NewCheck Project			
View Name:	Main Menu	View Type:	Display, Custom Layout	
File Name:	Transaction	File Type:	dBASE Mac	
Access Path:	Transaction			
Field Name:	Transaction Number			
Field Type:	Key, Ordered	Data Type:	Number	Required
Justify:	Right			
Format:	Fixed	Decimal Places:	0	
Decimal:	.	Thousands:		
Negative:	-n	Currency:		
Auto Sequenced By:	1			
Initial Value:	10			

Report Name:	View Definition		10/30/87	4:48 PM
			Page 3	
Project Name:	NewCheck Project			
View Name:	Main Menu	View Type:	Display, Custom Layout	
File Name:	Globals	File Type:	Globals	
File Name:	Transaction	File Type:	dBASE Mac	

Report Name:	View Definition		10/30/87	4:48 PM
			Page 4	
Project Name:	NewCheck Project			
View Name:	Main Menu	View Type:	Display, Custom Layout	
File Name:	Transaction	File Type:	dBASE Mac	
Field Name:	Balance			
Field Type:	Memory	Data Type:	Number	
Contents are:	Single Valued			
Justify:	Right			
Format:	Fixed	Decimal Places:	2	
Decimal:	.	Thousands:		
Negative:	-n	Currency:	$	
Initial Value:	$ 515.00			

Enter Transactions View

If you remember the Checkbook Entry view, you'll remember that it was fairly complex, and employed Tablets and some procedures. The Enter Transactions view is more complex still, and takes into account two subfile levels, split transactions, and error checking on budgets.

One of the key factors to observe is how this view writes records. It is important to understand how dBASE Mac handles a record when you press the **Enter** key.

When you press **Enter** to write a record to a file, dBASE Mac writes all records to their associated files—for all files at or below the hierarchy level of the file where the insertion point is located. For instance, if you were to press **Enter** from one of the Items fields in the Enter Transactions view, you would not be entering the whole transaction. That is because Items is at a lower level in the hierarchy than the Transactions file.

To save a record in the Enter Transactions view, the cursor must be at the Root level of the view. The exception is when you use **Command-Enter**, which will write records for all files in the hierarchy, regardless of the cursor position.

What happens when you press **Enter**, then, from the Root file level?

First, even though the files and subfiles are processed from the current level and down, the actual writing of data begins with the lowest level. So in this instance, the first file to be processed is the Budget file. However, you don't want people modifying budgets in this view, so a BREAK command has been placed in the Budget file pointer Write Record procedure, which disables the actual write capability to the Budget file.

> NOTE: Even though the Write Record procedure has been disabled for the Budget file, the posting still takes place. In fact, posting will take place on any open file in a project. The file does not need to be in the hierarchy, but does need to be open on the Structure Window.

After the Budget file, the Items Write Record procedure is executed. This processor first checks to see that the transaction is not a VOID check, and that it is a new record (using programming techniques that should be familiar to you). Then, depending on the transaction type, it sets the Transaction Amount equal to either the Withdrawal Amount or the Deposit Amount fields.

When it encounters the WRITE(SELF) command, it first writes the record to the file, then posts the appropriate values from either the Withdrawal Amount or the Deposit Amount field to the Actual Budget and the Balance fields. In the case of a VOID transaction, no Items record is written.

Next, the Transaction file Write Record processor executes. It checks to see if the transaction was a check, and if so, it updates the Check Count field to be equal to the current Check Number. If the transaction is a VOID check, it also sets it as reconciled. All three of these Write Record procedures are attached to the appropriate pointer fields. By now you should know how to add a procedure to a Pointer field (double-click the title bar of the file or subordinate file in the hierarchy).

In addition to the Write Record procedures, some other procedures are associated with the Enter Transactions view. Look at the Delete Record procedure. It does not allow you to delete a record in the Enter Transactions view. Because it does not contain a DELETE(SELF), no deletion will take place.

Similarly, a Post-Processor on the Type field prevents you from changing the transaction type of an existing record. This shouldn't really be necessary since the Enter Transactions Write Record procedures won't process an old record anyway. Still, it could get messy trying to change the type in the enter view.

The Date field shows another way to keep a running date (using a Global Memory field). You'll remember that the Checkbook Project used the Keep New Initial Value setting.

Notice that the Check Number is incremented in a field Pre-Processor. Although this system does the same thing as the Checkbook Project did, it does it in the opposite way. In this instance, the Check Number is given the value of Check Count + 1. Then, in the Write Record procedure, the Check Count field is equated with the Check Number.

Perhaps the most complex procedure in this view is the Pre-Processor on the Description field. This procedure first tests to see if the transaction type is a split check. If it is not, then it falls through the IF statement to the ELSE, where it creates a new Item record and REDISPLAYs the Item Number field.

In the case of a split check (Type = 6), the procedure enters a loop that brings up a dialog box. The total transaction amount is already entered, but the user may modify it here. Then, a new dialog box allows the user to enter each part of the split transaction—its amount, individual description, budget, and whether it is taxable or not.

The procedure then checks for an amount that exceeds the total check, takes appropriate action, then checks to see if the budget entered is valid. If everything is all right, the procedure updates the local variable arrays using the counter i as the subscript for the array. For instance, the first time through, i = 1. Thus, *check_amount[1]* is the first occurrence of the local variable *check_amount*. If the amount entered was 25, then the first occurrence of check_amount is 25. On the next loop, the occurrence of *check_amount* is 2 (written *check_amount[2]*). If the value entered this time was 10, then the second occurrence of *check_amount* (or *check_amount[2]*) would equal 10. Doing a *SUM(check_amount)* totals all the values contained in the array. In this case, *SUM(check_amount)* would yield 35 as a result.

The local variable, *estimate*, is the value of the total check (contained in the local variable total) minus *SUM(check_amount)*. Thus, *estimate* always represents the remaining amount of the check and is used as the default value for the edit text box in the dialog. Whenever the user goes to enter another split of the check, the default value will always show the amount remaining.

Once *estimate* is zero (meaning that the check has been completely allocated to its appropriate budgets), the procedure enters another loop in which it creates a new Items record and sets the values from the local variables to the appropriate fields, then writes the Items file. When it has written all but the last Item record, it sets *total* equal to the Transaction Amount and writes the Transactions record, which also activates the writing of the final Items record. Finally, it initializes a new record in the Transaction file and returns to the view.

Another useful procedure is a Post-Processor attached to the Budget ID# field. This procedure checks to see if the budget number you entered is a valid budget. If not, it brings up a dialog box allowing you to re-enter the budget number, see a list of available budgets (through the Budget Listing view), or enter a new budget (through the Budget Entry view).

The Enter Transactions view layout also has some interesting features. The fields are divided on the screen using boxes created with Fixed Graphic elements (Fill = None) and lines drawn for accents. The field elements are then placed on the graphic elements to produce fields within boxes. The Item Number, Budget Name, Monthly Budget, and Actual Budget fields are set to Display Only, and the SETNEXTFIELD Pre-Processor on Budget Name bypasses them anyway.

To keep the processing order correct, Memo, Description, and Tax are grouped on the layout. To group these three fields, highlight them by shift-clicking and select Group from the Design menu.

The Balance field is in bold. The Check Number field is actually in a small Tablet with the Selection set to Show If:

```
{Type•Transactions} = 1 OR {Type•Transactions} = 6
```

Keeping these details in mind, you should be able to recreate the layout from the picture. We've included some screen images of the Define Hierarchy screen to help you as well.

```
Report Name:    View Definition                                   10/30/87   4:49 PM
                                                                  Page  1
Project Name:   NewCheck Project
View Name:      Enter Transactions          View Type:     Display, Custom Layout

Procedure:
 Pre-Processor  NEW({Transaction Number•Transaction})

Root File:      Transaction                 File Type:     dBASE Mac
View Procedure:
 Write Record   IF {Transaction Number•Transaction} IN "Transaction" THEN
                   ALERT ("Sorry. You may only create NEW records here.  Use the 'Modify ":
                          "Transactions' view to update existing records.")
                ELSE
                   CASE {Type•Transaction} OF
                     WHEN 1 DO {Check Count•Transaction•Globals}= {Check Number•Transaction}
                     WHEN 6 DO {Check Count•Transaction•Globals}= {Check Number•Transaction}
                     WHEN 7 DO {Reconciled?•Transaction} = "T"
                  END
                 WRITE(SELF)
                END
                  REDISPLAY({Balance•Transaction•Globals})
 Delete Record  ALERT ("You may NOT Delete records in this view.")

File Name:      Globals                     File Type:     Globals
```

Report Name: View Definition 10/30/87 4:49 PM
Page 2

Project Name: NewCheck Project
View Name: Enter Transactions View Type: Display, Custom Layout
File Name: Transaction File Type: dBASE Mac

Access Path: Transaction

Field Name: Transaction Number
Field Type: Key, Ordered Data Type: Number Required
Justify: Right
Format: Fixed Decimal Places: 0
Decimal: . Thousands:
Negative: -n Currency:
Auto Sequenced By: 1
Initial Value: 10

Field Name: Type Modified
Field Type: Data Data Type: Choices
Contents are: Single Valued
Justify: Left
Format: Pop-Up
Values: Check
Bank Charges
Misc. Withdrawal
Deposit
Interest
Split Check
VOID
Initial Value: Check
View Procedure:
Post-Processor IF {Transaction Number•Transaction} IN "Transaction"
THEN ALERT ("You may NOT modify the 'Type' of an existing Transaction.")
ELSE ACCEPT
END

Field Name: Date Modified
Field Type: Data Data Type: Date
Contents are: Single Valued
Justify: Left
Format: mm/dd/yy
Year Length: 2 Separator: /
View Procedure:
Pre-Processor {Date•Transaction} = {Date•Globals}
REDISPLAY({Date•Transaction})
Post-Processor ACCEPT
{Date•Globals} = {Date•Transaction}

Field Name: Check Number Modified
Field Type: Data Data Type: Number

Report Name:	View Definition		10/30/87	4:49 PM
			Page 3	
Project Name:	NewCheck Project			
View Name:	Enter Transactions	View Type:	Display, Custom Layout	
File Name:	Transaction	File Type:	dBASE Mac	

Contents are:	Single Valued		
Justify:	Right		
Format:	Fixed	Decimal Places:	0
Decimal:	.	Thousands:	
Negative:	-n	Currency:	
View Procedure:			

Pre-Processor

```
IF {Check Number•Transaction} = "" THEN
    {Check Number•Transaction} = {Check Count•Transaction•Globals} + 1
END
```

Field Name:	Memo			
Field Type:	Data	Data Type:	Text	
Contents are:	Multiple Valued			
Justify:	Left			

Field Name:	Transaction Amount			
Field Type:	Data	Data Type:	Number	Required
Contents are:	Single Valued			
Justify:	Right			
Format:	Fixed	Decimal Places:	2	
Decimal:	.	Thousands:		
Negative:	-n	Currency:	$	
Range:	$ 0.00 To ...			

Field Name:	Items			Modified
Field Type:	Data	Data Type:	Number	Required
Contents are:	Multiple Valued			
Justify:	Right			
Format:	Fixed	Decimal Places:	0	
Decimal:	.	Thousands:		
Negative:	-n	Currency:		
Relations:	Two-way with Items			
View Procedure:				

Write Record

```
IF {Type•Transaction} <> 7 AND
    (NOT {Transaction Number•Transaction} IN "Transaction")
THEN
  IF {Type•Transaction} <= 3 THEN
      {Withdrawal Amount•Items•Transaction} = {Transaction Amount•Transaction}
  ELSE
    IF {Type•Transaction} <> 6 THEN
        {Deposit Amount•Items•Transaction} = {Transaction Amount•Transaction}
    END
  END
WRITE(SELF)
```

Report Name:	View Definition			10/30/87 4:49 PM Page 4
Project Name:	NewCheck Project			
View Name:	Enter Transactions	View Type:	Display, Custom Layout	
File Name:	Transaction	File Type:	dBASE Mac	

	END		
Relates File:	Items	File Type:	dBASE Mac

Field Name:	Reconciled?		
Field Type:	Data	Data Type:	Logical
Contents are:	Single Valued		
Justify:	Left		
Format:	Check Box		
Values:	No/Yes		
Initial Value:	No		

Report Name:	View Definition		10/30/87 4:49 PM Page 5	
Project Name:	NewCheck Project			
View Name:	Enter Transactions	View Type:	Display, Custom Layout	
File Name:	Items	File Type:	dBASE Mac	

Access Path: Items•Transaction

Field Name:	Item Number			Modified
Field Type:	Key, Ordered	Data Type:	Number	Required
Justify:	Left			
Format:	Fixed	Decimal Places:	0	
Decimal:	.	Thousands:		
Negative:	-n	Currency:		
Auto Sequenced By:	1			
Initial Value:	1			
View Procedure:				
Pre-Processor	SETNEXTFIELD({Transaction Amount•Transaction})			

Field Name:	Withdrawal Amount			
Field Type:	Data	Data Type:	Number	
Contents are:	Single Valued			
Justify:	Right			
Format:	Fixed	Decimal Places:	2	
Decimal:	.	Thousands:		
Negative:	-n	Currency:	$	
Post To:	Add to: Actual Budget•Budget Subtract from: Balance•Transaction			

Field Name:	Description			Modified
Field Type:	Data	Data Type:	Text	
Contents are:	Single Valued			
Justify:	Left			
View Procedure:				

Pre-Processor

```
IF {Type•Transaction} = 6 THEN
 REPEAT
   LOOP
      DIALOG 64,135,250,370
        BUTTON 1,150,145,170,195,"OK"
        BUTTON 2,150,40,170,100,"Cancel"
        FIXEDTEXT 55,10,70,240,"Enter Total Transaction Amount:"
        FIXEDTEXT 85,70,100,180,"Check # ":{Check Number•Transaction}
       FIXEDTEXT 20,56,40,300,"SPLIT TRANSACTIONS"
         EDITTEXT 1,120,70,136,165,{Transaction Amount•Transaction}
    END
     total = INTERNAL( TEXTVALUE(1), {Transaction Amount•Transaction} )
   WHEN (ERROR = 0 AND total > 0) OR BUTTONVALUE(2) LEAVE
     ALERT ("INVALID NUMBER ENTERED. Please enter valid amount.")
   END
 IF BUTTONVALUE(1) THEN
```

Report Name:	View Definition			10/30/87 Page 6	4:49 PM
Project Name:	NewCheck Project				
View Name:	Enter Transactions	View Type:	Display, Custom Layout		
File Name:	Items	File Type:	dBASE Mac		

```
check_amount = ""                    \ initialize array \
i = 0
estimate = total
REPEAT
    DIALOG 45,80,320,420
      BUTTON 1,240,215,260,265,"OK"
      BUTTON 7,240,60,260,120,"Cancel"
     FIXEDTEXT 10,100,25,300,"SPLIT TRANSACTIONS"
      FIXEDTEXT 40,80,55,240,"Enter split item values:"
      FIXEDTEXT 75,45,90,140,"Amount:"
      FIXEDTEXT 105,45,120,140,"Description:"
      FIXEDTEXT 135,45,150,140,"Budget:"
      EDITTEXT 1,75,145,91,240,estimate
      EDITTEXT 2,105,145,121,325,""
      EDITTEXT 3,135,145,151,210,""
      CHECKBOX 1,165,160,180,250,"F","Taxable"
      FIXEDTEXT 205,75,220,350,"Total Check Amount:  $":total
  END
  IF NOT BUTTONVALUE(7) THEN
IF (SUM(check_amount) + TEXTVALUE(1) )  > total THEN
        ALERT("The last entry exceeded the total check amount.":
            " Please re-enter...",STOP)
ELSE
     IF NOT TEXTVALUE(3) IN "Budget" THEN
        ALERT ("Invalid BUDGET # ... please re-enter.")
     ELSE
    i = i + 1
      check_amount[i]   = TEXTVALUE(1)
       description[i]   = TEXTVALUE(2)
           tax[i]   = CHECKBOXVALUE(1)
         budget_number[i]   = TEXTVALUE(3)
         estimate = total - SUM(check_amount)
     END
 END
END
  UNTIL estimate = 0 OR BUTTONVALUE(7)
 END
END
UNTIL BUTTONVALUE(2) OR estimate = 0 END
IF NOT BUTTONVALUE(2) AND total > 0 THEN
   LOOP                        \ * write 'Items' records * \
   n = n + 1
```

```
Report Name:    View Definition                                       10/30/87    4:49 PM
                                                                      Page 7

Project Name:   NewCheck Project
View Name:      Enter Transactions          View Type:     Display, Custom Layout
File Name:      Items                       File Type:     dBASE Mac

              NEW({Items•Transaction})
               {Withdrawal Amount•Items•Transaction} = check_amount[n]
               {Description•Items•Transaction}       = description[n]
              {Tax•Items•Transaction}                = tax[n]
              {Budget No.•Items•Transaction}         = budget_number[n]
           WHEN n >= i LEAVE
                WRITE({Item Number•Items•Transaction})
           END
                {Transaction Amount•Transaction} = total
                WRITE({Transaction Number•Transaction})
         END
              NEW({Transaction Number•Transaction})
             REDISPLAY({Transaction})
             SETNEXTFIELD({Transaction Number•Transaction})
        ELSE
           IF {Item Number•Items•Transaction} = ""
           THEN NEW({Item Number•Items•Transaction})      \* generate 'Items' key *\
               REDISPLAY({Item Number•Items•Transaction})
          END
        END

Field Name:     Tax
Field Type:     Data                        Data Type:     Logical
Contents are:   Single Valued
Justify:        Left
Format:         Check Box
Values:         No/Yes
Initial Value:  No

Field Name:     Budget No.                                                  Modified
Field Type:     Data                        Data Type:     Number           Required
Contents are:   Single Valued
Justify:        Right
Format:         Fixed                       Decimal Places: 0
Decimal:        .                           Thousands:
Negative:       -n                          Currency:
Relations:      Two-way with Budget
View Procedure:
 Write Record   BREAK
Relates File:   Budget                      File Type:     dBASE Mac

Field Name:     Deposit Amount
Field Type:     Data                        Data Type:     Number
Contents are:   Single Valued
```

Report Name:	View Definition		10/30/87 4:49 PM Page 8
Project Name:	NewCheck Project		
View Name:	Enter Transactions	View Type:	Display, Custom Layout
File Name:	Items	File Type:	dBASE Mac

Justify:	Right		
Format:	Fixed	Decimal Places:	2
Decimal:	.	Thousands:	
Negative:	-n	Currency:	$
Post To:	Add to: Balance•Transaction		
	Add to: Actual Budget•Budget		

```
Report Name:    View Definition                                          10/30/87    4:49 PM
                                                                         Page  9
Project Name:   NewCheck Project
View Name:      Enter Transactions             View Type:     Display, Custom Layout
File Name:      Budget                         File Type:     dBASE Mac

Access Path:    Budget No.•Items•Transaction

Field Name:     Budget ID#                                                Modified
Field Type:     Key,  Ordered                  Data Type:     Number      Required
Justify:        Right
Format:         Fixed                          Decimal Places:  0
Decimal:        .                              Thousands:
Negative:       -n                             Currency:
Initial Value:  1
View Procedure:
 Post-Processor IF NOT {Budget No.•Items•Transaction} IN "Budget"
                THEN BEEP(4)
                   DIALOG 100,60,220,440
                     BUTTON 1,95,25,115,80,"Cancel"
                     BUTTON 2,95,115,115,215,"ADD Budget"
                     BUTTON 3,95,255,115,355,"SEE Listing"
                    FIXEDTEXT 15,32,85,357,"You have entered a non-existent BUDGET code."
                     :"  Click 'Cancel' to re-enter a valid Budget number - OR":
                     " select another option to SEE Availble BUDGET categories, or":
                     " to ADD a new category."
                  END
                  CASE BUTTONPRESSED OF
                    WHEN 2 DO USE("Budget Entry",MODAL)
                    WHEN 3 DO PERFORM("Budget Listing",MODAL)
                  END
                  SETNEXTFIELD({Budget ID#•Budget No.•Items•Transaction})
                ELSE ACCEPT
                END

Field Name:     Budget Name                                               Modified
Field Type:     Data                           Data Type:     Text
Contents are:   Single Valued
Justify:        Left
View Procedure:
 Pre-Processor  SETNEXTFIELD({Transaction Amount•Transaction})

Field Name:     Monthly Budget
Field Type:     Data                           Data Type:     Number
Contents are:   Single Valued
Justify:        Right
Format:         Fixed                          Decimal Places:  2
Decimal:        .                              Thousands:
Negative:       -n                             Currency:      $
```

Report Name:	View Definition		10/30/87 4:49 PM Page 10
Project Name:	NewCheck Project		
View Name:	Enter Transactions	View Type:	Display, Custom Layout
File Name:	Budget	File Type:	dBASE Mac

Field Name:	Actual Budget		
Field Type:	Data	Data Type:	Number
Contents are:	Single Valued		
Justify:	Right		
Format:	Fixed	Decimal Places:	2
Decimal:	.	Thousands:	
Negative:	-n	Currency:	$

Report Name:	View Definition		10/30/87 4:49 PM Page 11
Project Name:	NewCheck Project		
View Name:	Enter Transactions	View Type:	Display, Custom Layout
File Name:	Globals	File Type:	Globals

Field Name:	Date		
Field Type:	Memory	Data Type:	Date
Justify:	Left		
Format:	mm/dd/yy		
Year Length:	2	Separator:	/
Initial Date	10/30/87		

File Name:	Transaction	File Type:	dBASE Mac

Report Name:	View Definition	10/30/87	4:49 PM
		Page	12
Project Name:	NewCheck Project		
View Name:	Enter Transactions	View Type:	Display, Custom Layout
File Name:	Transaction	File Type:	dBASE Mac

Field Name:	Balance		Modified
Field Type:	Memory	Data Type:	Number
Contents are:	Single Valued		
Justify:	Right		
Format:	Fixed	Decimal Places:	2
Decimal:	.	Thousands:	
Negative:	-n	Currency:	$
View Procedure:			
Pre-Processor	SETNEXTFIELD({Transaction Amount•Transaction})		

Field Name:	Check Count		
Field Type:	Memory	Data Type:	Number
Contents are:	Single Valued		
Justify:	Right		
Format:	Fixed	Decimal Places:	0
Decimal:	.	Thousands:	
Negative:	-n	Currency:	
Initial Value:	5		

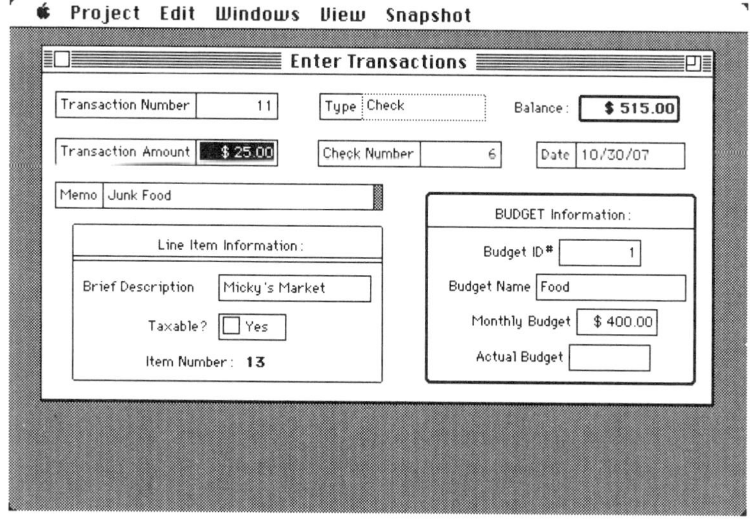

Figure 12-2 Enter Transactions Layout.

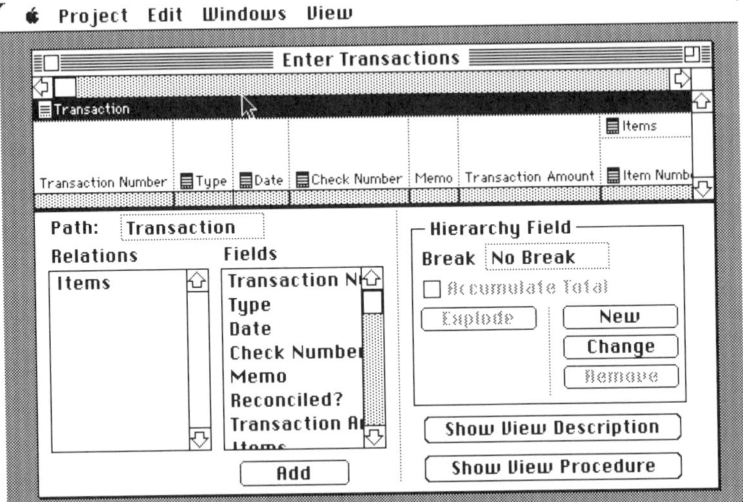

Figure 12-3 Enter Transactions Hierarchy1.

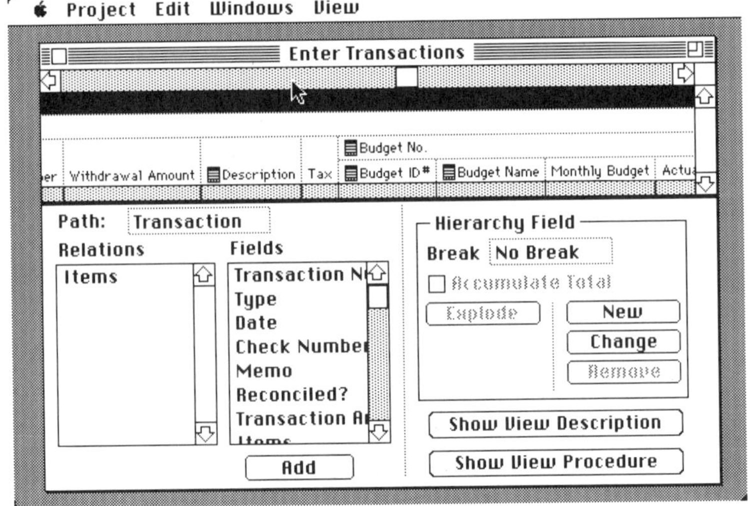

Figure 12-4 Enter Transactions Hierarchy2.

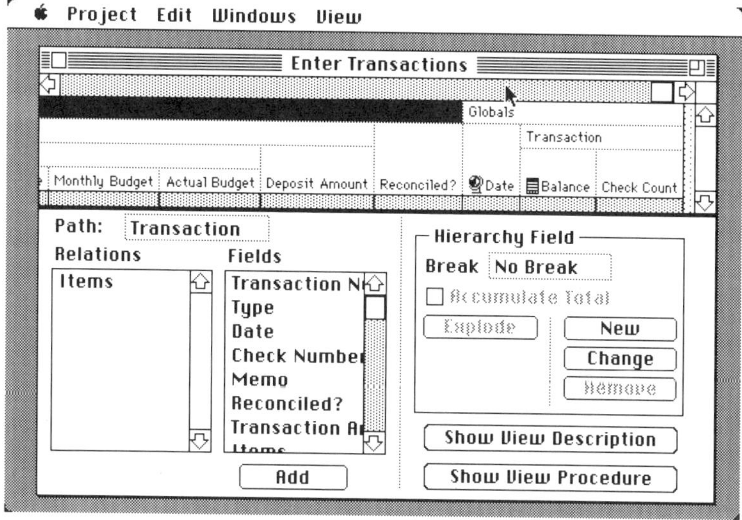

Figure 12-5 Enter Transactions Hierarchy3.

List Transactions View

The List Transactions view is essentially a duplication of the Enter Transactions view with columnar elements sized to fit onto one page. You should be able to create that view without much trouble. To save time, first Duplicate the Enter Transactions view as a Columnar layout.

Report Name:	View Definition		10/30/87 4:50 PM Page 1
Project Name:	NewCheck Project		
View Name:	List Transactions	View Type:	Display, Custom Layout
Root File:	Transaction	File Type:	dBASE Mac

Report Name:	View Definition		10/30/87 4:50 PM Page 2	
Project Name:	NewCheck Project			
View Name:	List Transactions	View Type:	Display, Custom Layout	
File Name:	Transaction	File Type:	dBASE Mac	
Access Path:	Transaction			
Field Name:	Transaction Number			
Field Type:	Key, Ordered	Data Type:	Number	Required
Justify:	Right			
Format:	Fixed	Decimal Places:	0	
Decimal:	.	Thousands:		
Negative:	-n	Currency:		
Auto Sequenced By:	1			
Initial Value:				
Field Name:	Type			
Field Type:	Data	Data Type:	Choices	
Contents are:	Single Valued			
Justify:	Left			
Format:	Pop-Up			
Values:	Check			
	Bank Ch			
	Misc Ck			
	Deposit			
	Interest			
	Split Ck			
	VOID			
Initial Value:	Check			
Field Name:	Date			
Field Type:	Data	Data Type:	Date	
Contents are:	Single Valued			
Justify:	Left			
Format:	mm/dd/yy			
Year Length:	2	Separator:	/	
Field Name:	Check Number			
Field Type:	Data	Data Type:	Number	
Contents are:	Single Valued			
Justify:	Right			
Format:	Fixed	Decimal Places:	0	
Decimal:	.	Thousands:		
Negative:	-n	Currency:		
Field Name:	Memo			
Field Type:	Data	Data Type:	Text	
Contents are:	Multiple Valued			
Justify:	Left			
Field Name:	Reconciled?			

Report Name:	View Definition		10/30/87	4:50 PM
			Page 3	
Project Name:	NewCheck Project			
View Name:	List Transactions	View Type:	Display, Custom Layout	
File Name:	Transaction	File Type:	dBASE Mac	

Field Type:	Data	Data Type:	Logical	
Contents are:	Single Valued			
Justify:	Left			
Format:	Check Box			
Values:	No/Yes			
Initial Value:	No			
Field Name:	Transaction Amount			
Field Type:	Data	Data Type:	Number	Required
Contents are:	Single Valued			
Justify:	Right			
Format:	Fixed	Decimal Places:	2	
Decimal:	.	Thousands:		
Negative:	-n	Currency:	$	
Range:	$ 0.00 To ...			
Field Name:	Items			
Field Type:	Data	Data Type:	Number	
Contents are:	Multiple Valued			
Justify:	Right			
Format:	Fixed	Decimal Places:	0	
Decimal:	.	Thousands:		
Negative:	-n	Currency:		
Relations:	Two-way with Items			
Relates File:	Items	File Type:	dBASE Mac	

Report Name:	View Definition		10/30/87 4:50 PM Page 4	
Project Name:	NewCheck Project			
View Name:	List Transactions	View Type:	Display, Custom Layout	
File Name:	Items	File Type:	dBASE Mac	
Access Path:	Items•Transaction			
Field Name:	Item Number			
Field Type:	Key, Ordered	Data Type:	Number	Required
Justify:	Right			
Format:	Fixed	Decimal Places:	0	
Decimal:	.	Thousands:		
Negative:	-n	Currency:		
Auto Sequenced By:	1			
Initial Value:	23			
Field Name:	Withdrawal Amount			
Field Type:	Data	Data Type:	Number	
Contents are:	Single Valued			
Justify:	Right			
Format:	Fixed	Decimal Places:	2	
Decimal:	.	Thousands:		
Negative:	-n	Currency:	$	
Post To:	Add to: Actual Budget•Budget			
	Subtract from: Balance•Transaction			
Field Name:	Deposit Amount			
Field Type:	Data	Data Type:	Number	
Contents are:	Single Valued			
Justify:	Right			
Format:	Fixed	Decimal Places:	2	
Decimal:	.	Thousands:		
Negative:	-n	Currency:	$	
Post To:	Add to: Balance•Transaction			
	Add to: Actual Budget•Budget			
Field Name:	Budget No.			
Field Type:	Data	Data Type:	Number	Required
Contents are:	Single Valued			
Justify:	Right			
Format:	Fixed	Decimal Places:	0	
Decimal:	.	Thousands:		
Negative:	-n	Currency:		
Relations:	Two-way with Budget			
Relates File:	Budget	File Type:	dBASE Mac	

Report Name:	View Definition		10/30/87	4:50 PM
			Page 5	
Project Name:	NewCheck Project			
View Name:	List Transactions	View Type:	Display, Custom Layout	
File Name:	Budget	File Type:	dBASE Mac	
Access Path:	Budget No.•Items•Transaction			
Field Name:	Budget ID#			
Field Type:	Key, Ordered	Data Type:	Number	Required
Justify:	Right			
Format:	Fixed	Decimal Places:	0	
Decimal:	.	Thousands:		
Negative:	-n	Currency:		
Initial Value:	1			
Field Name:	Monthly Budget			
Field Type:	Data	Data Type:	Number	
Contents are:	Single Valued			
Justify:	Right			
Format:	Fixed	Decimal Places:	2	
Decimal:	.	Thousands:		
Negative:	-n	Currency:	$	
Field Name:	Actual Budget			
Field Type:	Data	Data Type:	Number	
Contents are:	Single Valued			
Justify:	Right			
Format:	Fixed	Decimal Places:	2	
Decimal:	.	Thousands:		
Negative:	-n	Currency:	$	

Modify Transactions View

When dealing with split transactions and budgets, it is important to be sure that all values are accurately reflected when modifying values in existing records.

Modify Transactions allows the user to modify the records one at a time. Then, instead of simply pressing **Enter**, he or she uses the Modify button, a special view field with a Pre-Processor attached.

The trick in dealing with this view is to be sure that any changes made to split checks are reflected in the Transaction Amount field. To do so, the Write Record procedure contains a special routine to read each item in the Items Pointer field, total them, and set that total to the Transaction Amount field for the record. The re-posting of the Withdrawal Amount and Deposit Amount fields is handled automatically by dBASE Mac.

Notice how the two local variables, k and i, are used to create a loop that moves through each record in the multivalued Pointer field, Items•Transaction.

The mod_button field Pre-Processor first executes a WRITE command, then executes a NEXTBROWSE to display the next record.

The Post-Processor on the Transaction Number field is necessary to inform the user that new records are not allowed in the Modify Transactions view. However, due to an obscure bug in Release 1.0, a spurious transaction will be entered unless the Post-Processor also sets the Transaction Number to something else. We set it to zero, a record number nobody will use. To retrieve another record, the user simply enters the transaction number desired and **Tabs** out.

Another Post-Processor, this one on the Type field, prevents users from changing a transaction type to anything but VOID.

The Items Pointer field has a Post Processor, a New Record procedure, and a Write Record procedure attached to it.

NOTE: A subordinate file Pointer field can contain all five types of procedures. The Root can only contain New, Write, and Delete because (1) the Root is not a field, and (2) it can't be dragged onto the layout.

The Items Post-Processor prevents someone from modifying the Items number (which is the record number and can't be changed without corrupting the file data). The New Record procedure likewise prevents anyone from entering a new Items value.

The Items Write procedure first sets any VOID transaction values to zero (by assigning zero to the Withdrawal Amount and Deposit Amount fields). Next it sets Transaction Amount equal to the sum of Withdrawal Amount and Deposit Amount for all transactions except split checks. This means that even if you change the record, the Transaction Amount will be correct. The split check procedure is included in the Write Record procedure for the Transactions file, which is executed after the Items file Write Record procedure.

The rest of the view is self-explanatory.

The layout for this view is very useful. In addition to the small Tablet used in the Enter Transactions view (to control the appearance of the Check Number), another Tablet controls the appearance of the Withdrawal Amount or the Deposit Amount field. This Tablet contains the following selections for its two sheets—Show If:

```
{Type•Transactions} <= 3 OR {Type•Transactions} = 6
```

(for Withdrawal Amount) and

```
{Type•Transactions} = 4 OR {Type•Transactions} = 5
```

(for Deposit Amount).

The Modify button is created the same way the Help button was created for the MultiMail project in Chapter 10. When you work with this view, notice how smoothly everything works and how much information is contained in a small space.

```
Report Name:   View Definition                                      10/30/87   4:52 PM
                                                                    Page 1
Project Name:  NewCheck Project
View Name:     Modify Transactions        View Type:   Display, Custom Layout
================================================================================
Procedure:
 Pre-Processor SETNEXTFIELD({Transaction Number•Transaction})
--------------------------------------------------------------------------------
Root File:     Transaction                File Type:   dBASE Mac
View Procedure:
 Write Record  IF {Type•Transaction} = 6 THEN  k = COUNT({Items•Transaction})  \* split *\
                 SETBROWSE({Items•Transaction},1)
                FOR i = 1 TO k DO
                   READ({Items•Transaction})
                   temp_amount = temp_amount + {Withdrawal Amount•Items•Transaction}
                  NEXTBROWSE({Items•Transaction})
                END
                   {Transaction Amount•Transaction} = temp_amount
               END
               WRITE(SELF)
               REDISPLAY({Balance•Transaction•Globals})
 Delete Record ALERT ("You may NOT Delete records in this view.")
--------------------------------------------------------------------------------
Field Name:    mod_button                                           View Field
Field Type:    Memory                     Data Type:   Graphic
Scale:         None
Procedure:
 Pre-Processor WRITE({Transaction Number•Transaction})
               NEXTBROWSE({Transaction Number•Transaction})
               SETNEXTFIELD({Transaction Number•Transaction})
               REDISPLAY({Transaction})
               REDISPLAY({Items•Transaction})
               REDISPLAY({Budget No.•Items•Transaction})
--------------------------------------------------------------------------------
File Name:     Globals                    File Type:   Globals
--------------------------------------------------------------------------------
```

```
Report Name:    View Definition                                      10/30/87     4:52 PM
                                                                     Page  2

Project Name:   NewCheck Project
View Name:      Modify Transactions          View Type:     Display, Custom Layout
File Name:      Transaction                  File Type:     dBASE Mac

Access Path:    Transaction
--------------------------------------------------------------------------------------
Field Name:     Transaction Number                                   Modified
Field Type:     Key,  Ordered                Data Type:     Number   Required
Justify:        Right
Format:         Fixed                        Decimal Places:  0
Decimal:        .                            Thousands:
Negative:       -n                           Currency:
Auto Sequenced By:  1
Initial Value:  4
View Procedure:
  Post-Processor IF NOT ({Transaction Number•Transaction} IN "Transaction")
                 THEN ALERT ("You may NOT add NEW Transactions in this view - only MODIFY"
                         :" existing transactions.")
                   {Transaction Number•Transaction} = 0
                   SETNEXTFIELD({Transaction Number•Transaction})
                 END
                 ACCEPT
--------------------------------------------------------------------------------------
Field Name:     Type                                                 Modified
Field Type:     Data                         Data Type:     Choices
Contents are:   Single Valued
Justify:        Left
Format:         Pop-Up
Values:         Check
                Bank Ch
                Misc Ck
                Deposit
                Interest
                Split Ck
                VOID
Initial Value:  Check
View Procedure:
  Post-Processor IF {Type•Transaction} <> 7 THEN
                   ALERT ("You may only change TYPE to VOID.")
                 ELSE ACCEPT
                 END
--------------------------------------------------------------------------------------
Field Name:     Date
Field Type:     Data                         Data Type:     Date
Contents are:   Single Valued
Justify:        Left
Format:         mm/dd/yy
Year Length:    2                            Separator:     /
```

Report Name:	View Definition			10/30/87 4:52 PM
				Page 3
Project Name:	NewCheck Project			
View Name:	Modify Transactions	View Type:	Display, Custom Layout	
File Name:	Transaction	File Type:	dBASE Mac	

Field Name:	Check Number			
Field Type:	Data	Data Type:	Number	
Contents are:	Single Valued			
Justify:	Right			
Format:	Fixed	Decimal Places:	0	
Decimal:	.	Thousands:		
Negative:	-n	Currency:		
Field Name:	Memo			
Field Type:	Data	Data Type:	Text	
Contents are:	Multiple Valued			
Justify:	Left			
Field Name:	Reconciled?			
Field Type:	Data	Data Type:	Logical	
Contents are:	Single Valued			
Justify:	Left			
Format:	Check Box			
Values:	No/Yes			
Initial Value:	No			
Field Name:	Transaction Amount			Modified
Field Type:	Data	Data Type:	Number	Required
Contents are:	Single Valued			
Justify:	Right			
Format:	Fixed	Decimal Places:	2	
Decimal:	.	Thousands:		
Negative:	-n	Currency:	$	
Range:	$ 0.00 To ...			
View Procedure:				
Pre-Processor	SETNEXTFIELD({Transaction Number•Transaction})			
Field Name:	Items			Modified
Field Type:	Data	Data Type:	Number	
Contents are:	Multiple Valued			
Justify:	Right			
Format:	Fixed	Decimal Places:	0	
Decimal:	.	Thousands:		
Negative:	-n	Currency:		
Relations:	Two-way with Items			
View Procedure:				
Post-Processor	ALERT ("You may NOT change the item reference of an existing transaction.")			
New Record	ALERT ("You may NOT add a NEW occurrence (Line Item pointer) to an existing transaction.")			

Report Name:	View Definition		10/30/87 4:52 PM Page 4
Project Name:	NewCheck Project		
View Name:	Modify Transactions	View Type:	Display, Custom Layout
File Name:	Transaction	File Type:	dBASE Mac

```
Write Record   IF {Type•Transaction} = 7 THEN
                 {Withdrawal Amount•Items•Transaction} = 0
                 {Deposit Amount•Items•Transaction} = 0
               ELSE IF {Type•Transaction} <> 6 THEN  {Transaction Amount•Transaction} =
                 {Withdrawal Amount•Items•Transaction} + {Deposit Amount•Items•Transaction}
                 END
               END
               WRITE (SELF)
Delete Record  BREAK
```

Relates File:	Items	File Type:	dBASE Mac

Report Name:	View Definition			10/30/87 4:52 PM Page 5
Project Name:	NewCheck Project			
View Name:	Modify Transactions	View Type:	Display, Custom Layout	
File Name:	Items	File Type:	dBASE Mac	
Access Path:	Items•Transaction			
Field Name:	Item Number			
Field Type:	Key, Ordered	Data Type:	Number	Required
Justify:	Right			
Format:	Fixed	Decimal Places:	0	
Decimal:	.	Thousands:		
Negative:	-n	Currency:		
Auto Sequenced By:	1			
Initial Value:	23			
Field Name:	Description			
Field Type:	Data	Data Type:	Text	
Contents are:	Single Valued			
Justify:	Left			
Field Name:	Tax			
Field Type:	Data	Data Type:	Logical	
Contents are:	Single Valued			
Justify:	Left			
Format:	Check Box			
Values:	No/Yes			
Initial Value:	No			
Field Name:	Budget No.			Modified
Field Type:	Data	Data Type:	Number	Required
Contents are:	Single Valued			
Justify:	Right			
Format:	Fixed	Decimal Places:	0	
Decimal:	.	Thousands:		
Negative:	-n	Currency:		
Relations:	Two-way with Budget			
View Procedure:				
Pre-Processor	BREAK			
Relates File:	Budget	File Type:	dBASE Mac	
Field Name:	Withdrawal Amount			
Field Type:	Data	Data Type:	Number	
Contents are:	Single Valued			
Justify:	Right			
Format:	Fixed	Decimal Places:	2	
Decimal:	.	Thousands:		
Negative:	-n	Currency:	$	
Post To:	Add to: Actual Budget•Budget Subtract from: Balance•Transaction			

Report Name:	View Definition	10/30/87	4:52 PM
		Page 6	
Project Name:	NewCheck Project		
View Name:	Modify Transactions	View Type:	Display, Custom Layout
File Name:	Items	File Type:	dBASE Mac
Field Name:	Deposit Amount		
Field Type:	Data	Data Type:	Number
Contents are:	Single Valued		
Justify:	Right		
Format:	Fixed	Decimal Places:	2
Decimal:	.	Thousands:	
Negative:	-n	Currency:	$
Post To:	Add to: Balance•Transaction		
	Add to: Actual Budget•Budget		

Report Name:	View Definition	10/30/87	4:52 PM
		Page 7	
Project Name:	NewCheck Project		
View Name:	Modify Transactions	View Type:	Display, Custom Layout
File Name:	Budget	File Type:	dBASE Mac
Access Path:	Budget No.•Items•Transaction		
Field Name:	Budget Name		
Field Type:	Data	Data Type:	Text
Contents are:	Single Valued		
Justify:	Left		
Field Name:	Budget Type		
Field Type:	Data	Data Type:	Choices
Contents are:	Single Valued		
Justify:	Left		
Format:	Pop-Up		
Values:	Per Inc		
	Bus Inc		
	Per Exp		
	Bus Exp		
Initial Value:	Per Inc		
Field Name:	Actual Budget		
Field Type:	Data	Data Type:	Number
Contents are:	Single Valued		
Justify:	Right		
Format:	Fixed	Decimal Places:	2
Decimal:	.	Thousands:	
Negative:	-n	Currency:	$

Report Name:	View Definition		10/30/87 4:52 PM
			Page 8
Project Name:	NewCheck Project		
View Name:	Modify Transactions	View Type:	Display, Custom Layout
File Name:	Globals	File Type:	Globals
File Name:	Transaction	File Type:	dBASE Mac

Report Name:	View Definition		10/30/87 4:52 PM
			Page 9
Project Name:	NewCheck Project		
View Name:	Modify Transactions	View Type:	Display, Custom Layout
File Name:	Transaction	File Type:	dBASE Mac
Field Name:	Balance		Modified
Field Type:	Memory	Data Type:	Number
Contents are:	Single Valued		
Justify:	Right		
Format:	Fixed	Decimal Places:	2
Decimal:	.	Thousands:	
Negative:	-n	Currency:	$
Initial Value:	$ 300.00		
View Procedure:			
Pre-Processor	SETNEXTFIELD({Transaction Number•Transaction})		

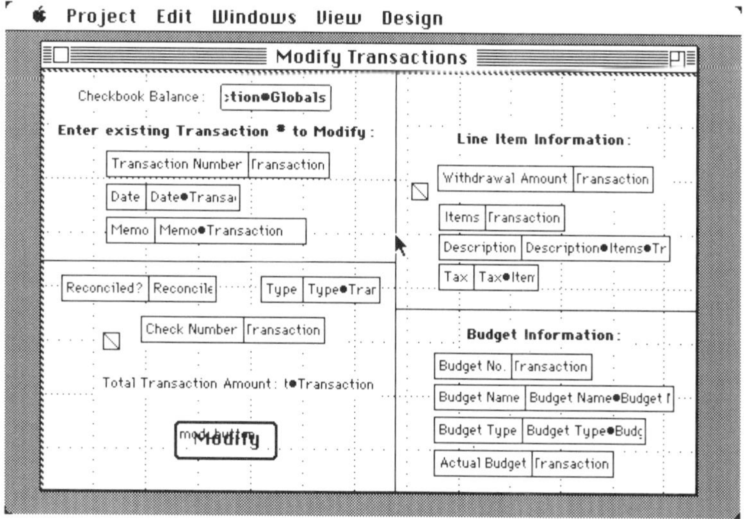

Figure 12-6 Modify Transactions Layout1.

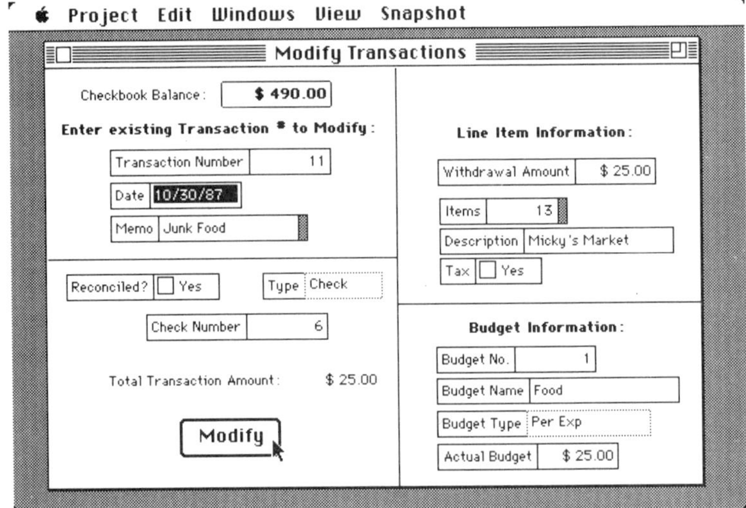

Figure 12-7 Modify Transactions Layout2.

Reconcile View

The Reconcile view efficiently checks to see if the NewCheck balance agrees with your bank statement balance. To use Reconcile, you will need to go into the Modify Transactions view and click on the reconcile field for each transaction that appears on the statement, then click Modify for each record. Then, return to the Main Menu and select Reconcile.

The key to the operation of the Reconcile view is the Selection criterion that reads Show Transaction If. . .

```
NOT {Reconciled?•Transaction}
```

You'll find the Selection criterion at the top of the Reconcile view listing.

When the Reconcile view is performed, a Pre-Processor on the Transaction Number field executes. A dialog box asks you to enter your ending balance, and the procedure takes it from there.

In a LOOP, the procedure reads each selected record, determines its type, and adds the appropriate amount to the local variables *withdrawal_sum* and *deposit_sum.* When the end of the file is reached, a trial balance (*trial_bal*) is created by adding the *deposit_sum* to and subtracting the *withdrawal_sum* from the balance you entered (stored in the local variable *real_bal*).

Notice that the REDISPLAY({Transaction}) command causes all fields in the layout to redisplay. What makes this so useful is that it shows the field values scrolling in the view as the records are processed. The user can see the activity of the procedure as it works.

Notice the way the concatenated ALERT box is created. The where variable is set to either "over." or "under." depending on the difference between *real_bal* and *trial_bal.* If the balances do match, then another ALERT box displays your total outstanding checks and deposits, and total balance.

That's about all there is to it. Once again, the layout is minimal. The Pre-Processor is attached to the Transaction Number Field; therefore, that field must occur first on the layout.

Report Name:	View Definition		10/30/87	4:51 PM
			Page 1	
Project Name:	NewCheck Project			
View Name:	Reconcile	View Type:	Display, Custom Layout	

Root File:	Transaction	File Type:	dBASE Mac
Show If:	NOT {Reconciled?•Transaction}		
File Name:	Globals	File Type:	Globals

```
Report Name:    View Definition                                  10/30/87    4:51 PM
                                                                 Page  2

Project Name:   NewCheck Project
View Name:      Reconcile                   View Type:    Display, Custom Layout
File Name:      Transaction                 File Type:    dBASE Mac

Access Path:    Transaction

Field Name:     Transaction Number                                    Modified
Field Type:     Key,  Ordered               Data Type:    Number      Required
Justify:        Right
Format:         Fixed                       Decimal Places:  0
Decimal:        .                           Thousands:
Negative:       -n                          Currency:
Auto Sequenced By:  1
Initial Value:  8
View Procedure:
 Pre-Processor  \* 'Reconcile' view; is 'called' (Performed) -  'selection criteria' attached
                   limits the snapfile (workfile) to only 'UN-reconciled' transactions.  *\
                LOOP
                  DIALOG 80,95,230,410
                    BUTTON 1,120,80,140,130,"OK"
                    BUTTON 2,120,190,140,250,"Cancel"
                    EDITTEXT 1,85,120,101,210,""
                  FIXEDTEXT 10,85,25,300,"RECONCILE CHECKBOOK"
                   FIXEDTEXT 40,30,75,310,"Please enter the ending balance from "
                                   :"your checking account statement:"
                 END
                   real_bal = INTERNAL(TEXTVALUE(1),{Transaction Amount•Transaction})
                WHEN ERROR = 0 LEAVE
                  ALERT ("INVALID amount entered.  Please enter valid numeric characters.")
                END
                IF NOT BUTTONVALUE(2) THEN
                 LOOP
                   REDISPLAY({Transaction})  \* this displays ALL fields in file on layout *\
                   IF {Type•Transaction} <= 3 OR {Type•Transaction} = 6
                   THEN withdrawal_sum = withdrawal_sum + {Transaction Amount•Transaction}
                   ELSE deposit_sum = deposit_sum + {Transaction Amount•Transaction}
                  END
                 WHEN ENDOF({Transaction}) LEAVE
                  NEXTBROWSE({Transaction Amount•Transaction})
                 END
                  trial_bal = real_bal + deposit_sum - withdrawal_sum
                  IF trial_bal = {Balance•Transaction•Globals} THEN
                     diff = TRUNC((real_bal - trial_bal),2)
                    ALERT ("Good job! The Checkbook balances! The difference between your"
                      :" statement ending balance and your present balance is $": diff
                      :"  You have $":withdrawal_sum:" in outstanding checks or charges."
```

```
Report Name:    View Definition                                    10/30/87   4:51 PM
                                                                   Page 3
Project Name:   NewCheck Project
View Name:      Reconcile                    View Type:     Display, Custom Layout
File Name:      Transaction                  File Type:     dBASE Mac
-------------------------------------------------------------------------------------
                    :" You have $":deposit_sum:" in outstanding depsits.",STOP)
                ELSE diff =  trial_bal - {Balance•Transaction•Globals}
                  IF diff > 0 THEN  where = " over.  "
                  ELSE  where = " short.  "
                 END
                 ALERT ("The checkbook does not balance.  Your account is $":
                          ABS(diff) : where  :
                     "Please check your records and try again.",STOP)
               END
               END
               EXIT
-------------------------------------------------------------------------------------
Field Name:     Type
Field Type:     Data                         Data Type:     Choices
Contents are:   Single Valued
Justify:        Left
Format:         Pop-Up
Values:         Check
                Bank Ch
                Misc Ck
                Deposit
                Interest
                Split Ck
                VOID
Initial Value:  Check
-------------------------------------------------------------------------------------
Field Name:     Date
Field Type:     Data                         Data Type:     Date
Contents are:   Single Valued
Justify:        Left
Format:         mm/dd/yy
Year Length:    2                            Separator:     /
-------------------------------------------------------------------------------------
Field Name:     Check Number
Field Type:     Data                         Data Type:     Number
Contents are:   Single Valued
Justify:        Right
Format:         Fixed                        Decimal Places: 0
Decimal:        .                            Thousands:
Negative:       -n                           Currency:
-------------------------------------------------------------------------------------
Field Name:     Memo
Field Type:     Data                         Data Type:     Text
Contents are:   Multiple Valued
```

Report Name:	View Definition		10/30/87	4:51 PM
			Page 4	
Project Name:	NewCheck Project			
View Name:	Reconcile	View Type:	Display, Custom Layout	
File Name:	Transaction	File Type:	dBASE Mac	
Justify:	Left			
Field Name:	Reconciled?			
Field Type:	Data	Data Type:	Logical	
Contents are:	Single Valued			
Justify:	Left			
Format:	Check Box			
Values:	No/Yes			
Initial Value:	No			
Field Name:	Transaction Amount			
Field Type:	Data	Data Type:	Number	Required
Contents are:	Single Valued			
Justify:	Right			
Format:	Fixed	Decimal Places:	2	
Decimal:	.	Thousands:		
Negative:	-n	Currency:	$	
Range:	$ 0.00 To ...			
Field Name:	Items			
Field Type:	Data	Data Type:	Number	
Contents are:	Multiple Valued			
Justify:	Right			
Format:	Fixed	Decimal Places:	0	
Decimal:	.	Thousands:		
Negative:	-n	Currency:		
Relations:	Two-way with Items			

Report Name:	View Definition		10/30/87	4:51 PM
			Page 5	
Project Name:	NewCheck Project			
View Name:	Reconcile	View Type:	Display, Custom Layout	
File Name:	Globals	File Type:	Globals	
File Name:	Transaction	File Type:	dBASE Mac	

Report Name:	View Definition		10/30/87 4:51 PM
			Page 6
Project Name:	NewCheck Project		
View Name:	Reconcile	View Type:	Display, Custom Layout
File Name:	Transaction	File Type:	dBASE Mac

Field Name:	Balance		
Field Type:	Memory	Data Type:	Number
Contents are:	Single Valued		
Justify:	Right		
Format:	Fixed	Decimal Places:	2
Decimal:	.	Thousands:	
Negative:	-n	Currency:	$
Initial Value:	$ 515.00		
Field Name:	Reconciled Amount		
Field Type:	Memory	Data Type:	Number
Contents are:	Single Valued		
Justify:	Right		
Format:	Fixed	Decimal Places:	2
Decimal:	.	Thousands:	
Negative:	-n	Currency:	$
Initial Value:	$ 0.00		

r•Transaction

t•Transaction

Date•Transa

Reconcile Transaction Layout with 3 fields: Transaction Number, Transaction Amount, and Date.

Income Statement View

The Income Statement view is a Columnar report sorted by Budget Type. The procedure that controls the view is the view Pre-Processor. This view allows the user to choose any time period for the report. Specific radio buttons allow any quarter of the year to be chosen, and specific data ranges can be entered. A Year-to-Date report is also available.

The Income Statement view prints with subtotals on the Budget Type for Withdrawal Amount, Deposit Amount, and Actual Budget. The entire Pre-Processor procedure is dedicated to handling the various date range options and contains several error checking routines.

Notice the Actual Formula field, a formula field, sets the value of the Actual Budget to a negative amount if the Budget Type is an expense category, and to positive if it is an income category. Use Actual Formula on the layout in place of Actual Budget.

```
Report Name:     View Definition                                    10/30/87    4:53 PM
                                                                    Page  1

Project Name:    NewCheck Project
View Name:       Income Statement            View Type:     Display, Custom Layout

Procedure:
 Pre-Processor   \* Income Statement - View pre-processor procedure *\
                 LOOP
                   DIALOG 60,20,290,490
                     EDITTEXT 1,200,50,216,130,""
                     EDITTEXT 2,200,220,216,300,""
                    FIXEDTEXT 10,35,60,360,"INCOME STATEMENT : please select a report choice "
                           :"and enter appropriate DATE values.  (current date is ":DATE:")"
                     FIXEDTEXT 165,50,180,160,"Starting Date:"
                     FIXEDTEXT 165,215,180,330,"Ending Date:"
                     BUTTON 1,200,385,220,440,"OK"
                     BUTTON 2,165,385,185,440,"Cancel"
                    RADIOLIST 1,2
                      RADIOBUTTON 80,20,95,380,
                                 "Quarterly (enter YEAR Start date & choose quarter)"
                       RADIOBUTTON 105,20,120,365, "Year-to-Date (enter YEAR Start Date only)"
                      RADIOBUTTON 130,20,145,365,"Date RANGE  (enter Start & Ending Dates)"
                   END
                      FIXEDTEXT 30,395,45,450,"QUARTER:"
                    RADIOLIST 2,0
                       RADIOBUTTON 50,390,65,460,"First"
                      RADIOBUTTON 70,390,85,460,"Second"
                       RADIOBUTTON 90,390,105,460,"Third"
                       RADIOBUTTON 110,390,125,460,"Fourth"
                   END
                  END
                   aDate = INTERNAL(TEXTVALUE(1),{Date A•Globals})
                  n = ERROR
                   bDate = INTERNAL(TEXTVALUE(2),{Date B•Globals})
                  n = n + ERROR
                 WHEN (n = 0 AND RADIOVALUE(1) >= 1) OR BUTTONVALUE(2) LEAVE
                  ALERT ("INVALID Date entered.  Please enter again.")
                 END
                 IF BUTTONPRESSED = 2 THEN EXIT
                 END
                 CASE RADIOVALUE(1) OF
                  WHEN 1 DO    {Date A•Globals} = (RADIOVALUE(2) - 1) * 90 + aDate
                               {Date B•Globals} = 90 + {Date A•Globals}
                  WHEN 2 DO    {Date B•Globals} = DAYS
                               {Date A•Globals} = aDate
                  WHEN 3 DO    {Date A•Globals} = aDate
                               {Date B•Globals} = bDate
                 END
```

Report Name:	View Definition			10/30/87 4:53 PM Page 2
Project Name:	NewCheck Project			
View Name:	Income Statement	View Type:	Display, Custom Layout	
Root File:	Budget	File Type:	dBASE Mac	
Sort By:	Budget Type•Budget			Ascending
File Name:	Globals	File Type:	Globals	

Report Name:	View Definition			10/30/87 4:53 PM
				Page 3
Project Name:	NewCheck Project			
View Name:	Income Statement	View Type:	Display, Custom Layout	
File Name:	Budget	File Type:	dBASE Mac	
Access Path:	Budget			
Field Name:	Budget ID#			
Field Type:	Key, Ordered	Data Type:	Number	Required
Justify:	Right			
Format:	Fixed	Decimal Places:	0	
Decimal:	.	Thousands:		
Negative:	-n	Currency:		
Initial Value:	1			
Field Name:	Budget Name			
Field Type:	Data	Data Type:	Text	
Contents are:	Single Valued			
Justify:	Left			
Field Name:	Budget Type			
Field Type:	Data	Data Type:	Choices	
Contents are:	Single Valued			
Justify:	Left			
Format:	Pop-Up			
Values:	Per Inc			
	Bus Inc			
	Per Exp			
	Bus Exp			
Initial Value:	Per Inc			
Control Break:	Line break			
Field Name:	Monthly Budget			
Field Type:	Data	Data Type:	Number	
Contents are:	Single Valued			
Justify:	Right			
Format:	Fixed	Decimal Places:	2	
Decimal:	.	Thousands:		
Negative:	-n	Currency:	$	
Field Name:	Actual Budget			
Field Type:	Data	Data Type:	Number	
Contents are:	Single Valued			
Justify:	Right			
Format:	Fixed	Decimal Places:	2	
Decimal:	.	Thousands:		
Negative:	-n	Currency:	$	
Field Name:	Trial Budget			
Field Type:	Data	Data Type:	Number	
Contents are:	Single Valued			

Report Name:	View Definition	10/30/87 Page 4	4:53 PM
Project Name:	NewCheck Project		
View Name:	Income Statement	View Type:	Display, Custom Layout
File Name:	Budget	File Type:	dBASE Mac
Justify:	Right		
Format:	Fixed	Decimal Places:	2
Decimal:	.	Thousands:	
Negative:	-n	Currency:	$
Field Name:	Items		
Field Type:	Data	Data Type:	Number
Contents are:	Multiple Valued		
Justify:	Right		
Format:	Fixed	Decimal Places:	0
Decimal:	.	Thousands:	
Negative:	-n	Currency:	
Relations:	Two-way with Items		
Relates File:	Items	File Type:	dBASE Mac
Show If:	{Date•Transaction No.•Items•Budget} >= {Date A•Globals} AND {Date•Transaction No.•Items•Budget} <= {Date B•Globals}		
Field Name:	Actual Formula		View Field
Field Type:	Formula	Data Type:	Number
Justify:	Right		
Format:	Fixed	Decimal Places:	2
Decimal:	.	Thousands:	,
Negative:	<n>	Currency:	$
Formula:	IF {Budget Type•Budget} <= 2 THEN {Actual Budget•Budget} ELSE {Actual Budget•Budget} * -1 END		Accumulate totals

Report Name:	View Definition		10/30/87 4:53 PM	
			Page 5	
Project Name:	NewCheck Project			
View Name:	Income Statement	View Type:	Display, Custom Layout	
File Name:	Items	File Type:	dBASE Mac	
Access Path:	Items•Budget			
Field Name:	Item Number			
Field Type:	Key, Ordered	Data Type:	Number	Required
Justify:	Right			
Format:	Fixed	Decimal Places:	0	
Decimal:	.	Thousands:		
Negative:	-n	Currency:		
Auto Sequenced By:	1			
Initial Value:	23			
Field Name:	Withdrawal Amount			
Field Type:	Data	Data Type:	Number	
Contents are:	Single Valued			
Justify:	Right			
Format:	Fixed	Decimal Places:	2	
Decimal:	.	Thousands:		
Negative:	-n	Currency:	$	
Post To:	Add to: Actual Budget•Budget			
	Subtract from: Balance•Transaction			Accumulate totals
Field Name:	Deposit Amount			
Field Type:	Data	Data Type:	Number	
Contents are:	Single Valued			
Justify:	Right			
Format:	Fixed	Decimal Places:	2	
Decimal:	.	Thousands:		
Negative:	-n	Currency:	$	
Post To:	Add to: Balance•Transaction			
	Add to: Actual Budget•Budget			Accumulate totals
Field Name:	Description			
Field Type:	Data	Data Type:	Text	
Contents are:	Single Valued			
Justify:	Left			
Field Name:	Transaction No.			
Field Type:	Data	Data Type:	Number	
Contents are:	Single Valued			
Justify:	Right			
Format:	Fixed	Decimal Places:	0	
Decimal:	.	Thousands:		
Negative:	-n	Currency:		
Relations:	Two-way with Transaction			
Relates File:	Transaction	File Type:	dBASE Mac	

Report Name:	View Definition			10/30/87 4:53 PM Page 6
Project Name:	NewCheck Project			
View Name:	Income Statement	View Type:	Display, Custom Layout	
File Name:	Transaction	File Type:	dBASE Mac	
Access Path:	Transaction No.•Items•Budget			
Field Name:	Transaction Number			
Field Type:	Key, Ordered	Data Type:	Number	Required
Justify:	Right			
Format:	Fixed	Decimal Places:	0	
Decimal:	.	Thousands:		
Negative:	-n	Currency:		
Auto Sequenced By:	1			
Initial Value:	10			
Field Name:	Type			
Field Type:	Data	Data Type:	Choices	
Contents are:	Single Valued			
Justify:	Left			
Format:	Pop-Up			
Values:	Check			
	Bank Ch			
	Misc Ck			
	Deposit			
	Interest			
	Split Ck			
	VOID			
Initial Value:	Check			
Field Name:	Date			
Field Type:	Data	Data Type:	Date	
Contents are:	Single Valued			
Justify:	Left			
Format:	mm/dd/yy			
Year Length:	2	Separator:	/	
Field Name:	Transaction Amount			
Field Type:	Data	Data Type:	Number	Required
Contents are:	Single Valued			
Justify:	Right			
Format:	Fixed	Decimal Places:	2	
Decimal:	.	Thousands:		
Negative:	-n	Currency:	$	
Range:	$ 0.00 To ...			

Report Name:	View Definition		10/30/87 4:53 PM Page 7
Project Name:	NewCheck Project		
View Name:	Income Statement	View Type:	Display, Custom Layout
File Name:	Globals	File Type:	Globals

Field Name:	Date A		
Field Type:	Memory	Data Type:	Date
Justify:	Left		
Format:	mm/dd/yy		
Year Length:	2	Separator:	/

Field Name:	Date B		
Field Type:	Memory	Data Type:	Date
Justify:	Left		
Format:	mm/dd/yy		
Year Length:	2	Separator:	/
Initial Date	10/30/87		

Budget										
					Items					
								Transaction Information		
Bdgt ID#	Budget Name	Budget Type	Monthly Budget	Actual Budget*	Item No.	Withdrawal Amount	Deposit Amount	Tx#	Type	Date
7	Dividends	Per Inc	$ 200.00	$ 2,000.00	7		$ 2000.00	5	Interest	10/30/87
6	Interest	Per Inc	$ 100.00							
				$ 2,000.00		$ 0.00	$ 2000.00			
4	Salary	Bus Inc	$ 1500.00	$ 500.00	2	$ 400.00		2	Check	10/30/87
					3	$ 100.00		3	Split Ck	10/30/87
5	Commisi...	Bus Inc	$ 1000.00	$ 1,350.00	1		$ 1000.00	1	Deposit	10/30/87
					4	$ 350.00		3	Split Ck	10/30/87
				$ 1,850.00		$ 850.00	$ 1000.00			
1	Food	Per Exp	$ 400.00	$ 0.00						
2	Rent	Per Exp	$ 350.00	$ <350.00>	12	$ 350.00		10	Misc Ck	10/30/87
3	Clothing	Per Exp	$ 150.00	$ <395.00>	5	$ 50.00		3	Split Ck	10/30/87
					6	$ 45.00		4	Bank Ch	10/30/87
					11	$ 300.00		9	Check	10/30/87
				$ <745.00>		$ 745.00	$ 0.00			
10	Misc. Ex...	Bus Exp	$ 100.00	$ <400.00>	10	$ 400.00		8	Check	10/30/87
8	Travel E...	Bus Exp	$ 50.00	$ <390.00>	8	$ 390.00		6	Misc Ck	10/30/87
9	Supplies	Bus Exp	$ 200.00	$ <100.00>	9	$ 100.00		7	Check	10/30/87
				$ <890.00>		$ 890.00	$ 0.00			
				$ 2,215.00		$ 2485.00	$ 3000.00			

Income Statement Sample Report

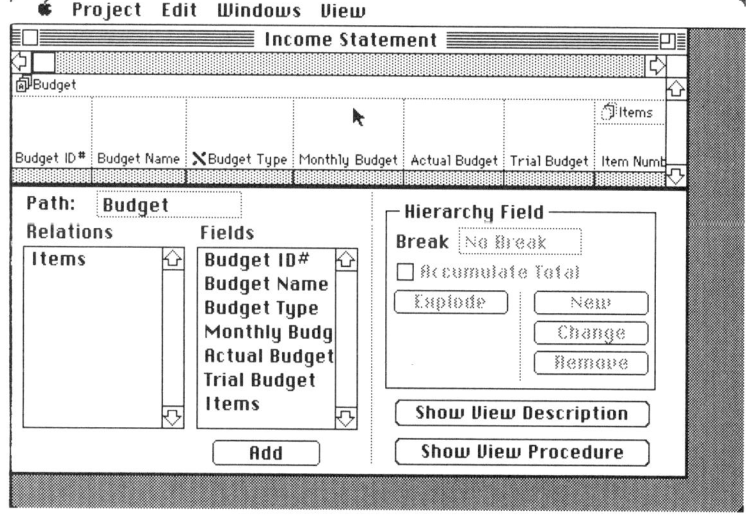

Figure 12-8 Income Statement Hierarchy1.

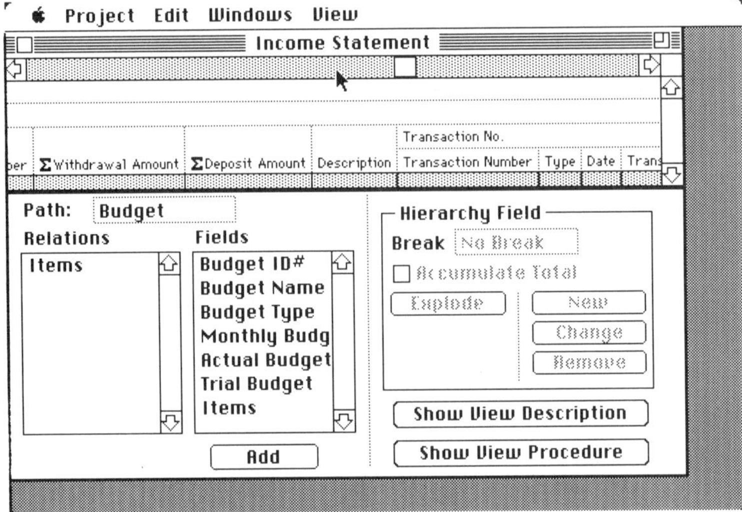

Figure 12-9 Income Statement Hierarchy2.

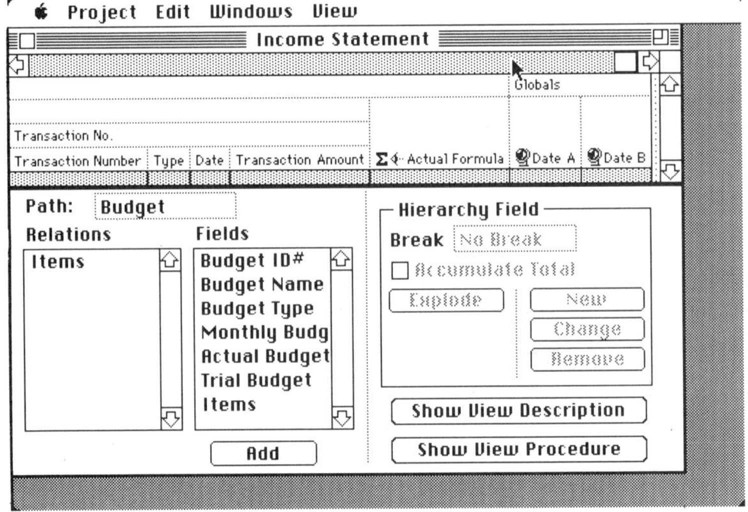

Figure 12-10 Income Statement Hierarchy3.

By now you know how to add Custom Menus and Protect your project. You can make the NewCheck project anything you want it to be. Or use the ideas presented in this and other applications to develop ideas of your own. Next, we've added a special application that demonstrates some things you can do with indexes. We'll finish the Tutorial with a brief look at file structures. Every so often you may receive a message stating File Needs Reorganization. The final section should help you understand some of what is going on in your files.

The States Project

As a final example, Tom Bodine has put together a handy application that demonstrates how you can choose from a list of values in a subordinate file and automatically insert one of those values into a Root File field. You might use this in many applications. For instance, suppose you often need to fill out a form that contains employee names, but you don't remember all the employee numbers. Using a system like the one presented here, you could choose from a pop-up list of employees in the Employee file, automatically inserting the chosen name where you need it.

This example uses a database of the states of the United States, an index file, and a Census file. The view uses the Census as the Root File. Below the Census file, the State Index file is next in the hierarchy, then the States file.

The State Index file is a special external index on the Dummy field in the States file. For each record in the States file, the Dummy field contains the number 1. This means that only one record will be contained in the State Index file, and that record will point back to every record in the States file.

A two-way relationship between Census and the State Index field forms the pathway for data sharing.

If you create the layout shown in the figure, you will notice that the Tablet contains the selection criterion, Show If. . .

```
{State Index•Census} = 1
```

The Tablet only shows when a 1 is entered in the State Index pointer field. When the Tablet shows, the States•State Index•Census pointer field contains each state code. The State Name•States•State Index•Census field contains the actual name of the state to go along with the state code. Finally, clicking on the State Chosen view

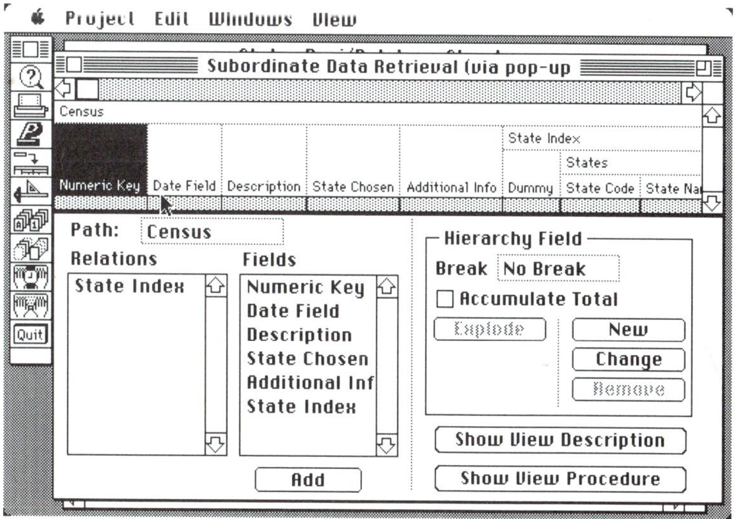

Figure 12-11 States Proj Hierarchy.

Graphic field initiates its Pre-Processor, which assigns the value of State Name to the State Chosen field.

This example is simply an interesting manipulation of data using indexes and subordinate file relationships. We put it in here at the end of the Tutorial to show you that you can have fun with dBASE Mac in many ways.

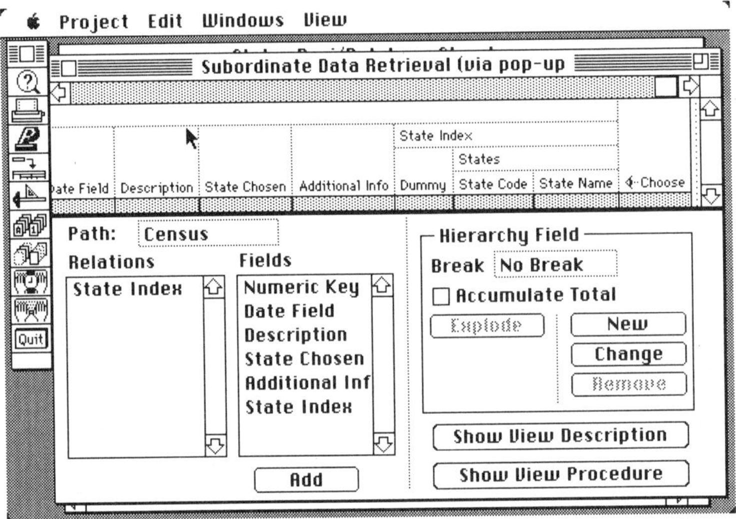

Figure 12-12 States Proj Hierarchy2.

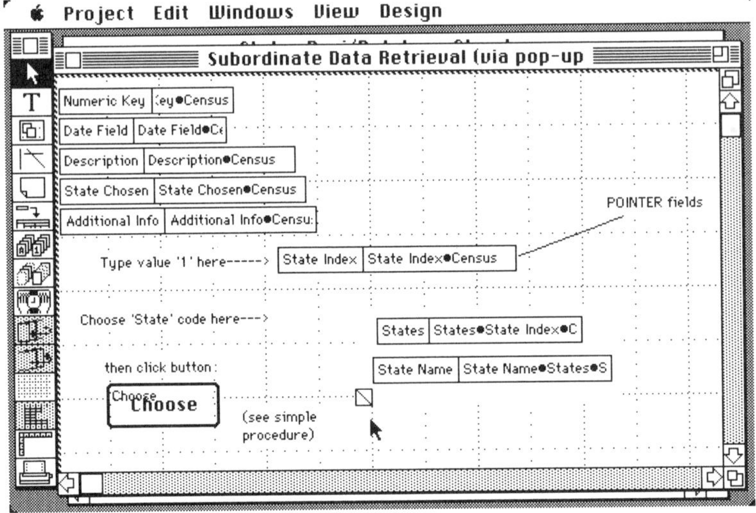

Figure 12-12a States Proj Layout.

Report Name:	File Structure			10/30/87 7:59 AM Page 1
File Name:	States	File Type:	dBASE Mac	

Field Name:	State Code			
Field Type:	Key, Ordered	Data Type:	Text	Required
Justify:	Left			
Pattern:	aa			
Field Name:	State Name			
Field Type:	Data	Data Type:	Text	
Contents are:	Single Valued			
Justify:	Left			
Field Name:	Attribute1			
Field Type:	Data	Data Type:	Text	
Contents are:	Single Valued			
Justify:	Left			
Field Name:	Size			
Field Type:	Data	Data Type:	Text	
Contents are:	Single Valued			
Justify:	Left			
Field Name:	# of people			
Field Type:	Data	Data Type:	Number	
Contents are:	Single Valued			
Justify:	Right			
Format:	Fixed	Decimal Places:	0	
Decimal:	.	Thousands:		
Negative:	-n	Currency:		
Field Name:	major industry			
Field Type:	Data	Data Type:	Text	
Contents are:	Single Valued			
Justify:	Left			
Field Name:	resources			
Field Type:	Data	Data Type:	Text	
Contents are:	Multiple Valued			
Justify:	Left			
Field Name:	Dummy			
Field Type:	Data	Data Type:	Text	
Contents are:	Single Valued			
Justify:	Left			
Pattern:	'1'			
Initial Text	1			
Relations:	Indexed by State Index			
Field Name:	People			
Field Type:	Data	Data Type:	Text	
Contents are:	Multiple Valued			

Report Name:	File Structure			10/30/87 7:59 AM
				Page 2
File Name:	States	File Type:	dBASE Mac	

Justify: Left

Report Name:	File Structure			10/30/87 7:58 AM
				Page 1
File Name:	Census	File Type:	dBASE Mac	

Field Name:	Numeric Key			
Field Type:	Key, Ordered	Data Type:	Number	Required
Justify:	Right			
Format:	Fixed	Decimal Places:	2	
Decimal:	.	Thousands:		
Negative:	-n	Currency:		
Auto Sequenced By:	1			
Initial Value:	1.00			

Field Name:	Date Field		
Field Type:	Data	Data Type:	Date
Contents are:	Single Valued		
Justify:	Left		
Format:	mm/dd/yy		
Year Length:	2	Separator:	/

Field Name:	Description		
Field Type:	Data	Data Type:	Text
Contents are:	Single Valued		
Justify:	Left		

Field Name:	State Chosen		
Field Type:	Data	Data Type:	Text
Contents are:	Single Valued		
Justify:	Left		

Field Name:	Additional Info		
Field Type:	Data	Data Type:	Text
Contents are:	Single Valued		
Justify:	Left		

Field Name:	State Index		
Field Type:	Data	Data Type:	Text
Contents are:	Multiple Valued		
Justify:	Left		
Pattern:	'1'		
Initial Text	1		
Relations:	One-way with State Index		

```
Report Name:    View Definition                                        10/30/87     8:00 AM
                                                                       Page  1

Project Name:   States Proj
View Name:      Subordinate Data Retrieval (via popView Type:     Display, Custom Layout

Procedure:
 Pre-Processor  NEW({Numeric Key•Census})

Root File:      Census                          File Type:      dBASE Mac

Field Name:     Choose                                                 View Field
Field Type:     Memory                          Data Type:      Graphic
Scale:          None
Procedure:
 Pre-Processor  {State Chosen•Census} = {State Name•States•State Index•Census}
                REDISPLAY({State Chosen•Census})
                SETNEXTFIELD({Numeric Key•Census})
```

```
Report Name:    File Structure                                         10/30/87     7:59 AM
                                                                       Page  1

File Name:      State Index                     File Type:      dBASE Mac

Field Name:     Dummy
Field Type:     Key, Ordered                    Data Type:      Text
Justify:        Left
Pattern:        '1'

Field Name:     States
Field Type:     Data                            Data Type:      Text
Contents are:   Multiple Valued
Justify:        Left
Pattern:        aa
Relations:                                                             Auto Delete
                Index to States
```

Report Name:	View Definition		10/30/87 8:00 AM Page 2	
Project Name:	States Proj			
View Name:	Subordinate Data Retrieval (via pop	View Type:	Display, Custom Layout	
File Name:	Census	File Type:	dBASE Mac	
Access Path:	Census			
Field Name:	Numeric Key			
Field Type:	Key, Ordered	Data Type:	Number	Required
Justify:	Right			
Format:	Fixed	Decimal Places:	2	
Decimal:	.	Thousands:		
Negative:	-n	Currency:		
Auto Sequenced By:	1			
Initial Value:	1.00			
Field Name:	Date Field			
Field Type:	Data	Data Type:	Date	
Contents are:	Single Valued			
Justify:	Left			
Format:	mm/dd/yy			
Year Length:	2	Separator:	/	
Field Name:	Description			
Field Type:	Data	Data Type:	Text	
Contents are:	Single Valued			
Justify:	Left			
Field Name:	State Chosen			
Field Type:	Data	Data Type:	Text	
Contents are:	Single Valued			
Justify:	Left			
Field Name:	Additional Info			
Field Type:	Data	Data Type:	Text	
Contents are:	Single Valued			
Justify:	Left			
Field Name:	State Index			
Field Type:	Data	Data Type:	Text	
Contents are:	Multiple Valued			
Justify:	Left			
Pattern:	'1'			
Initial Text	1			
Relations:	One-way with State Index			
Relates File:	State Index	File Type:	dBASE Mac	

Report Name:	View Definition		10/30/87 8:00 AM
			Page 3
Project Name:	States Proj		
View Name:	Subordinate Data Retrieval (via popView	View Type:	Display, Custom Layout
File Name:	State Index	File Type:	dBASE Mac
Access Path:	State Index•Census		
Field Name:	Dummy		
Field Type:	Key, Ordered	Data Type:	Text
Justify:	Left		
Pattern:	'1'		
Field Name:	States		
Field Type:	Data	Data Type:	Text
Contents are:	Multiple Valued		
Justify:	Left		
Pattern:	aa		
Relations:			Auto Delete
	Index to States		
Relates File:	States	File Type:	dBASE Mac

Report Name:	View Definition		10/30/87	8:00 AM
			Page 4	
Project Name:	States Proj			
View Name:	Subordinate Data Retrieval (via popView	View Type:	Display, Custom Layout	
File Name:	States	File Type:	dBASE Mac	
Access Path:	States•State Index•Census			
Field Name:	State Code			
Field Type:	Key, Ordered	Data Type:	Text	Required
Justify:	Left			
Pattern:	aa			
Field Name:	State Name			
Field Type:	Data	Data Type:	Text	
Contents are:	Single Valued			
Justify:	Left			

Optimizing File Performance

Often when you add many records to a file, or when you make modifications to the file as you have done in this chapter to the Checkbook file, the performance of the file may degrade. You can check that the file is running at its maximum efficiency by selecting Change File from the DataFile menu, or by double-clicking the title bar of the file in question in the Structure Window.

Understanding File Statistics

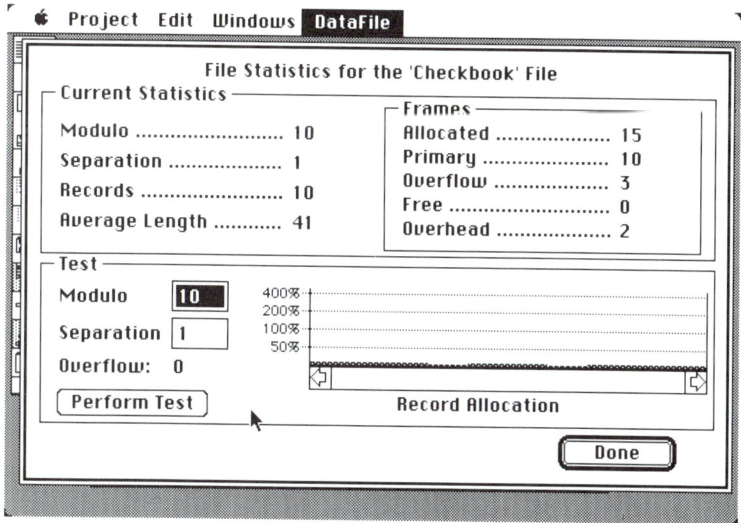

Figure 12-13 File Statistics Dialog Graphic.

- Highlight any file on the Structure Window and select Change File from the Datafile menu. (Or double-click the file's title bar.)
- Click the Show Statistics button.

You'll see a lot of numbers in the dialog box that follows. To understand their meaning, you need to have a basic understanding of how dBASE Mac organizes data.

Frame A Frame, in dBASE Mac, is a 512 byte block of data. The first 12 bytes contain internal data, the remaining 500 bytes contains file data.

Group A Group is a set of Frames that is treated as a single unit (normally a single record). Thus, you can think of a Group as being a record.

Primary Groups Primary Groups are the initial Groups created with your file. Remember when you estimated the file size? That told dBASE Mac how many Primary Groups to create.

Modulo The Modulo of a file is the number of Primary Groups.

Separation The Separation of a file is the number of Frames (512K blocks) in a single Primary Group.

dBASE Mac uses some formulas to calculate the Modulo and Separation. First, it must estimate the number of frames that will be needed to contain the file. Then it uses the estimated number of records, the approximate average record size, and the number of fields in each record to calculate the following formula:

```
TotalFrames = NumRecords * (AvgRecSize +
NumFields)\500
```

Now the program estimates the Separation:

```
Separation = 1 + (AvgRecSize DIV 500)
```

NOTE: DIV is an operator that uses only the integer portion of a division and is not in the dBASE Mac Procedural Interface.

Finally, Modulo is calculated:

```
Modulo = TotalFrames DIV Separation
```

Look at the data in the box labeled Frames:

Allocated The number of Frames currently allocated to the file.

Primary Frames allocated to the Primary Groups.

Overflow Frames to be used if you add more records to the file than estimated. This value will change dynamically, allowing you to enter as many records as your storage media will hold.

Free The number of Frames currently unused.

It is not really necessary to understand all the details of the dBASE Mac file structure to optimize the performance of the program.

Optimizing File Performance

NOTE: Before you begin to follow the steps in this section, you may wish to back up your current file or project.

Still in the Show Statistics dialog box, click the Perform Test button. The graph labeled Record Allocation will display a bar. If the bar is below 100 percent, your file should be operating efficiently. If it is over 100 percent, you should Reorganize.

To decide how to modify the file, change the Modulo to a higher number.

NOTE: You can use the information displayed in the dialog box to calculate values based on the formulas given above, or you can simply try different Modulo values. You are not changing the file at this point, so experiment freely.

NOTE: One suggested practice is to use Numeric Key Fields, and use only prime numbers for the Modulo. (A prime number is a number that can only be divided by itself and by 1.)

WARNING: Do not change the Separation. Separation controls the way the file is written to disk, and you do not want to change that unless you know exactly what you are doing, and why.

When you have set a Modulo that brings the Record Allocation graph down under 100 percent, look at the number of records you have in the file (displayed as Records under Current Statistics).

- Estimate how many more records you might be adding, if any.
- Now click **Done**, then click Reorganize File.
- Estimate the file size you will need.
- Click the Custom checkbox.
- Set the Modulo value you determined was best in the appropriate box, then click **OK** to perform the reorganization.

The file should perform faster now.

Summary

That concludes Part I, The Tutorial. You should have a pretty thorough knowledge of using dBASE Mac at this point. You can use Part II, The Reference, to find quick explanations of specific parts of the program. Part II is a complete alphabetical reference to dBASE Mac.

In this chapter you learned to create a new project from scratch, and how to use dBASE Mac file and view listings to do so.

You created a processor to handle split transactions, and another to handle budgets.

You created an entire system for reconciling the checkbook, including automatic validation of the Balance.

You created a flexible Income Statement.

You learned something about the way files are stored, and how to optimize them.

Congratulations. You're at the end of the Tutorial.

Have your hand stamped on the way out in case you decide to return.

PART II

dBASE Mac Reference

dBASE MAC REFERENCE

About dBASE Mac

About dBASE Mac is found in the Apple Menu. It tells you the version number you are using, and also how much memory is being used by your current application and how much remains free.

Add Button

The **Add** button is found in the Define Hierarchy screen, the procedure definition screens, the Define Sorts, the Define Selections, formula definition, and Show Selections screens. It is always used to add a field name to a hierarchy, procedure, or formula.

Add Field

From the Structure Window, you can add a field to a selected file. Pull down the Datafile menu and select Add Field.

Next, follow the procedures for creating a new, nonkey field.

TIP: The new field will be last on the structure screen. You can change the order any time by dragging that field to a new position.

NOTE: Repositioning a field on the Structure Window changes the display order for that field in the Field list boxes (in Define Hierarchy, procedures, etc.). If you've had to create a new field in a file, you can place it in a more advantageous position that way.

Align to Grid

You can use the Align to Grid command in the Design Menu to accurately place layout elements, whether the Grid is visible or not. Selected items will snap to the nearest grid line when this command is activated, thus allowing you more accuracy and consistency in the placement of layout elements. (For more, see Layout.)

Apple Menu

The Apple Menu contains, in addition to any Desk Accessories that you have added, About dBASE Mac, Help, and Picture This. . . .

For more, refer to each menu item by name.

Bring to Front

Layout elements can be placed in three dimensions, stacked one upon the other. Bring to Front from the Design menu will bring a highlighted layout element to the front of the stack, placing it on top of any other layout elements. (See also Layout, Send to Back.)

Change Field

You can change field characteristics at any time. You can't change the Field Type or the Data Type, but all other aspects of the field can be modified. Field characteristics can be changed at either the Structure Window or the Define Hierarchy screen. When you change the definition of a file field within the Define Hierarchy, the field is no longer considered a file field, but becomes a View Modified File Field, or VMFF. VMFFs can be changed back to file fields using the **Revert** button in the Change Field dialog box.

There are two ways to change a field. From the Structure Window, highlight the desired field and select Change Field from the Datafile menu, or double-click the field band on the desktop. The familiar field definition screen will appear. At this point, you can follow the same procedures used when creating a file.

> TIP: When you wish to create a procedure or formula for a field that uses the field name itself (i.e., fieldname = fieldname + 1), you will need to save the field definition first, then use Change Field to create the formula or procedure.

> TIP: When you are changing fields in a file, you can move from one to the next using the **Option** and **Command** keys. Holding **Option** and clicking **Done/P** moves to the previous file definition (if there is one), and clicking **Command-Done/N** moves to the next file definition (if any).

Change File

You might use Change File in a variety of circumstances. If dBASE Mac prompts you with a message that reads *File Needs Reorganization,* you need to use Change File. If you have removed some fields and want to make the removal permanent, Change File is necessary. To optimize performance in a file that has grown very large, that has added fields, or that had several individual records that contain a lot of data, use Change File to adjust the modulo of the file.

Select Change File also to add procedures that affect the entire file. Click the **Show Procedure** button in the Change File dialog box to open a standard procedure definition screen. You can attach New Record, Write Record, and Delete Record procedures to a file.

You can also use Change File to enter, edit, or remove a file's password.

Understanding File Organization and Optimization

A dBASE Mac file is organized into Frames and Groups. A basic understanding of this organization is helpful, but not mandatory, when trying to achieve optimized file performance.

Frame A Frame, in dBASE Mac, is a 512-byte block of data. The first 12 bytes contain internal data, and the remaining 500 contain file data.

Group A Group is a set of Frames that is treated as a single unit (normally a single record). Thus, you can think of a Group as being a record.

Primary Groups Primary Groups are the initial Groups created with your file. Remember when you estimated the file size? That told dBASE Mac how many Primary Groups to create.

Modulo The Modulo of a file is the number of Primary Groups.

Separation The Separation of a file is the number of Frames (512K blocks) in a single Primary Group.

dBASE Mac uses some formulas to calculate the Modulo and Separation. First, it must estimate the number of frames that will be needed to contain the file. Then it uses the estimated number of records, the approximate average record size, and the number of fields in each record to calculate the following formula:

```
TotalFrames = NumRecords * (AvgRecSize + NumFields)/500
```

Now the program estimates the Separation:

```
Separation = 1 + (AvgRecSize DIV 500)
```

NOTE: DIV is an operator that uses only the integer portion of a division and is not in the dBASE Mac Procedural Interface.

Finally, Modulo is calculated:

```
Modulo = TotalFrames DIV Separation
```

If you press the button labeled Show Statistics from the Change File dialog box, you will see the following information:

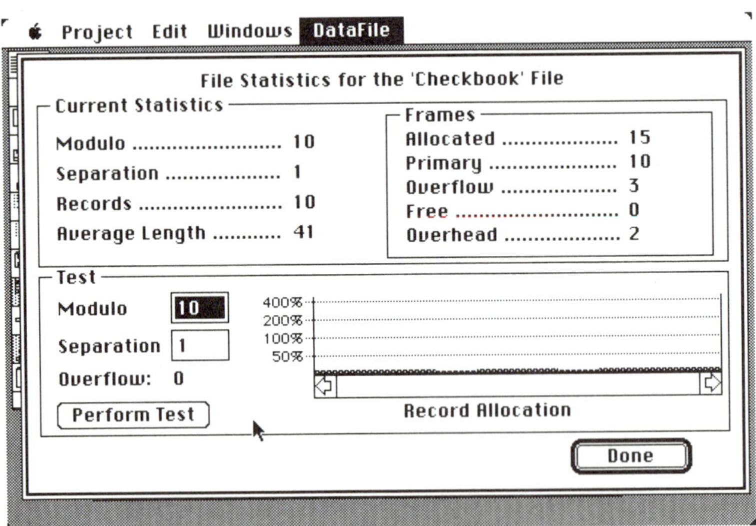

Figure R-1 Statistics Graphic.

Allocated The number of Frames currently allocated to the file.

Primary Frames allocated to the Primary Groups.

Overflow Frames to be used if you add more records to the file than estimated. This value will change dynamically, allowing you to enter as many records as your storage media will hold.

Free The number of Frames currently unused.

It is not really necessary to understand all the details of the dBASE Mac file structure to optimize the performance of the program.

Optimizing File Performance

Click the **Perform Test** button in the Show Statistics dialog box. The graph labeled Record Allocation will display a bar. If the bar is below 100 percent, your file should be operating efficiently. If it is over 100 percent, you should reorganize by changing the file.

To decide how to modify the file, change the Modulo to a higher number.

NOTE: You can use the information displayed in the dialog box to calculate values based on the formulas given above, or you can simply try different Modulo values. You are not changing the file at this point, so experiment freely.

NOTE: One suggested practice is to use Numeric Key fields, and use only prime numbers for the Modulo. (A prime number is a number that can only be divided by itself and by 1.)

WARNING: Do not change the Separation. Separation controls the way the file is written to disk, and you do not want to change that unless you know exactly what you are doing, and why.

When you have set a Modulo that brings the Record Allocation graph down under 100 percent, look at the number of records you have in the file (displayed as Records under Current Statistics).

- Estimate how many more records you might be adding, if any.
- Click **Done**, then click **Reorganize File**.
- Estimate the file size you will need.
- To set the new Modulo value, click the **Custom** checkbox.
- Set the Modulo value you determined was best in the appropriate box, then click **OK** to perform the reorganization.

Choices Field

You use a Choices field when you have a limited number of choices in a particular field, such as a list of salespeople in a particular department, a list of departments in a business, or a list of possible discount rates. A Choices field makes it easy to select a valid option when entering data into a record. By limiting options to a list of valid choices, you make data entry quicker and less prone to error.

Choices fields can display as pop-up lists:

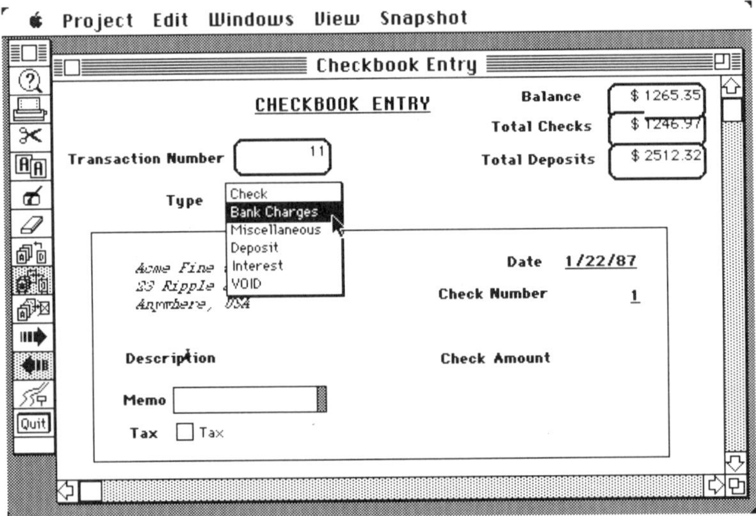

Figure R-2 Pop-up Graphic.

As horizontal buttons:

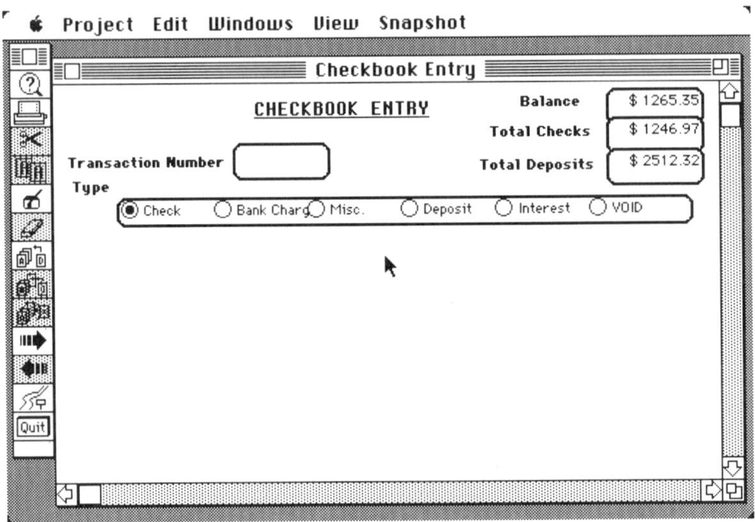

Figure R-3 Horizontal Buttons.

As vertical buttons:

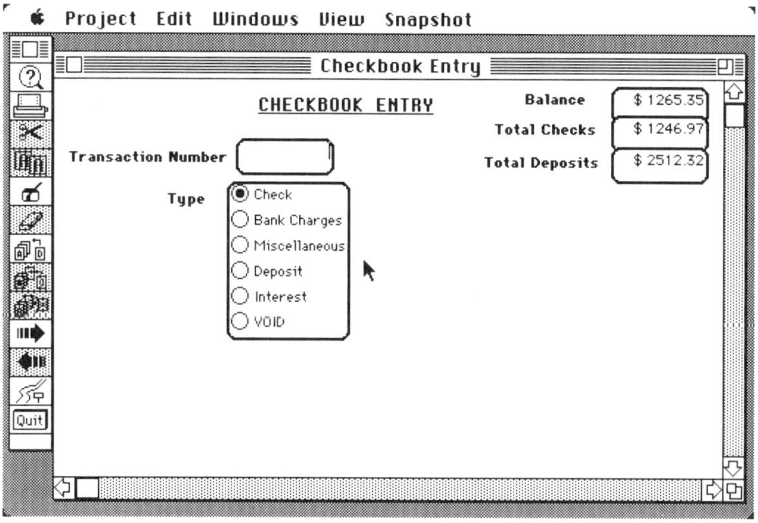

Figure R-4 Vertical Buttons.

or as a text box. If you choose the text box format, any entry into that text box must exactly match one of the choices defined in the field definition screen:

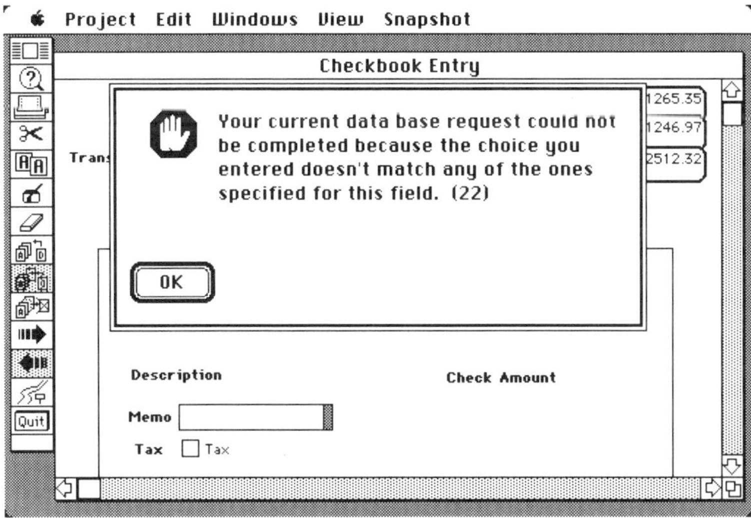

Figure R-5 Text Box and Matching Screen Graphic.

Define acceptable choices into the Choices box in the field definition dialog. Type **Return** after each choice. If you exceed six choices, the box will scroll to accept more.

If you want a particular value to be the default value, enter it in the Initial Choice box. If you do not choose one, the program assumes the first choice to be the default. If you check the Keep New Initial Choice box, the program will replace the default choice with any new choice entered during data entry. The new choice becomes the new default.

During programming, to refer to a particular value from a Choice Field you must use square brackets and the numeric position of the choice. For instance, look at the following list of choices from the Salesperson field in the Employee file:

Joe
Jane
Steve
Robert
Mary

Joe is referred to as {Employee•Salesperson}[1], while Mary is {Employee•Salesperson}[5].

In conditional programming, you can use the numeric position of the choice as its value:

```
IF {Type•Checkbook}= 1 THEN. . .
```

When you use a Choices field as a Sort criterion, the sort will be in numeric order (the order in which you defined the choices), not in alphabetical order.

A Choices field can contain up to 8,000 choices, up to 256 characters per choice, and a size maximum of 32,000 bytes.

Clear

Any time you see the **Clear** button, you can use it to erase all entries you have made in the dialog box, procedure, or formula you are currently writing, without placing it on the Clipboard.

WARNING: Pressing the **Clear** button before saving the contents of the current screen or dialog box may cause loss of new data.

Close DataFile

Choosing Close from the Datafile menu will cause the currently highlighted file to be closed and stored on the disk from which you retrieved it. The file is also removed from the current project. You cannot close a file if any of its fields are present in any view hierarchy.

Close Project

Choosing Close from the Project menu will close the active project, including all views, files, and relationships associated with it. If you have made changes to the project and have not saved them, you will be prompted to save changes. Any changes made to data in files have already been done, but saying **Yes** to the Save Changes dialog will save any changes to structure or view windows, any new indexes or relationships, and so on.

After you Close a project, you may Open an existing project, or select New. . . to begin a new one. If you wish to leave dBASE Mac after closing a project, choose Quit from the Project menu or click the **Exit** icon in the Palette.

Close View

To close an active view, click on the close box at the upper-left corner of the view. To select another view, leaving the current view open, select another view from the Windows menu or click in any visible portion of another view window.

Copy

The Copy command is the standard Macintosh Copy found in the Edit menu. Copy will save a copy of any highlighted text or graphics onto the Clipboard for later retrieval with the Paste command. The copied data will overwrite any existing data on the Clipboard.

The keyboard equivalent for Copy is **Command-C**.

For more information, see Appendix A.

Custom Menus

Use Custom Menus to create a set of pull-down menus for your project. Use these menus to allow controlled access to views during execution of a protected project (see Protect Project). By creating sophisticated view procedures, you can cause complex operations to be controlled by custom-designed menu items.

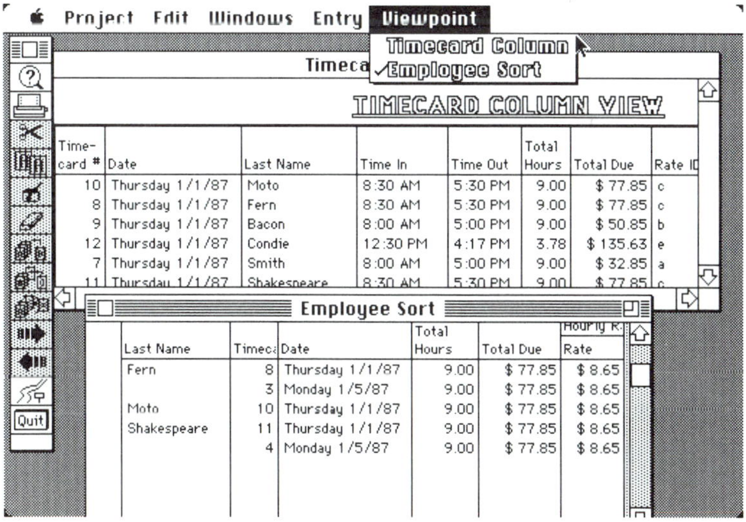

Figure R-6 Custom Menus Graphic.

First, in the layout of any view, select Custom Menus. . . from the Design menu. Click on the **Add New Title** button to create a new menu heading. A dialog box will open to allow you to enter the menu title. Hit **Return** or click **OK** to add that menu title to the list.

Now highlight a title from the Menu Titles list. When you click the **Add New Command** button, a list of available views is displayed. To add one of these view names to the menu highlighted, simply highlight the view name and click **OK**. Once a view has been used in a Custom Menu, it is no longer included in the list of available views.

Custom Menus will become active when the project has been protected (see Protect Project). If you click the Hide Window Menu checkbox, the standard Windows menu will be suppressed, and only those menu items you have defined will display, along with the standard Apple (Desk Accessory), Project, and Edit menus.

> HINT: If you do not hide Windows, the protected project will allow you to Perform and Use a view. If you hide the Windows menu, you might try adding the Perform and Use icon to the Use mode Palette if you will need to update records in a columnar view during operation of the protected project. However, the most common way to include a columnar view in a protected project is to create a controlling view with a procedure that PERFORMs the columnar view (most likely in conjunction with a dialog box menu choice).

Cut

Cut is the standard Macintosh Cut command found in the Edit menu. Choosing Cut removes highlighted text or graphics and saves them in the Clipboard. The most recently Cut material can be Pasted back into any appropriate place.

The keyboard equivalent for Cut is **Command-X**.

For more on standard Mac techniques, see Appendix A.

DataFile Menu

The DataFile menu appears when the Structure Window is active. It contains the basic commands for working with files and file fields.

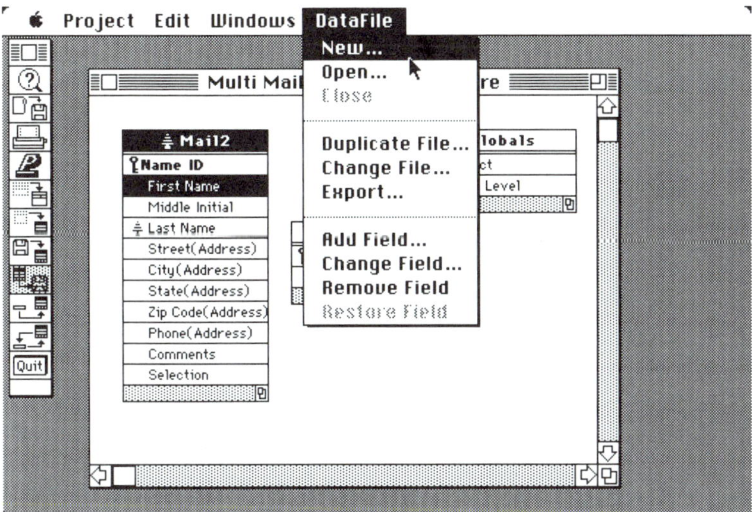

Figure R-7 Datafile Menu Graphic.

For more, see each individual DataFile command.

Data Type Field

A Data Type field is the most common file field type. You enter information to a Data field by typing from the keyboard, choosing from a Choices field or Logical field, or pasting from the Clipboard. Information in a Data field is stored conventionally in the file on a per-record basis. (See also Formula Fields, Memory Fields.)

Date Field

Date fields offer a wide variety of formats for storing dates. When you select Date from the Date Type: pop-up on a field definition screen, several new features appear. Look at the format types:

Format	Result
mm/dd/yy	9/14/87
mm/yy	9/87
yy	87

(continued)

Format	Result
dd/mm/yy	14/9/87
yy/mm/dd	87/9/14
dd m. . . yy	14 September 87
m. . . dd, yy	September 14, 87
m. . . yy	September 87
mmm dd, yy	Sep 14, 87
dd mmm yy	14 Sep, 87
mmm yy	Sep 87
Julian	1987257 (year and day of year)
Internal	2447052 (# of days since 1/1/4713 B.C.)
None	Whatever is entered

NOTE: Date-formatted fields can contain dates beginning with Jan. 1, 4713 B.C.

NOTE: To display the system date from the Macintosh calendar, you can use the DAYS function. For instance, to assign a Date field to the current system date: {Datefield•filename} = DAYS. To display a text or variable amount in date format, first assign the date information to a Date field, then assign the variable or text string using the form: D = FORMAT({Datefield•filename}). To convert a text string entered as a date to the dBASE Mac internal date format, use the form: Internal(textstring, {Datefield•filename}). See Chapter 11 for an example of this. These rules also apply to working with time values. The internal system time is represented by the function SECONDS.

The amount and kind of information available for display depends on the information entered. Put another way, if you store data in a format that uses only the month and year, the record information will not contain accurate data on the day of the month. If no day was entered, the internal format will default to the first day of the month. Because of this, you will not be able to change the display format to one that includes the day and receive an accurate portrayal of that date information. However, even if the display format is set to only month and year, you can enter the day information on a data entry form. If you do so, the information stored will be complete. Therefore, you can change from one display format to another with complete accuracy if all the data were entered in the first place.

For a complete chart of date formats and compatibilities, see your dBASE Mac manual.

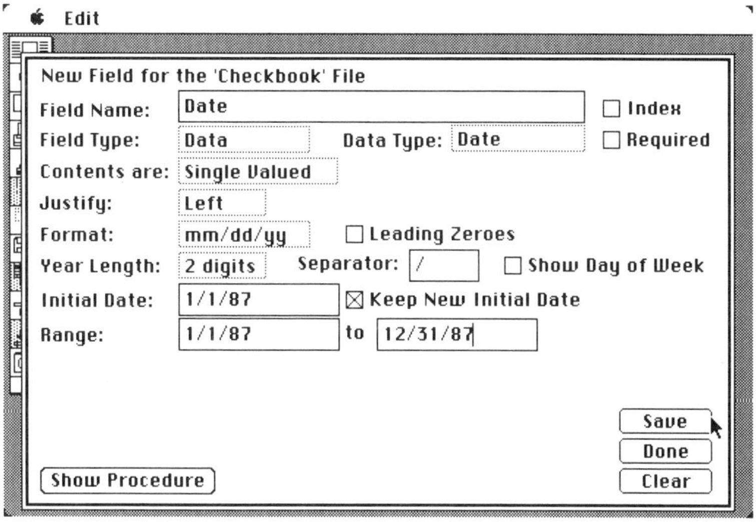

Figure R-8 Date Field Display.

dBASE Mac will automatically convert dates entered in compatible formats. Therefore, if the format is set to m... dd yy, and you enter 9/14/87, the display will change to read, September 14, 1987.

Other options available when defining a Date field include:

Leading Zeros checkbox Sets zeros before single digit numbers. For example, 3/4/87 is changed to 03/04/87.

Year Length Pop-up menu that chooses between a two-digit and a four-digit display, such as September 14, 87 or September 14, 1987.

Separator Selects the character to use to separate dates. The default separator is a slash (/), but you could use a dash (-) or a space, or any other character to separate date elements.

Show Day of Week checkbox Includes the day of the week in the date, for example, Monday 9/14/87.

Initial Date, Keep New Initial Date, and **Range** All work normally.

You can perform arithmetic using Date fields directly. For instance, to find the days between two Dates, create a Numeric Formula field, and enter a simple formula that subtracts one Date field from another. The result will be a numeric expression of the days between two dates. Or create a formula that adds a numeric value to a Date field to calculate a new date. For example, {Date•Datefile} + 3 adds three days to the value in the Date field in a file called Datefile.

- To enter the system date automatically on printed reports, use **Option-Shift-D** in a text element in the layout.

Define Selections

Often you will want to work with records that meet specific criteria. For instance, you might want to print employee records for the Sales Department only. Or you might want to display records for clients on the West Coast. Or you might want to display sales that exceeded $1,000. Whatever the criterion, you will use Define Selections to filter your records.

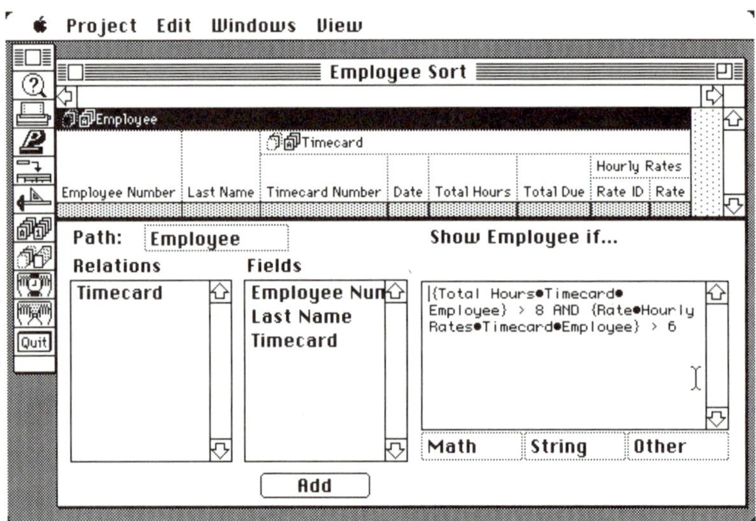

Figure R-9 Selection Screen Graphic.

Define Selections is found under the View menu. First, activate a view, then select Define Selections. The screen that appears is similar to the Define Hierarchy screen.

You can create a selection rule for any file or field in the hierarchy. Just remember that any selection applied to an element in the hierarchy will also affect all elements below that level. For instance, if you highlight a Pointer field in the hierarchy, all fields below that Pointer field will be affected. On the other hand, if you highlight a field at the lowest level of the hierarchy, then that field alone is affected by the selection rule you define.

In the box labeled Show If. . . , you will create an expression that defines your selection. You can highlight field names, change relations, use Global Memory fields, and use any of the expressions available within the Math, String, or Other pop-up menus. An example of a simple selection might be:

```
{Last Name•Employee} = "Smith"
```

This would select only those records in which the Last Name was Smith. To select records that were similar to the name Smith, use wildcard values, such as {Last

Name•Employee} MATCHES "Sm...th". This will find Smith, Smyth, or Smooth, but not Smythe, Smithe, and so on. MATCHES is found in the String pop-up.

More complex criteria are linked by logical operators like AND and OR. For instance:

```
            ({Last Name•Employee} = "Smith" AND
{Salary•Employee} > 10000) OR {City•Employee} =
"Baltimore"
```

The criteria above select all records in which an employee's last name is Smith and he makes more than $10,000. It also selects any employee who lives in Baltimore.

The same rules apply to creating Selection criteria as apply to procedures and formulas.

Define Sorts

At times you may want to sort the records in a view in different ways. For instance, you may want to list a name and address list by Zip Code or by last name, or even by city. You may want to sort financial transactions by date, amount, or budget code.

To change the order in which the records in a view are listed, use the Define Sorts command. First activate a view, then select Define Sorts from the View menu. The following screen appears:

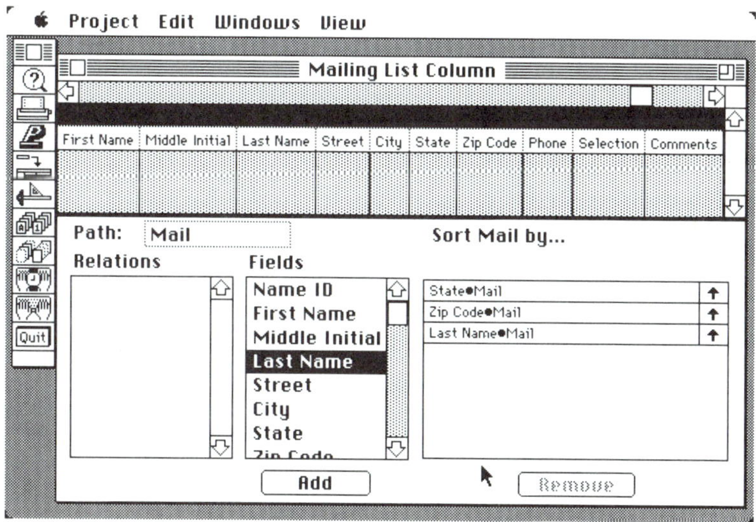

Figure R-10 Sort Screen Graphic.

Indicate the file to sort by highlighting a pointer field or field bar in the hierarchy. The pointer field name or field name should appear between the words Sort and by. . . , for example, Sort Employee by. . . .

NOTE: All fields below the selected level of the hierarchy are sorted, but fields above that level are unaffected.

NOTE: If you select a multivalued field, the values within that field will be sorted.

Next select the field or fields you wish to use as sort criteria. For instance, you might select Zip Code as your first sort criterion, then Last Name as a secondary sort. The file will be sorted by Zip Code first, then, within matching Zip Codes, by Last Name. Click on the arrow to select Ascending (A to Z) or Descending (Z to A) sorts. You can include up to eight fields within the criterion for a single sort, and you can define the sorts for as many files as you wish in the hierarchy.

Remember, the first sort field is the primary criterion, and each subsequent sort field is processed after those above. Thus, sort fields below the primary field are only sorted if there are duplicate entries in the primary field. For instance, in the example above, last name values are only sorted within equal Zip Code values.

When designing databases, keep in mind the various useful sorts that you might want to use, and create fields with data that can be sorted in the desired order.

Sorts are more efficient if the sorting is done on internally indexed fields.

Sorting Rules

1. You cannot sort a file based on the contents of a multivalued field.
2. You can, however, sort a multivalued field's contents.
3. You can sort using fields at the current level of the hierarchy. You cannot include subfields in a sort.
4. To create sorts that affect different levels of a hierarchy, create separate sort criteria for each level.
5. Sorts at higher levels of the hierarchy take precedence.
6. You can sort a file using a field that is not on the layout, as long as it is in the hierarchy.
7. You can drag sort criteria to change their processing order.
8. When you sort on a Choices field, the results are ordered according to the order of the Choices as defined in the field definition, not in alphabetical order.

Delete <name>

If the current insertion point is in the Key field or any single-valued file field in a form view, **Delete <name>** removes the record. If the cursor is in a multivalued field, **Delete <name>** removes the current occurrence in the multivalued field or Set.

WARNING: Be careful when you Delete records. They cannot be recovered. Also beware of deleting multivalued occurrences within Sets. All the data for that occurrence in each of the fields in the Set will be removed. If you only want to remove the value from an occurrence in an individual field—not the entire occurrence—use **Backspace** (**Delete**) or **Cut**.

Delete File

You can only delete a file from the Finder. Be sure to remove all relationships, views, and procedural references from any projects in which that file appears before deleting it. If you wish to remove a file from a project, you can Close the file from the Datafile menu.

NOTE: If you close a file that contains relationships, it will disappear from the Structure Window, but the pointer fields in any files to which it is related remain. Opening the file again will re-establish the relationships.

Delete Record Procedure

Delete Record procedures are invoked when a Delete Record command is issued (typically when a record is deleted from a file). Use Delete Record procedures to confirm deletions and to balance affected fields in other files. For instance, you might use a Delete Record procedure to reverse the effect of a Posting field on fields in other files. Delete Record is a special kind of processor—one that takes effect only when a record is about to be removed from a file.

A Delete Record procedure can be added to a file through the Show Procedure button in the Change File dialog box, or it can be added to a Pointer field (title bar) in a view hierarchy. It is invoked when you select Delete (**Command-D**) from the Edit menu or after a DELETE command is encountered in a procedure.

NOTE: A Delete Record procedure requires a DELETE command with the SELF parameter as its argument. The syntax is DELETE(SELF). If the DELETE(SELF) command is not encountered during a Delete Record procedure, the record will not be deleted.

Delete View

If you make a mistake creating a view or if you no longer need a view, first activate it, then choose Delete from the View menu. A dialog box will ask you to confirm the deletion. Clicking **OK** will remove the view permanently from the project. Be sure to remove any procedural references to that view.

You can't delete a view that is defined as one of the selections in a Custom Menu.

Remember, view deletions are not recoverable or Undo-able except with Revert to Saved.

Design Menu

The Design Menu appears when the layout is active. It contains most of the specific controls for laying out a view.

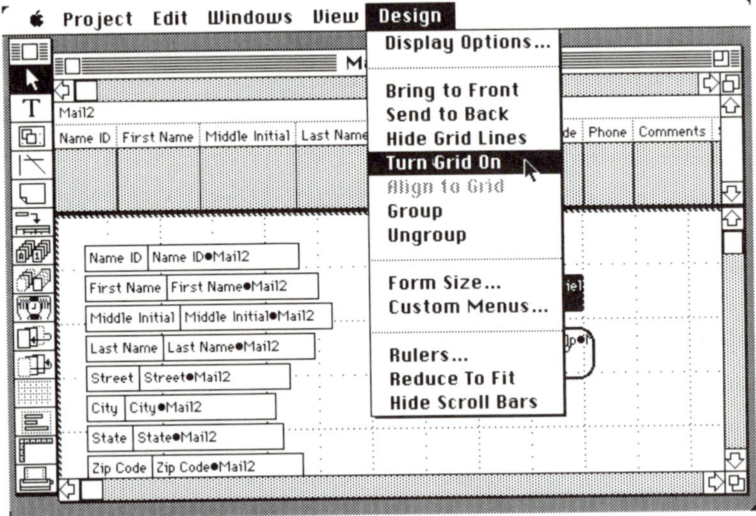

Figure R-11 Design Menu Graphic.

For more, refer to individual Design Menu elements.

Dialog Boxes

Dialog boxes used in dBASE Mac are typical Macintosh dialog boxes. They may include action buttons, choice buttons, checkboxes, text boxes, pop-up menus, and list boxes.

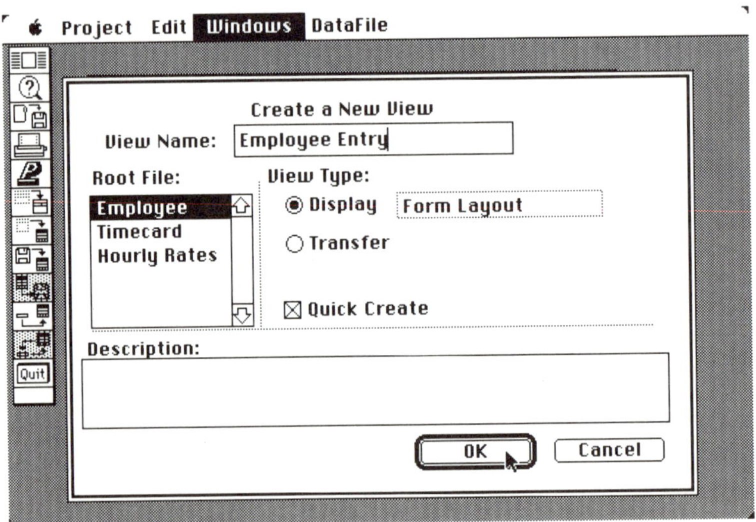

Figure R-12 Picture of a List Box Graphic.

The figure above contains a list box from which you choose an item, and action buttons, **OK** and **Cancel**.

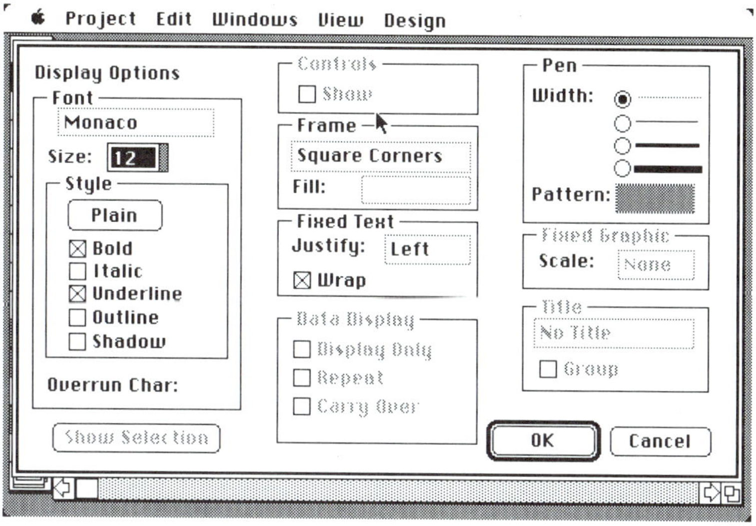

Figure R-13 Boxes, Buttons, etc.

Look at the Display Options dialog box. It contains almost all the different elements possible.

> Square boxes like Bold, Italic, and so on are checkboxes. You can click in a checkbox to select or deselect that option.
> Round buttons like those under Width are called radio buttons. You can click on one of these to choose the width of the boxes drawn in dBASE Mac.

TIP: The functional difference between a checkbox and a radio button is that you can usually choose as many checkboxes as you wish whereas you will choose one radio button only from a particular set of radio buttons. A dialog box can contain more than one set of unrelated radio buttons.

A typical pop-up menu is like that found under the Font heading. Notice that the outlines of the box are in grey instead of solid black. This indicates a pop-up menu. Holding down the mouse button opens the menu. Sliding the mouse up or down with the button held down moves the cursor to select an option from the pop-up menu.

Another kind of pop-up menu is found next to the Size title. Notice that there is a value displayed in the box, and a small grey sidebar next to it. Holding the mouse button down with the cursor on the grey sidebar opens a pop-up menu. This is also the way multivalued fields work.

Action buttons are buttons that cause immediate results when they are clicked. There are three action buttons on the screen in the figure above; **Show Selection, OK,** and **Cancel**. **Show Selection** opens yet another dialog box, **OK** accepts all settings made in the current box, **Cancel** closes the dialog box without accepting any new settings.

Note that the **OK** button is contained in a dark border. This means that it is the default button. Pressing the **Return** key on the keyboard will also select an action button if it is the default button. **Show Selection** is in a grey box. This means that it is not active. Clicking on it will accomplish nothing. **Show Selection** is activated when you select a Tablet in the layout (see Layout).

Display Options

To control the appearance of elements throughout a project, choose Preferences from the Edit menu. To set options for individual elements of a view, highlight those elements you wish to modify, then choose Display Options from the Design menu. Or double-click the desired layout elements to open the Display Options menu.

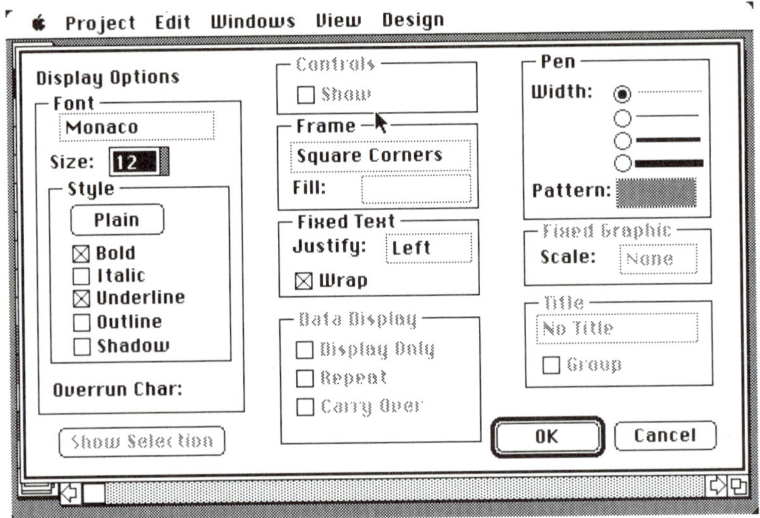

Figure R-14 Display Options Graphic.

Selecting Display Options opens a special dialog box. Most of the options available in the Display Options dialog box are available in the Preferences dialog box.

The Fonts pop-up menu allows you to set the font for particular display elements. The fonts that are available will vary depending on what fonts you have installed in your system or in the dBASE Mac program. You can also select the Size of the font from the Size box. Only valid sizes may be selected.

The Style section of Display Options allows you to set different special effects for text elements or your layouts. These effects are standard Macintosh effects—Bold, Italic, Underline, Outline, and Shadow. You can click on any combination of checkboxes to combine effects.

The Controls section affects the display of multivalued fields. Clicking on the Show checkbox will cause multivalued fields to display with pop-up menus in Form views. In Column views, special scroll boxes will be included with multivalued fields where the list of multivalued field occurrences extends beyond the bottom of the screen.

The Frame section allows you to set the kinds of boxes used to frame data elements in your view. You can set square or round corners. Set round corners by choosing from among several different curves. You can also use different fill patterns, choosing from a pop-up menu of patterns in the Frame section.

Under Fixed Text, you can set Left, Center, or Right justification for your text. This means that all text will be aligned with the appropriate edge, or centered in the field. You can select Wrap to wrap text within the field box much as word processor text does. By adjusting the size of the field box, you can create wrapped, multiple-lined text elements for any view. (See Layout for information on sizing field data boxes.)

The Data Display section of the Display Options dialog box replaces the Data Entry section in the Preferences dialog box. Data Display contains three checkboxes.

> The **Display Only** checkbox allows you to set any field element so that it will appear on the screen, but its data cannot be modified.
> The **Repeat** checkbox causes field contents to repeat on a following page if they do not all fit on the current page in a columnar layout.
> The **Carry Over** checkbox, when checked, causes the program to repeat (carry over) values from the previous record. This option supercedes any initial values defined in the field definitions.

Pen width and pattern affect the thickness and type of line used to draw field boxes. When combined with different types of corners and patterns, a variety of effects is possible.

> HINT: To eliminate boxes altogether, choose the upper pen width (the thin, grey line). This will allow the data to display as text only, and is useful in such applications as mailing labels, custom forms, and special preprinted forms. (See below for more on this).

The Fixed Graphic section allows you to set different scaling options. For more information about scaling graphics, see Graphic Fields.

The Titles section allows you to set the position of titles relative to the field data. Titles can be positioned to the right, left, above, or below the field data. If you select None, no titles will appear. For many printed applications, including mailing labels and special preprinted forms, it is desirable to eliminate titles. Also, clicking the Group checkbox causes dBASE Mac to tie the title with the data, thereby treating the two as one item. This is sometimes useful when you are moving layout elements.

Duplicate File

Choose Duplicate File. . . under the DataFile menu to create a copy of a file under a new name. If you choose, you can also duplicate the records from the old file, or you can duplicate only the file structure. This is a good way to create a backup of a file's contents before modifying the data. Also use Duplicate File to create new templates for applications that use the same file structure many times, such as monthly files for an accounting system.

Duplicate View

Choosing Duplicate View from the View menu creates a copy of the active view and activates the copy. This is especially useful when you have a view that is very similar to one you wish to create. You can use the copy as a starting point and make the modifications you desire.

Duplicate View reproduces the hierarchy, and all Sorts, Selections, procedures, Breaks, and totals from the original view. It does not duplicate the layout, however. Also, procedural references may need to be changed in the new view.

Edit Menu

The Edit menu is always active, although some of its commands may not be. The Edit menu is even active within a Protected project or when using many Desk Accessories.

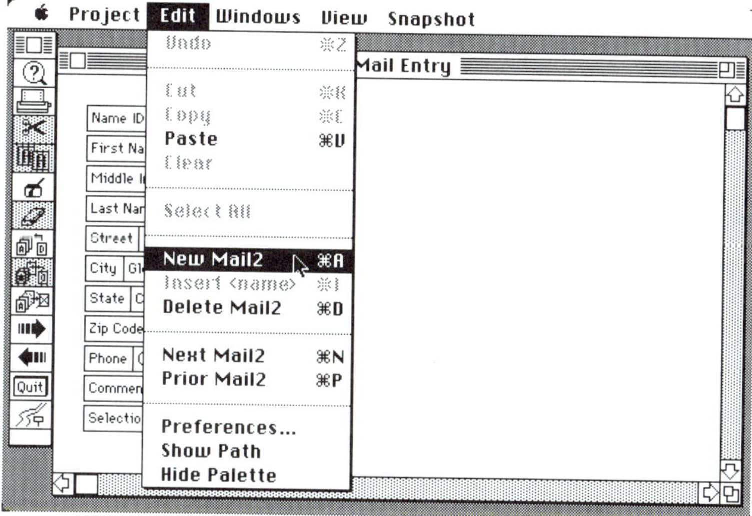

Figure R-15 Edit Menu Graphic.

For more, see individual Edit menu commands.

Explode

Exploded views are special cases of recursive relationships. They can be used to list items that can be categorized as part/subpart. An example is a bicycle. Spokes of a wheel are subparts of the wheel, the wheels are subparts of the bicycle, and so on.

To create an exploded view, you need to create a special kind of relationship between a field and its own file. You do this by dragging the field onto the title bar of the file. A one-way relationship is created, and the field becomes a pointer field.

Take another example—an exploded view of a guy named Joe. Joe is the whole thing. He contains all the parts that make him. He contains fingers and toes and arms, eyes, hair, teeth, and so on. But his hands have fingers and fingernails. His arms have hands, fingers, and fingernails.

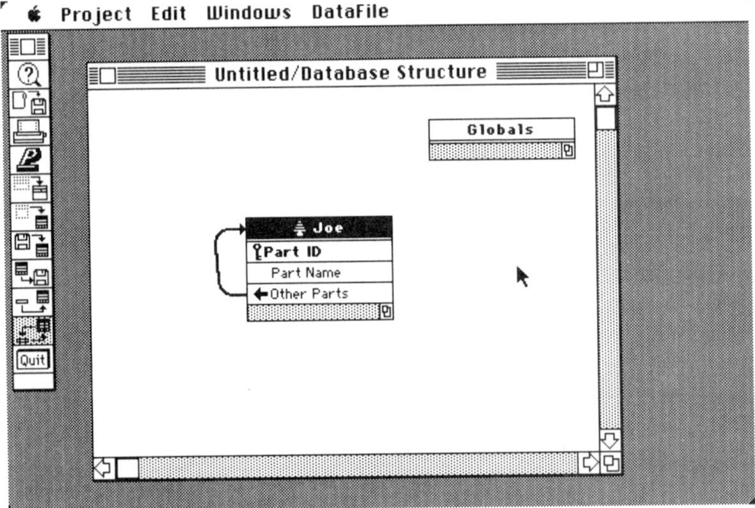

Figure R-16 Joe File Graphic.

To enter Joe into the database, create a file called Joe that contains the following fields:

Key field called Part ID
Text field called Part Name
Text field called Other Parts

Create a relationship between Other Parts and the title bar of Joe. Other Parts becomes a pointer field and an arrow is drawn from it to the title bar.

In a data entry screen, enter the information for fingernail.

Part ID:	**f1**
Part Name:	**fingernail**
Other Parts:	

Now enter data for finger:

Part ID:	**f2**
Part Name:	**finger**
Other Parts:	**f1**

Notice that the subpart ID, f1, is placed in the Pointer field. Now enter the data for the hand:

Part ID:	**h2**
Part Name:	**hand**
Other Parts:	**f1**
	f2

The hand contains both the finger (f2) and the fingernail (f1).

Keep going until you have all of Joe's parts defined.

Create a Column view, add the fields to the hierarchy, click once on the pointer field, Other Parts, and click **Explode**. A bomb symbol appears to let you know that this is an Exploded view.

Modify the layout if you wish, then Perform and Use the view.

NOTE: You can usually create the same effect using standard hierarchies and relationships, so you may not ever need to use Explode.

Export

The Export command is used to export the contents of a dBASE Mac file to an ASCII file. The convenience of the Export command is that it allows you to export records from a file without having to create a foreign file structure manually. However, there are some limitations to the Export command. The Export command only exports the first value of a multivalued field, and doesn't allow any selection or sort criteria to be applied to the file data. Therefore, it will often be preferable to export using a Transfer View.

TIP: You can create a foreign file structure using Export by beginning the process, naming the new file, then hitting **Cancel** before the records are actually exported. You will end up with an empty file structure perfect for use with a Transfer View.

Field Definition

The standard Field Definition screen consists of a series of text boxes, pop-up menus, checkboxes, and other options. You will see this screen whenever you (1) create a new file, or (2) modify a field.

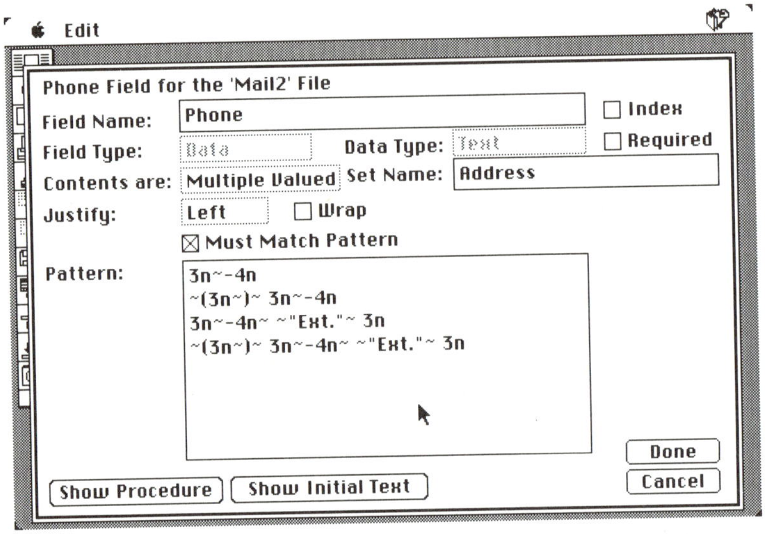

Figure R-17 Field Definition Graphic.

The first item in the Field Definition dialog box is the Field Name text box. Here you simply fill in the desired field name following the general Macintosh rules for names. You can include spaces and other punctuation. A name can be up to fifty characters long.

The Field Type pop-up menu contains four options: Key, Data, Formula, and Memory. Each Field Type has specific uses, and each is further explained in its own section.

The Data Type pop-up menu contains seven options: Text, Number, Date, Time, Logical, Choices, and Graphic. Each type is further explained under its own heading in the Reference.

The Required checkbox is checked if a valid entry is necessary in that field before a record can be processed. If the Required box is checked, and you try to enter a record leaving any Required fields blank, a warning message will be displayed, and you will be unable to process that record until valid data have been added to the field or fields in question.

The Contents Are: pop-up menu contains two choices: Single Valued and Multiple Valued. Single valued fields contain only one value per record. Multivalued fields can contain many values per record. An example of a multivalued field is a phone number field that contains more than one phone number for a particular record.

Multivalued fields can belong to sets. When you select Multiple Valued on the Field Definition screen, the Set Name text box appears. Multivalued fields that belong to the same set in the same file will act as if they were grouped together within each individual record. For instance, the first value in one field will be associated with the first value in another field of the same set. Displaying one field value within a set will automatically display all associated values.

The Justify pop-up menu allows you to control the alignment of the data in the field. You can align Left, Right, or Centered. Simply choose the appropriate option.

For information on field procedures, see the particular name of the procedure required (Pre-Processor, Post-Processor, New Record, etc.) in the reference.

Other options are dependent on the Data Type, and will be covered individually for each Data Type (Text, Number, Date, Time, Logical, Choices, Graphic).

File Types and File Icons

dBASE Mac can use several file types. Amoung the file types you may encounter are:

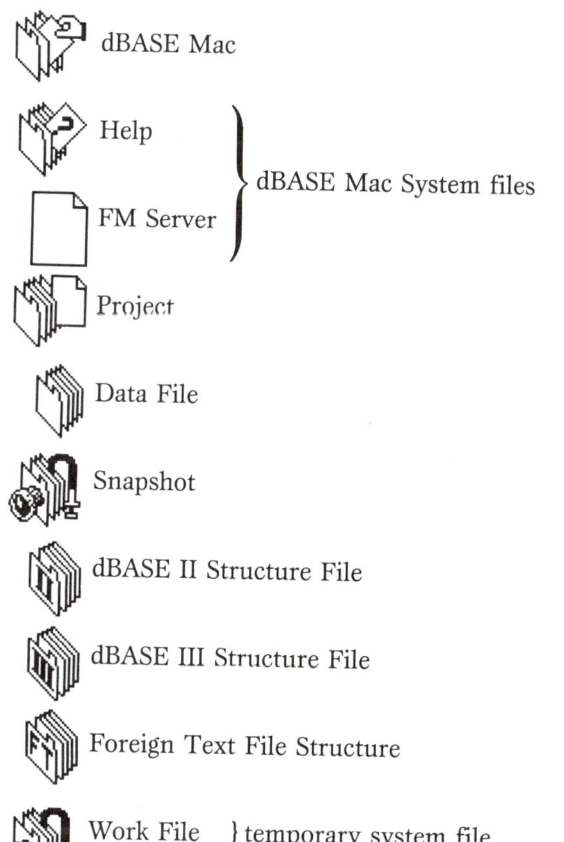

File Size

The File Size dialog box prompts you for the number of records you initially need for your application file. The default is 200 records, or fifty percent of the maximum number of records that can be contained on the application disk (whichever is less).

The number can be changed if more or fewer records are needed. Also, a custom dialog box is provided that allows you to specify a specific Modulo and Separation. Modulo and Separation are discussed under Change File.

> TIP: Don't specify more records than you actually need. Since the system actually reserves the amount of disk space needed for the file size you specify, you could waste a lot of disk space, especially if you are using a floppy-based system. dBASE Mac files will grow dynamically to the extent that disk space is available, so it does no harm if you underestimate the file size slightly. If a file grows too large, and its performance is affected, you may need to reorganize the file. See Change File for more information.

Foreign File

A foreign file is a non-dBASE Mac file like an ASCII text file from a word processor, spreadsheet, or other database. dBASE II, III, and III PLUS files are considered foreign files, too, but they are handled in a special way.

You can import the data from an ASCII file into a special foreign file structure, and use foreign files in almost all the ways you use a dBASE Mac file.

> NOTE: Foreign files can't contain Graphic fields or multivalued fields. Because they can't have multivalued fields, they can't be involved in two-way relationships or indexes. You can create a one-way relationship between a dBASE Mac file and a foreign file.

Create a foreign file structure by selecting New. . . from the DataFile menu and Foreign from the pop-up. Before you begin to create a foreign file, you should understand some of the structural elements in a database file.

Record Terminator Records are usually handled internally in dBASE Mac, but foreign files use special characters called Record Terminators. The Record Terminator is a character that is used to mark the end of a particular record. Usually the Record Terminator is a Carriage Return (Return on the keyboard). However the Record Terminator can also be a single blank line (single line feed), a Carriage Return (CR) followed by a blank line (CR followed by line feed), or a blank line followed by a Carriage Return (single line feed followed by CR).

Field Size There are two ways dBASE Mac can work with the size of a field. Some fields are fixed in length. These are called Fixed Length Fields. For instance, the Name field in a foreign file may be always fifteen characters long. In this case, dBASE Mac will always know where the field begins and ends. Other fields may be of varying lengths. These are called Variable Length Fields.

Like the Record Terminator, Variable Length Fields use a Field Terminator. In dBASE Mac foreign files, you can use one of six characters to terminate a Variable Length Field: comma (,), slash (/), period (.), colon (:), tab, or space.

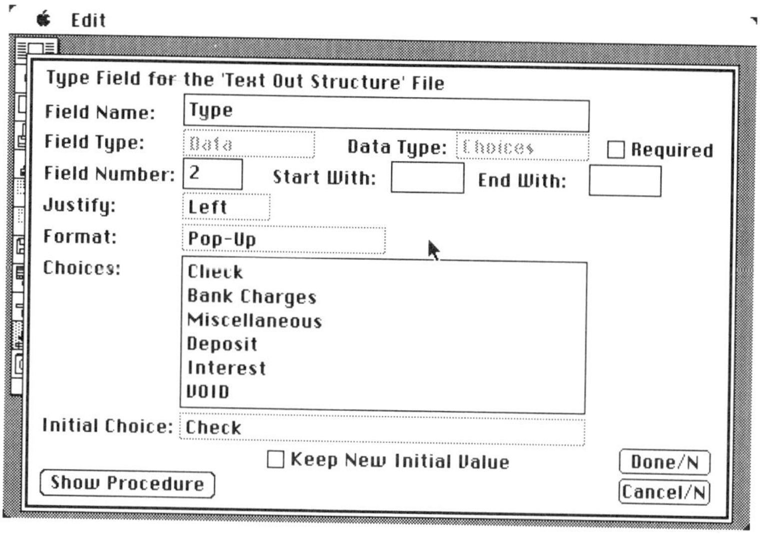

Figure R-18 Foreign File Field Definition Screen.

Choose the Record Terminator and Field Terminator to use, then proceed to the field definition form. Defining fields for a foreign file is similar to defining fields for a dBASE Mac field. The first field is the Record Number field. Other fields are assigned positions within the file. You can also define certain characters that will be written at the beginning or the end of the data (Start With: and End With:).

To import data to dBASE Mac, select New. . . from the DataFile menu, and check the Create Structure for Existing File checkbox. You can add a Header Record to the ASCII file to automate the creation of the file structure. The Header Record is the first record in the file, and it defines the file types. Header Records can only be used with Variable Length file structures.

Header Record Structure:

Character	Data Type
None	Text
#	Number
@	Date
!	Time
~	Logical

NOTE: You can't create a Header Record to import Graphics or Choices data types. If you wish to create a foreign file structure that contains Choices fields, you will have to create it manually (see section above). Foreign files can't contain Graphics fields.

The easiest way to export data from dBASE Mac to an outside file is to use the Export command, which builds the foreign structure for you. You can create a foreign file structure and use a Transfer View (see Transfer View) to send the data into the new structure. In some cases, you may gain control using the latter method. For more discussion of foreign files, see Chapter 11.

To import data from dBASE II, III, and III PLUS files, select Create Structure for Existing File, then select the appropriate dBASE version from the File Type pop-up.

For more on foreign files, see Chapter 11 of the Tutorial.

Form Size

The standard size of the layout drawing area is 7 1/2 inches by 10 inches, but you can create different size layouts by choosing Form Size from the Design menu. For preprinted forms, mailing labels, custom layouts—even greeting cards—you can use the Form Size command.

When you select Form Size, the following dialog box appears:

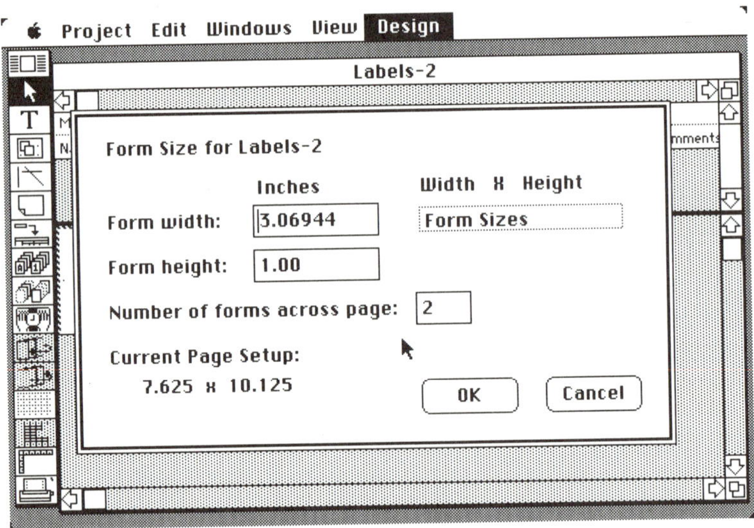

Figure R-19 Form Size Dialog Box Graphic.

Two text boxes contain the values for the current form width and length. You can change these values at will, or select from the pop-up menu entitled Some Common Sizes: In that menu you will find several preset form sizes, which will probably be useful for many of your needs.

To set more than one form to print across the page, enter the number of forms desired in the Number of Forms Across Page: text box. Remember that there must be at least one-sixteenth of an inch between forms. Also remember that your default form size is determined by the values entered in the Page Setup found under the Projects menu (see Page Setup). See also Reduce to Fit.

Formula Fields

A Formula field derives or calculates its value rather than obtaining data through keyboard entry or assignment through procedures (or Cut and Paste).

You can enter a formula for a field by selecting the **Show Formula** button. This will cause the Formula Field dialog box to appear. Formula fields can use four kinds of operations:

Arithmetic Calculates numeric values.

Logical (Boolean) Evaluates true or false conditions and then takes some action, if required.

Character Manipulates strings of characters.

Special Produces specific values for the field, such as a date or time, for instance.

The syntax for each function varies, but all functions involve some combination of (1) Selecting a field, (2) choosing operations, and/or (3) specifying values.

TIP: Formula fields do not contain data; therefore, some of the qualities of Data fields do not apply. Formula fields cannot be posted to, and they cannot post to other fields. Formulas do not have validation criteria such as a Range, and they cannot have an Initial Value. Data entry is not allowed in a Formula field, nor are procedures or Must Match Patterns.

Globals File

The Globals file is a special file that accompanies each project. It contains only Memory fields and, because it is a global file, its fields can be used by any view. The Globals file contains a single record, and no Key field or Finder icon. You cannot remove the Globals file although you can hide it on the Structure Window (off the visible portion or behind another file box).

A Globals field is a Memory field (see Memory Field) that resides in the Globals file. Globals Memory fields can be used to accumulate totals, to pass values from one view to another, and even to allow fields in one file to pass values to fields in another file.

Graphic Fields

A Graphic Field contains a Clipboard-compatible picture. You can obtain graphics by drawing them in MacPaint, MacDraw, or any other graphics program, by taking screen shots (Command Shift-3), or by using one of the many digitizers and scanners available for the Macintosh.

You create a Graphic Field in the same way you create any field. When you select Graphic from the Data Type menu, a graphic window appears on the field definition dialog box.

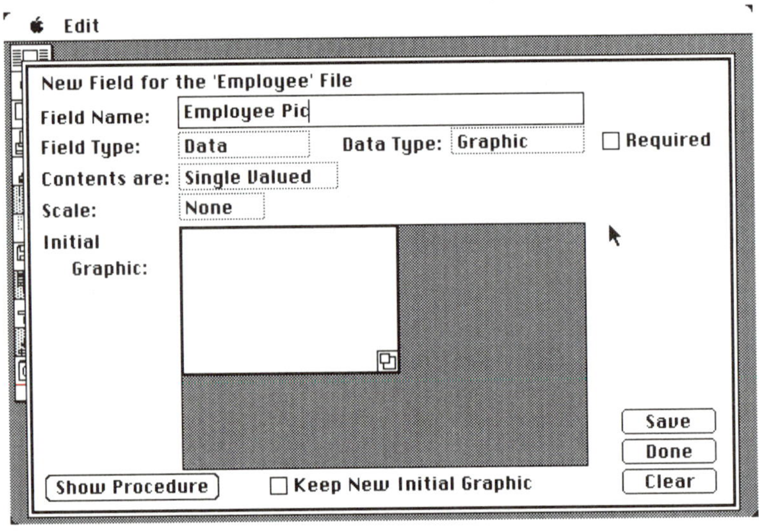

Figure R-20 Graphic Field Definition Graphic.

You can paste a graphic image in the Initial Graphic window. This image then becomes the default graphic image for the field. You can use the size control (at the bottom-right corner of the Initial Graphic box) to adjust the size of the display.

Use the Scale options to adjust the graphic display to fit into the box four ways:

1. Select None from the Scale menu to leave the graphic unmodified. The image will be cut off at the edges of the Initial Graphic box.
2. Select Width from the Scale menu to adjust the image to fit the width of the Initial Graphic box. Choosing Width may still truncate the picture lengthwise (adjusting to the height of the box), but it will proportion the picture so that it fits the width.
3. Select Height from the Scale menu to adjust the image to fit the height of the Initial Graphic box. Choosing Height may still truncate the picture lengthwise (adjusting to the width of the box), but it will proportion the picture so that it fits the height.
4. Select Both from the Scale menu to adjust the image to fit both height and width. The image will be proportioned to fit within the limits of the Initial Graphic box.

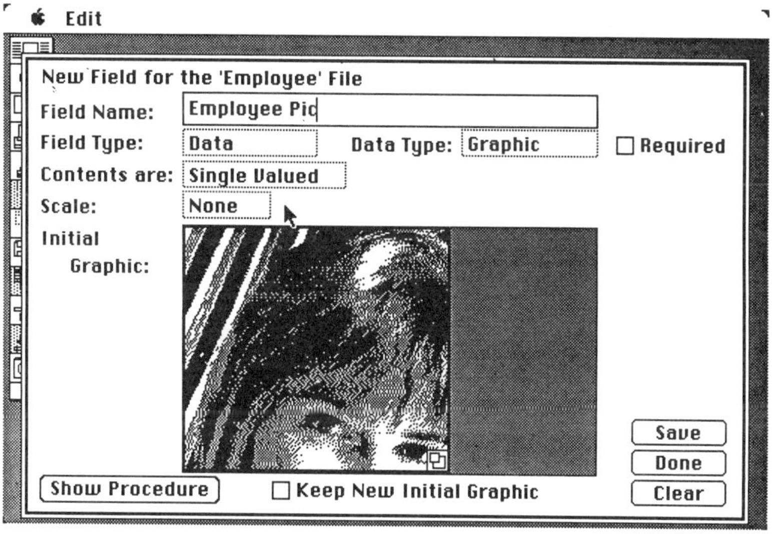

Figure R-21 None Scaling.

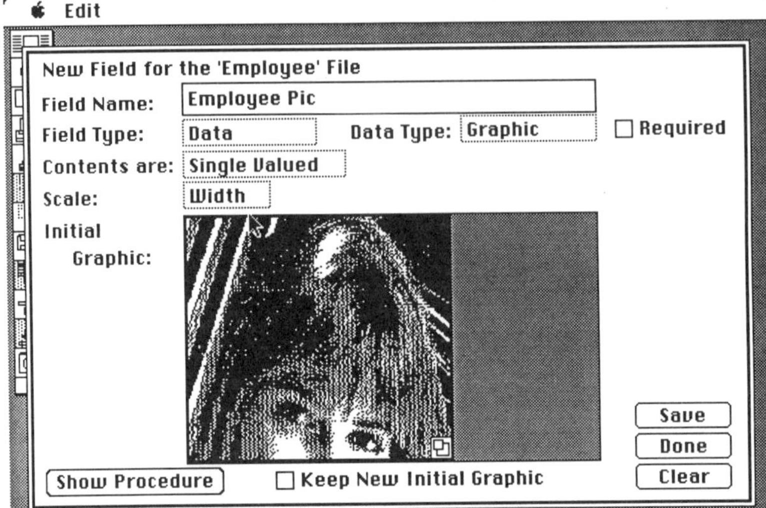

Figure R-22 Width Scaling.

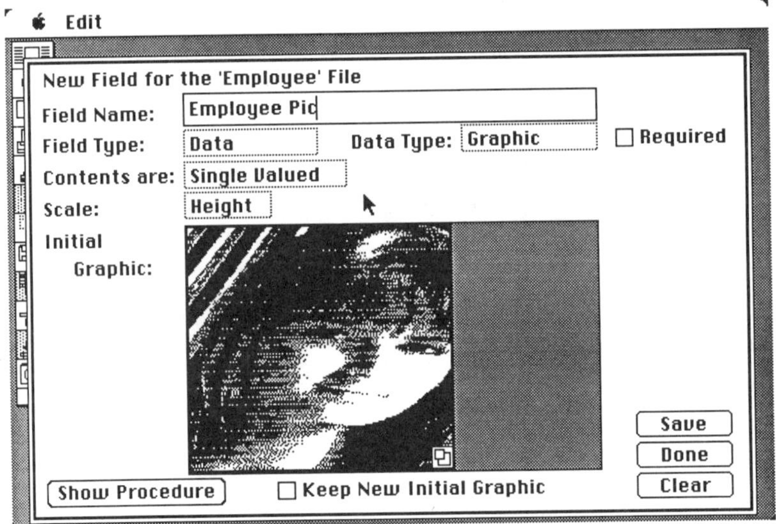

Figure R-23 Height Scaling.

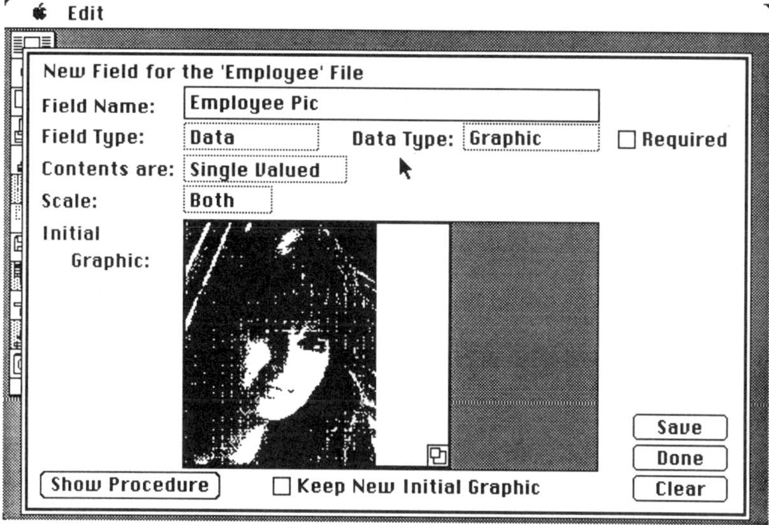

Figure R-24 Both Scaling.

Graphic fields can be multivalued, so more than one graphic image can be associated per field for each record. Also, you can check the Keep New Initial Graphic checkbox to tell dBASE Mac to use any new graphic as the new initial graphic.

Help

dBASE Mac Help is available as a Desk Accessory from the Apple menu. It is organized into a series of topics. Select one from the Topic Index, and then Read the appropriate entries. Help entries are often longer than one page. Use the scroll bar to display the rest of the information.

Topics may have several entries. You go from one to the next by clicking **Next**. Return to a previous entry by clicking **Previous**. Click **Done** when you are finished with Help.

Hierarchy

The View Hierarchy determines the Path for which dBASE Mac will retrieve and store information. Hierarchies allow you to utilize information from various related files. Understanding hierarchies is critical to the effective use of dBASE Mac.

At its simplest, a hierarchy defines the files and their associated fields that will be used in a view. It also graphically displays the ways those files and fields relate. The hierarchy graphically illustrates the data Path. The most simple of hierarchies contain a file represented by a pointer field with its associated fields beneath it.

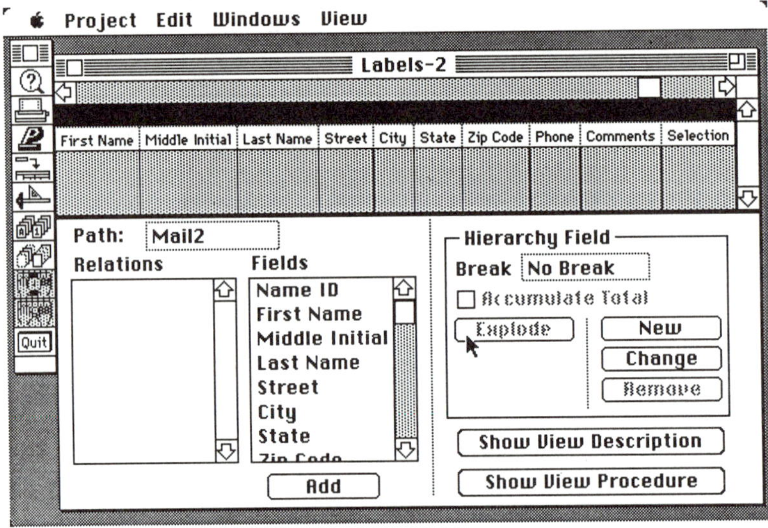

Figure R-25 Simple Hierarchy Graphic.

The path for the Last Name field reads {Last Name•Employee}. This means that the Last Name field is part of the Employee file. Note the long bar in the hierarchy labeled Employee. That is the pointer field or title bar. The smaller bars beneath it are field bars.

A more complex hierarchy contains related files and their associated fields.

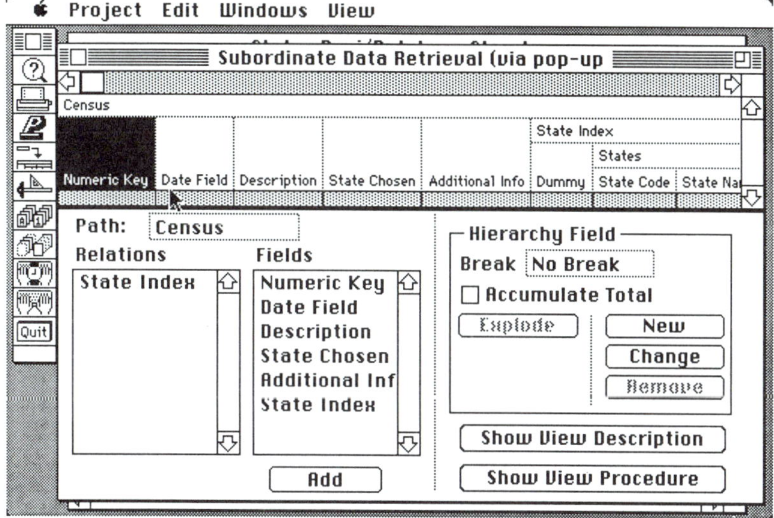

Figure R-26 Relational Hierarchy Graphic.

In the more complex example, the primary file, called the Root, is Transaction. The Root title bar for Transaction extends over the whole hierarchy. A secondary file is Items, and still lower in the hierarchy is Budgets. Under each pointer field are the field designators.

NOTE: A title bar in a hierarchy is also called a Pointer field. It is representative of the entire file and can contain procedures (New Record, Write Record, and Delete Record) that field and view procedures cannot contain. A subordinate file Pointer field (below the Root) can contain all five types of processor—Pre-Processor, Post Processor, New Record, Write Record, and Delete Record—and can be placed on a view layout.

To add a field to the hierarchy, highlight the desired field in the field list, then click the **Add** button. You can also double-click the desired field name. To add fields from a related file, click on the desired file in the Relations menu, then add any fields from that file that you wish to include.

As you add files to the hierarchy, the Path changes. You can see the full path if you open the Path pop-up menu. To shorten the path, open the Path menu, and select the file at the level you wish. Any files in the pop-up menu that are below the one you choose will be eliminated from the path.

Using the hierarchy with related files, you can display and process field information from various files at one time. You can create complex forms that automatically fill in necessary information from a few inputs. You can use Pointer fields to call information from related files. (For more on Pointer fields and Relational files, see Relationships).

You may **Remove** fields and files from the hierarchy by highlighting those elements and clicking **Remove**. If the field is in use on the layout, you cannot **Remove** it, but must first erase it from the design area.

You can also change a field definition by highlighting the field on the hierarchy, then clicking **Change**. (You can also double-click the field in question to achieve the same effect.) The dialog box that appears is the same one that appears when you define and change fields from the Structure Window. The difference is that any changes made on this dialog box affect the field only for the current view. Once you make any change to a file definition in a view, it becomes a View Modified File Field (VMFF). A VMFF can be changed back to its original file field definition by clicking the **Revert** button in the Change Field dialog box.

You can add procedures specific to the current VMFF or change default values.

You can also create view fields that exist only in the current view. To do so, click the **New** button on the hierarchy screen. View fields are Formula fields that allow you to further manipulate the values of the other fields in the hierarchy, or Memory fields that can store data needed within procedures associated with the view. Simple View fields include fields that concatenate names and other strings to eliminate unwanted spaces, and specific calculation fields that might, for instance, add sales tax to totals, or calculate reorder amounts for inventory items.

You also designate Break conditions, subtotals, and totals in the hierarchy. During reporting, you may want to divide the display based on the values in certain fields. If you want to insert a Break on a particular field, highlight that field, then select the type of Break you want from the Break menu. You can have No Break, Line Break, Blank Line Break, or Page Break. (For more on breaks, see Reporting.)

To accumulate totals and subtotals, highlight the field that you wish to total, then click the Accumulate Totals checkbox.

Breaks and totals only appear on printed reports, not on screen displays.

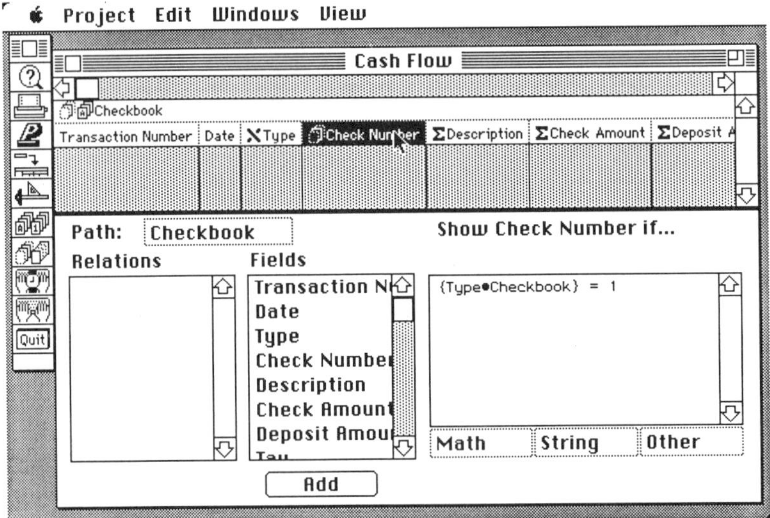

Figure R-27 Report Graphic Illustrating Breaks and Totals.

Exploded views are special views that show a hierarchical arrangement in full detail, that is, a list of parts and subparts that make up a whole item (a house, a car, a human body). Another use for this might be a geneological chart or an organizational chart of a large business (see Exploded Views, Relationships).

Fields in the Hierarchy can display several special graphics next to their names to indicate something about their status or contents. For instance, look at Figure R-27. Notice the symbols on the hierarchy that represent the sorts and selections as well as the Break on the Type field and the Totals on the Description, Check Amount, and Deposit Amount fields.

For more on hierarchies and how to use them, see Chapter 8 of the Tutorial.

Icons and Pointers

dBASE Mac file icons:

 dBASE Mac

 Help

 FM Server

 Project

 Data File

 Snapshot

 dBASE II Structure File

 dBASE III Structure File

 Foreign Text File Structure

 Work File

File box icons:

File ordered by key field

Key field

Formula field

Externally indexed field

Internally indexed field

Index pointer field

Memory field

Pointer field

Graphic field

View Hierarchy icons:

Sorting criteria placed on the field

Selection criteria placed on the field

Exploded report keyed on the field

Report breaks on this field

Σ Report totals on this field

View-modified file field

View field that exists only in the hierarchy

Globals file field

Pointer icons:

Arrow pointer

Spinning pointer

Insertion pointer

Crosshair pointer

Hand pointer

Field movement pointer

Horizontal size pointer

Vertical size pointer

Diagonal size pointer

Palette icons:

Add Field

Align to Grid

Bring to Front

Change Field

Change File

Clear

Close (File)

Close (Project)

Close (Snapshot)

Copy

Custom Menus

Define Hierarchy

Cut

Define Selections

Palette icons continued

 Define Sorts

 Delete View

 Display Options

 Duplicate File

 Duplicate View

 Form Size

 Group

 Hide/Show Grid Lines

 Help

 Import/Export

 Layout View

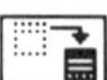 New (File)

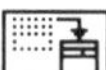 New View

 Open (File)

 Page Setup

 Paste

 Perform and Use

 Preferences

 Print to Disk

 Protect

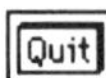

Quit

 Reduce to Fit

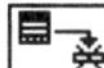 Remove Field

 Restore Field

 Revert

 Rulers

Save As (Project)

Save As (Snapshot)

Save (Project)

Save (Snapshot)

Select All

Send to Back

Show Path

Take

Turn Grid On/Off

Turn Trace On/Off

Ungroup

Use

Use View

Index Files

Sometimes you may want to order the contents of a file on a nonkey field. You can sort a view, but every time you perform the view, it must be sorted again. You can use Snapshots to freeze the order of a file after a sort or selection, but Snapshots are not dynamic—they do not change to accomodate changes in the file.

An Index file, or External Index file, is a special case of a relationship (see Relationships). You create an Index by dragging any nonkey field onto a blank area of the Structure Window. A dialog box will ask you to confirm the creation of an Index file for that field. Click **OK** or press **Return**.

The Index file contains the Key field values from the file in ascending order based on the value of the indexed, or nonkey, field. You can use the Index file in views just as you would use any other field, and the view will be automatically sorted in index order. After it is created, you can add other fields to an Index file, and even form additional relationships between it and other files.

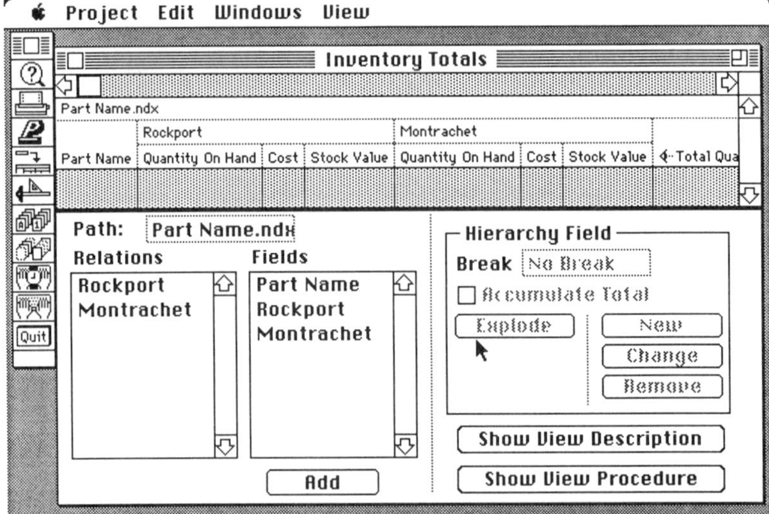

Figure R-28 Example Graphic of a Hierarchy Using Index Field.

When you add a new record to the primary file, a new record is automatically added to the index. When you change the value of the indexed field (for instance, Elizabeth Taylor changed her name to Elizabeth Burton), the change would also be reflected in the Index file and the file's contents are appropriately re-ordered (this assumes an index on last name). This is called dynamic updating.

In a special case of an index file, you can combine two or more field indexes in one file. This might be useful if you want a single alphabetical listing of information from more than one file. For instance, suppose you have separate files for customers and vendors. You want a single alphabetical listing of all customers and vendors with their phone numbers. You might set up a double index by first dragging the customer last name to the Structure Window, then dragging the vendor last name to the resulting Index file, thereby producing a two-way relationship between Vendor and the Index file.

Figure R-29 shows another example of a double index.

Because Index files are dynamically processed as you enter and modify data in the primary file, having one or more indexes may slow down processing of new or updated data. It will, however, speed up processing of display views and reports. You can use Index files whenever nonkey record order is important to your project.

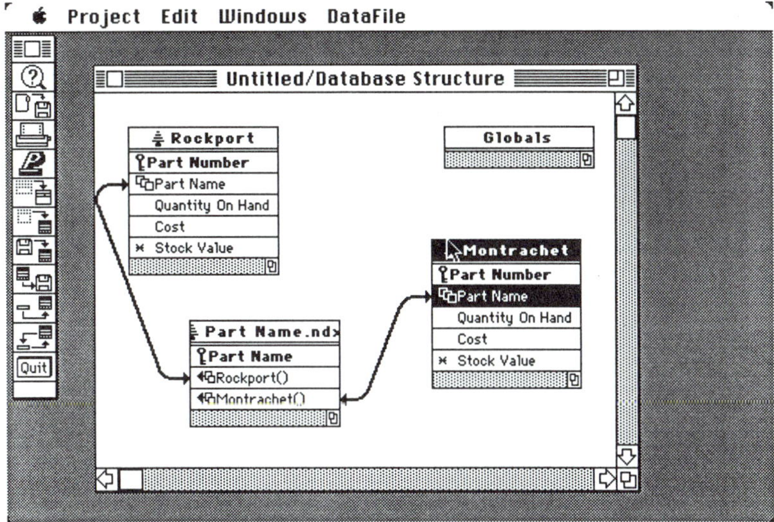

Figure R-29 Double Index Graphic (Structure Window).

You can also use Internal Indexes by checking the Index checkbox in the file definition dialog. This will speed up sorts and selections by creating an internal index on a nonkey field. However, Internal Indexes do not have the ability to form relationships, combine with other indexes, or perform any of the other file-based operations possible with External Index files.

Insert <name>

The **Insert <name>** command (**Command-I**) inserts a new occurrence in a multivalued field at the current position. If the multivalued field belongs to a Set, a new blank occurrence will be added to each member of the Set. (See also Multivalued Fields.)

Internal Index

An Internal Index is created on a field in a file by checking the Index checkbox (or the Order checkbox in a Key field). The internal index keeps a special index of the selected field within the file itself and aids in processing sorts and selections. However, internal indexes make the file larger and using an excessive number of internal indexes (or external Index files) could slow down file maintenance operations. (See also Index.)

Key Field

The Key field is a necessary part of each dBASE Mac file. The Key Field is the first field defined, and it must contain unique data entries. dBASE Mac uses the Key field to find records. The Key field is, in effect, an index field. You can use Text, Numeric, Date, or Time fields as Key fields.

The Key field definition screen is much like a standard field definition screen, but the Field Type is set to Key field and cannot be modified. Other specific options include the Order checkbox that tells the program to keep all data in Key field order. The Automatic Sequence checkbox is available if the Key field is Numeric. This option causes the value of the Key field to be adjusted by a preset amount for each new record.

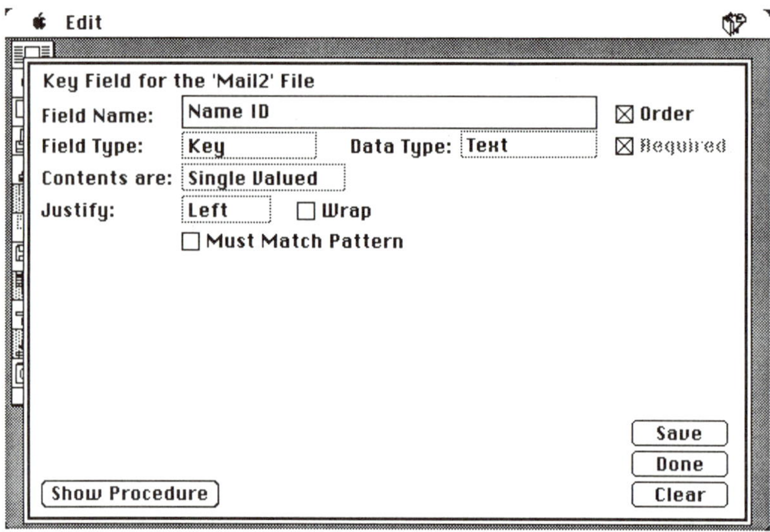

Figure R-30 Key Field Definition Screen Graphic.

Use the Key field value to retrieve specific records in Form Views. Also remember that Key field values are used as pointer values for files that are connected by Relationships (see Relationships).

Use Key field values that are unique and sensible. Don't use last names as Key field values in a name list if there might be duplicate last names. Try to avoid overly long and complicated key values. Devise a system that is easy to remember and easy to enter.

In some applications, the Key field values will be difficult to remember. You can create Custom Views that contain form elements and also a columnar list of Key field values with some associated information.

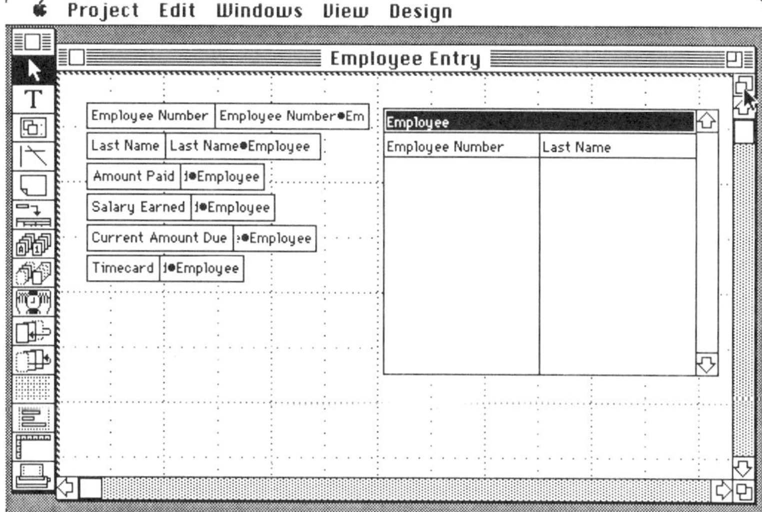

Figure R-31 Graphic of Combined View.

This method is handy, but the columnar element can slow down processing, especially in a large file. Another method is to have a separate View that contains the desired information. You can switch windows at any time to check for a needed Key field value, or size the windows so that you can still see the data in the inactive column list while entering data in a form.

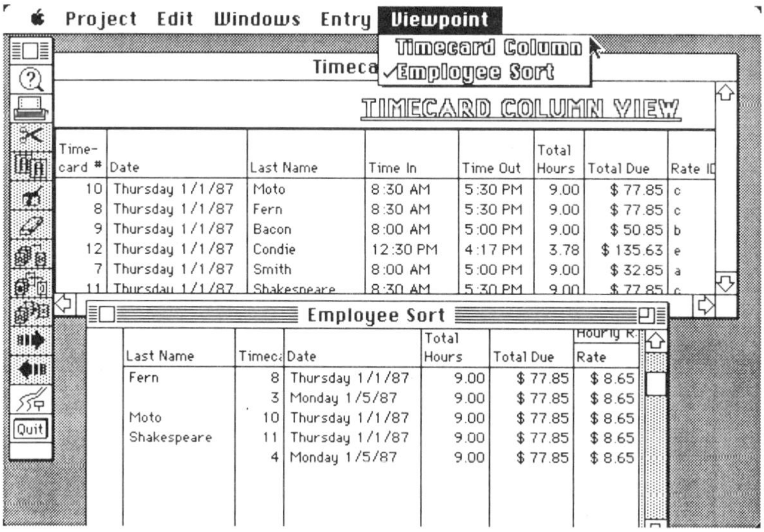

Project Edit Windows Entry Viewpoint

Timecard Column
✓Employee Sort

Timeca

TIMECARD COLUMN VIEW

Time-card #	Date	Last Name	Time In	Time Out	Total Hours	Total Due	Rate ID
10	Thursday 1/1/87	Moto	8:30 AM	5:30 PM	9.00	$ 77.85	c
8	Thursday 1/1/87	Fern	8:30 AM	5:30 PM	9.00	$ 77.85	c
9	Thursday 1/1/87	Bacon	8:00 AM	5:00 PM	9.00	$ 50.85	b
12	Thursday 1/1/87	Condie	12:30 PM	4:17 PM	3.78	$ 135.63	e
7	Thursday 1/1/87	Smith	8:00 AM	5:00 PM	9.00	$ 32.85	a
11	Thursday 1/1/87	Shakespeare	8:30 AM	5:30 PM	9.00	$ 77.85	c

Employee Sort

Last Name	Timeca	Date	Total Hours	Total Due	Hourly Rate
Fern	8	Thursday 1/1/87	9.00	$ 77.85	$ 8.65
	3	Monday 1/5/87	9.00	$ 77.85	$ 8.65
Moto	10	Thursday 1/1/87	9.00	$ 77.85	$ 8.65
Shakespeare	11	Thursday 1/1/87	9.00	$ 77.85	$ 8.65
	4	Monday 1/5/87	9.00	$ 77.85	$ 8.65

Quit

Figure R-32 Multiple Windows Graphic.

Layout

The layout is where your views take form. After creating a hierarchy for your view, you will want to position the various elements in useful and visually pleasing ways. In the layout section of dBASE Mac, a wide variety of tools are available that allow you to control the appearance and functional aspects of your projects.

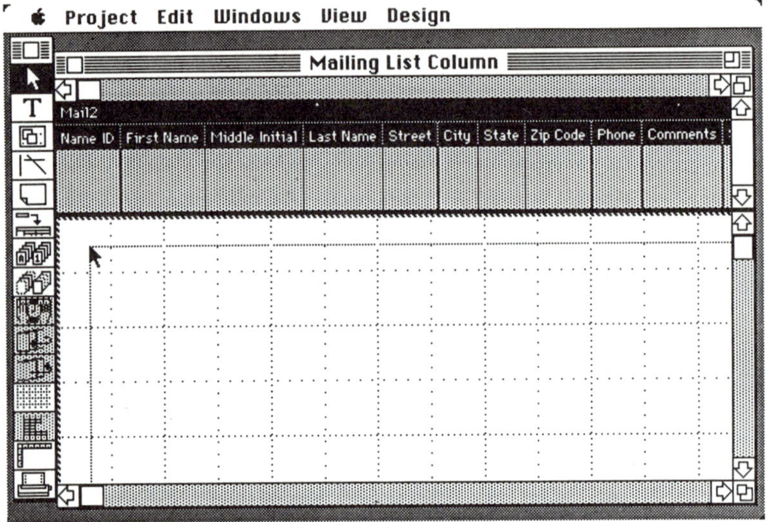

Figure R-33 Layout View Graphic.

At the top of the screen is the view hierarchy as defined on the Define Hierarchy screen. How you work with this screen is dependent on what kind of view you are creating—Form, Column, or Custom. Below the hierarchy is the design area. You can remove the hierarchy from the screen by selecting the Hide Hierarchy box in the upper-right corner (just above the scroll bar). Click it again to return the hierarchy to the screen.

Unless you change the form size (see Form Size), the design area is much larger than one screen. There are two ways to display hidden parts of the design area. One is to use the scroll bars. The other is to hold the **Option** key down while pushing the mouse button. The cursor changes to a hand and you can move the whole design area. This is like the hand in MacPaint.

To see the entire layout, choose Reduce to Fit from the Design menu. This is like the MacPaint Show Page command in that you can view the entire form but make no changes on it while Reduce to Fit is active. Click **Done** or press **Return** to close Reduce to Fit and return to the design area.

The Layout Palette

The Layout Palette has several icons that represent specific commands only available in the layout section, and only operational from the Palette.

The **Selection** icon changes the pointer to the familiar arrow for familiar operations such as highlighting, dragging, and selecting elements of the layout. Selection is the default mode for the layout.

The **Fixed Text** icon changes the cursor into a text icon for writing directly on the design area. Fixed text is independent of any fields or records. It is a permanent part of the form that can include titles, times and dates, and other textual material independent of the file data. You can change fonts and styles of fixed text the same way you do with any other text, through the Display Options command in the Design menu.

The **Fixed Graphics** icon allows you to create designated areas to contain graphics. The cursor changes to a crosshair. By dragging the mouse, you can draw a rectangular area to contain the graphic. Add graphics by Pasting (**Command-V**) from the Clipboard. Remember that these graphics are different from Graphic fields. Graphic fields are part of the file, and their value will change from record to record. Fixed Graphics are a permanent part of the form as it will print out.

The **Line** icon is a simple drawing tool. Again, the cursor changes to a crosshair. With the line icon, you can draw simple graphics and boxes to accent your forms. You can use the line icon to recreate forms you have used in noncomputer systems.

The **Tablet** icon allows you to create special areas on the form to contain multiple pages. The cursor changes to a crosshair and allows you to draw a rectangular area to contain the Tablet. (See Tablets.)

In addition to the special Palette icons, several specialized keyboard commands are available in the layout:

Option-Shift-D Places a fixed text display item at the cursor that shows the current system date (in mm/dd/yy format) when the report is printed.

Option-Shift-P Places a fixed text display item at the cursor that will print the current page number when a report is printed.

Option-Shift-T Places a fixed text display item at the cursor that will print the current system time (in hh:mm:ss format) when the report is printed.

The cursor changes shape when it is possible to change the size of a layout element. For instance, it changes to a pair of diagonal lines when placed at the lower-right corner of a form element. This means that you can change the size of the element by dragging up, down, or at a diagonal. The cursor changes shape when sizing columnar elements as well. Placing the cursor at the intersection of two columns or on a horizontal line in the column element will allow you to change the size of that element by dragging either vertically or horizontally, as the cursor indicates.

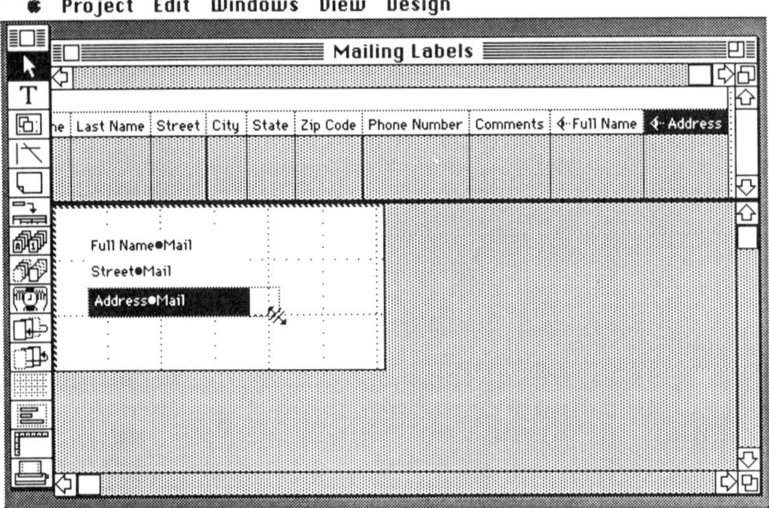

Figure R-34 Changing Size of Form Element.

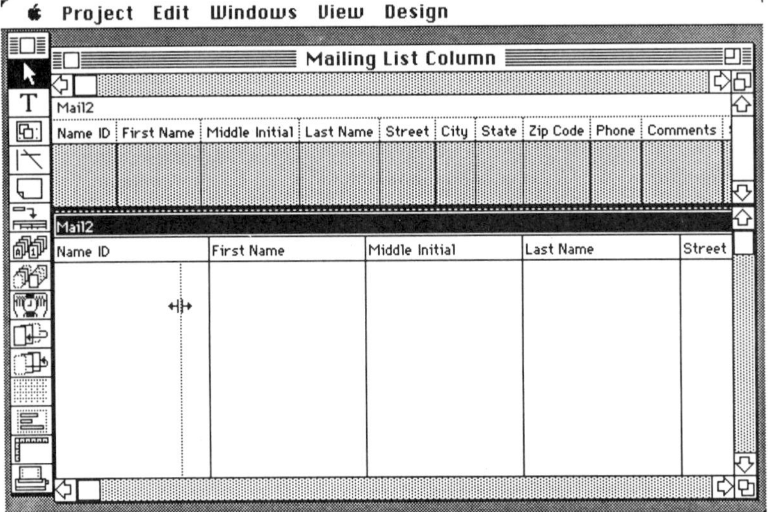

Figure R-35 Changing Size of Columnar Element.

Form View

If you are creating a Form view, select the fields you want and drag them down onto the layout design area. Depending on what Preferences you have set (see Preferences), you should see a representation of the field, with or without its title. Position that field anywhere you wish.

To set individual characteristics for the layout elements, highlight the elements desired, then select Display Options from the Design menu, or double-click the layout display elements you wish to modify (see Display Options). If you have highlighted several display elements, double-click on just one of them to set new Display Options for all.

If you have set the Group checkbox in the Preferences dialog box, titles and data boxes will move as if they were one item. You can also highlight several fields and select the Group command from the Design menu. This will cause all highlighted parts of the layout to move as one. Additionally, Grouped items will be processed together during data entry and modification.

You can change the size of a title or data box, or any other display item, by positioning the cursor at the bottom-right corner of the box. The cursor will change shape. Press and hold the mouse button and drag the cursor to change the box shape until satisfied. Release the mouse button.

> TIP: If a display item is very small, and you want to move, but not resize it, hold the **Command** key while you select and move it.

> HINT: If you highlight several boxes and size one, all highlighted boxes will change size at once. Sometimes, because of their relative positions, several fields may overlap after sizing. You can move them apart, or leave them overlapping. When you perform data entry, or browse the records, the active field will automatically come to the front.

A Text field can contain 255 characters, so it may be necessary to increase the size of the data box to show all or most of the field contents. If you click on the Wrap checkbox when defining the field, you can type data directly into the box as if on a miniword processor screen. The words will wrap at the edges of the box instead of scrolling out of sight.

When you first open the layout view, you'll notice a grid of one-half-inch squares covering the design area. The design area is actually divided into a grid of one-eighth inch squares. Although these smaller squares are invisible, they can aid you in aligning layout elements.

Five commands govern the operation of the grid. They are found under the Design menu:

Turn Grid On Toggles on the operation of the one-eighth-inch grid. Any item placed or moved upon the design area will align itself with the grid by lining up its upper-left corner with the nearest grid intersection.

Turn Grid Off Toggles off the operation of the grid. Items placed or moved upon the design area will remain exactly where they are left.

Align to Grid Will cause any items placed or moved upon the design area when the grid was off to move to align themselves with the nearest grid intersection.

Show Grid Turns on the display of the larger (one-half inch) grid lines.

Hide Grid Turns off the display of the larger (one-half inch) grid lines.

NOTE: The visible (one-half inch) grid lines act as guides, but do not actually affect the operation of the invisible (one-eighth inch) grid. Thus you can display the visible grid by Show Grid, but still have the grid deactivated (items will not align) by clicking **Turn Grid Off**. Conversely, you can hide the larger grid lines, but still have items align with the one-eighth-inch grid if you have **Turn Grid On** active.

Another layout aid is the Rulers command found on the Palette or under the Design menu. When you select this command, a dialog box appears. You can select a ruler scale from among three metric and three standard measures.

NOTE: If you choose a metric ruler measurement, the grid lines change from one-half-inch to one centimeter, and the invisible grid changes likewise.

Click on the **Show Ruler** checkbox and click **Done** or press **Return** to return to the layout. Rulers now appear along the left and upper edges of the layout screen. Use these rulers for more precise positioning of the layout elements.

Column View

If you are working with a Column view, select the Pointer field, then **Shift** click on each field you want included in the view. To include all fields, hold the **Command** key down and click on the Pointer field. Drag the highlighted fields onto the layout design area. The column layout will appear.

TIP: If you get a message that the form is too small to contain all the columns you wish to add, try again, but hold the **Option** key while you drag the column elements onto the layout. This places all columns completely within the visible portion of the window. To place the columns within the entire active page size, be sure the **Caps Lock** key is down when you use the **Option** key method.

You can easily change the order and size of column elements. To change the size, click the Selection icon in the Palette (if necessary) then position the cursor on either column dividing line. The cursor will change shape. Press the mouse button and drag the column line in the direction you wish. You will see the column change size. Release the mouse button when you are satisfied.

To change column order, highlight the column header, then drag the column to the desired position. The rules for moving columns are:

1. If you place the column on a field or Pointer field at the same or higher level, the field is placed to the right of that field or the Pointer field.

2. If you place the column on a Pointer field at the same hierarchy level, the column is placed to the left of that Pointer field, even if it contains several fields beneath it. A variant of that rule is that placing the column on the Root Pointer field places the column to the extreme left of the layout.

3. If you place the column on a Pointer field at a lower hierarchy level, the column is placed to the right of that Pointer field even if it contains several fields beneath it.

4. If you place a column on top of a field title at the same level, the column is placed to the right of that column.

5. If you place a column on top of a field title at a lower level, the column is placed to the right of the column, even splitting the Pointer field.

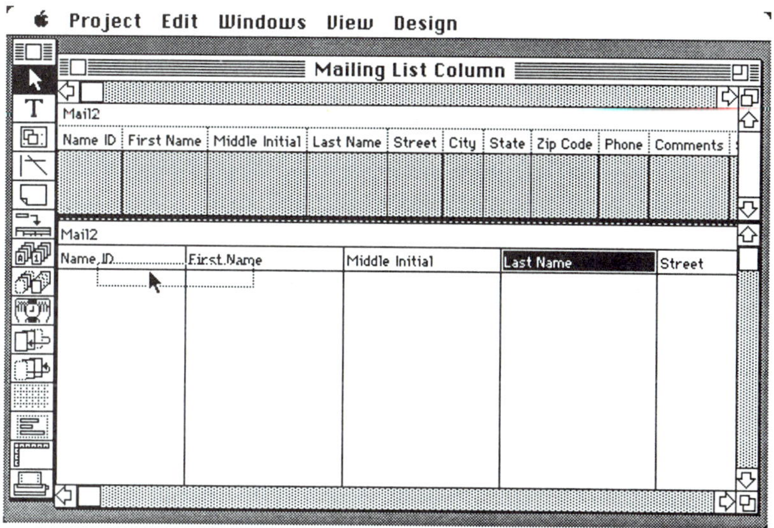

Figure R-36 Graphic for Column Positioning.

Custom View

Custom views can contain both form and column elements. Use the same rules of selection, sizing, and movement to arrange elements on the design area. In fact, any view is technically a Custom view if you modify any part of the view. Therefore, the only views that are not Custom views are those that contain default form or column elements that have not been modified.

TIP: Custom views are useful when you are creating mixed elements. However, there are times when using a Column or Form view is preferable. One such time is when you are creating a Column view that will need to include many files. You may not be able to select and drag the whole column hierarchy onto the layout (see **TIP**, above), whereas choosing Column view as the view type allows the columns to be created automatically. The other time is when you are duplicating a view. View layouts are not duplicated with the hierarchy and other information. If you select a Column or Form view, a layout of some sort will be created. Depending on the complexity of the original layout, this default layout may be close to the original.

Logical Data Type

A Logical field is a field whose value can be expressed as one of two values, such as True/False, Off/On, or Yes/No.

On the field definition screen, you choose the Logical Data Type. Next, choose the format to use—pop-up, checkbox, horizontal or vertical buttons, or text area. If you choose the checkbox, the true value is stored when the box is checked. If you choose the text box format, you must type in the value desired during data entry, but it must match exactly one of the values defined in the field definition.

After you choose the format, you must select the values from the Values: pop-up menu. You can choose from the preset values—False/True, No/Yes, Off/On, -/+, 0/1—or create your own pair of values by choosing Custom.

As with other fields, you can define the default value by entering it as the Initial Value. If you check the Keep New Initial Value checkbox, the most recent value entered will be carried over to the next record, regardless of the initial value you set in the field definition.

The internal representation of the logical field is "T" or "F" regardless of the display format chosen.

Memory Field

Memory fields contain values that apply to a whole file. Memory field values are not limited to just one record. Thus, Memory fields are good places to keep running totals or counters. Memory fields are better places to pass temporary values between different views.

You can create a Memory field by selecting Memory from the Field Type: pop-up menu on the field definition screen. A Memory field can be Text, Numeric, or even Graphic. A Memory field cannot be multivalued.

Values assigned to File Memory fields (Memory fields created within the file definition) are saved as the Initial Value when the file is closed. This is a good way to keep file totals between sessions. It also allows you to pass Memory field values between projects, since a file can be opened by different projects.

Memory fields (defined originally in a file) are not automatically added to the hierarchy of a Quick Create view. They can be added later, and can be found under the Globals Path designation.

Menus

There are eight standard menu headers and six menu configurations in dBASE Mac. The menus change depending on which window is active.

 Project Edit Windows DataFile

Figure R-37 Structure Window Menus Graphic.

 Project Edit Windows View

Figure R-38 Define Hierarchy, Sort, and Select Menu Graphic.

 Project Edit Windows View Design

Figure R-39 Layout Menu Graphic.

 Project Edit Windows View Snapshot

Figure R-40 Use Menu Graphic.

For more, see each individual menu title, or refer to each command by name.

Modulo

See Change File.

Multivalued Fields

Sometimes it is useful to include more than one item of data in a field. For instance, a person may have more than one telephone number, or a particular job description may have more than one employee.

Multivalued fields can contain unique entries for a single field. Each entry is a valid entry and can be used the same as any field data. You can also sort the values within a multivalued field (see Sort, elsewhere in the Reference).

Unless you change the Show Controls checkbox setting in the Preferences dialog box, all multivalued fields in Form views will have a pop-up menu of their values that opens up next to the field.

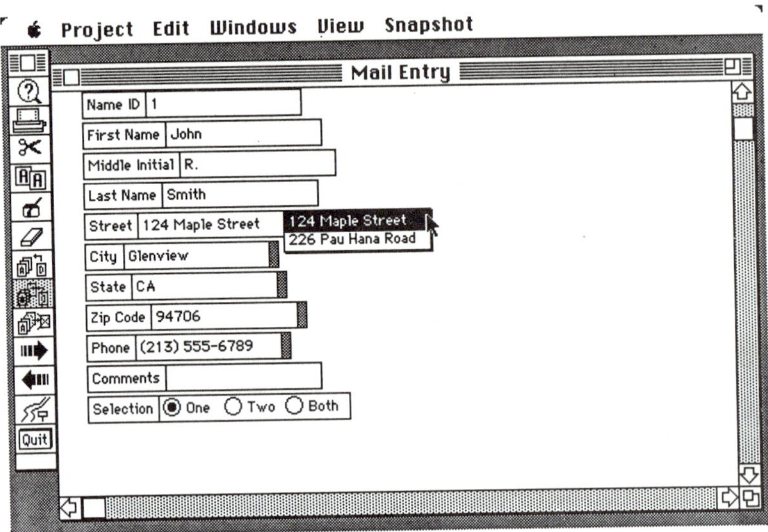

Figure R-41 Multivalued Field Graphic.

You can select and display any value from a multivalued field at any time.

In a Column view, the contents of multivalued fields display down the column.

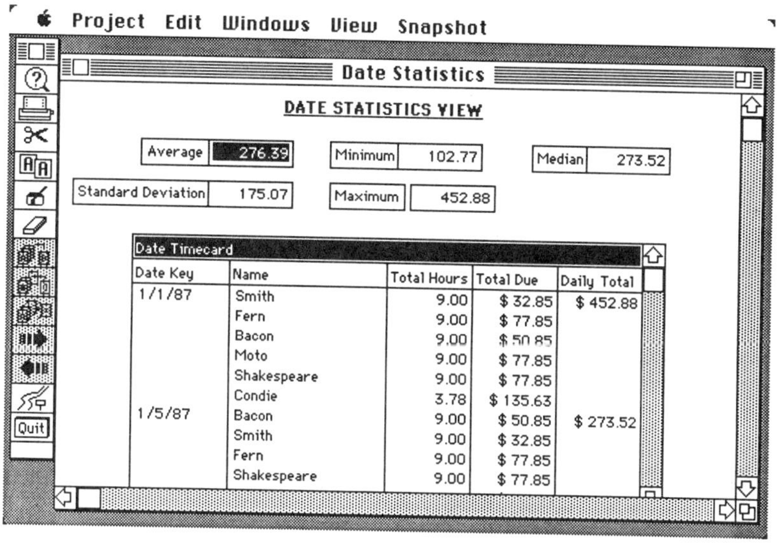

Figure R-42 Multivalued Field Column View Graphic.

You can Add, Delete, or Insert values in a multivalued field by selecting the appropriate command from the Edit menu, or by using the appropriate **Command** key combination or Palette selection.

To refer to a particular occurrence in a multivalued field, use the form {fieldname•filename} [n] where *n* is the number of the occurrence within the multivalued field array. (For more on multivalued fields (and sets), see Field Definitions.)

New File

When you select New from the Datafile menu (in the Structure view), you set in motion the chain of events for creating a new file.

You can create two types of new file— a standard dBASE Mac file, or a Foreign file. A Foreign file is imported from another source, possibly another database or an ASCII text file (see also Foreign File).

When you define a Foreign file, you must tell dBASE Mac whether the fields are fixed length, and if so, how long; or whether the fields are variable length. If they are variable length, you must tell dBASE Mac what character delimits the fields, and what character signals the end of each record.

Once this information is established, you name the new file, then proceed to field definition. The first field of a Foreign file, the Key field, is a Record Number field. You must define all subsequent fields in a manner similar to the field definition of all dBASE Mac fields. (See Field Definition and Foreign Files.)

To define a standard dBASE Mac file, select dBASE Mac from the pop-up menu if it is not already selected, then press **Return** or click **OK**. You will be asked to name the file, and define a password, if desired.

Next you will see the Key field definition screen, followed by the standard field definition screens. (See Key field, Field Definition.)

Finally, when all fields are defined, click **Done**. You will see the file size dialog box. Enter a value for the number of records you estimate your file will contain. (See File Size for more discussion of this topic.)

New Project

To begin a new project, you must first Close any existing projects. This will remove all files, views, and relationships from the Structure View. Then select New from the Projects menu. A new Structure View will appear in an Untitled project. Only the Globals file will appear on the Structure view of a new project. Now you can open existing files to include them in the new project, or select New from the Datafile menu to create new files (see New File).

New Record Procedure

New Record procedures take effect when a new record is added to a file or when Perform and Use is invoked in a Transfer View. Use New Record procedures to initialize values in various fields before data entry. New Record is like a special kind of Pre-Processor—one that takes effect only when a new record is added to a file. This makes it especially useful for setting conditions that must occur only when the record is first created, not when it is browsed or modified.

A New Record procedure can be added to a file through the **Show Procedure** button in the Change File dialog, or it can be added to a Pointer field (title bar) in a view hierarchy. It is invoked when you select New (**Command-A**) from the Edit menu or as a NEW command is encountered in a procedure.

NOTE: When a New Record procedure is invoked, it requires a specific NEW command using the SELF parameter as an argument. The syntax is NEW(SELF). If the NEW(SELF) command is not encountered during a New Record procedure, the action will not be completed.

New View

To create a new view, first select the file you wish to be the primary source of data processing for the new view. This file will be the Root File of the view. Any files included in a view other than the Root File are called Subordinate files.

Next select New View from the Windows menu. The New View dialog box appears. You must name the view, enter a description if you wish, and select the type of view to create—Custom, Column, or Form. You can also change the selection of the Root File from the list box on the left. Finally, check the Quick Create checkbox if you wish the program to select the basic hierarchy and layout for the new View (you can modify these settings later, if necessary). (For more, see Form View, Column View, Custom View, Layout, Hierarchy.)

Next <name>

Selecting the **Next <name>** command from the Edit menu, the right arrow Palette icon, or **Command-N** causes dBASE Mac to display the next item or record in a database. What item will be displayed depends on the selection criteria, if any. If dBASE Mac does not find a next occurrence, it will beep and display an error message.

If the cursor is in a multivalued field, **Next <name>** displays the next occurrence of the multivalued field.

Command-Shift-N will display the next Root File record regardless of the current cursor location.

Number Fields

Number fields are used primarily for numbers that must be mathematically manipulated. For instance, you might not use a Number field for zip codes, part numbers, and telephone numbers—numbers that should not be involved in mathematical operations. On the other hand, quantities, dollar amounts, and other numbers that may require calculation should be defined as Number fields.

Sometimes a Number field is preferable because it does error checking and doesn't allow nonnumeric characters to be entered. Thus, for a zip code, you might prefer a Number field to be sure that only numeric characters are entered.

To define a Number field, first select Number from the data type pop-up menu on a field definition screen. Key fields, Data fields, Formula fields, and Memory fields can all use the Number data type.

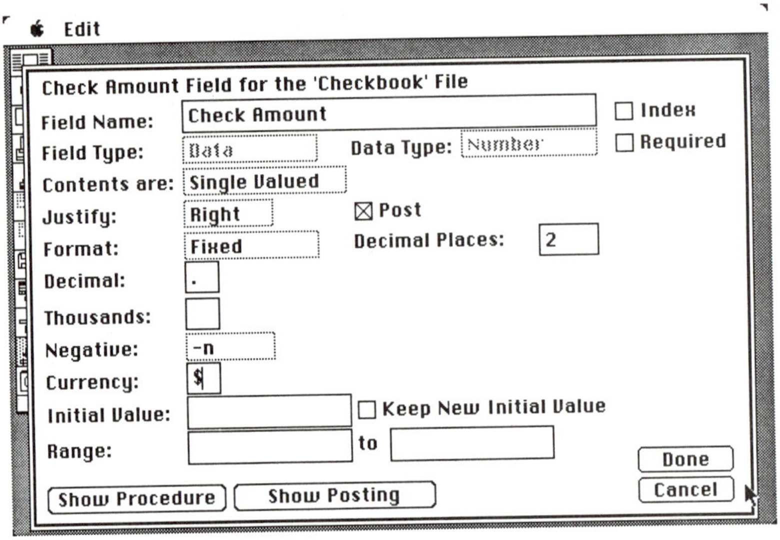

Figure R-43 Number Field Definition Screen.

When you select the Number data type, the field definition screen changes. You can select single or multivalued field in the Contents Are: pop-up. Next, notice that the Justify: menu has defaulted to Right. You can change this if you wish, but most number fields are better right justified. As with any field, you may check the Required checkbox to require a value in this field before a record can be processed.

If the field is a Key field, then you can check the Automatic Sequence checkbox. If you do so, the value of the Key field in each successive record will be updated by the amount you set in the Sequence Amount checkbox. (See Key field.)

Next you must decide what to fill in the remaining text boxes. First you must determine the number of decimal places. The program always defaults at two decimal places. Enter a zero for integer amounts.

NOTE: dBASE Mac number fields can contain a maximum of nineteen digits. If you want to display numbers with high precision, set a high number of decimal places, then set the Format to Floating. dBASE Mac will display as many digits after the decimal point as it can up to that limit. If you set the Format to Fixed, the number of decimal places will remain constant.

Decimal You can set the symbol you want to represent the decimal point (usually a period in the U.S., but sometimes a comma in other countries).

Thousands You can fill in the character you wish to use to separate thousands (usually a comma). If you do not enter a value, for instance, the number one thousand would read 1000. If you set a comma, the number reads 1,000.

Negative You can set the format for displaying negative numbers as follows:

/-n minus sign precedes the number (-100)

n/- minus sign follows the number (100-)

n CR credited (100 CR)

<n> places the number in brackets (<100>)

Currency Indicate the symbol to use for currency, if applicable. Although most uses may require the dollar sign, you could also enter the pound sign, the yen sign, or any other sign available from any Macintosh character set.

The Initial Value and Keep New Initial Value entries work the same as any other field. (See Field Definition.)

If the field is a Data type field, you can also set a Range of acceptable values, if applicable. Ranges can be set for Numeric, Date, and Time fields.

Finally, you can check the Post checkbox. If you check this box, the Show Posting button appears at the bottom of the screen. Click the **Show Posting** button to set the destination fields to which you want to post the values from this number field. (See Posting for more information.)

Open File

To add an existing file to a project, choose Open from the Datafile menu. A standard file-choosing dialog box appears. You can change drives by clicking the **Drive** button. You can open new directories using standard HFS procedures.

If the file you open already has relationships with any other files in the project, those relationships will be present when the file appears on the Structure Window. However, be careful of processing new information in a file that has relationships with other files if the others are not present.

You can also load a file by double-clicking its icon on the Finder desktop. This method will load the file in an unnamed project and will create default Form and Column views. However, if the file is already part of a project, the other views and files of the project will not load. To load a project, double-click the desired project icon.

Open Project

If you wish to load an existing project from within dBASE Mac, first Close any existing project, then choose Open from the Project menu. You can change drives by clicking the Drive button, or follow standard HFS techniques to change directories if necessary.

You can also open a project by double-clicking the project icon on the Finder desktop before loading dBASE Mac.

> TIP: If you highlight a group of files on the Finder desktop, then double-click one of them, dBASE Mac will create a new project, including all the highlighted files.

Page Breaks

You can set page breaks from the Define Hierarchy screen. First select the field that will trigger the break. Then select Page Break from the Break pop-up. Whenever the value of the selected field changes, a form feed will be issued to your printer, causing it to move to the next page.

Page Setup

If you choose Page Setup from the Projects menu, you will be presented with a dialog box containing various options for setting up your printing. This box will vary with the printer you are using.

If you are using an ImageWriter, you can choose from among five different page sizes:

1. U.S. Letter (8 1/2″ × 11″)
2. U.S. Legal (8 1/2″ × 14″)
3. Computer Paper (15″ × 11″)
4. A4 Letter (8 1/4″ × 11 2/3″)
5. International Fanfold (8 1/4″ × 12″)

In addition to the paper size, you can set certain special effects:

The **Tall Adjusted** option scales graphics to the dimensions of the page.

The **50% Reduction** option shrinks the entire page contents by half.

The **No Gaps Between Pages** option prints the page without including page breaks, headers, and footers that may have been included in the document.

Finally, the two Orientation icons determine normal printing or sideways printing (printing rotated ninety degrees).

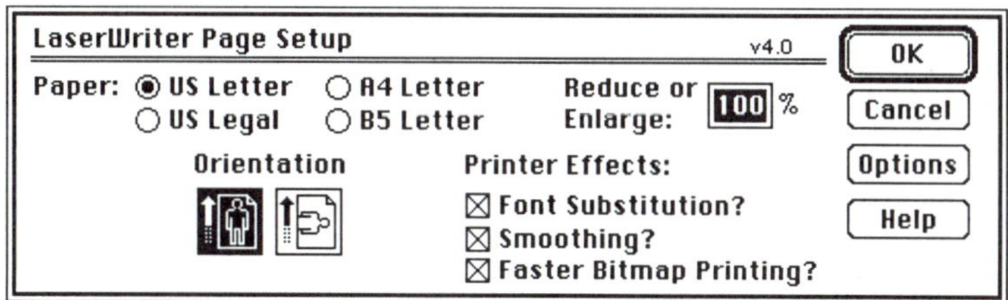

Figure R-44 LaserWriter Setup Graphic.

Palette

The Palette is a special window containing a stack of icons that perform useful menu commands. The standard Palette changes from one part of the program to another. If you wish, you can modify the Palette by changing, adding, or removing icons.

The Palette is like any window. You can drag it by its title bar to reposition it on the screen. You can close it by clicking its close window box at the top. You can also close it by selecting Close Palette from the Edit menu. If the Palette is currently closed, the command will read Show Palette, which you use to open it again.

When you click on a Palette icon, the corresponding menu command is activated. If the menu command is not currently executable, the icon will not highlight, and the program will beep. (If you look on the menu, the menu item associated with the icon that did not operate will be dimmed.)

The Custom Palette

To gain the greatest utility from the Palette, you may sometimes wish to change, add to, or reduce the standard Palette for a particular view or window.

To select an icon on the Palette, hold the **Command** key and click on the desired icon. If you wish to add to the Palette, hold the **Command** key and click on the blank space at the bottom of the Palette. If no blank space appears, the Palette is full and you will have to remove or modify one of the existing icons.

Once you have chosen an icon, or a blank space for one, the Palette definition dialog box appears.

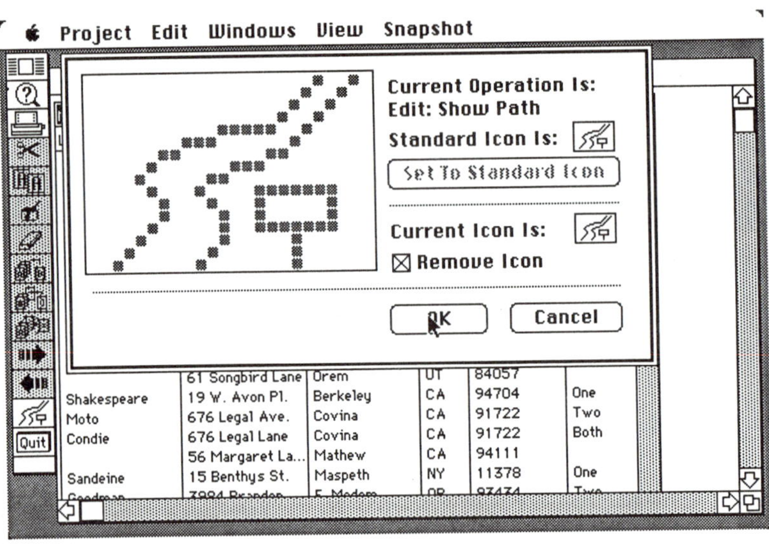

Figure R-45 Palette Definition Screen Graphic.

In this dialog box, you can draw or redraw an icon, set the standard icon shape, remove an icon from the Palette, or set or change the menu command the icon is to represent.

The large box to the left is a magnified view of the icon picture. Two smaller boxes show the Standard Icon for the current command and the Current Icon as it will display based on the contents of the large graphic box.

To set the Current Icon to its standard picture, click on the **Set to Standard Icon** button. This will cause the large box to contain an exploded view of the preset Standard Icon. You can modify this icon if you wish by selecting individual pixels with the mouse and reversing their color. The result of this modification will appear in the Current Icon Is: box.

HINT: If you click on a black pixel in the magnified view, it will change to white. If you hold and drag the mouse, any black pixels in the path of the cursor will also change. The opposite is true. Select a white pixel, turn it to black. Now hold the mouse button and drag. A line of black pixels will appear in the cursor's path.

To Remove an icon, **Command** click the desired icon, then check the Remove Icon box. Click **OK** or hit **Return**, and the icon will be removed.

To change the menu command associated with an icon, **Command** click on the desired icon (or on a blank space if you are adding an icon), then select any menu command, or operate a keyboard command. That command becomes the operational command for the current icon. The Standard Icon for that command will appear in the Standard Icon Is: box. You can click the **Set Standard Icon** button to change the Current Icon to the Standard Icon, or you can leave the current icon as is.

The Standard Icon Sets

In the following pages, the standard icons are presented. For more information about the operation of the associated commands, look them up by name elsewhere in the Reference.

The Database Structure Window Palette:

Help

Save

Print

Preferences

New View

New Datafile

Open Datafile

Close Datafile

Add Field

Change Field

Quit

Define View and Use Columnar View Palette:

- Help. . .
- Print
- Preferences
- Define Hierarchy
- Layout View
- Define Sorts
- Define Selections
- Perform and Use View
- Use View
- Quit

The Use View Palette:

- Help
- Print
- Cut
- Copy
- Paste
- Clear
- Add <Name>
- Insert <Name>
- Delete <Name>
- Next <Name>
- Prior <Name>
- Show Path
- Quit

Layout View Palette (for more see Layout):

NOTE: The first five icons on the Layout View Palette are special icons that do not have menu equivalents. Because of that, you cannot remove them. You can redraw them to suit your needs, however.

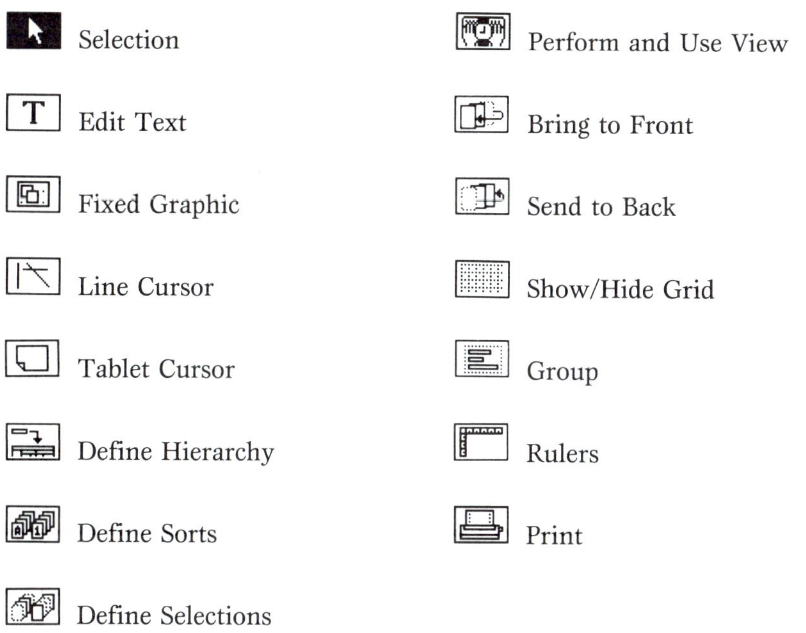

In addition to The Default Palette icons, other icons are available for customized Palettes:

Project Menu

Close Project

Save As

Revert

Protect/Modify

Page Setup

View Menu

Duplicate View

Delete View

Trace On/Off

Edit Menu

Select All

Design Menu

- Display Options
- Turn Grid On/Off
- Align to Grid
- Ungroup
- Form Size
- Custom Menus
- Reduce to Fit

Datafile Menu

- Duplicate File
- Change File
- Import/Export
- Remove Field
- Restore Field

Paste

Paste is the standard Macintosh Paste command (also **Command-V**). Use this command to move graphics or text from the Clipboard to your application. Use in conjunction with Cut and Copy to move material from one place to another. (See also Cut, Copy.)

Perform and Use

When you select Perform and Use from the View menu, dBASE Mac creates a memory-resident list of key values that conform to the view's sort and selection criteria definitions, then presents the Use view screen. Any changes that have been made to the files and fields of the view and any current sorts and selections will be reflected by Perform and Use. Internally dBASE Mac creates what is called a Work File, a listing of Key Field values in the current order. This Work File represents the order of the records in the view.

The Perform and Use command differs from the Use command in that it retrieves the information. The Use command simply activates the Use screen of the current view. Suppose you have two views, one a Form view for data entry and the other a Column view for displaying records. Suppose you activate the Column view and examine the existing records, then activate the Form view to add several new records. If you simply reactivate the Column view (with Use), the new records will not appear. You will have to select Perform and Use to update the information on the Column view.

TIP: If you often move from a data entry view to a data display view, add the Perform and Use icon to the Palette of the display view. In this way you will not have to open the View menu repeatedly. (To add a Palette icon, see Palette.)

The PERFORM command in the Procedural Interface is the equivalent of Perform and Use. The PERFORM command has some additional parameters that can be added to it:

> Syntax: PERFORM (view name [,MODAL][,INIT])
> The MODAL parameter disables the Palette and the menus during performance of the view.
> The INIT parameter invokes any Pre-Processor attached to the view (see Pre-Processor below).

Picture This. . .

When you load dBASE Mac, you automatically load two Desk Accessories—Help, and Picture This. . . . Picture This. . . allows you to grab parts of pictures from existing MacPaint compatible graphics (including SuperPaint and FullPaint images, and entire libraries of clip art).

- When you first open the Picture This. . . DA, you will be presented with a list of files in the current folder (change drives or folders as necessary). Find the graphics files you need, then double-click or highlight and click Open.
- Drag the mouse to select the part of the picture you want to grab, then **Command-C**, or Copy, to copy the image into the Clipboard.
- Close the Picture This. . . window and select a Graphic field or Fixed Graphic box on the layout.
- Press **Command-V** or Paste to insert the graphic into the Graphic field or Fixed Graphic.

Post-Processor

The Post-Processor is a type of procedure that can occur at the field or view level. Post-Processors take effect after leaving a field or view. They can be used for field validations, custom alerts for error conditions, and transferring control to another view.

Field Post-Processors only get executed after the contents of a field are modified and physically exited.

File-based field Post-Processors may also be invoked any time the contents of the field are modified (i.e., by a procedure).

> TIP: Use the Post-Processor for various housekeeping functions, such as posting control totals, validating field entries, or displaying a summary page after processing a view. It is also useful for presenting warning messages or defining exit criteria for your application, including calling other views and/or projects.

Posting

When you define a Number field, one of the options presented is the Post checkbox. If you check that box, it means that you wish to increment or decrement some other field with the contents of the current field.

dBASE Mac allows you to add (or subtract) the value of a Number field to (or from) a Numeric Memory field or Numeric Data field in the current or related file. Posting can be used to keep a running total for all the records in a file. It can also be used to pass the value of the current number field to one or more Number fields in a related file. Although you can't Post through one file using a common relation to another, you can Post to a field that itself Posts to a field in a third file.

NOTE: To use Posting to accumulate a total, post to a Memory field.

After you check the Post checkbox in the field definition dialog, a new button appears at the bottom of the screen. Click **Show Posting** to assign the destination of the posting.

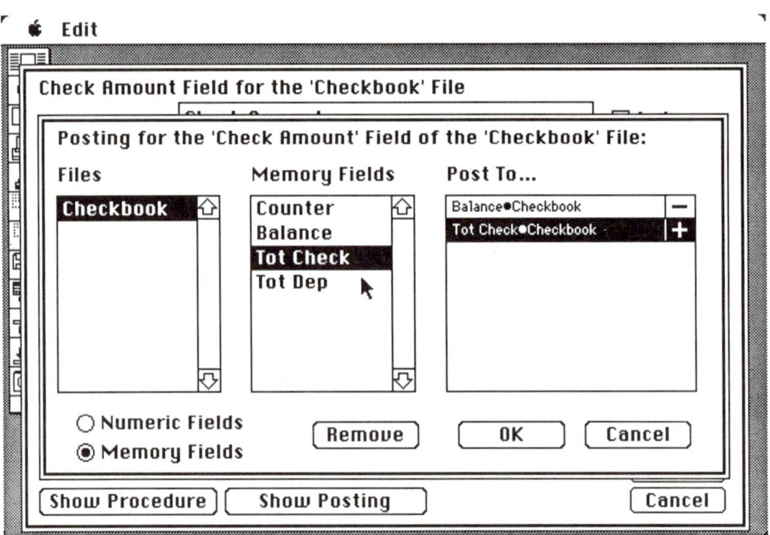

Figure R-46 Show Posting Dialog Box Graphic.

First select the kind of field to Post to—Numeric or Memory—by clicking the appropriate button at the bottom of the screen.

Next, select the file that contains the field to Post to. A list of available fields will appear in the choice list.

Select a field to Post to.

If you make a mistake, highlight the erroneous entry and click **Remove**.

Next, select the kind of operation you wish to perform while posting—addition or subtraction—by clicking on the right side of the field designator in the Post To box.

You can repeat these basic steps to post to other fields if you wish.

Pre-Processor

Pre stands for before. A Pre-Processor is a procedure that takes effect at the beginning of an operation. For instance, if the Pre-Processor is attached to a view, the procedure is run when you first Use or open the View—before any other operation takes place. A typical view Pre-Processor might be used to initialize, or preset certain values in the view, or to select certain records before data display. If the Pre-Processor is attached to a field, in a data entry form for instance, it is run before the cursor enters that field.

Preferences

The Preferences dialog box contains global settings for the current project. Select Preferences from the Edit menu to examine these options.

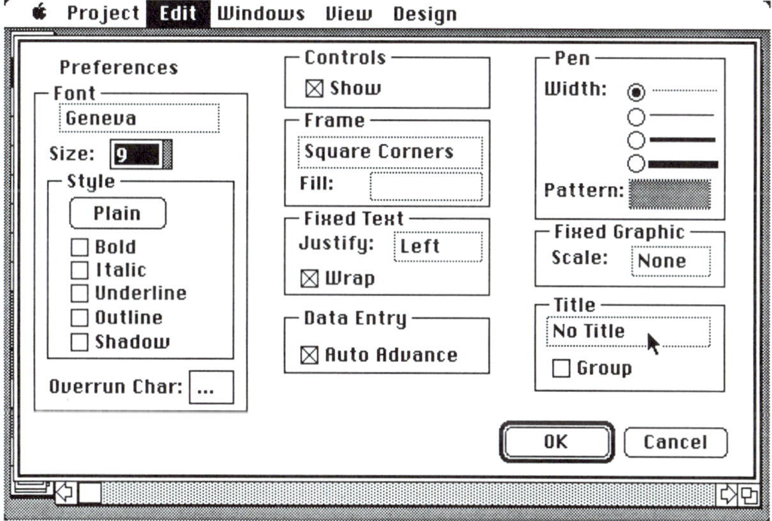

Figure R-47 Preferences Graphic.

In the Preferences dialog box you can select various display options like default font, default style, and so on. To modify a particular display element, choose the Display Options command in the Design menu (in the layout—see Design Options, Layout).

Look at the Preferences options one at a time:

The **Fonts** pop-up menu allows you to set the font for all text elements. The fonts that are available will vary depending on what fonts you have installed in your system or in the dBASE Mac program. You can also select the **Size** of the font from the Size box. Only valid sizes may be selected.

The **Style** section of Preferences allows you to set different special effects for text elements of your layouts. These are standard Macintosh effects—Bold, Italic, Underline, Outline, and Shadow. You can click on any combination of checkboxes to combine effects.

The **Controls** section effects the display of multivalued fields. Clicking on the **Show** checkbox causes multivalued fields to display with pop-up menus in Form type views. In Columnar views, special scroll boxes will be included with multivalued fields, where necessary.

The **Frame** section allows you to set the kinds of boxes used to frame data elements in your views. You can set square or round corners. Set round corners by choosing from among several different curves.

You can also use different fill patterns, choosing from a pop-up menu of patterns in the Frame section.

Under **Fixed Text**, you can set Left, Center, or Right justification for your text. This means that all text will be aligned with the appropriate edge, or centered in the field. Also you can select **Wrap** for text that wraps within the field box much as word processor text wraps. By adjusting the size of the field box, you can create wrapped, multiple-lined text elements for any view. (See Layout for more on sizing the field box.)

If you wish the program to present a blank record after each record is completed, check the **Auto Advance** checkbox under **Data Entry**. If you do not wish a new, blank record to appear after processing each record, do not check that box.

Pen Width and **Pattern** affect the thickness and type of line used to draw field boxes. When combined with different types of corners and patterns, a variety of effects is possible.

> HINT: To eliminate boxes altogether, choose the upper pen width (the thin, grey line). This will allow the data to display as text only, and is useful in such applications as mailing labels and special preprinted forms. (See below for more on this).

The **Fixed Graphic** section allows you to set different scaling options. (For more information about scaling graphics, see Graphic Fields.)

The **Titles** section allows you to set the position of titles relative to the field data. Titles can be positioned to the right, left, above, or below the field data. If you select None, no titles will appear. For many printed applications, including mailing labels and special preprinted forms, it is desirable to eliminate titles. Also, clicking the Group checkbox causes dBASE Mac to tie the title with the data, thereby treating the two as one item. This is sometimes useful when you are moving layout elements.

Print

The Print command in the Project menu (or on the Palette) performs multiple tasks, depending on what part of the program you are currently using. Each time you select Print, regardless of the kind of operation you are invoking, the standard Print dialog box appears:

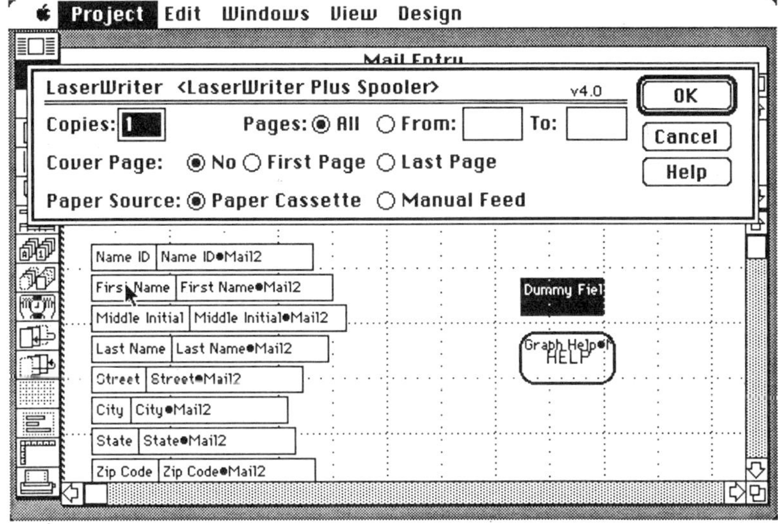

Figure R-48 Print Dialog Box Graphic.

Fill in the dialog box to proceed.

Database Structure Window

You can print three kinds of report from the Database Structure Window.

1. If no file or field is highlighted (click in a blank area), selecting Print will print a graphic image of the Structure Window.

2. If you highlight a field on the structure window, Print will print a listing of the field's structure, including any procedures associated with that field.

3. If you highlight the title bar of a file, Print will print a description of the file, including each field and its field type.

Hierarchy View

If the Hierarchy screen is active, Print will print out a detailed description of the current view, including any complete descriptions of all view fields, procedures, and path data.

Sort Criteria

If the Sort selection screen is active, Print will print a definition of the current sort settings.

Selection Criteria

If the Selection screen is active, Print will print a definition of the current selection information.

Layout

If the layout is active, Print will print a graphic image of the current layout.

> NOTE: Printing the layout does not print any current settings from the Display Options dialog, including Tablet selection criteria and such invisible values as Display Only, Carry Over, and Repeat. Also it gives you no information about Groups currently in effect.

Use View

If the Use screen is active, Print will print a report based on the current view hierarchy, layout, sort, and selection criteria, including any Breaks or totals defined in the Define Hierarchy screen. (For more on reports, see Reporting.)

Prior <name>

Selecting the **Prior<name>** command from the Edit menu, the left arrow palette icon, or **Command-P** causes dBASE Mac to display the next item or record in a database. What item will be displayed depends on the selection criteria, if any. If dBASE Mac does not find a next occurrence, it will beep and display an error message.

If the cursor is in a multivalued field, **Prior <name>** displays the previous occurrence in the multivalued field.

Command-Shift-P will display the previous Root File record.

Procedural Interface

The Procedural Interface (PI) in dBASE Mac operates through the processors—Pre-Processor, Post-Processor, New Record, Write Record, and Delete Record. For more on the processor types, look each up by name.

Other aspects of the PI involve the use of constants, variables, expressions, functions, and commands.

Constants Constants are values that do not change during the running of a procedure. These constants can be numbers, strings (text), dates, times, or logical values. All constants must be enclosed in quotation marks, with the exception of numbers. Number constants may optionally exclude the use of quotation marks.

"Ashton-Tate"—a string constant.
101—a numeric constant
"12/31/79"—a date constant
"8:30 AM"—a time constant
"T"—a logical constant meaning True

Variables You can use field names as if they were variables. You must use the proper syntax and include the full path name, such as {Description•Checkbook}. To designate the occurrence number in a multivalued field, enclose the number in brackets after the path, such as {Description•Checkbook}[3]. These field variables can be used freely in procedures.

Local Variable The other type of variable is called a local variable. You can define a local variable easily. Simply create a label for the variable and assign it a value, such as Test_Total = 3000. This sets the new variable Test_Total equal to 3000. You can use the variable anywhere within the current procedure. A local variable exists within the current procedure only. Its value is not carried over to other procedures. Notice that blank spaces are not allowed in local variable names.

Arrays Local variables can contain data in one- or two-dimensional arrays. Arrays are to local variables what multivalued fields are to single-valued fields. A one-dimensional array contains separate occurrences of values within a local variable. Notate the fourth occurrence in the array as Test_Total[4].

Two-dimensional arrays are actually data tables. Like a spreadsheet, these arrays are organized in rows and columns. For instance, to assign the value 1500 to the third row, ninth column of an array, the code reads, Test_Total[3,9] = 1500.

You can use arrays in many of the same ways that you would use multivalued fields. Arrays are especially useful for performing statistical analysis that otherwise could only be performed on the contents of a multivalued field.

Expressions and Functions The expressions used in dBASE Mac programming fall into four categories: mathematical, string, logical, or Date/Time. Expressions use constants, variables, functions, and even other expressions to evaluate information and return a constant as the result.

Math Functions

1. ABS

Syntax: ABS(operand1)

This returns the absolute value of operand1.

2. ACOS

Syntax: ACOS(operand1)

Operand1 represents the cosine of an angle. The result is the size of that angle in radians. To convert the result to degrees, multiply operand1 by 180/PI.

```
Example:   Degrees=ACOS(field)*180/PI
           Radian=ACOS(field)
```

3. ANNUITY

Syntax: ANNUITY(operand1,operand2)

Operand1 represents the periodic interest rate.
Operand2 is the number of periods.

4. ASIN

Syntax: ASIN(operand1)

Operand1 represents the sine of an angle. The result is the size of the angle in radians. To convert the result to degrees, multiply by 180/PI.

Example: Degree=ASIN(field)*180/PI
Radian=ASIN(field)

5. ATAN

Syntax: ATAN(operand1)

Operand1 represents the tangent of an angle. The result is the size of the angle in radians. To convert the result to degrees, multiply by 180/PI.

Example: Degree=ATAN(field)*180/PI
Radian=ATAN(field)

6. AVG

Syntax: AVG(operand1)

This averages the values contained in operand1, where operand1 is a multivalued field or an array.

NOTE: This is the same as:

average=SUM(field)/COUNT(file)

7. COS

Syntax: COS(operand1)

This finds the cosine of operand1 that is expressed in radians. To find the cosine of operand1 in degrees, multiply the number of degrees by PI/180.

Example: cosine=COS(field)
cosine=COS(degree field*PI/180)

8. **CV**

Syntax: CV (operand1)

This returns the current value number of the group containing operand1. Operand1 must be a multivalued field.
Example: CV({Budget•Checkbook}) = 3

9. **DEGREES**

Syntax: DEGREES(operand1)

This will convert operand1 from radians to degrees.

NOTE: This is the same as multiplying by 180 and dividing by PI.

10. **EXP**

Syntax: EXP(operand1)

This raises *e* to the power of operand1. The number *e* (which is approximately 2.718) is the base number for natural logarithms.
Example: EXP(1.258)= 3.5183777

11. **EXP2**

Syntax: EXP2(operand1)

This is the same as EXP except that it raises 2 to the power of operand1.

12. **FACT**

Syntax: FACT(operand1)

Return the factorial of operand1.

13. **LN**

Syntax: LN(operand1)

This returns the natural logarithm (base *e*) of a number. Natural logarithms use *e*, which is approximately 2.718, as a base. The EXP function is the exact opposite of this function.
Example: LN(EXP(4))=4

14. **LOG2**

Syntax: LOG2(operand1)

Returns the base 2 logarithm of a number. This number must be greater than 0.

15. MAX

Syntax: MAX(operand1)

This returns the maximum value contained in a multivalued or array variable.

16. MED

Syntax: MED(operand1)

This returns the median of a multivalued field, or an array variable.

17. MIN

Syntax: MIN(operand1)

Returns the minimum value of operand1, where operand1 is either a multivalued field or an array variable.

18. MOD

Syntax: Operand1 MOD Operand2

This returns the remainder of operand1 when it is divided by operand2. Operand1 must be an integer, and Operand2 must be a natural number. The sign (+ or -) of the result is always the same as the sign of operand1.
Example: 4 MOD 3 = 1
-14 MOD 3 = -2

19. PI

Syntax: PI

PI is the ratio of a circumference of a circle to its diameter (3.141592653589793285).

20. RADIANS

Syntax: RADIANS(operand1)

Converts operand1 from degrees to radians. This is the opposite of the DEGREES function. This will yield the same result as multiplying by PI and dividing by 180.
Example: Radian=RADIANS(degree)

21. RANDOM

Syntax: RANDOM(operand1)

Generates a pseudo-random number between 0 and operand1. To generate random numbers in other steps, add the lower limit of the range.
Example: RANDOM(100) generates a random number between 0 and 100.

22. ROUND

Syntax: ROUND(operand1,operand2)

Rounds operand1 to operand2 places. Operand2 must be an integer. dBASE MAC can round on either side of the decimal point. If operand2 is positive, then operand1 is rounded to operand2 digits to the right of the decimal point.
Example: ROUND(1234.5678,2)=1234.57

23. SIGN

Syntax: SIGN(operand1)

Determines the sign of a number and returns a result of 1 if operand1 is positive, -1 if operand1 is negative, and 0 if operand1 is 0.
Example: SIGN(1234)=1
SIGN(-1234)=-1
SIGN(0)=0

24. SIN

Syntax: SIN(operand1)

Returns the sign of operand1 that is expressed in radians. To convert a number of degrees to radians, multiply by PI/180.
Example: SIN(PI/6)=.5
SIN(90*PI/180)=1 (sine of 90 degrees)

25. SQRT

Syntax: SQRT(operand1)

This returns the positive square root of a number. Operand1 must be greater than or equal to 0.
Example: SQRT(12)=3.464101

26. STD

Syntax: STD(operand1)

Computes the standard deviation of values in operand1, where operand1 is a multivalued field or an array.

27. SUM

Syntax: SUM(operand1)

Produces a sum or total for operand1, where operand1 is a multivalued field or an array.

28. TAN

Syntax: TAN(operand1)

Returns the tangent of operand1 expressed in radians. To convert a number of degrees to radians, multiply by PI/180.
Example: TAN(PI/4)=1
TAN(.52)=.573

29. TRUNC

Syntax: TRUNC(operand1,operand2)

This function will truncate operand1 to the number of decimal points supplied in operand2. Operand2 must be an integer.
Example: TRUNC(12.34,0)=12

30. VAR

Syntax: VAR(operand1)

Computes the population variance of the items in operand1, where operand1 is a multivalued field or an array. (See also STD.)

Project Menu

The Project Menu contains the basic file handling commands of dBASE Mac. For information about those commands, see each in the Reference.

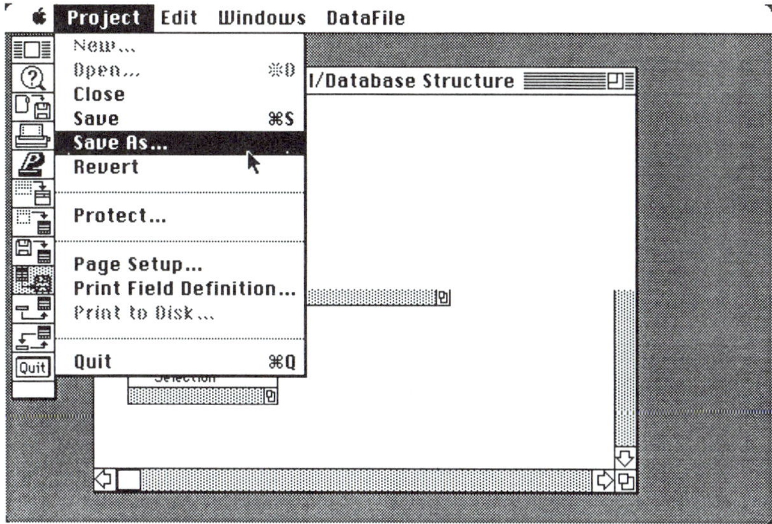

Figure R-48a Project Menu.

Protect Project

To Protect a project, select Protect from the Projects menu. On the dialog box that follows, enter a password. Click **OK**, and you will be returned to the project. If you have defined any Custom Menus (see Custom Menus) these will now be active. To make further changes in the project, select Modify from the Projects menu, enter the password, and you will be returned to the unprotected project.

WARNING: If you Protect a project, then Save it, you will be unable to make further modifications if you forget your password.

NOTE: You can also Protect a project when you first Save the project, or any time you use Save As. . . to save a new version of the current project. A checkbox at the bottom of the file-naming dialog box asks if you want to Save As Protected. If you check that box, you will be able to assign a password to the project before it is saved. When you retrieve the project, it will be in Protected mode.

Quick Create

Select the Quick Create check box when defining a Form or Column view to select all file fields for the hierarchy automatically, and create a simple layout using all fields. Quick Create leaves the view in the Use mode, ready for data entry or data display. You can modify a Quick Create view by choosing Define Hierarchy or Layout View from the View menu.

> NOTE: Any Memory fields in the file will not be included in the hierarchy or the layout using Quick Create. To include them, move to the Define Hierarchy screen, select Globals from the Path pop-up, and then select the Root file name under the Relations list box. Any Root file Memory fields should now be listed under Fields.

Quit

Select Quit from the Project menu, type **Command-Q**, or select the Exit icon from the Palette to close the current project and leave dBASE Mac. If you have not recently Saved your work, you will be prompted to Save it. If you chose **No**, any changes made to your project since the last time you Saved it will be abandoned. Select **Yes** to Save all changes. If you change your mind about exiting the program, select **Cancel** to return to the project.

Reduce to Fit

Because many layouts are too big to fit on the Macintosh screen all at once, you can select the Reduce to Fit command in the Design menu to see the whole layout in reduced form. Although you can't modify any element of the layout when the reduced image is present, you can see the overall effect of the layout as a whole. (See also Layout.)

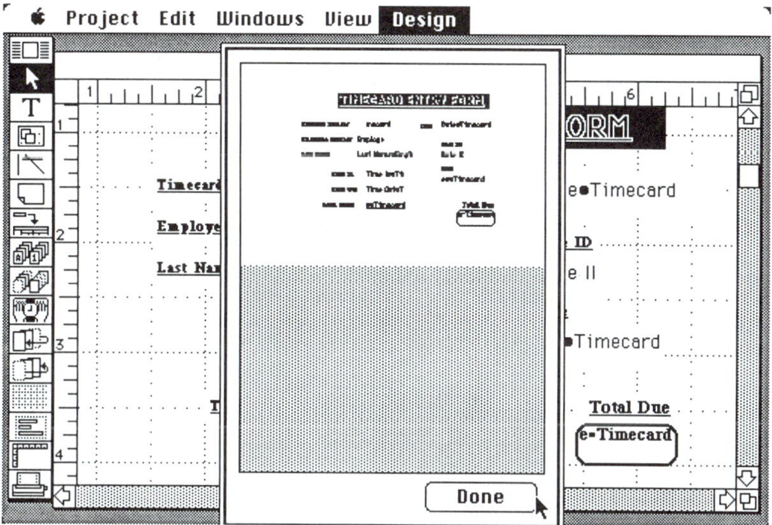

Figure R-49 Reduce to Fit Graphic.

Relationships

File Relationships allow different files to share information. There are, essentially, three kinds of file relationships: one-way relationships, two-way relationships, and External Indexes (for more on External Indexes, see Index).

One-Way Relationships

In a one-way relationship, one file can retrieve data from another, but not vice-versa. A good example of this kind of relationship is a reference file, sometimes called a lookup file. A reference file contains fixed data—tax tables, salary rates, possibly names and addresses—that must be used by other fields. The reference file does not use any information from other files. For instance, the tax rate file does not need to know what transactions used which tax rate, but the transactions file does need to know which tax rate to use. Thus, a one-way relationship is created between the transactions file and the tax rate file.

Two-Way Relationships

In a two-way relationship, both files can access information from each other. This kind of relationship is useful when two files use interdependent data. For instance, in the case of an employee timesheet application, the Employee Records file has a two-way relationship to the Timesheet file. Each individual timesheet is associated through the Key field value to an individual employee. From the Employee Records file, you can see which Timesheets belong to each employee, and using the relationship, you can find out how much each employee has earned. From the timesheet file, you can retrieve necessary information about each employee (for instance, special salary or other earning conditions, etc.)

How Relationships Work

All relationships are defined in the Structure Window. A file relationship is formed by dragging the Key field of a file onto some part of another file. In the case of a one-way relationship, you drag the Key field of the reference file onto the title bar of the other file.

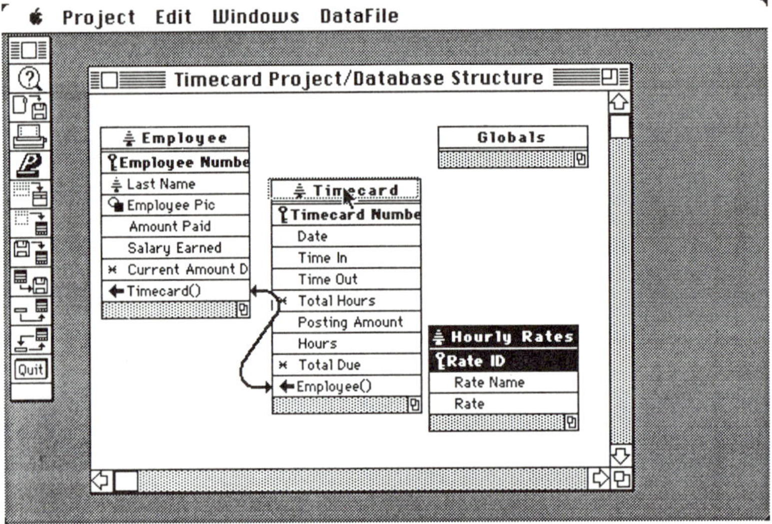

Figure R-50 Creating a One-Way Relationship Graphic.

HINT: In a one-way relationship, only the destination file contains a Pointer field. There is an easy way to remember how to create a one-way relationship. You are dragging a Key field from one file to another. Data will flow in that same direction. The Pointer field that will be created represents the Key field you are dragging. In a sense, the Key field you drag over becomes the Pointer field. As long as you remember that information flows in the same direction as you move the Key field, you should not become confused when creating one-way relationships.

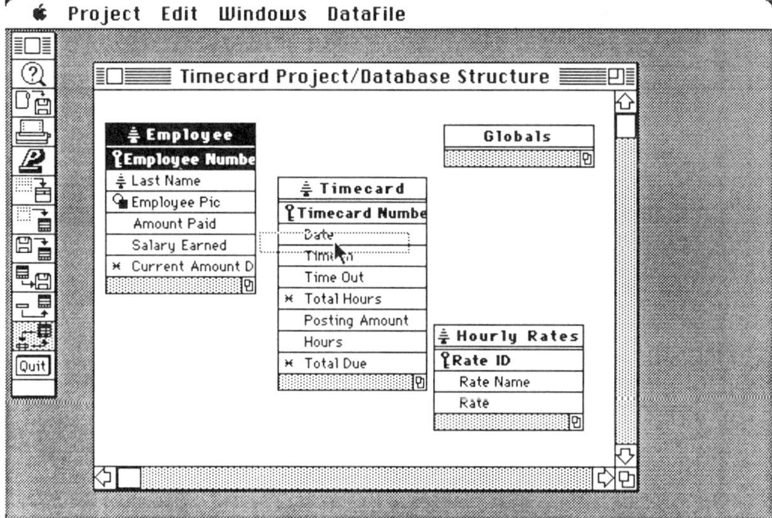

Figure R-51 Creating a Two-Way Relationship Graphic.

In the case of a two-way relationship, drag the Key field of one file onto the field area of another file.

In either case, two things happen. First, one or more new fields are created. These are called Pointer fields. Pointer fields are multivalued fields that contain the Key field values from the related file—they point to records in the other file using Key field values. In a one-way relationship, only the nonreference file gains a Pointer field. In a two-way relationship, both files gain Pointer fields. The name of the Pointer field is taken from the name of the source file, but you can change that name by double-clicking the Pointer field and modifying it as you would modify any field.

The second change that occurs when you create a file relationship is that Pointer arrows are drawn on the Structure Window screen showing the direction of the flow of data.

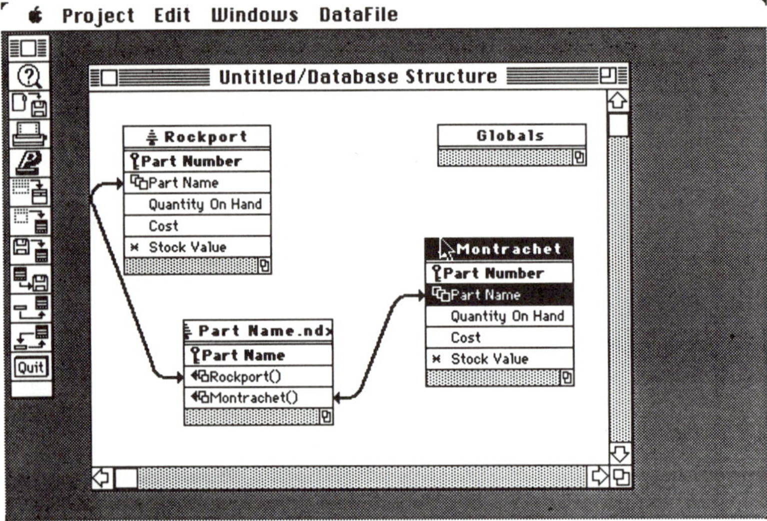

Figure R-52 Relationship Screen Graphic.

Recursive Relationships

There are some special cases of relationships involving recursive file relationships. It is possible to create a relationship between a file and itself. To create a one-way recursive relationship, drag the Key field of a file onto its title bar. A Pointer field will appear that relates back to the file. You can use such a relationship to relate individual records within the file to other records in the file.

To create a two-way recursive relationship, drag the Key field onto the field portion of the file. This process will create two Pointer fields. You can use this type of recursive relationship to create a hierarchical structure within the file (i.e., superior-subordinate, parent-child, master assembly-subassembly). (For more on recursive relationships, see Exploded Views.)

Remove Field

To remove a field, highlight a nonkey field on the Database Structure Window, then select Remove Field from the DataFile menu. Click **Remove Field** on the dialog box that appears. That field will be dimmed and will no longer be active in the project. However, the field will not be completely gone until you Reorganize the file (see Change File). This allows you to Restore the field if you change your mind (see Restore Field).

You cannot remove a Key field or any field that is referred to in any view in the active project. Also, any other projects containing views that refer to that field will be invalid, and you will not be able to open them.

You can also Remove a field from a hierarchy if it is not present on the current view's layout. To remove a field from a hierarchy, go to the Define Hierarchy screen, click on the field to remove (in the hierarchy) and then click **Remove**. If the **Remove** button is dimmed, it probably means the field is present on the layout.

Be very careful when Removing and Restoring fields from the Structure Window, as it is possible to corrupt the data in your files if the field is a Posting or indexed field.

Reorganize File

See Change File.

Reports

You can print reports from the Use mode of any view, but you may prefer to use some views for data entry and modification, and others for printing reports.

There are two basic kinds of reports you can print. One is based around a Column view; the other is based around a Form view. The Mailing Labels you created in Chapter Two and again in Chapter Seven are examples of a Form view report. If you print the Timecard Entry screen as a report, it will also print as a Form view report.

A report based on a Form view prints one form for each currently selected record, in the current sort order. What this means is that only those records that meet the current selection criteria will print in the report, and they will print in the sorted order. One form prints for each record.

> NOTE: When you print a Form view containing multivalued fields with multiple entries, a separate form prints for each occurrence in the multivalued field.

> HINT: If you wish to limit the report to print only selected occurrences in a multivalued field, you can use procedures and special view fields to represent specific occurrences in the multivalued field. Place these special view fields on the layout in place of the original field.

> NOTE: When you print a form report that contains multiple Tablet pages, only those pages that meet selection criteria for each individual form record will print. However, if you have multiple pages that meet selection criteria, a separate form will print for each page.

A column-based report prints each currently selected record in sorted order in a tabular listing. Each field in the report occupies a column, and the report prints the listing of records all on the same page, or on several pages if the report is long.

You would use different reports for different purposes. Form reports are good for mailing labels, complex forms like medical billing, personnel forms, or even 1040 tax forms.

Column reports are good for listing a lot of information. You might use a column format to create a balance sheet or an income statement, a listing of specific transactions, or a comprehensive name and address list.

You can set special conditions on columnar reports. These conditions include three kinds of Breaks (Line Break, Blank Line Break, and Page Break), and two kinds of Accumulated Totals (numeric and count of records).

Restore Field

To Restore a previously Removed file, highlight the dimmed file on the Database Structure Window, then select Restore from the DataFile menu. Confirm the restoration in the dialog box that appears by clicking **Restore**. The field will be restored.

It is a good idea to avoid Removing and Restoring files. If the restored file is a Posting or an indexed file, the contents of the file may become corrupted. Further, if the field was a Required field, you will have to reset that option after restoring the field.

Revert

Choose Revert from the Projects menu to return your project to the state it was in before the last time you Saved it. If you have made some mistakes in developing the project, or are simply not happy with your work, choosing Revert can often correct the problem.

Click **Revert** (in the Change File dialog box of a view) to change a View Modified File Field (VMFF) back to a File field (original definition).

> REMINDER: Unless a file field has been modified within a view hierarchy, it is still considered a File field. It becomes a VMFF only when it has been modified. Revert can remove the effect of modification, returning the field to its original definition.

Rulers

The Rulers command is found on the standard Layout Palette or under the Design menu. When you select this command, a dialog box appears. You can select a ruler scale from among three metric and three standard measures.

> NOTE: If you choose a metric ruler measurement, the grid lines change from one-half inch to one centimeter, and the invisible grid changes from one-eighth inch to one centimeter.

Click on the Show Ruler checkbox and click **Done** or press **Return** to return to the layout. Rulers now appear along the left and upper edges of the layout screen. Use these rulers for more precise positioning of the layout elements.

Save

To save the current state of a project, choose Save from the Projects menu. All current relationships, views, indexes, and other project data will be saved.

You can also Protect a project when you first Save the project, or any time you use Save As. . . to save a new version of the current project. A checkbox at the bottom of the file-naming dialog box asks if you want to Save As Protected. If you check that box, you will be able to assign a password to the project before it is saved. When you retrieve the project, it will be in Protected mode.

Save As

Choose Save As to save a project under a new name. This will create a new project icon on the Finder Desktop under the name you enter. The former project still exists.

Remember that because these projects share the same data files, changes to the data in the shared files will be reflected in both projects.

You can also Protect a project when you use Save As. . . . A checkbox at the bottom of the file-naming dialog box asks if you want to Save As Protected. If you check that box, you will be able to assign a password to the project before it is saved. When you retrieve the project, it will be in Protected mode.

Select All

The Select All command found in the Edit menu is the standard Macintosh command. Select All will highlight all items currently on a desktop. Select All is not always available, but when it is, you can use it to save time in selecting a large number of items for processing.

> TIP: You can use Select All to select all display elements in the layout design area.

Send to Back

Layout elements can be placed in three dimensions, stacked one upon the other. Send to Back from the Design menu will move a highlighted layout element to the bottom of the stack, placing it beneath any other layout elements. Sometimes this will result in the element in back being completely covered by the others. You can recover the invisible element in back by sending elements over it to the back (which brings the back element one level up). (See also Bring to Front.)

Separation

See Change File.

Show Path

Show Path displays information about a record or field. Selecting Show Path from the Palette or from the Edit Menu displays the position number of the current record (relative to other records in the current file), or the position number of field contents in a multivalued field—whatever is appropriate.

Show Path also displays the complete path, including all files and fields that the program must follow to display the current field or record, as determined by the current view hierarchy.

Show Procedure

The Show Procedure button appears in file definition screens (Structure Window or Define Hierarchy), the Change File dialog box (from Structure Window), and in the Define Hierarchy screen. Clicking **Show Procedure** opens the procedure definition dialog for the current file, field, or view.

Show Selections

Show Selections is used with Tablets to define the rules governing their display. Show Selections is found on the Display Options dialog box, which can be opened from the Design menu in the Layout. See Tablets and Layout for a more complete explanation.

Show Statistics

Show Statistics opens up a display of record allocation statistics for the current file. (For more, see Change File.)

Show/Hide Grid

Select Show Grid in the Design menu to display the one-half-inch lines on the layout. When the Grid is showing, select Hide Grid. (Show/Hide Grid changes depending on whether the Grid is visible or not).

> NOTE: The visual lines are not the entire Grid. The invisible Grid is divided into one-eighth-inch sections (or one centimeter if Rulers is set to metric). The visible grid serves as a visual guide. The invisible Grid is used when Align to Grid or Turn Grid On are selected.

Show/Hide Palette

You can hide the Palette by clicking on the close box at the top of the Palette window, or by selecting Hide Palette from the Edit menu. If the Palette is not visible, select Show Palette from the Edit menu. (See Palettes for more.)

Snapshot

A Snapshot is a list of Key field values for a Root file in a view that corresponds to current sort and selection criteria. For instance, if you have sorted and filtered the contents of a file, you can then take a Snapshot of the Key field contents in their present order. By selecting Use from the Snapshot menu, dBASE Mac will use the Snapshot to retrieve the records in the file.

Because a Snapshot is, in essence, a frozen view of the file at a particular point in time, you can save and reuse a Snapshot to process a file's contents in a particular order at any time. Because the Snapshot is simply a list of the Key field contents for that frozen moment, you can use a Snapshot with any view whose Root file shares the appropriate Key field values.

To Take a Snapshot, arrange the view by creating whatever sorts and selections you desire. Then open the Snapshot menu and choose Take. If you wish to keep the Snapshot, you must Save it by choosing Save or Save As. . . from the Snapshot menu.

After you Take the Snapshot, you must put it in operation by selecting Use from the Snapshot menu and selecting the desired Snapshot from the menu of choices available. The Snapshot will remain in operation until you select a new Snapshot to Use, Take another Snapshot, or Close the current Snapshot.

You can perform additional sorts and selections with a Snapshot active. If you wish to update the active Snapshot, choose Save from the Snapshot menu.

Snapshots differ from standard sorts and from Indexes in that they can be used with any view, even a view for a different file if it happens to have the same Key field values.

Structure Window

The Database Structure Window shows all files, fields, and relationships in the current project. Each file has its own window with fields defined in bands on the window. On the Structure Window, you can create New files, Open existing files, Change Field, Duplicate a file, Close a file, Add fields, Remove fields, Restore fields, create relationships and indexes, move or rearrange file or field locations, Print file or field structures, and so on.

The Globals file is always present in the Structure Window. A new project begins in the Structure Window.

Tablets

Tablets are multipage layout elements whose presence can be controlled by selection criteria. In appearance, a Tablet is similar to other Macintosh notepad-like programs. You move backward and forward through the Tablet pages by selecting the small bent corner at the bottom left to turn the page, or the unbent corner beneath it to page backwards.

To create a Tablet, first open the layout and click on the **Tablet** icon. Now position the cursor on the design area at either the upper-left or lower-left corner of the box you wish to create for the Tablet. A Tablet can be any rectangular shape. Drag the mouse to create a box of the desired size. When you let go of the mouse button, your Tablet will remain.

You can position field elements directly on any Tablet page. Turn the page to display a new, blank Tablet area. Using Tablets, you can create a multipage layout form.

To control the display of specific pages, first click on the Tablet page for which you wish to create a selection rule, then open the Design menu and select Display Options (or double-click the **Tablet** page). Now click on **Show Selections**. Here you can create the rules that will govern the display of the highlighted Tablet page.

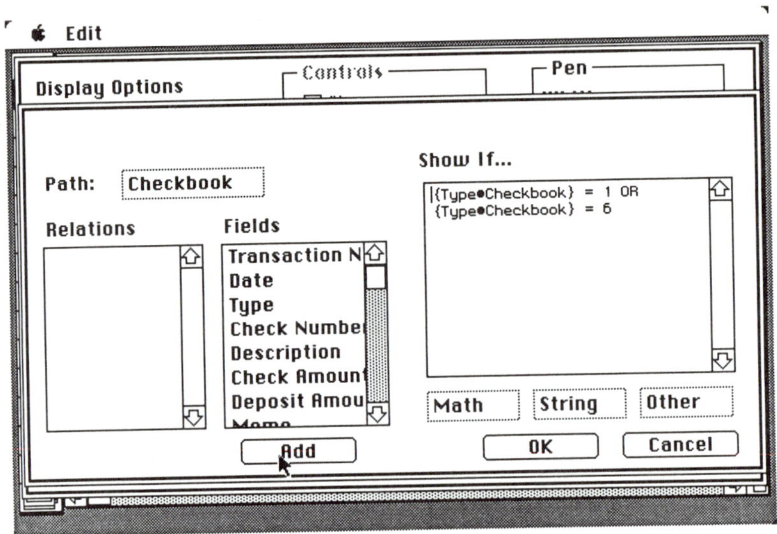

Figure R-53 Show Selection Graphic.

The rules governing the Tablet selections are the same as those governing view selections. Write a formula that describes the conditions under which the highlighted page should appear. If these conditions are not met, the page will not be available during Use mode, nor will that page print when you print a report.

Use Tablets to display different forms for different purposes. For instance, you may be filling in data on employees, but different job descriptions may require different data to be included. Use the job description as the selection criterion to determine the Tablet page or pages to display.

You can also create Tablets within Tablets. Thus, on a particular page, you could have other Tablets associated with still other selection criteria.

Text Data Type

The Text field can contain virtually any type of character, including letters, symbols, and numbers. Use Text fields for data such as names, addresses, zip codes, and phone numbers. A Text field can be up to 255 characters long, and you can set a text field to Wrap within its display area (see Layout for information on resizing field boxes).

Although 255 characters is not very long, you can get around this limit by making a Text field multivalued. Keep notes as separate entries in the multivalued field to circumvent the 255 character limit.

Text fields can also contain special formatting as determined by the Must Match Pattern box. Using special symbols, you can cause automatic entry of special characters such as parentheses and dashes in a phone number, or slashes in a date. Must Match Patterns can also prevent incorrect data from being entered.

Pattern matching uses the following rules for substitution:

Symbol	Meaning
a	Any alphabetical character
n	Any number
x	Any character
1–99 (a, n, or x)	Match the character the specified number of times.
∞(a, n, or x)	Match a, n, or x any number of times (Option 5 for the infinity symbol).
\‘text’	Match the text in single quotes exactly.
any text	Accept only data input that exactly matches the text, except a, n, x, or ~
~character	Accept the data whether or not they contain the character following the tilde (**Option-N**). If the data entered do not contain the character, insert them at that position.

(continued)

Symbol	Meaning
~\'text'	Accept the data whether or not it contains the text in single quotes that follows the tilde. If the data entered do not contain the text in single quotes, insert them at that position.

Following the rules above, you can create different patterns that the program will consider acceptable during data entry. The first entry is usually the preferred style, while later entries are alternates.

An example of a typical entry might be an inventory part number. If each part number begins with a four-letter code, followed by a dash, a number, another dash, and more numbers, acceptable patterns might be entered to prevent inaccurate codes:

ABCD~-4n~-3n
EFGH~-4n~-3n
etc.

Only valid codes are accepted, and the dashes are inserted automatically. In the example above, entering ABCD2345678 would be accepted and displayed as ABCD-2345-678. On the other hand, AZXY2323433 would be rejected because the code AZXY is not in the list of acceptable formats.

Time Field

Time fields are used to contain time information. You can display time in a variety of formats. All formats are compatible, but some display more information than others (depending on whether they display hours, minutes, and seconds, or just hours, or hours and minutes).

Acceptable formats:

Format	Resulting Display:
hh:mm:ss	2:25:27
hh:mm	2:25
hh	2
hh H mm	2 H 25
Minutes since Midnight	865
Seconds since Midnight	51900
Internal Time	Same as Seconds since Midnight
None	As entered

Selecting Time from the Data Type: pop-up of a field definition dialog adds some additional options. In addition to the various formats, there are:

Leading Zeros checkbox Adds zeros to single digit entries in the hours column, for example, 2:51:34 is changed to read 02:51:34.

NOTE: Entering a time in the form 2:2:3 will result in 2:02:03 even if Leading Zeros is not checked.

24 Hour Form pop-up You can select one of three types of time display, 24 hour (like military time), 12 hour, or AM/PM. Times are converted automatically to the appropriate form. For instance, entering 1 PM in field set for 24-Hour form will result in 13:00:00.

NOTE: The program assumes zeros for any part of a time not entered. So if you enter 1:30, the program assumes 00 seconds. Enter 4, and the program assumes 00 minutes and 00 seconds.

NOTE: Many times can be entered without the colon. For instance, entering 12345 results in 1:23:45, whereas entering 123456 results in 12:34:56. However, entering 5433 will produce an error message (although you might suppose it to mean 5:43:03). Experiment with entering times by the most convenient method.

Initial Time Sets the initial value for the field.

Keep New Initial Time checkbox Displays the time entered in the previous record when a new record is added.

Range Sets a range of acceptable times. If you enter only an ending time, the program assumes the beginning of the range to be 00:00:00.

You can perform arithmetic using time fields directly. For instance, to find the hours between two times, create a Numeric Formula field, and enter a simple formula that subtracts one time field from another. The result will be a numeric expression of the time between. Or create a formula that adds a numeric value to a time field to calculate a new time. {Time•Timefile} + 3 would add three hours to the value in the Time field in a file called Timefile. (For information on time functions in the Procedural Interface, see Procedural Interface.)

Transfer View

The Transfer View is really a method of moving data from one file to another (or from a file back to itself). It can be used for a variety of purposes. One way to use the Transfer View is to take data from several files and consolidate it all into one file. Another use is in batch processing, in which a whole session of record entry could be performed in a special entry file. Then, through the Transfer View, those records could be added to a master file.

Transfer Views can also be used to convert dBASE Mac data to Foreign file structures, and vice versa.

To create a Transfer View, first select New View from the Windows menu. Select the file to transfer from (the Source file). Next select Transfer under View Type and click **OK** or press **Return**.

A new dialog box appears. This dialog box contains a list of potential Destination files (the files available on the Structure Window). Select a Destination file. If the file is a dBASE Mac file, several new options will appear.

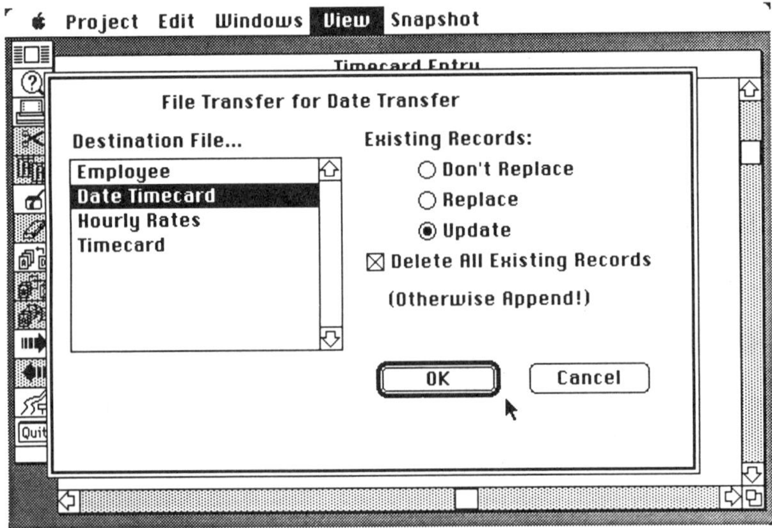

Figure R-54 Transfer View, dBASE Mac Type File Dialog Graphic.

On the right side of the Destination file-selection dialog box are three radio buttons and a check box. These represent the different ways the Transfer View has of dealing with existing records in the Destination file.

Don't Replace If you select Don't Replace, the Transfer View skips any records in the Destination file that have the same Key field value as records in the Source file. No data are changed in those records, but new records will be created in the Destination file where no match is found.

Replace If you select Replace, the Transfer View will replace selected field contents for each record it encounters with the same Key field value. Unmatched Key field values create new records in the Destination file just as with Don't Replace.

Update If you select Update, the Transfer View will update selected field information in the Destination file based on the contents of the Source fields. Update actually offers three possible options that are available in the Transfer View Layout (see below).

Delete All Existing Records The single checkbox in the dialog box allows you to clear an entire file of existing records before the transfer takes place. If there are incorrect data in the Destination file that need to be completely replaced by the data in the Source file, it may be a good idea to check the Delete All Existing Records checkbox.

NOTE: These options are preset. However, you can use processors in a Transfer View just as you can in a Display View. Use these processors to further refine the transfer process and/or create conditional transfers.

After you select the Destination file and the options for handling existing records, click **OK** to move to the Define Hierarchy screen. The Transfer View hierarchy is created exactly like any Display View hierarchy.

TIP: You can choose Duplicate View to use an existing hierarchy in a Transfer View. So if you have a view that uses a complex hierarchy, you can select Duplicate View from the View menu and select the Transfer View radio button. You then procede normally with the Destination file definition dialog, but when you click **OK**, the hierarchy will be a duplicate of the original view hierarchy. (If you do duplicate a view, remember that you also duplicate the procedures attached to that view and to its fields. You may need to **Clear** these processors before continuing with the transfer).

Once you have selected the destination file and the various options, you can click **OK** or press **Return** to proceed to the Transfer View Layout.

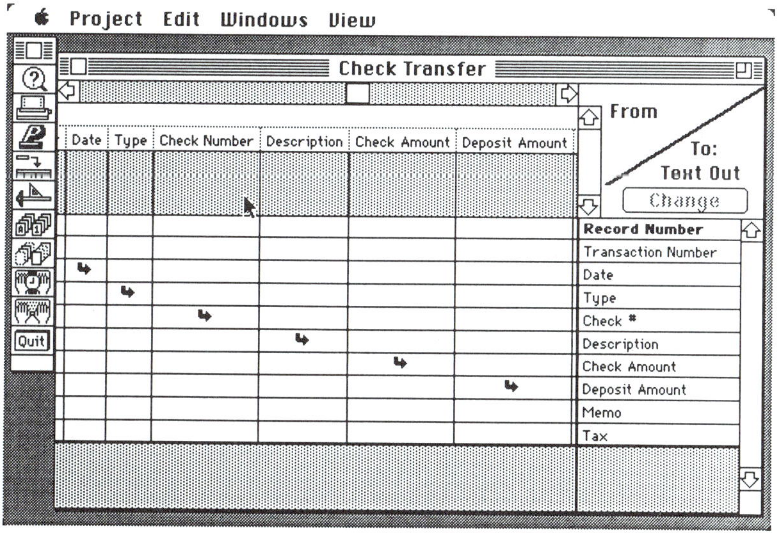

Figure R-55 Transfer View Layout Graphic.

The Transfer View Layout displays a grid of the fields available from the Source field in columns, and the Destination field in rows. By selecting one of the cells at the intersection of two fields, you tell the Transfer View to send the contents of the

Source field to the contents of the Destination field, using the replacement rules you have just established.

Rules for field processing are as follows:

Source Field	Destination Field
Single valued	Single valued Multivalued
Multivalued	Multivalued Key field
Several single valued	Multivalued Key field Single valued (foreign)

NOTE: When transferring several single valued fields to one Destination field, the effect depends on the type of Destination field. If you transfer several single valued fields to a Key field, a new record is created for each unique single field value. When transferring several single valued fields to a multivalued field, the values in the single valued fields are appended to the multivalued field. When transferring several single valued fields to one single valued field, a new record is created for each single field value in the Source file (this only operates when transferring to a foreign text file).

If you selected Update when choosing the Destination file, you can select any Destination field on the layout, then click the Change button to open the Update options dialog:

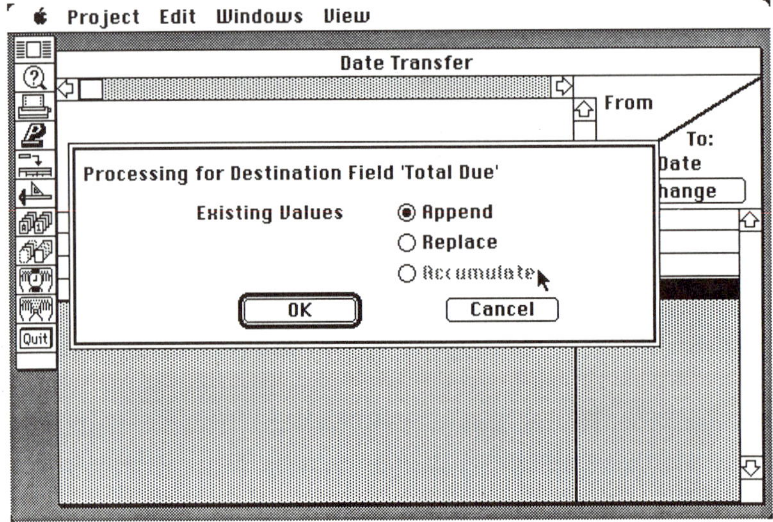

Figure R-56 Update Options Dialog Graphic.

Append Choosing the Append option adds all Source field values as new occurrences within a multivalued field array. If the Destination field is not multivalued, Append is dimmed and not available.

Replace Replace is the default selection. Choosing Replace instructs the Transfer View to replace all Destination field values with Source field values.

Accumulate Choosing Accumulate will add values from the Source field to the current value in the Destination field. You can only select Accumulate if the Destination field is a single valued Numeric Data field.

If you wish to return to the Hierarchy definition at any time, choose Define Hierarchy from the View menu.

When you have set all the field transfers you wish, select Use View, then **Start** to begin processing, or select Perform and Use View. If, at any time, you wish to pause or cancel the transfer, click the **Suspend** button. You will then be given the option to Resume or Cancel the transfer.

TIP: Any active sorts, selections, or snapshots will be implemented when the Transfer View processes your records. Therefore, you can have control over the processing order. Use the Transfer View to create a new master file of sorted and/or selected records. (See also Define Sorts, Define Selections, and Snapshots.)

Turn Trace On

When you are testing your applications, use Trace to watch the operation of any procedures you have written. Click **Turn Trace On** from the View menu. You can single step through procedures with the Trace on, allowing you to see the flow of logic in operation. This should make it easier to locate errors. To resume normal operations, choose Turn Trace Off from the View menu.

Trace will return error numbers for errors that it encounters. Look up the error number in the back of the dBASE Mac manual to see the source of the error.

NOTE: You can interrupt the operation of a procedure, even with Trace Off, by pressing **Shift-Option** before the procedure begins.

Undo

Undo is present in the Edit menu for use in Desk Accessories. It does not function within dBASE Mac itself.

Use

Selecting Use from the Palette or from the View menu places the current view in the Use mode. It does not automatically retrieve records.

The USE command in the PI allows you to call another view. With the INIT parameter, USE will implement any Pre-Processor attached to the view. MODAL will place the view in Use mode, but inactivate all menus and commands.

VMFF

A View Modified File Field (VMFF) is a field from a file that has been added to a view and then modified through the **Change** button. An unmodified field from a file is called a File field. A VMFF is different from a View field, which is a Formula or Memory field that has been created within the current view, and is found only within that view.

View Menu

The View Menu contains the commands for setting the current view mode. It is available when working with views. For more on the View Menu commands, see each command in the Reference.

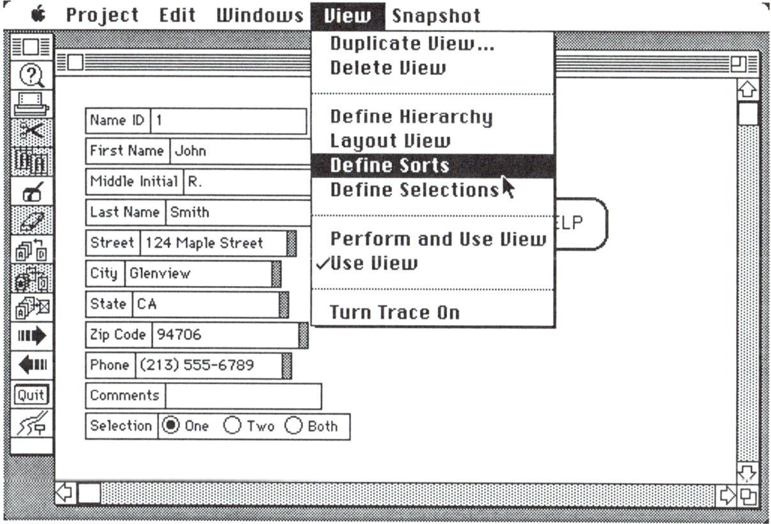

Figure R-57 View Menu.

View Type

There are two basic types of view:

1. Transfer Views are used primarily to transfer data from one file, or from several files, to another output file (see Transfer View).

2. Display Views input and display data. These can be Form Views, Column Views, or Custom Views. (For more information on these view types, look each up. See also Define Hierarchy, Layout.)

Windows Menu

It is from the Windows Menu that you can choose to create a new view or select any current view to activate. The Windows Menu is available at all times, except when hidden via Custom Menus in a protected project.

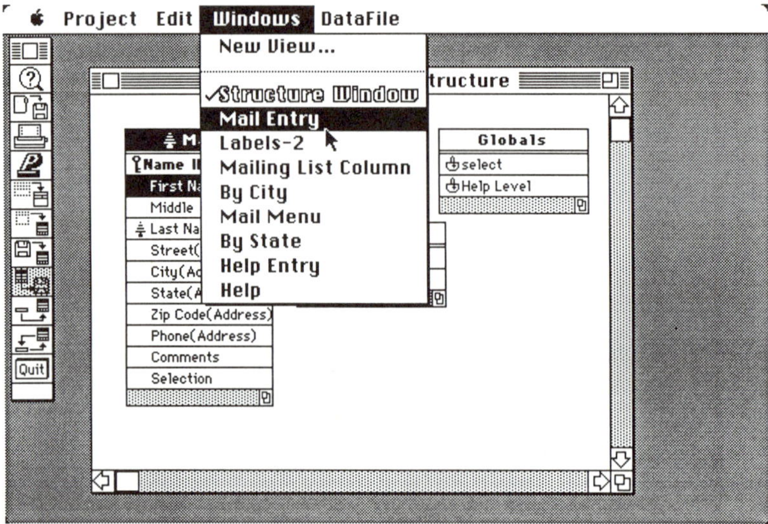

Figure R-58 Windows Menu Graphic.

Write Record Procedure

Write Record procedures take effect when a WRITE command is issued either from the keyboard or from a procedure, or whenever a record is written during the processing of a Transfer View. Use Write Record procedures to validate before writing a record. You might use a Write Record procedure to adjust the effect of a Posting field on fields in other files when data have been modified.

A Write Record procedure can be added to a file through the **Show Procedure** button in the Change File dialog at the Structure Window, or it can be added to a Pointer field (title bar) in a view hierarchy. It is invoked when you **Enter** a record or after a WRITE command is encountered in a procedure.

NOTE: A Write Record procedure is invoked when a WRITE command is issued via keyboard or procedural command. When you press the **Enter** key during record processing, a WRITE command is automatically issued. If a Write Record procedure exists, it will be activated. Once activated, a Write Record command requires a specific WRITE command (using the SELF parameter as an argument) in order to complete the WRITE command. If a WRITE(SELF) command is not encountered, the current record will not be saved.

PART III

APPLICATIONS

13

INTRODUCING APPLICATIONS

Part III of Working with dBASE Mac is an applications section. If you worked through Part I of this book, you have already created some of these applications. The Checkbook Project, the MultiMail project, the Timecard Project, and the NewCheck Project are examples of the type of application you can create.
Part III is divided into six chapters.

Chapter 13 presents the theory and practice of creating an application in dBASE Mac.
Chapter 14 serves two functions:
1. A Questionnaire application
2. A comparison of dBASE III and dBASE Mac

Chapter 15 contains the final description of the MultiMail project created in the Tutorial.
Chapter 16 contains the final description of the Checkbook Project created in the Tutorial.
Chapter 17 contains the Timecard Project, along with some suggested improvements.
Chapter 18 contains a tickler file for writers called Freelance. This is something we've used to keep track of magazine assignments, but it could be modified to keep track of other kinds of scheduled events.

Each of the applications in this book can serve as examples for other projects you may wish to create.

Applications Development

Chances are you already have some kind of project in mind, and you want to figure out how to go about creating it. Part III is designed to give you some idea of what goes into a finished application. Some of the applications in this book may be useful to you without modification. Others may need only a little customization. Some may be of no use to you at all, but the principles they represent may be very helpful. Take some time to try out these applications, and examine the relationships and procedures that make them run. Look at the reports they create. Use them. Modify them. Do whatever you wish with them.

Designing an Application

There is not necessarily one best way to accomplish goals. But you probably already know that, or you wouldn't have purchased an open-ended database like dBASE Mac. You would have purchased an off-the-shelf application that required you to do things according to its rules and limitations.

Using procedures and wellthought-out file structures, you can create an application that performs the way you want it to. You decide on the look and feel of your projects. And, in every project you develop, keep an ear cocked for the small voice of inspiration. You may discover wonderful enhancements to your projects by accident or by experimentation.

To design an application, it is necessary to decide what files you will need, what fields they must contain, and how the files will relate. It sometimes helps to begin with the end result and work backward. For instance, what reports do you wish to produce? What information is necessary in the end? Look at some of the final reports generated by the applications in this book. How would *you* have designed the projects based on the final result? Ask yourself some questions about your goals:

- Based on the expected results, what inputs are required?
- What is the minimum amount of data that you need to enter to calculate the results?
- Can you divide the data naturally into separate and distinct types? For instance, in an invoicing application, customers and vendors naturally require their own files. Tax tables, discount structures, and other reference data can be kept in files with one-way relationships. As often as is practical, divide information into separate files.
- Can you think of logical and practical ways to separate data and then relate the separated data files back to each other?
- Can you use these relations to prevent entering the same data more than once?
- Can you set up your data entry so that all connected files are kept updated through relations?
- Would fancy forms and procedures enhance the value of your project, or does a plain vanilla approach suffice?

- Do you need to design a project to run as a turn-key system (a Protected project), and do you need to selectively restrict access to parts of the project using passwords?
- If you plan to Protect the project, what is a logical organization for the Custom Menus?

Most of the difficulties in creating applications come when you try to modify data for specialized reports, and when you need to perform error-checking routines to be sure that data stays accurate. These problems are addressed in the applications that follow.

The Applications Chapters

Each application chapter contains a short description of the goal of the application, the key features it contains, and the reports and other views that it contains. Chapter 14 also contains a brief comparison of dBASE III and dBASE Mac, with annotated code from dBASE III illustrating some of the differences between the two programs.

At the end of each application chapter is the project listing. The project listing consists of up to five parts:

Structure Window printout A graphic representation of the project as seen from the Database Structure Window.

File Structure printout The complete file printout for each file in the project. This contains all the information needed to recreate the entire file structure.

View Structure printout A complete view printout for each view in the project. Includes all the data necessary to recreate the view hierarchy. (Sorts and Selections will be included here, if applicable.) Also, graphics of the view hierarchy will sometimes be included.

Layout Graphic Prints out a copy of the layout for each view. Annotations list any special Display Options that need to be set for the layout.

Sample Report A sample of the printed report for some of the report views.

From the data provided, you should have no difficulty recreating the applications in the chapters that follow. If you have trouble understanding the project printouts, refer to the Tutorial to refresh your understanding of file and view structures.

14

A COMPARATIVE VIEW OF dBASE MAC AND dBASE III And A QUESTIONNAIRE APPLICATION

Some of you have decided to make the transition to dBASE Mac from dBASE III on the IBM PC. If you have worked through the Tutorial in Part I, you have probably noticed the striking differences between the two products. In fact, there are more differences between these products than similarities.

Chapter 14 is designed to help the proficient dBASE III programmer create applications in dBASE Mac, and will identify certain functional differences by creating a similar application in each program. If you are not familiar with dBASE III programming concepts, much of what is discussed at the beginning of this chapter will be meaningless to you. If you are interested in the dBASE Mac application created in this chapter (The Questionnaire), you may wish to skip to the project listing later in this chapter. The Questionnaire application is quite interesting and shows ways to take advantage of some of dBASE Mac's mathematical functions.

Comparing dBASE Mac and dBASE III

The major difference between dBASE III and dBASE Mac can be seen in how dBASE Mac was designed. dBASE Mac is a significant departure from the traditional dBASE

IIx programming language that has been used in CP/M and IBM computers for many years. dBASE Mac really requires less thinking to develop applications but requires a greater knowledge of where every function may be located within the program structure.

Another interesting stylistic and functional difference is the Preprocessor/Post-Processor concept. dBASE IIx has always been an interpretive language. With the Pre-Processor and Post-Processor, a programmer must think in terms of events rather than routines. You may wish to think of it as before and after programming.

The Questionnaire Application

In this chapter you will develop a relatively simple but useful application that is designed around a survey of computer users. Schools or businesses frequently use questionnaires to poll students or customers. For example, a school may use a questionnaire to poll students about their outside interests in order to accommodate class scheduling. Businesses frequently use them to determine the types of customers who use their products. After completing the application in this section, you should have enough knowledge to design your own questionnaire database to meet your needs.

On the following pages is a complete listing of a dBASE III application and, following that, a similar application designed in dBASE Mac. If you have an IBM PC and dBASE III, you may wish to type in the application. **Do not** type in the line numbers that are included with the listing. These line numbers have been included as a guide to dBASE III programmers to reference specific differences between dBASE III and dBASE Mac. By using the line number method, you can look for specific examples from the following list rather than digging through the mounds of code to find what you want.

dBASE APPLICATION

```
1  * Menu: QUESTMNU
2  * Date: 01/22/87  Time: 22:55
3  set echo off
4  set talk off
5  set bell off
6  close databases
7  private exited
8  exited = .F.
9  do while .not. exited
10    clear
11    @  1, 0 say '╔═══════════════════════════════════════'
12    @  1,40 say '═══════════════════════════════════════╗'
13    @  2, 0 say '║ Royal Hawaiian Software'
14    @  2,55 say 'Questionaire Main Menu  ║'
15    @  3, 0 say '╚═══════════════════════════════════════'
16    @  3,40 say '═══════════════════════════════════════╝'
17    @  7,23 say '1.  Questionaire Maintenence'
18    @ 10,23 say '2.  Print Results of Questionaire'
```

dBASE APPLICATION, continued

```
19     @ 13,23 say '3.  Print mailing labels for those who'
20     @ 14,27 say 'want a copy of the research'
21     @ 20,14 say 'Enter a number or enter Q to exit the sy'
22     @ 20,54 say 'stem:'
23     choice = ' '
24     do while .not. choice $ 'Q123'
25       choice = 'Q'
26       @ 20,60 get choice picture '@!'
27       read
28     enddo
29     @ 24,00
30     @ 24,00 say 'Please wait'
31     do case
32       case choice = 'Q'
33         exited = .T.
34       case choice = '1'
35         if file('QUESTMNT.prg')
36           set procedure to QUESTMNT
37           do QUESTMNT
38         else
39           @ 23,00
40           wait 'Procedure file not found...'
41         endif
42       case choice = '2'
43         if file('QUESTTAL.prg')
44           set procedure to QUESTTAL
45           do QUESTTAL
46         else
47           @ 23,00
48           wait 'Procedure file not found...'
49         endif
50       case choice = '3'
51         if file('QUESTMAL.prg')
52           set procedure to QUESTMAL
53
54           do QUESTMAL
55         else
56           @ 23,00
57           wait 'Procedure file not found...'
58         endif
59     endcase
60   enddo (while .not. exited)
61   clear
62   return
63
64
65   * PROGRAM: QUESTMNT.PRG
66
67   * Description:  Questionaire Maintenance
68   * Date:         01/22/87    Time: 21:42
69
```

```
70  * MAINTENANCE OPTIONS:
71    * Duplic. keys: no
72    * Modify key:   yes
73    * Auto add:     yes
74    * Partial key:  no
75    * Comments:     yes
76    * Help screens: yes
77
78  PROCEDURE QUESTMNT
79
80  * FILES
81    * Questionaire File
82    database1 = 'QUESTION'
83    index_fil1 = 'QUESTION'
84
85  * VARIABLES
86   * Key in database QUESTION
87      questnum = 0
88    * Fields in database QUESTION
89      questdate = date()
90      income = 0
91      age = 0
92      sex = ''
93      magazines = 0
94      modem = 0
95      usage = 0
96      mstatus = 0
97      rpt = ''
98      firstname = ''
99      lastname = ''
100     addr1 = ''
101     addr2 = ''
102     city = ''
103
104     state = ''
105     zipcode = ''
106
107    * Flags
108     abort_rec = .F.
109     dupl_rec = .F.
110     empty = .F.
111     files_ok = .T.
112     del_rec = .F.
113     valid_rec = .T.
114     show_all = .T.
115     filter_on1 = .F.
116     set_filter = .F.
117    * Others
118     key1 = 'str(m->questnum,6,0)'
119     index1 = 'str(questnum,6,0)'
120     null_key1 = '     0'
121     comp_key1 = 'trim(str(m->questnum,6,0))'
122
123     list1 =
```

dBASE APPLICATION, continued

```
 124
'questnum,questdate,income,age,sex,magazines,modem,usage,
mstatus,rpt,firstname,l lastname'
 125
 126      pak1 = .F.
 127      choice = ''
 128      option = ''
 129      filt_str = ''
 130      filter1 = ''
 131      scr_num = 1
 132      num = '1'
 133      max_screen = 1
 134      record_no = 0
 135
 136   * ENVIRONMENT
 137     set exact off
 138     set heading off
 139     set bell off
 140     set deleted on
 141   * SCREEN
 142     do disp_scr
 143
 144   * OPEN FILES
 145     do chk_fils
 146     if .not. files_ok
 147       return
 148     endif
 149     index_str = index_fil1
 150     select 1
 151     use &database1 index &index_str
 152
 153     select question
 154     record_no = recno()
 155     * database is empty if eof() = .T.
 156     empty = eof()
 157     if empty
 158       do disp_msg with 'Database empty'
 159     endif
 160   * PROCESSING LOOP
 161     do while scr_num >= 1
 162       record_no = recno()
 163       * preserve option if in add mode
 164       if empty .or. (scr_num = max_screen .and. option = 'A')
 165         option = 'A'
 166       else
 167         do load_var
 168         do disp_rec
 169         option = 'M'
 170       endif
 171       do get_optn with
'Ret/Beg/End/Next/Prev/Skip/Modify/Add/Copy/' + ;
```

```
172
'Del/List/Filt/Tally/Help/Quit','RBENPSMACDLFTHQ',option
173
174         do case
175         * Add
176           case option = 'A'
177             do add
178         * Beginning
179           case option = 'B'
180             go top
181         * Copy
182           case option = 'C'
183             do add
184         * Delete
185           case option = 'D'
186             do delete
187         * End
188           case option = 'E'
189             go bottom
190         * Filter
191           case option = 'F'
192             do filter
193         * Help
194           case option = 'H'
195             do help
196             show_all = .T.
197             do disp_scr
198         * List
199           case option = 'L'
200             do list with list&num
201             show_all = .T.
202             do disp_scr
203
204             go record_no
205         * Modify
206           case option = 'M'
207             do modify
208         * Next
209           case option = 'N'
210             skip
211             if eof()
212               go bottom
213               do disp_msg with 'Last record'
214             endif
215         * Previous
216           case option = 'P'
217             skip -1
218             if bof()
219               go top
220               do disp_msg with 'First record'
221             endif
222         * Retrieve
223           case option = 'R'
224             do retrieve
```

dBASE APPLICATION, continued

```
225       * Skip
226         case option = 'S'
227           do skip
228       * Tally
229         case option = 'T'
230           do tally
231       endcase
232
233     * Quit
234       if option = 'Q'
235         scr_num = scr_num - 1
236         num = str(scr_num,1)
237         if scr_num <> 0
238           select &num
239           empty = .F.
240           show_all = .T.
241           do disp_scr
242         endif
243       endif
244     enddo (while scr_num >= 1)
245
246     if del_rec
247       do pack_all
248     endif
249     close databases
250   return
251
252   * PROCEDURES (listed alphabetically)
253
254   procedure add
255   * Add a new record (if option = 'A') or copy the current
256
257   * record (if option = 'C')
258     if option = 'A'
259       do init_key
260       do init_fld
261     endif
262     * The following "get record" loop can be exited either
when a valid
263     * record is entered (valid_rec = .T.), or when entry is
aborted by
264     * (1) blank key, (2) duplicate key (if not allowed), or
(3) abort
265     * request from the validation procedure (if called).
266     abort_rec = .F.
267     valid_rec = .F.
268     do while .not. (valid_rec .or. abort_rec)
269       do get_key
270       do get_flds
271       read
272       comp_key = comp_key&num
```

```
273      if null_key&num = &comp_key
274        * blank key
275        abort_rec = .T.
276      else
277        do chk_dupl
278        if dupl_rec
279          abort_rec = .T.
280        else
281          valid_rec = .T.
282        endif (dupl_rec)
283      endif (null_key = comp_key)
284    enddo (while .not. (valid_rec .or. abort_rec))
285    if valid_rec
286      do save_rec with .T.
287    else
288      * break out of "Add" if record invalid
289      if empty
290        option = 'Q'
291      else
292        option = 'M'
293        if .not. dupl_rec
294          go record_no
295        endif
296      endif (empty)
297    endif (valid_rec)
298  return
299
300  procedure chk_dupl
301  * Set dupl_rec to .F. if key is a duplicate, or to .T.
otherwise
302    key = key&num
303    if .not. empty
304      seek &key
305    endif
306    if option = 'M'
307      dupl_rec = record_no <> recno() .and. .not. eof()
308    else
309      dupl_rec = .not. eof()
310    endif
311
312    if dupl_rec
313      do disp_msg with chr(7) + 'Duplicate key not allowed'
314    else
315      if .not. empty
316        go record_no
317      endif
318    endif dupl_rec
319  return
320
321  procedure chk_fils
322  * Set files_ok to .F. and display a message if a file is
missing;
323  * create an index file if one does not exist.
324    close databases
```

dBASE APPLICATION, continued

```
325     file_num = 1
326     do while file_num <= max_screen .and. files_ok
327       seq = str(file_num,1)
328       if .not. file (database&seq + '.dbf')
329         do disp_msg with 'File ' + database&seq + ' not found'
330         files_ok = .F.
331       endif
332       if files_ok .and. .not. file (index_fil&seq + '.ndx')
333         @ 23,00
334         @ 23,00 say 'Indexing'
335         db = database&seq
336         ind = index_fil&seq
337         use &db
338         ind_key = index&seq
339         index on &ind_key to &ind
340         use
341       endif
342       file_num = file_num + 1
343     enddo (while file_num <= max_screen .and. files_ok)
344     @ 23,00
345     @ 24,00
346   return
347
348   procedure clr_flds
349   * Clear screen field areas
350     @  4,69 say space (8)
351     @  6,29 say space (10)
352     @  6,47 say space (3)
353     @  6,63 say space (1)
354     @  8,50 say space (2)
355     @ 10,30 say space (2)
356     @ 10,58 say space (2)
357     @ 12,65 say space (1)
358     @ 14,33 say space (1)
359     @ 18,14 say space (10)
360     @ 18,37 say space (20)
361     @ 19,14 say space (30)
362     @ 20,14 say space (30)
363     @ 21, 8 say space (15)
364     @ 21,32 say space (2)
365     @ 21,46 say space (10)
366
367   return
368
369   procedure delete
370   * Delete current record upon user approval
371     choice = 'N'
372     do get_optn with 'Delete (Y/N)','YN',choice
373     if choice = 'Y'
374       delete
375       * reposition to the next record
```

```
376       skip
377       * if last record deleted, go to beginning of database
378       if eof()
379         go top
380       endif
381       if eof() .and. filter_on&num
382         * if no records left in filter, remove the filter
383         filt_str = filter&num
384         set filter to &filt_str
385         filter_on&num = .F.
386         @ 0,0 say space(9)
387         go top
388       endif (eof() .and. filter_on&num)
389       if eof()
390         * quit if last record deleted and database becomes empty
391         option = 'Q'
392       endif
393       del_rec = .T.
394       pak&num = .T.
395     endif (choice = 'Y')
396   return
397
398   procedure disp_msg
399   parameters message
400   * Display "message" + '...' at line 23; wait for entry of
any key
401     @ 23,00
402     @ 22,79
403     wait message + '...'
404   return
405
406   procedure disp_rec
407   * Load fields from database and display record
408     do get_key
409     do get_flds
410     clear gets
411     show_all = .F.
412   return
413
414   procedure disp_scr
415   * Display stationary part of screen
416     clear
417     @  1, 0 say '╔═══════════════════════════════════════'
418     @  1,40 say '════════════════════════════════════════'
419     @  2, 0 say '║                           QUESTIONAIRE'
420     @  2,40 say 'MAINTENANCE                            ║'
421
422     @  3, 0 say '║'
423     @  3,79 say '║'
424     @  4, 0 say '║ Questionaire Number:'
425     @  4,50 say 'Questionaire Date:           ║'
426     @  5, 0 say '║'
427     @  5,79 say '║'
428     @  6, 0 say '║ What is the annual income:'
```

dBASE APPLICATION, continued

```
429     @  6,42 say 'Age:       Sex (M/F):                    ║'
430     @  7, 0 say '║'
431     @  7,79 say '║'
432     @  8, 0 say '║ How many computer magazines are read e'
433     @  8,40 say 'ach week:                               ║'
434     @  9, 0 say '║'
435     @  9,79 say '║'
436     @ 10, 0 say '║ How often is - Modem used:     hrs/wk.'
437     @ 10,42 say 'Computer used:     hrs/wk.           ║'
438     @ 11, 0 say '║'
439     @ 11,79 say '║'
440     @ 12, 0 say '║ Marital status - 1) Married 2) Single'
441     @ 12,40 say '3) Divorced 4) Widowed:                 ║'
442     @ 13, 0 say '║'
443     @ 13,79 say '║'
444     @ 14, 0 say '║ Final report to be sent (Y/N):'
445     @ 14,79 say '║'
446     @ 15, 0 say '║═══════════════════════════════════════'
447     @ 15,40 say '══════════════════╗                     ║'
448     @ 16, 0 say '║                        (Optional)'
449     @ 16,59 say '║                  ║'
450     @ 17, 0 say '║'
451     @ 17,59 say '║                  ║'
452     @ 18, 0 say '║ First Name:                 Last Name:'
453     @ 18,59 say '║                  ║'
454     @ 19, 0 say '║ Address #1:'
455     @ 19,59 say '║                  ║'
456     @ 20, 0 say '║ Address #2:'
457     @ 20,59 say '║                  ║'
458     @ 21, 0 say '║ City:                     State:     Zip'
459     @ 21,40 say 'Code:                ║                  ║'
460     @ 22, 0 say '╚═══════════════════════════════════════'
461     @ 22,40 say '════════════════════╩══════════════════╝'
462     if filter_on&num
463       @ 0,0 say 'FILTER ON'
464     else
465       @ 0,0 say space(9)
466     endif
467   return
468
469   procedure filter
470   * Set filter on database
471     choice = 'Y'
472     do get_optn with 'Set Filter (Yes/No/Cancel)','YNC',choice
473     if choice = 'Y'
474       set_filter = .T.
475       do init_key
476
477       do init_fld
478       do get_key
479       do get_flds
```

```
 480      read
 481      filt_str = ''
 482      if m->questnum <> 0
 483        questnum = str(m->questnum,6,0)
 484        filt_str = filt_str + 'questnum = &questnum .and.'
 485      endif
 486      if .not. (m->questdate <> m->questdate .or. .not. (m->
questdate = m-
 487  >questdate))
 488        questdate = dtoc(m->questdate)
 489        filt_str = filt_str + 'questdate = ctod("&questdate")
.and.'
 490      endif
 491      if m->income <> 0
 492        income = str(m->income,10,1)
 493        filt_str = filt_str + 'income = &income .and.'
 494      endif
 495      if m->age <> 0
 496        age = str(m->age,3,0)
 497        filt_str = filt_str + 'age = &age .and.'
 498      endif
 499      if '' <> trim(m->sex)
 500        filt_str = filt_str + 'sex = trim("&sex") .and.'
 501      endif
 502      if m->magazines <> 0
 503        magazines = str(m->magazines,2,0)
 504        filt_str = filt_str + 'magazines = &magazines .and.'
 505      endif
 506      if m->modem <> 0
 507        modem = str(m->modem,2,0)
 508        filt_str = filt_str + 'modem = &modem .and.'
 509      endif
 510      if m->usage <> 0
 511        usage = str(m->usage,2,0)
 512        filt_str = filt_str + 'usage = &usage .and.'
 513      endif
 514      if m->mstatus <> 0
 515        mstatus = str(m->mstatus,1,0)
 516        filt_str = filt_str + 'mstatus = &mstatus .and.'
 517      endif
 518      if '' <> trim(m->rpt)
 519        filt_str = filt_str + 'rpt = trim("&rpt") .and.'
 520      endif
 521      if '' <> trim(m->firstname)
 522        filt_str = filt_str + 'firstname = trim("&firstname")
.and.'
 523      endif
 524      if '' <> trim(m->lastname)
 525        filt_str = filt_str + 'lastname = trim("&lastname")
.and.'
 526      endif
 527      if '' <> trim(m->addr1)
 528        filt_str = filt_str + 'addr1 = trim("&addr1") .and.'
 529      endif
```

dBASE APPLICATION, continued

```
530      if '' <> trim(m->addr2)
531
532        filt_str = filt_str + 'addr2 = trim("&addr2") .and.'
533      endif
534      if '' <> trim(m->city)
535        filt_str = filt_str + 'city = trim("&city") .and.'
536      endif
537      if '' <> trim(m->state)
538        filt_str = filt_str + 'state = trim("&state") .and.'
539      endif
540      if '' <> trim(m->zipcode)
541        filt_str = filt_str + 'zipcode = trim("&zipcode")
.and.'
542      endif
543      if '' = trim(filt_str)
544        filt_str = filter&num
545        set filter to &filt_str
546        filter_on&num = .F.
547      else
548        if '' <> trim(filter&num)
549          filt_str = filter&num + '.and.' + filt_str
550        endif
551        filt_str = substr(filt_str,1,len(filt_str)-6)
552        set filter to &filt_str
553        go top
554        filter_on&num = .not. eof()
555        if .not. filter_on&num
556          do disp_msg with 'No records match the filter'
557          filt_str = filter&num
558          set filter to &filt_str
559          go record_no
560        endif
561      endif ('' = trim(filt_str))
562    endif (choice = 'Y')
563    if choice = 'C'
564      filt_str = filter&num
565      set filter to &filt_str
566      filter_on&num = .F.
567    endif (choice = 'C')
568    if filter_on&num
569      @ 0,0 say 'FILTER ON'
570    else
571      @ 0,0 say space(9)
572    endif
573    set_filter = .F.
574  return
575
576  procedure get_flds
577  * Get field variables
578    @  4,69 get m->questdate picture '@D'
579    @  6,29 get m->income picture '9999999.99'
```

```
580    @  6,47 get m->age picture '999'
581    @  6,63 get m->sex
582    @  8,50 get m->magazines picture '99'
583    @ 10,30 get m->modem picture '99'
584    @ 10,58 get m->usage picture '99'
585    @ 12,65 get m->mstatus picture '9'
586
587    @ 14,33 get m->rpt
588    @ 18,14 get m->firstname
589    @ 18,37 get m->lastname
590    @ 19,14 get m->addr1
591    @ 20,14 get m->addr2
592    @ 21, 8 get m->city
593    @ 21,32 get m->state
594    @ 21,46 get m->zipcode
595  return
596
597  procedure get_key
598  * Get key variables
599    @  4,23 get m->questnum picture '999999'
600  return
601
602  procedure get_optn
603  parameters message, choices, choice
604  * Display the string "message" on line 23; get a character
605  * (defaulted to "choice"), validate it against "choices" and
606  * return in "choice" (must be a memory variable, not
literal).
607  * If choice = 'A' display choice without accepting it.
608    @ 23,00 say message + '? '
609    @ 23,len(message)+3
610    char = ' '
611    do while .not. char $ choices
612      char = choice
613      @ 23,len(message) + 2 get char picture '!'
614      if choice <> 'A'
615        read
616      else
617        clear gets
618      endif
619    enddo (while .not. char $ choices)
620    choice = char
621  return
622
623  procedure help
624  * Display help screens
625    clear
626    @ 03,00
627    text
628                   Option    Database maintenance action
629                   ______    _____________________________
630                   Add       add a record to the database
631                   Beg       go to beginning of database
632                   Copy      duplicate current record
```

dBASE APPLICATION, continued

```
633                    Del      delete current record
634                    End      go to end of database
635                    Filt     set filter on database
636                    List     display records on screen
637                    Modify   edit current record
638                    Next     go to next record
639                    Prev     go to previous record
640                    Quit     terminate current activity
641
642                    Ret      retrieve a record by key
643                    Skip     move up or down by a specified
number of records
644                    Tally    count records
645     endtext
646     do disp_msg with 'More'
647     clear
648     @ 05,00
649     text
650                        White key     Screen editing action
651                        _________     _____________________
652                        -->           character right
653                        <--           character left
654                        up arrow      previous field
655                        down arrow    next field
656                        PgDn, PgUp    accept screen
657                        End           next word/field
658                        Home          previous word/field
659                        Del           delete character
660                        Ins           insert on/off toggle
661     endtext
662     do disp_msg with 'OK'
663     clear
664   return
665
666   procedure init_fld
667   * Clear field variables
668     questdate = ctod('  /  /  ')
669     income = 0.0
670     age = 0
671     sex = space(1)
672     magazines = 0
673     modem = 0
674     usage = 0
675     mstatus = 0
676     rpt = space(1)
677     firstname = space(10)
678     lastname = space(20)
679     addr1 = space(30)
680     addr2 = space(30)
681     city = space(15)
682     state = space(2)
```

```
683     zipcode = space(10)
684   return
685
686   procedure init_key
687   * Clear key variables
688     questnum = 0
689   return
690
691   procedure list
692   parameters list_items
693   * List records beginning from current record
694     do while .T.
695       clear
696
697       list off next 20 &list_items
698       if eof()
699         do disp_msg with 'OK'
700         exit
701       endif
702       choice = 'Y'
703       do get_optn with 'More','YN',choice
704       if choice = 'N'
705         exit
706       endif
707     enddo (while .T.)
708   return
709
710   procedure load_var
711   * Copy fields from database record to memory variables
712     questnum = questnum
713     questdate = questdate
714     income = income
715     age = age
716     sex = sex
717     magazines = magazines
718     modem = modem
719     usage = usage
720     mstatus = mstatus
721     rpt = rpt
722     firstname = firstname
723     lastname = lastname
724     addr1 = addr1
725     addr2 = addr2
726     city = city
727     state = state
728     zipcode = zipcode
729   return
730
731   procedure modify
732   * Modify current record
733   * The following "get record" loop is exited when either (1)
a valid record
734   * is entered (valid_rec = .T.), or (2) entry is aborted by a
duplicate
```

dBASE APPLICATION, continued

```
 735  * key (when not allowed), or a request from the validation
procedure.
 736    valid_rec = .F.
 737    abort_rec = .F.
 738    do while .not. (valid_rec .or. abort_rec)
 739      do get_key
 740      do get_flds
 741      read
 742      comp_key = comp_key&num
 743      if null_key&num = &comp_key
 744        abort_rec = .T.
 745      else
 746        do chk_dupl
 747        if dupl_rec
 748          abort_rec = .T.
 749        else
 750          valid_rec = .T.
 751
 752        endif (dupl_rec)
 753      endif (null_key = comp_key)
 754    enddo (while .not. (valid_rec .or. abort_rec))
 755    if valid_rec
 756      do save_rec with .F.
 757    else
 758      if .not. dupl_rec
 759        go record_no
 760      endif
 761      go record_no
 762    endif (valid_rec)
 763  return
 764
 765  procedure pack_all
 766  * Pack deleted records with user confirmation
 767    choice = 'N'
 768    do get_optn with 'Pack all deleted records
 (Y/N)','YN',choice
 769    if choice = 'Y'
 770      @ 23,00
 771      @ 23,00 say 'Packing, please wait'
 772      do while scr_num < max_screen
 773        scr_num = scr_num + 1
 774        num = str(scr_num,1)
 775        if pak&num
 776          select &num
 777          pack
 778        endif
 779      enddo (while scr_num < max_screen)
 780    endif
 781  return
 782
 783  procedure repl_rec
```

```
784  * Replace database fields with memory variables
785    replace questnum with m->questnum
786    replace questdate with m->questdate
787    replace income with m->income
788    replace age with m->age
789    replace sex with m->sex
790    replace magazines with m->magazines
791    replace modem with m->modem
792    replace usage with m->usage
793    replace mstatus with m->mstatus
794    replace rpt with m->rpt
795    replace firstname with m->firstname
796    replace lastname with m->lastname
797    replace addr1 with m->addr1
798    replace addr2 with m->addr2
799    replace city with m->city
800    replace state with m->state
801    replace zipcode with m->zipcode
802  return
803
804  procedure retrieve
805  * Accept key and seek record; if not found reposition to
record_no
806
807    do clr_flds
808    do init_key
809    do get_key
810    read
811    comp_key = comp_key&num
812    if null_key&num = &comp_key
813      * blank key
814      return
815    endif
816    key = key&num
817    seek &key
818    if eof()
819      do disp_msg with 'Not found'
820      go record_no
821    endif
822  return
823
824  procedure save_rec
825  parameters new_rec
826  * If new_rec: append record currently in memory to database;
827  * if .not. new_rec: replace database record record_no with
memory fields.
828    choice = 'Y'
829    do get_optn with 'Save (Y/N)','YN',choice
830    if choice = 'Y'
831      if new_rec
832        append blank
833      endif
834      do repl_rec
835      empty = .F.
```

dBASE APPLICATION, continued

```
836       if filter_on&num
837         * Check to see if record matches filter
838         record_no = recno()
839         skip
840         skip -1
841         if recno() <> record_no
842           go top
843           if eof()
844             * Remove filter
845             filt_str = filter&num
846             set filter to &filt_str
847             filter_on&num = .F.
848             @ 0,10 say space(9)
849             go record_no
850           endif
851         endif
852       endif (filter_on&num)
853     else
854       if .not. empty
855         go record_no
856       endif
857     endif (choice = 'Y')
858   return
859
860   procedure skip
861
862   * Move forward/backward several records
863     skip_no = 0
864     @ 23,70 say '  Recs' get skip_no picture '@Z 999'
865     read
866     skip skip_no
867     if eof()
868       go bottom
869       do load_var
870       do disp_rec
871       do disp_msg with 'Last Record'
872     endif
873     if bof()
874       go top
875       do load_var
876       do disp_rec
877       do disp_msg with 'First record'
878     endif
879   return
880
881   procedure tally
882   * Count and display number of records in database
883     @ 23,00
884     @ 23,00 say 'Counting, please wait'
885     count to number_
```

```
886     do disp_msg with 'Count: ' + str (m->number_,6) + '
records'
887     go record_no
888   return
889
890   * EOF QUESTMNT.PRG
891
892   * PROGRAM: QUESTMAL.PRG
893
894   * Description:  Questionaire Mailing Labels
895   * Date:         01/22/87    Time: 22:00
896
897   PROCEDURE QUESTMAL
898
899   * FILES
900     database = 'QUESTION'
901     index1 = 'QUESTION'
902
903   * MEMORY VARIABLES
904     page_no = 1
905     line_no = 1
906     record_no = 0
907     top_marg = 0
908     bot_marg = 0
909     max_line = 66
910     pg_ft_lins =  0
911     outp_dev = ' '
912     pr_ok = ' '
913     new_sort = ' '
914     files_ok = .T.
915     ok = .F.
916
917     break_on = .T.
918     top_record = 0
919     records = 0
920     recs_on_pg = 0
921
922   * ENVIRONMENT
923     set heading off
924     set scoreboard off
925     set safety off
926     set decimals to 10
927     set margin to 0
928
929   * SCREEN
930     clear
931     @ 01,00 say 'QUESTMAL.PRG'
932     @ 01,16 say 'Questionaire Mailing Labels'
933     @ 01,54 say 'Primary File: ' + database
934
935   * OPEN FILES
936     do chk_fils
937     if .not. files_ok
938       return
```

dBASE APPLICATION, continued

```
939     endif
940     select 1
941     use &database alias database
942   * INDEX
943     @ 04,00 say 'Special sort required?'
944     do while .not. new_sort $ 'YN'
945       new_sort = 'N'
946       @ 04,24 get new_sort picture '!'
947       read
948     enddo
949     if new_sort = 'Y'
950       sort_exp = '' + space(60)
951       legal_sort = .F.
952       do while .not. legal_sort
953         @ 06,00 say 'Index expression:' get sort_exp
954         read
955         if type(sort_exp) = 'U' .and. '' <> trim(sort_exp)
956           do disp_msg with 'Undefined sort expression'
957           @ 23,00
958         else
959           legal_sort = .T.
960           if '' <> trim(sort_exp)
961             index on &sort_exp to prim_ind
962           endif
963         endif
964       enddo
965     else
966       if file(index1+'.ndx')
967
968         set index to &index1
969       endif
970     endif (new sort = 'Y')
971
972   * FILTER
973     select database
974     filt_str = [rpt='y']
975     legal_filt = .F.
976     do while .not. legal_filt
977       @ 08,00 say 'Set Filter to' get filt_str
978       read
979       if type(filt_str) <> 'L' .and. '' <> trim(filt_str)
980         do disp_msg with 'Undefined filter expression'
981         @ 23,00
982       else
983         if '' <> trim(filt_str)
984           set filter to &filt_str
985         endif
986         legal_filt = .T.
987       endif
988     enddo
989   * DEVICE
```

```
990     do while .not. ok
991       @ 23,00
992       @ 23,00 say 'Printer/Screen/Quit?'
993       outp_dev = ' '
994       do while .not. outp_dev $ 'PSQ'
995         outp_dev = 'P'
996         @ 23,21 get outp_dev picture '!'
997         read
998       enddo
999       ok = .T.
1000       do case
1001         case outp_dev = 'P'
1002           @ 23,24 say 'Printer ready?'
1003           pr_ok = ' '
1004           do while .not. pr_ok $ 'YN'
1005             pr_ok = 'Y'
1006             @ 23,39 get pr_ok picture '!'
1007             read
1008           enddo
1009           if pr_ok = 'N'
1010             ok = .F.
1011           else
1012             @ 23,00 say 'Printing' + space(40)
1013             set device to print
1014             set console off
1015           endif
1016         case outp_dev = 'S'
1017           max_line = 23
1018           top_marg = 0
1019
1020           bot_marg = 0
1021           clear
1022         case outp_dev = 'Q'
1023           close databases
1024           return
1025       endcase
1026     enddo (while .not. ok)
1027
1028   * REPORT HEADER
1029     go top
1030     record_no = recno()
1031     line_no = top_marg
1032     top_record = recno()
1033     recs_on_pg = 0
1034
1035   * REPORT BODY
1036     do while .not. eof()
1037       record_no = recno()
1038       break_on = .F.
1039       do detail
1040       recs_on_pg = recs_on_pg + 1
1041       skip
1042     enddo (while .not. eof())
1043
```

dBASE APPLICATION, continued

```
1044  * REPORT FOOTER
1045    if outp_dev = 'S'
1046      @ 23,79
1047      wait 'Press any key'
1048    else
1049      eject
1050      set console on
1051      set device to screen
1052    endif (outp_dev = 'S')
1053
1054    close databases
1055  return
1056
1057  * PROCEDURES
1058
1059  procedure adv_line
1060    line_no = line_no + 1
1061    if line_no > max_line - bot_marg - pg_ft_lins
1062      do adv_page
1063    endif
1064  return
1065
1066  procedure adv_page
1067    page_no = page_no + 1
1068    if outp_dev = 'S'
1069      @ 23,79
1070      wait 'Press any key'
1071      clear
1072    else
1073
1074      eject
1075    endif
1076    top_record = recno()
1077    recs_on_pg = 0
1078    line_no = top_marg
1079    line_no = line_no + 1
1080  return
1081
1082  procedure chk_fils
1083  * Return files_ok = .T. if all required files exist .F.
otherwise.
1084  * Create index file if necessary.
1085    close databases
1086    if .not. file (database + '.dbf')
1087      do disp_msg with 'File &database..DBF not found'
1088      files_ok = .F.
1089    endif
1090  return
1091
1092  procedure detail
1093  * Compute and display line of information
```

```
1094    do adv_line
1095    @ line_no,  0 say firstname
1096    @ line_no, 11 say lastname
1097    do adv_line
1098    @ line_no,  0 say addr1
1099    do adv_line
1100    @ line_no,  0 say addr2
1101    do adv_line
1102    @ line_no,  0 say city
1103    @ line_no, 16 say state
1104    @ line_no, 19 say zipcode
1105    do adv_line
1106    do adv_line
1107  return
1108
1109  procedure disp_msg
1110  parameters message
1111    @ 23,00
1112    @ 22,79
1113    wait message + '...'
1114  return
1115
1116  * EOF QUESTMAL.PRG
1117
1118  * PROGRAM: QUESTTAL.PRG
1119
1120  * Description:  Tallies result of questionaire
1121  * Date:         01/22/87    Time: 22:01
1122
1123  PROCEDURE QUESTTAL
1124
1125  * FILES
1126    database = 'QUESTION'
1127    index1 = 'QUESTION'
1128
1129
1130  * MEMORY VARIABLES
1131    page_no = 1
1132    line_no = 1
1133    record_no = 0
1134    top_marg = 6
1135    bot_marg = 6
1136    max_line = 66
1137    pg_ft_lins =  2
1138    outp_dev = ' '
1139    pr_ok = ' '
1140    new_sort = ' '
1141    files_ok = .T.
1142    ok = .F.
1143    break_on = .T.
1144    top_record = 0
1145    records = 0
1146    recs_on_pg = 0
1147    gtotal = '(RECCOUNT())'
```

dBASE APPLICATION, continued

```
1148
1149  * ENVIRONMENT
1150    set heading off
1151    set scoreboard off
1152    set safety off
1153    set decimals to 10
1154    set margin to 0
1155
1156  * SCREEN
1157    clear
1158    @ 01,00 say 'QUESTTAL.PRG'
1159    @ 01,16 say 'Tallies result of questionaire'
1160    @ 01,54 say 'Primary File: ' + database
1161
1162  * OPEN FILES
1163    do chk_fils
1164    if .not. files_ok
1165      return
1166    endif
1167    select 1
1168    use &database alias database
1169
1170  * INDEX
1171    @ 04,00 say 'Special sort required?'
1172    do while .not. new_sort $ 'YN'
1173      new_sort = 'N'
1174      @ 04,24 get new_sort picture '!'
1175      read
1176    enddo
1177    if new_sort = 'Y'
1178      sort_exp = '' + space(60)
1179      legal_sort = .F.
1180      do while .not. legal_sort
1181        @ 06,00 say 'Index expression:' get sort_exp
1182        read
1183
1184        if type(sort_exp) = 'U' .and. '' <> trim(sort_exp)
1185          do disp_msg with 'Undefined sort expression'
1186          @ 23,00
1187        else
1188          legal_sort = .T.
1189          if '' <> trim(sort_exp)
1190            index on &sort_exp to prim_ind
1191          endif
1192        endif
1193      enddo
1194    else
1195      if file(index1+'.ndx')
1196        set index to &index1
1197      endif
1198    endif (new sort = 'Y')
```

```
1199
1200  * DEVICE
1201    do while .not. ok
1202      @ 23,00
1203      @ 23,00 say 'Printer/Screen/Quit?'
1204      outp_dev = ' '
1205      do while .not. outp_dev $ 'PSQ'
1206        outp_dev = 'P'
1207        @ 23,21 get outp_dev picture '!'
1208        read
1209      enddo
1210      ok = .T.
1211      do case
1212        case outp_dev = 'P'
1213          @ 23,24 say 'Printer ready?'
1214          pr_ok - ' '
1215          do while .not. pr_ok $ 'YN'
1216            pr_ok = 'Y'
1217            @ 23,39 get pr_ok picture '!'
1218            read
1219          enddo
1220          if pr_ok = 'N'
1221            ok = .F.
1222          else
1223            @ 23,00 say 'Printing' + space(40)
1224            set device to print
1225            set console off
1226          endif
1227        case outp_dev = 'S'
1228          max_line = 23
1229          top_marg = 0
1230          bot_marg = 0
1231          clear
1232        case outp_dev = 'Q'
1233          close databases
1234          return
1235      endcase
1236    enddo (while .not. ok)
1237
1238
1239  * REPORT HEADER
1240    go top
1241    record_no = recno()
1242    line_no = top_marg
1243    do rept_hd
1244    top_record = recno()
1245    recs_on_pg = 0
1246    do page_hd
1247
1248  * REPORT BODY
1249    do while .not. eof()
1250      record_no = recno()
1251      break_on = .F.
1252      do detail
```

dBASE APPLICATION, continued

```
1253      recs_on_pg = recs_on_pg + 1
1254      skip
1255    enddo (while .not. eof())
1256
1257  * REPORT FOOTER
1258    do rept_ft
1259    do page_ft
1260    if outp_dev = 'S'
1261      @ 23,79
1262      wait 'Press any key'
1263    else
1264      eject
1265      set console on
1266      set device to screen
1267    endif (outp_dev = 'S')
1268
1269    close databases
1270  return
1271
1272  * PROCEDURES
1273
1274  procedure adv_line
1275    line_no = line_no + 1
1276    if line_no > max_line - bot_marg - pg_ft_lins
1277      do adv_page
1278    endif
1279  return
1280
1281  procedure adv_page
1282    do page_ft
1283    page_no = page_no + 1
1284    if outp_dev = 'S'
1285      @ 23,79
1286      wait 'Press any key'
1287      clear
1288    else
1289      eject
1290    endif
1291    top_record = recno()
1292    recs_on_pg = 0
1293
1294    line_no = top_marg
1295    do page_hd
1296    line_no = line_no + 1
1297  return
1298
1299  procedure chk_fils
1300  * Return files_ok = .T. if all required files exist .F.
otherwise.
1301  * Create index file if necessary.
1302    close databases
```

```
1303     if .not. file (database + '.dbf')
1304       do disp_msg with 'File &database..DBF not found'
1305       files_ok = .F.
1306     endif
1307   return
1308
1309   procedure detail
1310   * Compute and display line of information
1311     do adv_line
1312     @ line_no,  0 say questnum picture '999999'
1313     @ line_no, 18 say questdate picture '@D'
1314     @ line_no, 27 say income picture '9999999.99'
1315     @ line_no, 40 say mstatus picture '9'
1316     @ line_no, 49 say magazines picture '99'
1317     @ line_no, 58 say modem picture '99'
1318     @ line_no, 66 say usage picture '99'
1319     @ line_no, 74 say age picture '999'
1320   return
1321
1322   procedure disp_msg
1323   parameters message
1324     @ 23,00
1325     @ 22,79
1326     wait message + '...'
1327   return
1328
1329   procedure page_hd
1330     * Print page header
1331     do adv_line
1332     @ line_no,  0 say 'PAGE'
1333     @ line_no,  5 say page_no picture '999'
1334     do adv_line
1335     do adv_line
1336     @ line_no,  0 say 'QUESTIONIARE #    DATE     INCOME    MAR'
1337     @ line_no, 40 say 'ITAL  MAGAZINES  MODEM   USAGE    AGE'
1338     do adv_line
1339     @ line_no,  0 say '--------------    -------- --------- -
--'
1340     @ line_no, 40 say '----  ---------  -----   -----    ---'
1341   return
1342
1343   procedure page_ft
1344     * Print page footer
1345     line_no = max_line - bot_marg - pg_ft_lins
1346     line_no = line_no + 1
1347     line_no = line_no + 1
1348
1349     @ line_no,  0 say '---------------------------------------
--'
1350     @ line_no, 40 say '-------------------------------------'
1351   return
1352
1353   procedure rept_hd
```

dBASE APPLICATION, continued

```
1354     * Print report header
1355     do adv_line
1356     @ line_no,  0 say date()
1357     @ line_no, 28 say 'USING DBASE MAC'
1358     return
1359
1360   procedure rept_ft
1361     * Print report footer
1362     do adv_line
1363     do adv_line
1364     @ line_no, 18 say 'AVERAGE:'
1365     average income to value
1366     go record_no
1367     @ line_no, 27 say value picture '9999999.99'
1368     average mstatus to value
1369     go record_no
1370     @ line_no, 40 say value picture '9'
1371     average magazines to value
1372     go record_no
1373     @ line_no, 49 say value picture '99'
1374     average modem to value
1375     go record_no
1376     @ line_no, 58 say value picture '99'
1377     average usage to value
1378     go record_no
1379     @ line_no, 66 say value picture '99'
1380     average age to value
1381     go record_no
1382     @ line_no, 74 say value picture '999'
1383     do adv_line
1384     do adv_line
1385     @ line_no,  0 say 'Total number of Questionaires:'
1386     @ line_no, 31 say &gtotal picture '99999'
1387   return
1388
1389   * EOF QUESTTAL.PRG
```

Line Number(s)	Description
1	This begins the menu procedure for the application. This entire procedure could be handled automatically through the dBASE Mac desktop. It uses numbers to reference choices the user has. In dBASE Mac, you could use radio buttons that the user clicks on as an alternative.

80	Files and fields are defined through the Structure Window, during the creation process of defining a new view for a file. You can select which fields to include in a view through the Define Hierarchy menu.
85	Variables are automatically set to nulls for data entry when you first perform and use a view.
136	There are no environment settings in the procedural language of dBASE Mac. You can, however, set preferences from the edit menu, which will affect the form that you are creating.
141–159	These two sections are performed automatically in dBASE Mac when you perform and use a view. Logically, this section would be a preprocessor step for dBASE Mac.
160	This section would be a Post-Processor procedure in dBASE Mac. The processing loop is handled automatically for this application, but if posting or some other function were required during this loop, you would add the procedure as a Post-Processor.
252	All of these procedures are handled automatically in dBASE Mac.
942–988	You can set specific sort and selection criteria from the view menu. However, once the project is protected, you cannot change the sort and selection criteria. Hence, the INDEX and FILTER sections cannot be implemented in dBASE Mac.
989	This section give the user an option to send the report to printer or screen. dBASE Mac will automatically send the output to screen unless you select **Print** from the project menu.
1028–1080	These sections are handled automatically when you create the view.
1360	This procedure is responsible for the calculations at the end of the report. In dBASE Mac, you would do this step as a preprocessor procedure.

The basic design consists of four modules of procedures.

1. The first module, **QUESTMNU**, displays a graphic menu that allows the user to make four choices. The choices are: maintaining the questionnaire database, printing a final result report, printing mailing labels of those who requested a copy of the resulting research, and quitting to the system. The first three choices call other modules to perform each function.

2. The second module, **QUESTMNT**, provides a graphic input form used to enter the data for each questionnaire answered. This is a general maintenance routine in which all file functions are performed, such as adding, deleting, changing, and setting filtering criteria.

3. The third module, **QUESTTAL**, tallies the questionnaire responses, computes an average, and then prints the results to the screen or printer.

4. Finally, the fourth module, **QUESTMAL**, selectively prints mailing labels for those who provided address information and requested a copy of the resulting research. The routine will print a mailing label for each 'y' answer provided to the question "Final report to be sent(Y/N)" of the **QUESTMNT** module.

The design of this application in dBASE III is relatively simple. A single file is used to store each questionnaire answered. An index is used to keep each questionnaire in order by number. The screens and menus use a double-line graphic border to give them visual appeal and flavor.

Report Name:	File Structure			10/30/87 4:22 PM
				Page 1
File Name:	Question	File Type:	dBASE Mac	
Field Name:	Question #			
Field Type:	Key, Ordered	Data Type:	Number	Required
Justify:	Right			
Format:	Fixed	Decimal Places:	0	
Decimal:	.	Thousands:		
Negative:	-n	Currency:		
Field Name:	Questionaire Date			
Field Type:	Data	Data Type:	Date	
Contents are:	Single Valued			
Justify:	Left			
Format:	mm/dd/yy			
Year Length:	2	Separator:	/	
Field Name:	Income			
Field Type:	Data	Data Type:	Number	
Contents are:	Single Valued			
Justify:	Right			
Format:	Fixed	Decimal Places:	2	
Decimal:	.	Thousands:		
Negative:	-n	Currency:		
Field Name:	Age			
Field Type:	Data	Data Type:	Number	
Contents are:	Single Valued			
Justify:	Right			
Format:	Fixed	Decimal Places:	0	
Decimal:	.	Thousands:		
Negative:	-n	Currency:		
Field Name:	Sex			
Field Type:	Data	Data Type:	Text	
Contents are:	Single Valued			
Justify:	Left			
Field Name:	Marital Status			
Field Type:	Data	Data Type:	Number	
Contents are:	Single Valued			
Justify:	Right			
Format:	Fixed	Decimal Places:	0	
Decimal:	.	Thousands:		
Negative:	-n	Currency:		
Field Name:	Modem Usage			
Field Type:	Data	Data Type:	Number	
Contents are:	Single Valued			
Justify:	Right			
Format:	Fixed	Decimal Places:	0	

Report Name:	File Structure	10/30/87 4:22 PM	
		Page 2	
File Name:	Question	File Type:	dBASE Mac

Decimal:	.	Thousands:	
Negative:	-n	Currency:	
Field Name:	Magazines		
Field Type:	Data	Data Type:	Number
Contents are:	Single Valued		
Justify:	Right		
Format:	Fixed	Decimal Places:	0
Decimal:	.	Thousands:	
Negative:	-n	Currency:	
Field Name:	Computer Usage		
Field Type:	Data	Data Type:	Number
Contents are:	Single Valued		
Justify:	Right		
Format:	Fixed	Decimal Places:	0
Decimal:	.	Thousands:	
Negative:	-n	Currency:	
Field Name:	Report		
Field Type:	Data	Data Type:	Text
Contents are:	Single Valued		
Justify:	Left		
Field Name:	First Name		
Field Type:	Data	Data Type:	Text
Contents are:	Single Valued		
Justify:	Left		
Field Name:	Last Name		
Field Type:	Data	Data Type:	Text
Contents are:	Single Valued		
Justify:	Left		
Field Name:	Address #1		
Field Type:	Data	Data Type:	Text
Contents are:	Single Valued		
Justify:	Left		
Field Name:	Address #2		
Field Type:	Data	Data Type:	Text
Contents are:	Single Valued		
Justify:	Left		
Field Name:	City		
Field Type:	Data	Data Type:	Text
Contents are:	Single Valued		
Justify:	Left		
Field Name:	State		

Report Name:	File Structure			10/30/87 4:22 PM
				Page 3
File Name:	Question	File Type:	dBASE Mac	
Field Type:	Data	Data Type:	Text	
Contents are:	Single Valued			
Justify:	Left			
Field Name:	Zip Code			
Field Type:	Data	Data Type:	Text	
Contents are:	Single Valued			
Justify:	Left			

Report Name:	View Definition			10/30/87 4:22 PM
				Page 1
Project Name:	Questionaire			
View Name:	Questionaire Maintenance	View Type:	Display, Custom Layout	
Root File:	Question	File Type:	dBASE Mac	

Report Name:	View Definition			10/30/87	4:22 PM
				Page 2	
Project Name:	Questionaire				
View Name:	Questionaire Maintenance	View Type:	Display, Custom Layout		
File Name:	Question	File Type:	dBASE Mac		

Access Path:	Question			
Field Name:	Question #			
Field Type:	Key, Ordered	Data Type:	Number	Required
Justify:	Right			
Format:	Fixed	Decimal Places:	0	
Decimal:	.	Thousands:		
Negative:	-n	Currency:		
Field Name:	Questionaire Date			
Field Type:	Data	Data Type:	Date	
Contents are:	Single Valued			
Justify:	Left			
Format:	mm/dd/yy			
Year Length:	2	Separator:	/	
Field Name:	Income			
Field Type:	Data	Data Type:	Number	
Contents are:	Single Valued			
Justify:	Right			
Format:	Fixed	Decimal Places:	2	
Decimal:	.	Thousands:		
Negative:	-n	Currency:		
Field Name:	Age			
Field Type:	Data	Data Type:	Number	
Contents are:	Single Valued			
Justify:	Right			
Format:	Fixed	Decimal Places:	0	
Decimal:	.	Thousands:		
Negative:	-n	Currency:		
Field Name:	Sex			
Field Type:	Data	Data Type:	Text	
Contents are:	Single Valued			
Justify:	Left			
Field Name:	Marital Status			
Field Type:	Data	Data Type:	Number	
Contents are:	Single Valued			
Justify:	Right			
Format:	Fixed	Decimal Places:	0	
Decimal:	.	Thousands:		
Negative:	-n	Currency:		
Field Name:	Modem Usage			

Report Name:	View Definition		10/30/87 4:22 PM
			Page 3
Project Name:	Questionaire		
View Name:	Questionaire Maintenance	View Type:	Display, Custom Layout
File Name:	Question	File Type:	dBASE Mac
Field Type:	Data	Data Type:	Number
Contents are:	Single Valued		
Justify:	Right		
Format:	Fixed	Decimal Places:	0
Decimal:	.	Thousands:	
Negative:	-n	Currency:	
Field Name:	Magazines		
Field Type:	Data	Data Type:	Number
Contents are:	Single Valued		
Justify:	Right		
Format:	Fixed	Decimal Places:	0
Decimal:	.	Thousands:	
Negative:	-n	Currency:	
Field Name:	Computer Usage		
Field Type:	Data	Data Type:	Number
Contents are:	Single Valued		
Justify:	Right		
Format:	Fixed	Decimal Places:	0
Decimal:	.	Thousands:	
Negative:	-n	Currency:	
Field Name:	Report		
Field Type:	Data	Data Type:	Text
Contents are:	Single Valued		
Justify:	Left		
Field Name:	First Name		
Field Type:	Data	Data Type:	Text
Contents are:	Single Valued		
Justify:	Left		
Field Name:	Last Name		
Field Type:	Data	Data Type:	Text
Contents are:	Single Valued		
Justify:	Left		
Field Name:	Address #1		
Field Type:	Data	Data Type:	Text
Contents are:	Single Valued		
Justify:	Left		
Field Name:	Address #2		
Field Type:	Data	Data Type:	Text
Contents are:	Single Valued		

Report Name:	View Definition		10/30/87 4:22 PM Page 4
Project Name:	Questionaire		
View Name:	Questionaire Maintenance	View Type:	Display, Custom Layout
File Name:	Question	File Type:	dBASE Mac
Justify:	Left		
Field Name:	City		
Field Type:	Data	Data Type:	Text
Contents are:	Single Valued		
Justify:	Left		
Field Name:	State		
Field Type:	Data	Data Type:	Text
Contents are:	Single Valued		
Justify:	Left		
Field Name:	Zip Code		
Field Type:	Data	Data Type:	Text
Contents are:	Single Valued		
Justify:	Left		

Report Name:	View Definition			10/30/87 4:24 PM
				Page 1
Project Name:	Questionaire			
View Name:	Compute Results	View Type:	Display, Custom Layout	
Root File:	Question	File Type:	dBASE Mac	
Field Name:	AVG INCOME			View Field
Field Type:	Memory	Data Type:	Number	
Justify:	Right			
Format:	Fixed	Decimal Places:	2	
Decimal:	.	Thousands:		
Negative:	-n	Currency:		
Initial Value:	26200.00			
Field Name:	MIN INCOME			View Field
Field Type:	Memory	Data Type:	Number	
Justify:	Right			
Format:	Fixed	Decimal Places:	2	
Decimal:	.	Thousands:		
Negative:	-n	Currency:		
Initial Value:	15000.00			
Field Name:	MAX INCOME			View Field
Field Type:	Memory	Data Type:	Number	
Justify:	Right			
Format:	Fixed	Decimal Places:	2	
Decimal:	.	Thousands:		
Negative:	-n	Currency:		
Initial Value:	45000.00			
Field Name:	MED INCOME			View Field
Field Type:	Memory	Data Type:	Number	
Justify:	Right			
Format:	Fixed	Decimal Places:	2	
Decimal:	.	Thousands:		
Negative:	-n	Currency:		
Initial Value:	23000.00			
Field Name:	AVG AGE			View Field
Field Type:	Memory	Data Type:	Number	
Justify:	Right			
Format:	Fixed	Decimal Places:	2	
Decimal:	.	Thousands:		
Negative:	-n	Currency:		
Initial Value:	28.60			
Field Name:	MIN AGE			View Field
Field Type:	Memory	Data Type:	Number	
Justify:	Right			
Format:	Fixed	Decimal Places:	2	
Decimal:	.	Thousands:		

Report Name:	View Definition			10/30/87 4:24 PM Page 2
Project Name:	Questionaire			
View Name:	Compute Results	View Type:	Display, Custom Layout	
Negative:	-n	Currency:		
Initial Value:	18.00			
Field Name:	MAX AGE			View Field
Field Type:	Memory	Data Type:	Number	
Justify:	Right			
Format:	Fixed	Decimal Places:	2	
Decimal:	.	Thousands:		
Negative:	-n	Currency:		
Initial Value:	45.00			
Field Name:	MED AGE			View Field
Field Type:	Memory	Data Type:	Number	
Justify:	Right			
Format:	Fixed	Decimal Places:	2	
Decimal:	.	Thousands:		
Negative:	-n	Currency:		
Initial Value:	25.00			
Field Name:	AVG MAGAZINES			View Field
Field Type:	Memory	Data Type:	Number	
Justify:	Right			
Format:	Fixed	Decimal Places:	2	
Decimal:	.	Thousands:		
Negative:	-n	Currency:		
Initial Value:	2.60			
Field Name:	MIN MAGAZINES			View Field
Field Type:	Memory	Data Type:	Number	
Justify:	Right			
Format:	Fixed	Decimal Places:	2	
Decimal:	.	Thousands:		
Negative:	-n	Currency:		
Initial Value:	1.00			
Field Name:	MAX MAGAZINES			View Field
Field Type:	Memory	Data Type:	Number	
Justify:	Right			
Format:	Fixed	Decimal Places:	2	
Decimal:	.	Thousands:		
Negative:	-n	Currency:		
Initial Value:	5.00			
Field Name:	MED MAGAZINES			View Field
Field Type:	Memory	Data Type:	Number	
Justify:	Right			
Format:	Fixed	Decimal Places:	2	

Report Name: View Definition 10/30/87 4:24 PM
Page 3

Project Name: Questionaire
View Name: Compute Results View Type: Display, Custom Layout

Decimal: . Thousands:
Negative: -n Currency:
Initial Value: 3.00

Field Name: AVG MODEM View Field
Field Type: Memory Data Type: Number
Justify: Right
Format: Fixed Decimal Places: 2
Decimal: . Thousands:
Negative: -n Currency:
Initial Value: 9.20

Field Name: MIN MODEM View Field
Field Type: Memory Data Type: Number
Justify: Right
Format: Fixed Decimal Places: 2
Decimal: . Thousands:
Negative: -n Currency:
Initial Value: 0.00

Field Name: MAX MODEM View Field
Field Type: Memory Data Type: Number
Justify: Right
Format: Fixed Decimal Places: 2
Decimal: . Thousands:
Negative: -n Currency:
Initial Value: 20.00

Field Name: MED MODEM View Field
Field Type: Memory Data Type: Number
Justify: Right
Format: Fixed Decimal Places: 2
Decimal: . Thousands:
Negative: -n Currency:
Initial Value: 5.00

Field Name: AVG MARITAL View Field
Field Type: Memory Data Type: Number
Justify: Right
Format: Fixed Decimal Places: 2
Decimal: . Thousands:
Negative: -n Currency:
Initial Value: 2.20

Field Name: MAX MARITAL View Field
Field Type: Memory Data Type: Number
Justify: Right

Report Name:	View Definition			10/30/87 4:24 PM Page 4
Project Name:	Questionaire			
View Name:	Compute Results	View Type:	Display, Custom Layout	

Format:	Fixed	Decimal Places:	2	
Decimal:	.	Thousands:		
Negative:	-n	Currency:		
Initial Value:	4.00			
Field Name:	MED MARITAL			View Field
Field Type:	Memory	Data Type:	Number	
Justify:	Right			
Format:	Fixed	Decimal Places:	2	
Decimal:	.	Thousands:		
Negative:	-n	Currency:		
Initial Value:	2.00			
Field Name:	MIN MARITAL			View Field
Field Type:	Memory	Data Type:	Number	
Justify:	Right			
Format:	Fixed	Decimal Places:	2	
Decimal:	.	Thousands:		
Negative:	-n	Currency:		
Initial Value:	1.00			
Field Name:	AVG USAGE			View Field
Field Type:	Memory	Data Type:	Number	
Justify:	Right			
Format:	Fixed	Decimal Places:	2	
Decimal:	.	Thousands:		
Negative:	-n	Currency:		
Initial Value:	20.00			
Field Name:	MIN USAGE			View Field
Field Type:	Memory	Data Type:	Number	
Justify:	Right			
Format:	Fixed	Decimal Places:	2	
Decimal:	.	Thousands:		
Negative:	-n	Currency:		
Initial Value:	1.00			
Field Name:	MAX USAGE			View Field
Field Type:	Memory	Data Type:	Number	
Justify:	Right			
Format:	Fixed	Decimal Places:	2	
Decimal:	.	Thousands:		
Negative:	-n	Currency:		
Initial Value:	40.00			
Field Name:	MED USAGE			View Field
Field Type:	Memory	Data Type:	Number	

Report Name:	View Definition		10/30/87 4:24 PM Page 5
Project Name:	Questionaire		
View Name:	Compute Results	View Type:	Display, Custom Layout
Justify:	Right		
Format:	Fixed	Decimal Places:	2
Decimal:	.	Thousands:	
Negative:	-n	Currency:	
Initial Value:	20.00		

Report Name:	View Definition			10/30/87 4:24 PM Page 6
Project Name:	Questionaire			
View Name:	Compute Results	View Type:	Display, Custom Layout	
File Name:	Question	File Type:	dBASE Mac	

Access Path:	Question			
Field Name:	Question #			Modified
Field Type:	Key, Ordered	Data Type:	Number	Required
Justify:	Right			
Format:	Fixed	Decimal Places:	0	
Decimal:	.	Thousands:		
Negative:	-n	Currency:		

View Procedure:

Pre-Processor

```
\ ** Compute Results view Pre-Processor ** \
I=1
SETBROWSE({Question #•Question},1)
LOOP
TINCOME[I]={Income•Question}
    TAGE[I]={Age•Question}
    TMAGAZINES[I]={Magazines•Question}
    TMODEM[I]={Modem Usage•Question}
      TMARITAL[I]={Marital Status•Question}
    TUSAGE[I]={Computer Usage•Question}
  I=I+1
 WHEN ENDOF({Question}) LEAVE
NEXTBROWSE({Question #•Question})
END
{AVG INCOME}=AVG(TINCOME)
{MIN INCOME}=MIN(TINCOME)
{MAX INCOME}=MAX(TINCOME)
{MED INCOME}=MED(TINCOME)
{AVG AGE}=AVG(TAGE)
{MIN AGE}=MIN(TAGE)
{MAX AGE}=MAX(TAGE)
{MED AGE}=MED(TAGE)
{AVG MAGAZINES}=AVG(TMAGAZINES)
{MIN MAGAZINES}=MIN(TMAGAZINES)
{MAX MAGAZINES}=MAX(TMAGAZINES)
{MED MAGAZINES}=MED(TMAGAZINES)
{AVG MODEM}=AVG(TMODEM)
{MIN MODEM}=MIN(TMODEM)
{MAX MODEM}=MAX(TMODEM)
{MED MODEM}=MED(TMODEM)
{AVG MARITAL}=AVG(TMARITAL)
{MIN MARITAL}=MIN(TMARITAL)
{MAX MARITAL}=MAX(TMARITAL)
```

Report Name:	View Definition		10/30/87 4:24 PM Page 7
Project Name:	Questionaire		
View Name:	Compute Results	View Type:	Display, Custom Layout
File Name:	Question	File Type:	dBASE Mac

{MED MARITAL}=MED(TMARITAL)
{AVG USAGE}=AVG(TUSAGE)
{MIN USAGE}=MIN(TUSAGE)
{MAX USAGE}=MAX(TUSAGE)
{MED USAGE}=MED(TUSAGE)

Field Name:	Income		
Field Type:	Data	Data Type:	Number
Contents are:	Single Valued		
Justify:	Right		
Format:	Fixed	Decimal Places:	2
Decimal:	.	Thousands:	
Negative:	-n	Currency:	

Field Name:	Age		
Field Type:	Data	Data Type:	Number
Contents are:	Single Valued		
Justify:	Right		
Format:	Fixed	Decimal Places:	0
Decimal:	.	Thousands:	
Negative:	-n	Currency:	

Field Name:	Sex		
Field Type:	Data	Data Type:	Text
Contents are:	Single Valued		
Justify:	Left		

Field Name:	Marital Status		
Field Type:	Data	Data Type:	Number
Contents are:	Single Valued		
Justify:	Right		
Format:	Fixed	Decimal Places:	0
Decimal:	.	Thousands:	
Negative:	-n	Currency:	

Field Name:	Modem Usage		
Field Type:	Data	Data Type:	Number
Contents are:	Single Valued		
Justify:	Right		
Format:	Fixed	Decimal Places:	0
Decimal:	.	Thousands:	
Negative:	-n	Currency:	

Field Name:	Magazines		
Field Type:	Data	Data Type:	Number
Contents are:	Single Valued		

Report Name:	View Definition		10/30/87 4:24 PM
			Page 8
Project Name:	Questionaire		
View Name:	Compute Results	View Type:	Display, Custom Layout
File Name:	Question	File Type:	dBASE Mac
Justify:	Right		
Format:	Fixed	Decimal Places:	0
Decimal:	.	Thousands:	
Negative:	-n	Currency:	
Field Name:	Computer Usage		
Field Type:	Data	Data Type:	Number
Contents are:	Single Valued		
Justify:	Right		
Format:	Fixed	Decimal Places:	0
Decimal:	.	Thousands:	
Negative:	-n	Currency:	

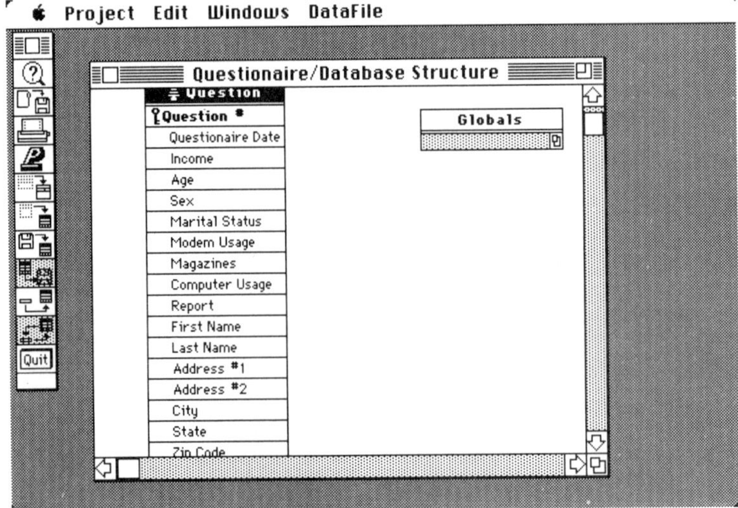

Figure 14-1 Questionnaire Structure.

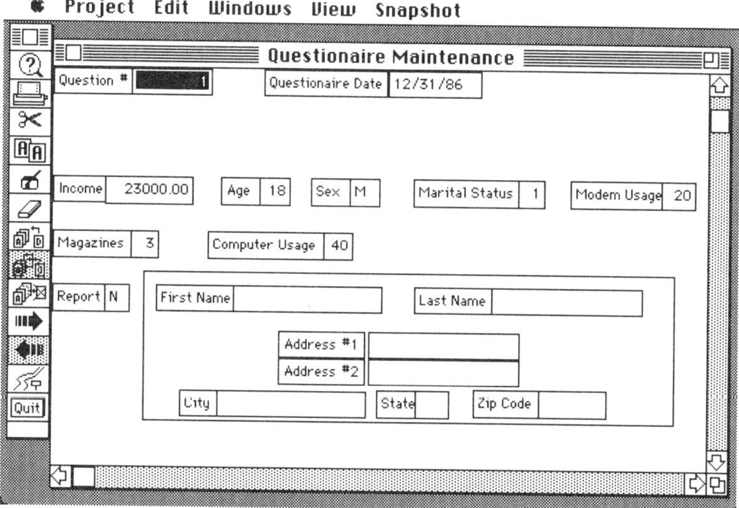

Figure 14-2 Question Entry.

Project Edit Windows View Snapshot

Compute Results

Question

	Income	Age	Marital Status	Modem Usage	Magazines	Computer Usage
	23000.00	18	1	20	3	40
	16000.00	45	2	0	1	1
	45000.00	25	4	5	5	34
	32000.00	34	3	20	3	20
	15000.00	21	1	1	1	5
Average	26200.00	28.60	2.20	9.20	2.60	20.00
Minimum	15000.00	18.00	1.00	0.00	1.00	1.00
Maximum	45000.00	45.00	4.00	20.00	5.00	40.00
Median	23000.00	25.00	2.00	5.00	3.00	20.00

Quit

Figure 14-3 Question Columns.

To design this application in dBASE Mac, first you need to define the Question file, which will contain each questionnaire answered. Since you should already be familiar with the procedures involved in creating new dBASE Mac data files, create the Question file as shown in the project listings (below).

After creating the Question file, create a data entry view—Add Question. Since you will be entering data for the entire file, select the Custom layout, and create the Add Question view by following the procedural listing for Add Question.

NOTE: Create a layout similar to the layout in the figure. Your layout may look somewhat different, depending on the fonts and font sizes you use.

Now you may wish to Use this view and add some data to the file. About seven records should be enough for this exercise, but you may enter as many as you wish. After you have finished entering your data, select New View from the Windows menu.

dBASE Mac only allows you to use the math functions on groups of data contained within a multivalued field or local variable array. Therefore, you have a choice: Create another file and use a Transfer View to send data from the original file to multivalued fields in the second file, or create a processor that uses local variable arrays to accumulate totals and perform statistical analysis on that data. In this application, you will use the latter approach.

- Create a view called Compute Results, so that you can accumulate the data and display the results of the research. Follow the procedure to create a Columnar view.
- You should now see the Define Hierarchy screen.
  Since you only want to accumulate totals and perform analysis on certain fields in the file, it is not necessary to select all the fields in the Question file.
- Add the following fields to the hierarchy: Question #, Income, Age, Marital Status, Modem Usage, Magazines, Computer Usage.
- Next, create twenty-four View Memory fields by clicking once on the **Question** title bar and then clicking **New**. The Memory fields should be named: AVG INCOME, MIN INCOME, MAX INCOME, MED INCOME, AVG AGE, MIN AGE, MAX AGE, MED AGE, AVG MAGAZINES, MIN MAGAZINES, MAX MAGAZINES, MED MAGAZINES, AVG MODEM, MIN MODEM, MAX MODEM, MED MODEM, AVG MARITAL, MIN MARITAL, MAX MARITAL, MED MARITAL, AVG USAGE, MIN USAGE, MAX USAGE, and MED USAGE.
  Remember to specify Numeric data types, and allow at least two decimal places for the calculations.

The next step is to write a Pre-Processor procedure that will transfer the values in each record to an array. This is necessary, since many of the statistical functions do not work with single-valued fields. The following procedure will load each field into six arrays and then perform the statistical analysis, which is then placed into the twenty-four Memory fields you just defined. This Pre-Processor procedure should be attached to the Question # field rather than the View itself.

```
\ ** Compute Results view Pre-Processor **\
I=1
SETBROWSE({Question #•Question},1)
LOOP
TINCOME[I]={Income•Question}
 TAGE[I]={Age•Question}
```

```
  TMAGAZINES[I]={Magazines•Question}
  TMODEM[I]={ModemUsage•Question}
   TMARITAL[I]={MaritalStatus•Question}
  TUSAGE[I]={ComputerUsage•Question}
  I=I+1
  WHEN ENDOF({Question}) LEAVE
NEXTBROWSE({Question #•Question})
END

{AVG INCOME}=AVG(TINCOME)
{MIN INCOME}=MIN(TINCOME)
{MAX INCOME}=MAX(TINCOME)
{MED INCOME}=MED(TINCOME)
{AVG AGE}=AVG(TAGE)
{MIN AGE}=MIN(TAGE)
{MAX AGE}=MAX(TAGE)
{MED AGE}=MED(TAGE)
{AVG MAGAZINES}=AVG(TMAGAZINES)
{MIN MAGAZINES}=MIN(TMAGAZINES)
{MAX MAGAZINES}=MAX(TMAGAZINES)
{MED MAGAZINES}=MED(TMAGAZINES)
{AVG MODEM}=AVG(TMODEM)
{MIN MODEM}=MIN(TMODEM)
{MAX MODEM}=MAX(TMODEM)
{MED MODEM}=MED(TMODEM)
{AVG MARITAL}=AVG(TMARITAL)
{MIN MARITAL}=MIN(TMARITAL)
{MAX MARITAL}=MAX(TMARITAL)
{MED MARITAL}=MED(TMARITAL)
{AVG USAGE}=AVG(TUSAGE)
{MIN USAGE}=MIN(TUSAGE)
{MAX USAGE}=MAX(TUSAGE)
{MED USAGE}=MED(TUSAGE)
```

Adjust the columns in the layout to the appropriate widths, and make any other modifications to the layout that you wish to make. Remember to include the Question # field before or next to the column portion of the layout. Since this field is only used to contain the controlling Pre-Processor, you may wish to make it invisible. For information on how to do this, refer to Chapter 10 of the tutorial.

Now Perform and Use the view to test the procedure. If you have made no mistakes in entering the procedure, your data should appear in the view. After analyzing the data from the questionnaire, you will need to send a copy of it to each of the participants that asked to receive results. To do so, you will print out one copy of the final report for each person who requested it, and you will also print out mailing labels, using a mailing label view.

To print out results for each participant who requested them, create a mailing label view and set the selection criteria in the Define Selections screen to read:

```
Report = "Y"
```

When you print the mailing labels, only those people who want a copy will have labels printed out.

NOTE: If you want to know how to create a mailing label View, see the Tutorial and look at the Mailing List Project or the MultiMail project.

Conclusion

Though this application is functional, you may be interested in other ways to do this procedure. You could easily have set up a Transfer View to transfer the data from the Question file into a accumulation file that contained multivalued fields. This would have required some additional steps such as creating an additional file and creating an additional view to perform the transfer. However, this method has advantages. For instance, once the transfer had been done, you could easily add different statistical procedures that would manipulate the data without writing a lengthy Pre-Processor procedure for each new view you wish to create.

You may want to add a procedure for archiving the data in the file, in case you decide to use the questionnaire again. To add flavor, you may also want to add some custom dialog boxes.

15

THE MULTIMAIL PROJECT

The MultiMail project is created in the Tutorial, Chapters 4–10. It contains a mailing list consisting of multivalued fields for the address fields. These multivalued fields are in sets, and a special field, Selection, allows the choosing of a default field for each record. Several views use this ability to select the field for listing in a report or for printing on mailing labels.

In addition to the files and reports, MultiMail gives an example of a menu-driven application complete with its own context-sensitive help system.

Report Name:	File Structure			10/30/87 4:10 PM Page 1
File Name:	Mail2	File Type:	dBASE Mac	
Field Name:	Name ID			
Field Type:	Key, Ordered	Data Type:	Text	Required
Justify:	Left			
Field Name:	First Name			
Field Type:	Data	Data Type:	Text	
Contents are:	Single Valued			
Justify:	Left			
Field Name:	Middle Initial			
Field Type:	Data	Data Type:	Text	
Contents are:	Single Valued			
Justify:	Left			
Field Name:	Last Name			
Field Type:	Data, Indexed	Data Type:	Text	Required
Contents are:	Single Valued			
Justify:	Left			
Field Name:	Street			
Field Type:	Data	Data Type:	Text	
Contents are:	Multiple Valued	Set Name:	Address	
Justify:	Left			
Field Name:	City			
Field Type:	Data	Data Type:	Text	
Contents are:	Multiple Valued	Set Name:	Address	
Justify:	Left			
Field Name:	State			
Field Type:	Data	Data Type:	Text	
Contents are:	Multiple Valued	Set Name:	Address	
Justify:	Left			
Field Name:	Zip Code			
Field Type:	Data	Data Type:	Text	
Contents are:	Multiple Valued	Set Name:	Address	
Justify:	Left			
Field Name:	Phone			
Field Type:	Data	Data Type:	Text	
Contents are:	Multiple Valued	Set Name:	Address	
Justify:	Left			
Pattern:	3n~-4n ~(3n~)~ 3n~-4n 3n~-4n~ ~"Ext."~ 3n ~(3n~)~ 3n~-4n~ ~"Ext."~ 3n			
Field Name:	Comments			
Field Type:	Data	Data Type:	Text	

Report Name:	File Structure			10/30/87 4:10 PM
				Page 2
File Name:	Mail2	File Type:	dBASE Mac	
Contents are:	Single Valued			
Justify:	Left, Wrapped			
Field Name:	Selection			
Field Type:	Data	Data Type:	Choices	
Contents are:	Single Valued			
Justify:	Left			
Format:	Horizontal Buttons			
Values:	One			
	Two			
	Both			
Initial Value:	One			

Report Name:	File Structure			10/30/87 4:10 PM
				Page 1
File Name:	Help Mail	File Type:	dBASE Mac	
Field Name:	Help ID			
Field Type:	Key, Ordered	Data Type:	Number	Required
Justify:	Right			
Format:	Fixed	Decimal Places:	0	
Decimal:	.	Thousands:		
Negative:	-n	Currency:		
Auto Sequenced By:	1			
Initial Value:	6			
Field Name:	Help Text			
Field Type:	Data	Data Type:	Text	
Contents are:	Single Valued			
Justify:	Left, Wrapped			

Report Name:	File Structure	10/30/87 4:10 PM	
		Page 1	
File Name:	Globals	File Type:	Globals
Field Name:	select		
Field Type:	Memory	Data Type:	Text
Justify:	Left		
Initial Text	NY		
Field Name:	Help Level		
Field Type:	Memory	Data Type:	Number
Justify:	Right		
Format:	Fixed	Decimal Places:	0
Decimal:	.	Thousands:	
Negative:	-n	Currency:	
Initial Value:	3		

Report Name:	View Definition	10/30/87 4:11 PM	
		Page 1	
Project Name:	Multi Mail		
View Name:	Mail Entry	View Type:	Display, Custom Layout
Procedure:			
Post-Processor EXIT			
Root File:	Mail2	File Type:	dBASE Mac
File Name:	Globals	File Type:	Globals

Report Name:	View Definition		10/30/87	4:11 PM
			Page 2	
Project Name:	Multi Mail			
View Name:	Mail Entry	View Type:	Display, Custom Layout	
File Name:	Mail2	File Type:	dBASE Mac	

Access Path:	Mail2			

Field Name:	Name ID			
Field Type:	Key, Ordered	Data Type:	Text	Required
Justify:	Left			

Field Name:	First Name		
Field Type:	Data	Data Type:	Text
Contents are:	Single Valued		
Justify:	Left		

Field Name:	Middle Initial		
Field Type:	Data	Data Type:	Text
Contents are:	Single Valued		
Justify:	Left		

Field Name:	Last Name			
Field Type:	Data, Indexed	Data Type:	Text	Required
Contents are:	Single Valued			
Justify:	Left			

Field Name:	Street		
Field Type:	Data	Data Type:	Text
Contents are:	Multiple Valued	Set Name:	Address
Justify:	Left		

Field Name:	City		
Field Type:	Data	Data Type:	Text
Contents are:	Multiple Valued	Set Name:	Address
Justify:	Left		

Field Name:	State		
Field Type:	Data	Data Type:	Text
Contents are:	Multiple Valued	Set Name:	Address
Justify:	Left		

Field Name:	Zip Code		
Field Type:	Data	Data Type:	Text
Contents are:	Multiple Valued	Set Name:	Address
Justify:	Left		

Field Name:	Phone		
Field Type:	Data	Data Type:	Text
Contents are:	Multiple Valued	Set Name:	Address
Justify:	Left		
Pattern:	3n~-4n		
	~(3n~)~ 3n~-4n		
	3n~-4n~ ~"Ext."~ 3n		

Report Name:	View Definition			10/30/87 4:11 PM
				Page 3
Project Name:	Multi Mail			
View Name:	Mail Entry	View Type:	Display, Custom Layout	
File Name:	Mail2	File Type:	dBASE Mac	
	~(3n~)~ 3n~-4n~ ~"Ext."~ 3n			
Field Name:	Comments			
Field Type:	Data	Data Type:	Text	
Contents are:	Single Valued			
Justify:	Left, Wrapped			
Field Name:	Selection			
Field Type:	Data	Data Type:	Choices	
Contents are:	Single Valued			
Justify:	Left			
Format:	Horizontal Buttons			
Values:	One			
	Two			
	Both			
Initial Value:	One			
Field Name:	Graph Help			View Field
Field Type:	Memory	Data Type:	Graphic	
Scale:	None			
Procedure:				
Pre-Processor	{Help Level•Globals} = 6			
	PERFORM("Help",MODAL)			
	SETNEXTFIELD({Name ID•Mail2})			
Field Name:	Dummy Field			View Field
Field Type:	Memory	Data Type:	Graphic	
Scale:	None			
Procedure:				
Pre-Processor	SETNEXTFIELD({Name ID•Mail2})			

Report Name:	View Definition			10/30/87 4:11 PM
				Page 4
Project Name:	Multi Mail			
View Name:	Mail Entry	View Type:	Display, Custom Layout	
File Name:	Globals	File Type:	Globals	
Field Name:	Help Level			
Field Type:	Memory	Data Type:	Number	
Justify:	Right			
Format:	Fixed	Decimal Places:	0	
Decimal:	.	Thousands:		
Negative:	-n	Currency:		
Initial Value:	3			

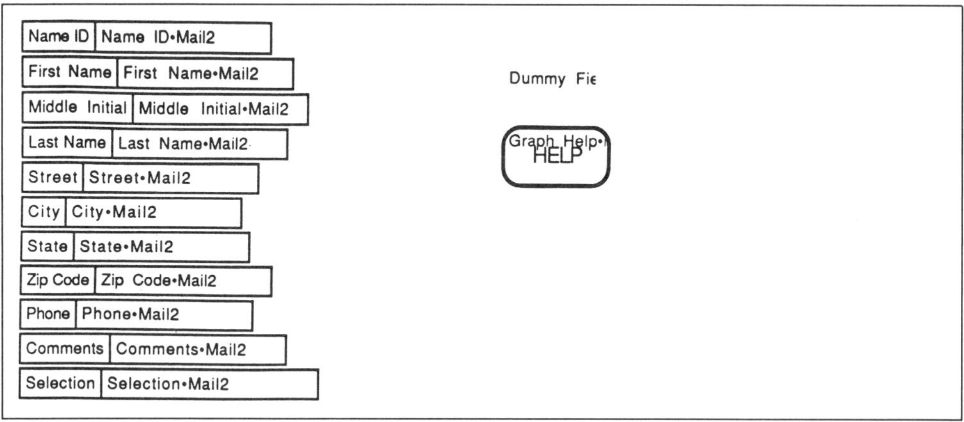

Mail Entry Layout

Report Name:	View Definition		10/30/87 4:12 PM Page 1
Project Name:	Multi Mail		
View Name:	Labels-2	View Type:	Display, Custom Layout

Procedure:

Post-Processor EXIT

Root File:	Mail2	File Type:	dBASE Mac

Report Name:	View Definition		10/30/87	4:12 PM
			Page 2	
Project Name:	Multi Mail			
View Name:	Labels-2	View Type:	Display, Custom Layout	
File Name:	Mail2	File Type:	dBASE Mac	

Access Path:	Mail2			
Field Name:	Name ID			
Field Type:	Key, Ordered	Data Type:	Text	Required
Justify:	Left			
Field Name:	First Name			
Field Type:	Data	Data Type:	Text	
Contents are:	Single Valued			
Justify:	Left			
Field Name:	Middle Initial			
Field Type:	Data	Data Type:	Text	
Contents are:	Single Valued			
Justify:	Left			
Field Name:	Last Name			
Field Type:	Data, Indexed	Data Type:	Text	Required
Contents are:	Single Valued			
Justify:	Left			
Field Name:	Street			
Field Type:	Data	Data Type:	Text	
Contents are:	Multiple Valued	Set Name:	Address	
Justify:	Left			
Show If:	CASE {Selection•Mail2} OF			
	WHEN 1 DO			
	{Street•Mail2} = {Street•Mail2}[1]			
	WHEN 2 DO			
	{Street•Mail2} = {Street•Mail2}[2]			
	OTHERWISE			
	"T"			
	END			
Field Name:	City			
Field Type:	Data	Data Type:	Text	
Contents are:	Multiple Valued	Set Name:	Address	
Justify:	Left			
Field Name:	State			
Field Type:	Data	Data Type:	Text	
Contents are:	Multiple Valued	Set Name:	Address	
Justify:	Left			
Field Name:	Zip Code			
Field Type:	Data	Data Type:	Text	
Contents are:	Multiple Valued	Set Name:	Address	

Report Name:	View Definition			10/30/87 4:12 PM
				Page 3
Project Name:	Multi Mail			
View Name:	Labels-2	View Type:	Display, Custom Layout	
File Name:	Mail2	File Type:	dBASE Mac	

Justify:	Left			
Field Name:	Phone			
Field Type:	Data	Data Type:	Text	
Contents are:	Multiple Valued	Set Name:	Address	
Justify:	Left			
Pattern:	3n~-4n			
	~(3n~)~ 3n~-4n			
	3n~-4n~ ~"Ext."~ 3n			
	~(3n~)~ 3n~-4n~ ~"Ext."~ 3n			
Field Name:	Comments			
Field Type:	Data	Data Type:	Text	
Contents are:	Single Valued			
Justify:	Left, Wrapped			
Field Name:	Selection			
Field Type:	Data	Data Type:	Choices	
Contents are:	Single Valued			
Justify:	Left			
Format:	Horizontal Buttons			
Values:	One			
	Two			
	Both			
Initial Value:	One			
Field Name:	Address			View Field
Field Type:	Formula	Data Type:	Text	
Justify:	Left			
Formula:	{City•Mail2}:", ":{State•Mail2}:" ":{Zip Code•Mail2}			
Field Name:	Full Name			View Field
Field Type:	Formula	Data Type:	Text	
Justify:	Left			
Formula:	{First Name•Mail2}:" ":{Last Name•Mail2}			

Report Name:	View Definition			10/30/87 4:13 PM
				Page 1
Project Name:	Multi Mail			
View Name:	Mailing List Column	View Type:	Display, Custom Layout	

Procedure:

Post-Processor EXIT

Root File:	Mail2	File Type:	dBASE Mac

Report Name:	View Definition		10/30/87	4:13 PM
			Page 2	
Project Name:	Multi Mail			
View Name:	Mailing List Column	View Type:	Display, Custom Layout	
File Name:	Mail2	File Type:	dBASE Mac	

Access Path:	Mail2			
Field Name:	Name ID			
Field Type:	Key, Ordered	Data Type:	Text	Required
Justify:	Left			
Field Name:	First Name			
Field Type:	Data	Data Type:	Text	
Contents are:	Single Valued			
Justify:	Left			
Field Name:	Middle Initial			
Field Type:	Data	Data Type:	Text	
Contents are:	Single Valued			
Justify:	Left			
Field Name:	Last Name			
Field Type:	Data, Indexed	Data Type:	Text	Required
Contents are:	Single Valued			
Justify:	Left			
Field Name:	Street			
Field Type:	Data	Data Type:	Text	
Contents are:	Multiple Valued	Set Name:	Address	
Justify:	Left			
Show If:	CASE {Selection•Mail2} OF WHEN 1 DO {Street•Mail2} = {Street•Mail2}[1] WHEN 2 DO {Street•Mail2} = {Street•Mail2}[2] OTHERWISE "T" END			
Field Name:	City			
Field Type:	Data	Data Type:	Text	
Contents are:	Multiple Valued	Set Name:	Address	
Justify:	Left			
Field Name:	State			
Field Type:	Data	Data Type:	Text	
Contents are:	Multiple Valued	Set Name:	Address	
Justify:	Left			
Field Name:	Zip Code			
Field Type:	Data	Data Type:	Text	
Contents are:	Multiple Valued	Set Name:	Address	

Report Name:	View Definition			10/30/87 4:13 PM
				Page 3
Project Name:	Multi Mail			
View Name:	Mailing List Column	View Type:	Display, Custom Layout	
File Name:	Mail2	File Type:	dBASE Mac	
Justify:	Left			
Field Name:	Phone			
Field Type:	Data	Data Type:	Text	
Contents are:	Multiple Valued	Set Name:	Address	
Justify:	Left			
Pattern:	3n~-4n			
	~(3n~)~ 3n~-4n			
	3n~-4n~ ~"Ext."~ 3n			
	~(3n~)~ 3n~-4n~ ~"Ext."~ 3n			
Field Name:	Comments			
Field Type:	Data	Data Type:	Text	
Contents are:	Single Valued			
Justify:	Left, Wrapped			
Field Name:	Selection			
Field Type:	Data	Data Type:	Choices	
Contents are:	Single Valued			
Justify:	Left			
Format:	Horizontal Buttons			
Values:	One			
	Two			
	Both			
Initial Value:	One			

Report Name:	View Definition			10/30/87 4:13 PM
				Page 1
Project Name:	Multi Mail			
View Name:	By City	View Type:	Display, Custom Layout	
Procedure:				
Post-Processor EXIT				
Root File:	Mail2	File Type:	dBASE Mac	
Show If:	{City•Mail2} = {select•Globals}			
File Name:	Globals	File Type:	Globals	

Report Name:	View Definition		10/30/87 4:13 PM
			Page 2
Project Name:	Multi Mail		
View Name:	By City	View Type:	Display, Custom Layout
File Name:	Mail2	File Type:	dBASE Mac

Access Path:	Mail2			
Field Name:	Name ID			
Field Type:	Key, Ordered	Data Type:	Text	Required
Justify:	Left			
Field Name:	First Name			
Field Type:	Data	Data Type:	Text	
Contents are:	Single Valued			
Justify:	Left			
Field Name:	Middle Initial			
Field Type:	Data	Data Type:	Text	
Contents are:	Single Valued			
Justify:	Left			
Field Name:	Last Name			
Field Type:	Data, Indexed	Data Type:	Text	Required
Contents are:	Single Valued			
Justify:	Left			
Field Name:	Street			
Field Type:	Data	Data Type:	Text	
Contents are:	Multiple Valued	Set Name:	Address	
Justify:	Left			
Show If:	CASE {Selection•Mail2} OF			
	WHEN 1 DO			
	{Street•Mail2} = {Street•Mail2}[1]			
	WHEN 2 DO			
	{Street•Mail2} = {Street•Mail2}[2]			
	OTHERWISE			
	"T"			
	END			
Field Name:	City			
Field Type:	Data	Data Type:	Text	
Contents are:	Multiple Valued	Set Name:	Address	
Justify:	Left			
Field Name:	State			
Field Type:	Data	Data Type:	Text	
Contents are:	Multiple Valued	Set Name:	Address	
Justify:	Left			
Field Name:	Zip Code			
Field Type:	Data	Data Type:	Text	
Contents are:	Multiple Valued	Set Name:	Address	

Report Name:	View Definition			10/30/87 4:13 PM
				Page 3
Project Name:	Multi Mail			
View Name:	By City	View Type:	Display, Custom Layout	
File Name:	Mail2	File Type:	dBASE Mac	
Justify:	Left			
Field Name:	Phone			
Field Type:	Data	Data Type:	Text	
Contents are:	Multiple Valued	Set Name:	Address	
Justify:	Left			
Pattern:	3n~-4n			
	~(3n~)~ 3n~-4n			
	3n~-4n~ ~"Ext."~ 3n			
	~(3n~)~ 3n~-4n~ ~"Ext."~ 3n			
Field Name:	Comments			
Field Type:	Data	Data Type:	Text	
Contents are:	Single Valued			
Justify:	Left, Wrapped			
Field Name:	Selection			
Field Type:	Data	Data Type:	Choices	
Contents are:	Single Valued			
Justify:	Left			
Format:	Horizontal Buttons			
Values:	One			
	Two			
	Both			
Initial Value:	One			

Report Name:	View Definition			10/30/87 4:13 PM
				Page 4
Project Name:	Multi Mail			
View Name:	By City	View Type:	Display, Custom Layout	
File Name:	Globals	File Type:	Globals	
Field Name:	select			
Field Type:	Memory	Data Type:	Text	
Justify:	Left			
Initial Text	NY			

Mail2

Name	Last Name	Street	City	State	Zip Code	Phone	Selection

Sample Column Layout for MultiMail

Report Name:	View Definition		10/30/87 4:15 PM Page 1
Project Name:	Multi Mail		
View Name:	Mail Menu	View Type:	Display, Custom Layout

Procedure:

Pre-Processor
```
REPEAT
\ **Auto Selection Pre-Processor** \
 DIALOG 100,100,250,400
  BUTTON 1,125,20,145,130,"OK"
  BUTTON 2,125,170,145,280,"Cancel"
   BUTTON 90,20,200,40,250,"HELP"
  FIXEDTEXT 20,25,40,190,"MAIL MENU"
  RADIOLIST 1,1
   RADIOBUTTON 50,55,65,380,"Enter Records"
   RADIOBUTTON 70,55,85,380,"View Records"
   RADIOBUTTON 90,55,105,380,"Print Labels"
   END
 END
IF BUTTONVALUE(90) THEN
 {Help Level•Globals} = 1
 PERFORM("Help",MODAL)
END
\ **If the user doesn't press the "Cancel" button **\
 IF BUTTONVALUE(1) THEN
  CASE RADIOVALUE(1) OF
   WHEN 1 DO
    USE ("Mail Entry")
   WHEN 2 DO
     REPEAT
     DIALOG 100,100,250,400
      BUTTON 1,125,20,145,130,"OK"
      BUTTON 3,125,170,145,280,"Cancel"
      BUTTON 90,20,200,40,250,"HELP"
     FIXEDTEXT 20,25,40,190,"VIEWING RECORDS"
      RADIOLIST 1,1
       RADIOBUTTON 50,55,65,380,"All Records"
       RADIOBUTTON 70,55,85,380,"By City"
       RADIOBUTTON 90,55,105,380,"By State"
        END
      END
    IF BUTTONVALUE(90) THEN
     CASE RADIOVALUE(1) OF
      WHEN 1 DO
       {Help Level•Globals} = 3
        PERFORM("Help",MODAL)
      WHEN 2 DO
       {Help Level•Globals} = 4
```

Report Name:	View Definition			10/30/87	4:15 PM
				Page 2	
Project Name:	Multi Mail				
View Name:	Mail Menu	View Type:	Display, Custom Layout		

```
PERFORM("Help",MODAL)
OTHERWISE
{Help Level•Globals} = 5
PERFORM("Help",MODAL)
END
END
\ **If the user doesn't press the "Cancel" button **\
IF BUTTONVALUE(1) THEN
CASE RADIOVALUE(1) OF
WHEN 1 DO
PERFORM("Mailing List Column", MODAL)
WHEN 2 DO
{select•Globals} = " "
DIALOG 100,100,250,400
BUTTON 1,125,20,145,130,"OK"
BUTTON 3,125,170,145,280,"Cancel"
FIXEDTEXT 20,105,40,280,"Enter the city:"
EDITTEXT 1,50,25,65,280,{select•Globals}
END
\ **Assign what the user has typed to the Globals field **\
{select•Globals} = TEXTVALUE(1)
\ **Perform the view to initialize the selection** \
PERFORM ("By City",MODAL)
WHEN 3 DO
{select•Globals} = " "
DIALOG 100,100,250,400
BUTTON 1,125,20,145,130,"OK"
BUTTON 3,125,170,145,280,"Cancel"
FIXEDTEXT 20,105,40,280,"Enter the state:"
EDITTEXT 1,50,25,65,280,{select•Globals}
END
\ **Assign what the user has typed to the Globals field **\
{select•Globals} = TEXTVALUE(1)
\ **Perform the view to initialize the selection** \
PERFORM("By State",MODAL)
END
END
UNTIL BUTTONVALUE(3)
END
WHEN 3 DO
PRINT("Labels-2")
END
END
```

Report Name:	View Definition		10/30/87 4:15 PM Page 3
Project Name:	Multi Mail		
View Name:	Mail Menu	View Type:	Display, Custom Layout
	UNTIL BUTTONVALUE(2) END SETNEXTVIEW("Mail Entry") EXIT		
Root File:	Mail2	File Type:	dBASE Mac
File Name:	Globals	File Type:	Globals

Report Name:	View Definition			10/30/87 4:15 PM
				Page 4
Project Name:	Multi Mail			
View Name:	Mail Menu	View Type:	Display, Custom Layout	
File Name:	Mail2	File Type:	dBASE Mac	
Access Path:	Mail2			
Field Name:	Name ID			
Field Type:	Key, Ordered	Data Type:	Text	Required
Justify:	Left			
Field Name:	First Name			
Field Type:	Data	Data Type:	Text	
Contents are:	Single Valued			
Justify:	Left			
Field Name:	Middle Initial			
Field Type:	Data	Data Type:	Text	
Contents are:	Single Valued			
Justify:	Left			
Field Name:	Last Name			
Field Type:	Data, Indexed	Data Type:	Text	Required
Contents are:	Single Valued			
Justify:	Left			
Field Name:	Street			
Field Type:	Data	Data Type:	Text	
Contents are:	Multiple Valued	Set Name:	Address	
Justify:	Left			
Field Name:	City			
Field Type:	Data	Data Type:	Text	
Contents are:	Multiple Valued	Set Name:	Address	
Justify:	Left			
Field Name:	State			
Field Type:	Data	Data Type:	Text	
Contents are:	Multiple Valued	Set Name:	Address	
Justify:	Left			
Field Name:	Zip Code			
Field Type:	Data	Data Type:	Text	
Contents are:	Multiple Valued	Set Name:	Address	
Justify:	Left			
Field Name:	Phone			
Field Type:	Data	Data Type:	Text	
Contents are:	Multiple Valued	Set Name:	Address	
Justify:	Left			
Pattern:	3n~-4n			
	~(3n~)~ 3n~-4n			
	3n~-4n~ ~"Ext."~ 3n			

Report Name:	View Definition		10/30/87 4:15 PM Page 5
Project Name:	Multi Mail		
View Name:	Mail Menu	View Type:	Display, Custom Layout
File Name:	Mail2	File Type:	dBASE Mac
	~(3n~)~ 3n~-4n~ ~"Ext."~ 3n		
Field Name:	Comments		
Field Type:	Data	Data Type:	Text
Contents are:	Single Valued		
Justify:	Left, Wrapped		
Field Name:	Selection		
Field Type:	Data	Data Type:	Choices
Contents are:	Single Valued		
Justify:	Left		
Format:	Horizontal Buttons		
Values:	One		
	Two		
	Both		
Initial Value:	One		

Report Name:	View Definition		10/30/87 4:15 PM Page 6
Project Name:	Multi Mail		
View Name:	Mail Menu	View Type:	Display, Custom Layout
File Name:	Globals	File Type:	Globals
Field Name:	select		
Field Type:	Memory	Data Type:	Text
Justify:	Left		
Initial Text	NY		
Field Name:	Help Level		
Field Type:	Memory	Data Type:	Number
Justify:	Right		
Format:	Fixed	Decimal Places:	0
Decimal:	.	Thousands:	
Negative:	-n	Currency:	
Initial Value:	3		

Report Name:	View Definition		10/30/87 4:16 PM Page 1
Project Name:	Multi Mail		
View Name:	By State	View Type:	Display, Columnar Layout
Procedure:			
Post-Processor EXIT			
Root File:	Mail2	File Type:	dBASE Mac
Show If:	{State•Mail2} = {select•Globals}		
File Name:	Globals	File Type:	Globals

Report Name:	View Definition		10/30/87 Page 2	4:16 PM
Project Name:	Multi Mail			
View Name:	By State	View Type:	Display, Columnar Layout	
File Name:	Mail2	File Type:	dBASE Mac	

Access Path:	Mail2			
Field Name:	Name ID			
Field Type:	Key, Ordered	Data Type:	Text	Required
Justify:	Left			
Field Name:	First Name			
Field Type:	Data	Data Type:	Text	
Contents are:	Single Valued			
Justify:	Left			
Field Name:	Middle Initial			
Field Type:	Data	Data Type:	Text	
Contents are:	Single Valued			
Justify:	Left			
Field Name:	Last Name			
Field Type:	Data, Indexed	Data Type:	Text	Required
Contents are:	Single Valued			
Justify:	Left			
Field Name:	Street			
Field Type:	Data	Data Type:	Text	
Contents are:	Multiple Valued	Set Name:	Address	
Justify:	Left			
Show If:	CASE {Selection•Mail2} OF WHEN 1 DO {Street•Mail2} = {Street•Mail2}[1] WHEN 2 DO {Street•Mail2} = {Street•Mail2}[2] OTHERWISE "T" END			
Field Name:	City			
Field Type:	Data	Data Type:	Text	
Contents are:	Multiple Valued	Set Name:	Address	
Justify:	Left			
Field Name:	State			
Field Type:	Data	Data Type:	Text	
Contents are:	Multiple Valued	Set Name:	Address	
Justify:	Left			
Field Name:	Zip Code			
Field Type:	Data	Data Type:	Text	
Contents are:	Multiple Valued	Set Name:	Address	

Report Name:	View Definition			10/30/87 4:16 PM
				Page 3
Project Name:	Multi Mail			
View Name:	By State	View Type:	Display, Columnar Layout	
File Name:	Mail2	File Type:	dBASE Mac	
Justify:	Left			
Field Name:	Phone			
Field Type:	Data	Data Type:	Text	
Contents are:	Multiple Valued	Set Name:	Address	
Justify:	Left			
Pattern:	3n~-4n			
	~(3n~)~ 3n~-4n			
	3n~-4n~ ~"Ext."~ 3n			
	~(3n~)~ 3n~-4n~ ~"Ext."~ 3n			
Field Name:	Comments			
Field Type:	Data	Data Type:	Text	
Contents are:	Single Valued			
Justify:	Left, Wrapped			
Field Name:	Selection			
Field Type:	Data	Data Type:	Choices	
Contents are:	Single Valued			
Justify:	Left			
Format:	Horizontal Buttons			
Values:	One			
	Two			
	Both			
Initial Value:	One			

Report Name:	View Definition			10/30/87 4:16 PM
				Page 4
Project Name:	Multi Mail			
View Name:	By State	View Type:	Display, Columnar Layout	
File Name:	Globals	File Type:	Globals	
Field Name:	select			
Field Type:	Memory	Data Type:	Text	
Justify:	Left			
Initial Text	NY			

Report Name:	View Definition			10/30/87 4:16 PM
				Page 1
Project Name:	Multi Mail			
View Name:	Help Entry	View Type:	Display, Custom Layout	
Root File:	Help Mail	File Type:	dBASE Mac	

Report Name:	View Definition			10/30/87 4:16 PM
				Page 2
Project Name:	Multi Mail			
View Name:	Help Entry	View Type:	Display, Custom Layout	
File Name:	Help Mail	File Type:	dBASE Mac	
Access Path:	Help Mail			
Field Name:	Help ID			
Field Type:	Key, Ordered	Data Type:	Number	Required
Justify:	Right			
Format:	Fixed	Decimal Places:	0	
Decimal:	.	Thousands:		
Negative:	-n	Currency:		
Auto Sequenced By:	1			
Initial Value:	6			
Field Name:	Help Text			
Field Type:	Data	Data Type:	Text	
Contents are:	Single Valued			
Justify:	Left, Wrapped			

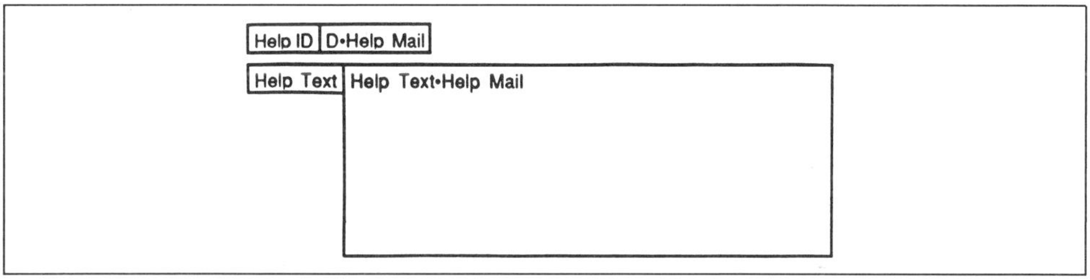

Help ID | D•Help Mail

Help Text | Help Text•Help Mail

Help Entry Layout

Report Name:	View Definition			10/30/87 4:17 PM
				Page 1
Project Name:	Multi Mail			
View Name:	Help	View Type:	Display, Custom Layout	
Root File:	Help Mail	File Type:	dBASE Mac	
File Name:	Globals	File Type:	Globals	

Report Name:	View Definition			10/30/87 4:17 PM
				Page 2
Project Name:	Multi Mail			
View Name:	Help	View Type:	Display, Custom Layout	
File Name:	Help Mail	File Type:	dBASE Mac	

Access Path: Help Mail

Field Name:	Help ID			Modified
Field Type:	Key, Ordered	Data Type:	Number	Required
Justify:	Right			
Format:	Fixed	Decimal Places:	0	
Decimal:	.	Thousands:		
Negative:	-n	Currency:		
Auto Sequenced By:	1			
Initial Value:	6			

View Procedure:

Pre-Processor

```
REPEAT
SETBROWSE({Help ID•Help Mail},{Help Level•Globals})
REDISPLAY({Help Text•Help Mail})
DIALOG 30,50,330,450
 BUTTON 90,260,150,280,240,"Exit"
 BUTTON 10,175,70,195,180,"Next"
 BUTTON 20,175,220,195,330,"Previous"
 BUTTON 50,225,150,245,240,"Help Index"
 FIXEDTEXT 20,150,40,260,"HELP SCREENS..."
 EDITTEXT 1,50,25,150,375,{Help Text•Help Mail}
END
IF BUTTONVALUE(50) THEN
DIALOG 50,50,350,500
 BUTTON 1,225,20,245,130,"OK"
 BUTTON 2,225,170,245,280,"Cancel"
 FIXEDTEXT 20,150,40,260,"HELP INDEX..."
 RADIOLIST 1,1
  RADIOBUTTON 50,10,70,140,"Mail Menu Dialog"
  RADIOBUTTON 75,10,95,120,"View Dialog"
  RADIOBUTTON 100,10,120,120,"All Records"
  RADIOBUTTON 125,10,145,120,"By City"
  RADIOBUTTON 150,10,170,120,"By State"
  RADIOBUTTON 175,10,195,120,"Mail Entry"
 END
END
CASE RADIOVALUE(1) OF
 WHEN 1 DO
  {Help Level•Globals} = 1
 WHEN 2 DO
  {Help Level•Globals} = 2
 WHEN 3 DO
```

Report Name:	View Definition			10/30/87 4:17 PM
				Page 3
Project Name:	Multi Mail			
View Name:	Help	View Type:	Display, Custom Layout	
File Name:	Help Mail	File Type:	dBASE Mac	

```
 {Help Level•Globals} = 3
 WHEN 4 DO
 {Help Level•Globals} = 4
 WHEN 5 DO
 {Help Level•Globals} = 5
 WHEN 6 DO
 {Help Level•Globals} = 6
 END
END
IF BUTTONVALUE(10) THEN
 {Help Level•Globals} = {Help Level•Globals} + 1
END
IF BUTTONVALUE(20) THEN
 {Help Level•Globals} = {Help Level•Globals} - 1
END
UNTIL BUTTONVALUE(90)
END
SETNEXTVIEW(CALLER)
EXIT
```

Field Name:	Help Text		
Field Type:	Data	Data Type:	Text
Contents are:	Single Valued		
Justify:	Left, Wrapped		

Report Name:	View Definition			10/30/87 4:17 PM
				Page 4
Project Name:	Multi Mail			
View Name:	Help	View Type:	Display, Custom Layout	
File Name:	Globals	File Type:	Globals	

Field Name:	Help Level		
Field Type:	Memory	Data Type:	Number
Justify:	Right		
Format:	Fixed	Decimal Places:	0
Decimal:	.	Thousands:	
Negative:	-n	Currency:	
Initial Value:	3		

16

THE CHECKBOOK PROJECT

The Checkbook Project illustrated in this chapter is the same as the project created in the Tutorial. It contains two files—Checkbook and Budget—and several views. If you followed the Tutorial chapters, you should already have this project created. If not, use the project printouts to recreate it. If you have any trouble, check Chapters 4–12 for more information.

Report Name:	File Structure			10/30/87 4:02 PM Page 1
File Name:	Checkbook	File Type:	dBASE Mac	

Field Name:	Transaction Number			
Field Type:	Key, Ordered	Data Type:	Number	Required
Justify:	Right			
Format:	Fixed	Decimal Places:	0	
Decimal:	.	Thousands:		
Negative:	-n	Currency:		
Auto Sequenced By:	1			
Initial Value:	10			

Field Name:	Date		
Field Type:	Data	Data Type:	Date
Contents are:	Single Valued		
Justify:	Left		
Format:	mm/dd/yy		
Year Length:	2	Separator:	/
Range:	1/1/87 To 12/31/87		
Initial Date	1/22/87	Keep New Initial Date	

Field Name:	Type		
Field Type:	Data	Data Type:	Choices
Contents are:	Single Valued		
Justify:	Left		
Format:	Pop-Up		
Values:	Check		
	Bank Charges		
	Miscellaneous		
	Deposit		
	Interest		
	VOID		
Initial Value:	Check	Keep new initial value	

Field Name:	Check Number		
Field Type:	Data	Data Type:	Number
Contents are:	Single Valued		
Justify:	Right		
Format:	Fixed	Decimal Places:	0
Decimal:	.	Thousands:	
Negative:	-n	Currency:	
Initial Value:	1		

Field Name:	Description		
Field Type:	Data	Data Type:	Text
Contents are:	Single Valued		
Justify:	Left		

Field Name:	Check Amount		
Field Type:	Data	Data Type:	Number

Report Name:	File Structure			10/30/87 4:02 PM Page 2
File Name:	Checkbook	File Type:	dBASE Mac	

Contents are:	Single Valued		
Justify:	Right		
Format:	Fixed	Decimal Places:	2
Decimal:	.	Thousands:	
Negative:	-n	Currency:	$
Post To:	Subtract from: Balance•Checkbook		
	Add to: Tot Check•Checkbook		
Field Name:	Deposit Amount		
Field Type:	Data	Data Type:	Number
Contents are:	Single Valued		
Justify:	Right		
Format:	Fixed	Decimal Places:	2
Decimal:	.	Thousands:	
Negative:	-n	Currency:	$
Post To:	Add to: Balance•Checkbook		
	Add to: Tot Dep•Checkbook		
Field Name:	Memo		
Field Type:	Data	Data Type:	Text
Contents are:	Multiple Valued		
Justify:	Left, Wrapped		
Field Name:	Tax		
Field Type:	Data	Data Type:	Logical
Contents are:	Single Valued		
Justify:	Left		
Format:	Check Box		
Values:	Custom		
False Value:	No Tax		
True Value:	Tax		
Initial Value:	No Tax		
Field Name:	Counter		
Field Type:	Memory	Data Type:	Number
Contents are:	Single Valued		
Justify:	Right		
Format:	Fixed	Decimal Places:	0
Decimal:	.	Thousands:	
Negative:	-n	Currency:	
Initial Value:	6		
Field Name:	Balance		
Field Type:	Memory	Data Type:	Number
Contents are:	Single Valued		
Justify:	Right		
Format:	Fixed	Decimal Places:	2

Report Name:	File Structure			10/30/87 4:02 PM
				Page 3
File Name:	Checkbook	File Type:	dBASE Mac	
Decimal:	.	Thousands:		
Negative:	-n	Currency:	$	
Initial Value:	$ 1265.35			
Field Name:	Tot Check			
Field Type:	Memory	Data Type:	Number	
Contents are:	Single Valued			
Justify:	Right			
Format:	Fixed	Decimal Places:	2	
Decimal:	.	Thousands:		
Negative:	-n	Currency:	$	
Initial Value:	$ 1246.97			
Field Name:	Tot Dep			
Field Type:	Memory	Data Type:	Number	
Contents are:	Single Valued			
Justify:	Right			
Format:	Fixed	Decimal Places:	2	
Decimal:	.	Thousands:		
Negative:	-n	Currency:	$	
Initial Value:	$ 2512.32			

Report Name:	View Definition			10/30/87 4:03 PM
				Page 1
Project Name:	Checkbook Project			
View Name:	Checkbook Entry	View Type:	Display, Custom Layout	
Root File:	Checkbook	File Type:	dBASE Mac	
View Procedure:				

Write Record

```
\** Checkbook Entry Write Record procedure **\
IF NOT {Transaction Number•Checkbook} IN "Checkbook" THEN
 IF {Type•Checkbook} = 1 OR {Type•Checkbook} = 6 THEN
  {Counter•Checkbook•Globals} = {Counter•Checkbook•Globals} + 1
END
\** Add the VOID check amount back into the Balance field and subtract it from the Tot
Check field **\
 IF {Type•Checkbook} = 6 THEN
  {Balance•Checkbook•Globals} = {Balance•Checkbook•Globals} + {Check
Amount•Checkbook}
  {Tot Check•Checkbook•Globals} = {Tot Check•Checkbook•Globals} - {Check
Amount•Checkbook}
 END
END
WRITE(SELF)
REDISPLAY({Balance•Checkbook•Globals})
REDISPLAY({Tot Check•Checkbook•Globals})
REDISPLAY({Tot Dep•Checkbook•Globals})
```

Delete Record

```
REDISPLAY({Balance•Checkbook•Globals})
REDISPLAY({Tot Check•Checkbook•Globals})
REDISPLAY({Tot Dep•Checkbook•Globals})
DELETE(SELF)
```

File Name:	Globals	File Type:	Globals

Report Name: View Definition 10/30/87 4:03 PM
Page 2

Project Name: Checkbook Project
View Name: Checkbook Entry View Type: Display, Custom Layout
File Name: Checkbook File Type: dBASE Mac

Access Path: Checkbook

Field Name: Transaction Number
Field Type: Key, Ordered Data Type: Number Required
Justify: Right
Format: Fixed Decimal Places: 0
Decimal: . Thousands:
Negative: -n Currency:
Auto Sequenced By: 1
Initial Value: 10

Field Name: Date
Field Type: Data Data Type: Date
Contents are: Single Valued
Justify: Left
Format: mm/dd/yy
Year Length: 2 Separator: /
Range: 1/1/87 To 12/31/87
Initial Date 1/22/87 Keep New Initial Date

Field Name: Type Modified
Field Type: Data Data Type: Choices
Contents are: Single Valued
Justify: Left
Format: Pop-Up
Values: Check
Bank Charges
Miscellaneous
Deposit
Interest
VOID
Initial Value: Check
View Procedure:
Post-Processor IF {Transaction Number•Checkbook} IN "Checkbook" THEN
ALERT("You can't change a transaction type once it has been entered into a file.",STOP)
ELSE ACCEPT
END

Field Name: Check Number Modified
Field Type: Data Data Type: Number
Contents are: Single Valued
Justify: Right
Format: Fixed Decimal Places: 0
Decimal: . Thousands:

Report Name:	View Definition		10/30/87 4:03 PM Page 3
Project Name:	Checkbook Project		
View Name:	Checkbook Entry	View Type:	Display, Custom Layout
File Name:	Checkbook	File Type:	dBASE Mac

Negative:	-n	Currency:	
Initial Value:	1		
View Procedure:			

Pre-Processor
```
IF {Type•Checkbook} = 1 OR {Type•Checkbook} = 6 THEN
 IF NOT {Transaction Number•Checkbook} IN "Checkbook" THEN
  {Check Number•Checkbook} = {Counter•Checkbook•Globals}
  REDISPLAY({Check Number•Checkbook})
  SETNEXTFIELD({Description•Checkbook})
 END
END
```

Field Name:	Description		
Field Type:	Data	Data Type:	Text
Contents are:	Single Valued		
Justify:	Left		

Field Name:	Check Amount			Modified
Field Type:	Data	Data Type:	Number	
Contents are:	Single Valued			
Justify:	Right			
Format:	Fixed	Decimal Places:	2	
Decimal:	.	Thousands:		
Negative:	-n	Currency:	$	
Post To:	Subtract from: Balance•Checkbook Add to: Tot Check•Checkbook			
View Procedure:				

Post-Processor
```
IF {Transaction Number•Checkbook} IN "Checkbook" THEN
 IF {Type•Checkbook} = 6 THEN
  ALERT("You can't change the value of a VOIDed check.",STOP)
 ELSE
  ACCEPT
 END
ELSE
ACCEPT
END
```

Field Name:	Deposit Amount		
Field Type:	Data	Data Type:	Number
Contents are:	Single Valued		
Justify:	Right		
Format:	Fixed	Decimal Places:	2
Decimal:	.	Thousands:	
Negative:	-n	Currency:	$
Post To:	Add to: Balance•Checkbook		

Report Name:	View Definition			10/30/87 4:03 PM Page 4
Project Name:	Checkbook Project			
View Name:	Checkbook Entry	View Type:	Display, Custom Layout	
File Name:	Checkbook	File Type:	dBASE Mac	
	Add to: Tot Dep•Checkbook			
Field Name:	Memo			
Field Type:	Data	Data Type:	Text	
Contents are:	Multiple Valued			
Justify:	Left, Wrapped			
Field Name:	Tax			
Field Type:	Data	Data Type:	Logical	
Contents are:	Single Valued			
Justify:	Left			
Format:	Check Box			
Values:	Custom			
False Value:	No Tax			
True Value:	Tax			
Initial Value:	No Tax			

Report Name:	View Definition			10/30/87 4:03 PM
				Page 6
Project Name:	Checkbook Project			
View Name:	Checkbook Entry	View Type:	Display, Custom Layout	
File Name:	Checkbook	File Type:	dBASE Mac	

Field Name:	Balance			Modified
Field Type:	Memory	Data Type:	Number	
Contents are:	Single Valued			
Justify:	Right			
Format:	Fixed	Decimal Places:	2	
Decimal:	.	Thousands:		
Negative:	-n	Currency:	$	
View Procedure:				
Pre-Processor	SETNEXTFIELD({Transaction Number•Checkbook})			

Field Name:	Tot Check			Modified
Field Type:	Memory	Data Type:	Number	
Contents are:	Single Valued			
Justify:	Right			
Format:	Fixed	Decimal Places:	2	
Decimal:	.	Thousands:		
Negative:	-n	Currency:	$	
Initial Value:	$ 0.00			
View Procedure:				
Pre-Processor	SETNEXTFIELD({Transaction Number•Checkbook})			

Field Name:	Tot Dep			Modified
Field Type:	Memory	Data Type:	Number	
Contents are:	Single Valued			
Justify:	Right			
Format:	Fixed	Decimal Places:	2	
Decimal:	.	Thousands:		
Negative:	-n	Currency:	$	
Initial Value:	$ 0.00			
View Procedure:				
Pre-Processor	SETNEXTFIELD({Type•Checkbook})			

Field Name:	Counter		
Field Type:	Memory	Data Type:	Number
Contents are:	Single Valued		
Justify:	Right		
Format:	Fixed	Decimal Places:	0
Decimal:	.	Thousands:	
Negative:	-n	Currency:	
Initial Value:	6		

Report Name:	View Definition			10/30/87 4:03 PM
				Page 5
Project Name:	Checkbook Project			
View Name:	Checkbook Entry	View Type:	Display, Custom Layout	
File Name:	Globals	File Type:	Globals	
File Name:	Checkbook	File Type:	dBASE Mac	

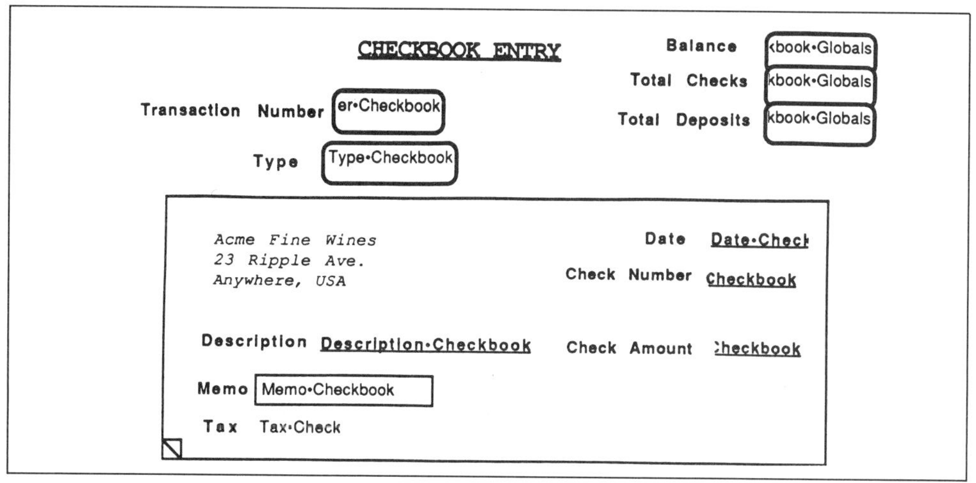
CHECKBOOK ENTRY
Balance
Total Checks
Total Deposits
kbook•Globals
kbook•Globals
kbook•Globals
Transaction Number
er•Checkbook
Type
Type•Checkbook
Acme Fine Wines
23 Ripple Ave.
Anywhere, USA
Date
Date•Check
Check Number
Checkbook
Description
Description•Checkbook
Check Amount
Checkbook
Memo
Memo•Checkbook
Tax
Tax•Check

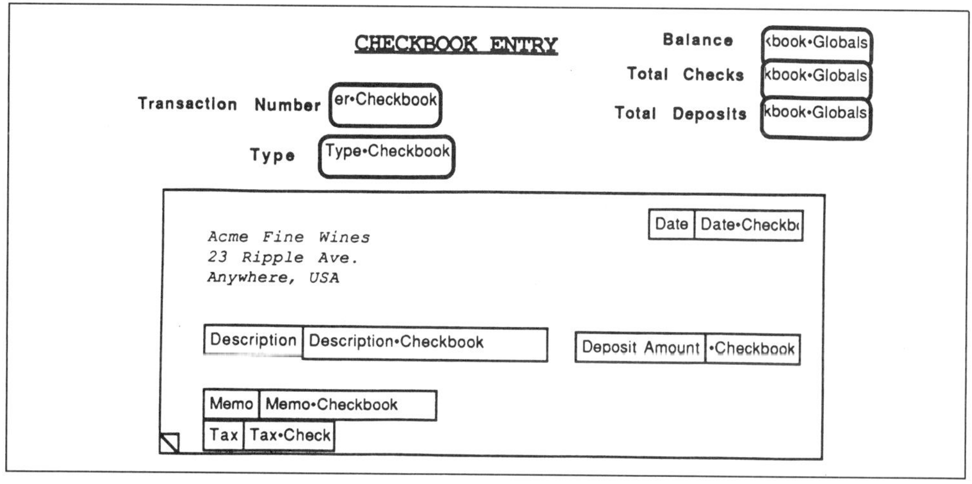
CHECKBOOK ENTRY
Balance
Total Checks
Total Deposits
kbook•Globals
kbook•Globals
kbook•Globals
Transaction Number
er•Checkbook
Type
Type•Checkbook
Acme Fine Wines
23 Ripple Ave.
Anywhere, USA
Date
Date•Checkb
Description
Description•Checkbook
Deposit Amount
•Checkbook
Memo
Memo•Checkbook
Tax
Tax•Check

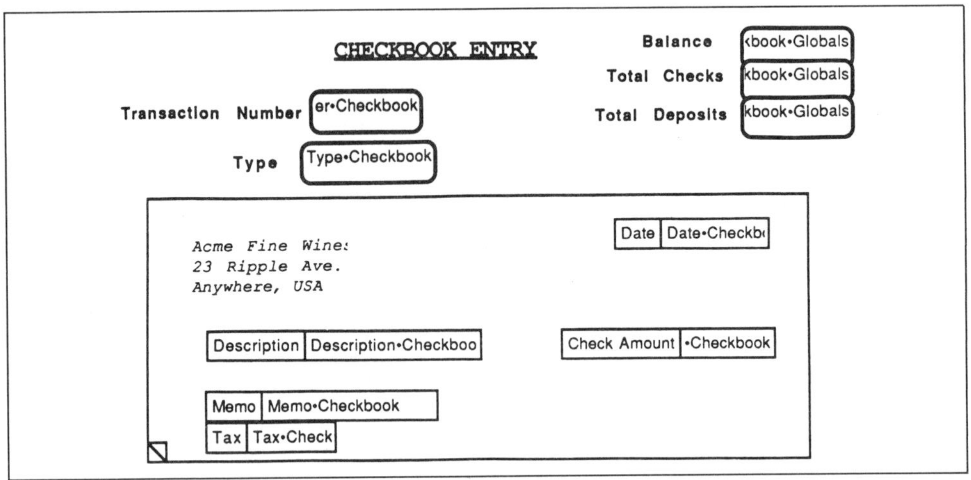

Check Entry Layout

Report Name:	View Definition			10/30/87 4:04 PM
				Page 1
Project Name:	Checkbook Project			
View Name:	Cash Flow	View Type:	Display, Custom Layout	
Root File:	Checkbook	File Type:	dBASE Mac	
Sort By:	Type•Checkbook			Ascending
	Date•Checkbook			Ascending
Show If:	{Type•Checkbook} ≠ 6			

Report Name:	View Definition		10/30/87	4:04 PM
			Page 2	
Project Name:	Checkbook Project			
View Name:	Cash Flow	View Type:	Display, Custom Layout	
File Name:	Checkbook	File Type:	dBASE Mac	

Access Path:	Checkbook			
Field Name:	Transaction Number			
Field Type:	Key, Ordered	Data Type:	Number	Required
Justify:	Right			
Format:	Fixed	Decimal Places:	0	
Decimal:	.	Thousands:		
Negative:	-n	Currency:		
Auto Sequenced By:	1			
Initial Value:	10			
Field Name:	Date			
Field Type:	Data	Data Type:	Date	
Contents are:	Single Valued			
Justify:	Left			
Format:	mm/dd/yy			
Year Length:	2	Separator:	/	
Range:	1/1/87 To 12/31/87			
Initial Date	1/22/87	Keep New Initial Date		
Field Name:	Type			
Field Type:	Data	Data Type:	Choices	
Contents are:	Single Valued			
Justify:	Left			
Format:	Pop-Up			
Values:	Check			
	Bank Charges			
	Miscellaneous			
	Deposit			
	Interest			
	VOID			
Initial Value:	Check	Keep new initial value		
Control Break:	Blank line break			
Field Name:	Check Number			
Field Type:	Data	Data Type:	Number	
Contents are:	Single Valued			
Justify:	Right			
Format:	Fixed	Decimal Places:	0	
Decimal:	.	Thousands:		
Negative:	-n	Currency:		
Initial Value:	1			
Show If:	{Type•Checkbook} = 1			
Field Name:	Description			

Report Name:	View Definition		10/30/87 4:04 PM
			Page 3
Project Name:	Checkbook Project		
View Name:	Cash Flow	View Type:	Display, Custom Layout
File Name:	Checkbook	File Type:	dBASE Mac
Field Type:	Data	Data Type:	Text
Contents are:	Single Valued		
Justify:	Left		Accumulate totals
Field Name:	Check Amount		
Field Type:	Data	Data Type:	Number
Contents are:	Single Valued		
Justify:	Right		
Format:	Fixed	Decimal Places:	2
Decimal:	.	Thousands:	
Negative:	-n	Currency:	$
Post To:	Subtract from: Balance•Checkbook		
	Add to: Tot Check•Checkbook		Accumulate totals
Field Name:	Deposit Amount		
Field Type:	Data	Data Type:	Number
Contents are:	Single Valued		
Justify:	Right		
Format:	Fixed	Decimal Places:	2
Decimal:	.	Thousands:	
Negative:	-n	Currency:	$
Post To:	Add to: Balance•Checkbook		
	Add to: Tot Dep•Checkbook		Accumulate totals
Field Name:	Tax		
Field Type:	Data	Data Type:	Logical
Contents are:	Single Valued		
Justify:	Left		
Format:	Check Box		
Values:	Custom		
False Value:	No Tax		
True Value:	Tax		
Initial Value:	No Tax		

CASH FLOW

#	Date	Type	Check	Desc.	Check Amt.	Deposit Amt	Tax
2	1/1/87	Check	1	Nick's Market	$ 25.66		No T...
3	1/1/87	Check	2	Sam's Paper Supply	$ 34.92		Tax
6	1/15/87	Check	3	Joe Landlord	$ 650.00		No T...
9	1/18/87	Check	4	Auto License	$ 59.39		Tax
10	1/22/87	Check	5	Computer Market	$ 350.00		Tax
				5	$ 1119.97	$ 0.00	
5	1/7/87	Bank Cha...		New Checks	$ 7.00		No T...
				1	$ 7.00	$ 0.00	
7	1/16/87	Miscella...		Bank Machine Withd...	$ 120.00		No T...
				1	$ 120.00	$ 0.00	
1	1/1/87	Deposit		Initial Deposit		$ 1000.00	No T...
8	1/18/87	Deposit		Paycheck		$ 1500.00	Tax
				2	$ 0.00	$ 2500.00	
4	1/5/87	Interest		Interest Payment		$ 12.32	Tax
				1	$ 0.00	$ 12.32	
				10	$ 1246.97	$ 2512.32	

Cash Flow Report

17

THE PERSONNEL PROJECT

Timecard Revisited

The Personnel Project in this chapter is an extension of the Timecard Project from the Tutorial. The Timecard Project contained a very minimal Employee file, an Hourly Rates lookup table, and the Timecard file itself. The Personnel Project adds a main employee file called History to the project. The History file is a complete personnel form in one file. It is quite large, and makes the project work very slowly, but it does represent some interesting features—particularly the History Entry view, which manages to use Tablets to cram a massive amount of data onto a small data entry screen. Other files that could be added include tax tables and calculations, as well as other sources of payments like salaries and commission calculations.

Notice that this is a modification of the original Timecard Project. Therefore, most of the Views remain. Notice also that the Employee Entry view has been replaced by a view called Payroll Summary, and that the History Entry view is new. In the Timecard Project, you entered new employees in the Employees file. That file is no longer the main employee file, and is therefore misnamed. Unfortunately, renaming a dBASE Mac file is very difficult, so we have opted to leave it alone for this example. If you were to create this application from scratch, a different name might be preferable.

The History Entry view is new, and it contains a number of Tablet pages. Several of these pages are linked to selections based on the values of the checkboxes on the first Tablet sheet. The Military Experience sheet has a Selection criterion that reads Show If. . . :

```
{Military?•History}
```

The Explanation of Physical Condition sheet has the Selection that reads Show If. . . :

```
{Physical Condition•History}
```

Finally, the Disposition of Felony Case sheet has the Selection that reads Show If. . . :

```
{Ever Convicted of a Felony?•History}
```

When any of these logical fields are true (because they were checked on the initial Tablet sheet), the associated sheet will display. Otherwise it is not available.

The History Entry view also makes use of several different multivalued field sets on different Tablet sheets. The Education sheet and the Prior Employment sheet are examples.

Report Name:	File Structure			10/30/87 3:35 PM Page 1
File Name:	History File	File Type:	dBASE Mac	
Field Name:	Employee ID			
Field Type:	Key, Ordered	Data Type:	Number	Required
Justify:	Right			
Format:	Fixed	Decimal Places:	0	
Decimal:	.	Thousands:		
Negative:	-n	Currency:		
Field Name:	First Name			
Field Type:	Data	Data Type:	Text	
Contents are:	Single Valued			
Justify:	Left			
Field Name:	Middle Name			
Field Type:	Data	Data Type:	Text	
Contents are:	Single Valued			
Justify:	Left			
Field Name:	Last Name			
Field Type:	Data	Data Type:	Text	
Contents are:	Single Valued			
Justify:	Left			
Relations:	Indexed by Last Name.ind			
Field Name:	Street			
Field Type:	Data	Data Type:	Text	
Contents are:	Single Valued			
Justify:	Left			
Field Name:	City			
Field Type:	Data	Data Type:	Text	
Contents are:	Single Valued			
Justify:	Left			
Field Name:	State			
Field Type:	Data	Data Type:	Text	
Contents are:	Single Valued			
Justify:	Left			
Field Name:	Zip Code			
Field Type:	Data	Data Type:	Text	
Contents are:	Single Valued			
Justify:	Left			
Field Name:	Telephone			
Field Type:	Data	Data Type:	Text	
Contents are:	Single Valued			
Justify:	Left			
Pattern:	~(3n~)~ 3n~-4n 3n~-4n			

Report Name:	File Structure			10/30/87 3:35 PM Page 2
File Name:	History File	File Type:	dBASE Mac	
Field Name:	Birthdate			
Field Type:	Data	Data Type:	Date	
Contents are:	Single Valued			
Justify:	Left			
Format:	mm/dd/yy			
Year Length:	2	Separator:	/	
Field Name:	Physical Condition?			
Field Type:	Data	Data Type:	Logical	
Contents are:	Single Valued			
Justify:	Left			
Format:	Check Box			
Values:	No/Yes			
Initial Value:	No			
Field Name:	Physical Data			
Field Type:	Data	Data Type:	Text	
Contents are:	Single Valued			
Justify:	Left, Wrapped			
Field Name:	Referrals			
Field Type:	Data	Data Type:	Text	
Contents are:	Multiple Valued			
Justify:	Left			
Field Name:	Relatives			
Field Type:	Data	Data Type:	Text	
Contents are:	Multiple Valued	Set Name:	Relations	
Justify:	Left			
Field Name:	Relation to You			
Field Type:	Data	Data Type:	Text	
Contents are:	Multiple Valued	Set Name:	Relations	
Justify:	Left			
Field Name:	Type of Employment			
Field Type:	Data	Data Type:	Choices	
Contents are:	Single Valued			
Justify:	Left			
Format:	Pop-Up			
Values:	Regular Part-Time Summer			
Initial Value:	Regular			
Field Name:	Shift Preferred			
Field Type:	Data	Data Type:	Choices	
Contents are:	Single Valued			

Report Name:	File Structure			10/30/87 3:35 PM Page 3
File Name:	History File	File Type:	dBASE Mac	
Justify:	Left			
Format:	Pop-Up			
Values:	1st			
	2nd			
	3rd			
	No Preference			
Initial Value:	1st			
Field Name:	Salary Desired			
Field Type:	Data	Data Type:	Number	
Contents are:	Single Valued			
Justify:	Right			
Format:	Fixed	Decimal Places:	2	
Decimal:	.	Thousands:		
Negative:	-n	Currency:	$	
Field Name:	Starting Salary			
Field Type:	Data	Data Type:	Number	
Contents are:	Single Valued			
Justify:	Right			
Format:	Fixed	Decimal Places:	2	
Decimal:	.	Thousands:		
Negative:	-n	Currency:	$	
Field Name:	Overtime?			
Field Type:	Data	Data Type:	Logical	
Contents are:	Single Valued			
Justify:	Left			
Format:	Check Box			
Values:	No/Yes			
Initial Value:	No			
Field Name:	Job Preferred			
Field Type:	Data	Data Type:	Text	
Contents are:	Multiple Valued	Set Name:	Jobs	
Justify:	Left			
Field Name:	Skills for Job			
Field Type:	Data	Data Type:	Text	
Contents are:	Multiple Valued	Set Name:	Jobs	
Justify:	Left			
Field Name:	Special Skills			
Field Type:	Data	Data Type:	Text	
Contents are:	Multiple Valued			
Justify:	Left			
Field Name:	Highest Grade Completed			

Report Name:	File Structure			10/30/87 3:35 PM
				Page 4
File Name:	History File	File Type:	dBASE Mac	
Field Type:	Data	Data Type:	Choices	
Contents are:	Single Valued			
Justify:	Left			
Format:	Pop-Up			
Values:	1			
	2			
	3			
	4			
	5			
	6			
	7			
	8			
	9			
	10			
	11			
	12			
	1 College			
	2 College			
	3 College			
	4 College			
	Bachelor's Degree			
	Master's Degree			
	Doctorate			
Initial Value:	1			
Field Name:	Schools Attended			
Field Type:	Data	Data Type:	Text	
Contents are:	Multiple Valued	Set Name:	School	
Justify:	Left			
Field Name:	School Location			
Field Type:	Data	Data Type:	Text	
Contents are:	Multiple Valued	Set Name:	School	
Justify:	Left			
Field Name:	Field of Study			
Field Type:	Data	Data Type:	Text	
Contents are:	Multiple Valued	Set Name:	School	
Justify:	Left			
Field Name:	Level Reached			
Field Type:	Data	Data Type:	Choices	
Contents are:	Multiple Valued	Set Name:	School	
Justify:	Left			
Format:	Pop-Up			
Values:	Graduated			

Report Name:	File Structure			10/30/87 3:35 PM
				Page 5
File Name:	History File	File Type:	dBASE Mac	
	Bachelor			
	Masters			
	Doctorate			
	Did not graduate			
Initial Value:	Graduated			
Field Name:	Military?			
Field Type:	Data	Data Type:	Logical	
Contents are:	Single Valued			
Justify:	Left			
Format:	Check Box			
Values:	No/Yes			
Initial Value:	No			
Field Name:	Military Branch			
Field Type:	Data	Data Type:	Choices	
Contents are:	Single Valued			
Justify:	Left			
Format:	Pop-Up			
Values:	Army			
	Air Force			
	Marines			
	Navy			
	Coast Guard			
	Merchant Marine			
Initial Value:	Army			
Field Name:	Military Start Date			
Field Type:	Data	Data Type:	Date	
Contents are:	Single Valued			
Justify:	Left			
Format:	mm/dd/yy			
Year Length:	2	Separator:	/	
Field Name:	Military Discharge Date			
Field Type:	Data	Data Type:	Date	
Contents are:	Single Valued			
Justify:	Left			
Format:	mm/dd/yy			
Year Length:	2	Separator:	/	
Field Name:	Beginning Rank			
Field Type:	Data	Data Type:	Choices	
Contents are:	Single Valued			
Justify:	Left			
Format:	Pop-Up			
Values:	Private			

Report Name:	File Structure			10/30/87 3:35 PM Page 6
File Name:	History File	File Type:	dBASE Mac	

	Corporal		
	Sergeant		
	Lieutenant		
	Captain		
Initial Value:	Private		
Field Name:	Ending Rank		
Field Type:	Data	Data Type:	Choices
Contents are:	Single Valued		
Justify:	Left		
Format:	Pop-Up		
Values:	Private		
	Corporal		
	Sergeant		
	Captain		
	Lieutenant		
	Captain		
	Colonel		
	General		
	Admiral		
	Dishonorable Discharge		
Initial Value:	Private		
Field Name:	Special Military Training		
Field Type:	Data	Data Type:	Text
Contents are:	Single Valued		
Justify:	Left		
Field Name:	Prior Employers		
Field Type:	Data	Data Type:	Text
Contents are:	Multiple Valued	Set Name:	Prior
Justify:	Left		
Field Name:	Beginning Date		
Field Type:	Data	Data Type:	Date
Contents are:	Multiple Valued	Set Name:	Prior
Justify:	Left		
Format:	mm/dd/yy		
Year Length:	2	Separator:	/
Field Name:	Ending Date		
Field Type:	Data	Data Type:	Date
Contents are:	Multiple Valued	Set Name:	Prior
Justify:	Left		
Format:	mm/dd/yy		
Year Length:	2	Separator:	/
Field Name:	Address		

Report Name:	File Structure			10/30/87 3:35 PM
				Page 7
File Name:	History File	File Type:	dBASE Mac	

Field Type:	Data	Data Type:	Text
Contents are:	Multiple Valued	Set Name:	Prior
Justify:	Left		
Field Name:	City_Emp		
Field Type:	Data	Data Type:	Text
Contents are:	Multiple Valued	Set Name:	Prior
Justify:	Left		
Field Name:	Phone_Emp		
Field Type:	Data	Data Type:	Text
Contents are:	Multiple Valued	Set Name:	Prior
Justify:	Left		
Field Name:	Job Title		
Field Type:	Data	Data Type:	Text
Contents are:	Multiple Valued	Set Name:	Prior
Justify:	Left		
Field Name:	Department		
Field Type:	Data	Data Type:	Text
Contents are:	Multiple Valued	Set Name:	Prior
Justify:	Left		
Field Name:	Supervisor		
Field Type:	Data	Data Type:	Text
Contents are:	Multiple Valued	Set Name:	Prior
Justify:	Left		
Field Name:	Starting Wage		
Field Type:	Data	Data Type:	Number
Contents are:	Multiple Valued	Set Name:	Prior
Justify:	Right		
Format:	Fixed	Decimal Places:	2
Decimal:	.	Thousands:	
Negative:	-n	Currency:	$
Field Name:	Ending Wage		
Field Type:	Data	Data Type:	Number
Contents are:	Multiple Valued	Set Name:	Prior
Justify:	Right		
Format:	Fixed	Decimal Places:	2
Decimal:	.	Thousands:	
Negative:	-n	Currency:	$
Field Name:	Reason for Leaving		
Field Type:	Data	Data Type:	Text
Contents are:	Multiple Valued	Set Name:	Prior
Justify:	Left		

Report Name:	File Structure		10/30/87 3:35 PM
			Page 8
File Name:	History File	File Type:	dBASE Mac
Field Name:	Ever Convicted of Felony?		
Field Type:	Data	Data Type:	Logical
Contents are:	Single Valued		
Justify:	Left		
Format:	Check Box		
Values:	No/Yes		
Initial Value:	No		
Field Name:	Felony Disposition		
Field Type:	Data	Data Type:	Text
Contents are:	Single Valued		
Justify:	Left, Wrapped		
Field Name:	Major Duties		
Field Type:	Data	Data Type:	Text
Contents are:	Multiple Valued	Set Name:	Prior
Justify:	Left		
Field Name:	Employee		
Field Type:	Data	Data Type:	Number
Contents are:	Multiple Valued		
Justify:	Right		
Format:	Fixed	Decimal Places:	0
Decimal:	.	Thousands:	
Negative:	-n	Currency:	
Relations:	Two-way with Employee		

Report Name:	File Structure		10/30/87 3:39 PM
			Page 1
File Name:	Last Name.ind	File Type:	dBASE Mac
Field Name:	Last Name		
Field Type:	Key, Ordered	Data Type:	Text
Justify:	Left		
Field Name:	History File		
Field Type:	Data	Data Type:	Number
Contents are:	Multiple Valued		
Justify:	Right		
Format:	Fixed	Decimal Places:	0
Decimal:	.	Thousands:	
Negative:	-n	Currency:	
Relations:			Auto Delete
	Index to History File		

Report Name:	File Structure			10/30/87 3:40 PM Page 1
File Name:	Employee	File Type:	dBASE Mac	
Field Name:	Employee Number			
Field Type:	Key, Ordered	Data Type:	Number	Required
Justify:	Right			
Format:	Fixed	Decimal Places:	0	
Decimal:	.	Thousands:		
Negative:	-n	Currency:		
Auto Sequenced By:	1			
Initial Value:	7			
Field Name:	Last Name			
Field Type:	Data	Data Type:	Text	
Contents are:	Single Valued			
Justify:	Left			
Field Name:	Amount Paid			
Field Type:	Data	Data Type:	Number	
Contents are:	Single Valued			
Justify:	Right			
Format:	Fixed	Decimal Places:	2	
Decimal:	.	Thousands:		
Negative:	-n	Currency:	$	
Field Name:	Total Earned			
Field Type:	Data	Data Type:	Number	
Contents are:	Single Valued			
Justify:	Right			
Format:	Fixed	Decimal Places:	2	
Decimal:	.	Thousands:		
Negative:	-n	Currency:	$	
Field Name:	Current Due			
Field Type:	Formula	Data Type:	Number	
Contents are:	Single Valued			
Justify:	Right			
Format:	Fixed	Decimal Places:	2	
Decimal:	.	Thousands:		
Negative:	-n	Currency:	$	
Formula:	{Total Earned•Employee} - {Amount Paid•Employee}			
Field Name:	Timecard			
Field Type:	Data	Data Type:	Number	
Contents are:	Multiple Valued			
Justify:	Right			
Format:	Fixed	Decimal Places:	0	
Decimal:	.	Thousands:		
Negative:	-n	Currency:		
Relations:	Two-way with Timecard			

Report Name:	File Structure			10/30/87 3:40 PM
				Page 2
File Name:	Employee	File Type:	dBASE Mac	
Field Name:	History File			
Field Type:	Data	Data Type:	Number	
Contents are:	Multiple Valued			
Justify:	Right			
Format:	Fixed	Decimal Places:	0	
Decimal:	.	Thousands:		
Negative:	-n	Currency:		
Relations:	Two-way with History File			

Report Name:	File Structure			10/30/87 3:42 PM
				Page 1
File Name:	Timecard	File Type:	dBASE Mac	

Field Name:	Timecard Number			
Field Type:	Key, Ordered	Data Type:	Number	Required
Justify:	Right			
Format:	Fixed	Decimal Places:	0	
Decimal:	.	Thousands:		
Negative:	-n	Currency:		
Auto Sequenced By:	1			
Initial Value:	16			

Field Name:	Date		
Field Type:	Data	Data Type:	Date
Contents are:	Single Valued		
Justify:	Left		
Format:	mm/dd/yy		
Year Length:	2	Separator:	/

Field Name:	Time In		
Field Type:	Data	Data Type:	Time
Contents are:	Single Valued		
Justify:	Left		
Format:	hh:mm		
24 Hour Form:	AM/PM		

Field Name:	Time Out		
Field Type:	Data	Data Type:	Time
Contents are:	Single Valued		
Justify:	Left		
Format:	hh:mm		
24 Hour Form:	AM/PM		

Field Name:	Total Hours		
Field Type:	Formula	Data Type:	Number
Contents are:	Single Valued		
Justify:	Right		
Format:	Fixed	Decimal Places:	2
Decimal:	.	Thousands:	
Negative:	-n	Currency:	
Formula:	({Time Out•Timecard} - {Time In•Timecard})/3600		

Field Name:	Posting Amount		
Field Type:	Data	Data Type:	Number
Contents are:	Single Valued		
Justify:	Right		
Format:	Fixed	Decimal Places:	2
Decimal:	.	Thousands:	
Negative:	-n	Currency:	$
Post To:	Add to: Total Earned•Employee		

Report Name:	File Structure			10/30/87 3:42 PM Page 2
File Name:	Timecard	File Type:	dBASE Mac	

Field Name:	Hours		
Field Type:	Data	Data Type:	Number
Contents are:	Single Valued		
Justify:	Right		
Format:	Fixed	Decimal Places:	2
Decimal:	.	Thousands:	
Negative:	-n	Currency:	
Field Name:	Total Timecard		
Field Type:	Formula	Data Type:	Number
Contents are:	Single Valued		
Justify:	Right		
Format:	Fixed	Decimal Places:	2
Decimal:	.	Thousands:	
Negative:	-n	Currency:	$
Formula:	{Total Hours•Timecard} * {Rate•Hourly Rates•Timecard}		
Field Name:	Hourly Rates		
Field Type:	Data	Data Type:	Number
Contents are:	Multiple Valued		
Justify:	Right		
Format:	Fixed	Decimal Places:	0
Decimal:	.	Thousands:	
Negative:	-n	Currency:	
Relations:	One-way with Hourly Rates		
Field Name:	Employee		
Field Type:	Data	Data Type:	Number
Contents are:	Multiple Valued		
Justify:	Right		
Format:	Fixed	Decimal Places:	0
Decimal:	.	Thousands:	
Negative:	-n	Currency:	
Relations:	Two way with Employee		

Report Name:	File Structure			10/30/87 3:43 PM
				Page 1
File Name:	Globals	File Type:	Globals	

Field Name:	Criterion		
Field Type:	Memory	Data Type:	Date
Justify:	Left		
Format:	mm/dd/yy		
Year Length:	2	Separator:	/
Initial Date	1/1/87		

Field Name:	Criterion1		
Field Type:	Memory	Data Type:	Date
Justify:	Left		
Format:	mm/dd/yy		
Year Length:	2	Separator:	/
Initial Date	1/6/87		

Field Name:	Average		
Field Type:	Memory	Data Type:	Number
Justify:	Right		
Format:	Fixed	Decimal Places:	2
Decimal:	.	Thousands:	
Negative:	-n	Currency:	$
Initial Value:	$ 169.14		

Field Name:	Standard Deviation		
Field Type:	Memory	Data Type:	Number
Justify:	Right		
Format:	Fixed	Decimal Places:	2
Decimal:	.	Thousands:	
Negative:	-n	Currency:	$
Initial Value:	$ 49.00		

Field Name:	Maximum		
Field Type:	Memory	Data Type:	Number
Justify:	Right		
Format:	Fixed	Decimal Places:	2
Decimal:	.	Thousands:	
Negative:	-n	Currency:	$
Initial Value:	$ 221.50		

Field Name:	Minimum		
Field Type:	Memory	Data Type:	Number
Justify:	Right		
Format:	Fixed	Decimal Places:	2
Decimal:	.	Thousands:	
Negative:	-n	Currency:	$
Initial Value:	$ 124.38		

Field Name:	Median		
Field Type:	Memory	Data Type:	Number

Report Name:	File Structure			10/30/87 3:43 PM
				Page 2
File Name:	Globals	File Type:	Globals	
Justify:	Right			
Format:	Fixed	Decimal Places:	2	
Decimal:	.	Thousands:		
Negative:	-n	Currency:	$	
Initial Value:	$ 161.55			

Report Name:	File Structure			10/30/87 3:43 PM
				Page 1
File Name:	Hourly Rates	File Type:	dBASE Mac	
Field Name:	Rate ID			
Field Type:	Key, Ordered	Data Type:	Number	Required
Justify:	Right			
Format:	Fixed	Decimal Places:	0	
Decimal:	.	Thousands:		
Negative:	-n	Currency:		
Auto Sequenced By:	1			
Initial Value:	5			
Field Name:	Rate Name			
Field Type:	Data	Data Type:	Text	
Contents are:	Single Valued			
Justify:	Left			
Field Name:	Rate			
Field Type:	Data	Data Type:	Number	
Contents are:	Single Valued			
Justify:	Right			
Format:	Fixed	Decimal Places:	2	
Decimal:	.	Thousands:		
Negative:	-n	Currency:	$	

Report Name:	View Definition			10/30/87 3:44 PM
				Page 1
Project Name:	Personnel			
View Name:	Rates Entry	View Type:	Display, Form Layout	
Root File:	Hourly Rates	File Type:	dBASE Mac	

Report Name:	View Definition			10/30/87	3:44 PM
				Page 2	
Project Name:	Personnel				
View Name:	Rates Entry	View Type:	Display, Form Layout		
File Name:	Hourly Rates	File Type:	dBASE Mac		
Access Path:	Hourly Rates				
Field Name:	Rate ID				
Field Type:	Key, Ordered	Data Type:	Number	Required	
Justify:	Right				
Format:	Fixed	Decimal Places:	0		
Decimal:	.	Thousands:			
Negative:	-n	Currency:			
Auto Sequenced By:	1				
Initial Value:	5				
Field Name:	Rate Name				
Field Type:	Data	Data Type:	Text		
Contents are:	Single Valued				
Justify:	Left				
Field Name:	Rate				
Field Type:	Data	Data Type:	Number		
Contents are:	Single Valued				
Justify:	Right				
Format:	Fixed	Decimal Places:	2		
Decimal:	.	Thousands:			
Negative:	-n	Currency:	$		

Report Name:	View Definition			10/30/87	3:44 PM
				Page 1	
Project Name:	Personnel				
View Name:	Timecard Entry	View Type:	Display, Custom Layout		
Root File:	Timecard	File Type:	dBASE Mac		
View Procedure:					
Write Record	REDISPLAY({Total Hours•Timecard})				
	REDISPLAY({Total Timecard•Timecard})				
	{Hours•Timecard} = {Total Hours•Timecard}				
	{Posting Amount•Timecard} = {Total Timecard•Timecard}				
	WRITE(SELF)				

Report Name:	View Definition		10/30/87	3:44 PM
			Page 2	
Project Name:	Personnel			
View Name:	Timecard Entry	View Type:	Display, Custom Layout	
File Name:	Timecard	File Type:	dBASE Mac	

Access Path:	Timecard			
Field Name:	Timecard Number			
Field Type:	Key, Ordered	Data Type:	Number	Required
Justify:	Right			
Format:	Fixed	Decimal Places:	0	
Decimal:	.	Thousands:		
Negative:	-n	Currency:		
Auto Sequenced By:	1			
Initial Value:	16			
Field Name:	Date			
Field Type:	Data	Data Type:	Date	
Contents are:	Single Valued			
Justify:	Left			
Format:	mm/dd/yy			
Year Length:	2	Separator:	/	
Field Name:	Time In			
Field Type:	Data	Data Type:	Time	
Contents are:	Single Valued			
Justify:	Left			
Format:	hh:mm			
24 Hour Form:	AM/PM			
Field Name:	Time Out			
Field Type:	Data	Data Type:	Time	
Contents are:	Single Valued			
Justify:	Left			
Format:	hh:mm			
24 Hour Form:	AM/PM			
Field Name:	Total Hours			
Field Type:	Formula	Data Type:	Number	
Contents are:	Single Valued			
Justify:	Right			
Format:	Fixed	Decimal Places:	2	
Decimal:	.	Thousands:		
Negative:	-n	Currency:		
Formula:	({Time Out•Timecard} - {Time In•Timecard})/3600			
Field Name:	Posting Amount			
Field Type:	Data	Data Type:	Number	
Contents are:	Single Valued			
Justify:	Right			
Format:	Fixed	Decimal Places:	2	

Report Name:	View Definition		10/30/87 3:44 PM Page 3
Project Name:	Personnel		
View Name:	Timecard Entry	View Type:	Display, Custom Layout
File Name:	Timecard	File Type:	dBASE Mac
Decimal:	.	Thousands:	
Negative:	-n	Currency:	$
Post To:	Add to: Total Earned•Employee		
Field Name:	Hours		
Field Type:	Data	Data Type:	Number
Contents are:	Single Valued		
Justify:	Right		
Format:	Fixed	Decimal Places:	2
Decimal:	.	Thousands:	
Negative:	-n	Currency:	
Field Name:	Total Timecard		
Field Type:	Formula	Data Type:	Number
Contents are:	Single Valued		
Justify:	Right		
Format:	Fixed	Decimal Places:	2
Decimal:	.	Thousands:	
Negative:	-n	Currency:	$
Formula:	{Total Hours•Timecard} * {Rate•Hourly Rates•Timecard}		
Field Name:	Hourly Rates		
Field Type:	Data	Data Type:	Number
Contents are:	Multiple Valued		
Justify:	Right		
Format:	Fixed	Decimal Places:	0
Decimal:	.	Thousands:	
Negative:	-n	Currency:	
Relations:	One-way with Hourly Rates		
Relates File:	Hourly Rates	File Type:	dBASE Mac
Field Name:	Employee		
Field Type:	Data	Data Type:	Number
Contents are:	Multiple Valued		
Justify:	Right		
Format:	Fixed	Decimal Places:	0
Decimal:	.	Thousands:	
Negative:	-n	Currency:	
Relations:	Two-way with Employee		
Relates File:	Employee	File Type:	dBASE Mac

Report Name:	View Definition		10/30/87	3:44 PM
			Page 4	
Project Name:	Personnel			
View Name:	Timecard Entry	View Type:	Display, Custom Layout	
File Name:	Hourly Rates	File Type:	dBASE Mac	
Access Path:	Hourly Rates•Timecard			
Field Name:	Rate ID			
Field Type:	Key, Ordered	Data Type:	Number	Required
Justify:	Right			
Format:	Fixed	Decimal Places:	0	
Decimal:	.	Thousands:		
Negative:	-n	Currency:		
Auto Sequenced By:	1			
Initial Value:	5			
Field Name:	Rate			
Field Type:	Data	Data Type:	Number	
Contents are:	Single Valued			
Justify:	Right			
Format:	Fixed	Decimal Places:	2	
Decimal:	.	Thousands:		
Negative:	-n	Currency:	$	

Report Name:	View Definition		10/30/87	3:44 PM
			Page 5	
Project Name:	Personnel			
View Name:	Timecard Entry	View Type:	Display, Custom Layout	
File Name:	Employee	File Type:	dBASE Mac	
Access Path:	Employee•Timecard			
Field Name:	Employee Number			
Field Type:	Key, Ordered	Data Type:	Number	Required
Justify:	Right			
Format:	Fixed	Decimal Places:	0	
Decimal:	.	Thousands:		
Negative:	-n	Currency:		
Auto Sequenced By:	1			
Initial Value:	7			
Field Name:	History File			
Field Type:	Data	Data Type:	Number	
Contents are:	Multiple Valued			
Justify:	Right			
Format:	Fixed	Decimal Places:	0	
Decimal:	.	Thousands:		
Negative:	-n	Currency:		
Relations:	Two-way with History File			
Relates File:	History File	File Type:	dBASE Mac	

Report Name:	View Definition			10/30/87 3:44 PM
				Page 6
Project Name:	Personnel			
View Name:	Timecard Entry	View Type:	Display, Custom Layout	
File Name:	History File	File Type:	dBASE Mac	
Access Path:	History File•Employee•Timecard			
Field Name:	Last Name			
Field Type:	Data	Data Type:	Text	
Contents are:	Single Valued			
Justify:	Left			
Relations:	Indexed by Last Name.ind			

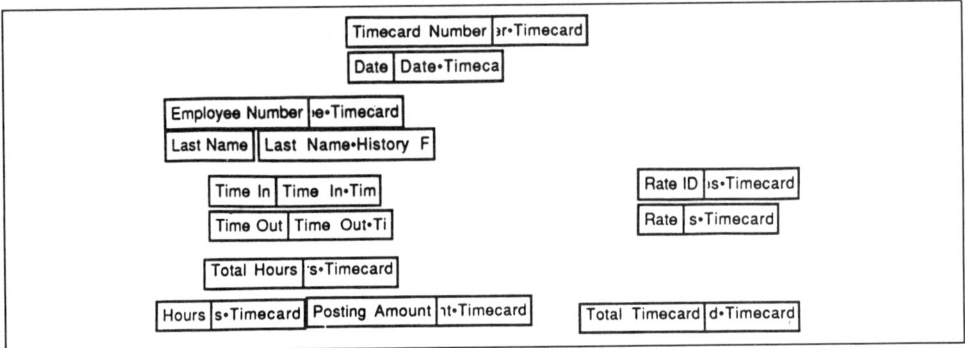

Simple Timecard Layout

Report Name:	View Definition			10/30/87 3:45 PM
				Page 1
Project Name:	Personnel			
View Name:	Timecard Columns	View Type:	Display, Custom Layout	
Root File:	Timecard	File Type:	dBASE Mac	
Sort By:	Date•Timecard			Ascending

Report Name:	View Definition		10/30/87	3:45 PM
			Page 2	
Project Name:	Personnel			
View Name:	Timecard Columns	View Type:	Display, Custom Layout	
File Name:	Timecard	File Type:	dBASE Mac	

Access Path:	Timecard			

Field Name:	Timecard Number			
Field Type:	Key, Ordered	Data Type:	Number	Required
Justify:	Right			
Format:	Fixed	Decimal Places:	0	
Decimal:	.	Thousands:		
Negative:	-n	Currency:		
Auto Sequenced By:	1			
Initial Value:	16			

Field Name:	Date		
Field Type:	Data	Data Type:	Date
Contents are:	Single Valued		
Justify:	Left		
Format:	mm/dd/yy		
Year Length:	2	Separator:	/

Field Name:	Time In		
Field Type:	Data	Data Type:	Time
Contents are:	Single Valued		
Justify:	Left		
Format:	hh:mm		
24 Hour Form:	AM/PM		

Field Name:	Time Out		
Field Type:	Data	Data Type:	Time
Contents are:	Single Valued		
Justify:	Left		
Format:	hh:mm		
24 Hour Form:	AM/PM		

Field Name:	Total Hours		
Field Type:	Formula	Data Type:	Number
Contents are:	Single Valued		
Justify:	Right		
Format:	Fixed	Decimal Places:	2
Decimal:	.	Thousands:	
Negative:	-n	Currency:	
Formula:	({Time Out•Timecard} - {Time In•Timecard})/3600		

Field Name:	Posting Amount			Modified
Field Type:	Data	Data Type:	Number	
Contents are:	Single Valued			
Justify:	Right			
Format:	Fixed	Decimal Places:	2	

Report Name:	View Definition	10/30/87	3:45 PM
		Page 3	
Project Name:	Personnel		
View Name:	Timecard Columns	View Type:	Display, Custom Layout
File Name:	Timecard	File Type:	dBASE Mac
Decimal:	.	Thousands:	
Negative:	-n	Currency:	$
Post To:	Add to: Total Earned•Employee		
View Procedure:			
Pre-Processor	{Posting Amount•Timecard} = {Total Timecard•Timecard}		
	REDISPLAY({Posting Amount•Timecard})		
Field Name:	Hours		
Field Type:	Data	Data Type:	Number
Contents are:	Single Valued		
Justify:	Right		
Format:	Fixed	Decimal Places:	2
Decimal:	.	Thousands:	
Negative:	-n	Currency:	
Field Name:	Total Timecard		
Field Type:	Formula	Data Type:	Number
Contents are:	Single Valued		
Justify:	Right		
Format:	Fixed	Decimal Places:	2
Decimal:	.	Thousands:	
Negative:	-n	Currency:	$
Formula:	{Total Hours•Timecard} * {Rate•Hourly Rates•Timecard}		
Field Name:	Hourly Rates		
Field Type:	Data	Data Type:	Number
Contents are:	Multiple Valued		
Justify:	Right		
Format:	Fixed	Decimal Places:	0
Decimal:	.	Thousands:	
Negative:	-n	Currency:	
Relations:	One-way with Hourly Rates		
Relates File:	Hourly Rates	File Type:	dBASE Mac
Field Name:	Employee		
Field Type:	Data	Data Type:	Number
Contents are:	Multiple Valued		
Justify:	Right		
Format:	Fixed	Decimal Places:	0
Decimal:	.	Thousands:	
Negative:	-n	Currency:	
Relations:	Two-way with Employee		
Relates File:	Employee	File Type:	dBASE Mac
Sort By:	Last Name•Employee		Ascending

Report Name:	View Definition			10/30/87 3:45 PM
				Page 4
Project Name:	Personnel			
View Name:	Timecard Columns	View Type:	Display, Custom Layout	
File Name:	Hourly Rates	File Type:	dBASE Mac	
Access Path:	Hourly Rates•Timecard			
Field Name:	Rate ID			
Field Type:	Key, Ordered	Data Type:	Number	Required
Justify:	Right			
Format:	Fixed	Decimal Places:	0	
Decimal:	.	Thousands:		
Negative:	-n	Currency:		
Auto Sequenced By:	1			
Initial Value:	5			
Field Name:	Rate			
Field Type:	Data	Data Type:	Number	
Contents are:	Single Valued			
Justify:	Right			
Format:	Fixed	Decimal Places:	2	
Decimal:	.	Thousands:		
Negative:	-n	Currency:	$	

Report Name:	View Definition		10/30/87 3:45 PM	
			Page 5	
Project Name:	Personnel			
View Name:	Timecard Columns	View Type:	Display, Custom Layout	
File Name:	Employee	File Type:	dBASE Mac	
Access Path:	Employee•Timecard			
Field Name:	Employee Number			
Field Type:	Key, Ordered	Data Type:	Number	Required
Justify:	Right			
Format:	Fixed	Decimal Places:	0	
Decimal:	.	Thousands:		
Negative:	-n	Currency:		
Auto Sequenced By:	1			
Initial Value:	7			
Field Name:	Last Name			
Field Type:	Data	Data Type:	Text	
Contents are:	Single Valued			
Justify:	Left			

Report Name:	View Definition		10/30/87 3:46 PM	
			Page 1	
Project Name:	Personnel			
View Name:	Employee sort	View Type:	Display, Custom Layout	
Root File:	Employee	File Type:	dBASE Mac	
Sort By:	Last Name•Employee			Ascending
Show If:	{Total Hours•Timecard•Employee} > 8.5 AND {Rate•Hourly Rates•Timecard•Employee} > 5			

Report Name:	View Definition		10/30/87	3:46 PM
			Page 2	
Project Name:	Personnel			
View Name:	Employee sort	View Type:	Display, Custom Layout	
File Name:	Employee	File Type:	dBASE Mac	

Access Path:	Employee			
Field Name:	Employee Number			
Field Type:	Key, Ordered	Data Type:	Number	Required
Justify:	Right			
Format:	Fixed	Decimal Places:	0	
Decimal:	.	Thousands:		
Negative:	-n	Currency:		
Auto Sequenced By:	1			
Initial Value:	7			
Field Name:	Last Name			
Field Type:	Data	Data Type:	Text	
Contents are:	Single Valued			
Justify:	Left			
Field Name:	Timecard			
Field Type:	Data	Data Type:	Number	
Contents are:	Multiple Valued			
Justify:	Right			
Format:	Fixed	Decimal Places:	0	
Decimal:	.	Thousands:		
Negative:	-n	Currency:		
Relations:	Two-way with Timecard			
Relates File:	Timecard	File Type:	dBASE Mac	
Sort By:	Date•Timecard			Ascending
Show If:	{Total Hours•Timecard•Employee} > 8.5 AND {Rate•Hourly Rates•Timecard•Employee} > 5			
Field Name:	History File			
Field Type:	Data	Data Type:	Number	
Contents are:	Multiple Valued			
Justify:	Right			
Format:	Fixed	Decimal Places:	0	
Decimal:	.	Thousands:		
Negative:	-n	Currency:		
Relations:	Two-way with History File			
Relates File:	History File	File Type:	dBASE Mac	

Report Name:	View Definition		10/30/87 3:46 PM	
			Page 3	
Project Name:	Personnel			
View Name:	Employee sort	View Type:	Display, Custom Layout	
File Name:	Timecard	File Type:	dBASE Mac	
Access Path:	Timecard•Employee			
Field Name:	Timecard Number			
Field Type:	Key, Ordered	Data Type:	Number	Required
Justify:	Right			
Format:	Fixed	Decimal Places:	0	
Decimal:	.	Thousands:		
Negative:	-n	Currency:		
Auto Sequenced By:	1			
Initial Value:	16			
Field Name:	Date			
Field Type:	Data	Data Type:	Date	
Contents are:	Single Valued			
Justify:	Left			
Format:	mm/dd/yy			
Year Length:	2	Separator:	/	
Field Name:	Total Hours			
Field Type:	Formula	Data Type:	Number	
Contents are:	Single Valued			
Justify:	Right			
Format:	Fixed	Decimal Places:	2	
Decimal:	.	Thousands:		
Negative:	-n	Currency:		
Formula:	({Time Out•Timecard} - {Time In•Timecard})/3600			
Field Name:	Total Timecard			
Field Type:	Formula	Data Type:	Number	
Contents are:	Single Valued			
Justify:	Right			
Format:	Fixed	Decimal Places:	2	
Decimal:	.	Thousands:		
Negative:	-n	Currency:	$	
Formula:	{Total Hours•Timecard} * {Rate•Hourly Rates•Timecard}			
Field Name:	Hourly Rates			
Field Type:	Data	Data Type:	Number	
Contents are:	Multiple Valued			
Justify:	Right			
Format:	Fixed	Decimal Places:	0	
Decimal:	.	Thousands:		
Negative:	-n	Currency:		
Relations:	One-way with Hourly Rates			
Relates File:	Hourly Rates	File Type:	dBASE Mac	

Report Name:	View Definition			10/30/87 3:46 PM
				Page 4
Project Name:	Personnel			
View Name:	Employee sort	View Type:	Display, Custom Layout	
File Name:	Hourly Rates	File Type:	dBASE Mac	
Access Path:	Hourly Rates•Timecard•Employee			
Field Name:	Rate ID			
Field Type:	Key, Ordered	Data Type:	Number	Required
Justify:	Right			
Format:	Fixed	Decimal Places:	0	
Decimal:	.	Thousands:		
Negative:	-n	Currency:		
Auto Sequenced By:	1			
Initial Value:	5			
Field Name:	Rate			
Field Type:	Data	Data Type:	Number	
Contents are:	Single Valued			
Justify:	Right			
Format:	Fixed	Decimal Places:	2	
Decimal:	.	Thousands:		
Negative:	-n	Currency:	$	

Report Name:	View Definition			10/30/87 3:46 PM
				Page 5
Project Name:	Personnel			
View Name:	Employee sort	View Type:	Display, Custom Layout	
File Name:	History File	File Type:	dBASE Mac	
Access Path:	History File•Employee			
Field Name:	Last Name			
Field Type:	Data	Data Type:	Text	
Contents are:	Single Valued			
Justify:	Left			
Relations:	Indexed by Last Name.ind			

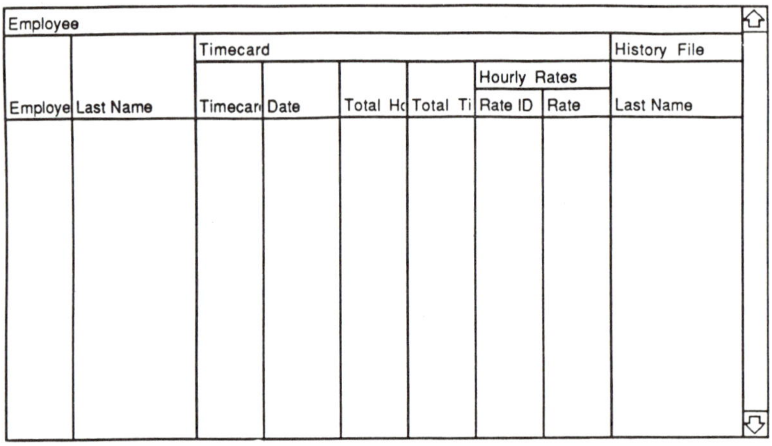

Employee									
		Timecard						History File
						Hourly Rates		
Employe	Last Name	Timecar	Date	Total Hc	Total Ti	Rate ID	Rate	Last Name

Employee Sort Layout

Report Name:	View Definition		10/30/87 3:47 PM Page 1
Project Name:	Personnel		
View Name:	Date Statistics	View Type:	Display, Custom Layout

Procedure:

Post-Processor
```
DIALOG  100,100,250,400
 BUTTON  1,125,20,145,130,"Yes"
 BUTTON  2,125,170,145,280,"No"
 FIXEDTEXT 20,25,40,380,"PRINT REPORT?"
 END
IF BUTTONVALUE(1) THEN
PRINT("Statistics Report")
{Criterion•Globals} = 1
ELSE
EXIT
END
```

Root File:	Date Timecard	File Type:	dBASE Mac
Show If:	{Date Key•Date Timecard} ≥{Criterion•Globals} AND {Date Key•Date Timecard} ≤ {Criterion1•Globals}		

File Name:	Globals	File Type:	Globals

Report Name:	View Definition		10/30/87 3:47 PM
			Page 2
Project Name:	Personnel		
View Name:	Date Statistics	View Type:	Display, Custom Layout
File Name:	Date Timecard	File Type:	dBASE Mac

Access Path:	Date Timecard			
Field Name:	Date Key			
Field Type:	Key, Ordered	Data Type:	Date	Required
Justify:	Left			
Format:	mm/dd/yy			
Year Length:	2	Separator:	/	
Field Name:	Name			
Field Type:	Data	Data Type:	Text	
Contents are:	Multiple Valued	Set Name:	Time	
Justify:	Left			
Field Name:	Total Hours			
Field Type:	Data	Data Type:	Number	
Contents are:	Multiple Valued	Set Name:	Time	
Justify:	Right			
Format:	Fixed	Decimal Places:	0	
Decimal:	.	Thousands:		
Negative:	-n	Currency:		
Field Name:	Total Due			
Field Type:	Data	Data Type:	Number	
Contents are:	Multiple Valued	Set Name:	Time	
Justify:	Right			
Format:	Fixed	Decimal Places:	2	
Decimal:	.	Thousands:		
Negative:	-n	Currency:	$	
Field Name:	Daily Total			
Field Type:	Formula	Data Type:	Number	
Contents are:	Single Valued			
Justify:	Right			
Format:	Fixed	Decimal Places:	2	
Decimal:	.	Thousands:		
Negative:	-n	Currency:	$	
Formula:	SUM({Total Due•Date Timecard})			

Report Name:	View Definition			10/30/87 3:47 PM Page 3
Project Name:	Personnel			
View Name:	Date Statistics	View Type:	Display, Custom Layout	
File Name:	Globals	File Type:	Globals	

Field Name:	Criterion			
Field Type:	Memory	Data Type:	Date	
Justify:	Left			
Format:	mm/dd/yy			
Year Length:	2	Separator:	/	
Initial Date	1/1/87			
Field Name:	Criterion1			
Field Type:	Memory	Data Type:	Date	
Justify:	Left			
Format:	mm/dd/yy			
Year Length:	2	Separator:	/	
Initial Date	1/6/87			
Field Name:	Average			Modified
Field Type:	Memory	Data Type:	Number	
Justify:	Right			
Format:	Fixed	Decimal Places:	2	
Decimal:	.	Thousands:		
Negative:	-n	Currency:	$	
Initial Value:	$ 0.00			
View Procedure:				

Pre-Processor

```
i = 1
LOOP
T[i] = {Daily Total•Date Timecard}
i = i +1
WHEN ENDOF ({Date Timecard})
LEAVE
NEXTBROWSE({Date Key•Date Timecard})
END
{Average•Globals} = AVG(T)
{Standard Deviation•Globals} = STD(T)
{Maximum•Globals} = MAX(T)
{Minimum•Globals} = MIN(T)
{Median•Globals} = MED(T)
```

Field Name:	Standard Deviation		
Field Type:	Memory	Data Type:	Number
Justify:	Right		
Format:	Fixed	Decimal Places:	2
Decimal:	.	Thousands:	
Negative:	-n	Currency:	$
Initial Value:	$ 0.00		

Report Name:	View Definition		10/30/87 3:47 PM
			Page 4
Project Name:	Personnel		
View Name:	Date Statistics	View Type:	Display, Custom Layout
File Name:	Globals	File Type:	Globals

Field Name:	Maximum		
Field Type:	Memory	Data Type:	Number
Justify:	Right		
Format:	Fixed	Decimal Places:	2
Decimal:	.	Thousands:	
Negative:	-n	Currency:	$
Initial Value:	$ 2.00		

Field Name:	Minimum		
Field Type:	Memory	Data Type:	Number
Justify:	Right		
Format:	Fixed	Decimal Places:	2
Decimal:	.	Thousands:	
Negative:	-n	Currency:	$
Initial Value:	$ 2.00		

Field Name:	Median		
Field Type:	Memory	Data Type:	Number
Justify:	Right		
Format:	Fixed	Decimal Places:	2
Decimal:	.	Thousands:	
Negative:	-n	Currency:	$
Initial Value:	$ 0.00		

Report Name:	View Definition		10/30/87 3:48 PM Page 1
Project Name:	Personnel		
View Name:	Do Statistics	View Type:	Display, Custom Layout

Procedure:

Pre-Processor

```
LOOP
ALERT("In the dialog box that follows, please enter the beginning date and the ending date
for the period you wish to examine.",STOP)
LOOP
DIALOG 100,100,350,400
 BUTTON 1,225,20,245,130,"OK"
 BUTTON 2,225,170,245,280,"Cancel"
 FIXEDTEXT 20,25,40,380,"DATE STATISTICS"
 FIXEDTEXT 60,55,75,380,"Enter Beginning Date (mm/dd/yy):"
EDITTEXT 1, 90,55,110,155,""
FIXEDTEXT 120,55,140,380,"Enter Ending Date (mm/dd/yy):"
EDITTEXT 2, 150,55,170,155,""
END
n1 = INTERNAL(TEXTVALUE(1),{Date Key•Date Timecard})
e1 = ERROR
n2 = INTERNAL(TEXTVALUE(2),{Date Key•Date Timecard})
e2 = ERROR
WHEN e2 = 0 AND e1 = 0
LEAVE
ALERT("Invalid date have been entered. Please re-enter.",STOP)
END
WHEN BUTTONVALUE(2) LEAVE
{Criterion•Globals} = n1
{Criterion1•Globals} = n2
PERFORM("Date Statistics",INIT,MODAL)
END
SETNEXTVIEW("Timecard Entry")
EXIT
```

Root File:	Date Timecard	File Type:	dBASE Mac
File Name:	Globals	File Type:	Globals

Report Name:	View Definition			10/30/87 3:48 PM
				Page 2
Project Name:	Personnel			
View Name:	Do Statistics	View Type:	Display, Custom Layout	
File Name:	Date Timecard	File Type:	dBASE Mac	

Access Path:	Date Timecard			
Field Name:	Date Key			
Field Type:	Key, Ordered	Data Type:	Date	Required
Justify:	Left			
Format:	mm/dd/yy			
Year Length:	2	Separator:	/	
Field Name:	Name			
Field Type:	Data	Data Type:	Text	
Contents are:	Multiple Valued	Set Name:	Time	
Justify:	Left			
Field Name:	Total Hours			
Field Type:	Data	Data Type:	Number	
Contents are:	Multiple Valued	Set Name:	Time	
Justify:	Right			
Format:	Fixed	Decimal Places:	0	
Decimal:	.	Thousands:		
Negative:	-n	Currency:		
Field Name:	Total Due			
Field Type:	Data	Data Type:	Number	
Contents are:	Multiple Valued	Set Name:	Time	
Justify:	Right			
Format:	Fixed	Decimal Places:	2	
Decimal:	.	Thousands:		
Negative:	-n	Currency:	$	
Field Name:	Daily Total			
Field Type:	Formula	Data Type:	Number	
Contents are:	Single Valued			
Justify:	Right			
Format:	Fixed	Decimal Places:	2	
Decimal:	.	Thousands:		
Negative:	-n	Currency:	$	
Formula:	SUM({Total Due•Date Timecard})			

Report Name:	View Definition		10/30/87	3:48 PM
			Page 3	
Project Name:	Personnel			
View Name:	Do Statistics	View Type:	Display, Custom Layout	
File Name:	Globals	File Type:	Globals	

Field Name:	Criterion		
Field Type:	Memory	Data Type:	Date
Justify:	Left		
Format:	mm/dd/yy		
Year Length:	2	Separator:	/
Initial Date	1/1/87		

Field Name:	Criterion1		
Field Type:	Memory	Data Type:	Date
Justify:	Left		
Format:	mm/dd/yy		
Year Length:	2	Separator:	/
Initial Date	1/6/87		

Field Name:	Average		
Field Type:	Memory	Data Type:	Number
Justify:	Right		
Format:	Fixed	Decimal Places:	2
Decimal:	.	Thousands:	
Negative:	-n	Currency:	$
Initial Value:	$ 0.00		

Field Name:	Standard Deviation		
Field Type:	Memory	Data Type:	Number
Justify:	Right		
Format:	Fixed	Decimal Places:	2
Decimal:	.	Thousands:	
Negative:	-n	Currency:	$
Initial Value:	$ 0.00		

Field Name:	Minimum		
Field Type:	Memory	Data Type:	Number
Justify:	Right		
Format:	Fixed	Decimal Places:	2
Decimal:	.	Thousands:	
Negative:	-n	Currency:	$
Initial Value:	$ 2.00		

Field Name:	Median		
Field Type:	Memory	Data Type:	Number
Justify:	Right		
Format:	Fixed	Decimal Places:	2
Decimal:	.	Thousands:	
Negative:	-n	Currency:	$
Initial Value:	$ 0.00		

Report Name:	View Definition			10/30/87 3:48 PM
				Page 4
Project Name:	Personnel			
View Name:	Do Statistics	View Type:	Display, Custom Layout	
File Name:	Globals	File Type:	Globals	
Field Name:	Maximum			
Field Type:	Memory	Data Type:	Number	
Justify:	Right			
Format:	Fixed	Decimal Places:	2	
Decimal:	.	Thousands:		
Negative:	-n	Currency:	$	
Initial Value:	$ 2.00			

Report Name:	View Definition			10/30/87 3:48 PM
				Page 1
Project Name:	Personnel			
View Name:	Statistics Report	View Type:	Display, Custom Layout	

Procedure:

Post-Processor
```
DIALOG 100,100,250,400
 BUTTON 1,125,20,145,130,"Yes"
 BUTTON 2,125,170,145,280,"No"
 FIXEDTEXT 20,25,40,380,"PRINT REPORT?"
 END
IF BUTTONVALUE(1) THEN
PRINT("Date Statistics",INIT)
ELSE
EXIT
END
```

Root File:	Date Timecard	File Type:	dBASE Mac
Show If:	{Date Key•Date Timecard} ≥{Criterion•Globals} AND {Date Key•Date Timecard} ≤ {Criterion1•Globals}		
File Name:	Globals	File Type:	Globals

Report Name:	View Definition			10/30/87	3:48 PM
				Page 2	
Project Name:	Personnel				
View Name:	Statistics Report	View Type:	Display, Custom Layout		
File Name:	Date Timecard	File Type:	dBASE Mac		
Access Path:	Date Timecard				
Field Name:	Date Key				
Field Type:	Key, Ordered	Data Type:	Date	Required	
Justify:	Left				
Format:	mm/dd/yy				
Year Length:	2	Separator:	/		
Field Name:	Name				
Field Type:	Data	Data Type:	Text		
Contents are:	Multiple Valued	Set Name:	Time		
Justify:	Left				
Field Name:	Total Hours				
Field Type:	Data	Data Type:	Number		
Contents are:	Multiple Valued	Set Name:	Time		
Justify:	Right				
Format:	Fixed	Decimal Places:	0		
Decimal:	.	Thousands:			
Negative:	-n	Currency:			
Field Name:	Total Due				
Field Type:	Data	Data Type:	Number		
Contents are:	Multiple Valued	Set Name:	Time		
Justify:	Right				
Format:	Fixed	Decimal Places:	2		
Decimal:	.	Thousands:			
Negative:	-n	Currency:	$		
Field Name:	Daily Total				
Field Type:	Formula	Data Type:	Number		
Contents are:	Single Valued				
Justify:	Right				
Format:	Fixed	Decimal Places:	2		
Decimal:	.	Thousands:			
Negative:	-n	Currency:	$		
Formula:	SUM({Total Due•Date Timecard})				

Report Name: View Definition 10/30/87 3:48 PM
Page 3

Project Name: Personnel
View Name: Statistics Report View Type: Display, Custom Layout
File Name: Globals File Type: Globals

Field Name: Criterion
Field Type: Memory Data Type: Date
Justify: Left
Format: mm/dd/yy
Year Length: 2 Separator: /
Initial Date 1/1/87

Field Name: Criterion1
Field Type: Memory Data Type: Date
Justify: Left
Format: mm/dd/yy
Year Length: 2 Separator: /
Initial Date 1/6/87

Field Name: Average Modified
Field Type: Memory Data Type: Number
Justify: Right
Format: Fixed Decimal Places: 2
Decimal: . Thousands:
Negative: -n Currency: $
Initial Value: $ 0.00
View Procedure:
Pre-Processor

```
i = 1
T = 0
REPEAT
T[i] = {Daily Total•Date Timecard}
NEXTBROWSE({Date Key•Date Timecard})
i = i +1
UNTIL ENDOF ({Date Timecard})
END
{Average•Globals} = AVG(T)
{Standard Deviation•Globals} = STD(T)
{Maximum•Globals} = MAX(T)
{Minimum•Globals} = MIN(T)
{Median•Globals} = MED(T)
```

Field Name: Standard Deviation
Field Type: Memory Data Type: Number
Justify: Right
Format: Fixed Decimal Places: 2
Decimal: . Thousands:
Negative: -n Currency: $
Initial Value: $ 0.00

Report Name:	View Definition			10/30/87 3:48 PM Page 4
Project Name:	Personnel			
View Name:	Statistics Report	View Type:	Display, Custom Layout	
File Name:	Globals	File Type:	Globals	
Field Name:	Maximum			
Field Type:	Memory	Data Type:	Number	
Justify:	Right			
Format:	Fixed	Decimal Places:	2	
Decimal:	.	Thousands:		
Negative:	-n	Currency:	$	
Initial Value:	$ 2.00			
Field Name:	Minimum			
Field Type:	Memory	Data Type:	Number	
Justify:	Right			
Format:	Fixed	Decimal Places:	2	
Decimal:	.	Thousands:		
Negative:	-n	Currency:	$	
Initial Value:	$ 2.00			
Field Name:	Median			
Field Type:	Memory	Data Type:	Number	
Justify:	Right			
Format:	Fixed	Decimal Places:	2	
Decimal:	.	Thousands:		
Negative:	-n	Currency:	$	
Initial Value:	$ 0.00			

Report Name:	View Definition			10/30/87 3:49 PM Page 1
Project Name:	Personnel			
View Name:	History Entry	View Type:	Display, Custom Layout	
Root File:	History File	File Type:	dBASE Mac	

Report Name:	View Definition		10/30/87 3:49 PM	
			Page 2	
Project Name:	Personnel			
View Name:	History Entry	View Type:	Display, Custom Layout	
File Name:	History File	File Type:	dBASE Mac	
Access Path:	History File			
Field Name:	Employee ID			
Field Type:	Key, Ordered	Data Type:	Number	Required
Justify:	Right			
Format:	Fixed	Decimal Places:	0	
Decimal:	.	Thousands:		
Negative:	-n	Currency:		
Field Name:	First Name			
Field Type:	Data	Data Type:	Text	
Contents are:	Single Valued			
Justify:	Left			
Field Name:	Middle Name			
Field Type:	Data	Data Type:	Text	
Contents are:	Single Valued			
Justify:	Left			
Field Name:	Last Name			
Field Type:	Data	Data Type:	Text	
Contents are:	Single Valued			
Justify:	Left			
Relations:	Indexed by Last Name.ind			
Field Name:	Street			
Field Type:	Data	Data Type:	Text	
Contents are:	Single Valued			
Justify:	Left			
Field Name:	City			
Field Type:	Data	Data Type:	Text	
Contents are:	Single Valued			
Justify:	Left			
Field Name:	State			
Field Type:	Data	Data Type:	Text	
Contents are:	Single Valued			
Justify:	Left			
Field Name:	Zip Code			
Field Type:	Data	Data Type:	Text	
Contents are:	Single Valued			
Justify:	Left			
Field Name:	Telephone			
Field Type:	Data	Data Type:	Text	
Contents are:	Single Valued			

Report Name:	View Definition	10/30/87 3:49 PM	
		Page 3	
Project Name:	Personnel		
View Name:	History Entry	View Type:	Display, Custom Layout
File Name:	History File	File Type:	dBASE Mac

Justify:	Left		
Pattern:	~(3n~)~ 3n~-4n		
	3n~-4n		
Field Name:	Birthdate		
Field Type:	Data	Data Type:	Date
Contents are:	Single Valued		
Justify:	Left		
Format:	mm/dd/yy		
Year Length:	2	Separator:	/
Field Name:	Physical Condition?		
Field Type:	Data	Data Type:	Logical
Contents are:	Single Valued		
Justify:	Left		
Format:	Check Box		
Values:	No/Yes		
Initial Value:	No		
Field Name:	Physical Data		
Field Type:	Data	Data Type:	Text
Contents are:	Single Valued		
Justify:	Left, Wrapped		
Field Name:	Referrals		
Field Type:	Data	Data Type:	Text
Contents are:	Multiple Valued		
Justify:	Left		
Field Name:	Relatives		
Field Type:	Data	Data Type:	Text
Contents are:	Multiple Valued	Set Name:	Relations
Justify:	Left		
Field Name:	Relation to You		
Field Type:	Data	Data Type:	Text
Contents are:	Multiple Valued	Set Name:	Relations
Justify:	Left		
Field Name:	Type of Employment		
Field Type:	Data	Data Type:	Choices
Contents are:	Single Valued		
Justify:	Left		
Format:	Pop-Up		
Values:	Regular		
	Part-Time		

Report Name:	View Definition	10/30/87	3:49 PM
		Page 4	
Project Name:	Personnel		
View Name:	History Entry	View Type:	Display, Custom Layout
File Name:	History File	File Type:	dBASE Mac

	Summer		
Initial Value:	Regular		
Field Name:	Shift Preferred		
Field Type:	Data	Data Type:	Choices
Contents are:	Single Valued		
Justify:	Left		
Format:	Pop-Up		
Values:	1st		
	2nd		
	3rd		
	No Preference		
Initial Value:	1st		
Field Name:	Salary Desired		
Field Type:	Data	Data Type:	Number
Contents are:	Single Valued		
Justify:	Right		
Format:	Fixed	Decimal Places:	2
Decimal:	.	Thousands:	
Negative:	-n	Currency:	$
Field Name:	Starting Salary		
Field Type:	Data	Data Type:	Number
Contents are:	Single Valued		
Justify:	Right		
Format:	Fixed	Decimal Places:	2
Decimal:	.	Thousands:	
Negative:	-n	Currency:	$
Field Name:	Overtime?		
Field Type:	Data	Data Type:	Logical
Contents are:	Single Valued		
Justify:	Left		
Format:	Check Box		
Values:	No/Yes		
Initial Value:	No		
Field Name:	Job Preferred		
Field Type:	Data	Data Type:	Text
Contents are:	Multiple Valued	Set Name:	Jobs
Justify:	Left		
Field Name:	Skills for Job		
Field Type:	Data	Data Type:	Text
Contents are:	Multiple Valued	Set Name:	Jobs

Report Name:	View Definition		10/30/87 3:49 PM Page 5
Project Name:	Personnel		
View Name:	History Entry	View Type:	Display, Custom Layout
File Name:	History File	File Type:	dBASE Mac
Justify:	Left		
Field Name:	Special Skills		
Field Type:	Data	Data Type:	Text
Contents are:	Multiple Valued		
Justify:	Left		
Field Name:	Highest Grade Completed		
Field Type:	Data	Data Type:	Choices
Contents are:	Single Valued		
Justify:	Left		
Format:	Pop-Up		
Values:	1		
	2		
	3		
	4		
	5		
	6		
	7		
	8		
	9		
	10		
	11		
	12		
	1 College		
	2 College		
	3 College		
	4 College		
	Bachelor's Degree		
	Master's Degree		
	Doctorate		
Initial Value:	1		
Field Name:	Schools Attended		
Field Type:	Data	Data Type:	Text
Contents are:	Multiple Valued	Set Name:	School
Justify:	Left		
Field Name:	School Location		
Field Type:	Data	Data Type:	Text
Contents are:	Multiple Valued	Set Name:	School
Justify:	Left		
Field Name:	Field of Study		
Field Type:	Data	Data Type:	Text

Report Name:	View Definition		10/30/87 3:49 PM
			Page 6
Project Name:	Personnel		
View Name:	History Entry	View Type:	Display, Custom Layout
File Name:	History File	File Type:	dBASE Mac

Contents are:	Multiple Valued	Set Name:	School
Justify:	Left		

Field Name:	Level Reached		
Field Type:	Data	Data Type:	Choices
Contents are:	Multiple Valued	Set Name:	School
Justify:	Left		
Format:	Pop-Up		
Values:	Graduated		
	Bachelor		
	Masters		
	Doctorate		
	Did not graduate		
Initial Value:	Graduated		

Field Name:	Military?		
Field Type:	Data	Data Type:	Logical
Contents are:	Single Valued		
Justify:	Left		
Format:	Check Box		
Values:	No/Yes		
Initial Value:	No		

Field Name:	Military Branch		
Field Type:	Data	Data Type:	Choices
Contents are:	Single Valued		
Justify:	Left		
Format:	Pop-Up		
Values:	Army		
	Air Force		
	Marines		
	Navy		
	Coast Guard		
	Merchant Marine		
Initial Value:	Army		

Field Name:	Military Start Date		
Field Type:	Data	Data Type:	Date
Contents are:	Single Valued		
Justify:	Left		
Format:	mm/dd/yy		
Year Length:	2	Separator:	/

Field Name:	Military Discharge Date		
Field Type:	Data	Data Type:	Date

Report Name:	View Definition	10/30/87	3:49 PM
		Page 7	
Project Name:	Personnel		
View Name:	History Entry	View Type:	Display, Custom Layout
File Name:	History File	File Type:	dBASE Mac

Contents are:	Single Valued		
Justify:	Left		
Format:	mm/dd/yy		
Year Length:	2	Separator:	/

Field Name:	Beginning Rank		
Field Type:	Data	Data Type:	Choices
Contents are:	Single Valued		
Justify:	Left		
Format:	Pop-Up		
Values:	Private		
	Corporal		
	Sergeant		
	Lieutenant		
	Captain		
Initial Value:	Private		

Field Name:	Ending Rank		
Field Type:	Data	Data Type:	Choices
Contents are:	Single Valued		
Justify:	Left		
Format:	Pop-Up		
Values:	Private		
	Corporal		
	Sergeant		
	Captain		
	Lieutenant		
	Captain		
	Colonel		
	General		
	Admiral		
	Dishonorable Discharge		
Initial Value:	Private		

Field Name:	Special Military Training		
Field Type:	Data	Data Type:	Text
Contents are:	Single Valued		
Justify:	Left		

Field Name:	Prior Employers		
Field Type:	Data	Data Type:	Text
Contents are:	Multiple Valued	Set Name:	Prior
Justify:	Left		

Field Name:	Beginning Date

Report Name:	View Definition		10/30/87 3:49 PM Page 8
Project Name:	Personnel		
View Name:	History Entry	View Type:	Display, Custom Layout
File Name:	History File	File Type:	dBASE Mac

Field Type:	Data	Data Type:	Date
Contents are:	Multiple Valued	Set Name:	Prior
Justify:	Left		
Format:	mm/dd/yy		
Year Length:	2	Separator:	/
Field Name:	Ending Date		
Field Type:	Data	Data Type:	Date
Contents are:	Multiple Valued	Set Name:	Prior
Justify:	Left		
Format:	mm/dd/yy		
Year Length:	2	Separator:	/
Field Name:	Address		
Field Type:	Data	Data Type:	Text
Contents are:	Multiple Valued	Set Name:	Prior
Justify:	Left		
Field Name:	City_Emp		
Field Type:	Data	Data Type:	Text
Contents are:	Multiple Valued	Set Name:	Prior
Justify:	Left		
Field Name:	Phone_Emp		
Field Type:	Data	Data Type:	Text
Contents are:	Multiple Valued	Set Name:	Prior
Justify:	Left		
Field Name:	Job Title		
Field Type:	Data	Data Type:	Text
Contents are:	Multiple Valued	Set Name:	Prior
Justify:	Left		
Field Name:	Department		
Field Type:	Data	Data Type:	Text
Contents are:	Multiple Valued	Set Name:	Prior
Justify:	Left		
Field Name:	Supervisor		
Field Type:	Data	Data Type:	Text
Contents are:	Multiple Valued	Set Name:	Prior
Justify:	Left		
Field Name:	Starting Wage		
Field Type:	Data	Data Type:	Number
Contents are:	Multiple Valued	Set Name:	Prior
Justify:	Right		

Report Name:	View Definition	10/30/87	3:49 PM
		Page 9	
Project Name:	Personnel		
View Name:	History Entry	View Type:	Display, Custom Layout
File Name:	History File	File Type:	dBASE Mac
Format:	Fixed	Decimal Places:	2
Decimal:	.	Thousands:	
Negative:	-n	Currency:	$
Field Name:	Ending Wage		
Field Type:	Data	Data Type:	Number
Contents are:	Multiple Valued	Set Name:	Prior
Justify:	Right		
Format:	Fixed	Decimal Places:	2
Decimal:	.	Thousands:	
Negative:	-n	Currency:	$
Field Name:	Reason for Leaving		
Field Type:	Data	Data Type:	Text
Contents are:	Multiple Valued	Set Name:	Prior
Justify:	Left		
Field Name:	Major Duties		
Field Type:	Data	Data Type:	Text
Contents are:	Multiple Valued	Set Name:	Prior
Justify:	Left		
Field Name:	Ever Convicted of Felony?		
Field Type:	Data	Data Type:	Logical
Contents are:	Single Valued		
Justify:	Left		
Format:	Check Box		
Values:	No/Yes		
Initial Value:	No		
Field Name:	Felony Disposition		
Field Type:	Data	Data Type:	Text
Contents are:	Single Valued		
Justify:	Left, Wrapped		

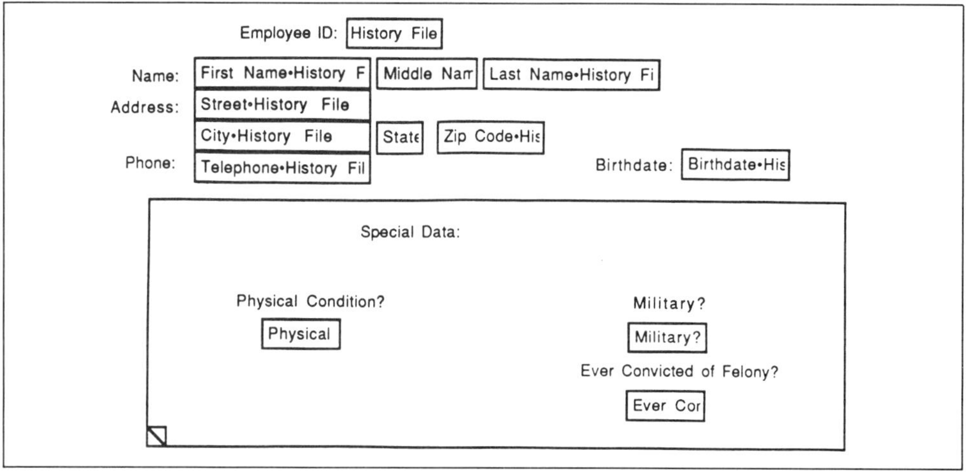

History Entry Number 1

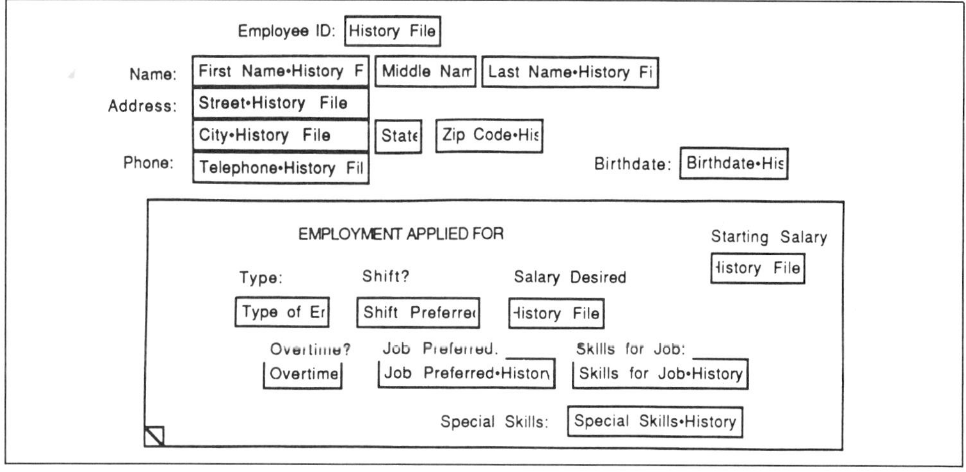

History Entry Number 2

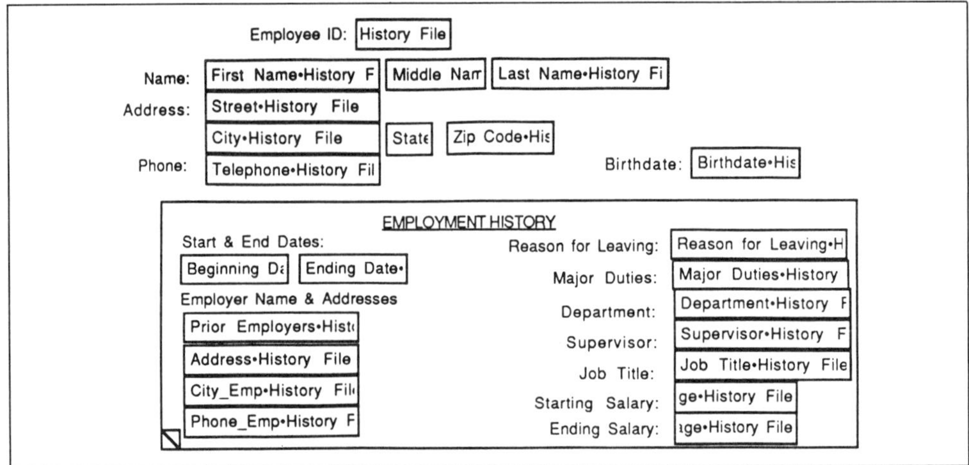

History Entry Number 3

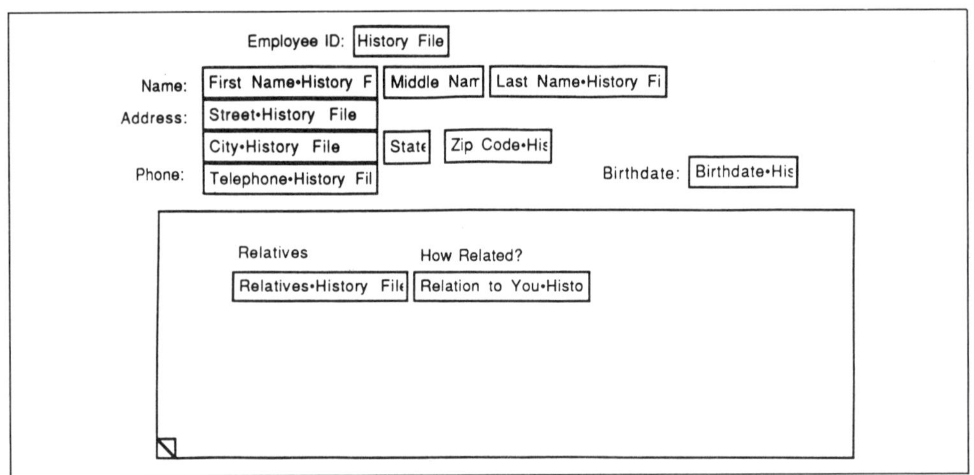

History Entry Number 4

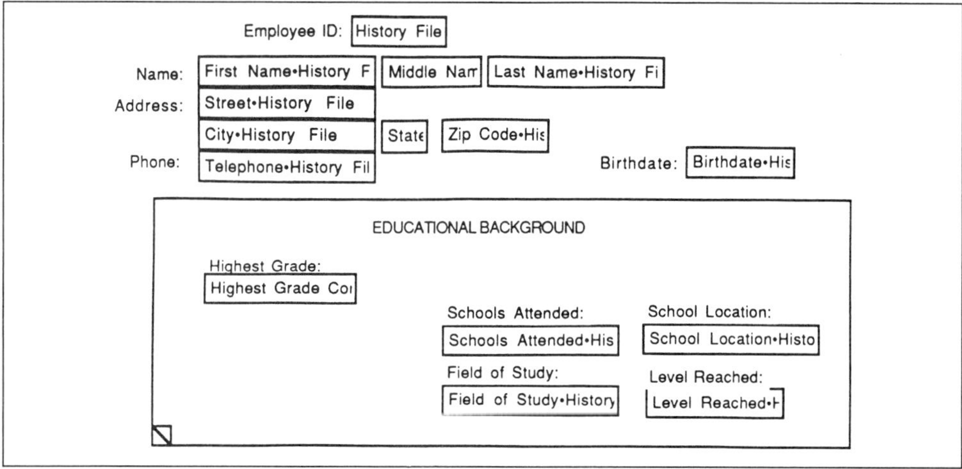

History Entry Number 5

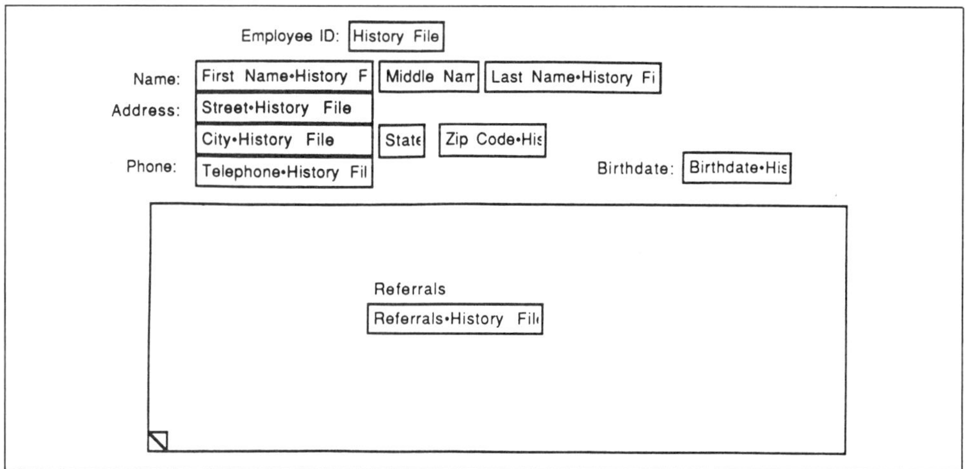

History Entry Number 6

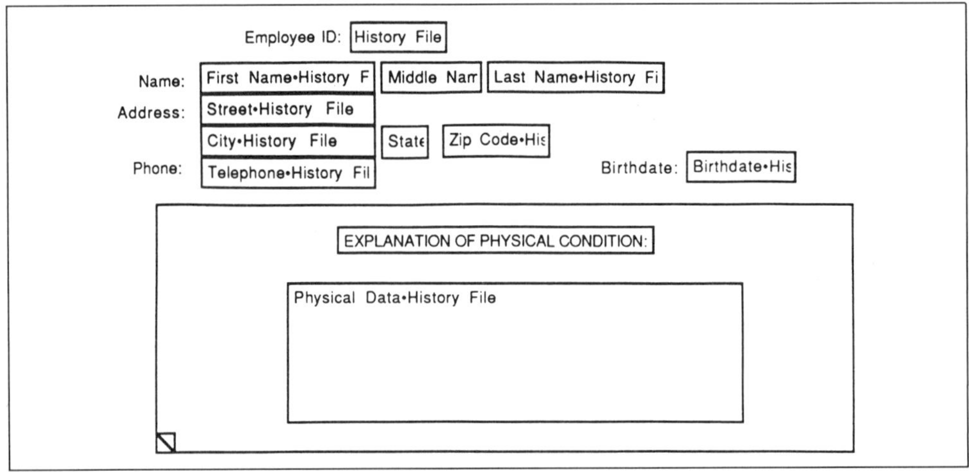

History Entry Number 7

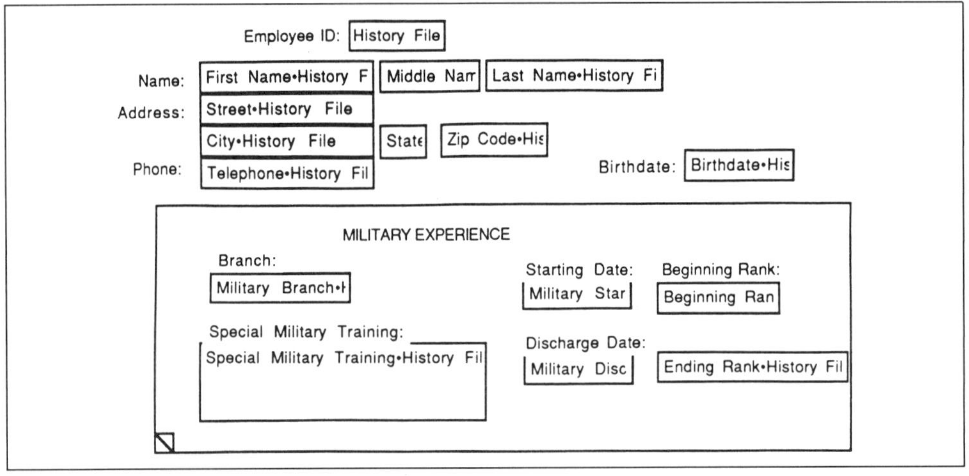

History Entry Number 8

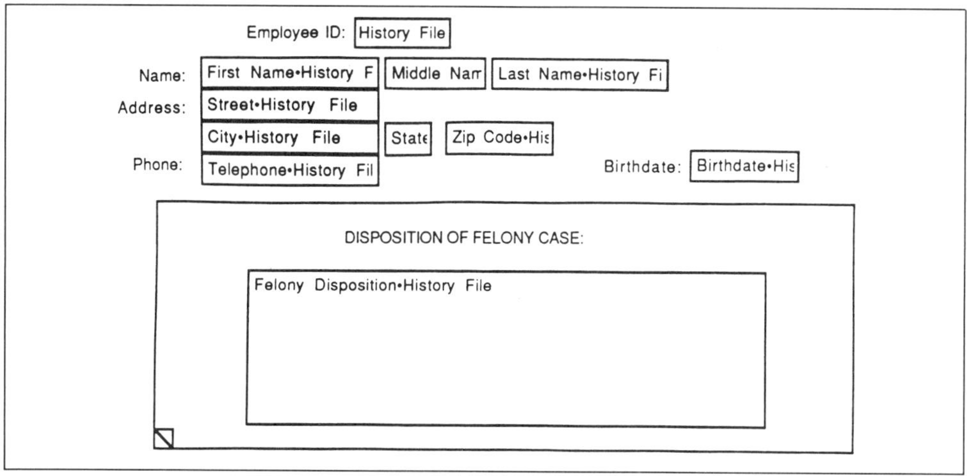

History Entry Number 9

Report Name:	View Definition		10/30/87 3:50 PM Page 1
Project Name:	Personnel		
View Name:	Payroll Summary	View Type:	Display, Custom Layout

Description:	Payroll Summary

Root File:	History File	File Type:	dBASE Mac
View Procedure:			
New Record	ALERT("You can't enter new employee records here. To enter a new employee into the system, Use the Enter History view.") SETNEXTFIELD({Employee ID•History File})		

Report Name:	View Definition		10/30/87	3:50 PM
			Page 2	
Project Name:	Personnel			
View Name:	Payroll Summary	View Type:	Display, Custom Layout	
File Name:	History File	File Type:	dBASE Mac	
Access Path:	History File			
Field Name:	Employee ID			
Field Type:	Key, Ordered	Data Type:	Number	Required
Justify:	Right			
Format:	Fixed	Decimal Places:	0	
Decimal:	.	Thousands:		
Negative:	-n	Currency:		
Field Name:	Last Name			
Field Type:	Data	Data Type:	Text	
Contents are:	Single Valued			
Justify:	Left			
Relations:	Indexed by Last Name.ind			
Field Name:	Employee			
Field Type:	Data	Data Type:	Number	
Contents are:	Multiple Valued			
Justify:	Right			
Format:	Fixed	Decimal Places:	0	
Decimal:	.	Thousands:		
Negative:	-n	Currency:		
Relations:	Two-way with Employee			
Relates File:	Employee	File Type:	dBASE Mac	

Report Name:	View Definition			10/30/87 3:50 PM
				Page 3
Project Name:	Personnel			
View Name:	Payroll Summary	View Type:	Display, Custom Layout	
File Name:	Employee	File Type:	dBASE Mac	

Access Path:	Employee•History File		
Field Name:	Amount Paid		
Field Type:	Data	Data Type:	Number
Contents are:	Single Valued		
Justify:	Right		
Format:	Fixed	Decimal Places:	2
Decimal:	.	Thousands:	
Negative:	-n	Currency:	$
Field Name:	Total Earned		
Field Typo:	Data	Data Type:	Number
Contents are:	Single Valued		
Justify:	Right		
Format:	Fixed	Decimal Places:	2
Decimal:	.	Thousands:	
Negative:	-n	Currency:	$
Field Name:	Current Due		
Field Type:	Formula	Data Type:	Number
Contents are:	Single Valued		
Justify:	Right		
Format:	Fixed	Decimal Places:	2
Decimal:	.	Thousands:	
Negative:	-n	Currency:	$
Formula:	{Total Earned•Employee} - {Amount Paid•Employee}		
Field Name:	Timecard		
Field Type:	Data	Data Type:	Number
Contents are:	Multiple Valued		
Justify:	Right		
Format:	Fixed	Decimal Places:	0
Decimal:	.	Thousands:	
Negative:	-n	Currency:	
Relations:	Two-way with Timecard		

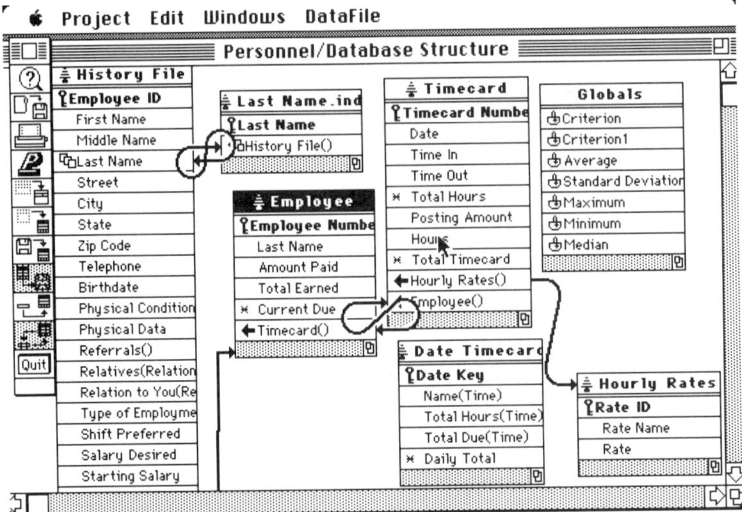

Figure 17-1 Structure Window for Payroll.

18

FREELANCE

The Tickler

Every freelance writer who gets busy eventually has to perform the same juggling act. Keeping track of assignments can be difficult. You must know who they are for, how long they are, when they are due, and what they are about. You must know how much you will be paid, and you must keep track of assignments in progress. When an assignment is complete, you need to note that, and then when it actually prints, you want to note the print date and issue number.

The Freelance project is one I wrote for myself. It is simple. No fancy views or special effects. It does a utilitarian job, and it does it well. I can see at a glance, through various views, what I have going, and in what state each assignment currently exists.

I can also track payments, and can, at a glance, tell what is still unpaid.

As you'll see, in this application there are several related files. One for each magazine or publisher, one for software vendors (since I write about computer software most of the time), one for software products, and one for the freelance job itself. All the views are either basic Form layouts or slightly modified Column views.

The Freelance project is specific to writers, but it may suggest a use in other fields, too. Feel free to tinker with it to produce something useful in other areas.

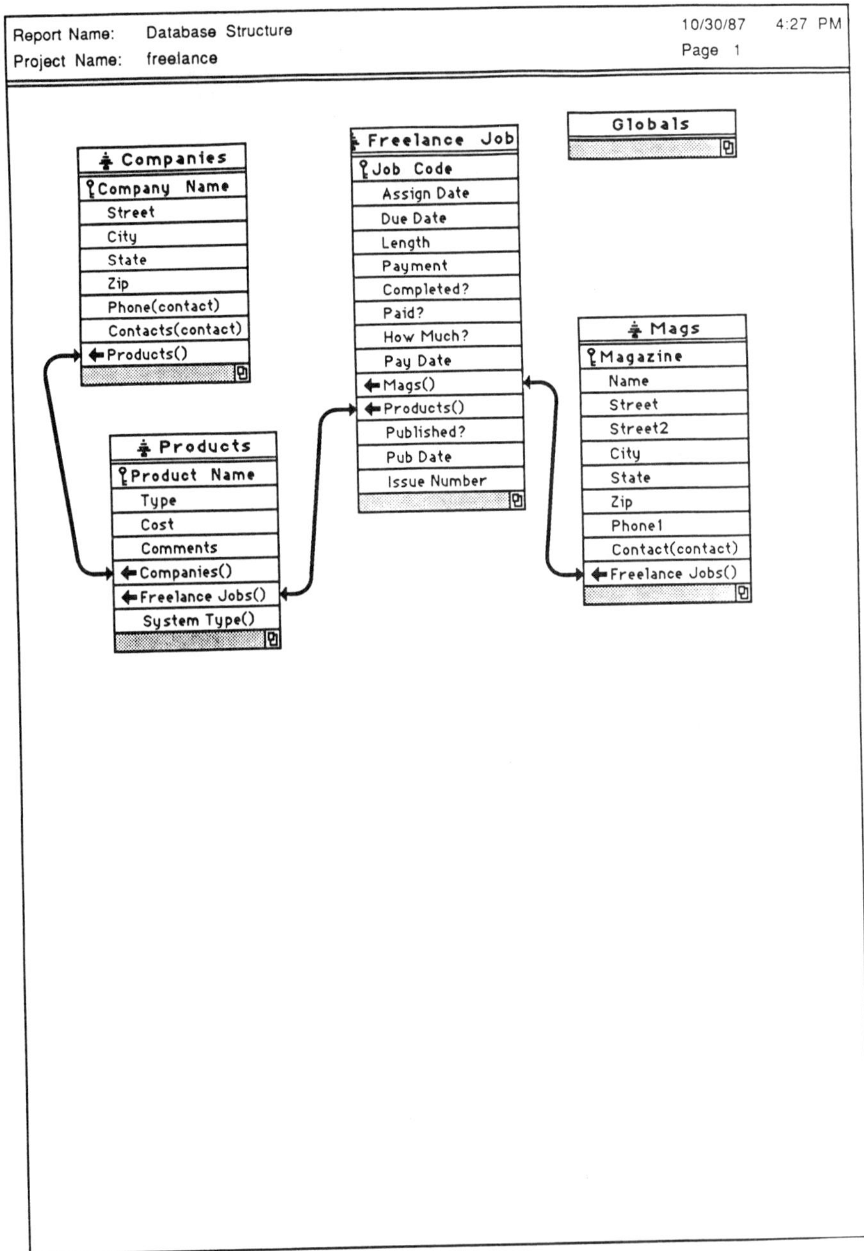

Freelance Structure Window

Report Name:	File Structure			10/30/87 4:28 PM
				Page 1
File Name:	Companies	File Type:	dBASE Mac	

Field Name:	Company Name			
Field Type:	Key, Ordered	Data Type:	Text	Required
Justify:	Left			
Field Name:	Street			
Field Type:	Data	Data Type:	Text	
Contents are:	Single Valued			
Justify:	Left			
Field Name:	City			
Field Type:	Data	Data Type:	Text	
Contents are:	Single Valued			
Justify:	Left			
Field Name:	State			
Field Type:	Data	Data Type:	Text	
Contents are:	Single Valued			
Justify:	Left			
Field Name:	Zip			
Field Type:	Data	Data Type:	Text	
Contents are:	Single Valued			
Justify:	Left			
Field Name:	Phone			
Field Type:	Data	Data Type:	Text	
Contents are:	Multiple Valued	Set Name:	contact	
Justify:	Left			
Field Name:	Contacts			
Field Type:	Data	Data Type:	Text	
Contents are:	Multiple Valued	Set Name:	contact	
Justify:	Left			
Field Name:	Products			
Field Type:	Data	Data Type:	Text	
Contents are:	Multiple Valued			
Justify:	Left			
Relations:	Two-way with Products			

Report Name:	File Structure			10/30/87 4:28 PM Page 1
File Name:	Products	File Type:	dBASE Mac	

Field Name:	Product Name			
Field Type:	Key, Ordered	Data Type:	Text	Required
Justify:	Left			

Field Name:	Type		
Field Type:	Data	Data Type:	Text
Contents are:	Single Valued		
Justify:	Left		

Field Name:	Cost		
Field Type:	Data	Data Type:	Number
Contents are:	Single Valued		
Justify:	Right		
Format:	Fixed	Decimal Places:	2
Decimal:	.	Thousands:	
Negative:	-n	Currency:	$

Field Name:	Comments		
Field Type:	Data	Data Type:	Text
Contents are:	Single Valued		
Justify:	Left		

Field Name:	Companies		
Field Type:	Data	Data Type:	Text
Contents are:	Multiple Valued		
Justify:	Left		
Relations:	Two-way with Companies		

Field Name:	Freelance Jobs		
Field Type:	Data	Data Type:	Text
Contents are:	Multiple Valued		
Justify:	Left		
Relations:	Two-way with Freelance Jobs		

Field Name:	System Type		
Field Type:	Data	Data Type:	Text
Contents are:	Multiple Valued		
Justify:	Left		

Report Name:	File Structure			10/30/87 4:29 PM Page 1
File Name:	Mags	File Type:	dBASE Mac	
Field Name:	Magazine			
Field Type:	Key, Ordered	Data Type:	Text	Required
Justify:	Left			
Field Name:	Name			
Field Type:	Data	Data Type:	Text	
Contents are:	Single Valued			
Justify:	Left			
Field Name:	Street			
Field Type:	Data	Data Type:	Text	
Contents are:	Single Valued			
Justify:	Left			
Field Name:	Street2			
Field Type:	Data	Data Type:	Text	
Contents are:	Single Valued			
Justify:	Left			
Field Name:	City			
Field Type:	Data	Data Type:	Text	
Contents are:	Single Valued			
Justify:	Left			
Field Name:	State			
Field Type:	Data	Data Type:	Text	
Contents are:	Single Valued			
Justify:	Left			
Field Name:	Zip			
Field Type:	Data	Data Type:	Text	
Contents are:	Single Valued			
Justify:	Left			
Field Name:	Phone1			
Field Type:	Data	Data Type:	Text	
Contents are:	Single Valued			
Justify:	Left			
Field Name:	Contact			
Field Type:	Data	Data Type:	Text	
Contents are:	Multiple Valued	Set Name:	contact	
Justify:	Left			
Field Name:	Freelance Jobs			
Field Type:	Data	Data Type:	Text	
Contents are:	Multiple Valued			
Justify:	Left			
Relations:	Two-way with Freelance Jobs			

Report Name:	File Structure			10/30/87 4:28 PM
				Page 1
File Name:	Freelance Jobs	File Type:	dBASE Mac	

Field Name:	Job Code			
Field Type:	Key, Ordered	Data Type:	Text	Required
Justify:	Left			
Field Name:	Assign Date			
Field Type:	Data	Data Type:	Date	
Contents are:	Single Valued			
Justify:	Left			
Format:	mm/dd/yy			
Year Length:	2	Separator:	/	
Field Name:	Due Date			
Field Type:	Data	Data Type:	Date	
Contents are:	Single Valued			
Justify:	Left			
Format:	mm/dd/yy			
Year Length:	2	Separator:	/	
Field Name:	Length			
Field Type:	Data	Data Type:	Number	
Contents are:	Single Valued			
Justify:	Right			
Format:	Fixed	Decimal Places:	0	
Decimal:	.	Thousands:		
Negative:	-n	Currency:		
Field Name:	Payment			
Field Type:	Data	Data Type:	Number	
Contents are:	Single Valued			
Justify:	Right			
Format:	Fixed	Decimal Places:	2	
Decimal:	.	Thousands:		
Negative:	-n	Currency:	$	
Field Name:	Completed?			
Field Type:	Data	Data Type:	Logical	
Contents are:	Single Valued			
Justify:	Left			
Format:	Check Box			
Values:	No/Yes			
Initial Value:	No			
Field Name:	Paid?			
Field Type:	Data	Data Type:	Logical	
Contents are:	Single Valued			
Justify:	Left			
Format:	Check Box			
Values:	No/Yes			

Report Name:	File Structure			10/30/87 4:28 PM
				Page 2
File Name:	Freelance Jobs	File Type:	dBASE Mac	

Initial Value:	No		

Field Name:	How Much?		
Field Type:	Data	Data Type:	Number
Contents are:	Single Valued		
Justify:	Right		
Format:	Fixed	Decimal Places:	2
Decimal:	.	Thousands:	
Negative:	-n	Currency:	$

Field Name:	Pay Date		
Field Type:	Data	Data Type:	Date
Contents are:	Single Valued		
Justify:	Left		
Format:	mm/dd/yy		
Year Length:	2	Separator:	/

Field Name:	Mags		
Field Type:	Data	Data Type:	Text
Contents are:	Multiple Valued		
Justify:	Left		
Relations:	Two-way with Mags		

Field Name:	Products		
Field Type:	Data	Data Type:	Text
Contents are:	Multiple Valued		
Justify:	Left		
Relations:	Two-way with Products		

Field Name:	Published?		
Field Type:	Data	Data Type:	Logical
Contents are:	Single Valued		
Justify:	Left		
Format:	Check Box		
Values:	No/Yes		
Initial Value:	No		

Field Name:	Pub Date		
Field Type:	Data	Data Type:	Date
Contents are:	Single Valued		
Justify:	Left		
Format:	mm/dd/yy		
Year Length:	2	Separator:	/

Field Name:	Issue Number		
Field Type:	Data	Data Type:	Text
Contents are:	Single Valued		
Justify:	Left		

Report Name:	View Definition			10/30/87	4:30 PM
				Page 1	
Project Name:	freelance				
View Name:	Mags Entry	View Type:	Display, Form Layout		
Root File:	Mags	File Type:	dBASE Mac		

Report Name:	View Definition		10/30/87	4:30 PM
			Page 2	
Project Name:	freelance			
View Name:	Mags Entry	View Type:	Display, Form Layout	
File Name:	Mags	File Type:	dBASE Mac	
Access Path:	Mags			
Field Name:	Magazine			
Field Type:	Key, Ordered	Data Type:	Text	Required
Justify:	Left			
Field Name:	Name			
Field Type:	Data	Data Type:	Text	
Contents are:	Single Valued			
Justify:	Left			
Field Name:	Street			
Field Type:	Data	Data Type:	Text	
Contents are:	Single Valued			
Justify:	Left			
Field Name:	Street2			
Field Type:	Data	Data Type:	Text	
Contents are:	Single Valued			
Justify:	Left			
Field Name:	City			
Field Type:	Data	Data Type:	Text	
Contents are:	Single Valued			
Justify:	Left			
Field Name:	State			
Field Type:	Data	Data Type:	Text	
Contents are:	Single Valued			
Justify:	Left			
Field Name:	Zip			
Field Type:	Data	Data Type:	Text	
Contents are:	Single Valued			
Justify:	Left			
Field Name:	Phone1			
Field Type:	Data	Data Type:	Text	
Contents are:	Single Valued			
Justify:	Left			
Field Name:	Contact			
Field Type:	Data	Data Type:	Text	
Contents are:	Multiple Valued	Set Name:	contact	
Justify:	Left			
Field Name:	Freelance Jobs			
Field Type:	Data	Data Type:	Text	

Report Name:	View Definition			10/30/87 4:30 PM
				Page 3
Project Name:	freelance			
View Name:	Mags Entry	View Type:	Display, Form Layout	
File Name:	Mags	File Type:	dBASE Mac	
Contents are:	Multiple Valued			
Justify:	Left			
Relations:	Two-way with Freelance Jobs			

Report Name:	View Definition			10/30/87 4:30 PM
				Page 1
Project Name:	freelance			
View Name:	Company Entry	View Type:	Display, Form Layout	
Root File:	Companies	File Type:	dBASE Mac	

Report Name:	View Definition		10/30/87	4:30 PM
			Page 2	
Project Name:	freelance			
View Name:	Company Entry	View Type:	Display, Form Layout	
File Name:	Companies	File Type:	dBASE Mac	
Access Path:	Companies			
Field Name:	Company Name			
Field Type:	Key, Ordered	Data Type:	Text	Required
Justify:	Left			
Field Name:	Street			
Field Type:	Data	Data Type:	Text	
Contents are:	Single Valued			
Justify:	Left			
Field Name:	City			
Field Type:	Data	Data Type:	Text	
Contents are:	Single Valued			
Justify:	Left			
Field Name:	State			
Field Type:	Data	Data Type:	Text	
Contents are:	Single Valued			
Justify:	Left			
Field Name:	Zip			
Field Type:	Data	Data Type:	Text	
Contents are:	Single Valued			
Justify:	Left			
Field Name:	Phone			
Field Type:	Data	Data Type:	Text	
Contents are:	Multiple Valued	Set Name:	contact	
Justify:	Left			
Field Name:	Contacts			
Field Type:	Data	Data Type:	Text	
Contents are:	Multiple Valued	Set Name:	contact	
Justify:	Left			
Field Name:	Products			
Field Type:	Data	Data Type:	Text	
Contents are:	Multiple Valued			
Justify:	Left			
Relations:	Two-way with Products			

Report Name:	View Definition		10/30/87	4:31 PM
			Page 1	
Project Name:	freelance			
View Name:	Product Entry	View Type:	Display, Custom Layout	
Root File:	Products	File Type:	dBASE Mac	

Report Name:	View Definition			10/30/87 4:31 PM Page 2
Project Name:	freelance			
View Name:	Product Entry	View Type:	Display, Custom Layout	
File Name:	Products	File Type:	dBASE Mac	
Access Path:	Products			
Field Name:	Product Name			
Field Type:	Key, Ordered	Data Type:	Text	Required
Justify:	Left			
Field Name:	Type			
Field Type:	Data	Data Type:	Text	
Contents are:	Single Valued			
Justify:	Left			
Field Name:	Cost			
Field Type:	Data	Data Type:	Number	
Contents are:	Single Valued			
Justify:	Right			
Format:	Fixed	Decimal Places:	2	
Decimal:	.	Thousands:		
Negative:	-n	Currency:	$	
Field Name:	Comments			
Field Type:	Data	Data Type:	Text	
Contents are:	Single Valued			
Justify:	Left			
Field Name:	Companies			
Field Type:	Data	Data Type:	Text	
Contents are:	Multiple Valued			
Justify:	Left			
Relations:	Two-way with Companies			
Field Name:	Freelance Jobs			
Field Type:	Data	Data Type:	Text	
Contents are:	Multiple Valued			
Justify:	Left			
Relations:	Two-way with Freelance Jobs			
Field Name:	System Type			
Field Type:	Data	Data Type:	Text	
Contents are:	Multiple Valued			
Justify:	Left			

Report Name:	View Definition			10/30/87 4:32 PM Page 1
Project Name:	freelance			
View Name:	Jobs Entry	View Type:	Display, Form Layout	
Root File:	Freelance Jobs	File Type:	dBASE Mac	

Report Name:	View Definition		10/30/87	4:32 PM
			Page 2	
Project Name:	freelance			
View Name:	Jobs Entry	View Type:	Display, Form Layout	
File Name:	Freelance Jobs	File Type:	dBASE Mac	
Access Path:	Freelance Jobs			
Field Name:	Job Code			
Field Type:	Key, Ordered	Data Type:	Text	Required
Justify:	Left			
Field Name:	Assign Date			
Field Type:	Data	Data Type:	Date	
Contents are:	Single Valued			
Justify:	Left			
Format:	mm/dd/yy			
Year Length:	2	Separator:	/	
Field Name:	Due Date			
Field Type:	Data	Data Type:	Date	
Contents are:	Single Valued			
Justify:	Left			
Format:	mm/dd/yy			
Year Length:	2	Separator:	/	
Field Name:	Length			
Field Type:	Data	Data Type:	Number	
Contents are:	Single Valued			
Justify:	Right			
Format:	Fixed	Decimal Places:	0	
Decimal:	.	Thousands:		
Negative:	-n	Currency:		
Field Name:	Payment			
Field Type:	Data	Data Type:	Number	
Contents are:	Single Valued			
Justify:	Right			
Format:	Fixed	Decimal Places:	2	
Decimal:		Thousands:		
Negative:	-n	Currency:	$	
Field Name:	Completed?			
Field Type:	Data	Data Type:	Logical	
Contents are:	Single Valued			
Justify:	Left			
Format:	Check Box			
Values:	No/Yes			
Initial Value:	No			
Field Name:	Paid?			
Field Type:	Data	Data Type:	Logical	

Report Name:	View Definition		10/30/87 4:32 PM Page 3
Project Name:	freelance		
View Name:	Jobs Entry	View Type:	Display, Form Layout
File Name:	Freelance Jobs	File Type:	dBASE Mac

Contents are:	Single Valued		
Justify:	Left		
Format:	Check Box		
Values:	No/Yes		
Initial Value:	No		

Field Name:	How Much?		
Field Type:	Data	Data Type:	Number
Contents are:	Single Valued		
Justify:	Right		
Format:	Fixed	Decimal Places:	2
Decimal:	.	Thousands:	
Negative:	-n	Currency:	$

Field Name:	Pay Date		
Field Type:	Data	Data Type:	Date
Contents are:	Single Valued		
Justify:	Left		
Format:	mm/dd/yy		
Year Length:	2	Separator:	/

Field Name:	Mags		
Field Type:	Data	Data Type:	Text
Contents are:	Multiple Valued		
Justify:	Left		
Relations:	Two-way with Mags		

Field Name:	Products		
Field Type:	Data	Data Type:	Text
Contents are:	Multiple Valued		
Justify:	Left		
Relations:	Two-way with Products		

Field Name:	Published?		
Field Type:	Data	Data Type:	Logical
Contents are:	Single Valued		
Justify:	Left		
Format:	Check Box		
Values:	No/Yes		
Initial Value:	No		

Field Name:	Pub Date		
Field Type:	Data	Data Type:	Date
Contents are:	Single Valued		
Justify:	Left		
Format:	mm/dd/yy		

Report Name:	View Definition			10/30/87 4:32 PM
				Page 4
Project Name:	freelance			
View Name:	Jobs Entry	View Type:	Display, Form Layout	
File Name:	Freelance Jobs	File Type:	dBASE Mac	
Year Length:	2	Separator:	/	
Field Name:	Issue Number			
Field Type:	Data	Data Type:	Text	
Contents are:	Single Valued			
Justify:	Left			

Report Name:	View Definition			10/30/87 4:32 PM
				Page 1
Project Name:	freelance			
View Name:	Product List	View Type:	Display, Columnar Layout	
Root File:	Products	File Type:	dBASE Mac	

Report Name:	View Definition		10/30/87 4:32 PM Page 2
Project Name:	freelance		
View Name:	Product List	View Type:	Display, Columnar Layout
File Name:	Products	File Type:	dBASE Mac
Access Path:	Products		
Field Name:	Product Name		
Field Type:	Key, Ordered	Data Type:	Text Required
Justify:	Left		
Field Name:	Type		
Field Type:	Data	Data Type:	Text
Contents are:	Single Valued		
Justify:	Left		
Field Name:	Cost		
Field Type:	Data	Data Type:	Number
Contents are:	Single Valued		
Justify:	Right		
Format:	Fixed	Decimal Places:	2
Decimal:	.	Thousands:	
Negative:	-n	Currency:	$
Field Name:	Comments		
Field Type:	Data	Data Type:	Text
Contents are:	Single Valued		
Justify:	Left		
Field Name:	Companies		
Field Type:	Data	Data Type:	Text
Contents are:	Multiple Valued		
Justify:	Left		
Relations:	Two-way with Companies		
Field Name:	Freelance Jobs		
Field Type:	Data	Data Type:	Text
Contents are:	Multiple Valued		
Justify:	Left		
Relations:	Two-way with Freelance Jobs		
Field Name:	System Type		
Field Type:	Data	Data Type:	Text
Contents are:	Multiple Valued		
Justify:	Left		

Report Name:	View Definition		10/30/87 4:33 PM Page 1
Project Name:	freelance		
View Name:	Job List	View Type:	Display, Custom Layout
Root File:	Freelance Jobs	File Type:	dBASE Mac

Report Name:	View Definition		10/30/87	4:33 PM
			Page 2	
Project Name:	freelance			
View Name:	Job List	View Type:	Display, Custom Layout	
File Name:	Freelance Jobs	File Type:	dBASE Mac	

Access Path:	Freelance Jobs			

Field Name:	Job Code			
Field Type:	Key, Ordered	Data Type:	Text	Required
Justify:	Left			Accumulate totals

Field Name:	Assign Date		
Field Type:	Data	Data Type:	Date
Contents are:	Single Valued		
Justify:	Left		
Format:	mm/dd/yy		
Year Length:	2	Separator:	/

Field Name:	Due Date		
Field Type:	Data	Data Type:	Date
Contents are:	Single Valued		
Justify:	Left		
Format:	mm/dd/yy		
Year Length:	2	Separator:	/

Field Name:	Length		
Field Type:	Data	Data Type:	Number
Contents are:	Single Valued		
Justify:	Right		
Format:	Fixed	Decimal Places:	0
Decimal:	.	Thousands:	
Negative:	-n	Currency:	

Field Name:	Payment			
Field Type:	Data	Data Type:	Number	
Contents are:	Single Valued			
Justify:	Right			
Format:	Fixed	Decimal Places:	2	
Decimal:	.	Thousands:		
Negative:	-n	Currency:	$	Accumulate totals

Field Name:	Completed?			
Field Type:	Data	Data Type:	Logical	
Contents are:	Single Valued			
Justify:	Left			
Format:	Check Box			
Values:	No/Yes			
Initial Value:	No			Accumulate totals

Field Name:	Paid?		
Field Type:	Data	Data Type:	Logical

Report Name:	View Definition			10/30/87 4:33 PM
				Page 3
Project Name:	freelance			
View Name:	Job List	View Type:	Display, Custom Layout	
File Name:	Freelance Jobs	File Type:	dBASE Mac	
Contents are:	Single Valued			
Justify:	Left			
Format:	Check Box			
Values:	No/Yes			
Initial Value:	No			Accumulate totals
Field Name:	How Much?			
Field Type:	Data	Data Type:	Number	
Contents are:	Single Valued			
Justify:	Right			
Format:	Fixed	Decimal Places:	2	
Decimal:	.	Thousands:		
Negative:	-n	Currency:	$	Accumulate totals
Field Name:	Pay Date			
Field Type:	Data	Data Type:	Date	
Contents are:	Single Valued			
Justify:	Left			
Format:	mm/dd/yy			
Year Length:	2	Separator:	/	
Field Name:	Mags			
Field Type:	Data	Data Type:	Text	
Contents are:	Multiple Valued			
Justify:	Left			
Relations:	Two-way with Mags			
Field Name:	Products			
Field Type:	Data	Data Type:	Text	
Contents are:	Multiple Valued			
Justify:	Left			
Relations:	Two-way with Products			
Field Name:	Published?			
Field Type:	Data	Data Type:	Logical	
Contents are:	Single Valued			
Justify:	Left			
Format:	Check Box			
Values:	No/Yes			
Initial Value:	No			Accumulate totals

Report Name:	View Definition			10/30/87 4:35 PM
				Page 1
Project Name:	freelance			
View Name:	Completed and Paid	View Type:	Display, Custom Layout	
Root File:	Freelance Jobs	File Type:	dBASE Mac	
Show If:	{Completed?•Freelance Jobs} AND {Paid?•Freelance Jobs}			

Report Name:	View Definition		10/30/87	4:35 PM
			Page 2	
Project Name:	freelance			
View Name:	Completed and Paid	View Type:	Display, Custom Layout	
File Name:	Freelance Jobs	File Type:	dBASE Mac	

Access Path:	Freelance Jobs			
Field Name:	Job Code			
Field Type:	Key, Ordered	Data Type:	Text	Required
Justify:	Left			Accumulate totals
Field Name:	Mags			
Field Type:	Data	Data Type:	Text	
Contents are:	Multiple Valued			
Justify:	Left			
Relations:	Two-way with Mags			
Relates File:	Mags	File Type:	dBASE Mac	
Field Name:	Payment			
Field Type:	Data	Data Type:	Number	
Contents are:	Single Valued			
Justify:	Right			
Format:	Fixed	Decimal Places:	2	
Decimal:	.	Thousands:		
Negative:	-n	Currency:	$	Accumulate totals
Field Name:	Completed?			
Field Type:	Data	Data Type:	Logical	
Contents are:	Single Valued			
Justify:	Left			
Format:	Check Box			
Values:	No/Yes			
Initial Value:	No			
Field Name:	Paid?			
Field Type:	Data	Data Type:	Logical	
Contents are:	Single Valued			
Justify:	Left			
Format:	Check Box			
Values:	No/Yes			
Initial Value:	No			
Field Name:	How Much?			
Field Type:	Data	Data Type:	Number	
Contents are:	Single Valued			
Justify:	Right			
Format:	Fixed	Decimal Places:	2	
Decimal:	.	Thousands:		
Negative:	-n	Currency:	$	Accumulate totals

Report Name:	View Definition		10/30/87	4:35 PM
			Page 3	
Project Name:	freelance			
View Name:	Completed and Paid	View Type:	Display, Custom Layout	
File Name:	Mags	File Type:	dBASE Mac	
Access Path:	Mags•Freelance Jobs			
Field Name:	Magazine			
Field Type:	Key, Ordered	Data Type:	Text	Required
Justify:	Left			

Report Name:	View Definition		10/30/87	4:35 PM
			Page 1	
Project Name:	freelance			
View Name:	All Jobs	View Type:	Display, Custom Layout	
Root File:	Freelance Jobs	File Type:	dBASE Mac	

Report Name:	View Definition		10/30/87	4:35 PM
			Page 2	
Project Name:	freelance			
View Name:	All Jobs	View Type:	Display, Custom Layout	
File Name:	Freelance Jobs	File Type:	dBASE Mac	

Access Path:	Freelance Jobs			
Field Name:	Job Code			
Field Type:	Key, Ordered	Data Type:	Text	Required
Justify:	Left			
Field Name:	Mags			
Field Type:	Data	Data Type:	Text	
Contents are:	Multiple Valued			
Justify:	Left			
Relations:	Two-way with Mags			
Relates File:	Mags	File Type:	dBASE Mac	
Field Name:	Payment			
Field Type:	Data	Data Type:	Number	
Contents are:	Single Valued			
Justify:	Right			
Format:	Fixed	Decimal Places:	2	
Decimal:	.	Thousands:		
Negative:	-n	Currency:	$	Accumulate totals
Field Name:	Completed?			
Field Type:	Data	Data Type:	Logical	
Contents are:	Single Valued			
Justify:	Left			
Format:	Check Box			
Values:	No/Yes			
Initial Value:	No			
Field Name:	Paid?			
Field Type:	Data	Data Type:	Logical	
Contents are:	Single Valued			
Justify:	Left			
Format:	Check Box			
Values:	No/Yes			
Initial Value:	No			
Field Name:	How Much?			
Field Type:	Data	Data Type:	Number	
Contents are:	Single Valued			
Justify:	Right			
Format:	Fixed	Decimal Places:	2	
Decimal:	.	Thousands:		
Negative:	-n	Currency:	$	Accumulate totals

Report Name:	View Definition			10/30/87 4:35 PM
				Page 3
Project Name:	freelance			
View Name:	All Jobs	View Type:	Display, Custom Layout	
File Name:	Mags	File Type:	dBASE Mac	
Access Path:	Mags•Freelance Jobs			
Field Name:	Magazine			
Field Type:	Key, Ordered	Data Type:	Text	Required
Justify:	Left			

Report Name:	View Definition			10/30/87 4:36 PM
				Page 1
Project Name:	freelance			
View Name:	Unfinished Jobs	View Type:	Display, Custom Layout	
Root File:	Freelance Jobs	File Type:	dBASE Mac	
Sort By:	Due Date•Freelance Jobs			Ascending
Show If:	NOT {Completed?•Freelance Jobs}			

Report Name:	View Definition		10/30/87	4:36 PM
			Page 2	
Project Name:	freelance			
View Name:	Unfinished Jobs	View Type:	Display, Custom Layout	
File Name:	Freelance Jobs	File Type:	dBASE Mac	
Access Path:	Freelance Jobs			
Field Name:	Job Code			
Field Type:	Key, Ordered	Data Type:	Text	Required
Justify:	Left			
Field Name:	Mags			
Field Type:	Data	Data Type:	Text	
Contents are:	Multiple Valued			
Justify:	Left			
Relations:	Two-way with Mags			
Relates File:	Mags	File Type:	dBASE Mac	
Field Name:	Payment			
Field Type:	Data	Data Type:	Number	
Contents are:	Single Valued			
Justify:	Right			
Format:	Fixed	Decimal Places:	2	
Decimal:	.	Thousands:		
Negative:	-n	Currency:	$	Accumulate totals
Field Name:	Completed?			
Field Type:	Data	Data Type:	Logical	
Contents are:	Single Valued			
Justify:	Left			
Format:	Check Box			
Values:	No/Yes			
Initial Value:	No			
Field Name:	Paid?			
Field Type:	Data	Data Type:	Logical	
Contents are:	Single Valued			
Justify:	Left			
Format:	Check Box			
Values:	No/Yes			
Initial Value:	No			
Field Name:	How Much?			
Field Type:	Data	Data Type:	Number	
Contents are:	Single Valued			
Justify:	Right			
Format:	Fixed	Decimal Places:	2	
Decimal:	.	Thousands:		
Negative:	-n	Currency:	$	Accumulate totals
Field Name:	Assign Date			

Report Name:	View Definition		10/30/87 4:36 PM
			Page 3
Project Name:	freelance		
View Name:	Unfinished Jobs	View Type:	Display, Custom Layout
File Name:	Freelance Jobs	File Type:	dBASE Mac
Field Type:	Data	Data Type:	Date
Contents are:	Single Valued		
Justify:	Left		
Format:	mm/dd/yy		
Year Length:	2	Separator:	/
Field Name:	Due Date		
Field Type:	Data	Data Type:	Date
Contents are:	Single Valued		
Justify:	Left		
Format:	mm/dd/yy		
Year Length:	2	Separator:	/
Field Name:	Length		
Field Type:	Data	Data Type:	Number
Contents are:	Single Valued		
Justify:	Right		
Format:	Fixed	Decimal Places:	0
Decimal:	.	Thousands:	
Negative:	-n	Currency:	

Report Name:	View Definition		10/30/87 4:36 PM	
			Page 4	
Project Name:	freelance			
View Name:	Unfinished Jobs	View Type:	Display, Custom Layout	
File Name:	Mags	File Type:	dBASE Mac	
Access Path:	Mags•Freelance Jobs			
Field Name:	Magazine			
Field Type:	Key, Ordered	Data Type:	Text	Required
Justify:	Left			

Report Name:	View Definition		10/30/87 4:37 PM
			Page 1
Project Name:	freelance		
View Name:	Unpaid Jobs Completed	View Type:	Display, Custom Layout
Root File:	Freelance Jobs	File Type:	dBASE Mac
Show If:	{Completed?•Freelance Jobs} AND NOT {Paid?•Freelance Jobs} OR ({Payment•Freelance Jobs} > {How Much?•Freelance Jobs} AND {How Much?•Freelance Jobs} > 0)		

Report Name:	View Definition		10/30/87 4:37 PM Page 2	
Project Name:	freelance			
View Name:	Unpaid Jobs Completed	View Type:	Display, Custom Layout	
File Name:	Freelance Jobs	File Type:	dBASE Mac	
Access Path:	Freelance Jobs			
Field Name:	Job Code			
Field Type:	Key, Ordered	Data Type:	Text	Required
Justify:	Left			
Field Name:	Mags			
Field Type:	Data	Data Type:	Text	
Contents are:	Multiple Valued			
Justify:	Left			
Relations:	Two-way with Mags			
Relates File:	Mags	File Type:	dBASE Mac	
Field Name:	Payment			
Field Type:	Data	Data Type:	Number	
Contents are:	Single Valued			
Justify:	Right			
Format:	Fixed	Decimal Places:	2	
Decimal:	.	Thousands:		
Negative:	-n	Currency:	$	Accumulate totals
Field Name:	Completed?			
Field Type:	Data	Data Type:	Logical	
Contents are:	Single Valued			
Justify:	Left			
Format:	Check Box			
Values:	No/Yes			
Initial Value:	No			
Field Name:	Paid?			
Field Type:	Data	Data Type:	Logical	
Contents are:	Single Valued			
Justify:	Left			
Format:	Check Box			
Values:	No/Yes			
Initial Value:	No			
Field Name:	How Much?			
Field Type:	Data	Data Type:	Number	
Contents are:	Single Valued			
Justify:	Right			
Format:	Fixed	Decimal Places:	2	
Decimal:	.	Thousands:		
Negative:	-n	Currency:	$	Accumulate totals
Field Name:	Assign Date			

Report Name:	View Definition			10/30/87	4:37 PM
				Page 3	
Project Name:	freelance				
View Name:	Unpaid Jobs Completed	View Type:	Display, Custom Layout		
File Name:	Freelance Jobs	File Type:	dBASE Mac		
Field Type:	Data	Data Type:	Date		
Contents are:	Single Valued				
Justify:	Left				
Format:	mm/dd/yy				
Year Length:	2	Separator:	/		
Field Name:	Due Date				
Field Type:	Data	Data Type:	Date		
Contents are:	Single Valued				
Justify:	Left				
Format:	mm/dd/yy				
Year Length:	2	Separator:	/		
Field Name:	Length				
Field Type:	Data	Data Type:	Number		
Contents are:	Single Valued				
Justify:	Right				
Format:	Fixed	Decimal Places:	0		
Decimal:	.	Thousands:			
Negative:	-n	Currency:			

Report Name:	View Definition			10/30/87	4:37 PM
				Page 4	
Project Name:	freelance				
View Name:	Unpaid Jobs Completed	View Type:	Display, Custom Layout		
File Name:	Mags	File Type:	dBASE Mac		
Access Path:	Mags•Freelance Jobs				
Field Name:	Magazine				
Field Type:	Key, Ordered	Data Type:	Text	Required	
Justify:	Left				

Report Name:	View Definition			10/30/87	4:37 PM
				Page 1	
Project Name:	freelance				
View Name:	All Jobs by Mag	View Type:	Display, Custom Layout		
Root File:	Mags	File Type:	dBASE Mac		
Sort By:	Name•Mags			Ascending	

Report Name:	View Definition			10/30/87 4:37 PM Page 2
Project Name:	freelance			
View Name:	All Jobs by Mag	View Type:	Display, Custom Layout	
File Name:	Mags	File Type:	dBASE Mac	
Access Path:	Mags			
Field Name:	Magazine			
Field Type:	Key, Ordered	Data Type:	Text	Required
Justify:	Left			
Field Name:	Name			
Field Type:	Data	Data Type:	Text	
Contents are:	Single Valued			
Justify:	Left			
Control Break:	Blank line break			
Field Name:	Freelance Jobs			
Field Type:	Data	Data Type:	Text	
Contents are:	Multiple Valued			
Justify:	Left			
Relations:	Two-way with Freelance Jobs			
Relates File:	Freelance Jobs	File Type:	dBASE Mac	

Report Name:	View Definition			10/30/87 4:37 PM Page 3
Project Name:	freelance			
View Name:	All Jobs by Mag	View Type:	Display, Custom Layout	
File Name:	Freelance Jobs	File Type:	dBASE Mac	
Access Path:	Freelance Jobs•Mags			
Field Name:	Job Code			
Field Type:	Key, Ordered	Data Type:	Text	Required
Justify:	Left			
Field Name:	Payment			
Field Type:	Data	Data Type:	Number	
Contents are:	Single Valued			
Justify:	Right			
Format:	Fixed	Decimal Places:	2	
Decimal:	.	Thousands:		
Negative:	-n	Currency:	$	Accumulate totals
Field Name:	Completed?			
Field Type:	Data	Data Type:	Logical	
Contents are:	Single Valued			
Justify:	Left			
Format:	Check Box			
Values:	No/Yes			
Initial Value:	No			
Field Name:	Paid?			
Field Type:	Data	Data Type:	Logical	
Contents are:	Single Valued			
Justify:	Left			
Format:	Check Box			
Values:	No/Yes			
Initial Value:	No			
Field Name:	How Much?			
Field Type:	Data	Data Type:	Number	
Contents are:	Single Valued			
Justify:	Right			
Format:	Fixed	Decimal Places:	2	
Decimal:	.	Thousands:		
Negative:	-n	Currency:	$	Accumulate totals

Report Name:	View Definition			10/30/87 4:38 PM Page 1
Project Name:	freelance			
View Name:	Mag list	View Type:	Display, Columnar Layout	
Root File:	Mags	File Type:	dBASE Mac	

Report Name:	View Definition		10/30/87	4:38 PM
			Page 2	
Project Name:	freelance			
View Name:	Mag list	View Type:	Display, Columnar Layout	
File Name:	Mags	File Type:	dBASE Mac	
Access Path:	Mags			
Field Name:	Magazine			
Field Type:	Key, Ordered	Data Type:	Text	Required
Justify:	Left			
Field Name:	Name			
Field Type:	Data	Data Type:	Text	
Contents are:	Single Valued			
Justify:	Left			
Field Name:	Street			
Field Type:	Data	Data Type:	Text	
Contents are:	Single Valued			
Justify:	Left			
Field Name:	Street2			
Field Type:	Data	Data Type:	Text	
Contents are:	Single Valued			
Justify:	Left			
Field Name:	City			
Field Type:	Data	Data Type:	Text	
Contents are:	Single Valued			
Justify:	Left			
Field Name:	State			
Field Type:	Data	Data Type:	Text	
Contents are:	Single Valued			
Justify:	Left			
Field Name:	Zip			
Field Type:	Data	Data Type:	Text	
Contents are:	Single Valued			
Justify:	Left			
Field Name:	Phone1			
Field Type:	Data	Data Type:	Text	
Contents are:	Single Valued			
Justify:	Left			
Field Name:	Contact			
Field Type:	Data	Data Type:	Text	
Contents are:	Multiple Valued	Set Name:	contact	
Justify:	Left			
Field Name:	Freelance Jobs			
Field Type:	Data	Data Type:	Text	

Report Name:	View Definition			10/30/87 4:38 PM Page 3
Project Name:	freelance			
View Name:	Mag list	View Type:	Display, Columnar Layout	
File Name:	Mags	File Type:	dBASE Mac	
Contents are:	Multiple Valued			
Justify:	Left			
Relations:	Two-way with Freelance Jobs			

Report Name:	View Definition			10/30/87 4:38 PM Page 1
Project Name:	freelance			
View Name:	Completed by Mag	View Type:	Display, Custom Layout	
Root File:	Mags	File Type:	dBASE Mac	
Sort By:	Name•Mags			Ascending

Report Name:	View Definition			10/30/87 4:38 PM Page 2
Project Name:	freelance			
View Name:	Completed by Mag	View Type:	Display, Custom Layout	
File Name:	Mags	File Type:	dBASE Mac	
Access Path:	Mags			
Field Name:	Magazine			
Field Type:	Key, Ordered	Data Type:	Text	Required
Justify:	Left			
Field Name:	Name			
Field Type:	Data	Data Type:	Text	
Contents are:	Single Valued			
Justify:	Left			
Control Break:	Blank line break			
Field Name:	Freelance Jobs			
Field Type:	Data	Data Type:	Text	
Contents are:	Multiple Valued			
Justify:	Left			
Relations:	Two-way with Freelance Jobs			
Relates File:	Freelance Jobs	File Type:	dBASE Mac	
Show If:	{Completed?•Freelance Jobs•Mags}			

Report Name:	View Definition		10/30/87	4:38 PM
			Page 3	
Project Name:	freelance			
View Name:	Completed by Mag	View Type:	Display, Custom Layout	
File Name:	Freelance Jobs	File Type:	dBASE Mac	
Access Path:	Freelance Jobs•Mags			
Field Name:	Job Code			
Field Type:	Key, Ordered	Data Type:	Text	Required
Justify:	Left			
Field Name:	Completed?			
Field Type:	Data	Data Type:	Logical	
Contents are:	Single Valued			
Justify:	Left			
Format:	Check Box			
Values:	No/Yes			
Initial Value:	No			
Field Name:	Paid?			
Field Type:	Data	Data Type:	Logical	
Contents are:	Single Valued			
Justify:	Left			
Format:	Check Box			
Values:	No/Yes			
Initial Value:	No			Accumulate totals
Field Name:	How Much?			
Field Type:	Data	Data Type:	Number	
Contents are:	Single Valued			
Justify:	Right			
Format:	Fixed	Decimal Places:	2	
Decimal:	.	Thousands:		
Negative:	-n	Currency:	$	Accumulate totals

Report Name:	View Definition		10/30/87	4:39 PM
			Page 1	
Project Name:	freelance			
View Name:	Incomplete by Mag	View Type:	Display, Custom Layout	
Root File:	Mags	File Type:	dBASE Mac	
Sort By:	Name•Mags			Ascending

Report Name:	View Definition		10/30/87 4:39 PM Page 2	
Project Name:	freelance			
View Name:	Incomplete by Mag	View Type:	Display, Custom Layout	
File Name:	Mags	File Type:	dBASE Mac	
Access Path:	Mags			
Field Name:	Magazine			
Field Type:	Key, Ordered	Data Type:	Text	Required
Justify:	Left			
Field Name:	Name			
Field Type:	Data	Data Type:	Text	
Contents are:	Single Valued			
Justify:	Left			
Control Break:	Blank line break			
Field Name:	Freelance Jobs			
Field Type:	Data	Data Type:	Text	
Contents are:	Multiple Valued			
Justify:	Left			
Relations:	Two-way with Freelance Jobs			
Relates File:	Freelance Jobs	File Type:	dBASE Mac	
Show If:	NOT {Completed?•Freelance Jobs•Mags}			

Report Name:	View Definition		10/30/87	4:39 PM
			Page 3	
Project Name:	freelance			
View Name:	Incomplete by Mag	View Type:	Display, Custom Layout	
File Name:	Freelance Jobs	File Type:	dBASE Mac	
Access Path:	Freelance Jobs•Mags			
Field Name:	Job Code			
Field Type:	Key, Ordered	Data Type:	Text	Required
Justify:	Left			
Field Name:	Assign Date			
Field Type:	Data	Data Type:	Date	
Contents are:	Single Valued			
Justify:	Left			
Format:	mm/dd/yy			
Year Length:	2	Separator:	/	
Field Name:	Due Date			
Field Type:	Data	Data Type:	Date	
Contents are:	Single Valued			
Justify:	Left			
Format:	mm/dd/yy			
Year Length:	2	Separator:	/	
Field Name:	Length			
Field Type:	Data	Data Type:	Number	
Contents are:	Single Valued			
Justify:	Right			
Format:	Fixed	Decimal Places:	0	
Decimal:	.	Thousands:		
Negative:	-n	Currency:		
Field Name:	Payment			
Field Type:	Data	Data Type:	Number	
Contents are:	Single Valued			
Justify:	Right			
Format:	Fixed	Decimal Places:	2	
Decimal:	.	Thousands:		
Negative:	-n	Currency:	$	Accumulate totals
Field Name:	Completed?			
Field Type:	Data	Data Type:	Logical	
Contents are:	Single Valued			
Justify:	Left			
Format:	Check Box			
Values:	No/Yes			
Initial Value:	No			
Field Name:	Products			
Field Type:	Data	Data Type:	Text	

Report Name:	View Definition			10/30/87 4:39 PM
				Page 4
Project Name:	freelance			
View Name:	Incomplete by Mag	View Type:	Display, Custom Layout	
File Name:	Freelance Jobs	File Type:	dBASE Mac	
Contents are:	Multiple Valued			
Justify:	Left			
Relations:	Two-way with Products			
Field Name:	How Much?			
Field Type:	Data	Data Type:	Number	
Contents are:	Single Valued			
Justify:	Right			
Format:	Fixed	Decimal Places:	2	
Decimal:	.	Thousands:		
Negative:	-n	Currency:	$	Accumulate totals

APPENDIX A

MACINTOSH CONVENTIONS, TIPS, AND TECHNIQUES

Introduction to the Mac

Appendix A is for those who are new to the Mac. Some of you may be familiar with IBM PCs and other computer operating systems. For others, the Mac may be your first computer. In any case, understanding the various conventions and techniques discussed in this appendix will help you get the most out of this book, dBASE Mac, and the Mac.

Basic Equipment

Keyboard The keyboard is like any other computer keyboard. It contains the alphanumeric keys found on a typewriter, plus some special keys for specific uses:

The **Tab** key is used to move from one item to another in a screen full of items. It is also used in word processors to move to the next tab stop. Use the **Tab** key to indent procedural elements for more readable code.

Caps Lock is used to set the keyboard to all capital letters. It is also recognized by the Mac in some special operations.

The **Shift** keys function much like the shift keys on a typewriter, but they also combine with other keys for more complex operations. For instance, **Shift-Tab** moves to a previous form element. **Shift**-clicking the mouse selects additional elements in a hierarchy or layout without removing the highlight from anything already highlighted.

The **Option** key is used to modify the effect of keyboard entries. Most Macintosh fonts have special character sets that are accessed by using the **Option** key. (If you have the Desk Accessory called Key Caps, you can use it to see what characters look like in a particular font.) The **Option** key sometimes combines with other keys for more complex operations. If you are used to IBM-compatible systems, the **Option** key functions like the **Alt** key.

The **Command** key is very important in Macintosh applications. Many menu commands have keyboard equivalents that use the **Command** key (i.e. **Command-C** for Copy). The **Command** key often combines with **Shift** or **Option** to achieve more complex effects. If you are used to other computer systems, the **Command** key functions like the **Control** key.

Backspace is used to erase backwards. **Backspace** alone erases one letter or character behind the cursor. On a Macintosh, you can select a block of text, then begin typing to replace it. If you press **Backspace** with a block of text selected, the text is erased. **Shift-Backspace** highlights the word behind the cursor.

NOTE: On newer keyboards, the **Backspace** key has been replaced by a **Delete** key.

The **Return** key is used to finish an operation. Sometimes it is used to begin a new paragraph. Often you can use the **Return** key in place of the mouse to select an operation (if that operation is considered the default operation).

Some Macintoshes have direction arrow keys. These keys can be used in place of the mouse to move the cursor.

The **Enter** key is used in dBASE Mac to write the current record to disk. It can also be used in place of the **Return** key where the **Return** key has another function. For instance, when you are entering a new field definition, pressing **Return** does not Save the definition, but pressing **Enter** does. You can try using **Enter** to activate the default button on many dBASE Mac dialog boxes.

The **Space Bar** inserts a space at the cursor. It can also be used to move down through a Choices field list or to check a Logic field check box.

Mouse The Mouse is used in all Macintosh applications to position the cursor, to open menus, and to select items on the screen. Using the mouse takes practice, but soon becomes second-nature.

NOTE: For more on using the keyboard with dBASE Mac, see Appendix B.

Basic Terms and Techniques

The Cursor

The Cursor often changes in a Macintosh application. An arrow usually indicates the current position of the mouse. Sometimes the cursor changes into a vertical line. This is the text cursor and indicates that keyboard entry is required. The watch cursor indicates that the Mac is busy, so please wait. Other cursors appear within an application as needed.

The Finder

The Finder is the basic Macintosh desktop screen. It is the Finder that you first see when you start the Mac. Use the Finder to launch applications, to move files from one disk or folder to another, to delete files by dragging them into the Trashcan, and so on.

Icons

Icons are the standard Macintosh representation for a file or folder. Icons tell you what kind of file you are using. For instance, dBASE Mac uses several different icons:

 dBASE Mac Icon

 dBASE Mac FM•Server Icon

 dBASE Mac Help Icon

 Project Icon

 File Icon

 Snapshot Icon

 Foreign Text File Structure Icon

 dBASE II Icon

 dBASE III Icon

Each icon tells you immediately what it is for. Other applications use special icons to represent different types of files as well.

Mouse Techniques

There are several common mouse techniques, and terms to describe them:

Click Whenever you are asked to click on something, you move the mouse until the cursor is on the item named, then press the mouse button once. This will usually cause the item to change color (highlight), or will set in motion an operation (as with the **OK** and **Cancel** buttons).

Shift-Click To select more than one item on the screen, click on the first, then hold the **Shift** key down while clicking on any additional items. The original item(s) will remain selected and the new ones added.

Double-Click Double clicking is clicking the mouse button twice in rapid succession. Often you can select an item and perform the action required in one operation. For instance, to select a file from a list of files, you might click on the file name. But to select the file and load it at the same time, you would double-click the file name.

Select To Select a menu item, open the menu at the top of the Mac screen, place the mouse cursor on the menu title, press and hold the mouse button, then drag the mouse down until the menu command you desire is highlighted. Letting go of the button selects the currently highlighted command.

Selection Box Marquee To highlight, or select several items from a Mac screen, you can often click once on an unoccupied portion of the screen and drag the mouse. A dotted box will surround the items on the screen as you move the mouse. When you let go, any items within the box will be selected. You can now operate on all items at the same time. Sometimes using a selection box is quicker and easier than **Shift**-clicking.

TIP: You can **Shift**-select. If you have selected some items, and want to use a selection box to select additional items, hold the **Shift** key and create a selection box around the new items. The originally selected items will remain selected.

Drag To Drag an item on the Mac screen, first highlight it by clicking on it once (or **Shift**-click or use a selection box for multiple items), then press and hold the mouse button. With the button down, move the mouse. The item or items currently highlighted will move.

Menus and Dialog Boxes

For those already familiar with other computers, the Macintosh presents an ever more familiar user interface. Menus and pop-up dialog boxes have become more familiar on other computers such as the IBM PC and its compatibles, the Apple II, and newer computers such as the Atari ST and the Amiga. For some of these computers, menus and dialog boxes are recent additions, placed there through software programming. In others, notably the newer products, this kind of interface is a direct result of the influence of the Mac. In the Macintosh environment, menus and dialog boxes *are* the interface.

Menus are found at the top of the screen. Some are always present—notably the Apple menu and the Edit menu. Others appear and disappear as the program changes. You will notice several menus at different points within dBASE Mac. You open a menu by placing the mouse cursor on the menu name, pressing and holding the mouse button, then dragging the mouse downward to select the desired command.

Much of your interaction on the Macintosh will take place through dialog boxes. These are special instructional windows that appear at specific times within a program. They may contain boxes for you to fill with text, checkboxes or buttons to click on and select options, or buttons to click on to move to the next part of the program.

Almost all dialog boxes contain the **OK** and **Cancel** buttons (or some derivative of them). **OK** proceeds with an operation. **Cancel** backs out of the current operation.

TIP: Often there is one button with dark borders. This is the default selection. Pressing **Return** or **Enter** on the keyboard will select the default selection.

Desk Accessories and Fonts

One of the unique and powerful aspects of the Macintosh is its versatility. This versatility is part of the design of the machine. Desk Accessories and Fonts are a case in point.

A Desk Accessory (DA, for short) is always available from the Apple menu. DAs range from standard items like the Control Panel, Alarm Clock, and Chooser, to more complex applications like dBASE Mac's Help screens and Picture This... utility. Many excellent and useful DAs are available in the public domain and commercially. For more information on the standard DAs, see your Macintosh manuals.

Fonts allow great versatility in text display. You can use many font styles and sizes within dBASE Mac layouts. There are many excellent fonts in the public domain, and several collections are available commercially.

Working with Windows

In addition to dialog boxes and menus, windows are an essential part of the Macintosh environment. You can open and close, scroll, move, size, and zoom windows on the Mac. You can have many windows open at one time.

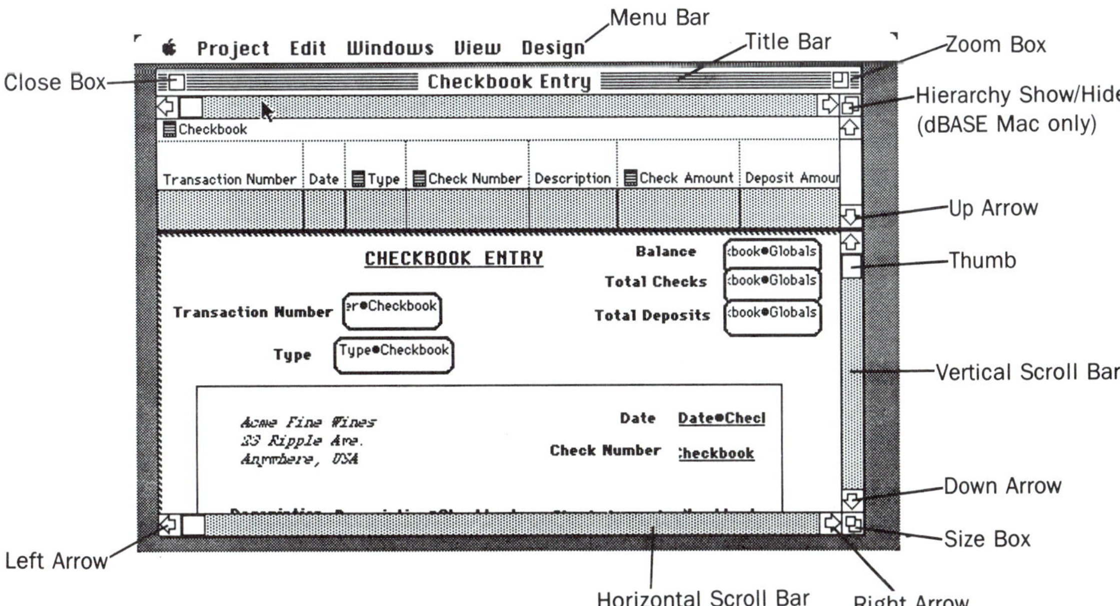

Figure A-1 Labeled Window Graphic.

To open a window, you generally need to select the appropriate command from a menu. For instance, selecting Structure Window from the Windows menu in dBASE Mac opens the Database Structure Window. Selecting Define Hierarchy opens the hierarchy definition screen for the current view (itself a window).

On the Finder screen, you can open new windows by opening folders or drives. Each open folder or drive displays in its own window. Each separate disk has its own Finder window as well. Amost all Macintosh windows have the same controls.

Title Bar The title bar is the area that contains the window name. It is filled with horizontal lines. You can move an entire window by dragging the title bar.

Close Window Box At the upper-left corner of a window is a small box. Click once on this box to close the window.

Scroll Bars On the right side and often along the bottom of a window are the scroll bars. The scroll bar is a long, narrow rectangle in a grey pattern. A small white box within the scroll bar indicates your relative position within the current window. You can scroll the window in one of three ways: by the arrows, by clicking in the grey area of the scroll bar, or by dragging the white indicator box.

Clicking on an arrow moves the window one line or column at a time. Clicking anywhere in the scroll bar above (or to the left of) the indicator box will move one screen up (or left). Clicking below (or to the right of) the indicator box (also known as thumb) will move one screen down (or right). Dragging the indicator box will move to the point in the window where the box is placed.

Size Controls You can change the size of a window by dragging the small box at the lower-right corner of a window (at the intersection of the bottom and right scroll bars).

Zoom Box Some windows can be Zoomed to fill the entire screen. The Zoom box, if present, is above the right scroll bar. To unzoom, click the Zoom box again.

Working with HFS

The original Macintosh used a flat filing system that did not make use of folders and sub-folders (to IBM users—directories and subdirectories). The Hierarchical Filing System is a newer system, and does take advantage of multilevel disk filing.

You can create a new folder on the Finder desktop by selecting **Command-N** (or New Folder from the Edit menu). Rename the folder by typing its name with the folder highlighted.

You can move files in and out of folders by dragging their icons, but how do you find files in other folders and drives when selecting from dialog boxes?

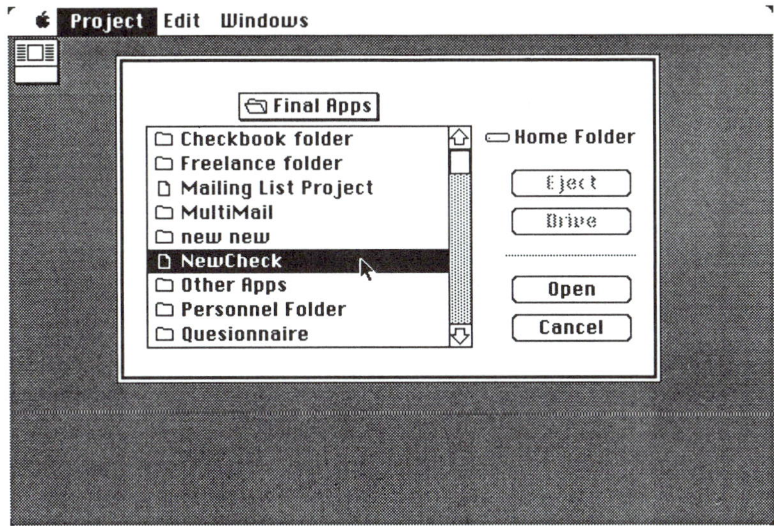

Figure A-2 Open File Dialog Graphic.

Look at the Open File dialog box in dBASE Mac. To open a folder that is above your current level in the hierarchy, select it from the files list (use the scroll bar if necessary), and click **Open** (or double click the folder name). Once the folder is open, a list of the files and/or folders it contains is displayed. You can select more folders, or select files at that point. Notice the folder name above the files list. If you are not in the Root Folder (the main Finder desktop), you can open the folder selections like any menu, by pressing and dragging. Select the folder level that you desire to move back up the hierarchy.

If the file or folder is on a disk other than the one currently displayed, click the **Drive** button (or the **Tab** key in some systems) to select another disk. If the disk is a floppy that is not in a drive, and the drive currently contains a disk, click **Eject** to remove the current disk, then replace it with the one you want to use.

TIP: Whenever you are presented with a list of files in a dialog box, you can type the beginning of the file or folder name to select it. The first file that begins with the characters you type will be selected. The more characters you type, the more accurate the selection will be. The speed you have to type depends on the keyboard settings in the Control Panel.

File Naming Conventions

Macintosh disk names can contain up to twenty-seven characters. A folder or application can contain up to thirty-three characters, including spaces and other symbols. You cannot begin a file name with a period, and you should not use colons (:) in file names.

On disks that do not use HFS, you can have up to sixty-three characters in a file, folder, or application name.

Longer names can be inconvenient, and will often be cut off in dialog boxes and will be obscured by other icons on the Finder. Therefore, it is best to keep names relatively short. For IBM users, you can go far beyond the eight character limit, and create much more descriptive names. You can also use upper and lower case in file names.

Edit Commands

Another of the Mac's built-in features is the Clipboard. The Clipboard is a place where information can be stored temporarily. It is the place where all data that are Cut or Copied are placed. When you select Paste, the contents of the Clipboard are copied into the current application at the current cursor location (if possible). If the data from the Clipboard are not compatible with the input area where the cursor is (for instance, you try to Paste a graphic into a text input area, or vice versa), the Mac will beep and nothing will happen. You can use the Clipboard to move graphics and text from one application to another, or from one window to another.

Standard Edit menu commands are Cut (**Command-X**), Copy (**Command-C**), Paste (**Command-V**), Select All, and Clear (**Command-B** in some applications).

Cut Removes highlighted text or graphics and places them in the Clipboard, replacing current Clipboard contents. You can then Paste them into another application or window, or into a new location within the current application or window.

Copy Places a copy of the currently highlighted text or graphics into the Clipboard, replacing current Clipboard contents without disturbing the original data. You can then Paste the Clipboard contents elsewhere.

Paste Places a copy of the current Clipboard contents into the current application or window (if possible). Does not erase Clipboard contents, so you can Paste the same data over and over until it is replaced by a new Cut or Copy.

Clear Removes highlighted data without placing it in the Clipboard (same as **Backspace**).

Select All When available, selects (highlights) all items in the current window. You can use Select All to select all layout elements in the design area of a dBASE Mac layout.

If you have more questions about using the Macintosh, consult your Apple user manuals. There are also several excellent books written about the Mac, and they are full of useful tips and information. For some more hints on using the Mac keyboard with dBASE Mac, see Appendix B.

APPENDIX B

USING THE KEYBOARD AND OTHER TRICKS

The Keyboard

The Macintosh and the mouse are synonymous. You don't think of one without the other. Almost all Macintosh applications make extensive use of the mouse, and it is difficult to imagine trying to use the Mac without one.

dBASE Mac is no exception to this rule. The mouse is often essential in dBASE Mac. You can't, for instance, create relations and indexes, click on radio buttons and checkboxes, or draw Tablets and fixed graphic boxes without the mouse. You can't add columns and form fields to a layout, or fields to a hierarchy, without the mouse.

You can, however, use the keyboard in several places. First, look at the keyboard commands available for Edit menu commands in dBASE Mac:

Keyboard Command	Edit Menu Command	Performance Result
Command-A	Add <name>	Add record or multivalued field occurrence.
Command-C	Copy	Copy highlighted text or graphics to the Clipboard.
Command-D	Delete <name>	Delete record or multivalued field occurrence.
Command-I	Insert <name>	Insert multivalued field occurrence.
Command-N	Next <name>	Display next record or multivalued field item.

Command-P	Prior <name>	Display previous record or multivalued field item.
Command-V	Paste	Paste contents of Clipboard to cursor location.
Command-Z	Undo	Undo changes made while using a desk accessory.

Other commands using the keyboard:

Command	**Result**
Command-H	Moves pointer to first form display item in view.
Command-O	Open Project (Project menu).
Command-Q	Quit dBASE Mac (Project menu).
Command-S	Save project (Project menu).
Command-Shift-N	Display next Root File record.
Command-Shift-P	Display previous Root File record.
Command-Shift-Cancel	Move to next file definition screen without completing present one.
Command-Shift-Done	Move to next file definition screen after saving current one.
Option-Shift-D	Create fixed text display showing system date as mm/dd/yy.
Option-Shift-D	Create fixed text display showing current page number.
Option-Shift-T	Create fixed text display showing system time as hh:mm:ss.
Option-Shift-Done	Complete and move to previous file definition screen.
Option-Shift-Cancel	Move to previous file definition screen without completing present one.
Tab	Move pointer to next form display item.
Shift-Tab	Move pointer to previous form display item.
Option-Tab	Enter current data in field without moving to another field in Form view.
Enter	Post current record to current file*.
Command-Enter	Post information in current record to all files in view.
Return	Insert Carriage Return in Wrapping Text field.

Space Bar	Move to next entry in Choices field, select value in Logic field.
Shift-Space Bar	Move to previous entry in Choices field.
Right Arrow	Move one character right in text box.
Left Arrow	Move one character left in text box.
Up Arrow	Move to beginning of text box.
Down Arrow	Move to end of text box.

* **Enter** can also be used in place of **Return** to select the default button. Use **Enter** in field definition dialog boxes, procedure definition boxes, and other places where Return has another function.

NOTE: All commands above apply to Use mode and data entry or modification only, with the exception of **Option-Shift-D**, **Option-Shift-P**, and **Option-Shift-T**, which are active in the layout.

NOTE: When using **Spacebar** to select in a Choices field, or to select a value in a Logic field, you must **Tab** to the field. If you enter the field using the mouse, the **Spacebar** cannot be used.

Other Tips

- To print bidirectionally in the Faster mode using an ImageWriter II, press **Caps Lock-Shift-Option** when you click **OK** to begin printing. The ImageWriter will print in both directions until you turn off the Macintosh, change start-up disk, or press **Command** with **OK**.
- Don't forget, you can select a file or folder from a dialog box list (like the Open Project or Open DataFile dialogs) by typing the first few characters of the file or folder name. You can also move one item at a time by pressing the **Up** and **Down Arrow** keys. To open a folder using the keyboard, press **Command-Down Arrow**. To move to the folder higher in the hierarchy, press **Command-Up Arrow**.
- Press **Return** or **Enter** in most dialog boxes in place of **OK**.
- Press **Tab** to change Drives in dialog boxes that choose a file from the Finder.
- Of course, use **Backspace** (**Delete** on newer keyboards) to erase data without sending them to the Clipboard. And remember, when you **Tab** into a text box, the entire contents are highlighted. Backspacing will remove the contents (having the same effect as Clear).
- **Backspace** (**Delete**) also removes fields and other highlighted display elements from the layout.

There are no particular keyboard shortcuts when writing procedures, but you can alway type any part of a procedure directly and bypass all mouse techniques. Press **Enter** when done with a procedure (in place of clicking **OK**). There are no keyboard command equivalents for Verify, Clear, or Cancel.

Remember to keep a Scrapbook, or other DA listing of common procedures, to Paste into dBASE Mac processors. It will save you time, especially when creating dialog boxes, which can be easily standardized.

Remember also, you can use Cut, Copy, and Paste to move compatible data in and out of any text entry box, graphic field, or fixed graphic. You may find ways to use the Clipboard to save keystrokes during data entry.

You may find other ways to use the keyboard—other shortcuts and techniques—but, as you can see, the keyboard has many uses during data entry and modification (using Form views), and some other uses at other points in the program.

APPENDIX C

OTHER RESOURCES

Many users of dBASE Mac will want to take full advantage of the program. This may mean making extensive use of graphic fields in applications or sending data back and forth either from dBASE II, III, or III PLUS, or from other IBM software. To do these things, you may need other resources such as image scanners and Mac-to-IBM networks. What follows is a very brief discussion of some of those options.

dBASE Toolbox

The first addition you'll want is called dBASE Toolbox. Although current versions of dBASE Mac may already include it, at the time of this writing, it is a public domain desk accessory written by Kent Irwin of Ashton-Tate's Software Product Center. This invaluable tool allows you to create dialog boxes the same way you create layouts—by placing, sizing, and dragging buttons, checkboxes, radio buttons, fixed text, and fixed graphic elements at will. You can turn your graphic display into a script with a single command. Or, you can import your own dialog box scripts into the Toolbox, convert them to a graphic display, modify the placement and/or size of the elements, convert back to script, and finally cut, then paste, back to the original application. Frankly, this should have been part of dBASE Mac from the beginning, but, since dBASE Toolbox is a public domain utility, it can be part of anyone's system.

dBASE Toolbox can be found on major BBS systems, such as CompuServe and GEnie; however, as of this writing, we expect Ashton-Tate to bundle dBASE Toolbox with the next release of dBASE Mac. Be sure to send in your registration cards to receive word about updates! If you don't already have dBASE Toolbox, get it!

Getting the Picture

With today's desktop publishing phenomenon in full swing, graphics have gained importance in the business community. To get pictures into a computer requires devices that digitize the image. Such devices are generally pretty expensive, but they are becoming more affordable.

There are several different kinds of devices for importing images to computers. Some digitize a picture, others digitize using a video camera. Some also incorporate OCR (Optical Character Reader) technology to import printed text into ASCII files or word processor formats.

One of the most economical solutions for digitizing a still picture is Thunderscan from Thunderware, Inc. Thunderscan sells for $249 and connects to an ImageWriter. You can then digitize a picture easily by placing it into a MacPaint format. This enables you to further edit the graphic. From there, it is easy to incorporate the graphic into dBASE Mac. Two camera-based solutions are MacViz and MacVision, which sell for $595 and $349.95, respectively.

ThunderScan
Thunderware, Inc.
21 Orinda Way
Orinda, CA 94563
(415) 254-6581

Price: $249

MacViz
Microvision Co.
38 Montvale Ave.
Stoneham, MA 02180
(617) 438-5520

Price: $595
$1,295: Desktop publishing system

MacVision
Koala Technologies
269 Mt. Herman Road
Scotts Valley, CA 95066
(408) 438-0946

Price: $349.95

Operating Systems, Networks, and Add-Ons

Moving data from one operating system to another is often full of headaches and usually involves multiple modem transfers and frustrating reformatting. But the marketplace is beginning to move in the direction of increased portability, if not compatibility. New networks and peripherals are able to link IBM (PC DOS and MS DOS) computers with Macintoshes, and new software makes the translations easier. The result is a much improved method of converting and/or moving information between the two machine types.

Apple's newer systems include Apple File Exchange software that allows conversion of Mac files to other formats. Currently, a fine set of translation utilities between PC and Mac file types is offered by DataViz.

DataViz MacLink Plus Translators for AFE and MacLink Plus MacLink Plus is a direct-connect file transfer system that can send and translate files at up to 57,600 baud. It uses a special cable to connect the modem port of the Mac with a standard serial port on the PC. The DataViz translators are able to convert many DOS and Mac file types, and are the best currently available. MacLink Plus Translators work with the MacLink Plus software as well as with Apple File Exchange.

DataViz
16 Winfield St.
Norwalk, CT 06855
(203) 866-4944

Price: $195 (with cables and software)
$159 (without cables)

There are two newer solutions similar to MacLink Plus. These include QuickShare and LAP-LINK Mac.

LAP-LINK Mac LAP-LINK Mac offers file exchanges at up to 57,000 baud and can support multiple file transfers. It comes with a universal cable for connecting between a variety of Macs and PCs.

Traveling Software
North Creek Corporate Center
19310 North Creek Parkway
Bothell, WA 98011
(206) 483-8088

Price: $139.95 (with software and cables)

QuickShare QuickShare takes a different approach from that of MacLink Plus and LAP-LINK Mac. Instead of using serial connections, it uses an SCSI connection. The package includes software and a plug-in board for the PC. In addition to very high-speed transfers (at 1,400,000 baud or greater), QuickShare allows Mac users to use PC hard disks from their desktops and even allows a PC hard disk to act as an AppleShare file server. You can even boot up your Mac on the PC disk.

Compatible Systems Corporation
P.O. Drawer 17220
Boulder, CO 80308
(303) 444-9532

Price: $465

Translating graphics is facilitated using The Graphics Link from PC Quik-Art, Inc. This product will convert to and from MacPaint format and several common PC paint formats.

PC Quik-Art, Inc.
394 S. Milledge Ave., Suite 200
Athens, GA 30606
(404) 543-1799

Price: $99.95

Add-On Drives

One of the easiest ways to move data between formats is to use an add-on disk drive.

Apple 5.25-inch Drive The Apple drive is a simple 5.25-inch IBM-type drive that fits onto a Mac SE or a Mac II through a special controller card. It will read, write, and format IBM-style drives, but at this time it is limited to working with Apple File Exchange and the Mac286 coprocessor board from AST.

Apple Computer
20525 Mariani Avenue
Cupertino, CA 95014
(408) 996-1010

Prices: PC Drive alone—$399.00
Mac II interface card—$129.00
SE interface card—$129.00

DaynaFile DaynaFile is an add-on SCSI disk drive for any Macintosh above 512K. It comes with a case for two drives, but is sold in any configuration of 5.25-inch and DOS 3.5-inch drives. It will work with any Mac application, and so is more versatile than the drive from Apple. DaynaFile is a very useful product for converting between PC and Mac formats, and optionally includes its own set of the DataViz translation utilities.

Dayna Communications
50 South Main Street, Suite 530
Salt Lake City, UT 84144-9901
(801) 531-0600

Prices: Single 360K drive—$595.00
Single 1.2 meg drive—$695.00
Single 720K 3.5"—$695.00
Single 1.44 meg 3.5"—$735.00
Dual 360K/1.2 meg—$849.00
Dual 360K/720K—$849.00

MatchMaker MatchMaker is a half-card for the IBM PC or compatible that allows you to connect a standard Mac 3.5-inch drive to the PC. You can share files and even initialize a Mac disk using MatchMaker.

Micro Solutions, Inc.
132 West Lincoln Hwy.
DeKalb, IL 60115
(815) 756-3411

Price: $149.00

AppleShare Apple is offering an AppleTalk board that fits in an IBM or compatible. Using this board, Macintoshes and IBMs can be included in the same networks. AppleShare uses a dedicated file server—a Mac Plus and hard disk that runs the network and is not used as a work station. Using AppleShare's sophisticated networking software, medium to large offices and businesses can link many computer systems into one network. Data from IBM programs such as dBASE III can be accessed directly by applications such as dBASE Mac. In January 1988, Apple introduced its AppleShare PC product, which directly links DOS computers to the AppleShare network. This product is similar to the TangentShare product mentioned below.

Prices: AppleShare File Server Software—$799
AppleShare PC Software $149
LocalTalk PC Card—$249
Macintosh II EtherTalk Interface Card—$699

TOPS AppleShare, with its dedicated file server and relatively high-priced software, may be beyond the means and needs of some users. If this is true, you can still link several Macs and IBMs inexpensively using TOPS. TOPS is software only on the Mac side but, like AppleShare, it uses a special board in the IBM side to emulate the AppleTalk network. TOPS software for one Mac plus software/hardware for one IBM costs under $600.

Centram Systems West, Inc.
2560 9th St., Suite 220
Berkeley, CA 94710
(415) 549-5900

Price: $189 for Mac
$349 for PC

TangentShare Tangent Technologies has another solution. This one uses either the AppleTalk PC board or Tangent's own board to make an IBM PC or compatible a working member of an AppleShare network. This solution is good for those who already have AppleShare up and running, since TangentShare fits well into such a scheme.

Using an IBM-to-Mac network allows you to share disks between the different systems, and move documents around between computers. If you plan to use data in both dBASE Mac and dBASE II or III, you will probably find a network to be a reasonable solution.

Tangent Technologies
5720 Peachtree Parkway, Suite 100
Norcross, GA 30092
(404) 662-0366

Price: $150 for software alone
$350 with PC MacBridge board

3Plus for the Mac 3Com also has a powerful networking product for connecting Macs with PCs and with other Macs. 3Plus is, perhaps, a more high-end product since it requires a dedicated server and contains all the features of the full-blown 3Com networks already in service in many companies worldwide. The Mac connection can be made via AppleTalk or EtherTalk. 3Plus is a natural choice for companies that already have 3Com networks installed since it adds the Macs to the existing system with minimal fuss. 3Com is also the most logical choice for very large networks with hundreds of workstations. It also may be a good choice for networks that include many remote branches, since 3Com networks are proven performers in such environments.

3Com Corporation
3165 Kifer Road
Santa Clara, CA 95052-8145
(408) 562-6400

Prices: 3S/200 fully configured server with 3Plus Share—$7,995
3Plus for Mac—$495 (unlimited users on server)

3Plus Mail for Mac—$595 up to 5 users
EtherLink N/B (EtherTalk board for Mac II)—$595

Two coprocessing solutions are also available—MacCharlie from Dayna, and AST286, a set of plug-in cards for the Mac II from AST Research. These coprocessing units effectively turn a Mac into a combination Mac/PC. A software-only DOS emulator called Soft PC—in production at the time of this writing—was unavailable for testing.

Mac Charlie Mac Charlie sells for under $1,000 and is available from Dayna (see above). MacCharlie places a specially designed 8088-based PC clone onto a Mac Plus or Mac SE and allows easy switching between PC and Mac sessions. Unfortunately, MacCharlie does not have the ability to share the hard drive of a Mac, and is limited to using the two floppy drives built in. An expansion chassis could be added, but the cost is prohibitive in most cases.

Mac286 The Mac286 boards have been called "an AT in a Mac II." That is an accurate description. Plugging the Mac286 into a Mac II effectively makes it a dual machine. It will run just about any software that runs on an IBM PC clone and, other than some video limitations, it does so as well as or better than most clones. Can share hard-disk space with Mac, or run from floppies. It is especially useful with MultiFinder. With a little extra memory, Mac286 can allow easy switching between DOS and Mac sessions (Clipboard data can be transferred).

Requires: A Mac II and Apple PC 5.25-inch drive for installation.

AST Research Inc
Apple Products Division
2121 Alton Ave.
Irvine, CA 92714
(714) 553-0340

Price: $1499

Mac-VAX Connectivity

Another "foreign" environment that some Mac users will want to work with is the VAX minicomputer from Digital Equipment Corporation. A variety of products are available providing various features and functionality.

pcLink and PacerShare pcLink and PacerShare, both from Pacer Software, Inc., provide a Macintosh (or a PC) user with a wide range of options in integrating with a Digital Equipment VAX minicomputer, including file transfer, terminal emulation, virtual disk support, and print spooling services. Since pcLink is available for both the Macintosh and PC environments, files can be transferred between these to environments using the VAX as a gateway. Ashton-Tate has demonstrated that dBASE Mac can use dBASE III/III Plus files transferred from the PC environment as well as the reverse (dBASE III Plus using files generated by dBASE Mac). pcLink supports both asynchronous RS-232 and Ethernet connections.

Pacer Software, Inc.
7911 Herschel Ave., Suite 402
La Jolla, CA 92037
(619) 454-0565

Price: $2000–$37500, depending on the number of concurrent users

AlisaTalk Produced by Alisa Systems, AlisaTalk is the family name of a group of products that allow a Digital VAX to become a very useful host to a network of Macintosh computers. The product provides file server capabilities, allowing files to be opened across a network and used (including both read and write capabilities) as if they were on a locally connected disk. AlisaTalk also provides print spooling capabilities. Similar to Pacer's pcLink and PacerShare products, AlisaTalk allows dBASE Mac users to access dBASE III Plus files created on a PC via a VAX acting as a gateway.

Alisa Systems, Inc.
221 E. Walnut Street, Suite 230
Pasadena, CA 91101
(818) 792-9474

Price: Available from vendor

Fastpath, EtherSC, Etherport SE Kinetics, Inc. makes several hardware products that allow Macs to become full-fledged members of an Ethernet-based network configuration. Fastpath is the name of an external box that acts as a bridge between Macs on an AppleTalk network and a VAX running on an Ethernet network. EtherSC is a similar bridge box that allows Macs to connect directly to an Ethernet network via the Mac's SCSI port. Etherport SE is an internal card for the Mac SE that offers the same functionality as EtherSC. Kinetics has also recently introduced a card that fits inside a Mac II system. All of these products can be used with both Alisa Systems and Pacer Software's products.

Kinetics, Inc.
2500 Camino Diablo, Suite 110
Walnut Creek, CA 94596
(415) 947-0998

Price: Available from vendor

CL/1 CL/1 is a Mac-VAX communications tool developed by Network Innovations (now an Apple Computer subsidiary) that provides Macintosh users with the ability to access VAX DBMS files, extract desired data, and download data to be used by popular Macintosh applications. VAX DBMS files that can be accessed include Oracle, DEC Rdb, Relational Technology's Ingres, and Informix. At a recent DEXPO (a Digital VAX-oriented trade show), several vendors demonstrated prototype implementations of CL/1 technology incorporated with their products. Ashton-Tate showed a special version of dBASE Mac. At the time of this writing, there are not many more details regarding Ashton-Tate's implementation of CL/1 technology.

Network Innovations
20863 Stevens Creek Blvd., Suite 200
Cupertino, CA 95014
(408) 257-6800

Price: Available from vendor

Mac-UNIX Connectivity

Both Pacer Software and Network Innovations' products work with UNIX host computers as well as VAX minicomputers. For details on these products, please see the write-ups in the previous section, "Mac-VAX Connectivity." Ethernet connections can also be used to connect Macs to UNIX systems. Those who need UNIX compatibility may also want to investigate how TOPS connects with Sun Microsystems networks and workstations (see TOPS, above)

Mac-IBM Mainframe Connectivity

MacIRMA The Macintosh can also act as an IBM 3270 terminal and conduct sessions with an IBM mainframe. MacIRMA is a communications board that provides this functionality.

Digital Communications Associates (DCA)
1000 Alderman Drive
Alpharetta, GA 30201
(800) 442-4522
(404) 241-4762

Price: Available from vendor

Other Sources

The area of communications is expanding very quickly, with many new products becoming available. This section has provided a selection of the products that, at the time of writing, are most relevant to dBASE Mac. Other sources of information provide much greater detail on these products; among them are:

- *Apple Business Solutions Guide for Communications* (produced by Apple Computer)
- *Apple Desktop Solutions Reference Guide* (produced by Apple Computer)
- *Digital Review Magazine*, February 8, 1988 issue

dBASE Mac/ dBASE III Plus File Sharing

Hardware/Software Needed

Macintosh
DEC VAXMate or IBM PC with DEC Network Integration Kit
VAX
Kinetics FastPath
DEC DESTA
AppleTalk cabling
Ethernet cabling
VAX VMS Services for MS-DOS (DEC product)
Pacer Software's pcLink and PacerShare software
dBASE III Plus
dBASE III Plus LAN Pack
dBASE Mac

Setup

Install VAX VMS Services for MS-DOS on VAX; create shared volume.
Install PacerShare on Mac and VAX.
Install dBASE Mac on Macintosh.
Install dBASE III Plus and dBASE III Plus LAN Pack on VAX under VAX VMS Services for MS-DOS.

Exchanging Files Between dBASE III Plus and dBASE Mac

(Note: dBASE Mac can handle additional file types that are not valid with dBASE III Plus. It is strongly recommended that a file be created in dBASE III Plus first and then sent to dBASE Mac rather than the other way around.)

- Start-up dBASE from the VAX file server.
- Create dBASE III Plus file in dBASE III Plus.
- Close file by typing: **Close <Return>**.

(If not done already, open PacerShare volume via Chooser.)

- The file created in dBASE III Plus should appear in PacerShare volume area.
- Copy the dBASE III Plus file into the same work area as dBASE Mac, that is, onto the Mac hard disk.
- Open dBASE Mac.

Importing the dBASE III Plus File into dBASE Mac

- Choose *New* under the Datafile menu.
- Choose *Create Structure for Existing File.*
- Choose *dBASE III* under file type options (click on the word "foreign" to see options).
- Click **OK**.
- Select file created in dBASE III Plus from list of folders, programs, data files, etc.; click **Open** (you should now see the structure of the file on the screen).
- Select *New View* under the "Windows" menu.
- Type in the name of a view, for example, Testview1.
- Select *Columnar Layout* under "Display" options.
- Click **Quick Create**.
- Click **OK**.
- Select *Perform and Use View* under "View" menu.
- You should now see the records in the file that was created in dBASE III Plus.

To Edit/Append Records in dBASE Mac

- Create another view by selecting *New View* on the "Windows" menu.
- Type in new view name.
- Select *Form Layout* under "Display" options.
- Select *Quick Create*; press *OK.*

- Select *Perform and Use View* on the "View" menu. (You should now see the first record in the file; records cannot be edited or appended.)
- Move through the records by using the forward/backward arrows found on the left-hand side of the screen. Press **Tab** to go to the next field or **Shift-Tab** to go to the previous field. (Note: Hitting <**Return**> will erase what has been typed in the field.)
- To add records, fill in data in the fields as desired, moving to the next field via the **Tab** key. After data in the last field of a record have been entered, press **Enter** to load the new record into the file on the disk.

Move Data Between dBASE Mac and dBASE III Plus

- Select *Structure Window* under "Windows" menu.
- Select *New* under the "Datafile" menu.
- Select *Create New File* (the default option).
- Select *Foreign* under "File Type" options.
- Select *Carriage Return & Line Feed* under "Record Terminator" options.
- Select *Variable Size Delimited* under "Field Size."
- Select *Comma* as the field delimiter (the default option).
- Click **OK**.
- Give name to file. (Limit name to eight characters to accommodate MS-DOS limitations.)
- Click **Save**.
- In next dialog box, select *Save* at lower right corner.
- In next dialog box, fill in the name of the first field that was in the dBASE III Plus file; click **Save** at the lower right corner.
- Repeat previous step until you have created all of the fields that were in the dBASE III Plus file structure; click **Done** in the lower right corner.
- Select *New View* under the "Windows" menu.
- Type in name for the view.
- Select dBASE Mac version of dBASE III Plus file as the "root" file (the file will have the name:
  "<dBASE III Plus file name> Structure.")

- Select *Transfer.*
- Select *Quick Create.*
- Click **OK**.
- Pick file name given above as the "destination file."
- Click **OK**.
- Click in the boxes in the grid (along the diagonal) that exactly match the field names of the "root" file with the same field names in the To: ("destination") file.
- Select *Perform and Use View* under the "View" menu.
- Exit dBASE Mac.
- Copy "destination file" into PacerShare volume. (This will have an icon that looks like a memo.)
- On the PC or VAXMate, rename the "destination" file to have the MS-DOS extension .TXT:

```
rename <filename> <filename>.TXT
```

- Create a new dBASE III Plus file structure by typing:

```
use <original dBASE III Plus filename>  <CR>
copy structure to <new filename>  <CR>
use <new filename>  <CR>
append from <"destination" file name.TXT>
delimited  <CR>
```

- Type **list** to see records in new dBASE III Plus file.

INDEX

About dBASE Mac, 363
ACCEPT, 148, 228
Access Path, 214
Add button, 363
Add Field, 363
Add-on drives, 660-65
ALERT box, 148, 334, 335
Align to Grid, 364
Allocated, 359, 367
ANNUITY, 231
Apple Menu, 38, 176, 364
  Help, 398
Application
  Creating, 12-34
  Designing, 468-69
  Development, 468
  Error-check, 50
  File creation, 13-26
  Loading dBASE Mac, 13
  Main elements, 34
  Questionnaire application, 471-518
  Save, 32
  see also Checkbook project, Mailing List project, MultiMail project, NewCheck project, States project, Timecard project
Arrow, 42, 116
ASCII text files, 36, 39
Ashton-Tate, 232, 246, 288
Automatic Sequence, 78-79, 88, 122, 163, 193

Basic equipment, 647-48
Basic techniques, 649-50
Basic terms, 649-54
Batch processing, 275-76
BBS system, 232
Bleed-through effect, 170
Bodine, Tom, 288, 356
BREAK, 306
Breaks, 215-16
  Conditions, 46
Bring to Front/Send to Back, 176, 364
BUTTON, 231, 235
Buttons, 37, 232
  Description, 38
B-tree, 65

Cap Locks key, 163
CASE, 222, 231
Cash flow report, 218-21
Change button, 138, 144
Change Field, 65, 138, 365
Change File, 365-67
Checkbook project, 53, 155
  Add data, 186-89
  Create file, 78-92
  Fields, 78-90
  File, 78, 187-89
  Final description, 544-47
  Graphics, 176-77
  Hierarchies, 135, 141-51
  Key field, 166-77
Checkboxes, 37
  Description, 38
Choices fields, 9, 36, 67-68, 81-83, 146-47, 367-70
  Keyboard entry, 40
  Number of choices, 82
Clear, 185, 370
Clipboard, 40, 170, 171, 176, 208
Close, datafile, 370
Close, project, 370-71
Close, view, 371
Color layouts, 174
Column view, 50, 68
  Description, 44
  Reports, 211
  To create, 24, 47, 162
  Use mode, 50
  Working with, 161-65
Columnar format, 9
Columnar Layout, 24, 26
Command-A, 70, 71, 187
Command-C, 170, 176, 208, 224
Command-D, 197
Command-Done, 91
Command-Done/N, 297
Command-Enter, 182, 194, 306
Command-N, 72
Command-P, 72, 221
Command-Shift-3, 212, 225
Command-V, 176, 208
Commands, 231
Compound, 231
Constants, 230
Control break, 10
Copy, 72, 165, 185, 210, 371
Cross-referencing, 7
Custom Layout, 19

Custom Menus, 227, 240, 371-72
 Function of, 52
 To create, 241-44
Custom view, 191
 Description, 44
Cut, 185, 210, 372

da Vinci, 3
Data
 Add to Checkbook, 186-89
 Add to file, 18-24
 Entry, 70-76
 Manipulating, 185-86
 Numeric, 39
 Posting, 90-92
 Viewing, 24-26, 76-77
Data field, 41, 373
 Description, 39
Data types, 39-41, 373
Database, 5
 Computer advantage, 5-6
 Concepts, 3-11
 Design, 10-11
 Displaying, 9-10
 Field types, 8-9
 Programming, 10
 Relational, 6-8, 11
 Reporting, 9-10
 Sorting, 5-6
 What it is, 4
Database concepts, 3-5
 Design, 10-11
 Field types, 8-9
 Relational databases, 6-8
Database design, 10-11
Database Structure Window
 see Structure Window
Datafile menu, 373, 430
 Add Field, 17, 18, 67, 232, 363
 Change Field, 82, 90, 365
 Change File, 131, 365-67
 Close, 370
 Duplicate File, 54, 123, 383-84
 Export, 387
 New, 14, 18, 55, 78, 122, 420
 Open, 424
 Remove Field, 129, 130, 131, 448-49
 Restore, 130, 450
Date field, 8-9, 36, 373-75
 Description, 40
dBASE Mac
 Estimate file size, 64
 Files, 39-41
 Loading, 13
 Preferences, 43-52
 Specifications, 36
 Starting, 54
 Structure Window, 41-42
 Structures, 35-52
 Ways to communicate, 36-38
dBASE Mac and dBASE III, 470-518
dBASE Mac Runtime, 246
dBASE Toolbox, 659
dBASE II, 36, 39
dBASE III, 36, 39, 670-71
 And dBASE Mac, 470-518
dBASE III Plus, 36, 668-69
Define Hierarchy mode, 46
Define Hierarchy Palette, 136-41
Define Layout Palette, 155-56
Define Selection Palette, 205
Define Selections, 376-77
Define Sorts, 214, 377-78
Define Sorts screen, 211
DELETE, 229
Delete File, 379
Delete‹name›, 185, 378-79
DELETE(SELF), 51, 229, 307
Delete Record, 52, 227, 229, 379
 When to use, 51
Delete View, 379
Design menu, 379-80, 430
 Align to Grid, 159, 180, 364
 Bring to Front, 364
 Custom menus, 371-72
 Display Options, 49-50, 157, 158, 168, 221, 382-83
 Form Size, 49, 158, 178, 392-93
 Group, 49, 181
 Reduce to Fit, 445
 Rulers, 48, 178, 450
 Send to Back, 176, 225, 451
 Show Selections, 452
 Show/Hide Grid, 180, 452
 Turn Grid On/Off, 49, 159, 178
 Ungroup, 49
Desk Accessory, 38, 40, 651
 Help, 398, 431
 Picture This. . . , 431
Destination file, 42, 47, 260-61
DIALOG, 231, 235
Dialog boxes, 232-36, 380-82, 650-51
 Description, 37
 Display setting, 43
 Post-Processor, 51
 Programs, 10
 To create, 51
Display information, 9-10
Display Only, 182
Display Options, 48, 49-50, 168, 170, 179, 214, 382-83
 Design menu, 157, 158
Display settings, 43
Display View, 44, 142
 Kinds of, 43
Drawing program, 176
Duplicate File, 54, 383-84
Duplicate View, 384
Dynamic, 5

Edit, 654
Edit masks, 9
Edit menu, 385, 429
 Close, 428
 Close Palette, 426
 Copy, 371
 Cut, 372
 Delete, 51, 185, 378-79
 Hide Palette, 452
 Insert, 185, 407
 New, 185
 New Record procedure, 420-21
 Next, 185, 186, 421
 Paste, 170, 430
 Preferences, 43, 382, 433-34
 Prior, 185, 186, 436

Select All, 185, 451
Show Palette, 452
Show Path, 240, 451-52
Undo, 462
Edit Text boxes, 38
EDITTEXT, 231, 235, 236
Ellipses, 50
ELSE, 307
END, 235
Enter key, 148
Equipment, basic, 647-48
Error checking, 10, 50
EXIT, 231, 252
Explode, 385-87
Export, 387
Expressions, 231
External Index files, 42, 121

Fat Bits, 240
Field Data types
Choice field, 9, 36, 40, 67-68, 81-83, 146-47, 367-70
Date field, 9, 36, 40, 373-75
Graphic field, 9, 36, 40, 97-100, 394-97
Logical field, 9, 36, 40, 416
Number field, 9, 36, 39, 58-59, 101-02, 421-23
Text field, 9, 39, 455-56
Time field, 36, 40, 456-57
Field Definition screen, 388-89
Field types, 8-9
Data, 39, 41, 373
Formula, 9, 39, 41, 45, 102-05, 393
Key, 15, 39, 42, 56-57, 157, 408-09
Memory, 9, 39, 40, 41, 45, 121, 417
Fields, 4
Adding, 17
Changing definitions, 91
Defining, 56-58
Display only, 181-82
Lookup, 182
Maximum occurrences, 36
Maximum size, 36
Password protection, 52
Posting, 54
Removing, 129-32
Resize, 32
File Field Procedure, 229
File icons, 389
File name conventions, 653-54
File Procedures, 229
Files, 4
Add data, 18-24
Destination file, 42, 44
External index, 42
Foreign, 39, 260, 276-80, 390-92
Icons, 389
List, 46
Maximum file size, 36
Maximum open files, 36
Optimizing performance, 357-60, 367
Organization, 365-67
Password, 52
Pointer field, 40
Protect, 52
Relationships, 42
Reorganize, 130
Size, 36, 390
Source file, 42, 44
Statistics, 358-59
Structure, 39, 54
Types, 389
Understanding statistics, 358
View data, 24-26
Files, creating, 13-26, 93
Checkbook, 53, 77-92
Design, 55-56
Export command, 387
Fields, 56-58
Key field, 55, 56-57
MultiMail, 53
Multivalued fields, 58-59
Palette, 66-68
Pattern matching, 60-64
Selection field, 67-68
Sets, 58, 59-60
Size, 58
Special instructions, 54
Structure Window, 65-66, 67
View, 68-77
Files, foreign, 39, 260, 276-86, 390-92
Files, related
External Index files, 42
Pointer fields, 40, 42
Files, types of, 389
ASCII text, 36, 39
dBASE Mac, 36
dBASE II, 36, 39
dBASE III, 36, 39
dBASE III Plus, 36
Filter, 6
Finder, 35, 54, 151
Load application, 32
Load dBASE Mac, 13
FIXEDTEXT, 235
Floppy disks, 64
Fonts, 43, 158, 180, 651
Form, 9
Reducing, 180-81
Form Layout, 19, 24
Form Size, 48, 49, 155, 392-93
Form view, 44, 50, 68, 215
Description, 43
Manipulating data, 185-86
To create, 18-24
To design, 47
FORMAT, 147
Formula fields, 9, 39, 41, 102-05, 393
Description, 39
View fields, 45
Frame, 358, 365
Allocated, 359, 367
Free, 359, 367
Overflow, 359, 367
Primary, 359, 367
Freelance project, 613-46
Functions, 231

Galileo, 3
Global fields, 148
Globals file, 39, 65, 92, 150, 394
Used for, 41
Globals Memory field, 39
Not saved, 92
Uses of, 41
Graphic field, 9, 36, 94, 97-100, 394-97
Description, 40
Graphics, 160, 176-77
Grid, 48, 49, 159, 180
Hiding, 180

Grouping, 48, 49
Groups, 181, 358, 365

Helix, 260
Help, 38, 252, 398
HFS, 652-53
Hide Grid, 452
Hide Palette, 452
Hierarchical Filing System see HFS
Hierarchy, 42, 398-401
  Add Fields, 46
  Creating, 135-54
  Define, 45-46
  Define Hierarchy Palette, 136-41
  Path, 45
  Procedures in, 141-51
  Remove a field, 138
  Root, 138
  Root level, 127
  Show/Hide, 172-75
  Sorting, 200-05
  Title bar, 138
  With relationships, 151-54

IBM mainframe, 667
Icons, 402-05
  Adding, 239-40
  dBASE Mac file, 402
  File box, 402
  Palette, 38, 403-05
  Pointer, 403
  Removing, 239
  Standard, 427-30
  View Hierarchy, 402-03
IF, 237, 307
IF . . . THEN, 146, 150
IF . . . THEN . . . ELSE, 231
IN, 147, 150
Index, 42, 58, 405-07
  Remove from field, 65
Index box, 57
Index files, 42, 405-07
  Creating, 121-29
Information flow, 35
Insert, 210
Insert‹name›, 185, 407
Internal index, 42, 52, 53, 407
Irwin, Kent, 232

Justify, 84

Key field, 56-57, 408-09
  Description, 39
  Layout, 157
  Pointer field, 42
  Why it is necessary, 15
Keyboard, 655-57
  Choices Field, 40

Layout, 9, 45, 410-15
  Aids to design, 48
  Checkbook, 166-77
  Column, 414-15
  Custom view, 415
  Default Palette, 155
  Define, 46-47
  Display View, 47
  Features, 183
  Form view, 412-14
  Mailing label, 156-65
  Palette, 155-56, 410-11
  Tablet, 155
  Timecard, 177-83
  Transfer View, 47, 262-65
  Window, 155
Layout, creating
  Checkbook, 166-77
  Mailing label, 156-65
  Palette, 155-56
  Timecard, 177-83
Layout View screen, 211, 220, 224
  Title bar, 42
Leading zeroes, 80
LENGTH, 231
Line Break, 216
List, 9
Loading, 13
Logical field, 9, 36, 416
  Description, 40
LOOP, 231, 238, 334

MacDraw, 176
MacPaint, 176, 212, 240
Mac-IBM, 667
Mac-UNIX, 667
Mac-VAX, 665-67
Mail Menu, 252-54
Mailing label application, 27-34
  Create the file, 13-26
  Load dBASE Mac, 13
  Printing, 222-25
  Purpose of, 26
  see also Mailing List project
Mailing label forms, 156-60
  Column view, 161-65
Mailing List project, 53, 54
  Hierarchies, 135, 136-38
  Special instructions, 197-98
  To load, 32
  View field, 138-41
  see also MultiMail project
MATCHES, 50
Matching patterns, 9
Memory, in use, 363
Memory fields, 9, 417
  Description, 39
  Globals Memory field, 40, 41
  Posting, 121
  View field, 45
Menus, 417, 650
  Basic technique, 36
  Custom, 227
  Description, 36
  Pop-up, 36-37
  Pull-down, 36
  To view contents, 36
  see also Apple Menu, Datafile menu, Design menu, Edit menu, Projects menu, Snapshot menu, View menu, Windows menu
Modal, 236
Modulo, 358, 360, 366, 418
Mouse, 36
  Techniques, 649-50
MultiMail project, 53, 54, 519-20, 522-31, 533-42
  Completing, 246-58
  Create file, 55-58
  Create Mailing label forms, 156-65
  Data entry, 70-76
  Delete view, 77
  File structure, 521-22
  Final description, 519-43
  Help entry layout, 541
  How sets work, 59-60
  Mail entry layout, 525
  Multivalued fields, 58-59, 221-25

Palette, 66-68
Pattern matchings, 60-64
Reports, 220-25
Sample column layout, 532
Structure window, 65-66
To save, 77
View creation, 136-41
View data, 76-77
Multivalued fields, 9, 221-25, 418-19
Add an occurrence, 70
Examples of, 40
Pointer fields, 40
Must Match Patterns, 60, 71

Networks, 660-62
NEW, 228
New button, 28, 139
New file, 420
New project, 420
New Record, 227, 228, 229
Description, 420-21
When to use, 51
New‹name›, 185
NEW(SELF), 51, 228, 229
New view, 421
NewCheck project, 288, 289, 296
Budget file, 290-92
Entering budgets, 298-303
Globals file, 297
Income Statement View, 339-48
Items file, 295-97
Reconcile View, 334-39
Transaction file, 292-95
Transactions view, 306-34
NEXTBROWSE, 325
Next‹name›, 185, 186, 421
Number field, 9, 36, 101-02, 421-33
Description, 39
Posting, 39
Reason for, 58-59
Numbers, 8-9
Numeric data, 39

Occurrences, 36
Omnis, 260
One-way arrow, 42
Open file, 424
Open project, 424
Operating systems, 660-62
Option-Done, 91
Option key, 163, 167, 201
Option-Tab, 73
Order box, 56
Other menu
IN, 150
REDISPLAY, 150
SELF, 150
WRITE, 150
Overflow, 359

Page Breaks, 425
Page flippers, 169, 170
Page Setup, 425
Page Setup selection, 49
Page Size, 49
Palette, 38, 66-68, 426-30
Customizing, 238-40
Standard icons, 427-30
Passwords, 52, 227-28
Change File, 365
Paste, 176, 185, 210, 430
Path, 45, 119, 153
Add a file, 46
Path menu, 137
Pattern matching, 60-64
Symbols, 61
Pen Width, 31, 34, 157, 165, 168
PERFORM, 231, 236
Personnel project, 558-612
Picture menu, 176
Picture This . . . , 40, 431
Pictures, 40
Pointer field, 40, 42, 94, 113, 114, 117
Naming, 45
To another file, 119-21
To place in set, 116
Pop-up menu, 36, 37, 56
Posting, 39, 54, 90-92, 148, 432
Post-Processor, 148, 227, 228, 431
When to use, 51
Preferences, 43-52, 157-58, 161-62, 433-34
Preferences dialog box, 49, 165, 168
Preferences menu, 187
Pre-Processor, 145-47, 182, 227, 228
Description, 433
When to use, 51
Primary, 359, 367
Primary Group, 358, 366
Printing, 211-18, 226, 434-36
Cash Flow Report, 218-21
Kinds of, 225
MultiMail, 221-25
Multivalued fields, 221-25
Reports, 214-18
Totals, 217-18
View definitions, 213-14
Prior‹name›, 185, 186, 436
Procedural Interface (PI), 36, 50, 228-30, 436-42
Elements of, 230-31
MATCHES, 50
Procedures, 10, 35, 227
Delete Record, 51, 52, 227, 229, 379
Description, 50-51
New Record, 51, 227, 228, 229, 420-21
Pre-Processor, 51, 52, 227, 228, 433
Post-Processor, 51, 52, 148, 227, 228, 431
Stopping, 237
Types of, 51-52
Write Record, 51, 52, 120, 148-51, 227, 228, 229, 464
PROJECT, 231, 245
Projects, 35
As an application, 52
How to customize, 227
Password protect, 52, 227-28
Protecting, 244-46, 443
To create, 78
Projects menu, 429, 442-43
Close, 77, 136, 141, 142, 165, 370-71
New, 78, 420
Open, 68, 136, 141, 142, 151, 161, 166, 424
Page Setup, 49, 425
Page Size, 49
Print, 225, 434-36
Print Field Definition, 212

Print File Definition, 212
Print File Structure, 212
Print Layout, 214
Print Report, 32, 34, 221
Print Structure Window, 213
Print View Definition, 213
Protect, 52, 443
Quit, 68, 92, 133, 141, 161, 165, 444
Revert, 77, 450
Revert to Saved, 68, 171
Save, 32, 133, 141, 154, 161, 177, 451
Save As, 451
Save Changes, 136
Protected mode, 245
Pull-down menu, 36

Questionnarie application, 471-518
Quick create, 19, 24, 69, 76, 161, 162, 190, 193, 444
Quick Create Columnar view, 198
Quit, 68, 444

Radio buttons, 37, 232
Description, 38
RADIOLIST, 231, 235
Reconciliation routine, 288
Records, 4
Adding, 184, 186-96, 210
Browse, 161
Columnar format, 9
Data transfer, 47
Delete, 185
Maximum fields, 36
Maximum number per file, 36
Maximum size, 36
Print, 161
Selecting, 50, 161, 205-08
Sorting, 50, 161, 196-205
REDISPLAY, 147, 150-51, 307, 334
Reduce to Fit, 180-81, 445
Reflex, 260
Relational databases, 6-8
Relational system, 11
Relationships, 116-20, 134, 445-48
Creating, 94-134
How they work, 446-47
Index, 58, 121-29
Kinds of, 42
Modifying, 132
One-way, 42, 115, 117, 445
Pointer field, 42, 113, 114, 116, 117
Recursive, 448
Remove a field, 129-32
Removing, 132-33
Structure Window, 42
Timecard project, 94-113
Two-way, 42, 114, 116, 117, 133, 445-46
What is it?, 113-15
Remove button, 138
Remove Field, 448-49
Reorganize File, 449
REPEAT, 231, 238, 252
Reports, 9-10, 449
Basic kinds, 214
Cash flow, 218-21
Form based, 9-10
List based, 9-10
Printing, 214-18
Width's limit, 36
Restore Field, 450
Revert, 450
Revert button, 138, 147
Revert to Saved, 161
Root File, 69, 152, 208, 210, 214, 356
Rulers, 178, 450
Description, 48
Grid, 49

Save, 68, 451
Save As, 68, 451
Scroll, 72
Select All, 185, 451
Select records, 50, 205-08
Selection criteria, 6
SELF, 150
Separation, 358, 366, 451, 458
SETNEXTFIELD, 181, 182, 308
SETNEXTVIEW, 231
Sets, 58
Deleting, 185-86
How they work, 59-60
Setting, 43
Sharing
see Relationships
Show Formula button, 28, 29, 33, 119
Show Grid, 452
Show/Hide Grid, 452
Show/Hide Palette, 452
Show Palette, 452
Show Path, 240, 451-52
Show Procedure, 452
Show Procedure button, 148
Show Selections, 166, 170, 171, 452
Show Selections button, 50, 168
Show Statistics, 452
Show View Description dialog, 52
Sine(SIN), 231
Snapshot, 209-10, 452-53
Snapshot menu, 209, 452-53
Sort, 5, 50, 198-205
Change criteria, 199
Designing, 197
External Index files, 42
Internal Index, 42
Multilevel, 6
Number of levels, 36
Palette, 196
Primary sort field, 6
Printing, 211
Records, 196-205
Rules, 205
Secondary sort field, 6
Set criteria, 198
Snapshots, 209-10
Widths, 36
Sort definition screen, 50
Source file, 42, 44, 47, 260-61
Special effects, 43
Square Root (SQRT), 231
Standard Deviation (STD), 231
SUBSTR, 231
States Project, 349-57
Strings, 8
Structural elements, 35
File types, 39-41

Preferences, 43-52
Specifications, 36
Structural Window, 41-42
Ways to communicate, 36-38
Structure Window, 13, 41, 453
Loading dBASE Mac, 13
Mailing list, 65-66
Printing, 211, 212-13
Relationships, 42
SUM, 231, 307

Tablet pages, 50
Tablets, 48, 49, 166-74, 454-55
Bleed, 170
Description, 49, 155
Terms, basic, 649-54
Text, 8
Text boxes, 37
Description, 38
Text data type, 455-56
Text field, 8-9, 36
Description, 39
Time field, 94, 456-57
Description, 40
Timecard project, 53, 558-612
Add records, 189-95
Create a relational system, 94-113
Employee Pic, 97
Hierarchies, 135, 151-54
Layout, 177-83
Number of files, 94
Printing, 212-14
Related files, 95-96
Remove a field, 129-32
Saving, 113, 133
Snapshot, 210
Title bar, 42, 138, 153, 162, 228
Topic list, 38
Total definitions, 46
Trace, 236-38
Transfer View, 43, 44, 457-61
Batch processing, 275-76
Date timecard file, 266-75
Destination file, 260-62
Files, 260-87
Foreign files, 276-86
Inventory example, 275-76
Layout, 47, 262-65
New Record, 51
Source file, 260-62
Used for, 44
Write Record, 51, 148
Turn Grid On/Off, 49, 159
Turn Trace On, 461
Turnkey system, 10, 228
Two-way arrow, 42

Undo, 462
UNIX, 667
UPPER, 231
USE, 231
Use, 186-89, 462
Use mode, 50, 181, 186, 211, 214, 240
Use mode Palette, 184-86, 245
Use View, 50

Variables, 230-31
Variance (VAR), 231
VAX, 665-67
Verify button, 146, 147, 151
View, 9, 43
Column view, 44, 47, 50
Creating, 26-34, 45-48, 135-54
Custom view, 44
Default, 142
Define Hierarchy Palette, 136-41
Delete, 77
Descriptive text, 52
Display View, 43-44
Fields, 28, 45, 138-41
Form view, 43, 44, 50
Hierarchy with Relationships, 151-54
Interactive mode, 50
Make-up of a, 35
Password protection, 52
Path, 45
Pointer field, 138
Procedures in the Hierarchy, 141-51
Purpose of, 43
Root, 138, 148
Selection modules, 50
Sorting records, 50
Transfer View, 43-44
Types of, 43-44
see also Layout, Hierarchy
View definitions, 213-14
View menu, 429, 463
Define Hierarchy, 213, 215
Define Selections, 206, 220, 376-77
Define Sorts, 198, 204, 215, 219, 377-78
Delete, 77, 161, 379
Duplicate view, 200, 233, 384
Layout View, 30, 33, 129, 156, 162, 166, 177, 190, 200
Perform, 50, 77
Perform and Use, 430-31
Sort, 202
Turn Trace Off, 238
Turn Trace On, 237, 461
Use, 77, 186, 193, 462
View Modified File Fields (VMFF), 138, 147, 229, 230, 365, 463
View Procedure, 229-30
View Type, 463
View Type:pop-up menu, 26, 76

WHILE, 231, 238
Window, 38, 651-52
Window menu, 464
Checkbook entry, 166
Mailing List Column, 161, 198, 233
New, 233
New View, 19, 24, 421
Timecard Column, 215
Timecard entry, 210, 213
When to use, 51
Work file, 186
Wrap checkbox, 17, 18, 66
Wrap feature, 67
Write Record, 120, 148-51, 227, 228, 229
Description, 464
When to use, 51
WRITE, 51, 148, 150, 325
WRITE(SELF), 51, 150, 229, 306

Zoom, 172

About the Authors

Rusel DeMaria writes a weekly computer column for *The Maui News* and a monthly column for *Nikkei Byte* in Japan. He is MS DOS editor for *Macazine* and a regular contributor to other magazines including *Byte*, *PC Week*, and *Business Software Magazine*. His articles and product reviews have also appeared in *Macworld*, *Mac User*, *Mac Today*, *Mac Week*, *PC Magazine*, *A+*, *ST Log*, and *The Whole Earth Catalog*. In his infrequent spare time, he plays flamenco and classical guitar and dreams of writing novels again. He is the co-sysop of the RHS RBBS in Hawaii.

George Fontaine is a programmer, writer, and pilot. His programming experience spans more than ten years. He is currently a Sergeant with the Maui Police Department and holds a degree in Administration of Justice. He is the primary sysop of the RHS RBBS.

Together, DeMaria and Fontaine have written several magazine articles, as well as the book *Public Domain Software: Untapped Resources for the Business User* for M&T Publishing.